J2EE™

Paul R. Allen, Joseph J. Bambara, Mark Ashnault,
Ziyad Dean, Thomas Garben, Sherry Smith

SAMS

J2EE Unleashed

Copyright © 2002 by Sams Publishing

International Standard Book Number: 0-672-32180-7

Library of Congress Catalog Card Number: 2001095490

Printed in the United States of America

First Printing: October 2001

04 03 02 4 3 2

Trademarks

All terms mentioned in this book that are known to be trademarks or service marks have been appropriately capitalized. Sams Publishing cannot attest to the accuracy of this information. Use of a term in this book should not be regarded as affecting the validity of any trademark or service mark.

Warning and Disclaimer

Every effort has been made to make this book as complete and as accurate as possible, but no warranty or fitness is implied. The information provided is on an "as is" basis. The authors and the publisher shall have neither liability nor responsibility to any person or entity with respect to any loss or damages arising from the information contained in this book.

Executive Editor
Michael Stephens

Acquisitions Editor
Carol Ackerman

Development Editor
David Fox

Managing Editor
Matt Purcell

Project Editor
Christina Smith

Production Editors
Seth Kerney
Emylie Morgan
Rhonda Tinch-Mize
Matt Wynalda

Indexer
Cheryl Landes

Proofreader
Harvey Stanbrough

Technical Editor
David Fox

Team Coordinator
Lynne Williams

Media Developer
Dan Scherf

Interior Designer
Gary Adair

Cover Designer
Aren Howell

Page Layout
Ayanna Lacey

Contents at a Glance

Introduction **1**

Chapter 1 Java, Distributed Computing, and J2EE **7**

2 The Design and Development of a J2EE Application **41**

3 Designing the J2EE Application **63**

4 Task List for Building J2EE Applications **97**

5 Build Resource Access: JNDI and LDAP **123**

6 Build Data Access: JDBC **137**

7 Build Control Flow: Servlets **181**

8 JavaServer Pages: Introduction **225**

9 JavaServer Pages: Practical Development with Tag Libraries **257**

10 Building the User Interface to the Application **289**

11 Enterprise JavaBeans: Introduction **327**

12 Enterprise JavaBeans: Building Session Beans **357**

13 Enterprise JavaBeans: Building Entity Beans **411**

14 Messaging with E-mail: JavaMail **445**

15 Messaging with Applications: Java Message Service (JMS) **487**

16 Data Exchange with XML **525**

17 Validating the Application **569**

18 Making the Application Perform **605**

19 Deploying the Application **631**

Appendix A Documentation for Sample Applications **691**

B Related Tools **709**

C Quick Reference Material **755**

Index 783

Contents

Introduction 1

1 Java, Distributed Computing, and J2EE 7

Background on Java 12
Widespread Capabilities for Application Development 12
Java Is the Glue for Application Development 13
Companies Must Re-Invent Themselves for the Web 14
Companies Increasingly Need the Internet to Compete 16
Challenges of Application Development for the Enterprise 17
Requirements of Web Architecture 20
The Speed to Compete 20
Service Availability 20
Connecting to Existing Data 21
Expanded User Definition: Customers, Employees, and Partners 21
Flexible User Interaction 21
Flexible Business Component Model 22
Web Application Life Cycle 22
Multiple Developer Roles 23
Iterative Development 24
Simplified Architecture and Development 25
Maps Easily to Application Functionality 26
Component-Based Architecture 27
Support for Client Components 28
Support for Business Logic Components 28
J2EE APIs and Certification 30
Java 2 Platform, Enterprise Edition Specification 31
J2EE Compatibility Test Suite 32
Sun BluePrints Design Guidelines for J2EE 32
The Enterprise Standard with a Future 32
XML and J2EE 32
Why Use XML? 34
Electronic Data Exchange and E-Commerce 35
Electronic Data Interchange (EDI) 35
Enterprise Application Integration (EAI) 36
Software Development and XML 36
XML Technology and the Java Platform 37
Java Platform Standard Extension for XML Technology 37
The Packaging of J2EE Applications 38
Applications Studied in This Book 39
Summary 40

2 The Design and Development of a J2EE Application 41

J2EE Layers 42

The Client Layer 42

The Presentation Layer 43

The Business Logic Layer....44

The Data Layer 44

J2EE Application Components....45

Client Components 45

Web Components....47

Business Components 48

J2EE Architecture 49

Containers and Services 49

Container Types....50

Development Methodology and Process 51

Modeling Tools 51

Development Tools 52

Contents of a J2EE Application 53

Development Phases of J2EE Applications 54

Sample Applications Introduced....61

Summary....61

3 Designing the J2EE Application 63

History of Modeling Tools 64

Overview....64

Designing an Application 64

Why Create a Model? 65

Entity Relationship Basics....67

CASE Tools "Lite" 69

Reverse Engineering 70

Entity Modeling....72

Relationship Modeling 73

Supported Databases 76

Modeling a Web Application 77

Overview 77

System Modeling 79

Web Application Architecture....81

The Unified Modeling Language 82

Goals and Principles of the UML 83

Conventions and Terminology....84

Modeling Web Pages 87

Forms....91

Frames 92

EJB UML Mapping 92
Need of the Java Community Addressed by the Proposed Specification 93
Specification to be Developed and How It Addresses the Need....94
Tool Support 94
Summary....95

4 Task List for Building J2EE Applications 97

Completing Prerequisite Tasks 98
Logistic Prerequisites 98
Physical Prerequisites 101
Designing the Database 102
Determining the Application Entities 102
Refining Each Entity and Attribute 103
Determining Relationships 103
Creating Tables and Columns....104
Choosing Data Types....105
Creating Keys 106
Completing Database Physical Design 106
Estimating the Size of the Database 107
Setting Up the Development Database Environment 108
Defining the Application....108
The Application Standards 109
Creating a Back-End Interface 110
Initial Data Loading....111
Creating EJB Classes and Database Stored Procedures 111
Batching Utilities for Database Tuning and Repair 112
Batching Utilities for Backup and Recovery 112
Creating the Interface 112
Choosing an Application User Interface Style 112
Setting Up the TAGLIB Class Library for the Interface Style 114
Building Pages 114
Determining the Type of Page....115
Adding Controls to a Page or a Subpage 116
Designing Menu Interaction 117
Creating Data Access Objects....117
Building Data Access Objects with Completed Database Entities 118
Validating Your Code 118
Determining When to Use the Debugger 118
Selecting the Code to Breakpoint 119
Refining Your Code....119
Creating an Executable 120
Summary....121

5 Build Resource Access: JNDI and LDAP 123

Naming and Directory Services 124
What is JNDI? 124
Finding Sample Application Resources 124
Benefits of JNDI 125
JNDI and J2EE 125
JNDI Service Providers 127
JNDI Architecture 128
JNDI Packages 128
Naming 129
Contexts 129
Namespaces 131
JNDI Operations 131
Lightweight Directory Access Protocol 132
JNDI/LDAP Practical Examples 133
Summary 135

6 Build Data Access: JDBC 137

Introduction 138
What Is JDBC? 139
Benefits of JDBC 139
JDBC Architecture: API and Drivers 139
Database Drivers 141
The JDBC API 143
JDBC 2.1 Core API: The `java.sql` Package 143
Retrieving and Updating Data 148
Statements 148
`ResultSet` 152
SQL-to-Java Data Types 153
Handling Nulls 155
Stored Procedures 155
JDBC Exception Types 157
`SQLException` 157
`SQLWarning` 157
`DataTruncation` Warnings 158
Metadata 158
The `ResultSetMetaData` Object 158
The `DatabaseMetaData` Interface 159
Scrollable Resultsets 159
Scrollable `ResultSet` Methods 160
Scrollable `ResultSet` Example 161
Updateable Resultsets 161
Creating Updateable Resultsets 161

Updating Rows 162
Deleting Rows 163
Inserting Rows 163
Transaction Support 163
Batch Statements 164
JDBC 2.1 New Data Types 166
`BLOB` and `CLOB` 166
`ARRAY` 167
`STRUCT` 168
`REF` 168
JDBC 2.0 Optional Package API: `javax.sql` 168
Database Access with JNDI 169
Connection Pooling 169
Distributed Transactions 170
JDBC `RowSets` 171
Case Study: The SilverStream Application Server 171
Database Connectivity in SilverStream 172
JDBC Within SilverStream 172
Accessing JDBC from a Session Bean in a SilverStream Database 174
Accessing JDBC from a Session Bean 175
Defining a Resource Reference Lookup in the Session Bean 176
Constructing the JDBC Calls 176
Getting a Connection 176
Constructing, Compiling, and Executing an SQL Select Statement 176
Creating an Environment Entry 177
Mapping the Resource Reference to a SilverStream Database 178
Summary 179

7 Build Control Flow: Servlets 181

What Are Servlets? 182
First Generation—CGI 182
Second Generation—ISAPI/NSAPI 183
The Java Alternative—Servlets 184
Benefits of Servlets 184
Use as Controller in MVC and the Sample Application 184
Basic HTTP 185
Servlet Container 188
Servlet API 188
Servlet Exceptions 189

Service Method Detail 189
Streaming Data to the Client 190
Setting MIME Type 190
HTML Clients 192
Forms 192
Commonly Used <FORM> Tag Attributes 192
Servlet Life Cycle 195
Initialization 195
Service 196
Destruction 196
ServletContext 196
HTTP Request Header 197
Parameters 197
Content 197
Connection 198
Cookies 200
Header 200
HTTP Response Header 203
Setting Response Status 204
Session Management 205
Hidden Form Fields 205
URL Rewriting 205
Persistent Cookies 206
The Session Tracking API 208
Dispatching Requests 209
Servlets with JDBC 211
Web Applications 213
Web Application Archive (WAR) 213
Directory Structure 213
Deployment Descriptor/Mapping Requests to Servlets 215
Multi-MIME Types 217
Using Servlets in the SilverStream Application Server 218
Developing Standard Servlets 218
Servlet 2.3 API 223
Summary 224

8 JavaServer Pages: Introduction 225

Features of JSP Pages 229
The Efficient Use of Server-Side Java 229
Web Development, Deployment, and Maintenance 229
Components That Are Reusable 230
Separating Business Logic and Presentation 230
Large Development Community and Widespread Support 230

Platform Independence ...230
Next Generation Page Development with Tags...231
The Components of a JSP Page ...231
JSP Directives ...231
JSP Tags...232
Scripting Elements...233
Developing and Deploying JSP Pages ...233
Writing JSP Pages ...234
Samples of JSP 1.1 Pages ...237
JSP Architectures ...240
Simple Application ...241
Mature Architecture: Redirecting Requests ...244
Model-View-Controller (MVC) Design ...248
Conclusion: JSP Pages Are a Big Part of the Enterprise Java Solution ...254
JSP Pages: Advantages Over Servlets Alone ...255
Working with Your Existing Servlets ...256

9 JavaServer Pages: Practical Development with Tag Libraries 257

JSP Syntax ...258
JSP Comments...258
HTML Comments ...258
Hidden Comments...259
JSP Directives ...259
JSP Scripting Elements ...265
JSP Actions ...267
Object Scope ...280
Implicit Objects ...280
Error Handling...281
Tag Libraries...282
Declaring Tag Libraries...282
Tag Handler ...283
Creating a Corporation Banner Custom Tag...286
Summary...288

10 Building the User Interface to the Application 289

The Model-View-Controller Paradigm...290
Advantages ...292
Disadvantages ...293
The Struts Framework ...293
Installing Struts ...294
Prerequisite Software...294
Struts Framework Overview ...295

JavaBeans and Scope 302
Building Model Components 302
Building View Components....304
Building Controller Components 313
Accessing Relational Databases 323
Summary....326

11 Enterprise JavaBeans: Introduction 327

Enterprise JavaBeans Overview 328
Distributed Programming Overview....330
EJB Framework 330
Containers 331
Session and Entity Beans 333
Session Beans 333
Entity Beans....334
Encapsulating Entity Beans with Session Beans 335
Bean Relativity 335
Attributes of a Bean 335
Stateless Beans 336
Stateful Beans 336
Parts of a Bean 336
`Home` Interface 337
`EJBObject` Interface....337
Deployment Descriptor 337
`SessionContext` and `EntityContext` Objects 337
Dependent and Fine-Grained Objects 338
Container-Managed Persistence (CMP) and Bean-Managed Persistence (BMP) 338
Container-Managed Persistence (CMP) 339
Bean-Managed Persistence (BMP) 340
The Life Cycle of Enterprise JavaBeans 340
Java Message Service (JMS) and Message-Driven Beans (MDB) 341
Java Message Service (JMS)....341
Message-Driven Beans (MDB) 342
Distributed Programming Services....346
Naming and Registration....346
Remote Method Invocation (RMI) 346
Protocols 346
Common Object Request Broker Architecture (CORBA) and Remote Method Invocation (RMI) 347
CORBA 347
Java/RMI 347
Transactions and Transaction Management 349
Distributed Transactions 349
Multiple Transactions 350

Java Transaction Service (JTS) 350
Java Transaction API (JTA) 351
Entity Bean Methods and Transaction Attributes 351
Session Bean Methods and Transaction Attributes 351
Security 352
Security Not Covered by the EJB Specification 352
Deployment 352
Deployment Descriptors 352
Packaging Hierarchies 353
Personal Roles for EJB Development 353
Entity Bean Developer 354
Bean Writer 354
Application Assembler 355
Bean Deployer 355
Corporate Roles 355
Component Provider 356
Application Server Provider 356
EJB Container Provider 356
Summary 356

12 Enterprise JavaBeans: Building Session Beans 357

Creating Session Beans 358
Stateful Versus Stateless Session Beans 358
Defining the Session Bean Class 359
Session Beans and Inheritance 360
Session Bean Interface 360
Session Bean Class Methods 366
Sample Session Bean Component Code 367
Stub, Tie, and Object Sample Code 373
Packaging and Deploying a Session Bean 400
JAR Contents 400
Deployment 402
Changes to Bean Code 402
Finding Session Beans from a Client 402
`InitialContext` 403
Type-Narrowing 403
Finding Objects and Interfaces: The Java Naming and Directory Interface (JNDI) 404
Creating an Instance Using `EJBHome` 405
Calling Session Beans from a Client 405
Coding Clients to Call EJBs 405
Different Types of Clients 406
Summary 409

13 Enterprise JavaBeans: Building Entity Beans 411

Defining Entity Beans....412
  Uses of Entity Beans....413
  Entity Bean Life Cycle States....413
Container- and Bean-Managed Persistence....415
  Bean-Managed Persistence....415
  Container-Managed Persistence....416
The Anatomy of a CMP Entity Bean....416
  Bean Writer–Created Components....417
  Container-Created Objects....420
Developing Entity Beans....421
  Step 1—Set Up A Data Source to a Database....421
  Step 2—Develop a Primary Key Class....422
  Step 3—Develop the Entity Bean Class....422
  Step 4—Define the Home or Local Home Interface....425
  Step 5—Define the Local or Remote Interface....426
  Step 6—Define a Deployment Descriptor....426
  Step 7—Deploy Using Container-Provided Tools....428
  Step 8—Creating a Client Application....428
A Closer Look at Developing Entity Beans....428
  Primary Keys....428
  Mapping to a Single Field....428
  The `EntityBean` Class and Life Cycle Event Methods....430
  Home Interfaces and `create()` Methods....433
  Home Interfaces and `finder()` Methods....434
  Home Interfaces and `remove()` Methods....435
  Home Interfaces and `getEJBMetaData()` Methods....436
  Remote Interfaces....436
  Local Interfaces....436
EJB Clients....437
  Remote Clients....437
  Local Clients....438
Using a GUI Tool to Configure, Package, and Deploy Entity Beans....439
  Assembling, Configuring, and Packaging Entity Beans....439
  Deploying Entity Bean Jar Files....443
Summary....444

14 Messaging with E-mail: JavaMail 445

E-mail Messaging in General....446
What Does JavaMail Do?....447
The Provider Registry....448

JavaMail Architecture and Primary Classes 450
Java Activation Framework 451
`javax.mail.Session` 452
`javax.mail.Store` 453
`javax.mail.Folder` 454
`javax.mail.search` 456
`javax.mail.Address` 459
`javax.mail.internet.InternetAddress` 459
`javax.mail.Message` 460
`javax.mail.internet.MimeMessage` 460
`javax.mail.Transport` 466
Sending and Receiving Messages 466
Sending Internet Messages 467
Receiving Internet Messages 468
Working with Multipart Messages 469
Sending `MimeMultipart` Messages 469
Receiving `MimeMultipart` Messages 470
Sending Binary Data in a Message 471
Receiving Binary Data in a Message 472
Using JavaMail in JavaServer Pages 474
Summary Instructions 474
Detailed Instructions 478
Code Solution 483
Summary 486

15 Messaging with Applications: Java Message Service (JMS) 487

Messaging Basics 488
Messages 488
Middleware 488
Message-Oriented Middleware 489
Communication Modes 489
Where Does JMS Fit In? 490
JMS in Applications 491
Handling Exceptions 494
Session Management 494
Messages 495
JMS Components 498
Administered Objects 498
Interface Classes 499
Producing and Consuming Messages 500
`MessageProducer` 500
`MessageConsumer` 500
`MessageListener` 501
`MessageSelector` 501

JMS Examples 501
A Simple Point-to-Point Example...502
A Simple Publish/Subscribe Example...504
A Point-to-Point Browsing Example...507
A MessageListener Example 510
A MessageSelector Example 514
Queue and Topic Destination Maintenance Examples 518
JMS Implementation and Deployment Issues 522
What Else Needs to Be Implemented? 522
Deployment 523
Summary...523

16 Data Exchange with XML 525

What Is XML? 526
Brief History of XML 526
Structure of an XML Document..527
Prolog...528
Instance Section..528
Elements 528
Tags 529
Empty Elements..529
Attributes 529
Entities..530
Escape Characters 532
Unparsed Data..533
Comments 533
CDATA 533
Processing Instructions 534
Character References...534
Character Range 535
Whitespace..535
Document Type Definitions (DTDs) 535
DTD Basics 536
XML Schema 540
Schemas Versus DTDs...540
Schema Constraints 541
Features of XML Schema 542
Schema Vocabulary 543
Schema Examples 543
The Future of Schema Representation 548
XML Parsers...549
Xerces 549

Document Object Model (DOM) 549
The DOM Structure Model 549
Memory Management 551
Naming Conventions 552
DOM Objects 552
Simple API for XML (SAX) 553
Java API for XML Processing (JAXP) 556
XML Output 556
Cascading Style Sheets (CSS) 556
XSL 557
XSL Transformations (XSLT) 558
XSL Formatting Objects (XSL-FO) 558
XML Path Language (XPath) 558
XSLT Namespace 559
Style Sheet Structure 560
`stylesheet` Elements 560
Template Elements 563
Applying Style Sheets 564
XML Linking Language (XLink) 564
XLink Structure 565
XML Security 566
XML Key Management Specification (XKMS) 566
Security Assertion Markup Language (SAML) 566
Relationship Between XKMS and SAML 567
Summary 567

17 Validating the Application 569

Java and Testing 570
Involve Team Members Early 571
Quality Control Through Debugging 572
Debugging and Experience 572
Debugging Techniques 574
Test Without Ego 574
Step Away and Regroup 574
Adding Science to the Art of Debugging 575
Syntax Errors 578
Correcting an Error 579
Improving Reliability 581
The Importance of Being a Good Debugger 582
Testing and Development Phases 582
Alpha Phase 583
Beta Phase 583
FCS 584

Testing Methods and Techniques 584
Unit Testing 584
Stress Testing and Volume Data Generation 584
Code Complexity Analysis 584
Benchmarking/Performance Testing 584
Stability Testing 584
Regression Testing 585
Black Box Testing 585
White Box Testing 585
Usability Testing 585
Cross-Platform Testing 585
Security Testing 585
Installation Testing 585
Interrupt Testing 586
Parallel Processing 586
Test Coverage Analysis 586
Web Site Test Tools and Site Management Tools 586
Load and Performance Test Tools 587
Java Test Tools 595
Link Checking Tools 596
HTML Validators 597
Web Functional/Regression Test Tools 598
Web Site Security Test Tools 599
External Site Monitoring Services 600
Web Site Management Tools 601
Other Web Test Tools 602
Summary 603

18 Making the Application Perform 605

Overview 606
Writing High-Performance Applications 607
Sizing Factors 607
Performance Sizing 608
Component Design 608
Environmental Factors 610
Reducing Network Traffic 610
Coding Guidelines 611
Pool Management 612
J2EE Component Performance 615
Design and Performance 617
Preparing for Performance Tuning 618
Scope, Objectives, and Metrics 618
Load Testing 619
Profilers 620

Guide to Diagnosis and Cure 621
Low-Hanging Fruit 622
Deployment Strategies....................622
Improving Applet Download Speed 623
Packaging Images into One Class 623
Using JAR Files....................623
Thread Pooling 624
What Affects Server Performance?....................624
Central Processing Unit (CPU) 624
Volatile Storage (Memory) 625
Persistent Storage (Disk)....................625
Database Performance....................625
Database Monitoring and Tuning Tools 627
ShowPlan (SQL Server) or Explain Plan (Oracle) 627
INDEX Tuning Wizard 628
Oracle Tuning Pack 628
Oracle SQL_TRACE....................628
Optimizeit 628
Summary....................629

19 Deploying the Application 631

Java's Write Once, Run Anywhere Promise....................632
The Assembly Process 633
Assembly Overview 633
Assembling Applications and Components....................634
The Deployment Process 648
Deployment Using the J2EE Reference Implementation 649
Deployment Using the SilverStream Application Server 654
Deployment Using the BEA WebLogic Server....................660
Summary....................689

A Documentation for Sample Applications 691

SilverBooks....................692
Tour of the SilverBooks Site 693
Technologies Used in SilverBooks 699
E-mail Verification....................702
Internationalization 702
Java Pet Store 702
Technologies Used in Java Pet Store....................703
The Version of Java Pet Store That We Used 703
Files Provided 703
Running the Command Files....................704
Running the Java Pet Store Application 705
Summary....................707

B Related Tools 709

Development Tools 710
SilverStream eXtend Workbench 710
Artistic Systems' JCanvas Studio 711
Borland JBuilder 5....712
Compoze's Harmony Component Suite 714
Elixir IDE 715
Flashline.com's Component Manager....716
IBM VisualAge for Java 717
VA Assist Enterprise 718
Macromedia Dreamweaver UltraDev 719
Pramati Studio 2.5....720
Sitraka's JClass Enterprise Suite....722
WebGain Studio 4.5 Professional Edition....724
Application Servers....725
SilverStream Application Server....726
Allaire-Macromedia JRun 3.0....727
BEA WebLogic Server 6.1 727
Gemstone/J Application Server....728
IBM WebSphere 730
IONA iPortal Application Server 3.0 731
iPlanet Application Server....731
Pramati Java Application Server 732
Sitraka DeployDirector 733
Unify eWave Engine 734
Modeling and Object/Report Generation Tools 736
Cape Clear CapeConnect XML Business Server 736
Cerebellum eCom Integrator and Portal Integrator....737
Embarcadero Technologies' DBArtisan 738
Computer Associates' ERwin 4.0 738
HiT's Allora for Java....739
PointBase Network Server and Embedded Server 740
Rational Rose....740
Together ControlCenter....741
Elixir Report 742
InetSoft Style Report....742
Tidestone Technologies' Formula One iReporting Engine....743
Quadbase Systems' EspressChart 743
Messaging and XML Tools 744
FioranoMQ 5 Message Server....745
SonicMQ 745
SilverStream jBrokerMQ....746

Softwired's iBus//MessageServer 746
XERCES and XALAN 747
Java API for XML Processing 1.1 (JAXP) 748
Altova's XML Spy..748
Validation and Performance Monitoring Tools..748
VMGEAR's Optimizeit..749
ParaSoft's Jtest..750
RadView Software's WebLoad 751
Empirix Bean-test 752
Segue Software's SilkPilot 752
Sitraka Software's JProbe 753

C Quick Reference Material 755

J2EE APIs..756
Required APIs 756
Optional Packages 757
J2EE Software Development Kit (SDK) Installation Instructions......759
Installation for Windows 760
Installation for Linux..761
Common Installation Notes for All Platforms 763
Naming Conventions for J2EE 763
Required Access to the JNDI Naming Environment..763
Enterprise JavaBeans (EJB) References 768
Resource Manager Connection Factory 772
Resource Environment References 778
`UserTransaction` References 780

Index 783

About the Authors

Paul R. Allen is a principal of UCNY, Inc., an international consulting firm that helps Fortune 500 companies improve operations through the use of database and object technology. His e-mail address is `pallen@ucny.com`. He has been developing applications systems for over 15 years. He has been developing database applications for the last eight years, using SilverStream WEBLOGIC and WEBSPHERE and Java for Web development the past three years. (SilverStream is a J2EE certified application server.) Paul is a Certified SilverStream Trainer, WEBLOGIC and WEBSPHERE Developer, and FAE. His professional experience includes work with the financial, brokerage, pharmaceutical, and manufacturing industries. He specializes in transitioning clients to Web-based, object-oriented database technology. He has taught numerous courses in computing at Columbia University in New York. He has co-authored the following books: *PowerBuilder: A Guide To Developing Client/Server Applications* (McGraw-Hill, 1995), *Informix: Client/Server Application Development* (McGraw-Hill, 1997), *Informix: Universal Data Option* (McGraw-Hill, 1998), *SQL Server Developer's Guide* (IDG, 2000), and *SilverStream Success Volumes I and II* (SilverStream Journal Inc, 2000 & 2001). He has also written several *SilverStream Journal* articles. He a regular presenter at SilverSummit user conferences and the New York metropolitan area SilverStream user group. Over the past seven years, he has taught numerous courses and given many presentations on computing in several cities worldwide, including Los Angeles, San Deigo, Vienna, Paris, Berlin, Orlando, Nashville, New York, Washington, D.C., Copenhagen, Oslo, and Stockholm.

Joseph J. Bambara is a principal of UCNY, Inc. His e-mail address is `jbambara@ucny.com`. He has been developing applications systems for over 25 years including relational database development for the last 15 years and Java application server for Web development the past four years. He is a Certified SilverStream WEBLOGIC and WEBSPHERE Trainer, Developer, and FAE. His professional experience includes work with the financial, brokerage, manufacturing, medical, and entertainment industries. Mr. Bambara has a Bachelor's and a Master's degree in Computer Science. He also holds a Juris Doctorate in Law and has been admitted to the New York Bar. He has taught various computer courses for CCNY's School of Engineering. He has co-authored the following books: *PowerBuilder: A Guide To Developing Client/Server Applications* (McGraw-Hill, 1995), *Informix: Client/Server Application Development* (McGraw-Hill, 1997), *Informix: Universal Data Option* (McGraw-Hill, 1998), *SQL Server Developer's Guide* (IDG, 2000), and volumes I and II of *SilverStream Success* (SilverStream Journal Inc., 2000 & 2001). He has also written several *SilverStream Journal* articles. Over the past seven years, he has taught numerous courses and given many presentations for SilverStream and Sybase in several cities worldwide, including Los Angeles, San Diego, Vienna, Paris, Berlin, Orlando, Nashville, New York, Copenhagen, Oslo, and Stockholm.

Mark Ashnault is a Java consultant working for UCNY, Inc. He has been specializing in Java-based business applications, with emphasis on the SilverStream Application Server, Servlets, EJB, and JSP for the past two years. His background includes developing applications for client/server, Web, and SQL Server databases. He is a SilverStream Certified Developer and Instructor. Mark studied at Scranton University in Pennsylvania, attaining a Bachelor of Science in Computer Science.

Thomas Garben is a Java consultant working for UCNY, Inc. and is a principal of J-Class Solutions, Inc. He has been specializing in Java-based business applications, with emphasis on the SilverStream Application Server, Servlets, EJB, and JSP for the past five years. His background includes developing applications for client/server, Web, and SQL databases. He is a SilverStream, WebLogic and Precise Business Partner. Tom studied at SUNY in Freedonia and holds a Bachelor of Science in Physics and Mathematics. Tom also studied at SUNY in Buffalo, where he earned a Bachelor of Science degree in Electrical and Computer Engineering. Tom received a Master of Science in Electrical and Computer Engineering from the Polytechnic Institute in Brooklyn.

Ziyad Dean is a Java consultant working for UCNY, Inc. He has been specializing in Java-based business applications, with emphasis on the SilverStream Application Server, Servlets, EJB, and JSP for the past four years. His background includes developing applications for client/server, Web, and Oracle databases. He is a PowerBuilder Certified Developer and Instructor. Ziyad studied at Odessa University in Ukraine, where he earned a Bachelor of Science in Mathematics.

Sherry Smith resides in New York City and works for UCNY, Inc. She received her Bachelor of Science degree from the University of Wisconsin-Madison in 1992. She has a strong background in computer-aided design and has worked with a wide variety of computer tools used to publish technical manuscripts, books, and magazine articles. She has developed training material for Java, HTML, and XML. She has written several articles for *CoreBit News*, a corporate technology newsletter, and has been a technical editor for Paul Allen and Joe Bambara for the past 6 months. She is a member of MENSA.

Dedications

In memory of all the innocent people who lost their lives in the World Trade Center tragedy on September 11, 2001. We hope and pray that this never happens anywhere again.

To Martha, Francesca, Freddie, George, Olivia, Eden, Dakota, and Ethan
—Paul R. Allen

To Roseanne, Vanessa, and Michael
—Joseph J. Bambara

To my wife, Dawn, and my son, Connor. Thanks to my parents for dedicating their lives to raising a great family
—Mark Ashnault

To Ellen, Seth, Rachel, Bruce, June, Lynn, Gregory, Douglas, and Helen
—Thomas Garben

To my lovely wife, Natalie, and our children, Samir and Sarah
—Ziyad Dean

To Jack and Pat Smith
—Sherry Smith

Acknowledgments

I would like to thank Michael Stephens, Carol Ackerman, and our agent Chris Van Buren for presenting the opportunity to write this book. I would also like to thank Christina Smith, Matt Wynalda, and all of the people at Sams Publishing for their hard work and dedication in producing this book. Very special thanks to my co-author, Joseph J. Bambara, especially for his encouragement, strength, and perseverance, which make it possible to succeed at all of our endeavors.

Thanks to Gary Salamone and Bill Gillen at the Bank of New York Clearing and Don LaGuardia at PurchaseSoft for providing us with opportunities to work with them on great projects.

I would also like to thank Sandra and Goran Jovicic, Vicki and Larry Kramer, Lisa and Tom Jardine, Vicki DiSalvo, Sheila Ruddigan and Lenny Appleton, Kailash Chanrai, Jim Burns, Peter Naughton, and Ian Stokes for their friendship and support.

Thanks to Brian Holmes for his sound advice and for taking good care of my mother. Thanks to my mother, Carole, my sister, Lorisa, and the rest of the family for their never-ending love, optimism, and support. To my nieces, Francesca, Olivia, Eden, and

Dakota, and my nephews, Freddie, George, and Ethan, always believe in your dreams. Foremost, I would like to thank my wife, Martha, for being patient, loving, and supportive in our adventures.

Paul R. Allen
New York, New York

I would like to thank Michael Stephens, Carol Ackerman, and our agent Chris Van Buren for presenting the opportunity to write this book. I would also like to thank Christina Smith, Matt Wynalda, and all of the folks at Sams Publishing for their hard work and dedication in producing the book. Thanks to CNA Insurance (Shaati), Bank of New York Clearing (Gary Salamone and Bill Gillen), PurchaseSoft (Don LaGuardia) and Professor G. Schwartz for providing us with opportunities to develop our material. A very special thanks to my co-author Paul R. Allen, especially for his friendship and for being a great partner no matter what we try.

Thanks to my dad, Joseph, my mom, Carmela, my brothers, Vincent and Richard, my sister, Patricia, my father-in-law, Joseph, and the rest of my family who are always there when I need them. Foremost, I thank my wife, Roseanne, and my children, Vanessa and Michael, who are and have always been patient, loving, helpful, and encouraging no matter what I pursue.

Joseph J. Bambara
Greenvale, New York

First, I would like to thank Joseph Bambara and Paul Allen for giving me the opportunity to work on this book with them and for challenging me to grow both technically and personally. I would like to thank Sherry Smith for her careful reading and practical suggestions and Tom Garben for being my sounding board.

I would like to thank my parents, Nancy and William, who have always supported me and provided me with all the opportunities I could ask for. Thanks to my brothers, William and Robert, and my sister, Kimberly, for your guidance and encouragement. Thanks to Susan, Lisa, John, Billy, Brian, Carly, Kelly, Anthony, and Zachary, cousins, aunts, uncles, in-laws, and friends who have helped me in many different aspects of my development. Thanks to Bank of New York Clearing (Gary Salamone, Bill Gillen, Charlie Dugan, and Steve Tunney), CNA Insurance (Shaati and Mark), and Viacom (Brad Burke, Joe Leggio, and Trish Baer) for providing me with the opportunity to grow. Primarily, I would like to thank my wife for her support and patience as I worked on this book while we awaited the birth of our child. Dawn, thanks for being a great partner. Dawn gave birth to Connor Mark Ashnault on Monday, August 13 at 7:37 p.m. Mother and baby are doing great. Connor weighs 8 pounds 9 ounces and is 21 inches long.

Mark Ashnault
Greenbrook, New Jersey

I would like to take this opportunity to thank my co-authors Joseph J. Bambara and Paul R. Allen for inviting me to participate in this project. I consider it an honor to be able to work with two people who are held in such high regard in their field. I would also like to thank Sherry Smith for all of her help and the rest of the authors for their support and the team spirit they maintained for the duration of this project.

I would like to thank Peter Heller for sharing his extraordinary knowledge with me and for always being available to discuss the ever-changing directions of technology.

I would also like to thank Lenny Ilizarov for holding the business together while I was busy working on this book and Michael Grasso for his inspiration.

I would like to thank my Grandmother Helen and my late Grandfather Eddie for paying for my college books and my parents, June and Bruce, for their never-ending love and support, and for getting me that Commodore 64 computer for Christmas.

Most of all I would like to thank my wife, Ellen, for her love and support and our children, Seth and Rachel, for keeping me company while I worked in the "dungeon" night after night.

Thomas Garben
Scarsdale, New York

I would like to thank Paul Allen, Joe Bambara, and Sams Publishing for giving me the opportunity to write this book. I would also like to thank Sherry Smith for helping out with the editing and formatting of my chapters. Foremost, I would like to thank my wife, Natalie, and our children, Samir and Sarah, for allowing me the time to dedicate to this book.

Ziyad Dean
East Brunswick, New Jersey

I would like to thank Paul Allen and Joe Bambara for giving me the opportunity to contribute to this book. It has been an invaluable experience that has influenced multiple facets of my life. I would also like to thank Mark Ashnault and Tom Garben for the patience and kindness they exude every day. Additionally, I would like to thank everyone at Sams Publishing for their commitment and diligence in producing this book.

Special thanks to Alison McCarthy and Patty Moley for providing all the support, encouragement, and friendship that one could ever hope for. Lastly, I would like to thank all those who never doubted I could accomplish anything I set my mind to.

Sherry Smith
New York, New York

Tell Us What You Think!

As the reader of this book, *you* are our most important critic and commentator. We value your opinion and want to know what we're doing right, what we could do better, what areas you'd like to see us publish in, and any other words of wisdom you're willing to pass our way.

As an executive editor for Sams Publishing, I welcome your comments. You can fax, e-mail, or write me directly to let me know what you did or didn't like about this book—as well as what we can do to make our books stronger.

Please note that I cannot help you with technical problems related to the topic of this book, and that due to the high volume of mail I receive, I might not be able to reply to every message.

When you write, please be sure to include this book's title and the authors' names as well as your name and phone or fax number. I will carefully review your comments and share them with the authors and editors who worked on the book.

Fax: 317-581-4770

E-mail: `feedback@samspublishing.com`

Mail: Michael Stephens
Executive Editor
Sams Publishing
201 West 103rd Street
Indianapolis, IN 46290 USA

Introduction

Developing applications with *Java 2 Enterprise Edition (J2EE)* is much like developing other types of applications; however there are advantages. It is similar because the iterative steps of the developmental process are the same. The true advantage is that J2EE provides a process standard to accompany the database standard, SQL.

J2EE marks a point where a technology becomes a standard. Much like SQL for database development, the majority of development software vendors have embraced J2EE as a standard for developing Enterprise applications.

Scope

We, the authors of this book, are consultants serving as computer-based solution providers for the financial sector in New York, with an average of 12 years experience each. As technologies advance, we are required to absorb new technology as well as apply it.

In this book, we will try to address J2EE on many levels, providing a hands-on practical guide for building Web-enabled and distributed enterprise systems using J2EE.

The Organization of This Book

The book begins with a background on Java technology and a description of the enterprise system development process. It then looks at the tasks required for J2EE application development and covers the key technologies, including Java Naming and Directory Interface (JNDI), Lightweight Directory Access Protocol (LDAP), Java Database Connectivity (JDBC), Java Servlets, JavaServer Pages (JSP), Model-View-Controller, and Enterprise JavaBeans. The next several chapters cover specialized components of J2EE applications, focusing primarily on JavaMail, Java Message Service (JMS), and the eXtensible Markup Language (XML). The last few chapters discuss many of the issues involved with validating and deploying an application. The appendixes consist of reference materials that support the content of this book (including instruction for configuring the commercial and sample software used with this book) and provide additional references that you can use to augment the book's material. A more detailed description of the content of each chapter follows:

Chapter 1, "Java, Distributed Computing, and J2EE," begins with a background on Java. The chapter talks about current requirements for Web application development and also covers the J2EE Specification and Certification tests, which are used to verify compatibility of the vendor's platform. The chapter summary looks at how J2EE applications are packaged, introducing the sample applications that are studied in the remainder of the book.

Chapter 2, "The Design and Development of a J2EE Application," begins with an overview of the J2EE Architecture and then moves into an examination of the development methodology and process. It covers the development environment including the various *IDE (Integrated Development Environment)* tools available today. It covers the security aspects of J2EE applications as well as the various roles required when designing, building, assembling, and deploying a J2EE application.

Chapter 3, "Designing the J2EE Application," begins by discussing the history of modeling tools, including database, process, and object modeling tools. It continues by examining why modeling is important and how well modeling and Java fit together. The chapter looks at how EJBs and other types of classes can be generated from a model. It also examines the models utilized in the sample applications.

Chapter 4, "Task List for Building J2EE Applications," is, as its title suggests, a task list that can be used when starting a J2EE development project. The chapter covers the steps involved in establishing access to the database and developing *Data Definition Language (DDL)* and *Data Manipulation Language (DML)*. It covers the steps involved in building the business logic and data access of an application, including utility classes, session beans, and entity beans. It covers the mapping of the navigation and flow of the application, including the use of Struts, XML files, Servlets, and JSP pages.

Chapter 5, "Build Resource Access: JNDI and LDAP," describes naming services in general and *Java Naming and Directory Interface (JNDI)* in particular. It discusses the architecture and interfaces of JNDI, providing explanations and examples that demonstrate how a distributed application's components can locate one another using the JNDI. Additionally, the chapter introduces directory services, discussing the *Lightweight Directory Access Protocol (LDAP)* in detail.

Chapter 6, "Build Data Access: JDBC," examines *Java Database Connectivity (JDBC)* technology, an integral part of the Java Platform. This chapter discusses JDBC in terms of the Core package, including driver types, database connections, processing query results, mapping SQL types to Java, and getting information about the database. The chapter also discusses the JDBC 2.0 Optional Package API, including Database Naming via JNDI, connection pools, distributed transactions, RowSets, and advanced data types. The chapter also introduces code examples using JDBC within the SilverStream Application Server, including SilverStream Connection pooling and accessing JDBC from a session bean in the SilverStream Application Server.

Chapter 7, "Build Control Flow: Servlets," covers Java Servlets, which are currently a very popular choice for the construction of interactive Web applications. This chapter introduces Java Servlets, discussing their role in the J2EE framework for enterprise Web application development and deployment. The chapter looks into the servlet API, focusing on building Java Servlets to generate responses to HTTP requests.

Chapter 8, "JavaServer Pages: Introduction," introduces the *JavaServer Page (JSP)*, beginning with an explanation of what they are and the architecture in which they live. The chapter covers the variety of models in which JSPs can be used, including Model 1 and Model 2. The chapter covers the Model-View-Controller architecture, with the View portion relating to the JavaServer Page. The chapter also compares a JSP to a Java Servlet.

Chapter 9, "JavaServer Pages: Practical Development with Tag Libraries," covers the syntax of a JSP page, including object scope, implicitly created objects, comments, declarations, expressions, scriptlets, and directives. The chapter covers the steps required to create a JSP, including those that use JavaBean components. The chapter also looks at exception handling and HTML forms processing. The chapter concludes with an examination of tag libraries, which are encapsulations of behavior that can be reused on many pages.

Chapter 10, "Building the User Interface to the Application," covers the user interface aspects of the sample applications used in the book. The chapter also provides additional information with respect to the Model-View-Controller and how it is implemented within the tag libraries of Struts.

Chapter 11, "Enterprise JavaBeans: Introduction," begins with an overview of *Enterprise JavaBeans (EJB)* and distributed programming. It demonstrates how EJBs fit into the distributed computing architecture and how objects can be organized into appropriate package hierarchies. The chapter introduces the EJB container, EJB session beans, EJB entity beans, and EJB message-driven beans. It examines the attributes of an EJB, including persistence, state, and transactional capability. The chapter also covers the various roles (developer, assembler, and deployer) involved in the creation and deployment of EJBs.

Chapter 12, "Enterprise JavaBeans: Building Session Beans," concentrates on the steps and issues involved with building EJB session beans. This includes a comparison of stateful and stateless implementations of a session bean. This chapter takes the reader through the creation of the bean and its supporting Home and Remote interfaces. The chapter also provides example code that calls a session bean.

Chapter 13, "Enterprise JavaBeans: Building Entity Beans," looks at the steps and issues involved with building EJB entity bean. This includes defining the entity bean, creating a primary key class, creating the entity bean class, implementing the Home and Remote interfaces, and implementing the methods for the entity bean. The chapter compares *bean-managed persistence (BMP)* with *container-managed persistence (CMP)* and then discusses the packaging and deployment of an entity bean.

Chapter 14, "Messaging with E-mail: JavaMail," gives an overview of messaging in general before covering the specific and major capabilities of the JavaMail API. The chapter covers the JavaMail architecture and the major classes involved with sending and receiving mail. In doing so, the chapter covers service providers, the *Java Activation Framework (JAF)*, and the Message and MimeMessage objects.

Chapter 15, "Messaging with Applications: Java Message Service (JMS)," examines the *Java Message Service (JMS)*, an API that provides a common way for Java programmers to create, send, receive, and read an enterprise messaging system's messages. The chapter covers messaging basics as well as the JMS components required to produce and consume messages. The chapter also provides many real-world examples of Point-to-Point and Publish/Subscribe JMS applications.

Chapter 16, "Data Exchange with XML," discusses the fundamentals of *eXtensible Markup Language (XML)*, including the structure of an XML document, parsed data, processing instructions, *Document Type Definitions (DTDs)*, schemas, and displaying XML data using style sheets. The chapter also covers the *Document Object Model (DOM)*, *Simple API for XML (SAX)*, and parsers for both formats.

Chapter 17, "Validating the Application," discusses the fundamentals of testing. Topics include problem determination and resolution, the items that should be considered when locating problems, and some of the tools available for testing software.

Chapter 18, "Making the Application Perform," examines the performance and tuning aspects of an application, beginning with the steps involved in preparation for performance tuning. It includes a guide for diagnosing and curing performance issues. It gives some performance hints for Java Servlets, JSPs, and EJBs. The chapter also discusses what factors affect Java performance as well as what Java syntax to avoid. Some examples of database monitoring and tuning tools are also discussed.

Chapter 19, "Deploying the Application," examines the various steps with deploying a J2EE application to a J2EE application server. This includes discussing Java's *Write Once, Run Anywhere (WORA)* aspects. All the archive types are discussed, including JAR, WAR, CAR, and EAR. The chapter looks at the XML deployment descriptor, which is used for defining resource references and the XML deployment plan, which is used for resolving resource references. The chapter also looks at the tools used to deploy a J2EE application, including a comparison of a few of the J2EE application servers available.

Appendix A, "Documentation for Sample Applications," supplies information and documentation for the sample applications used in this book.

Appendix B, "Related Tools," consists of information on third-party software vendors and the tools that they provide.

Appendix C, "Quick Reference Material," serves as a reference guide, including references for J2EE APIs, J2EE setup, naming conventions, and other guidelines.

CHAPTER 1

Java, Distributed Computing, and J2EE

In This Chapter

- Background on Java *12*
- Companies Must Re-Invent Themselves for the Web *14*
- Requirements of Web Architecture *20*
- Web Application Life Cycle *22*
- J2EE APIs and Certification *30*
- XML and J2EE *32*
- The Packaging of J2EE Applications *38*
- Applications Studied in This Book *39*

Often in the world of corporate information technology a new development paradigm arises:

- In the 60s, IBM brought us a multitasking operating system called OS MVT/MFT. For the first time, an enterprise could run multiple batch jobs on the same machine. This heralded the beginning of what we affectionately called the "batch night cycle." All transactions for an entire firm, whatever the business happened to be, for example, brokerage/trades, would be collected daily and then keyed into punch cards. This information was then fed to one or more of these batch COBOL jobs, which would record the information to create the firm's "books and records." This was fine, but the information was always out of date by a day.
- In the 70s, IBM brought us online data entry. This functionality was made possible by software called CICS and VSAM. CICS provided for terminal access and entry of data. VSAM provided a way to store the data with indexes and keys to facilitate access. This was fine, and now the information was fairly up-to-date, even intraday.
- In the 80s, Microsoft improved on the IBM "greenscreen" and brought us the Personal Computer equipped with a mouse and a personal drive space for storing information locally. Additionally, a host of other vendors (including IBM) brought us SQL. Because it was done by committee, SQL became the de facto standard for working with data and databases.
- In the 90s, Microsoft popularized the client server platform. This seemed like a good idea, and it certainly provided an example for so called "user-friendly" ways of combining business transactions and computers. The problem here was distribution. If an organization had 1000 workstations, it would be difficult if not impossible to maintain each of these workstations at the same level of software.
- In the 2000s, Sun Microsystems (symbol:SUNW) and other vendors brought us the Java 2 Enterprise Edition (J2EE). Here again, a committee has created a standard way to build business processes that run on most any platform. This is powerful because these computer classes are portable and interoperable.

From a development perspective, the major revolutions involved only SQL and J2EE because these are standards to which most everyone has adhered.

Just as SQL defines the standard for querying multiuser relational databases, The Java 2 Platform, Enterprise Edition (J2EE) defines the standard for developing multitier enterprise applications. J2EE, much like the SQL paradigm, simplifies enterprise applications by basing them on standardized, modular components, by providing a complete set of services to those components, and by handling many details of application behavior automatically, without complex programming.

The Java 2 Platform, Enterprise Edition takes advantage of many features of standard Java 2 such as Write Once, Run Anywhere portability; the JDBC API for database access; CORBA technology for interaction with existing enterprise resources; and a security model. Building on this base, Java 2 Enterprise Edition adds support for Enterprise JavaBeans components, the Java Servlets API, JavaServer Pages and XML technology. The J2EE standard includes complete specifications and compliance tests to ensure portability of applications across the wide range of existing enterprise systems capable of supporting J2EE. This portability was also a key factor in the success of SQL.

Standards such as SQL and J2EE help enterprises gain competitive advantage by facilitating quick development and deployment of custom applications. Whether they are internal applications for staff use or Internet applications for customer or vendor services, this timely development and deployment of an application is key to success.

Portability and scalability are also essential for long-term viability. Our company has ported a single SQL application database using five different vendors: Oracle, Sybase, Informix, MS SQL Server, and IBM DB/2. Enterprise applications must scale from small working prototypes and test cases to complete 24×7, enterprise-wide services that are accessible by tens, hundreds, or even thousands of clients simultaneously. 24×7 is especially important in the global finance market.

Multitier applications are difficult to architect. They require merging a variety of skill sets and resources, perhaps also including legacy data and legacy code. In today's heterogeneous environment, enterprise applications must integrate services from a variety of vendors with a diverse set of application models and other standards. Existing daily cycle applications at Merrill Lynch use all of the database vendors in addition to legacy databases such as IDMS, ADABAS, IMS, and a host of others. Industry experience shows that integrating these resources can take up to 50% of application development time. As a single standard that can sit on top of a wide range of existing enterprise systems—database management systems, transaction monitors, naming and directory services, and more.

J2EE attempts to break the barriers inherent to current enterprise systems. The unified J2EE standard permits an API set which in full maturity (perhaps by 2003) will wrap and embrace existing resources required by multitier applications with a unified, component-based application model. This will initiate the next generation of components, tools, systems, and applications for solving the strategic requirements of the enterprise. See Figure 1.1. for a glimpse of how a J2EE server fits into the frame of a net-enabled enterprise application. The good news is that it can salvage and extend life to legacy systems that have been in production and are sensitive to change.

Although Sun Microsystems invented the Java programming language, the J2EE standard represents a collaboration between leaders from throughout the enterprise software arena. Partners include OS and database management system providers IBM and Microsoft, middleware and tool vendors BEA and SilverStream, and vertical market applications and component developers such as UCNY, Inc. Sun has defined a robust, flexible platform that can be implemented on the wide variety of existing enterprise systems currently available. This platform supports the range of applications IT organizations need to keep their enterprises competitive.

A major part of the J2EE architecture is Enterprise JavaBeans (EJBs). That is because the EJB server-side component model simplifies development of middleware components that are transactional, scalable, and portable.

Consider transaction management. In the past, developers have had to either write and maintain transaction management code, or rely on third-party transaction management systems, generally provided through proprietary, vendor-specific APIs. This second-generation Web development helped to promote Java and highlighted the need for a standard. In contrast, Enterprise JavaBeans technology enables components to participate in transactions, including distributed transactions. The EJB server itself handles the underlying transaction management details, while developers focus specifically on the business purpose of the objects and methods. EJB components can be deployed on any platform and operating system that supports the Enterprise JavaBeans standard. The list of these J2EE-compliant application servers is growing and can be checked at the Sun Web site (`http://java.sun.com/j2ee/`).

FIGURE 1.1
The J2EE Application Server is at the heart of e-business.

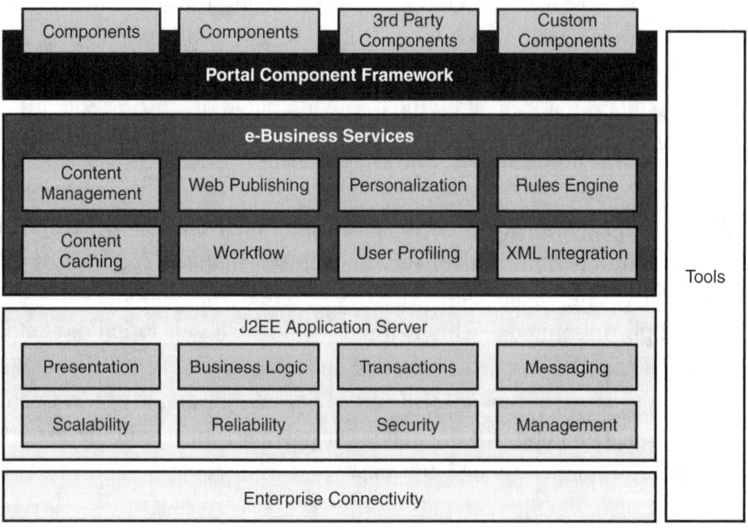

Scheduled for release in the fall of 2001, J2EE 1.3 defines the current standard for developing and deploying enterprise applications. With the latest versions of the now familiar J2EE 1.2 API's for Enterprise JavaBeans (EJB), JavaServer Pages (JSP), and Java Servlet API component technologies, the existing J2EE platform is enhanced. In addition, J2EE 1.3 adds support for the J2EE Connector Architecture, the Java API for XML Parsing (JAXP), and the Java Authentication and Authorization Service (JAAS) API. J2EE 1.3 also increases the level of support for the Java Message Service (JMS) API from optional to required.

In addition to supporting JavaBeans (which is a Java 2, Standard Edition technology), J2EE provides three kinds of components: Web, Enterprise JavaBean, and Client. Web applications consist of Web components and other resources bundled together.

One type of Web component is a Java servlet. Java servlets extend the functionality of a Web server, much like Common Gateway Interface (CGI) programs. Servlets are a better choice than CGI programs because, unlike CGI programs, they are portable (because they are written in Java), scale well, and are easy to maintain. Servlets describe how to process an HTTP request and generate a response. You can use them to deliver dynamic content.

Another Web component is the JavaServer Page (JSP). Like servlets, JSPs describe how to process and respond to HTTP requests. Unlike servlets, which are written in Java, JSPs are text-based documents that include a combination of HTML and JSP tags, Java code, and other information.

JSPs and servlets both solve the same problem, but JSPs have the advantage of separating presentation (expressed in HTML) from application logic, coded in Java. JSPs can include limited imprint declarative statements which can invoke java beans or tag library objects to perform server side processing. Tag libraries can include Java components which can perform central flow logic or access to build page content. With servlets, the presentation and application logic are mixed together in the same Java file. By using JSPs, UI developers can work on presentation of information while Java programmers separately develop the application's logic.

To separate the business model from the presentation, a J2EE application's business logic resides in Enterprise JavaBeans (also called enterprise beans). Enterprise beans provide the link between the presentation of your application, viewed in a Web browser, and the transactions which access and modify data that is in your back-end enterprise information systems.

Session beans implement logic that is specific to one client session. For example, in a shopping cart application, you would maintain a client's state, such as the items in a client's shopping cart, in a session bean. Session beans are not shared across clients.

Entity beans represent persistent business data, such as a row in a relational database. Entity beans are object models—they encapsulate the data along with the methods that act on the data. Entity beans can be shared across application clients and persist as long as the data they represent persists.

Although most J2EE applications will use a standard Web browser as the primary or sole client, J2EE also supports the clients in the form of applets as well as standalone Java application clients. These clients execute a Java Virtual Machine on the client machine. Java applications and applets run in the client space. Class file transport only occurs for initial download.

Background on Java

Seven years into its life, Java is now the acceptable and mature technology most commonly behind the strategic plans for the enterprise. After years in which Java development seemed to be reserved primarily for Internet applications, the bigger firms in the corporate world are using Java as the language of choice over C and COBOL for most of their new development including but not limited to messaging, back end night cycle functions like database repair and warehousing, and data capture from external data feeds.

Java's appeal lies not only in its affinity for the network and distributed computing (although intranet, extranet, and Internet applications remain the major focus of Java development) but in Java's other qualities such as ease of programming and cross-platform capabilities—the *Write Once, Run Anywhere* promise.

But even as corporate developers increasingly opt for Java, some concern remains about the readiness of the environment for J2EE. We should remember that SQL, another standard, also required some early pioneering to reach maturity.

Widespread Capabilities for Application Development

A large portion of the appeal of Java is the ease it allows in creating Web-based, self-service applications that enable customers to do the work and perform other tasks over the Internet through a browser. Most applications are HTML on the Web-server front end and Java servlets on the application-server back end that run on the company's Web server.

However, Java isn't just for e-business, either. Many organizations with a large user base are reengineering client server because the deployment/distribution is cumbersome and expensive. Some are developing Java applications for internal use, occasionally deploying Java clients to employee desktops.

Many issues stand in the way of J2EE adoption by corporate application-development groups. These include concerns about the maturity of the development environment, the need to find or train more Java developers, the complexity of Enterprise JavaBeans (EJB), and the need to upgrade to the new generation of J2EE application servers to take full advantage of the technology.

An undercurrent of concern also exists about what Microsoft is doing with its .NET initiative and what impact, if any, those actions will have on a development group's Java plans.

"If you believe all the hype, Java for the enterprise is here now," said Mike Gilpin, vice president and research leader at Giga Information Group. "But if you look at the fine print, you'll see that it comes close, but it's not quite all the way there." See the article "A Framework for Evaluating and Choosing Application Integration Solutions"; it can be procured from `http://www.simc-inc.org/meetings98-99/Apr20-1999/gilpin/`.

The fine print, however, doesn't appear to be discouraging Java adoption, judging from the J2EE application server market. Giga projects the application server market will reach $1.64 billion in 2000 and $9 billion by 2003, up from about $585 million in 1999.

Java Is the Glue for Application Development

J2EE application servers are key to developing and deploying scalable enterprise Java applications. Application servers provide infrastructure to execute and maintain business-critical applications, especially e-business applications. J2EE defines the programming model and provides underlying services such as security, transaction management, and messaging to enable developers to quickly build networked Java applications and effectively deploy them in the distributed world.

"The Enterprise JavaBeans component model and associated Java 2 Enterprise Edition standards will dominate the application server market and drive a potential market growth rate of almost 180 percent year to year," Gilpin said. A rush to deploy the latest J2EE application servers in the business environment is fueling this growth. Observers count upward of 200 application servers being offered today, with more appearing weekly. However, Gilpin said he expects only a few to dominate the market.

"We see potentially as few as two or three companies each claiming 20 percent or more of the market and several smaller vendors that specialize in market niches claiming less than 10 percent each," he said.

Most industry experts believe the J2EE application servers likely to emerge on top include BEA Systems' WebLogic, IBM's WebSphere, Sun's own iPlanet, and Sybase's EAserver. Additional players include Allaire Corp., Bluestone Software Inc., and SilverStream Software Inc. More specialized players include Iona Technologies, which provides a J2EE application server with strong CORBA object-broker capabilities, and Enhydra, an open-source application server.

The application server is emerging as the focal point of the new distributed, networked, corporate development. The application server acts as middleware, making the necessary back-end connections, running business logic and messaging, as well as managing functions such as transaction management and security.

The latest application servers are adding support for wireless computing with built-in transcoding and integrated XML capabilities.

You can build distributed applications without an application server, but you'll end up building much of the functionality it would otherwise provide by yourself. For example, one of our UCNY, Inc. (`www.ucny.com`) clients has Lotus Domino as its Web server. It has no application server.

"We've already built a lot of the functionality we'd get in an application server," reasoned the application manager.

The company is now considering acquiring IBM's WebSphere J2EE application server.

WebSphere is the most controversial of the leading J2EE application servers. The controversy revolves around IBM's decision not to seek formal J2EE certification for the product, a business decision reflecting the dynamics of the industry as much as a technical issue.

From a practical point of view, IBM's J2EE customizations provide backward compatibility with legacy IBM Corp. systems, better enterprise scalability, and better management across diverse systems environments, essentially building on IBM's historic strengths in legacy enterprise computing.

In any event, J2EE will be given a fair shot, as we see many major application server vendors (IBM notwithstanding) hastily moving to J2EE certify their products.

Companies Must Re-Invent Themselves for the Web

In any market economy, the rules of competition define who wins and who loses—this is true of countries, businesses, and people. In the Internet Economy, where knowledge, information, and time are the prevailing currencies of competition, a new set of rules is emerging. These reflect the basic nature of the Internet Economy. As it is based on technology standards, the Internet Economy promotes broad and massive market participation while encouraging market anarchy. These rules are becoming tenets of competitive success and guideposts to prosperity for companies and people in market economies.

The prevailing model of competition in the Internet Economy is more like a web of interrelationships than the hierarchical, command-and-control model of the Industrial Economy. Unlike the value chain, which rewarded exclusivity, the Internet Economy is inclusive and has low barriers to entry. Just like an ecosystem in nature, activity in the Internet Economy is self-organizing. The process of natural selection is centered around profit to companies and value to customers. Development standards like J2EE have been selected and are evolving. As J2EE evolves, both technologically and in population, it will be even easier and more likely for countries, companies, and individuals to participate in the Internet Economy. The Internet has $1 trillion in technical infrastructure in place, ready and available for anyone to use at any time—free of charge, so far. That's why new ideas and ways of doing things can come from anywhere at any time in the Internet Economy. The old rules don't work anymore. The Internet Ecosystem is the new business model of the Internet Economy.

The quality of an ecosystem determines the potential of advancing the standard of living for a country, the shareholder value of a company, and the participation of individuals in the economy. Some companies take advantage of the Internet as a business medium. They have developed a qualitative formula for measuring the quality of an ecosystem. The Internet Quotient self-assessment test is a measure of an organization's potential to create and leverage the Internet Ecosystem. Based on the book *Net Ready* by Amir Hartman and John Sifonis, IQ Expertise self-assessment tool is a qualitative measure for determining your business potential in the Internet Economy. By responding to a series of 20 Internet Business-related statements you can determine your own Internet Quotient (IQ), consisting of your

- Overall Expertise
- Critical Success Factors
- Leadership
- Ability to Govern Your Industry
- Organizational Competency
- Technology

Visit the site `http://www.netreadiness.com` for more details. The IQ test is the product of two metrics: operations ecosystem, or how a company uses the Internet to optimize its internal operations, and market ecosystem, or a company's ability to expand and create value for the entire ecosystem. The text correlates with the most important measures by which Wall Street assesses the fitness of a company to compete successfully on the Internet: return on invested capital (ROIC). It is a blueprint for success in the Internet Economy of how well people will live in countries, how much value in the marketplace companies can build, what people should look for where they work, and what skills they should learn. To survive, business must measure up with respect to their Web IQ.

Companies Increasingly Need the Internet to Compete

Over the next ten years virtually every business transaction will be conducted over the Internet. To do so on a grand scale, standards will be critical. The success of J2EE is important. This will ensure that the Internet is the most cost-effective media to promote the services of your business. Conducting your business with a user-friendly, reliable, speedy, and attractive set of Web pages supported by reliable "back end" business logic and transactions makes a difference in the success of your business.

The entire business must be Internet enabled. The business site must engage the customer and enable them to transact without the necessity of human interaction. Moreover, it will feed the organization's "fulfillment" engine as well as provide a place to go for post-transaction services (see Figure 1.2).

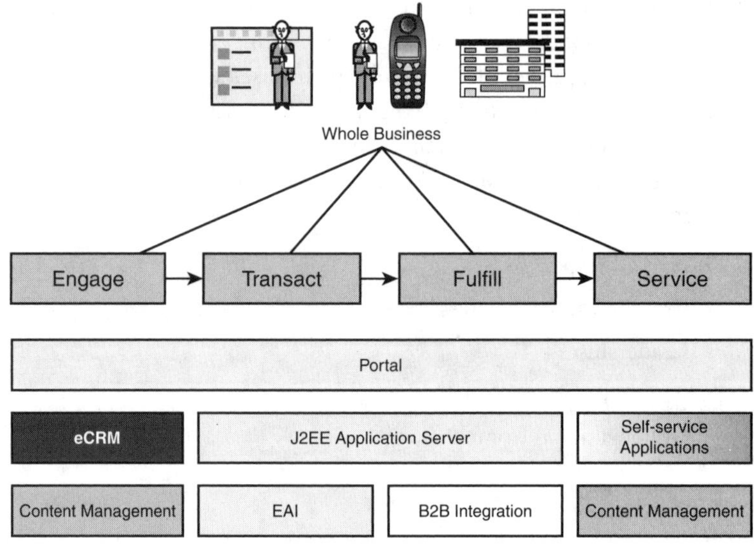

FIGURE 1.2
The e-business must provide Internet access to the whole business.

Corporations will need development standards such as J2EE to facilitate the construction of Web sites that clearly communicate the business objectives of its clients, whether they want to direct functionality to local, national, or international markets.

Roles are now more important. The marketing, technical, and graphic design personnel must work together to ensure that the Web pages not only meet your business needs but that they also maintain a perfect balance between performance and professional graphic work. The design of each component must follow a standard such as J2EE to ensure that the end product looks professional, loads faster, and effectively communicates your business objectives to the world.

Challenges of Application Development for the Enterprise

Timing has always been a critical factor to adopting new technologies, but the accelerated pace inherent in a virtual, information-driven business model has put even greater emphasis on response times. To leverage Internet economics, it is imperative not only to project, build, and display enterprise systems, but to do so repeatedly and in a timely manner, with frequent updates to both information and services. Just as the SQL standard facilitated data access, widespread acceptance and inherited experience with the J2EE standard will make it easier to construct enterprise systems. Therefore, the principal challenge is one of keeping up with the Internet's hyper-competitive pace while maintaining and leveraging the value of existing business systems. In this environment, timeliness is absolutely critical in gaining and maintaining a competitive edge. A number of factors can enhance or impede an organization's capability to deliver custom enterprise applications quickly and to maximize their value over their lifetime. Hopefully, IT development with J2EE will progress quickly so that the RAD (Rapid Application Development) capability we grew fond of in client/server will be present for the Internet.

Increasing Programmer Productivity

The ability to develop and deploy applications is a key to success in the information economy. Applications must go quickly from prototype to production, and must continue evolving even after they are deployed.

Productivity, therefore, is vital to responsive application development. J2EE provides application development teams with a set of standard APIs, that is, the means to access the services required by multitier applications, and standard ways to support a variety of clients. This can contribute to both responsiveness and flexibility.

In contrast to data access that is standardized and stabilized by SQL, a destabilizing factor in Internet and other distributed computing applications is the divergence of programming models. Historically (in Web terms), technologies such as HTML and CGI have provided a front-end mechanism for distributing dynamic content, while back-end systems such as transaction processors are based on IBM CICS, Tuxedo, IBM MQ, Lotus Notes, and other access systems for data. These technologies present a diversity of non-standard programming models based on proprietary architectures.

With no single application model, it can be difficult for teams to communicate application requirements effectively and productively. As a result, the process of architecting applications becomes more complex. What's more, the skill sets required to integrate these technologies aren't well organized for effective division of labor.

Another complicating factor in application development time is the choice of clients. Although many applications can be distributed to Web browser clients through static or dynamically generated HTML, others may need to support a specific type of client, or to support several types of clients simultaneously (for example, WAP). The programming model should support a variety of client configurations with minimal consequence to basic application architecture or the core business logic of the application.

J2EE enables development to be role oriented. Components are built by one group, assembled by another, and deployed by still another.

Ability to Respond to Consumer Demand

Imagine a multilocation retail business trying to increase its customer base by a factor of 10. How much time and effort would be expended on remodeling storefronts, building new warehouses, and so on, to keep up? Realistically, constant rework would impact their ability to serve the customers.

This holds for businesses in the information economy as well. The ability for applications to scale easily to accommodate growth is the key to achieving the goals. To scale effectively, systems require mechanisms for efficient management of system resources and services such as database connections and transactions. They need access to features such as automatic load balancing without any effort on the part of the application developer. Applications should be able to run on any server appropriate to anticipated client volumes and to easily switch server configurations when the need arises. J2EE-compliant application servers such as WebLogic and SilverStream provide these features in the form of database pooling, server clustering, and fail-over functionality.

Legacy Systems More Easily Integrate When Using Standards

In many enterprises we work with, the data of value to organizations, also called "books and records," has been collected over the years by existing information systems. The programming investment resides in applications on those same systems. The business rules, the procedures, and Y2K code all work, perform the business functionality properly, and cost a great deal of time and money to produce. The challenge for developers of enterprise applications is how to reuse and capitalize on this value by betting on middleware, which can converse with the legacy systems.

It is time for a systems development standard such as J2EE to help application developers by providing standard ways to access middle-tier and back-end services such as database management systems and transaction monitors.

Standards Promote Competition and Choices

RAD client/server development environments advance programmer productivity by obviating and facilitating the assembly of software components. Eventually, as J2EE matures, Integrated Development Environments (IDEs) will resemble their client/ server counterparts. The remaining challenge will be deployment. Application developer productivity requires the capability to mix and match solutions to come up with the optimum configuration for the task at hand. As the vendor shakeout continues, freedom of choice in enterprise application development should soon extend from servers to tools to components.

As vendors adhere to the J2EE standard, choices among server products will give an organization the ability to select configurations tailored to their application requirements. Much like SQL, the J2EE standard provides the capability to move quickly and easily from one configuration to another (SQL: Sybase DB converted to ORACLE), as internal and external demand requires.

Access to the appropriate tools for the job is another important choice. Development teams should be able to adopt new tools as new needs arise, including tools from server vendors and third-party tool developers. What's more, each member of a development team should have access to the tools most appropriate to their skill set and contribution.

Finally, developers should be able to choose from a ready market of off-the-shelf application components to take advantage of external expertise and to enhance development productivity. J2EE standardization over the coming years will advance systems development just as SQL advanced database development. See Appendix B, "Related Tools," for a survey and review of the tools currently available.

What About Security?

Somewhat ironically, making your systems and data available to extract their value can jeopardize that very value. Ultimately, enterprise technology departments have been able to maintain a relatively high level of control over the environment of both servers and clients, but with a price. When information assets are projected into less-protected environments, it becomes increasingly important to maintain tight security over the most sensitive assets, while allowing seemingly unencumbered access to others.

One of the difficulties in integrating disparate systems is providing a unified security model. Single sign-on across internal application and asset boundaries is important to creating a positive user experience with the applications. Security must be compatible with existing mechanisms. In cases where customers need to access secure information, the mechanisms must maintain high security (and user confidence) while remaining as unobtrusive and transparent as possible.

Requirements of Web Architecture

The Web architecture required for J2EE again is somewhat analogous to the architecture required to run vendor-based SQL database servers. The same qualities of performance, reliability, and security must be present for Web application servers to provide a host for an application.

The Speed to Compete

Speed is key. The competition will win out every time if it is able to provide faster response to the client. The user can click away to a competitor if a response is too slow. This is a difficult task because the user base can change rapidly. Not only are we concerned with domestic customers and business hours, we must consider the effects of globalization. J2EE application servers need to be efficient and scalable. These qualities will pare down the field to only those venders who can provide the speed to handle a local customer base with thousands of simultaneous hits.

Service Availability

Users want the application to be available 24×7. This is the attraction of doing business on the Web. Users don't have to worry about the doors being closed after hours. Whatever is convenient to them should be available. Additionally, users want to be able to speak to customer service representatives without having to wait until Monday. In addition to general availability, the reliability of the application server and the application software it runs is critical. There should be no downtime. The business depends on the application being up and ready to serve. J2EE application server vendors must provide reliable server configurations (clustering) as well as safe and clear fail-over procedures. J2EE application server vendors also must consider privacy issues. They must be able to maintain passwords and log-ins and to hide sensitive data. The data must be tamper proof, and they must be able to allow for encrypted communication for sensitive portions of the business transactions.

Connecting to Existing Data

Having been part of the development of large scale mainframe systems to maintain the books and records of large enterprises such as Merrill Lynch, Goldman Sachs, Phillip Morris, and most of the banks located in New York, it is easy for me to understand why most of these systems are still in operation 25 years later.

Specialized access to enterprise resource planning and mainframe systems such as IBM's CICS and IMS will be provided in future versions of J2EE through the Connector architecture. Because each of these systems is highly complex and specialized, each requires unique tools and support to ensure utmost simplicity to application developers. As J2EE evolves, enterprise beans will be able to combine the use of connector access objects and service APIs with middle-tier business logic to accomplish their business functions (see Figure 1.3).

FIGURE 1.3
J2EE combines presentation and business processes as well as enterprise connectivity.

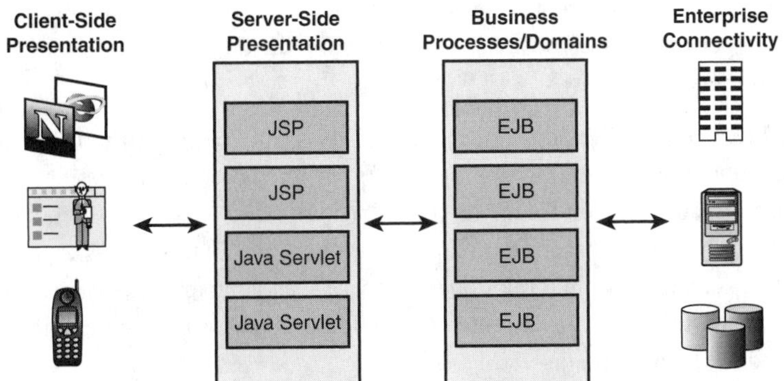

Expanded User Definition: Customers, Employees, and Partners

In the past, a desktop was the sole means of interfacing with an enterprise system. Those days are gone. Users today want to connect from virtually anywhere. The access begins during their commute and might continue through the workday and while traveling to remote business sites.

Flexible User Interaction

J2EE provides choices for graphical user interfaces across a company's intranet or on the World Wide Web. Clients can run on desktops, laptops, PDAs, cell phones, and other devices. Pure client-side user interfaces can use standard HTML and Java applets.

Support for simple HTML means quicker prototypes and support for a broader range of clients. Additionally, J2EE supports automatic download of the Java Plug-In to add applet support where it's lacking. J2EE also supports standalone Java application clients.

For server-side deployment of dynamic content, J2EE supports both the Java Servlets API and JavaServer Pages (JSP) technology. The Java Servlets API enables developers to easily implement server-side behaviors that take full advantage of the power of the rich Java API. JavaServer Pages technology combines the ubiquity of HTML with the power of server-side scripting in the Java programming language. The JSP 1.0 specification supports static templates, dynamic HTML generation, and custom tags.

Flexible Business Component Model

Since its introduction, Enterprise JavaBeans (EJB) technology has developed significant momentum in the middleware marketplace. It enables a simplified approach to multitier application development, concealing application complexity and enabling the component developer to focus on business logic. J2EE is the natural evolution of Enterprise JavaBeans technology.

EJB technology gives developers the ability to model the full range of objects useful in the enterprise by defining two distinct types of EJB components: Session Beans and Entity Beans. Session Beans represent behaviors associated with client sessions—such as a user purchase transaction on an e-commerce site. Entity Beans represent collections of data—such as rows in a relational database—and encapsulate operations on the data they represent. Entity Beans are intended to be persistent, surviving as long as the data they're associated with remains viable.

J2EE extends the power and portability of EJB components by defining a complete infrastructure that includes standard clients and service APIs for their use.

Web Application Life Cycle

One of the strengths of the J2EE platform is that the implementation process is divided naturally into roles, which can be performed by different individuals with different skills.

Because of this role-based development, you can use your staff efficiently. Your developers can do what they do best—code high-performance applications—without worrying about the details of the UI, and your designers can do what they do best—design attractive, easy-to-use interfaces—without having to be involved in the application's coding.

Multiple Developer Roles

Before the emergence of SQL as a standard for data access, the role of the developer included the applications, files, and data access. SQL-facilitated distributed application data and the added requirement of database, design, creation, and maintenance required new development administration roles. Therefore, with a set of features designed specifically to expedite the process of distributed application development, the J2EE platform offers several benefits, but requires additional developer roles (see Figure 1.4 and Table 1.1).

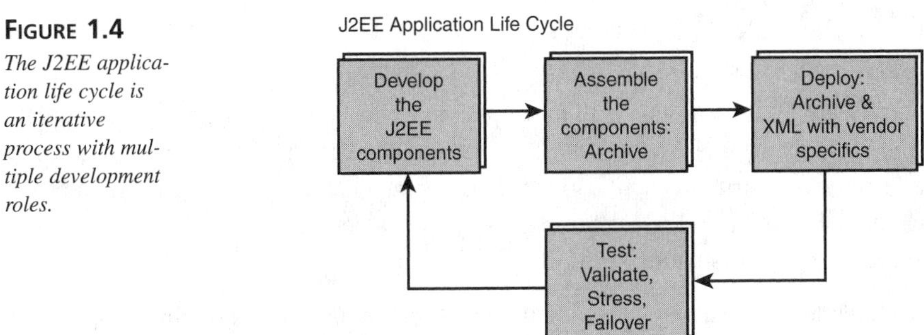

FIGURE 1.4 *The J2EE application life cycle is an iterative process with multiple development roles.*

TABLE 1.1 The J2EE Roles

Role	*Function*
J2EE Product Provider	Provides the J2EE platform. Examples are WebLogic and SilverStream.
Application Component Provider	Creates Web components (JSPs, servlets) and enterprise beans for use in J2EE applications. You can develop your own components or purchase components from others.
Application Assembler	Takes the application components from the component providers and assembles them into the J2EE Enterprise Archive (EAR) file. During this process, the assembler verifies that the components are defined properly to work together. The assembler also creates or modifies the application's deployment descriptor.
Deployer	Deploys the application in the runtime environment—that is, deploys the application onto the runtime server. Defines final security and transaction mappings as needed.

TABLE 1.1 continued

Role	*Function*
System Administrator	Configures and administers the runtime environment.
Tool Provider	Provides J2EE development, assembly, and deployment tools. You can also use third-party development tools to build your application, and then deploy the application to the application server using deployment tools.

Iterative Development

The authors of this book have been developing enterprise systems for an average of 15 years, and we are all too familiar with the application life cycle. Throughout the remainder of this book, the Model-View-Controller (MVC) application architecture is used to analyze features of distributed applications. This abstraction helps in the process of dividing an application into logical components that can be built more easily. This section explores the general features of MVC.

The MVC architecture is a way to divide the functionality involved in maintaining and presenting data (see Figure 1.5). The MVC architecture is not new, appearing in IBM CICS implementations as well as in client server with PowerBuilder. It was originally developed to map the traditional input, processing, and output tasks to the user interaction model. However, it is straightforward to map these concepts into the domain of multitier Web-based enterprise applications.

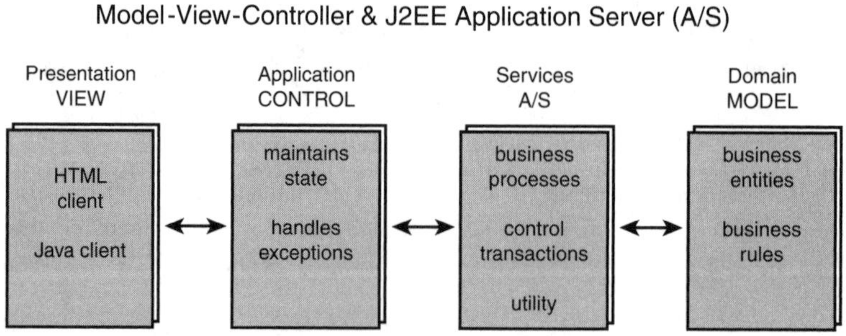

FIGURE 1.5
The Model-View-Controller provides an application development breakout for developing with J2EE.

In the MVC architecture, the Model represents application data and the business rules that govern access and modification of this data. The Model maintains the persistent state of the business. It also provides the Controller with the ability to access application functionality encapsulated by the Model.

A View component renders the contents of a particular part of the Model. It accesses data from the Model and specifies how that data should be presented. When the Model changes, it is the View's responsibility to maintain consistency in its presentation. The View forwards user actions to the Controller.

A Controller defines application behavior; it interprets user actions and maps them into processing to be performed by the Model. In a Web application client, these user actions could be button clicks or menu selections. The actions performed by the Model include activating business processes or changing the state of the Model. Based on the user action and the outcome of the Model processing, the Controller selects a View to be rendered as part of the response to this user request. There is usually one Controller for each set of related functionality.

Simplified Architecture and Development

The J2EE platform supports a simplified, component-based development model. Because it is based on the Java programming language and the Java 2 Platform, Standard Edition (J2SE platform), this model offers Write Once, Run Anywhere portability, supported by any server product that conforms to the J2EE standard.

J2EE applications have a standardized, component-based architecture. J2EE applications consist of components (including JavaServer Pages, Enterprise JavaBeans, and servlets) that are bundled into modules. Because J2EE applications are component based, you can easily reuse components in multiple applications, saving time and effort, and enabling you to quickly deliver applications. Also, this modular development model supports clear division of labor across development, assembly, and deployment of applications so you can best leverage the skills of individuals at your site.

J2EE applications are distributed and multitier. J2EE provides server-side and client-side support for enterprise applications. J2EE applications present the user interface on the client (typically, a Web browser), perform their business logic and other services on the application server in the middle tier, and are connected to enterprise information systems on the back end (these three tiers are described in more detail later). With this architecture, functionality exists on the most appropriate platform.

J2EE applications are standards-based and portable. J2EE defines standard APIs, which all J2EE-compatible vendors must support. This assures you that your J2EE development is not tied to a particular vendor's tools or server.

This means that you have your choice of tools, components, and servers. Because J2EE components use standard APIs, you can develop them in any J2EE development tool, develop components or purchase them from a component provider, and deploy them on any J2EE-compatible server. You pick the tools, components, and server that make the most sense for you.

J2EE applications are scalable. J2EE applications run in containers, which are part of a J2EE server. The containers themselves can be designed to be scalable, so that the J2EE server provider can handle scalability without any effort from the application developer.

J2EE applications can be easily integrated with back-end information systems. The J2EE platform provides standard APIs for accessing a wide variety of enterprise information systems, including relational database management systems, e-mail systems, and CORBA systems. Additional connector APIs are being developed for J2EE.

Maps Easily to Application Functionality

Component-based application models map easily and with flexibility to the functionality desired from an application. As the examples presented throughout this book illustrate, the J2EE platform provides a variety of ways to configure the architecture of an application, depending on factors such as client types required, level of access required to data sources, and other considerations. Component-based design also simplifies application maintenance. Because components can be updated and replaced independently, new functionality can be shimmed into existing applications simply by updating selected components.

Components can expect the availability of standard services in the runtime environment, and can be connected dynamically to other components providing well-defined interfaces. As a result, many application behaviors can be configured at the time of application assembly or deployment, without any modification. Component developers can communicate their requirements to application deployers through specific settings stored in XML files. Tools can automate this process to further expedite development. (See the discussion of third-party tools in Appendix B.)

Components help divide the labor of application development among specific skill sets, enabling each member of a development team to focus on his or her ability. For example, JavaServer Pages (JSP) templates can be created by graphic designers, their behavior by Java programming language coders, the business logic by domain experts, and application assembly and deployment by the appropriate team members. This division of labor also helps expedite application maintenance. For example, the user interface is the most dynamic part of many applications, particularly on the Web. With the J2EE platform, graphic designers can modify the look and feel of JSP-based user interface components without the need for programmer intervention.

A number of generic roles are discussed in the J2EE specifications, including Application Component Provider, Application Assembler, and Application Deployer. On some development teams, one or two people can perform all these roles, while other teams can subdivide these tasks into even more specific skill sets (such as user interface designers, programmers, and so on). This role assignment will evolve as development with J2EE becomes popular.

Component-Based Architecture

Central to the J2EE component-based development model is the notion of containers. Containers are standardized runtime environments that provide specific component services. Components can expect these services to be available on any J2EE platform from any vendor. For example, all J2EE Web containers provide runtime support for responding to client requests, performing request-time processing (such as invoking JSP or servlet behavior), and returning results to the client. All EJB containers provide automated support for transaction and life cycle management of EJB components, as well as bean lookup and other services. Containers also provide standardized access to enterprise information systems; for example, providing RDBMS access through the JDBC API (see Figure 1.6).

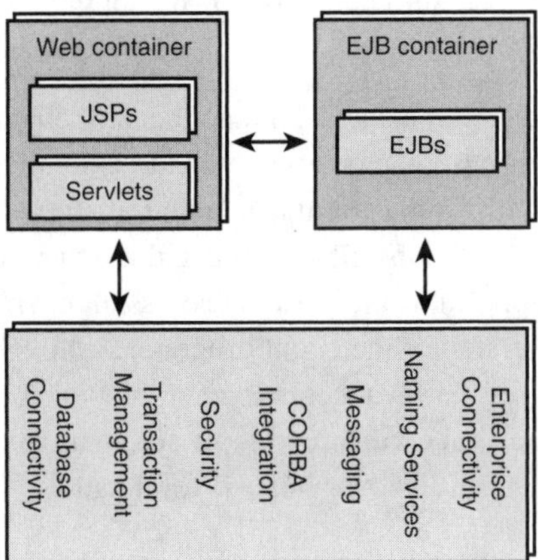

FIGURE 1.6
J2EE components for Web and EJB are run from containers.

In addition, containers provide a mechanism for selecting application behaviors at assembly or deployment time. Through the use of deployment descriptors (text files that specify component behavior in terms of well-defined XML tags), components can be configured to a specific container's environment when deployed, rather than in component code. Features that can be configured at deployment time include security checks, transaction control, and other management responsibilities.

Although the J2EE specification defines the component containers that must be supported, it doesn't specify or restrict the configuration of these containers. Thus, both container types can run on a single platform, Web containers can live on one platform and EJB containers on another, or a J2EE platform can be made up of multiple containers on multiple platforms.

Support for Client Components

The J2EE client tier provides support for a variety of client types, both within the enterprise firewall and outside. Clients can be offered through Web browsers by using plain HTML pages, dynamic HTML generated with JavaServer Pages (JSP) technology, or Java applets. Clients can also be offered as standalone Java language applications. J2EE clients are assumed to access the middle tier primarily using Web standards, namely HTTP, HTML, and XML.

Although use of the J2EE client tier has been difficult to perfect and it is therefore rarely used, it can be necessary to provide functionality directly in the client tier. Client-tier JavaBeans components would typically be provided by the service as an applet that is downloaded automatically into a user's browser. To eliminate problems caused by old or nonstandard versions of the Java virtual machine in a user's browser, the J2EE application model provides special support for automatically downloading and installing the Java Plug-in.

Client-tier beans can also be contained in a standalone application client written in the Java programming language. In this case, the enterprise would typically make operating system-specific installation programs for the client available for users to download through their browsers. Users execute the installation file and are then ready to access the service. Because Java technology programs are portable across all environments, the service need only maintain a single version of the client program. Although the client program itself is portable, installation of the Java technology client typically requires code specific to the operating system. Several commercial tools automate the generation of these OS-specific installation programs. See Appendix B for details.

Support for Business Logic Components

In the J2EE platform, business logic is implemented in the middle tier as Enterprise JavaBeans components (EJBs). Enterprise beans enable the component or application developer to concentrate on the business logic while the complexities of delivering a reliable, scalable service are handled by the EJB server.

The J2EE platform and EJB architecture have complementary goals. The EJB component model is the backbone of the J2EE programming model. The J2EE platform complements the EJB specification by fully specifying the APIs that an enterprise bean developer can use to implement enterprise beans.

This defines the larger, distributed programming environment in which enterprise beans are used as business logic components. Application servers such as SilverStream, WebLogic and WebSphere provide the environment, which must be scalable, secure, and reliable.

The J2EE application is packaged in an archive or "zip" file known as an Enterprise Archive (EAR). The EAR contains the Web, EJB and client components (see Figure 1.7).

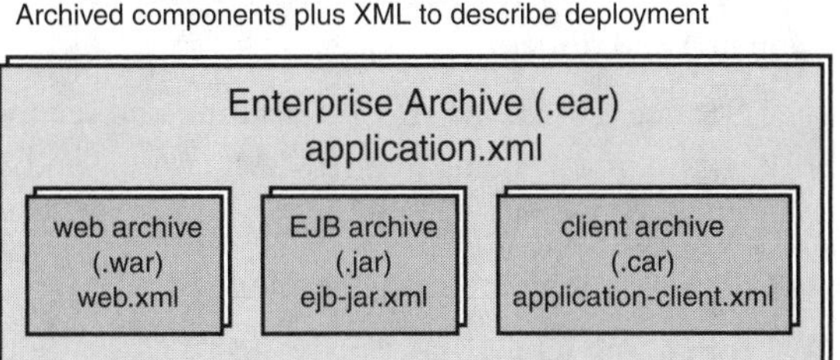

FIGURE 1.7
The J2EE enterprise application equals the enterprise archive plus the deployment XML file.

The Web, EJB, and Client components are encased in their own archive files (WAR, JAR, and CAR respectively) as shown in Figure 1.8.

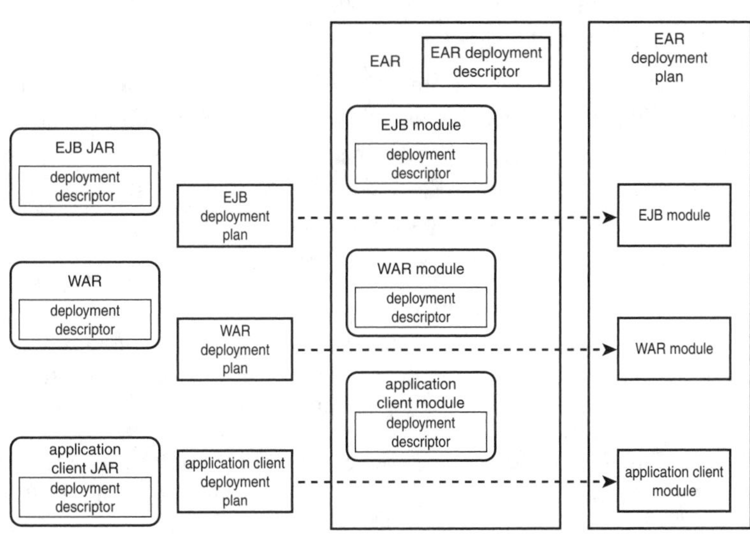

FIGURE 1.8
The enterprise archive file encapsulates the Web archive, client archive, and EJB archive.

The archives are accompanied by XML files that describe the deployment specifics of the EAR, WAR, JAR, and CAR archives.

J2EE APIs and Certification

The J2EE platform, together with the J2SE platform, includes a number of industry-standard APIs for access to these existing enterprise information systems. Basic access to these systems is provided by the following APIs:

- JDBC, the API for accessing relational data from Java
- The Java Transaction API (JTA), the API for managing and coordinating transactions across heterogeneous enterprise information systems
- The Java Naming and Directory Interface (JNDI), the API for accessing information in enterprise name and directory services
- The Java Message Service (JMS), the API for sending and receiving messages through enterprise-messaging systems like IBM MQ Series and TIBCO Rendezvous
- JavaMail, the API for sending and receiving e-mail
- Java IDL, the API for calling CORBA services

The J2EE standard is defined through a set of related specifications; key among these are the EJB specification, the Servlet specification, and the JSP specification. Together, these specifications define the architecture described in this book. In addition to the specifications, several other offerings are available to support the J2EE standard, including the J2EE Compatibility Test Suite and the J2EE SDK.

The J2EE Compatibility Test Suite (CTS) helps maximize the portability of applications by validating the specification compliance of a J2EE platform product. This test suite begins where the basic Java Conformance Kit (JCK) ends. The CTS tests conformance to the Java standard extension APIs not covered by the JCK. In addition, it tests a J2EE platform's ability to run standard end-to-end applications.

The J2EE SDK is intended to achieve several goals. First, it provides an operational definition of the J2EE platform, used by vendors as the "gold standard" to determine what their product must do under a particular set of application circumstances. It can be used by developers to verify the portability of an application, and it is used as the standard platform for running the J2EE Compatibility Test Suite.

The J2EE SDK exists to provide the developer community with a free implementation of the J2EE platform. This is Sun's way to expedite adoption of the J2EE standard.

The J2EE specifications have, by design, set the bar for platform compatibility. Owing to the collaborative way in which the platform specifications have been developed thus far, Sun gave platform vendors the opportunity to supply implementations of the J2EE platform. Obvious and unreasonable implementation hurdles were avoided. For example, no restrictions exist on vendors adding value to J2EE products by supporting services not defined in the specifications.

J2EE-component portability is primarily a function of the dependency a component has on the underlying container. The rule is (as it was with SQL), where possible, follow the standard to ensure portability, else mark the divergent parts of the application. Components using a vendor-specific feature that falls outside of the J2EE requirements can have limitations in the area of portability. J2EE specifications, however, spell out a base set of capabilities that a component can count on; hence, there is a minimum cross-container portability that an application should be able to achieve. An application developer expecting to deploy on a specific vendor implementation of the J2EE platform should carefully engineer the design to implement the application across a wide range of operating systems and hardware architectures.

Sun Microsystems set a new standard for client-side computing with the Java 2 Platform, Standard Edition. That experience coupled with input from enterprise software vendors and developers has led to a full support program for the Java 2 Platform, Enterprise Edition standard. This program includes four specific deliverables: the Java 2 Platform, Enterprise Edition specification; a complete J2EE reference implementation; the J2EE Sun BluePrint; and a Compatibility Test Suite to validate the J2EE brand.

Java 2 Platform, Enterprise Edition Specification

Based on input and feedback from a variety of enterprise technology leaders and the industry at large, the Java 2 Platform, Enterprise Edition Specification is the beginning of a definition for a consistent yet flexible approach to implementing the platform. The J2EE specification enumerates the APIs to be provided with all J2EE platforms and includes full descriptions of the support levels expected for containers, clients, and components. It defines a standard that can be built on either a single system or deployed across several servers, each providing a specific set of J2EE support services. Hopefully, this will mean that a wide range of existing enterprise systems in use throughout industry will be able to support the Java 2 Platform, Enterprise Edition.

The J2EE Reference Implementation provides all the specified technologies, plus a range of sample applications, tools, and documentation. This basic implementation of the J2EE standard is provided for two purposes. First, it provides system vendors with a standard by which to compare their implementations. Second, it provides application developers with a way to become familiar with J2EE technology as they explore commercial products for full-scale deployment of J2EE applications. We will review this application along with a more comprehensive one through this text.

J2EE Compatibility Test Suite

By providing a means to fully test implementations of the platform standard, the Compatibility Test Suite ensures consistent implementation across various vendor offerings. For application developers, this means the hope for full portability for enterprise applications. The suite includes tests for all classes and methods required by the J2EE specification. It also includes end-to-end tests to check that all layers of a J2EE application will interact correctly and consistently.

Sun BluePrints Design Guidelines for J2EE

Provided as both documentation and complete examples, the Sun BluePrints Design Guidelines for J2EE will describe and illustrate "best practices" for developing and deploying component-based enterprise applications in J2EE. Topics explored will include component design and optimization, division of development labor, and allocation of technology resources.

The Enterprise Standard with a Future

Although J2EE defines a model for implementing enterprise applications, the world of enterprise computing continues to evolve. J2EE must advance to keep pace. Proposed additions include full Java Message Service API support, additional integration of XML, the capability to interact with business objects developed in COM, and a connector API for building J2EE services on an expanding variety of existing information systems.

XML and J2EE

Prior to 1998, the exchange of data and documents was limited to proprietary or loosely defined document formats. The advent of Hypertext Markup Language (HTML), the presentation markup language for displaying interactive data in a Web browser, offered the enterprise a standard format for exchange with a focus on interactive visual content. Adversely, HTML is rigidly defined and cannot support all enterprise data types; therefore, those shortcomings provided the impetus to create the eXtensible Markup Language (XML). The XML standard enables the enterprise to define its own markup languages with emphasis on specific tasks, such as electronic commerce, supply-chain integration, data management, and publishing.

For these reasons, XML is rapidly becoming the strategic instrument for defining corporate data across a number of application domains. The properties of XML make it suitable for representing data, concepts, and contexts in an open, platform-, vendor-, and language-neutral manner. It uses *tags*, identifiers that signal the start and end of a related block of data, to create a hierarchy of related data components called *elements*. In turn, this hierarchy of elements provides encapsulation and context, implied meaning based on location. As a result, there is a greater opportunity to reuse this data outside of the application and data sources from which it was derived.

XML technology has already been used successfully to furnish solutions for mission-critical data exchange, publishing, and software development. Additionally, XML has become the incentive for groups of companies within a specific industry to work together to define industry-specific markup languages (sometimes referred to as vocabularies). These initiatives create a foundation for information sharing and exchange across an entire domain rather than on a one-to-one basis.

Sun Microsystems, IBM, Novell, Oracle, and even Microsoft support the XML standard. Sun Microsystems coordinated and underwrote the World Wide Web Consortium (W3C) working group that delivered the XML specification. Sun also created the Java platform, a family of specifications that form a ubiquitous application development and runtime environment.

XML and Java technologies have many complementary features, and when used in combination they enable a powerful platform for sharing and processing data and documents. Although XML can clearly define data and documents in an open and neutral manner, there is still a need to develop applications that can process it. The Java platform offers a homogeneous computing environment with portable code that can be downloaded over a network to any Java virtual machine. XML and Java technologies provide the potential for enterprises to apply Write Once, Run Anywhere fundamentals to the processing of data and documents generated by both Java and non-Java technology. By extending the Java platform standards to include XML technology, companies will obtain a long-term secure solution for including support for XML technologies in their applications written in the Java programming language.

Because XML is a recommendation of the W3C (World Wide Web Consortium), the group responsible for creating and maintaining all core Web technical specifications, it reflects a true industry accord that provides the first real opportunity to liberate the business intelligence that is trapped within disparate data sources found in the enterprise. XML does this by providing a format that can represent structured and unstructured data, along with rich descriptive delimiters, in a single atomic unit. In other words, XML can represent data found in common data sources, such as databases and applications, but also in non-traditional data sources, such as word processing documents and spreadsheets. Previously, non-traditional data sources were constrained by proprietary data formats and hardware and operating system platform differences.

Why Use XML?

XML technology enables companies to develop application-specific languages that better describe their business data. This section provides a brief overview of what it means to use XML data and what an XML document looks like.

By applying XML technology, one is essentially creating a new markup language. For example, an application of the XML language would produce the likes of an Invoice Markup Language or a Book Layout Markup Language. Each markup language should be specific to the individual needs and goals of its creator.

Part of creating a markup language includes defining the elements, attributes, and rules for their use. In the XML language, this information is stored inside of a document type definition (DTD). DTDs can be included within XML documents or the DTD can be external to it. If the DTD is stored externally then the XML document must provide a reference to the DTD. If a document does provide a DTD and the document adheres to the rules specified in the DTD then it is considered valid.

SAX (Simple API for XML) is a Java technology interface that enables applications to integrate with any XML parser to receive notification of parsing events. Every major Java technology-based parser available now supports this interface.

Here are some other ways that the Java platform supports the XML standard:

- The Java platform intrinsically supports the Unicode standard, simplifying the processing of an international XML document. For platforms without native Unicode support, the application must implement its own handling of Unicode characters, which adds complexity to the overall solution.
- The Java technology binding to the W3C Document Object Model (DOM) provides developers with a highly productive environment for processing and querying XML documents. The Java platform can become a ubiquitous runtime environment for processing XML documents.
- The Java platform's intrinsic support of the object-oriented programming means that developers can build applications by creating hierarchies of Java objects. Similarly, the XML specification offers a hierarchical representation of data. Because the Java platform and XML content share this common underlying feature, they are extremely compatible for representing each other's structures.

- Applications written in the Java programming language that process XML can be reused on any tier in a multitiered client/server environment, offering an added level of reuse for XML documents. The same cannot be said of scripting environments or platform-specific binary executables.

Electronic Data Exchange and E-Commerce

Given the industry's vast knowledge of communications, networking, and data processing, processing data from other departments and/or enterprises should be a simple task. Unfortunately, that's not the case. Validating data formats and ensuring content correctness are still major hurdles to achieving simple, automated exchanges of data. Using XML technology as the format for data exchange can quickly remedy most of these problems for the following reasons:

- Electronic data exchange of nonstandard data formats requires developers to build proprietary parsers for each data format. XML technology eliminates this requirement by using a standard XML parser.
- An XML parser can immediately provide some content validation by ensuring that all the required fields are provided and are in the correct order. This function, however, requires the availability of a DTD. Additional content validation is possible by developing applications using the W3C Document Object Model, an application programming interface that facilitates exploration of XML documents that apply field validation rules to content by element.

Additionally, content and format validation can be completed outside of the processing application and perhaps even on a different machine. The effect of this approach is twofold: It reduces the resources used on the processing machine and speeds up the processing application's overall throughput because it does not need to first validate the data. Secondly, the approach offers companies the opportunity to accept or deny the data at time of receipt instead of requiring them to handle exceptions during processing.

Electronic Data Interchange (EDI)

EDI is a special category of data exchange that nearly always uses a VAN (Value-Added Network) as the transmission medium. It relies on either the X12 or EDIFACT standards to describe the documents that are being exchanged. Currently, EDI is a very expensive environment to install and possibly requires customization depending on the terms established by the exchanging parties. For this reason, a number of enterprises and independent groups are examining the XML language as a possible format for X12 and EDIFACT documents, although no decisions have been reached.

Enterprise Application Integration (EAI)

Enterprise Application Integration (EAI) is best described as making one or more disparate applications act as one single application. This is a complex task that requires that data to be replicated and distributed to the correct systems at the correct time. For example, when integrating accounting and sales systems, it can be necessary for the sales system to send sales orders to the accounting system to generate invoices. Furthermore, the accounting system must send invoice data into the sales system to update data for the sales representatives. If done correctly, a single sales transaction will generate the sales order and the invoice automatically, thus eliminating the potentially erroneous manual re-entry of data.

Software Development and XML

XML has impacted three key areas of software development: the sharing of application architectures, the building of declarative environments, and scripting facilities.

In February 1999, the OMG (Object Management Group) publicly stated its intention to adopt the XMI (XML Metadata Interchange) specification. XMI is a XML-based vocabulary that describes application architectures designed using the Unified Modeling Language (UML). UML is a standard set of rules that describe system elements and the relationships between them. With the adoption of XMI, it is possible to share a single UML model across a large-scale development team that is using a diverse set of application development tools. This level of communication over a single design makes large-scale development teams much more productive. Also, because the model is represented in XML, it can easily be centralized in a repository, which makes it easier to maintain and change the model as well as provide overall version control. See the object Management Group site at `www.omg.org` for detailed specifications on UML.

XMI illustrates how XML simplifies the software development process, but it also can simplify design of overall systems. Because XML content exists within a document that must be parsed to provide value, it is a given that that a XML technology-based application will be a declarative application. A declarative application decides what a document means for itself. In contrast, an imperative application will make assumptions about the document it is processing based on predefined logic. The Java compiler is imperative because it expects any file it reads to be a Java class file. A declarative environment would first parse the file, examine it, and make a decision about what type of document it is. Then, based on this information, the declarative application would take a course of action.

The concept of declarative environments is extremely popular right now, especially when it comes to business rules processing. These applications enable developers to declare a set of rules that then are submitted to a rules engine, which will match behavior (actions) to rules for each piece of data they examine. XML technology can also provide developers with the ability to develop and process their own action (scripting) languages. The XML language is a metalanguage; it can be used to create any other language, including a scripting language. This is a powerful use of XML technology that the industry is just starting to explore.

XML Technology and the Java Platform

Since early 1998, early adopters of the XML specification have been using Java technology to parse XML and build XML applications for a variety of reasons. Java technology's portability provides developers with an open and accessible market for sharing their work and XML data portability provides the means to build declarative, reusable application components.

Development efforts within the XML community clearly illustrate this benefit. In contrast to many other technology communities, those building on XML technology always have been driven by the need to remain open and facilitate sharing. Java technology has enabled these communities to share markup languages as well as code to process markup languages across most major hardware and operating system platforms.

Java Platform Standard Extension for XML Technology

The Java Platform Standard Extension for XML technology proposes to provide basic XML functionality to read, manipulate, and generate text. This functionality will conform to the XML 1.0 specification and will leverage existing efforts around Java technology APIs for XML technology, including the W3C Document Object Model (DOM) Level 1 Core Recommendation and the SAX (Simple API for XML) programming interface version 1.0.

The intent of supporting an XML technology standard extension is to

- Ensure that it easy for developers to use XML and XML developers to use Java technologies
- Provide a base from which to add XML features in the future
- Provide a standard for the Java platform to ensure compatible and consistent implementations
- Ensure a high-quality integration with the Java platform

The Java Community Process gives Java technology users the opportunity to participate in the active growth of the Java platform. The extensions created by the Process will eventually become supported standards within the Java platform, thus providing consistency for applications written in the Java programming language going forward. The Java Platform Standard Extension for XML technology will offer companies a standard way to create and process XML documents within the Java platform.

The XML language provides a data-centric method of moving data between Java and non-Java technology platforms. Although CORBA represents the method of obtaining interoperability in a process-centric manner, it is not always possible to use CORBA connectivity.

XML defines deployment descriptors for the Enterprise JavaBeans (EJB) architecture. Deployment descriptors describe for EJB implementations the rules for packaging and deploying an Enterprise JavaBeans component. XML is an industry-wide recognized language for building representations of semistructured data that could be shared intra- and inter-enterprise. However, XML enables companies to describe only the data and its structure. Additional processing logic must be applied to ensure document validity, transportation of the documents to interested parties, and for transforming the data into a form more useful to everyday business systems. See Figure 1.7 for an example of how SML is used as a deployment descriptor for J2EE components.

The Packaging of J2EE Applications

As in any distributed environment, multitier servers combine to answer the business questions. J2EE in like fashion runs on this n-tier environment, typically consisting of a client tier, a middle tier app server, and multiple servers at the third tier providing services such as data and possibly legacy functionality (see Table 1.2).

TABLE 1.2 J2EE Applications Run on Three Tiers

Tier	*Description*
Client tier	Web browsers or standalone application clients. The J2EE BluePrint document recommends using Web browsers as clients whenever possible.
Middle tier	Consists of two subtiers: Web tier—The J2EE BluePrint document recommends using JSPs (with supporting servlets) to provide the core of the user interface of your application.

Table 1.2 continued

Tier	*Description*
	EJB tier (sometimes called the business tier)—Here is where the business logic, including data access, resides.
Enterprise Information System tier	The back-end databases and other information sources.

As mentioned, containers are the heart of the J2EE component model. Containers are the runtime environments provided by J2EE platform providers. J2EE applications are delivered in archive files. A J2EE application consists of one or more J2EE modules (described in the following text) and one J2EE deployment descriptor, packaged in an Enterprise Archive (EAR) file, which is a JAR file with the .EAR extension.

A deployment descriptor is an XML document that describes how to assemble and deploy an application or application module in the runtime environment. J2EE modules consist of one or more J2EE components of the same type and one component deployment descriptor (see Table 1.3).

Table 1.3 Three Kinds of J2EE Modules

Module	*Description*
Web modules	Consist of JSP files, classes for servlets, HTML or XML files, a deployment descriptor, and graphics files, all in a Web Archive (WAR) file, which is a JAR file with the .WAR extension
EJB modules	Consist of EJB classes and interfaces, plus a deployment descriptor, in a JAR file with the .JAR extension
Application Client modules	Consist of class files and a deployment descriptor, in a JAR file with the .JAR extension (included only if the application is providing a standalone Java client)

Applications Studied in This Book

We will use two sample applications in the book to illustrate and provide code examples for J2EE development (refer to Appendix A to find documentation for these applications). Both are e-commerce applications. One will resemble the Amazon business model and the other will be the Java Pet Store, which vendors use to display compliance and J2EE certification. We will provide code snippets and analysis of the sample application components to illustrate the various J2EE APIs and their implementation and deployment. The sample applications reflect a multitier application model. This decision assumes the presence of both a Web container and an EJB container. The following enterprise requirements are reflected in the sample applications:

- The need to make rapid and frequent changes to the "look" of the application.
- The need to partition the application along the lines of presentation and business logic to increase modularity.
- The need to simplify the process of assigning suitably trained human resources to accomplish the development task such that work can proceed along relatively independent but cooperating tracks.
- The need to have developers familiar with back-office applications unburdened from GUI and graphic design work, for which they may not be ideally qualified.
- The need to have the necessary vocabulary to communicate the business logic to teams concerned with human factors and the aesthetics of the application.
- The ability to assemble back-office applications using components from a variety of sources, including off-the-shelf business logic components.
- The ability to deploy transactional components across multiple hardware and software platforms independent of the underlying database technology.
- The ability to externalize internal data without having to make many assumptions about the consumer of the data and to accomplish this in a loosely coupled manner.

These requirements influence the application-level decisions and choices that a designer would make. The J2EE programming model takes the approach that it is highly desirable to engineer a 3-tier application such that the migration to a future multitier architecture is simplified through component reusability.

Summary

In summary, the J2EE programming model promotes a model that anticipates growth, encourages component-oriented code reusability, and leverages the strengths of inter-tier communication. It is the tier integration that lies at the heart of the J2EE programming model. We will first present it at a very high level and then drill down into each part of the J2EE standard to provide the information needed to facilitate the develop/deploy J2EE application life cycle.

CHAPTER

The Design and Development of a J2EE Application

In This Chapter

- **J2EE Layers** *42*
- **J2EE Application Components** *45*
- **J2EE Architecture** *49*
- **Development Methodology and Process** *51*
- **Sample Applications Introduced** *61*

J2EE Layers

The J2EE platform uses a multitiered distributed application model, where application logic is divided into components according to its function. The various components that a J2EE application consists of are installed on different machines. A component's location depends on which tier in the multitiered J2EE environment that component belongs to. Figure 2.1 shows two multitiered J2EE applications divided into the tiers described here:

- Client tier components run on the client machine.
- Web tier components run on the J2EE server.
- Business tier components run on the J2EE server.
- Enterprise information system (EIS) tier software runs on the EIS server.

While a J2EE application can consist of three or more tiers as shown in Figure 2.1, J2EE multitiered applications are generally considered to be three-tiered applications because they are distributed over three different locations: client machines, J2EE server machine, and the database or legacy machines at the back end. Three-tiered applications that run in this way extend the standard two-tiered client and server model by placing a multithreaded application server between the client application and back-end storage.

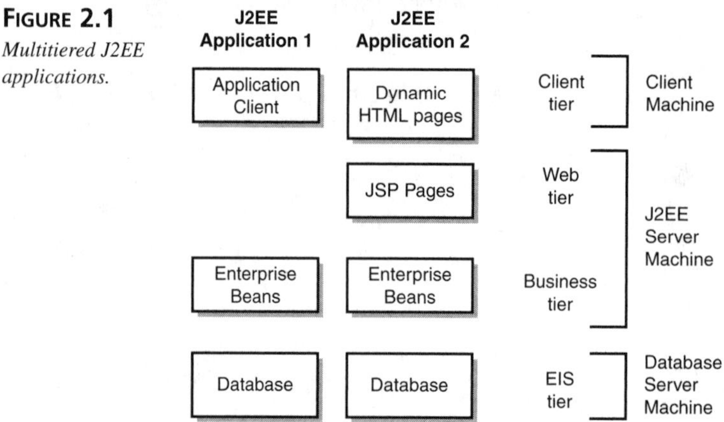

FIGURE 2.1
Multitiered J2EE applications.

The Client Layer

The client layer of a Web application is implemented as a Web browser running on the user's machine. Its function is to display data, providing the user with a place to enter and update data. Generally, one of two common approaches is used for building the client layer:

- A pure HTML-only client—In this scenario, virtually all of the intelligence is placed in the middle tier. When the user submits the Web pages, all the validation is done on the J2EE server (the middle tier). Errors are then posted back to the client.
- A hybrid HTML/Dynamic HTML (DHTML)/JavaScript client—In this scenario, some intelligence is included in the Web pages, which run on the client. The client will do some basic validations (for example, ensuring that mandatory columns are completed before allowing users to submit information). The client may also include some DHTML (for functions such as hiding fields when they are no longer applicable due to earlier selections).

The pure HTML approach is less efficient for end users because all operations require the server for even the most basic functions. On the other hand, as long as the browser understands HTML, it will generally work with this basic approach, making it possible to work on basic wireless or text-only browsers. The second argument in favor of this approach is that it provides a better separation of business logic and presentation.

The hybrid client approach is more user-friendly, requiring fewer trips to the server. Typically, DHTML and JavaScript are written to work with more recent versions of mainstream browsers.

The Presentation Layer

The presentation layer generates Web pages and any dynamic content in the Web pages. The dynamic content is typically obtained from a database; for example, content may consist of a list of transactions conducted over the last month. The other major job of the presentation layer is to package requests contained on the Web pages coming back from the client.

The presentation layer can be built with a number of different tools. The presentation layers for the first Web sites were built as Common Gateway Interface (CGI) programs. Netscape servers also offered server-side JavaScript for Web sites. Contemporary Web sites generally have presentation layers built using the Microsoft solution, Active Server Pages (ASP), which may be generated by Visual InterDev, or the Java solution, which utilizes some combination of servlets and JavaServer Pages (JSP).

Tools provide methods to facilitate embedding dynamic content inside other static HTML in the Web page. They also provide tools for simple parsing of the Web pages coming back from the client in order to extract the user-entered information.

The presentation layer is generally implemented inside a Web server (such as Microsoft IIS, SilverStream WebServer, or IBM Websphere). The Web server typically handles requests for several applications in addition to requests for the site's static Web pages. Based on the initial configuration, the Web server knows which application to forward the client-based request to (or which static Web page to serve up).

The Business Logic Layer

The bulk of the application logic is written in the business logic layer. The challenge here is to allocate adequate time and resources to identify and implement this logic. Business logic includes

- Performance of all required calculations and validations
- Workflow management (including keeping track of session data)
- Management of all data access for the presentation layer

In modern Web applications, business logic is frequently built using the Java solution, with Enterprise JavaBeans (EJB) that are built to carry out the business operations. Language-independent Common Object Request Broker Architecture (CORBA) objects can also be built and accessed effortlessly with a Java presentation tier. The main component of CORBA is the Object Request Broker (ORB). It encapsulates the communication infrastructure necessary to locate objects, manage connections, and deliver data. The ORB core is the critical part of the Object Request Broker; it is responsible for the communication of requests. The basic functionality provided by the ORB consists of passing the requests from clients to the object implementations on which they are invoked. The ORB then transfers the request to the object implementation, which receives the request, processes it, and returns an object result.

Much like the presentation layer, the business logic layer is generally implemented inside the application server. The application server automates many services such as transactions, security, persistence/connection pooling, messaging, and name services. Isolating the business logic from the need to manage resources allows the developer to focus on building application logic. In the application server marketplace, vendors differentiate their products based on manageability, security, reliability, scalability, and tools support.

The Data Layer

The data layer is responsible for data management. A data layer may be as simple as a modern relational database; on the other hand, it may include data access procedures to other data sources such as hierarchical databases or legacy flat files. The data layer provides the business logic layer with required data when needed and stores data when requested.

To avoid making an application less interoperable, the architect should strive to keep validation and business logic out of the data layer; that logic belongs in the business logic layer. Sometimes basic database design rules can overlap with business logic. There is usually some basic business logic in the data tier. For example, both *not null* constraints and *foreign key* constraints, which designate that certain columns must have a value and that the value must match an existing foreign row's corresponding key value, could be considered "business rules" that should only be known to the business logic layer. Most product designers would agree that it is necessary to include such simple constraints in the database to maintain data integrity, changing them as the business rules evolve.

J2EE Application Components

J2EE applications are made up of *components*: self-contained functional software units assembled into J2EE applications with their related classes and files. These components communicate with other components. The J2EE specification defines the following components:

- Client components—application clients and applets
- Web components—Java Servlet and JavaServer Pages (JSP) technology
- Business components—Enterprise JavaBeans (EJB) components

These components are written in the Java programming language and compiled in the same manner as any other program written in Java. When working with the J2EE platform, the difference is that J2EE components are assembled into a J2EE application where it is verified that they are well formed and compliant with the J2EE specification. They are then deployed to production, where they are run and managed by the J2EE server.

Client Components

A J2EE application can either be Web-based or non-Web-based. Non-Web-based components are an extension of the heretofore common client server applications. In a non-Web-based J2EE application, an application client executes on the client machine. For a Web-based J2EE application, the Web browser downloads Web pages and applets to the client machine.

Application Clients

Application clients run on a client machine, providing a way for users to handle tasks such as J2EE system or application administration. There is usually a graphical user interface (GUI) created using Swing or Abstract Windowing Toolkit (AWT) APIs; however, a command-line interface is also possible.

Application clients directly access enterprise beans that run in the business tier. On the other hand, an application client can open an HTTP connection establishing communication with a servlet running in the Web tier if warranted by the J2EE application.

Web Browsers

The user's Web browser downloads static or dynamic Hypertext Markup Language (HTML), Wireless Markup Language (WML), eXtensible Markup Language (XML), or pages in other formats from the Web tier. Servlets and JSP pages running in the Web tier will generate dynamic Web pages.

Applets

Web pages downloaded from the Web tier can include embedded applets. These are small client applications, written in the Java programming language, which execute in the Java Virtual Machine (JVM) installed in the Web browser. Client systems often need an additional Java Plug-in and perhaps even a security policy file so the applet can successfully execute in the Web browser.

JSP pages are the preferred API for the creation of Web-based client programs, where plug-ins and security policy files are not necessary on the client system. In addition, JSP pages enable cleaner, more modular application designs because they provide a way to separate application programming from Web page design. This means Web page designers do not need to know Java to do their jobs.

Applets running in other network-based systems such as handheld devices and cell phones are able to render Wireless Markup Language (WML) pages generated by a JSP page or servlets running on the J2EE server. The WML page is delivered using the Wireless Application Protocol (WAP). The network configuration requires a gateway to translate WAP to HTTP and back again. This gateway translates the WAP request from the handheld device to an HTTP request for the J2EE server, translating the HTTP server response and WML page to a WAP server response and WML page for display on the device.

JavaBeans Component Architecture

The client tier sometimes includes a component based on the JavaBeans component architecture for managing data flow between the application client or applet and components running on the J2EE server. The J2EE specification does not regard JavaBeans components as components. As will be explained later in this book, JavaBeans are not the same as Enterprise JavaBeans (EJBs).

JavaBeans components have instance variables as well as `get` and `set` methods for accessing the data in those instance variables. When used in this manner, JavaBeans components tend to be simple in design and implementation. They should, however, conform to the naming and design conventions specified in the JavaBeans component architecture.

J2EE Server Communications

Figure 2.2 shows the various elements that make up the client tier. The client communicates with the business tier running on the J2EE server either directly (as in the case of a client running in a browser) or by going through JSP pages or servlets running in the Web tier.

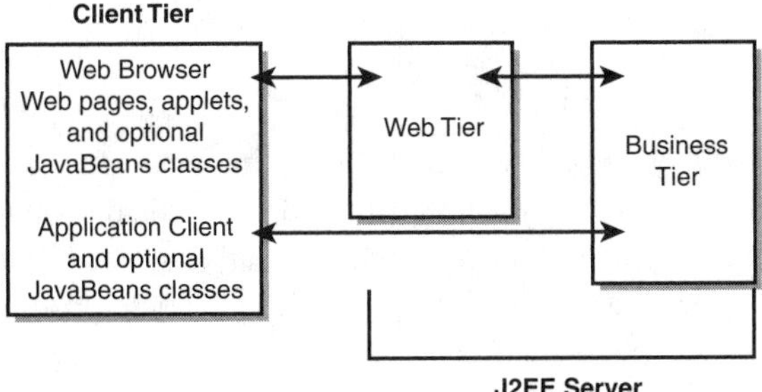

FIGURE 2.2
Elements of the client tier.

Thin Clients

J2EE applications use a lightweight interface to the application, known as a thin client, which does not perform functions such as querying databases, executing complex business rules, or connecting to legacy applications. Instead, these operations are off-loaded to Web or enterprise beans that execute on the J2EE server. Here, the security, speed, services, and reliability of J2EE server-side technologies are maximized.

Web Components

J2EE Web components are either JSP pages or servlets. Servlets are Java classes that dynamically process requests and construct responses. JSP pages are text-based documents containing static content along with snippets of Java code in order to generate dynamic content. When a JSP page loads, a background servlet executes the code snippets, returning a response.

Although static HTML pages and applets are bundled with Web components during application assembly, they are not considered Web components by the J2EE specification. In the same manner, server-side utility classes are often bundled with Web components yet are not themselves considered Web components.

The Web tier, shown in Figure 2.3, might include JavaBeans objects for managing user input, sending that input to enterprise beans running in the business tier to be processed.

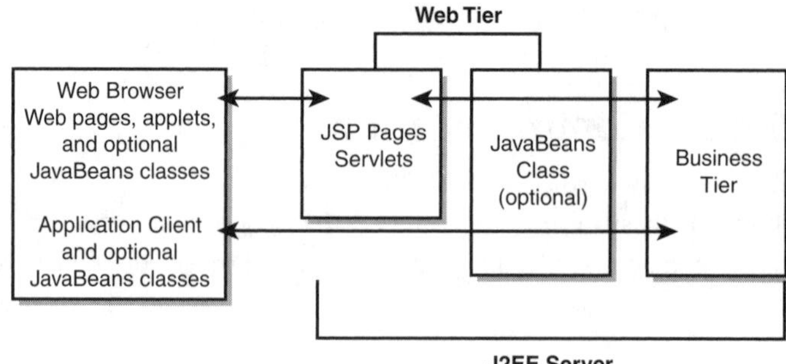

FIGURE 2.3
Elements of the Web tier.

Business Components

Business code is logic that solves the functional requirements of a particular business domain such as banking, retail, or finance. This code is handled by enterprise beans that run in the business tier. Figure 2.4 demonstrates how an enterprise bean receives data from client programs, processes it, and then sends it to the enterprise information system tier to be stored. In addition, an enterprise bean retrieves data from storage, processes it, and then sends it back to the client program.

There are three kinds of enterprise beans: session beans, entity beans, and message-driven beans. Session beans represent transient conversations with a client. When the client completes execution, the session bean and its accompanying data are gone. On the other hand, entity beans represent persistent data, which is stored in one row of a database table. If the client ends or the server shuts down, underlying services ensure that the entity bean data is saved. Message-driven beans combine features of a session bean and a Java Message Service (JMS) message listener. They allow business components to receive asynchronous JMS messages.

Enterprise Information System Tier

The enterprise information system (EIS) tier is a giant "catch-all" handling EIS software. It includes enterprise infrastructure systems such as Enterprise Resource Planning (ERP), mainframe transaction processing, database systems, and other legacy information systems. J2EE application components access enterprise information systems for functions such as database connectivity.

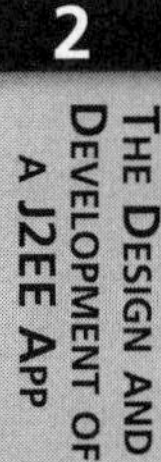

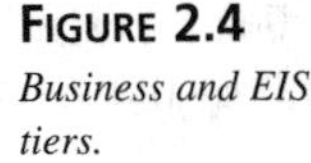

Business and EIS tiers.

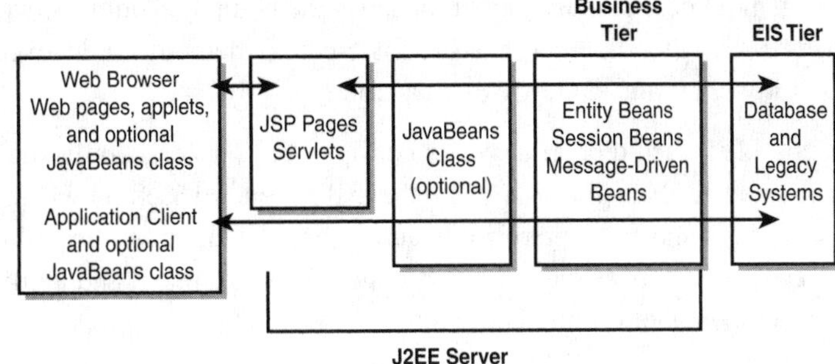

J2EE Architecture

Typically, thin-client multitiered applications are difficult to write because they involve complex programming for handling transaction management, multithreading, database connection pooling, and other low-level details. The component-based and platform-independent J2EE architecture makes J2EE applications desirable and easier to develop because business logic is organized into reusable components and the J2EE server provides underlying services in the form of a container for every component type.

Containers and Services

Components are installed in their containers during deployment. Containers are the interface between a component and the platform-specific functionality supporting that component. Before a Web component can be executed, it must first be assembled into a J2EE application and then deployed into its container.

The process of assembly involves specifying container settings for each component within the J2EE application as well as for the application itself. These settings customize the underlying support provided by the J2EE server, including services such as security, transaction management, JNDI lookups, and remote connectivity. The following are some examples:

- The J2EE security model allows configuration of a Web component or enterprise bean so that only authorized users can access system resources.
- The J2EE transaction model provides for relationships among methods that make up a single transaction; therefore, all methods in one transaction are treated as a single unit of work.
- JNDI lookup services provide an interface to multiple naming and directory services in the enterprise, allowing application components to access naming and directory services.

The J2EE remote connectivity model manages the communication between clients and enterprise beans. After an enterprise bean is created, methods are invoked on it by the client as if it were in the same virtual machine.

Because the J2EE architecture provides configurable services, application components within the same J2EE application can behave differently based on where they are deployed. For instance, an enterprise bean can have security settings allowing it a certain level of access to database data in one production environment and a different level of database access in another production environment.

Containers also manage non-configurable services such as enterprise bean and servlet life cycles, database connection resource pooling, data persistence, and access to the J2EE platform APIs. Although data persistence is a non-configurable service, the J2EE architecture allows you to include code in your enterprise bean implementation in order to override container-managed persistence (CMP) when more control is desired than the default provided by container-managed persistence. For example, bean-managed persistence (BMP) may be used to implement your own finder methods or to create a customized database cache.

Container Types

The deployment process installs J2EE application components in the J2EE containers as shown in Figure 2.5.

- An EJB container manages the execution of all enterprise beans for a single J2EE application. Enterprise beans and their accompanying container run on the J2EE server.
- A Web container manages the execution of all JSP and servlet components for a single J2EE application. Web components and their accompanying container run on the J2EE server.
- An application client container manages the execution of all application client components for a single J2EE application. Application clients and their accompanying container run on the client machine.
- An applet container is the Web browser and Java Plug-in combination that runs on the client machine.

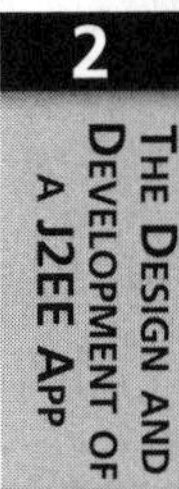

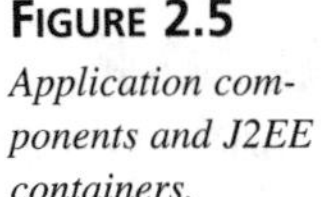

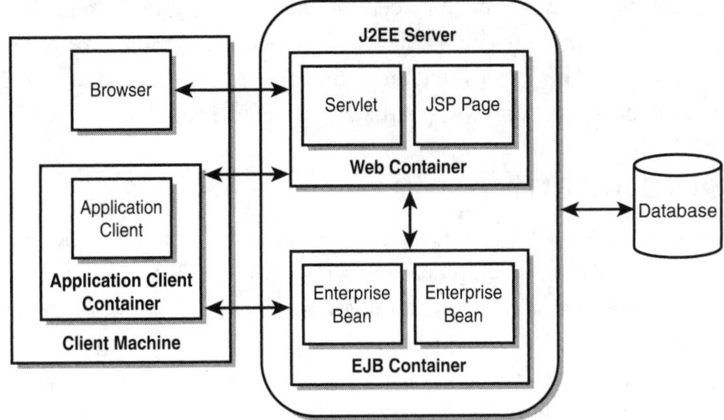

FIGURE 2.5
Application components and J2EE containers.

Development Methodology and Process

A J2EE application is assembled from two different types of modules: enterprise beans and Web components. Both of these modules are reusable; therefore, new applications can be built from pre-existing enterprise beans and components. The modules are also portable, so the application that comprises them will be able to run on any J2EE server conforming to the specifications. In order to build these modules you will first need to consider designing the application using a modeling tool before using a development tool to actually implement code. The remainder of this section will take a look at each of these areas before moving into a discussion of what makes up a J2EE application and the development phases of a J2EE project.

Modeling Tools

Modeling is the visual process used for constructing and documenting the design and structure of an application. The model is an outline of the application, showing its interdependencies and relationships between the components and subsystems. There are tools available to facilitate this process, showing a high-level view of many objects. The Unified Modeling Language (UML) was created to unify the many proprietary and incompatible modeling languages that existed beforehand.

The use of modeling tools makes sense with the increasing complexity of Enterprise Java applications and components. However, learning to model comes from experience and from sharing knowledge about best practices and bad practices. Today, modeling involves the use and reuse of patterns. A *pattern* is commonly defined as a three-part rule that expresses a relationship between a certain context, a problem, and a solution. In other words, a pattern can represent a solution to a recurring problem or issue. For more information on the modeling tools that are available, see the "Modeling and Object/Report Generation Tools" section in Appendix B, "Related Tools."

Development Tools

In order to be productive with technology such as J2EE, analysts and programmers will inevitably need visual development tools for building J2EE applications and components. When constructing a J2EE application, a developer must not only create Java code, but also build an archive file to house the classes and other supporting files including XML deployment descriptors and reference resolutions. This archive must then be deployed to a server and tested. These sets of tasks will be repeated several times over before the application is finally ready to be deployed to a production environment. All of these tasks typically need to be coordinated among multiple developers. The tools available at this time are still maturing and tool vendors frequently release newer versions of these tools to ease the development process.

In addition to the tools themselves, there are application frameworks that provide components and services based on the best patterns, practices, and standards available. The ideal framework would implement extendable design patterns on the presentation, business, and data/services layers. These implementations should work for any J2EE-certified server. At the time of this book's publication, the following frameworks and guidelines were available:

- realMethods framework
- Struts framework
- Sun's J2EE BluePrints (Pet Store)

The realMethods framework supports all of the major J2EE technologies, on all tiers (Web, EJB, and data access). See `http://www.realmethods.com/` for more information regarding this framework.

The Struts framework is an implementation of the Model-View-Controller (MVC) pattern. This framework can be used when developing Web components consisting of JSP pages and servlets. See `http://www.apache.org/` for more information regarding this framework.

Sun's J2EE BluePrints is a set of best practice guidelines for developing J2EE applications. Along with the guidelines is a practical implementation of them, known as the Pet

Store application. This application is the classic Web shopping cart for buying a pet. For more information on the Pet Store application, see Appendix A, "Documentation for Sample Applications."

Contents of a J2EE Application

The hierarchy of a J2EE application is demonstrated in Figure 2.6. A J2EE application may contain any number of enterprise beans, Web components, and J2EE application clients. The DD in Figure 2.6 refers to a *deployment descriptor*, a file that defines structural information such as class names, location, and other attributes to facilitate the deployment of the Web or enterprise application.

Enterprise beans are composed of three class files: the `EJB` class, the `remote` interface, and the `home` interface. Web components may contain files such as `servlet` classes, JSP pages, HTML files, and GIFs. A J2EE application client is a Java application that runs in a container, so it is allowed access to J2EE services.

Each J2EE application, Web component, and enterprise bean has a .xml file called a deployment descriptor (DD) that describes the component. An EJB deployment descriptor has functions to declare transaction attributes and security authorizations for an enterprise bean. This information is declarative; it can be changed without subsequent modification to the bean's source code. The J2EE server reads this information at runtime, acting upon the bean accordingly.

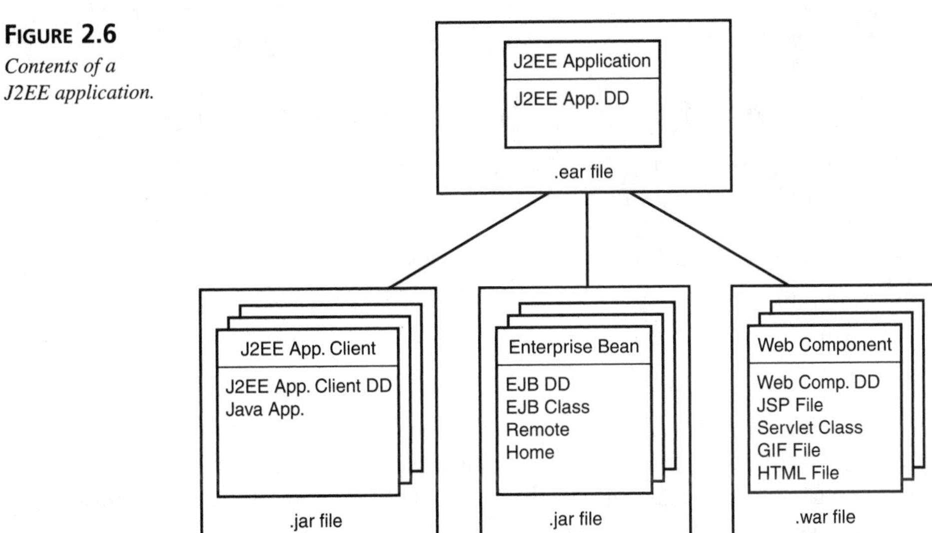

FIGURE 2.6
Contents of a J2EE application.

Each module is bundled into a file with a particular format as seen in Table 2.1.

TABLE 2.1 Files Used in J2EE Applications

File Content	*File Extension*
J2EE Enterprise Application	.ear
J2EE application deployment descriptor	.xml
Enterprise JavaBean	.jar
EJB deployment descriptor	.xml
`EJB` class	.class
`remote` interface	.class
`home` interface	.class
Web application component	.war
Web component deployment descriptor	.xml
JSP file	.jsp
`servlet` class	.class
Image files	.gif and .jpg
HTML file	.html
J2EE application client	.jar
J2EE application client deployment descriptor	.xml
Java class	.class

Development Phases of J2EE Applications

J2EE applications pass through the following developmental phases:

- Enterprise Bean Creation
- Web Component Creation
- Application Assembly
- Application Deployment

In larger organizations, different individuals or teams may perform each of these phases. This division of labor is made more feasible by the creation of a portable file output by each phase. This file contains the input for the subsequent phase. In the Enterprise Bean Creation phase, for example, a developer delivers EJB .jar files. During the application phase, another developer combines these files into a J2EE application, saving it in a .ear file. Lastly, a system administrator at the customer site uses that .ear file to install the

J2EE application into an application server at deployment time. These final stages are illustrated in Figure 2.7. Depending on the size of the organization, these different phases may or may not be executed by different people.

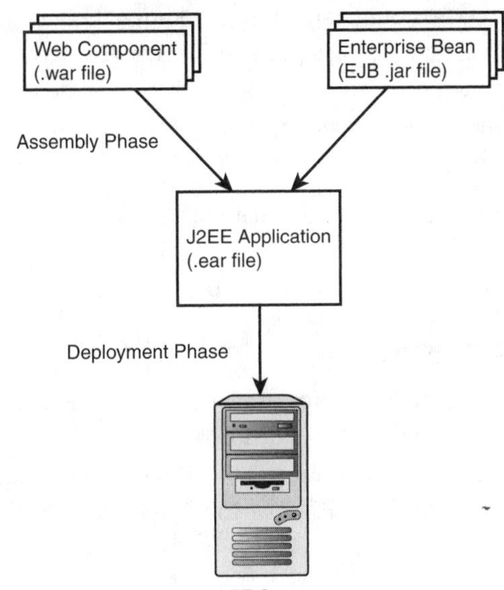

FIGURE 2.7
Development phases of a J2EE application.

How Does XML Fit into the J2EE Environment?

XML, the eXtensible Markup Language, is the preferred technology in many information-transfer scenarios because of its ability to encode information in a way that is easy to read, process, and generate. Java is an ideal companion to XML: both languages share a similar historical background (C++, SGML); both have goals of simplicity, portability, and flexibility; and both continue to be developed in groups that involve industry, development community, and academia (W3C, JCP). Not surprisingly, Java is the overwhelmingly preferred language for server and client-side XML application development.

The Java software platform has a comprehensive collection of core APIs specifically targeted at building XML-based applications:

- Java API for XML Processing (JAXP)
- Java Architecture for XML Binding (JAXB)
- Long Term JavaBeans Persistence
- Java API for XML Messaging (JAXM)

- Java API for XML RPC (JAX RPC)
- Java API for XML Registry (JAXR)

Java and XML are a natural match for the creation of applications that exploit the web of information where different classes of clients, from a traditional phone to the latest smart refrigerator, consume and generate information that is exchanged between different servers that run on varied system platforms. The portability and extensibility of both XML and Java make them the ideal choices for the flexibility and wide availability requirements of this new web.

The following sections summarize the development phases for J2EE applications. Because a J2EE application does not necessarily need both enterprise beans and Web components, one of the first two phases is often skipped; all other phases are required.

Enterprise Bean Creation

Enterprise bean creation is performed by software developers. They are responsible for coding and compiling the Java source code needed by the enterprise bean, specifying the deployment descriptor for the enterprise bean, and bundling the .class files and deployment descriptor into an EJB .jar file. That EJB .jar file is subsequently delivered to facilitate the next step.

Web Component Creation

Web component creation can be performed by Web designers, who create the JSP components, along with software developers, who are responsible for the servlets. Java source code for the servlet is coded and compiled, .jsp and .html files are written, the deployment descriptor for the Web component is specified, and the .class, .jsp, .html, and deployment descriptor files are bundled into the .war file. That .war file is delivered to facilitate the next step.

J2EE Application Assembly

The application assembler is the person who takes Enterprise JavaBeans (EJB .jar) and Web components (.war) and assembles them into a J2EE Enterprise Archive, or EAR, file. The next step is to resolve any references, which include

- Database connection pools
- Mail sessions
- URL connections
- JMS queues and topics
- EJB references

This process is handled by defining elements in one or more additional XML documents, also known as deployment descriptors or deployment plans. The assemblers or deployers can edit the deployment properties directly or use tools that add these XML tags. These additional files map internal references along with server-specific properties to JNDI or other names that exist in the destination J2EE application server. The application assemblers perform the following tasks to deliver an EAR file containing the J2EE application:

- Assemble EJB JAR and Web components (WAR) files created in the previous phases into a J2EE application (EAR) file.
- Specify the deployment descriptor for the J2EE application.
- Verify that the contents of the EAR file are well formed and comply with the J2EE specification.

The final deliverable for this stage is the completed Enterprise Archive (.ear) file containing the J2EE Enterprise Application.

Packager

The packager tool is a command-line script that allows you to package J2EE components. The packager enables you to create the component packages listed in Table 2.2.

TABLE 2.2 Component Packages Created with the Packager

Component	*File Extension*
EJB component	.jar
Web component	.war
Application client	.jar
J2EE Enterprise Application	.ear

The syntax for packaging an EJB follows:

```
packager -ejbJar <root-directory> <list-of-files>
<ejb-deployment-descriptor> <ejb.jar>
```

The following example packages the `EJB` classes and the deployment descriptor into a file named repEjb.jar:

```
packager -ejbJar /com/ucny/app/classes/
repHome.class:repEJB.class:repRemote.class:Util.class
rep-ejb.xml repEjb.jar
```

The syntax for packaging a Web component is as follows:

```
packager -webArchive [-classpath servlet-or-jspbean/classes
[-classFiles <list-of-files> ] ]
<content-root> [-contentFiles <list-of-files>]
<web-deployment-descriptor> <web-war-file>
```

The following example packages pages in a directory (currently only one file exists: ucny.html) along with the deployment descriptor into a file named tradingArea.war:

```
packager -webArchive ucnyWebPageDir web.xml tradingArea.war
```

Let's say you want to add two new JSP files to the directory ucnyWebPageDir and no longer want the HTML page ucny.html. If you modify your deployment descriptor accordingly, you can now individually specify the content files to add using the `-contentFiles` option. Here is an example:

```
packager -webArchive ucnyWebPageDir -contentFiles first.jsp:other.jsp
web.xml tradingArea.war
```

Now if you have a servlet and compile it into your classes directory (with the result being classes/mypack1/Servlet1.class) and then modify the deployment attributes of the Web deployment descriptor file, the following command includes the `servlet` class file because it is under the classes directory:

```
packager -webArchive -classpath classes ucnyWebPageDir -contentFiles
first.jsp:other.jsp web.xml tradingArea.war
```

The following command specifies that only the mypack1/Servlet1.class and mypack2/Servlet2.class files are to be included:

```
packager -webArchive -classpath classes
-classFiles mypack1/Servlet1.class:mypack2/Servlet2.class
ucnyWebPageDir -contentFiles first.jsp:other.jsp web.xml tradingArea.war
```

The next example adds the ucny.html file back into the .war file:

```
packager -webArchive -classpath classes
-classFiles mypack1/Servlet1.class:mypack2/Servlet2.class
ucnyWebPageDir -contentFiles first.jsp:other.jsp:ucny.html
web.xml tradingArea.war
```

The syntax for packaging an application client is as follows:

```
packager -applicationClient <root-directory> <list-of-files>
<main-class> <client-deployment-descriptor> <client-jar>
```

The following example creates the tradingClient.jar file:

```
packager  -applicationClient classes trade/trading.class
package.Main client.xml tradingClient.jar
```

The syntax for packaging a J2EE Enterprise Archive is as follows:

```
packager -enterpriseArchive <list-of-files>
[-alternativeDescriptorEntries <list-of-files>]
[-libraryJars <list-of-files>] <app-name> <earfile>
```

The following example creates the petStore.ear file:

```
packager -enterpriseArchive
trading.war:tradingEJB.jar
-alternativeDescriptorEntries
myTrading/web.xml:myTrading/tradingEjb.xml
trade trading.ear
```


Verifier

The verifier validates the J2EE component files shown in Table 2.3.

TABLE 2.3 Component Files Validated by the Verifier

Component	*File Extension*
J2EE Enterprise Application	.ear
EJB component	.jar
Web component	.war
Application client	.jar

Note that this tool is only useful for verifying components that will be deployed to Sun's J2EE Reference Implementation server.

There are three different ways to run the verifier:

- From within the J2EE Reference Implementation's deploytool utility
- As a command-line utility
- As a standalone GUI utility

To run the verifier from within the Application Deployment Tool, select Verifier from the Tools menu.

The syntax of the command-line verifier is as follows:

```
verifier [options] <filename>
```

The `filename` argument is the name of a J2EE component file. The options are listed and described in Table 2.4.

TABLE 2.4 Verifier Options

Option	*Description*
`-v`	Displays the verbose version of the output
`-o<output-file>`	Results are written to `<output-file>`; overrides default Results.txt file
`-u`	Runs GUI version of the utility
`-<report-level>`	Determines whether warnings or failures are reported, where `<report-level>` may be `a` (all results), `w` (warnings only), or `f` (failures only); by default, all results are reported

Here are the steps required to run the standalone GUI verifier:

1. From the command line, type

   ```
   verifier -u
   ```
2. Select a file for verification by clicking Add.
3. Select the radio button to indicate the report level; choose All Results, Failures Only, or Warnings Only.
4. Click OK.
5. The verifier will run and list the results in the lower portion of the screen.

See Chapter 19, "Deploying the Application," for additional information on packaging an application.

J2EE Application Deployment

The deployer is the person who configures and deploys the J2EE application, administers the computing and networking infrastructure where J2EE applications run, and oversees the runtime environment. Duties include setting security attributes, setting transaction controls, and specifying database connection pools.

During configuration, the deployer follows instructions supplied by the application component provider to resolve external dependencies, specify security settings, and assign transaction attributes. During installation, the deployer is responsible for moving the components to the server and generating the classes and interfaces specific to the destination container.

A deployer performs the following tasks to install and configure a J2EE application:

- Add the J2EE application (EAR) file created in the preceding phase to the J2EE server.
- Configure the J2EE application for the operational environment by modifying the deployment descriptor of the J2EE application.
- Verify that the contents of the EAR file are well formed and comply with the J2EE specification.
- Deploy (install) the J2EE application EAR file into the J2EE server.

See Chapter 19 for more detailed information on deploying an application.

Sample Applications Introduced

Throughout this book, where possible, we use and refer to a couple of sample applications. These applications help to present certain aspects of J2EE development and deployment. The applications are named and described here:

- SilverBooks is an application provided by SilverStream. SilverBooks is a Web-based application for an online bookstore. The application implements the Model-View-Controller (MVC) design paradigm by using the Struts Framework architecture.
- Java Pet Store is the standard J2EE sample application from Sun Microsystems.

Both of these applications were developed according to J2EE specifications and as such provide good J2EE programming sample code examples. See Appendix A for more information on the sample applications.

Summary

This chapter covered the architecture of a J2EE application, the development methodology, and the process involved in setting up and deploying a J2EE application. It covered the modeling tools and development tools and the phases of a project ultimately leading to the packaging and deployment of an application. The chapter concluded by introducing the sample applications.

CHAPTER

Designing the J2EE Application

IN THIS CHAPTER

- History of Modeling Tools *64*
- Overview *64*
- Designing an Application *64*
- Modeling a Web Application *77*
- System Modeling *79*
- The Unified Modeling Language *82*
- Modeling Web Pages *87*
- EJB UML Mapping *92*
- Tool Support *94*

History of Modeling Tools

Modeling is a visual process used for constructing and documenting the design and structure of an application. It is a good idea to make at least some outline of an application, showing interdependencies and relationships between the components and subsystems, during development. Modeling tools facilitate this process; as one change is made in the model, the ripple effect of that change is shown. Use of modeling tools gives developers a high-level view of what could amount to thousands of individual lines of code. Modeling can be introduced at any point in an existing project, as most modeling tools will read existing code, creating a visual model based on that code.

The standard language used by most modeling tools on the market is called the Unified Modeling Language (UML). This language was developed to unify the many proprietary and incompatible modeling languages, creating one modeling specification.

Use of modeling tools for Java development projects is increasing. With the increasing complexity of enterprise Java applications and components, modeling will become a necessity, reducing development time while ensuring that a program is well written the first time around.

Overview

Throughout the history of designing computer applications, some things have changed drastically while others have remained the same. To illustrate, the tools and methodologies for development have changed (that is, they are refined and plentiful), but the problem (or opportunity, depending on your viewpoint) is the same (that is, we need to design smart but not necessarily clever business systems to provide accurate and timely information).

Designing an Application

Whether the object is to understand and modify an existing computer-based business system or to create an entirely new one, a large obstacle to successful engineering is our inability to analyze and communicate the numerous interacting activities that make up our business process. Conversational languages such as English prove too ambiguous to be effective. More formal languages are unintelligible to most functional (business) experts. What is needed instead is a technique that structures conversational language to eliminate ambiguity, facilitating effective communication and understanding.

Database modeling has progressed exponentially in recent years. There are many good tools available, creating competition, which further moves the techniques along. On the other hand, process modeling has not progressed as well. Database modeling tools cater to the current Relational Database Management Systems standard SQL (Structured Query Language). We still have only the beginnings of process models because there is no standard process language. We have Third Generation Languages (3GLs) and Fourth Generation Languages (4GLs) being used in a myriad of combinations (A 3GL is a high-level programming language that is structured, modular, and usually procedural. A 4GL is a high-level programming language that is non-procedural and declarative). We have COBOL, C, and Java mixed with PowerBuilder, Visual Basic, and various Web development tools used in the same shop and sometimes on the same project. Currently, many vendors are working to create process-modeling tools that will generate target code for many popular process program languages. Be aware that a good database design is not just a nice relational model but also one that supports the business processes with data manipulation SQL that provides for fast access coupled with integrity.

Why Create a Model?

Modeling is an effective technique for understanding and communicating that has been used for centuries. In a process model, extraneous detail is eliminated, thus reducing the apparent complexity of the system under study. The remaining detail is structured to eliminate any ambiguity while highlighting important information. Graphics (pictures, lines, arrows, graphic standards) are used to provide much of the structure, so most people consider process models to be pictorial representations. However, well-written definitions of the objects appearing in the model, as well as supporting text, are also critical to the model.

In engineering disciplines, the model is typically constructed before an actual working system is built. In most cases, modeling the target business process is a necessary first step in developing a database application. It becomes a road map that will establish the final destination. Deciding the exact functionality of the target destination is essential. It must be captured and represented in as much detail as possible. Figure 3.1 shows a sample model illustrating a database connected to multiple servers with MS SQL Server 7 databases.

A Model Is a Tool to Facilitate the Design Process

Once a model is created (see Figure 3.2 for an example of a database model) and is made available to the developers, refinement of the product can be accomplished at a more logical level, increasing the likelihood of a successful software product. Even though there are tools available to facilitate the construction of a model, no tool is able to tell you what you want to do. Formulating your requirements with a tool such as Visio, which can be used to create graphical representations of almost anything, can be helpful (see Figure 3.1). Although you will still need to do the modeling with the business experts, these tools can help with presentation and control. For more information regarding the Visio product, visit `http://www.microsoft.com/office/visio/`.

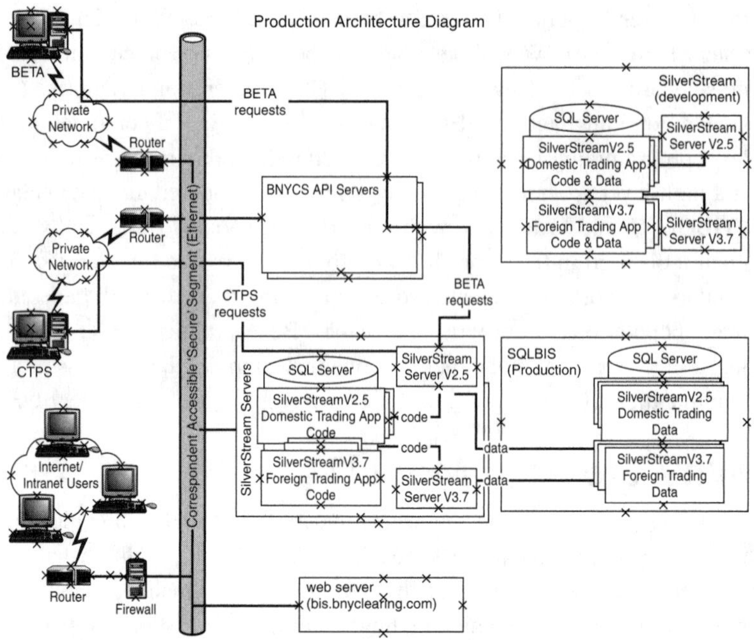

FIGURE 3.1
Model of database/server configuration.

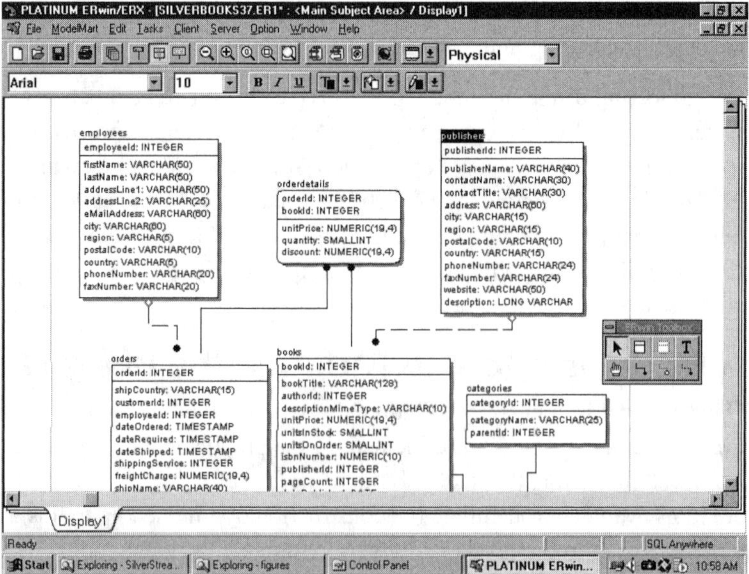

FIGURE 3.2
Model of a database for a sample Web application.

With process modeling, you can look at a system of interest in depth. This allows you to analyze, understand, and communicate to others the subtle nuances of the organization.

There are several reasons to begin a process-modeling project. First, it is an excellent way to document a multiple-step business process. One of the rules of thumb of business is that the longer a document is, the less it will be read. You can look over a short document with a Visio or PowerPoint diagram in a reasonable amount of time. Process modeling is also a valuable technique for gaining consensus on what is being accomplished and quickly proposing alternative approaches. It costs much less to develop a model than it does to develop a whole information system, especially if the new approach merely creates a new set of problems and inefficiencies.

Develop an Entity Relationship

Once you have a basic model of the business process functionality, you should gather information about the data requirements to support that functionality. Before computer aided software engineering (CASE) tools became available, this was a tedious process. Even CASE was sometimes too large to handle. Thankfully, tools have evolved and now there are a host of viable alternatives (for example, ERwin, Together, Rational Rose).

Entity Relationship Basics

Database design is critical. The degree to which it is completed before full-scale development can make or break the development process. The process of designing an application database is unique to each development environment. We will discuss it in general terms and then we will explore how CASE tools can facilitate the process. The specifics of the process may vary from shop to shop.

Determine the Application Entities

An *entity* is a person, place, object, event, or activity that is of interest to the functionality being created. It can be thought of as any noun that can represent information of importance to the organization. In logical database design, an entity/relationship model is built by identifying the entities and their attributes as well as the relationships between the different entities.

Database logical design begins as soon as you meet the users. Entities can be determined through interviews with the users. As an example, when developing a database to track the schedules at a television station, entities may include series and episodes. The attributes of an entity are the things that describe and define it; for example, a series has a descriptive name, so *name* is an attribute of *series*. The date it was originally produced may also be an attribute.

Relationships can also be revealed through user interviews. To further define a relationship, if an entity cannot exist without a parent, it is dependent (that is, it belongs to another entity). This is a relationship.

Subentities are important subsets of an entity with special attributes. To continue the example of a television station, a TV series may be of type *special* with attributes that only pertain to a *special* series. We might have a subentity called *special*. *Special* is a part of a series (that is, it could be merged with *series* and has the same primary key), while a dependent entity, such as an episode belonging to a series, has a primary key that contains the parent key and an additional key to identify the dependent.

Refine Each Entity and Attribute

After you have collected the business entities and attributes from interviews with the user, the project standards should be checked for naming conventions. When applicable, these objects should be checked using firm-wide abbreviations to ensure consistent naming. Next, description and validation criteria for each entity and attribute should be captured. If the project has a data dictionary, the description and validation criteria should be entered in it. In addition, the dictionary should be checked to determine whether the attribute or entity exists already.

PowerBuilder has its own catalog tables that can house descriptions and validation rules. These attributes can be populated from CASE tools such as ERwin or PowerDesigner. (For more information about ERwin, go to `http://www.cai.com/products/alm/erwin.htm`; for more information about PowerDesigner, go to `http://www.sybase.com/products/enterprisemodeling/powerdesigner`.) The primary key for each entity should be determined. The primary key of an entity uniquely identifies entity instances (rows). The primary key of a dependent entity includes parent key and descriptive column. In our television series example, the primary key for the *episode* entity is the `series_code` and `episode_code` concatenated. You can document past or future states in detail by adding `last_update_timestamp`. The primary key will promote database integrity by preventing table row duplication and the creation of database orphans (that is, rows in a dependent table with no parent).

Determine Relationships

Relationships can be determined through interviews with the user. The roles of entities in recursive relationships should be documented. A series may be a part of another series. Determine the cardinality of the relationship, which is the number of instances of one entity associated with the instances of another entity. For example, how many episodes are there in a series? This will facilitate the choice of keys or indices to access the entity.

Relationships should not be confused with entities or attributes. Attributes that designate entities are relationships. If the primary key of an entity consists of other primary keys, it may be a relationship. In our example, the TV episode entity would have a primary key consisting of the TV series identifier and the episode identifier. The TV series identifier is the primary key of the series entity.

CASE Tools "Lite"

So how do you create an entity relationship diagram in the new world? ERwin and PowerDesigner are generally considered to be the best choices for serious developers when it comes to CASE tools. They are similar and both perform the really important functions. In this book, we will use ERwin for illustrating the capabilities of these newer CASE tools. ERwin's stated focus is on quickly creating high quality, robust physical databases. ERwin is sold as a database design tool. ERwin does not create processing modeling diagrams, just entity relationship diagrams (these are known as ER diagrams; hence the name ERwin). ERwin's specialization is on the physical side. Around the time of this book's publication, ERwin 3.5 was released with support for MS SQL Server 7 and several other database management systems. When you finish modeling the database, you can have ERwin build the data definition language. This is essentially what has been missing from upper CASE tools.

Using old, heavy, and complex CASE tools such as ADW, you may have found that even after spending a couple of years designing something, you still didn't know much more about good relational database design, which is critical for client/server success. The newer, more lightweight tools, such as ERwin and PowerDesigner, show you the physical definition right from the start, not hiding it like these older CASE tools do. To build a good database model for physical implementation using MS SQL Server 7, you have to think like a relational database.

Benefits of "Lite" CASE

We can break the benefits of "lite" CASE into two categories. The first one you will notice is increased productivity. This is true for those projects that already have an existing database, and also for new projects with a blank slate for a data model.

The second benefit you will see after you create your database. The quality and robustness of the physically generated SQL DDL (Data Definition Language) is unsurpassed by even the largest and most expensive CASE tools on the market. An interesting point to note is the duration of ERwin's usefulness on a project. I have found that when tools such as ERwin are chosen, they are used throughout the entire project, without exception. Where upper CASE tools (LBMS, ADW, and so on) are used, the tool is usually abandoned somewhere during the initial development phase. I've never seen a project that adopted an upper CASE tool in the middle of development. However, on many occasions, I've seen projects that weren't using any form of CASE tool easily pick up ERwin in midstream and keep with it to the end.

Data Modeling Using ERwin

ERwin uses a traditional methodology called IDEF1X. IDEF1X is a method for designing relational databases (see `http://www.idef.com/idef1x.html` for more information). Not unlike other tools, with ERwin you start creating an ER diagram by placing entities (tables) on your diagram and adding relationships between them. Figure 3.3 shows the ERwin environment, which allows you to do this. MS SQL Server has its own diagramming tool, but it is immature at this stage and as such is unusable.

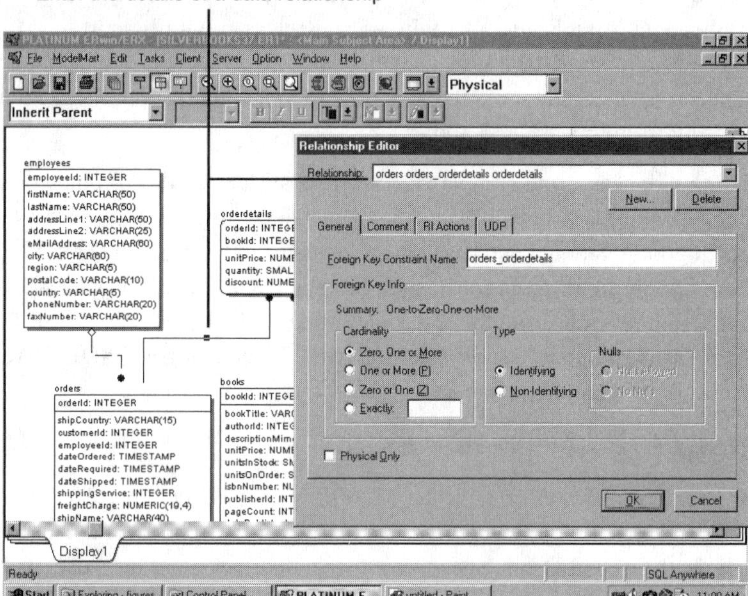

FIGURE 3.3
ERwin environment depicted with a sample application database.

Reverse Engineering

Sometimes the data we will use is contained in a legacy data model. Both ERwin and PowerDesigner include the capability to reverse engineer from any of the supported databases. Reverse engineering is the process of examining the previously existing table structure and getting your ERwin data model up to date with what's going on in the real database. In previous versions of ERwin, reverse engineering required you to have the original SQL DDL that was used to create your tables. However, quite often you can find yourself with a DDL that is out of date, or, in the worst case, you may have no DDL. ERwin 4.0 solves this problem by providing a reverse engineering option in the Tasks/Reverse Engineer menu. Figure 3.4 is the first in a series of wizard-like dialogs for the reverse engineering process.

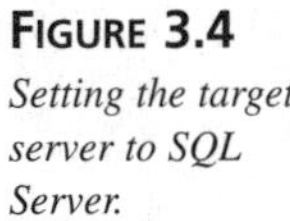

FIGURE 3.4
Setting the target server to SQL Server.

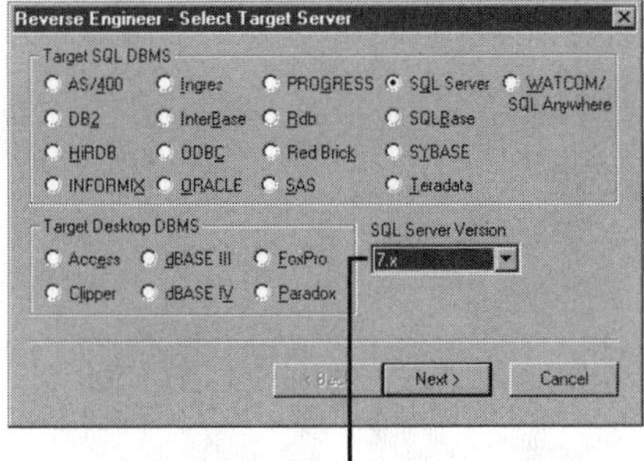

If you prefer, you can still use the traditional approach in the latest version. You are basically using the Open option from the File menu to read in SQL and create a model. Here are the steps involved:

- Start ERwin.
- From the Tasks menu, select Reverse Engineer.
- Specify the DBMS type that the SQL syntax is written for.

In the Reverse Engineer window, you now have several options. You can specify which components of SQL you want to capture. You must reverse engineer tables for obvious reasons, but you can capture foreign keys and indexes as well. You also have the ability to set case conversion options. Lastly, you can display the parse of the SQL as it is happening. When all options are set, press the Next button. Now would be a good time to calculate how much time you are saving by letting ERwin do the reverse engineering as opposed to doing it yourself! Unfortunately, you may not even have time to do that—it's pretty fast. It even runs in the background, so you can minimize and go do something else.

ERwin 4.0 has a much better method of reverse engineering than previous versions offered. With this capability, ERwin will actually connect to your DBMS and read directly from the system catalogs. This is not a one-time process, but an ongoing synchronization. Basically, you connect to the MS SQL Server 7 database you want to re-engineer. Then you choose Update Model or Alter Database from the Tasks menu bar item. The ERwin tool will read the database system catalog and build the model based on the tables, columns, indices, and so on found in the system catalog. (See Figures 3.5 and 3.6.) If a developer makes a change directly on the database, it is very easy to pick that up the next time you synchronize. This capability can only strengthen ERwin's projected longevity.

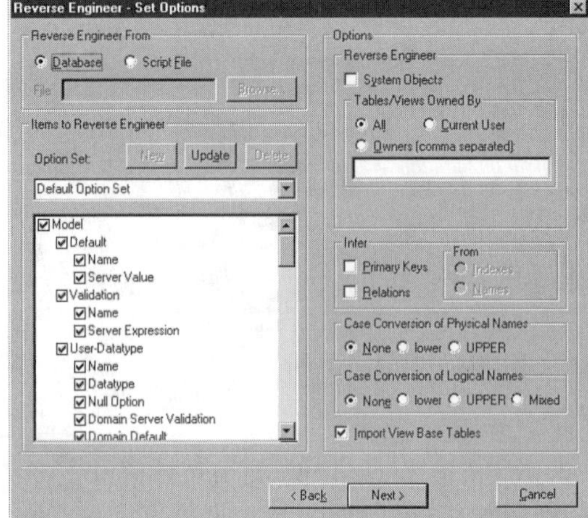

FIGURE 3.5
ERwin setting options for Reverse Engineer.

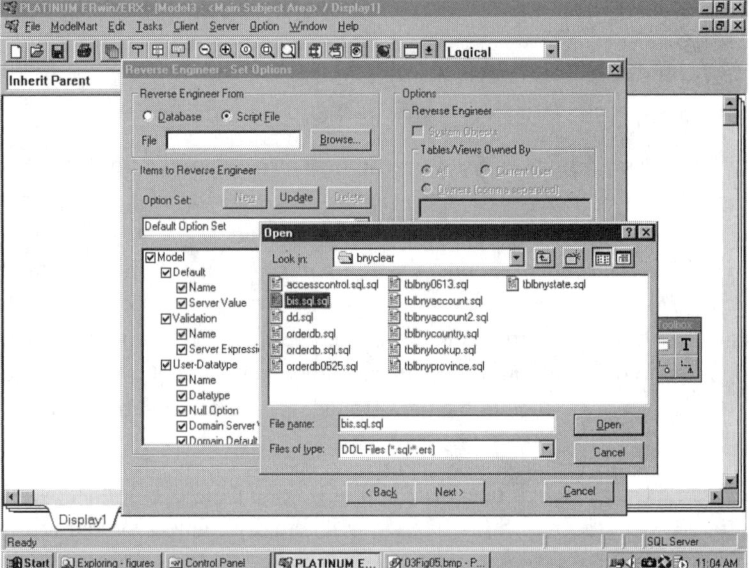

FIGURE 3.6
Choosing the file containing the DDL to be reverse engineered.

Entity Modeling

Whether you are starting from scratch or working with an existing database, there are two types of entities: independent and dependent. Independent entities are those that can be uniquely identified without depending on relationships with other entities. Conversely, dependent entities cannot be identified uniquely without depending on relationships with other entities. Both types are available within the ERwin environment shown in Figure

3.3. Sharp cornered entities are independent; entities with rounded corners are dependent. To add an entity to your diagram, select the appropriate icon from the toolbox and click anywhere on your diagram. ERwin will give your entity a default name. To change the name, you will need to use the right mouse button and click on the entity to bring up the list of available editors for that entity. Invoke the Entity-Attribute Editor.

The Entity-Attribute Editor (shown in Figure 3.7) allows you to enter not only the entity name, but also the attributes (fields, columns) for the entity. When you enter an attribute, you need to decide whether it forms part of the primary key or not, and enter it into the appropriate window. Keep in mind that what we are entering so far are only logical names for the attributes and the entity. These names can have spaces in them. The logical names will be used to generate default physical names. It might be wise to limit your logical names according to the specifications of your particular database. That way, you may never need to adjust your physical names.

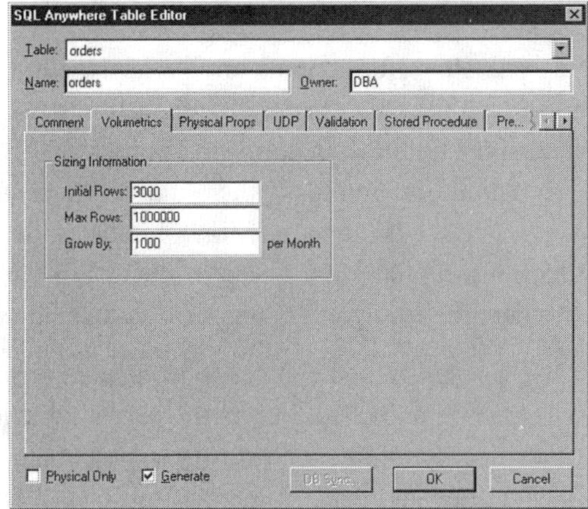

FIGURE 3.7
Entity-Attribute Editor.

The Column Editor (shown in Figure 3.8) allows you to enter the data type and other physical properties of the particular attribute (table column) within each entity.

Relationship Modeling

One of the nicest features of ERwin is its foreign key migration capability. This is a feature you really need to understand before you start adding relationships between entities. In the IDEF1X terminology, there are two types of relationships between entities: identifying and non-identifying. Identifying relationships are used when a child entity is identified through its association with the parent entity. In other words, the foreign key column of the child table is also part of the primary key. Non-identifying relationships indicate that the child entity is not identified by its relationship to the parent entity. Identifying relationships and non-identifying relationships are represented by solid and dashed lines, respectively.

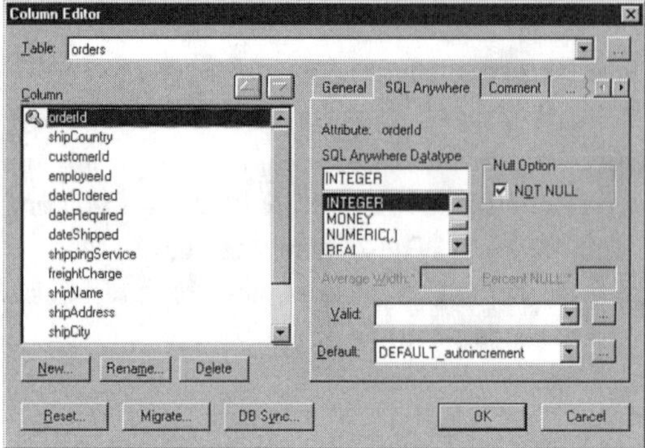

FIGURE 3.8
Column Editor.

Relationships in ERwin are generally referred to as foreign keys on the physical level. Normally, when you create foreign keys you first define the parent table (with a primary key) and the child table (with some columns in common). Afterwards, you add a foreign key on the child table's related columns, and make that point to the primary key of the parent table. You'll always get an error if the number of columns in the foreign key is not the same as the number of columns in the primary key of the parent table (or if the data types don't match). This is where the foreign key migration comes into play.

To create a relationship in ERwin, select the appropriate icon (Identifying or Non-Identifying) from the ERwin toolbox and click first on the parent table and then on the child table. ERwin will automatically migrate the primary key attributes of the parent table into the child table. If you draw an identifying relationship (solid line), the primary key attributes of the parent table will migrate into the primary key section of the child entity. Conversely, non-identifying relationships will migrate the primary key columns of the parent table into the non-key area of the child entity.

Take a look at Figure 3.9. It shows a dialog that is defining a non-identifying relationship. When completed, the non-identifying relationship causes the employeeId number to be automatically inserted in the non-primary key area of the employees table.

The best part about this foreign key migration is that it is dynamic. If you change the data type of a primary key column in a parent table, the change is reflected in all child tables. If you add columns to the primary key of a parent table, they are migrated down to the child tables.

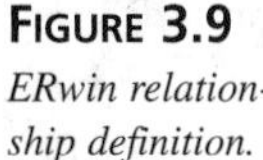

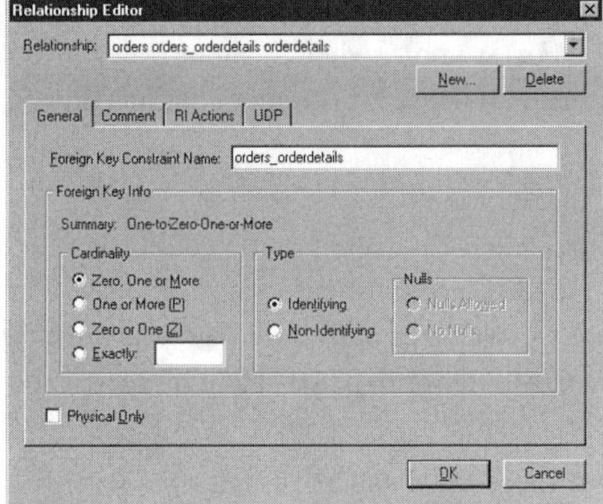

FIGURE 3.9
ERwin relationship definition.

Referential Integrity

After a relationship has been added between tables, ERwin lets you control the referential integrity between them. To access this feature, you need to right-click on the relationship line to bring up the relationship's menu, and select RelationshipEditor. This will display the referential integrity actions (RI Actions) tab of the Relationship Editor (see Figure 3.10).

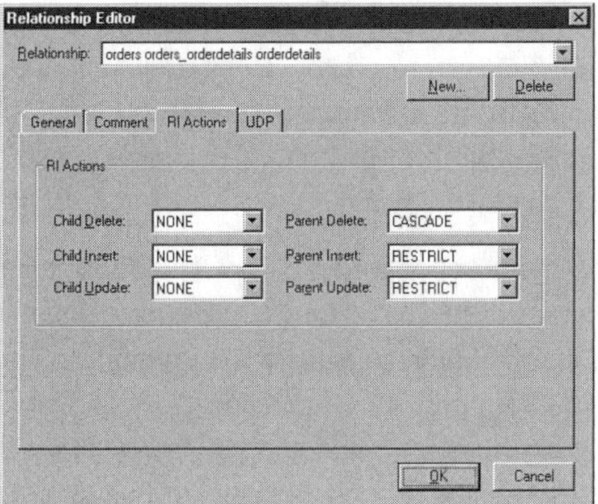

FIGURE 3.10
The Relationship Editor's referential integrity actions.

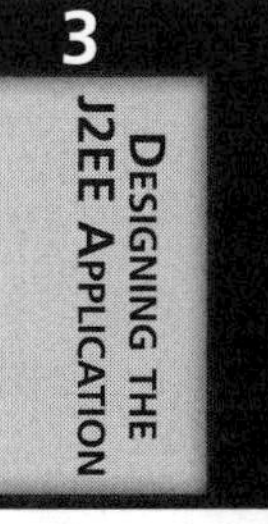

Once in the RI Actions table of the Relationship Editor, ERwin will display the name of the relationship. The first thing you can do is change the verb phrase and physical name of the relationship. This will be used for the name of the foreign key.

ERwin allows you to control the behavior for an insert, delete, or update on either the parent or the child. Your options for any given action are *Restrict*, *Cascade*, *Set Null*, *Set Default*, and *None*:

- The *Restrict* option will cause the database to return an error if the action will violate referential integrity. For example, when a Parent Delete–Restrict setting is in effect, if an attempt is made to delete a customer who has orders, the deletion will fail.
- The *Cascade* option will cause the database to apply any changes between the related entities. A Parent Delete–Cascade setting would cause an attempt to delete a customer with orders to also delete the associated orders. A Parent Update–Cascade setting would result in any attempt to change a customer number (the primary key of the Customer table) also changing the customer number for all orders that belong to this customer.
- The *Set Null* option will cause the database to make the foreign key columns in the child table null during a deletion or an update. For example, a Parent Delete–Set Null option would result in Order records having a null customer number for any orders that once belonged to a deleted customer.
- The *Set Default* option is very similar to Set Null, but instead of setting the foreign key columns to null, it resets them to their original default values.
- The *None* option means that no action is taken to ensure referential integrity.

Not all of the options are available for each action. For example, a Child Update–Set Null setting doesn't make much sense if you think about it for a minute; why would you want to set columns in the child to null just because an update to the parent occurs? Also, not all of the options are available for foreign key declaration syntax in your particular DBMS. In fact, most of the options are not supported by the popular DBMSes. However, ERwin provides physical support for all of its options through the use of triggers. If your DBMS supports triggers, you can take advantage of most, if not all, of the options.

ERwin accomplishes this through a set of trigger templates. These templates are created with a large and feature-filled set of macros. You can customize and even create your own triggers—however, the macro language is poorly documented. This same macro language has now been extended to support stored procedures and ad hoc scripts. You can create your own stored procedure templates and apply them to tables or to the schema as a whole. This can be a powerful means for creating standard `select`, `insert`, `update`, and `delete` stored procedures to use in your DataWindows.

Supported Databases

One of ERwin's strengths is its support for a wide variety of databases. Figure 3.11 shows the Reverse Engineer—Select Target Server dialog with all of the supported databases. ERwin doesn't make a big deal out of it, but you can easily change databases on the fly. ERwin maintains a datatype map between databases, so the process of porting from one database to another is only a few clicks away.

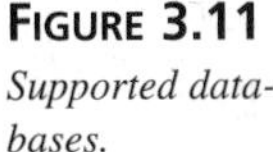

FIGURE 3.11
Supported data-bases.

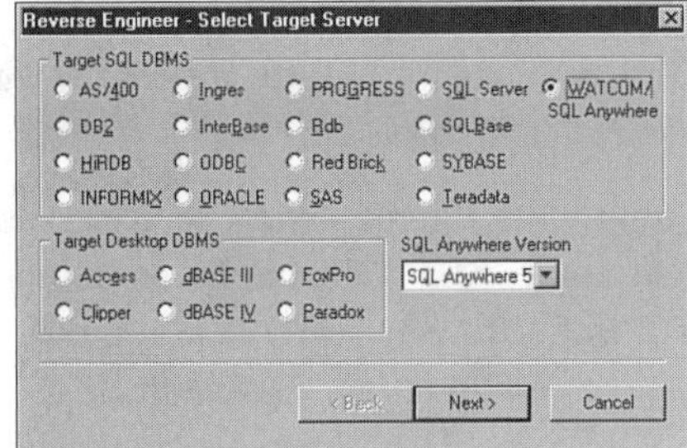

It may also be noteworthy to mention that ERwin/ERX now supports physical storage parameters for most DBMSes including MS SQL Server 7, Informix, DB2, Oracle, and Sybase to name just a few.

Modeling a Web Application

Web applications are becoming progressively more intricate as well as mission critical. Modeling can help to manage this growing complexity. The current standard for modeling software-intensive systems is the Unified Modeling Language (UML).

Unfortunately, when modeling a Web application with UML, it becomes apparent that some components don't automatically fit into standard UML modeling elements. In order to utilize a single modeling notation for an entire system that includes Web components and traditional middle-tier components, UML must be extended.

This chapter introduces and discusses an extension to the UML, making use of its formal extension mechanism. The extension has been designed so that Web-specific components can be integrated with the remainder of the system's model. It is meant to exhibit a level of abstraction and detail suitable for application designers and implementers.

Overview

Nowadays, it seems that everyone involved with business software, and even many involved in non-business-related software efforts, has plans to build Web applications. Web applications have evolved from small successful Web site add-ons to robust *n*-tiered applications. Many Web applications service tens of thousands of concurrent users distributed all over the world. Building Web applications is serious business.

The actual term "Web application" has different meanings to different people. Some believe Web applications to be anything that utilizes the Java programming language, while others consider them to be anything that uses a Web server. For the purpose of this chapter, we will consider a Web application to be a Web system (Web server, network,

HTTP, browser) in which user input (navigation and data input) affects the state of the business. With this definition, a Web application is a software system with a business state and a front end that is delivered via a Web system.

Generally, a Web application has the architecture of a client server system, with a few notable differences. A significant advantage of a Web application is deployment. Deploying a Web application consists of setting up server-side components on a network. The client needs no special software or configuration. The nature of client and server communication is also significantly different. The principal communication protocol of a Web application is HTTP, a connectionless protocol designed for robustness and fault tolerance instead of maximum communication throughput. Client-server communication in Web applications revolves around the navigation of Web pages instead of direct communications between server-side and client-side objects. Messaging in a Web application is best described as the request for and reception of Web page entities.

The architecture of a Web application is really not very different from the architecture of a dynamic Web site; the difference involves usage. A Web application implements business logic; use of the application changes the state of the business (as captured by the system). Since Web applications execute business logic, the most important models of the system focus on that logic as well as the business state instead of focusing on presentation details. This concept defines the focus of the modeling effort.

Presentation is not entirely unimportant, as the system won't be effective without it. When dealing with Web applications, a clear separation between business and presentation is essential. If presentation issues are important or complex, they should also be modeled.

A methodology often associated with the design, construction, and maintenance of intranet and Internet Web systems is known as Relationship Management Methodology (RMM). The goal of RMM is a reduction in the cost of maintaining dynamic, database-driven Web sites. A visual representation of the system is used to facilitate design discussions. It is a repetitive process that includes breaking down the visual elements in the Web pages, along with their associations with database entities.

RMM is not adequate for building most Web applications as they include a number of technological mechanisms for the implementation of business logic that are not covered by RMM notation. These technologies include client-side scripting, applets, and ActiveX controls, which often make significant contributions to the execution of the business rules.

Additionally, Web applications are often used as delivery mechanisms for distributed object systems. Applets and ActiveX controls contain components that interact asynchronously with server-side components via Remote Method Invocation (RMI) or Distributed Component Object Model (DCOM), independent of the Web server. Sophisticated applications also frequently use multiple browser instances and frames on the client, establishing and maintaining their own communication mechanisms.

Since all of these mechanisms contribute to the business logic of the system, they require modeling. Because they represent only a portion of the business logic, they also need to be integrated with the other models in the system.

In many Web applications, most of the business logic is executed behind the Web server in one of the server-side tiers. The needs of this side of the application typically lead to the choice of modeling language and notation. Since UML has been accepted as the de facto object modeling language, systems are expressed with UML notation to a greater extent than ever before. UML has become the language of choice for modeling software-intensive systems.

This chapter provides an introduction to the issues and possible solutions for modeling Web applications. It focuses on the architecturally significant components particular to Web applications, along with instructions on modeling them with UML. You should already be familiar with UML, object-oriented principles, and general Web application development. Throughout the remainder of this chapter, the following assumptions should be kept in mind:

- Web applications are software-intensive systems that are becoming more complex, and are playing more mission-critical roles.
- The complexity of software systems can be managed by abstracting and modeling them.
- It is typical for a software system to have multiple models, with each representing a different level of abstraction and detail.
- The exact level of that abstraction and detail depends on the artifacts and activities in the development process.
- Unified Modeling Language (UML) is the standard modeling language for software-intensive systems.

System Modeling

Models help to simplify details of a system, therefore making it easier to understand. Choosing exactly what to model can have an enormous effect on your understanding of the problems at hand. Web applications, much like other software-intensive systems, are normally represented with a set of models. Model types include use case models, implementation models, deployment models, and security models. Site maps, which are abstractions of the Web pages and navigation routes throughout the system, are models used exclusively by Web systems.

Determining the correct level of abstraction and detail is crucial in order to benefit the users of the model. It is often best to model the artifacts of the system, meaning the entities that will be constructed and manipulated to produce the final product. Modeling pages, hyperlinks, and dynamic content on the client and server is very important. Modeling internals of the Web server or details of the browser are not very helpful to the designers and architects of a Web application.

The artifacts should be mapped to modeling elements. Hyperlinks map to association elements in the model and represent navigational paths between pages. Pages might also map to classes in the logical view of the model. If a Web page were a class in the model, the page's scripts would map to operations of the class. Any variables in the scripts that are page-scoped would map to class attributes.

A problem arises when you consider that a Web page may contain a set of scripts that execute on the server in order to prepare the dynamic content of the page along with a completely different set of scripts that execute on the client. A perfect example of this is JavaScript. When using JavaScript, there can be confusion as to which operations, attributes, and relationships are active on the server and which are active on the client. In addition, a Web page as delivered in a Web application is best modeled as a component of the system. Simply mapping a Web page to a UML class does not help us understand the system any better.

The creators of the UML realized that it is not always sufficient to capture the relevant semantics of a particular domain or architecture. To address this problem, a formal extension mechanism was defined in order for practitioners to extend the semantics of the UML. This mechanism allows the defining of stereotypes, tagged values, and constraints that can be applied to model elements.

A *stereotype* allows you to define a new semantic meaning for a modeling element. *Tagged values* are key value pairs that can be associated with a modeling element. These allow you to attach any value to a modeling element. *Constraints* are rules defining the best way to express a model: as free-form text or with the more formal Object Constraint Language (OCL).

In modeling, a very clear distinction needs to be made between business logic and presentation logic. In typical business applications, presentation details such as animated buttons, fly-over help, and other UI enhancements do not normally belong in the model unless a separate UI model is constructed for the application.

Web Application Architecture

Basic Web application architecture includes browsers, a network, and a Web server. Browsers request the Web pages from the server. Each page contains a mix of content and formatting instructions, expressed in HTML. Some pages include client-side scripts defining additional dynamic behaviors for the display page. These scripts (which are interpreted by the browser) interact with the browser, page content, and additional controls such as applets, ActiveX controls, and plug-ins that are contained in the page.

Users view and interact with the content in the page. Often there are field elements in the page that are filled in and submitted to the server by the user for processing. Users also interact with the system by navigating to different pages in the system via hyperlinks. In both cases, the user supplies input to the system that may alter the business state of the system.

The client sees a Web page as an HTML formatted document. On the server, however, a Web page may manifest itself in several different ways. Early Web applications utilized the common gateway interface (CGI) for dynamic Web pages. CGI defines an interface for scripts and compiled modules to utilize in order to gain access to the information passed along with a page request. In a CGI-based system, a special directory is usually configured on the Web server to be able to execute scripts in response to page requests. When a CGI script is requested, instead of just returning the contents of the file (as it would for any HTML formatted file), the server processes or executes the file with the correct interpreter (usually a Perl shell). The output is streamed back to the requesting client. The end result of this processing is an HTML formatted stream, which is sent back to the requesting client. Business logic is executed in the system while the file is being processed. During that time, it has the potential to interact with server-side resources such as databases and middle-tier components.

Web servers have improved on this basic design over time, becoming more security aware, and including features such as client state management, transaction processing integration, remote administration, and resource pooling. The latest generation of Web servers addresses issues that are important to architects of mission-critical, scalable, and robust applications.

Today's Web servers can be divided into three major categories: scripted pages, compiled pages, and hybrids of the two. In scripted pages, each Web page that can be requested by a client browser is represented on the Web server's file system as a scripted file. This file is often a mix of HTML and another scripting language. Upon page request, the Web server delegates the task of processing the page to an engine that recognizes it and results in an HTML formatted stream that is sent back to the requesting client. Prime examples are Microsoft's Active Server Pages, JavaServer Pages, and Allaire Cold Fusion.

In compiled pages, the Web server loads and executes a binary component that has access to all of the information accompanying the page request, such as the values of form fields and parameters. The compiled code uses the request details and accesses server-side resources to produce the HTML stream that is returned to the client. Compiled pages often offer more functionality than do scripted pages. Different functionality can be obtained by passing parameters to the compiled page request. Any single compiled component has the ability to include all of the functionality of an entire directory's scripted pages. Examples of this architecture include Microsoft's ISAPI and Netscape's NSAPI.

The third category is a hybrid of the previous categories, representing scripted pages that are compiled on request, with the compiled version then being used by all subsequent requests. When the original page's contents change, the page will undergo another compile. This category is a compromise between the flexibility of scripted pages and the efficiency of compiled pages.

The Unified Modeling Language

The strength of UML is rooted in its semantics as well as the metamodel that forms a foundation for future methods. The metamodel is one layer of a four-layer metamodeling architecture. In a metacircular manner, it specifies itself using a subset of UML object-oriented notation.

Through the unification of leading object-oriented methods founded on a wide base of user experience, UML provides the basis for an object-oriented analysis and design standard. Standardization of a language can become the foundation for tools and processes as well. The Unified Modeling Language is an object-oriented modeling language for specifying, visualizing, and documenting the artifacts of an object-oriented system during development. It combines concepts including `Booch-93`, OMT-2, and OOSE, resulting in a single, common, and widely usable modeling language for users of these and other methods.

Users of any object-oriented method can usually learn enough to achieve the same level of expressiveness fairly quickly. UML is appropriate for real-time systems, providing support for modeling classes, objects, and the relationships among them. These relationships include association, aggregation, inheritance, dependency, and instantiation. Use cases are directly supported with scenarios for detailed descriptions of required system behavior. Model scenarios are graphically represented through interaction diagrams that can include both timing and message synchronization annotations. Real-time features are supported through enhanced finite state machine modeling, including concurrency, event propagation, and nested states. The UML is extensible through the definition of additional stereotypes.

Many CASE tool vendors have committed to supporting the UML, so it will likely remain the standard notation for object-oriented systems development for the foreseeable future.

Goals and Principles of the UML

Devising a notation for use in object-oriented analysis and design is somewhat like designing a programming language. First, the author must define the problem, answering questions such as Should the notation encompass requirements specification? and Should the notation extend to the level of a visual programming language? Secondly, a balance between expressiveness and simplicity must be achieved. A notation that is too simple will limit the breadth of problems that can be solved, while one that is too complex can be overwhelming for the developer. If the methods already exist, too many changes may confuse existing users. On the other hand, not advancing the notation may eliminate the possibility of engaging a broader set of users.

The UML has seven goals:

1. To provide users with a ready-to-use, expressive visual modeling language for the development and exchange of meaningful models
2. To provide mechanisms for extensibility and specialization in order to extend the central concepts
3. To be independent from specific programming languages and development processes
4. To provide a formal foundation for understanding the modeling language
5. To encourage further development in the OO tools market
6. To support higher-level development concepts including collaborations, frameworks, patterns, and components
7. To integrate best practices

A metamodel was created in order to offer a common, clear-cut statement of the method's semantic model. Once this metamodel was developed, decisions about the surface graphical syntax for the visual elements of this model were taken. A number of principles to guide these efforts have been established:

- Simplicity—A method should only require a few concepts and symbols.
- Expressiveness—A method should be applicable to a wide variety of production-quality systems.

- Usefulness—A method should only focus on elements that are meaningful to practical system and software engineering.
- Common problems—These should be simple to model. More rare problems should still be expressible, but may require some complexity corresponding with their frequency of use.
- Self-consistency—The same concept and symbol should be used in the same manner throughout the method.
- Orthogonality—Unrelated concepts should be modeled independently.
- Advanced concepts—Layers of advanced concepts should be treated as additions to the method for more basic concepts.
- Stability—Concepts and symbols that are already commonly understood and used should be adopted.
- Printability—The approach to visualization should be based on a format that can be extended. Users should be able to sketch out the method manually or display it as a printed image.
- Adaptability—Extensible users and tool builders should have the ability to extend and adapt the method.

Devising real methods requires balancing each of these principles.

Conventions and Terminology

In UML, the explanation of each element follows a simple pattern. The semantics of the concept are described, followed by its graphical syntax. The following subsections may be found within each section:

- Semantics—This subsection provides a brief summary of semantics. For a fuller explanation and discussion, locate the UML Semantics document by searching for it by keyword on OMG's document search page at `http://cgi.omg.org/cgi-bin/doclist.pl`.
- Notation—This subsection explains the notational representation of the semantic concept, not always in a separated subsection.
- Presentation options—This subsection describes various options in presenting the model information, such as the ability to suppress or filter information, alternate ways of showing things, and alternate ways of presenting information within a tool.

We will discuss the underlying principles and/or relevance of each element that is explained and will provide a simple example of its use, an explanation of any recommended idioms, and hints that will help both users and tool builders.

This section is arranged according to diagram types, including the model elements found on that diagram as well as their representation. Many model elements can be used in more than one diagram; therefore, the description has been placed where it is used the most.

The metamodel layer can be thought of as a framework of subsections describing concepts of the underlying layer. The metamodel layer describes the subsections that will be used to describe the features of the UML concepts for object-oriented modeling on the model layer. In this case, metaclasses forming top-level packages on the metamodel level along with classes on the model level can be described as using the subsections Attributes (class attributes) and Associations (relationships between class instances).

The UML metamodel can be broken down into several top-level packages. The Foundation and Behavioral Elements packages are described in the following sections.

The Foundation Package

The Foundation package is composed of the Core, Auxiliary Elements, Extension Mechanisms, and Data Types subpackages, which are defined here:

- Core—This includes a Model Element, Generalizable Element, and Classifier. Specified constructs include Class, Attribute, Operation, and Association. This package specifies the core constructs required for a basic metamodel, defining an architectural backbone for the attachment of additional language constructs such as metaclasses, meta-associations, and meta-attributes.
- Auxiliary Elements—This package defines additional constructs that extend the core to support advanced concepts such as dependencies, templates, physical structures, and view elements.
- Extension Mechanisms—This package specifies how model elements are customized and extended with new semantics.
- Data Types—This package defines basic data structures for the language.

The Behavioral Elements Package

The Common Behavior package is the most fundamental of the subpackages that make up the Behavioral Elements package. This package specifies core concepts that are required for dynamic elements and provides the infrastructure to support the Collaborations package, the State Machine/Activity package and the Use Cases package. The Collaborations package specifies concepts required for expressing how different elements of a model interact with each other from a structural point of view. The State Machine package specifies a set of concepts that can be utilized for modeling behavior through finite state-transition systems. It also relies on concepts that are defined in the

Common Behavior package, allowing integration with the other subpackages within Behavioral Elements. The Use Cases package specifies concepts utilized for defining the functionality of an entity such as a system. The elements in the Use Cases package are used mainly to define the behavior of an entity such as a system or a subsystem without specifying the internal structure. The key elements in this package are `UseCase` and `Actor`. See Figure 3.12 for a use case diagram of the SilverBooks sample application including the actors (portrayed as stick figures).

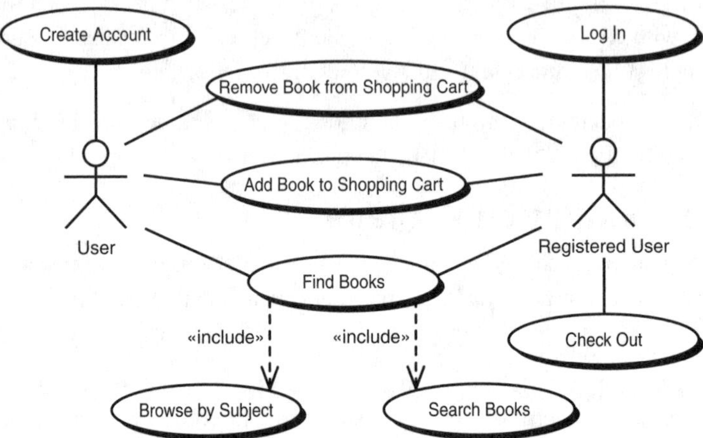

FIGURE 3.12
Sample application use case diagram.

Rational Rose 2000, by Rational Software Corporation, is a visual modeling tool that assists teams practicing iterative software development. The tool features multiuser support for round-trip engineering supporting C++, Java, and J2EE/EJB1.1. It supports the UML, including use cases, the `Booch` method, and the Object Modeling Technique (`OMT`). With the information contained in an application model, Rational Rose can generate both relational database schemas and `CORBA` 2–compliant IDL source code. Rational Rose 2000 includes portions of BEA's WebLogic Products for implementation of EJB 1.1. Go to `http://www.rational.com` for more information on Rational Rose.

Together ControlCenter by TogetherSoft (`http://www.togethersoft.com/`) is the development platform for building enterprise solutions. Its platform and building blocks technologies feature an end-to-end development environment that attempts to integrate the design, deployment, debugging, and administration of complex applications. See Figure 3.13 for an example of the tool's look and feel.

The latest version of ControlCenter has several new features and improvements. They are listed here:

- Diagram editor advances—new folded compartments, snap-to-grid, Web application diagrams, robustness diagrams
- Programming editor advances—new deep-search usage, JSP and HTML syntax, javadoc code completions, keyboard shortcuts for bookmarks
- JSP advances—new JSP/HTML editor, plus deployment and debugging with Tomcat
- Servlet advances—complete servlet modeling and generation
- EJB advances—new 2.0 support, EJB verification, works with over a dozen leading application server products
- Audit and metrics—results to HTML, plus new C++ support
- XML Metadata Interchange (XMI)—full and complete coverage in accordance with the Unisys standard

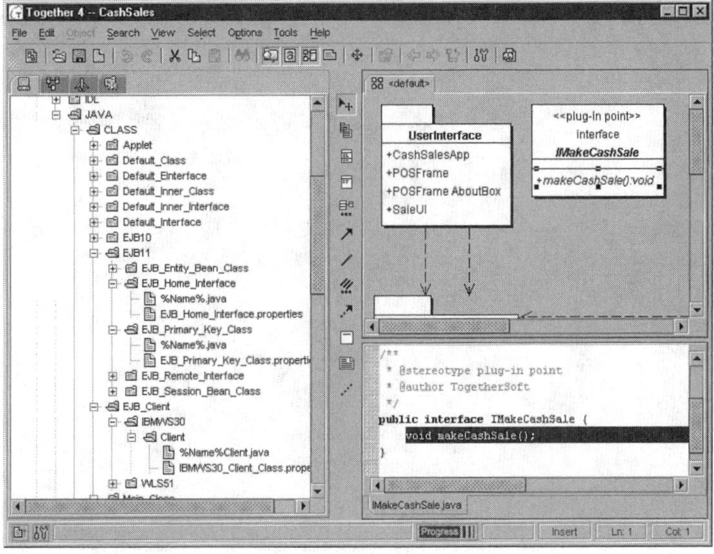

FIGURE 3.13
Together modeling tool.

Modeling Web Pages

Web pages, whether scripted or compiled, map one-to-one to components in UML. Components are physical and replaceable parts of the system. The Implementation view of the model, also known as the Component view, describes the components of the system along with their relationships. See Figure 3.14 for a look at the diagramming types used in UML. In a Web application, this view describes all of the Web pages of the system along with their relationships with each other (such as hyperlinks). At one level, the component diagram of a Web system is much like a site map.

Since components represent only the physical packaging of interfaces, they are not suitable for modeling the collaborations inside the pages. This level of abstraction, which is extremely important to the designer and implementer, still needs to be part of the model. We could say that each Web page is a UML class in the model's Design view, also known as the Logical view, and that its relationships/associations to other pages represent hyperlinks. This abstraction tends to break down when you consider that any given Web page can potentially represent a set of functions and collaborations existing only on the server, while a completely different set may exist only on the client. Any server-scripted Web page that employs Dynamic HTML (client-side scripting) as a portion of its output is an example of this type of page.

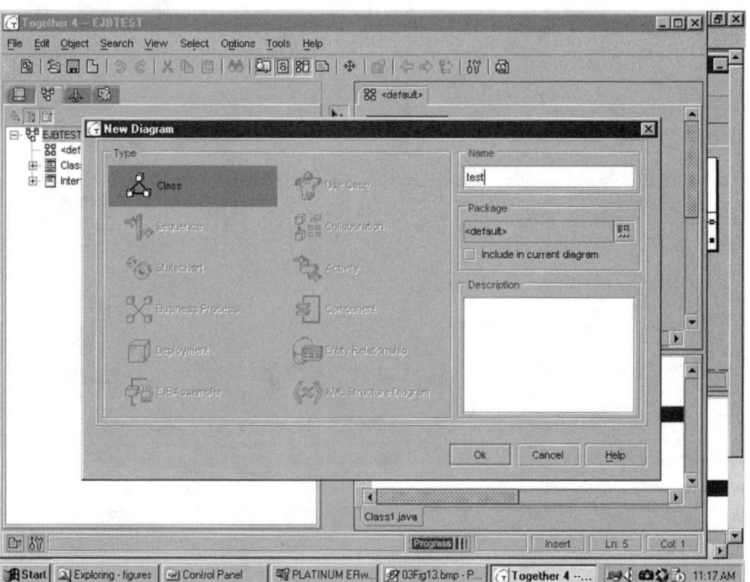

FIGURE 3.14
Diagramming UML.

The immediate reaction to this problem might be to stereotype each attribute or operation in the class to indicate whether or not it is valid on the server or client side. It is at this point that our model, originally intended to help simplify things, starts getting quite complicated.

A better approach to the problem is the principle of *separation of concerns*. The behavior of a Web page on the server is completely different from its behavior on the client. While executing on the server, it has access to and relationships with server-side resources such as middle-tier components, databases, and file systems. That same page, or the streamed HTML output of the page, has a completely different behavior and set of relationships when on the client. On the client, a scripted page has relationships with the browser itself via the Document Object Model (DOM) as well as with any Java applets, ActiveX controls, or plug-ins that the page specifies. For serious designers, there can be additional relationships with other active pages on the client that appear in another HTML frame or browser instance.

Separating concerns, the server-side aspect of a Web page can be modeled with one class, while the client-side aspect is modeled with another. The two are distinguished through use of UML's extension mechanism defining stereotypes and icons for each server page and client page. Stereotypes in UML allow the defining of new semantics for a modeling element.

For Web pages, stereotypes indicate that the class is an abstraction of the logical behavior of a Web page on either the client or the server. The two abstractions are related to each other with a directional relationship between them. This association is stereotyped as `«build»`, since server pages build client pages. In other words, every dynamic Web page whose content is determined at runtime is constructed with a server page. Every client page is built by a single server page at most; however, it's possible for a server page to build multiple client pages.

Hyperlinks are a common relationship between Web pages. Hyperlinks in a Web application represent navigation paths through the system. These relationships are expressed in the model with the `«link»` stereotyped association. As a rule, this association originates from a client page and points to either a client or server page. See Figure 3.15 for the `makeASale` relationships that can be diagrammed with the TogetherSoft tool.

Hyperlinks are implemented as a request for a Web page. Those Web pages are modeled as components in the Implementation view. Typically, a link association to a client page is equivalent to a link association to the server page that builds the client page. This is because a link is in reality a request for a page, not either of the class abstractions.

Because a Web page component realizes both page abstractions, a link to any of the classes realized by the page component is equivalent. Tagged values are utilized for defining the parameters that are passed along with a link request. The `«link»` association tagged value `Parameters` is a list of parameter names along with optional values that are expected and used by the server page processing the request.

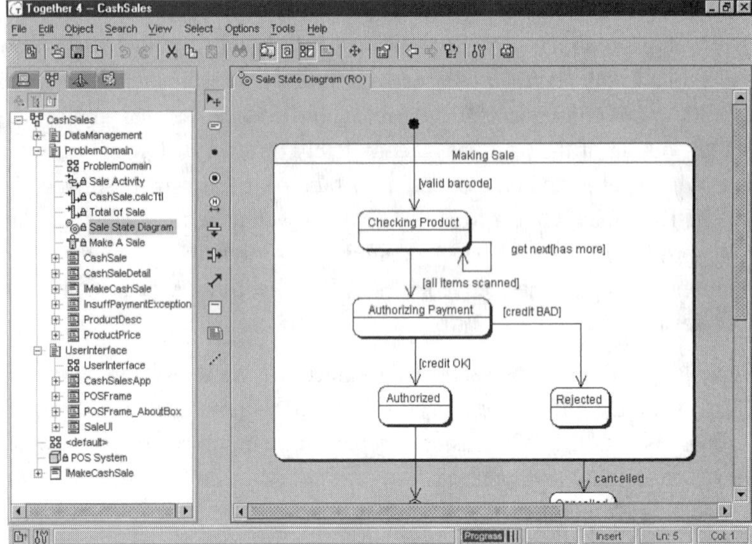

FIGURE 3.15
Relationships in UML.

These stereotypes make it easier to model a page's scripts and relationships. The `«server page»` class's operations become functions in the page's server-side scripts; its attributes become page-scoped variables that are globally accessible by the page's functions. The `«client page»` class's operations and attributes also become functions and variables visible on the client.

The key advantage to separation of the server- and client-side aspects of a page into different classes is in the relationships between pages and other classes of the system. Client pages are modeled with relationships to client-side resources such as DOM, Java applets, ActiveX controls, and plug-ins. Server pages are modeled with relationships to server-side resources such as middle-tier components, database access components, and server operating system.

One of the biggest advantages of using class stereotypes when modeling the logical behaviors of Web pages is that their collaborations with server-side components can be expressed in much the same way as any other server-side collaborations. The `«server page»` is just another class participating in the business logic of the system. On a more conceptual level, generally server pages take on the role of controllers. They orchestrate the necessary business object activity to accomplish the business goals initiated by the browser's page request. See Figure 3.16 for an activity view of shopping within the SilverBooks sample application.

FIGURE 3.16
Sample application activity diagram.

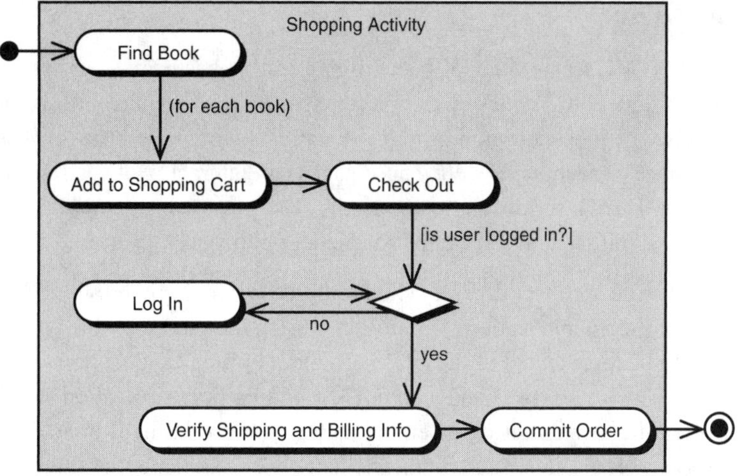

On the client side, collaborations tend to be more complicated, partially due to the wide variety of technologies that can be employed. In the simplest form, a client page is an HTML document containing both content and presentation information.

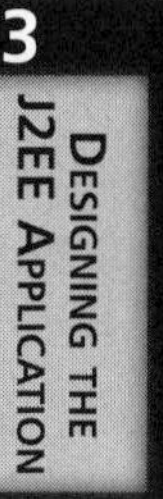

Browsers render HTML pages using formatting instructions in the page or in a separate style sheet. In the logical model, this relationship would be expressed with a dependency from a client page to a «`Style Sheet`» stereotyped class. Since style sheets are primarily a presentation issue, they are often left out of the Application Design Model (ADM).

Forms

The principal mechanism for entering data in Web pages is the form. In an HTML document, forms are defined with `<form>` tags. Each form specifies the page to which it should submit itself. A form also contains a number of input elements that are expressed as HTML tags. The most common of these tags are `<input>`, `<select>`, and `<textarea>`. The `<input>` tag can be a text field, check box, radio button, push button, image, hidden field, or one of a few other less common types.

Modeling forms is achieved through the «`Form`» class stereotype. A «`Form`» has no operations because any operations that might be defined in a `<form>` tag are really owned by the client page. The input elements of the form are all stereotyped attributes of the «`Form`» class. A «`Form`» can have relationships with applets or ActiveX controls acting as input controls. Each form also has a relationship with a server page, which is the page that processes the form's submission. This relationship is stereotyped as «`submit`». Since forms are contained entirely in an HTML document, they are expressed in a UML diagram with a strong form of aggregation.

Frames

Use of HTML frames in a Web site or application has been a subject of debate since their introduction. Frames allow multiple pages to be simultaneously active and visible to the user. The most common browsers today allow multiple browser instances to be active on the user's machine as well. These pages can interact with each other through use of Dynamic HTML scripts and components. The potential for complex interactions on the client is significant, and the need for modeling this even greater.

The software architect decides whether frames or multiple browser instances are employed in an application. If frames are used, the model of this client-side behavior needs to be represented in the ADM. To model frame usage, define two more class stereotypes, `«frameset»` and `«target»`, as well as the association stereotype `«targeted link»`. A frameset class representing a container object maps directly to the HTML `<frameset>` tag. This class contains client pages and targets. A target class is either a named frame or browser instance that is referenced by other client pages. A targeted link association is a hyperlink to another page that is rendered in a specific target. The actual presentation specifics are, for the most part, captured by tagged values in the frameset and the associations. Two tagged values on the aggregation relationship between a frameset and a target, or client page, identify the frameset row and column in which the target, or page, belong. The tagged value `Target` on the targeted link association specifies the `«target»` where the page should be rendered.

In cases where a target is not aggregated with a frameset, a separate browser instance is used to render the pages. It should be kept in mind that this notation is expressing a single instance of a client machine. It is assumed that all multiple independent targets are running on the same machine, with the diagram expressing the client-side behavior of one client instance. Any other deployment configuration would need to be heavily documented in the model to be better understood.

EJB UML Mapping

For more than a decade, development and use of object technology has been increasing. Database administrators, who controlled the mainframe and client/server development fields, have been increasingly forced to share authority as developers are moving quickly to adopt object-oriented (OO) languages such as C++ and Java. Recently, object and data professionals have been required to cooperate, especially when it comes to technology such as Enterprise JavaBeans (EJB) that are written in Java but are typically stored in relational databases such as Oracle or IBM's DB2, which use non-object technology.

Relational DBMSes have a well-known flaw: the application programmer is forced to work in languages such as Java or C++ that have a syntax, semantics, and type system different from the data manipulation language (that is, SQL) of the DBMS. Many developers overcome this by using object-relational mapping.

The UML specification provides a specialized use of UML known as a profile. In addition, the Java Community Process is involved in the creation of an EJB UML-mapping profile. The JSR-000026 UML profile for EJB, which can be found at `http://jcp.org/jsr/detail/26.jsp`, defines a set of UML extensions for use when modeling software implemented with Enterprise JavaBeans in UML. These extensions allow the Java IDE, application server, and other enterprise tool vendors to provide EJB modeling capabilities using UML within their tools. They also facilitate forward and reverse engineering between UML models and EJB implementations. an XML DTD for a file placed within the EJB-JAR that identifies a UML model stored in that EJB-JAR is defined within the specification, as well as that model's relationship to other EJBs in the same EJB-JAR. This enables use of Java's automation and reflection APIs to access UML models stored in EJB-JARs.

This is especially compelling because it gives EJB components the capability to self-describe their contents and capabilities, through use of case or other UML diagrams. XML Metadata Interchange (XMI), the widely used metadata representation format based on XML, will also be supported by this profile.

Need of the Java Community Addressed by the Proposed Specification

UML models must represent EJBs, capturing both their structure and semantics in order to describe software implemented with EJB. The model elements that express this structure and semantics are not contained in UML, since it predates EJB architecture. Because UML was designed to be extensible, it provides standard extension mechanisms for defining new model elements. These extension mechanisms can be used to define new model elements to represent EJBs.

In order for tools and frameworks from different vendors to interoperate, these extensions must be standardized. As it stands, some vendors may use nonstandard proprietary mappings between UML and EJB, some may use nonstandard proprietary metamodels rather than UML, and still others will not support modeling or model-based reflection and automation for EJB at all.

In addition, UML models describing EJBs with the EJB implementations in an EJB-JAR must be associated in order to use the models for automation and reflection. Without a standard way to achieve this association, tools and frameworks will be unable to use the UML models in EJB-JARs from different vendors.

Specification to be Developed and How It Addresses the Need

The following items express a new specification, defining a set of standard UML extensions that will define new model elements to represent EJBs. The UML profile for EJBs

- Describes the relationship of logical and physical EJB constructs to UML model elements using the standard UML extension mechanisms
- Describes the relationship between the EJB deployment descriptor and UML model elements using the standard UML extension mechanisms
- Describes the forward engineering transformation from UML model elements using the standard UML extension mechanisms to EJB implementation artifacts
- Describes the reverse engineering transformation from EJB implementation artifacts to UML model elements using the standard UML extension mechanisms

In addition, the specification defines a mechanism for the association of UML models stored in an EJB-JAR with the implementations of the EJBs they describe. The UML descriptor for EJB defines an XML DTD for a file placed within the EJB-JAR identifying UML models stored in the same EJB-JAR as well as their relationship to EJBs in the EJB-JAR.

Tool Support

The high cost of UML modeling tools has kept the majority of developers from adopting object-oriented analysis and design techniques. With the advent of open source modeling tool efforts such as ArgoUML (see `http://argouml.tigris.org/`), this is about to change. Thorn is a UML modeling tool written in Java that enables the use of XML to save the models you create. The Thorn modeling tool was created to help develop and manage increasingly sophisticated open source development efforts.

ArgoUML is a modular and extensible open source Java/UML project that focuses on developing better tools for collaborative software development. ArgoUML is based on the UML 1.3 specification and is licensed in much the same way as the Apache Web server. It provides comprehensive support for the XML Metadata Interchange (XMI) format and the Object Constraint Language (OCL).

Several UML tool vendors including Rational are getting involved in collaborative tools. The Rational Suite set of software development life cycle tools integrates the Rational

Rose platform with its ClearCase change management solution and a collection of other requirements (RequisitePro), testing (QualityArchitect, Purify, Quantify, and TestManager), and verification (PureCoverage) tools. For more information about Rational products, visit `http://www.rational.com/products/index.jsp`.

UML has been a blessing for developers eager to work at a higher level of abstraction because it offers standardization for modeling artifacts and semantics. In addition to EJB component-based and object-oriented software projects, UML also facilitates non-OO software development. Despite the fact that database systems have been around for many years, industry analysts estimate that 80% of the electronic data in companies is unstructured, residing in forms such as text files. With the rapid evolution of the World Wide Web and the availability of content-based search engines, it is becoming even more clear that data can be accessed successfully even in the absence of a database.

Because much of the data found on the Web is fragmented, it seems unnecessary to store this data in a bunch of RDBMS tables accessing it with relational connectors. With XML organizing content in a more structured and semantically meaningful form than HTML, it is likely that developers will increasingly take a more responsibility-driven or object-oriented (as opposed to data-centric) approach to their applications.

Because developers are no longer willing to store all the data in one vulnerable RDBMS basket, it is also increasingly likely that they will turn to UML to raise the level of abstraction of their Web-based systems, especially if those systems consist of societies of collaborating objects. Although the concept of relational models was powerful and useful in its time, the future will be about objects and Internet-based UML applications and tools.

Summary

The ideas and concepts discussed in this chapter are an introduction to issues and solutions for modeling Web application–specific elements with UML. The goal was to present a brief introduction to the ways and means of integrating the modeling of Web-specific elements with the rest of the application, such that the levels of detail and abstraction are appropriate for designers, implementers, and architects of Web applications.

CHAPTER 4

Task List for Building J2EE Applications

In This Chapter

- Completing Prerequisite Tasks *98*
- Designing the Database *102*
- Creating Tables and Columns *104*
- Defining the Application *108*
- Creating a Back-End Interface *110*
- Creating the Interface *112*
- Building Pages *114*
- Creating Data Access Objects *117*
- Validating Your Code *118*
- Refining Your Code *119*

Developing an application is one of those catch phrases that can mean different things. For the purposes of this reference, we will focus on the tasks (as well as the relative sequence of the tasks) that make up the average application development life cycle. Each of these steps takes place during the course of development. Some will need to be done more than once. In fact, sometimes a whole group of steps will be performed iteratively. This is not unique to developing with J2EE and a relational database management system (RDBMS), but is common in most development efforts. Effective planning and hard work can keep these reiterations to a minimum, saving time and money, and perhaps maintaining the integrity of the objects developed.

In any event, this chapter will first provide a quick overview and later a basic checklist of the steps involved in J2EE application development.

Completing Prerequisite Tasks

Before you begin the actual construction portion of the development life cycle, certain prerequisite tasks should either be complete or in an advanced state of preparation. The project team should have a development approach and an accompanying plan that includes skilled players to carry it to fruition. They will also need an application and perhaps a database logical model and the physical manifestation of the model (file directories and a database with adequate space as well as workstation resources). These are the components that provide for successful development.

Logistic Prerequisites

The developers must decide on the separation of the application components. The lead development team, which on a larger project may consist of more than 30 people, will incorporate an application design based upon a three-tier (3T) approach. The developers must decide how to break out the functional requirements into logical tiers that promote a consistent, reusable, and maintainable application system that performs to the user's satisfaction. The developers must consider how this can be accomplished. There are many aspects of development to consider. They will dictate the type of developers you will staff the effort with (that is, which skills are required to implement the architecture).

The classic two-tier (2T) approach, implemented ad infinitum, uses the Visual Basic or PowerBuilder client server architecture, or in the old days, the CICS/COBOL/MVS client with DB2/MVS server sometimes residing on the same host platform MVS.

Table 4.1 shows the structure of the two-tier model.

TABLE 4.1 Two-Tier Development

Level	*Function*	*Description*
TIER 1	Server	Database server stores and requests data
TIER 2	Client	Application objects receive and present data

The majority of the application is on the client, including the database access language (SQL). Another approach is to put the data access (for example, stored procedures) and database on the server and use the client as a presentation tool only. The best implementations are flexible and include the proper mix of client SQL with presentation pages and the use of stored procedures for functions where performance demands are severe. The appropriateness of this approach must be evaluated on a case-by-case basis.

To complicate the issue further, the three-tier (3T) development explicitly breaks out everything in the application into a separate layer. The architecture includes the tiers listed and described in Table 4.2.

TABLE 4.2 Three-Tier Development

Level	*Function*	*Description*
TIER 1	Presentation logic	Developers build the application presentation objects (pages or JSP pages) to provide application presentation and navigation.
TIER 2	Business rules	Developers implement application servers and handle business rules and processes using non-visual objects.
TIER 3	Database management	EJB developers implement access modules in the form of session or entity beans. DBAs develop database design and access modules in the form of stored procedures.

The 3T approach requires separate teams of developers and better coordination of effort than is required by the 2T approach. It also breaks out the types of objects developed by RDBMS vendor database systems such as SQL Server 7, as well as which external items will have to interface with a GUI presentation tool. For example, the GUI presentation tool object's JSP pages may call server-based taglibs and beans for business logic or page switching.

Figure 4.1 depicts the two-tier architecture, which consists of integrated business rules and database access.

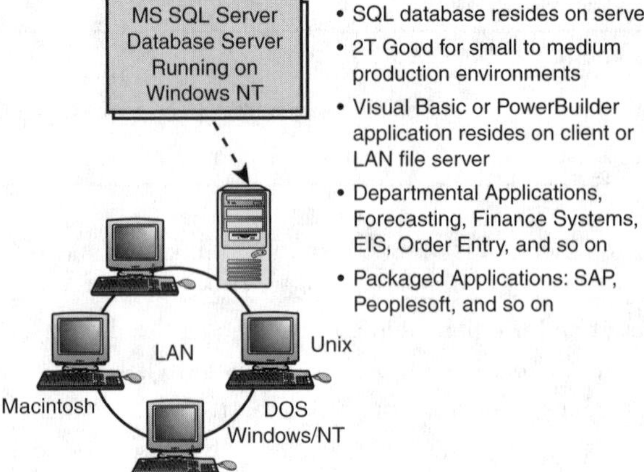
MS SQL Server
Database Server
Running on
Windows NT
• SQL database resides on server
• 2T Good for small to medium production environments
• Visual Basic or PowerBuilder application resides on client or LAN file server
• Departmental Applications, Forecasting, Finance Systems, EIS, Order Entry, and so on
• Packaged Applications: SAP, Peoplesoft, and so on
LAN
Unix
Macintosh
DOS
Windows/NT

FIGURE 4.1
Two-tier architecture.

This arrangement of server and client can cause the following interactions:

- The client1 workstation uses JSP to issue a request for server-based resources and starts a shopping session.
- The server1/client2 issues a remote call to an EJB entity bean to access an RDBMS database such as SQL Server.
- The server2 accesses a mainframe CICS transaction to select from an NT-based SQL Server database server and returns the data down the chain to the client for final presentation.

The legacy system is viewed mainly as a database server, with the business rules of the application moved onto an intermediate server and presentation placed on the end-user client machine. Placing the business rules on the client machine can result in what is physically a 2T system having a 3T architecture, except that security and performance concerns have mandated an intermediate server to effect load balancing between database and file servers. This frees up a lot of expensive mainframe (database server) time, producing a much more efficient system.

Three-tier development is more complex and expensive. It also requires faster network communication to support the increase in messaging between the three tiers. Extensive planning, design, and coordination are also required. Note that in Figure 4.2, we see the typical back office mainframe using IBM's MVS operating system with database access software such as ADABAS, IDMS, and IMS. Also, the mainframe would house a CICS transaction server using IBM's relational database DB2. Care must be taken so that 3T systems come in on budget and on schedule. Setbacks are usually caused by a lack of appropriate planning and undereducated and miscast management and developers.

The three-tiered/multitiered environment is what J2EE is designed to facilitate. Information and services must be available for external as well as internal users with a wide range of clients (for example, HTML- and WAP-based interfaces).

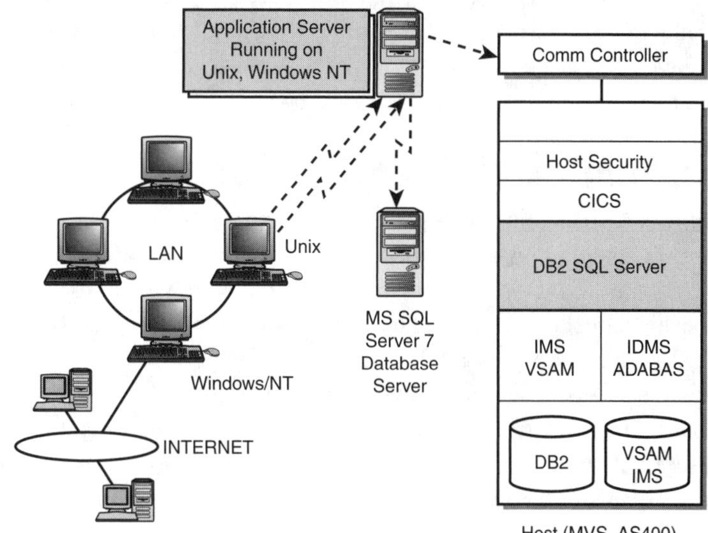

FIGURE 4.2
Three-tier architecture.

Physical Prerequisites

Before you begin the physical construction of the application components, certain prerequisite physical items must be in place for use by the development team. Besides an adequate workstation and the appropriate server(s), the J2EE project libraries (GUI presentation tool) accessible to developers should also be available, with the appropriate permissions in place. Access to the RDBMS application database with current maintenance and whatever third-party or in-house J2EE development software is needed should be available from each workstation. Developers should be aware of the guidelines and naming standards the project team has agreed to use to develop both the database and the application.

These suggestions may seem a bit pedantic, but they will save precious time later in the process. They will also reduce the confusion that accompanies the start of a project. Developers can work efficiently when these conditions are met. They can be certain that objects such as database tables are named properly, follow suggested guidelines (for example, having a unique index for each table), and are stored in the correct database.

Designing the Database

The design process for the application database is unique to each development environment but will be discussed in general terms here. The specifics of the process may vary from shop to shop. The design process is a critical item, and the degree to which it is completed before the commencement of full-scale development is critical to the success of the project.

Determining the Application Entities

An *entity* is a person, place, object, event, or activity that is relevant to the functionality you are creating. For instance, any noun that can represent information of interest to the organization is an entity. In the logical database design, you try to build an entity-relationship model by identifying the entities and their attributes as well as the relationships between the different entities. The database logical design effort begins as soon as you meet the users. Listen for entities in interviews with the user. If you are developing a database to track employee expenses, the entities will include employee and employee expense detail. Figure 4.3 illustrates a database logical design using a popular tool known as ERwin, which was discussed in Chapter 3, "Designing the J2EE Application."

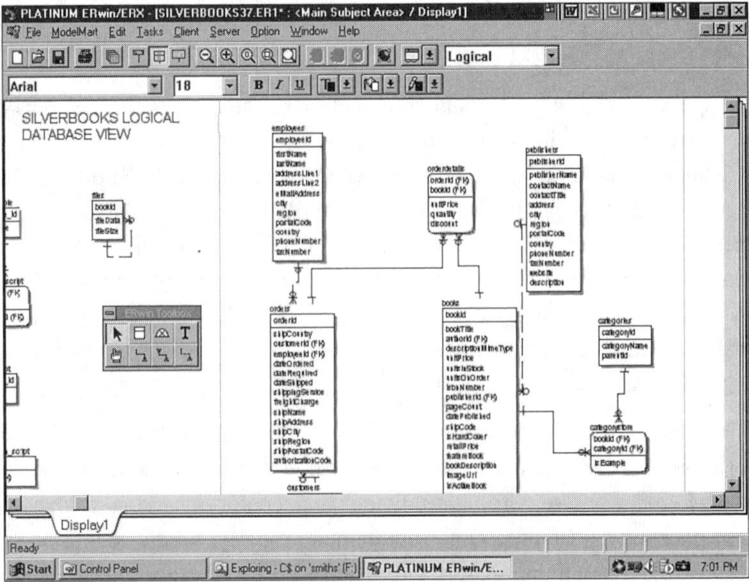

FIGURE 4.3
Database logical model.

The *attributes* of an entity are the things that describe and define it. For example, a book has a descriptive name, which is an attribute of the book. The date it was originally published may also be an attribute. Also, listen for relationships in the user interviews. What is a relationship? If an entity cannot exist without a parent, it is dependent, which means it belongs to another entity. This is a relationship.

Important subsets of an entity that have special attributes are called *subentities*. For example, a book may be of type `hardcover` with attributes that only pertain to a hardcover series, while a dependent entity (`orderdetails`, for example) belongs to an order and has a primary key that contains the parent key and an additional key to identify the dependent entity.

Refining Each Entity and Attribute

After you have collected the business entities and attributes from interviews with the user, check the project standards for naming conventions. If applicable, use firm-wide abbreviations to ensure consistent naming. Next, attempt to capture description and validation criteria for each entity and attribute. Does the project have a data dictionary? If so, enter the description and validation criteria here. Also check the dictionary to determine if the attribute or entity already exists. An RDBMS such as SQL Server 7 usually has its own catalog tables, or extended attributes, which can house descriptions and validation rules. These attributes can be populated from computer aided software engineering (CASE) tools such as ERwin or PowerDesigner and eventually can help define the SQL Server database diagram. These tools facilitate design efforts for database and business application systems.

Determine the primary key for each entity. The primary key of an entity uniquely identifies entity instances (rows). The primary key of a dependent entity includes the parent key and descriptive column. For example, the primary key for the `orderdetails` entity is the `orderId` and `bookId` concatenated. In database design, it is also important to document the past or future states of all data, that is, to add a `last_update_timestamp`. This will facilitate garbage collection of old data. The primary key will promote database integrity, as you will inhibit table row duplication and the creation of database orphans (that is, rows in a dependent table with no parent). Moreover, there will be integrity with respect to any parent-child relationships. No child rows will exist without a parent.

Determining Relationships

Again, listen for relationships in interviews with the user. Document the roles of entities in recursive relationships. A series may be a part of another series. Determine the cardinality of the relationship. A relationship describes a business rule about two or more entities. Cardinality refers to a statement of how many of one item relate to another. A relationship may be optional or mandatory. Cardinality is represented by “crow’s feet” (see Figure 4.3) as follows: zero or one, exactly one, zero, one or more. Examples of relationship/business rules are "Each customer must place one or more orders" and "Each order must include exactly one orderdetail."

This will facilitate the choice of keys or indices to access the entity. Does the identifying key to the relationship have many different values? Decide on a formal name by checking the standards for naming keys. Don't confuse relationships with entities or attributes. Attributes that designate entities are relationships. If the primary key of an entity consists of other primary keys, it may be a relationship. For example, in Figure 4.3, the `orderdetails` entity would have a primary key consisting of the `orderId` and `bookId` concatenated. The `bookId` identifier is the primary key of the `books` entity.

Creating Tables and Columns

Typically, when you are using the completed logical design, independent entities are cast as independent tables. Similarly, dependent entities become dependent tables. See Figure 4.4 for an example of a physical design of the logical model that was depicted in Figure 4.3. Before defining the database in the development RDBMS, the designers should verify that tables are in third normal form (3NF), which means that every non-key column depends on the key, the whole key, and nothing but the key, as is the case with the orderdetails entity in Figure 4.3. The designers should attempt to retain normalized subtables unless the cost of application-required table joins is unacceptable or merging with the supertable creates few inapplicable nulls.

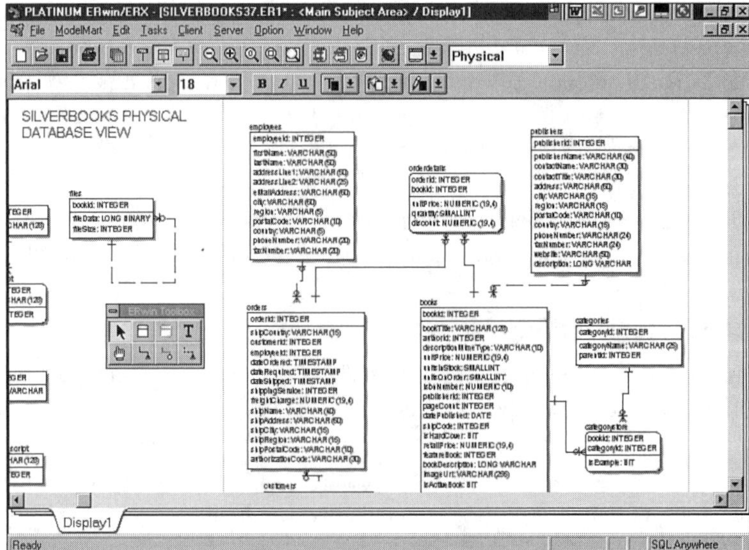

FIGURE 4.4
Physical database design.

Consider merging tables linked by one-to-one relationships. This merger works best if minimum cardinality is also one-to-one, and cardinality is stable. Denormalize for performance as a last resort. You should exhaust physical solutions first, denormalize selectively, and apply updates directly to third normal form (3NF) tables.

Briefly, 3NF means that you

- Eliminate repeating groups—Make a separate table for each set of related attributes, and give each table a primary key.
- Eliminate redundant data—If an attribute depends on only part of a multi-valued key, remove it to a separate table.
- Eliminate columns not dependent on the key—If attributes do not contribute to a description of the key, remove them to a separate table.

The attributes of each entity usually become table columns. These table columns should be well-thought-out data types. For instance, do not use a decimal for a number that is always an integer. These table columns should be specified as `NOT NULL` for required attributes and relationships. You can cause the DBMS to enforce unique attributes/columns by defining them as an index. Attributes of relationships then go with a foreign key. Implement vectors column-wise unless physical size, user access, or number of tables forces row-wise design. Where possible, avoid alternating, encoded, or overlapping columns.

Choosing Data Types

The RDBMS has had real impact in the area of data type choices; there are a host of new data types such as date and time. In the example of a bookstore database, we want to store more than the fundamental data types, such as numbers, characters, and dates. This application would not have been practical using older nonrelational technology.

Essentially, the SQL-92 data types are

- `integer`
- `floating-point number`
- `character string` *(fixed or variable length)*
- `day-time`, `time interval`
- `numeric` and `decimal`

Consider the following additional new wave data as well. Images and large text data types are becoming increasingly popular.

- Geographic locations—The information for viewer locations, although available, can be efficiently stored or queried in a traditional RDBMS. This type of activity has historically been done in a global information system (GIS), but this is a very expensive approach, and the tools don't integrate well.
- Images—Again, these are at best stored as Binary Large Objects or BLOBs within a traditional RDBMS. Technology to search for images that are similar to one another has been available only as a client implementation, and searching an entire image base for particular images just has not been practical.

Imagine that you want to expand the bookstore system, and let's say that the following technical requirements must be met:

- Image storage and retrieval—This requirement is for storage and management of book covers and other images.
- Text search—Screening reports always contain text descriptions, which have valuable content that is hard to access. A text search might enable you to find books about J2EE and RDBMS by searching for the words "J2EE" and "RDBMS" near each other.
- Geospatial analysis—Consider the issue of finding which products sell well in or near a specific location. Unless both the text information and the geospatial information are in the same server with efficient search optimization, such analysis is impractical.
- Web integration—The bookstore Web site is fully dynamic; what you see and interact with must adapt to the type of inquiry.

Creating Keys

Besides the primary key and index, secondary keys and indices may be required. In a many-to-one relationship, place the foreign key in the many-side table. In a one-to-one relationship, place foreign keys in the table with fewer rows. The many-to-many relationship becomes an associative or junction table. Consider an artificial primary key such as a random number when there are many incoming foreign keys and the natural key is null, not unique, unstable, complex, or meaningful.

Completing Database Physical Design

Now you have tables and columns and a cluster index, but you are not done yet. To *cluster* means to define indices such that like valued rows are stored in close proximity to each other, allowing for quicker retrieval. To really know whether your design will perform, you must list, examine, and explain critical queries and transactions. Critical queries are high-volume, require quick response, or are frequently executed. They are the points of reference for physical design. Create and use critical queries (the SQL used most frequently in the application) for reference and access a clustered index for most if not all tables (usually on the primary key). Occasionally some other column is more important for access and gets the clustered index. Small or temporary tables may have no clustered index.

Create nonclustered indexes (consider foreign key columns) for other columns that are used to search or order the data. Review critical queries after you have assigned a clustered index. Are any of these queries unable to utilize the clustered indices for access? If so, consider nonclustered indexes on column(s) specified in a `where` clause, particularly join columns. Create a nonclustered index only when the hit ratio is low. Usually, it is best to create at most three or four indices per table (unless they're read-only). The rest are DBMS-dependent. The DBAs usually determine partitions, locking, granularity, and device assignments. Whoever is responsible for completing the physical design should notify the developers at each significant milestone.

Estimating the Size of the Database

It is a good idea to find out how much traffic your database is expected to have for the first years of production. This will help in the physical design of the database and SQL access as well. Toward this end, it is wise to build a spreadsheet to estimate and finalize storage requirements. The steps in this process are as follows:

1. Estimate the number of tables.
2. Estimate the length of each row.
3. Estimate the number of rows for each table (including a year's worth of growth).
4. Procure additional storage, if needed.
5. Build a spreadsheet to estimate and finalize access requirements.
6. Estimate the number of users.
7. Determine user transaction types—Enterprise Information System (EIS), Decision Support System (DSS), or Online Transaction Processing (OLTP).
8. Calculate the cost and frequency of each access.

Setting Up the Development Database Environment

It is also good practice to set up your development database to have simulated data for the first year of production loaded. This will help to certify the physical design of the database and SQL access as well. The steps in this process are as follows:

1. Create the database, tables, indices, and user permissions.
2. Use ERwin to generate the database schema.
3. Use RDBMS Enterprise Manager to administer and maintain database objects.
4. Build batch and online procedures to populate and access the database.
5. Use flat-file extracts to load the initial test bed of data.
6. Develop procedures for periodic mass updates (embedded SQL, Java, J2EE session and entity beans).
7. Develop OLTP using stored procedures and SQL.
8. Build ad hoc query tools (dynamic data pages).
9. Procure warehousing tools.
10. Use the DBMS EXPLAIN utility for all SQL with problematic performance.
11. Refine the database physical design.
12. Add secondary indexes to aid access and improve performance.
13. Repartition and relocate physical components.

Defining the Application

After the development environment has been established, the first step in defining the application is to create the application libraries and the point of entry. Defining the application not only includes setting up and defining the application object, but also establishing the rules of interaction between developers. The developers must buy into the idea of sharing objects they will jointly develop. They should "check in" and "check out" development objects, using basic teamwork to maximize project productivity.

The basic items required to set up a J2EE Web application development environment are listed here and shown in Figure 4.5:

- Command line and DOS prompt to run batch files
- The Java Development Kit (javac.exe and jar.exe) or jikes.exe
- An archiving tool for Java, such as Winzip

- Deployment tools to add .ear files to the application server (for example, SilverCmd.exe from \SilverStream37\bin\)
- Java, XML, and HTML editors such as JBuilder, Forte, Visual Café, and Dreamweaver

Once you have these items, you should complete the following steps:

1. Set up the J2EE directory structure (see Figure 4.6).
2. Create JSP pages, JavaBeans, and servlet classes in the appropriate directory; place all of the Web-based Java .class files in WEB-INF\classes.
3. Set up the CLASSPATH.
4. Compile the servlets, JSP pages, EJBs, and other Java classes.
5. Edit application.wml and web.xml.
6. Create the archives to house the classes and application components: EAR, WAR, EJB JARs.
7. Create a deployment plan.
8. Deploy the application EAR and deployment description to the target servers.
9. Validate the application.

FIGURE 4.5
Basic J2EE and Web application components.

Client	Presentation	Business Logic	Integration	Resources
HTML JavaScript CSS	Servlet	EJB	JDBC 2.0	RDBMS
	JSP	Session	JMS	Message Queue Topic
XHTML WML	MVC/Struts	Entity Beans	SOAP	
Swing	XML Parser	Data Accessors		XML
	XSL Processor			JCA
E-mail	JavaMail - SMTP, IMAP, POP3			
EDI/B2B SOAP				

The Application Standards

At this point, you and your developer colleagues should be familiar with certain application defaults. The standard font and size can be set in the cascading style sheets (CSS). Libraries and store objects can be set up according to application functionality or by object type. Defining an application library set for an application is usually done once, but the application object may be copied onto each developer's workstation so that the developer can include his or her own UI presentation tool in the library list (usually first). This is a good technique for setting up a development environment where object sharing is accomplished (library list 2–N contains project-wide UI presentation tools) and developers can test new objects (library list item 1, which contains an individual developer's new and amended classes).

The application standard may also involve the use of the Model-View-Controller (MVC) methodology. The goal of the MVC design pattern is to separate the application object (Model) from the way it is represented to the user (View) from the way in which the user controls it (Controller). This design allows support for multiple presentations of the same information. It allows providers and developers to focus on their areas of expertise.

The MVC design breaks out the components as follows:

- View—manages the graphical and/or textual output to the portion of the bitmapped display that is allocated to its application
- Controller—interprets the mouse and keyboard inputs from the user, commanding the Model and/or the View to change as appropriate
- Model—manages the behavior and data of the application domain, responds to requests for information about its state (usually from the View), and responds to instructions to change state (usually from the Controller)

Creating a Back-End Interface

Even a J2EE Web-based system will usually require some form of back-end interface. By back-end interface, we mean jobs and processes consisting of a command language (for example, NT command script) that executes a sequential series of utilities and application programs (for example, EMBEDDED SQL) to access and manipulate the application database. For example, you might have a data transfer from a mainframe (for example, IBM MVS or AS/400) containing reference data. The flat ASCII reference data or XML, when received, is then loaded into a table in an RDBMS vendor database system such as SQL Server 7 for use by the OLTP. The load might be followed by a script call to an RDBMS database to execute a stored procedure to update other tables in accordance with the downloaded data. For example, an ASCII price file is downloaded from an IBM DB2 database and used to update an SQL Server 7 price table. The new prices are then used by an SQL Server 7 stored procedure to update client positions in an SQL Server 7 portfolio table.

Initial Data Loading

Every table has to start drawing content from somewhere. If you have an existing system, you may have a conversion where the old system's data is downloaded and used to seed and populate the new system tables. RDBMS vendor database systems such as SQL Server 7 provide a variety of utilities and options to load flat ASCII data into a RDBMS table. The choice between utilities is based on speed and flexibility.

Creating EJB Classes and Database Stored Procedures

When you have the database designed and you know the set of accesses required by the application, you can begin to build Enterprise JavaBeans (EJBs) and perhaps database procedures to access the RDBMS database. A powerful option available with J2EE is the EJB entity bean. An entity bean (EB) is an EJB that models data typically stored in a relational database. Usually, it will exist for as long as the data associated with the bean exists. Entity beans allow data to be persisted as Java objects. They enable the bean writer to abstractly associate Java objects with relational database components. Entity beans are most often used for representing a set of data, such as the columns in a database table, with each entity bean instance containing one element of that data set, such as a row from a database table.

Another avenue provided by most RDBMS vendor database systems such as SQL Server 7 is the stored procedure. Using stored procedures, SQL statements and control-of-flow stored procedure language (SPL) can be grouped in one object to improve the performance of SQL Server. Stored procedures are collections of SQL statements and SPLs. They are stored in the database, and the SQL is parsed and optimized. An execution plan is prepared and cached when a procedure is run so that subsequent execution is very fast. The SQL is only reoptimized at execution if necessary.

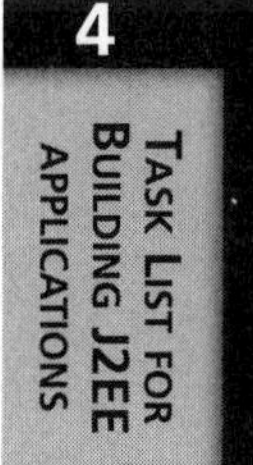

Stored procedures can

- Receive parameters passed by the calling object
- Call other procedures
- Return a status value to a calling procedure or GUI front end to indicate success or failure, and, in the event of failure, the reason
- Return values of parameters to a calling procedure or GUI front end
- Be executed on remote SQL Server 7 as remote procedures calls (RPC)

In summary, both EJBs and stored procedures can be executed if your server and the remote server are both set up to allow remote logins. You can write triggers on your local RDBMS vendor database systems such as SQL Server 7 that execute procedures on a remote server whenever certain events such as deletions, updates, or inserts take place locally.

Batching Utilities for Database Tuning and Repair

Sometimes a table can become fragmented and unorganized, degrading your performance. It is best to know about this as soon as possible. Other times, a table can become corrupted and you would like to be able to amend it as soon as possible. RDBMS vendor database systems such as SQL Server 7 typically provide a host of utilities to reorganize and repair disorganized and damaged tables.

Batching Utilities for Backup and Recovery

Every serious database application should include a scenario for backup and recovery in the case of a system failure that destroys the database. RDBMS vendors provide various solutions that can support each particular environment.

Creating the Interface

After you have developed the basic presentation/navigation of the application and received user approval, you can build the HTML and JSP pages and navigation/menus that present the data. They are stored in a directory setup similar to Figure 4.6. You also develop the menu(s) or navigation pages that allow the user to move from page to page and perform application tasks. Internet-based OLTP applications should provide easy-to-understand, user-approved data entry characteristics as well as a quick, understandable response to each user action.

The user-approved application presentation and navigation can and should be done at or near the beginning of the development cycle. Make sure the user has seen and used a prototype or example of how the basic system components will look and feel, and make sure the user signs off on the design for that application version.

Choosing an Application User Interface Style

As Web sites such as Amazon.com increased in popularity, their look and feel became the de facto standard. A growing number of users are accustomed to using Amazon's application interface. Moreover, the predominant development style is the Model-View-Controller (MVC) style. MVC uses one Controller to determine the View presented to the user after the Model processing has been completed (see Figure 4.7 for an example). In Figure 4.7, the first request goes to the Controller, which initializes the context/session for the overall transaction. It then alerts Page A's Model (business logic) and forwards execution to Page A's View (a JSP). Page A posts the flow back to the Controller, which invokes Model A to validate the posted form data. If the input is invalid, Model A returns a result that the Controller uses to forward or redisplay the View Page A. The Controller determines what happens next in the application using the classic if/then/else syllogism or perhaps by parsing an XML document, matching against database records, or invoking a more complex rules engine. The Controller is the centralized dispatcher that is aware of when all required steps in a transaction are complete.

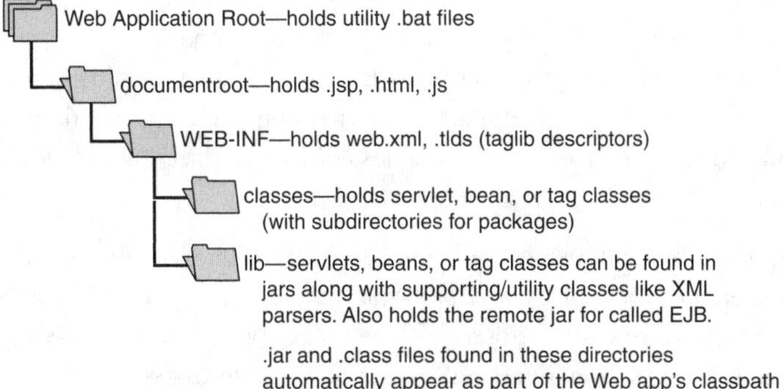

FIGURE 4.6
Basic J2EE Web application directory structure.

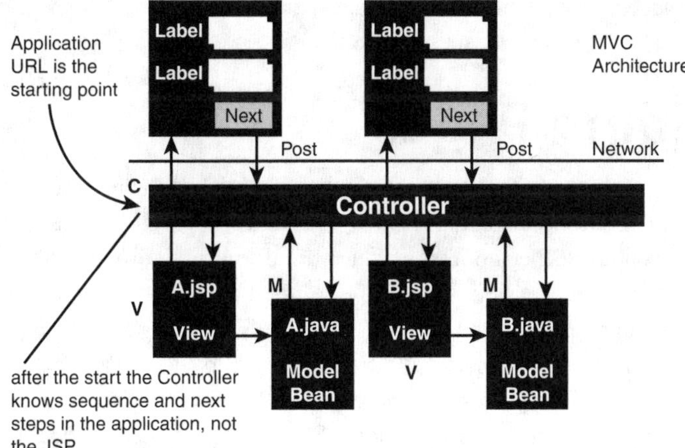

FIGURE 4.7
Basic MVC-based Web application flow.

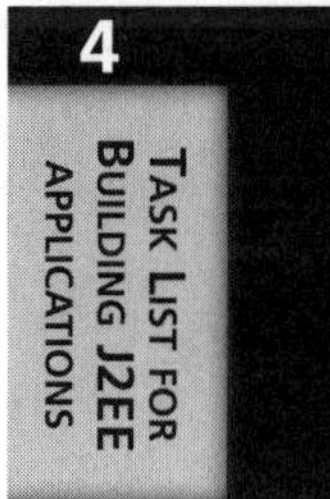

Setting Up the TAGLIB Class Library for the Interface Style

Web sites need people with varied skills working on the front end of an application. Tag libraries allow the page developer and Java programmer to add a layer of abstraction to the solution. This helps since the logic code, like JavaBeans, can be separated from the presentation.

Tag libraries take the `useBean` approach one step further, as the page developer often knows nothing at all about the underlying Java code and can simply use a set of predefined tags that most HTML writers find natural to add to the presentation.

In simple terms, a class or tag library is a collection of objects (pages, menus, business objects) that have generic functionality that the developer can use by inheriting the class object. Inheriting this class object provides all pages that use this menu with a consistent print interface. Moreover, the interface is only coded once. Each time you inherit it, you save time and money because it is one less object you need to develop and maintain. Eventually, the class/tag library will pay for itself.

Assuming that we will use the Model-View-Controller (MVC) interface, the organization will have either procured a class/tag library, including an MVC implementation kit, or developed its own class/tag libraries. This will obviate a redo of the application launching objects (`page frame` and `menu`) on the part of aggressive developers. Once the base frame, menu, and pages are created, the developers need only inherit the page to be able to create pages, place controls in the pages, and build scripts that specify the processing that will occur when events are triggered.

Building Pages

Pages are the main interface between the user and the application. Pages can display information, request information from a user, and respond to mouse or keyboard actions. Pages can contain JSP custom tags, which are useful in defining new beans (in any desired scope) from a variety of possible sources, as well as a tag to render a particular bean (or bean property) to the output response. JSP pages with an embedded Struts taglib can include the use of localization (a Struts internal bean). Java Servlets are designed to handle requests made by browsers. JavaServer Pages are designed to create pages that can turn static sites into live applications. Struts uses a special Servlet as a dispatcher to route requests from Web browsers to the appropriate JSP page. Struts combines Java Servlets, JavaServer Pages, custom tags, and message resources into a unified framework. The end result is a cooperative, synergistic platform, suitable for development teams and independent developers. See Chapter 10, "Building the User Interface to the Application," for a more detailed discussion of building pages.

Struts is useful in creating dynamic HTML user interfaces, including input forms. Struts can bridge the gap between the Form class and the JSP page. Struts contains tags that are useful in managing conditional generation of output text, looping over object collections for repetitive generation of output text, and application flow management.

Determining the Type of Page

The type of page you use to implement a particular feature of the application is an important decision when you are trying to make your application consistent with other Web applications. Table 4.3 lists page types and their properties.

TABLE 4.3 Page Types

Type	*Properties*
Main/page	This is a standalone page; it has no dependencies.
	The page has a title bar. (Is there a project standard for setting the title?)
	This is sometimes called a parent or overlapped page.
	The page has its own menu. (Is there a standard class-library menu?)
Child/subpage	The page is always subordinate to its parent page (for example, drop-down data access pages).
	the page moves with the parent page because its position is always relative to the parent page.
Response	The page obtains information from and provides information to the user (for example, "The row you are trying to add already exists! Continue? Yes or No"). This remains the active page until the user responds by clicking a control. The page is application modal. That is, fixed-path menu items are disabled. The user must respond before any other action can be taken. When the response page is open, the user cannot go to other pages in the application from which the response page was opened. The page cannot be minimized but can be moved.

Using MVC JSP Pages

In an MVC application, a main page is used for both the frame and pages. This is probably the most common page type you will create. Child/subpage pages are useful when an application needs to display a variable number of subordinate entities, tables, and data views. If an application's style calls for heavy use of response pages, it is best to find an open solution using a menu if possible. Response pages often have the downside of making the applications modal or less open. In other words, the user must go down a predefined path to perform a task. There are few options for change. When deciding how to use response pages, look at other Web applications for some precedents before you commit to an approach.

Using the BASE or Frame Page of an MVC Application

Every application needs a frame page. This is usually the first page you see when you invoke the application or after you have supplied login information. This page usually remains on the screen throughout the application session. In a combination interface application, the first page that appears usually has a menu on it.

Adding Controls to a Page or a Subpage

After the page type is chosen, one or more controls are added to enhance the functionality. In the MVC style, the number of controls should be kept to a minimum. The menu should be used for carrying out application tasks. The most common control will probably be the database page control. For determining an option or value, the external source data access control can be used. Table 4.4 provides a brief summary of controls.

TABLE 4.4 Page Controls

Control	*Determines Option or Value*	*Notes*
CheckBox	Yes	
Button	No	Try to use the menu instead; this control is commonly used on response pages.
Data access	Yes	This is a control that accesses the database to select, insert, update, or delete base or system metadata. This *should be* the most common control; you can use it as a better alternative to almost all of the other controls. The data access control includes its own control styles, such as a drop-down list box.
DropDownListBox	Yes	
Edit mask	No	This control is used to display and enter formatted data.
Graph	No	
Group presentation tool box	No	This control is used to group available selections.

TABLE 4.4 continued

Control	*Determines Option or Value*	*Notes*
Horizontal ScrollBar and Vertical ScrollBar	No	
ListBox	Yes	
MultiLineEdit	No	Use this control to enter data; try an external data access page instead.
Picture	Yes	This control is cosmetic; it's expensive and large.
RadioButton	Yes	
SingleLineEdit	No	Use this control to enter data; try an external (nondatabase) data access page instead.
SpinBox	Yes	
Static text	No	Use this control to display text information.
User object	Yes	

The data access page control should be the most common control utilized. Use it with a menu to trigger event processing on the page and the data access page object currently associated with the control.

Designing Menu Interaction

Menu development should be done carefully. Poorly designed menu handling can cause latent problems that may only be detected when the application is used heavily. Poor planning with menus can also cause problems that manifest themselves as inconsistent responses to user actions. These errors are hard to detect, reproduce, and correct.

Creating Data Access Objects

Create data access objects to retrieve data from the database. This will facilitate the functions that format and validate data, analyze data through graphs and crosstabs, create reports, and update the database. A data access object is typically an object that enables the user to display and manipulate database information using SQL statements in scripts or stored procedures developed for the particular function. You can build a data access object using a J2EE EJB session or entity bean and save it in a place that is available to the application. To build serious data access objects (for example, EJB entity beans in J2EE) that are used for data entry and mission-critical applications, the database design should be roughly 90% complete; otherwise, developers will have to recode and retest too many parts of the application.

Building Data Access Objects with Completed Database Entities

A good database design will make data access object creation easy. Good design will provide column names that are consistent, data types that are not overly exotic, unique indexes that provide uniform data distribution, and primary and foreign keys creating relationships that promote integrity and facilitate "full statement" information joins. When the database is completed, you will probably know all of the accesses required to provide the desired functionality.

These are the database qualities that enable developers to easily build a usable data access object. If your database has these qualities, you are ready to proceed. The database design is the most critical component; the presentation can be easily changed and modified, but the database cannot. A poor database design can cause integrity problems as well as performance problems.

At some point, the database design becomes workable. The developers are granted permissions and are ready to build data access objects. Data access objects usually take the form of EJB entity beans (add/update single rows), session beans (multiple database rows), or sometimes RDBMS stored procedures to speed up and simplify the processing. To use a data access object, you place a data access control in the page and then associate a data access object with the control. During execution, RDBMS vendor database systems such as SQL Server 7 create an instance of the data access object.

Validating Your Code

You can run your application at any time during development. If you discover problems, you can debug your application by setting breakpoints, stepping through your code statement by statement, and looking at variable and structure values during execution.

Determining When to Use the Debugger

When you compile a Java class, the compiler detects obvious errors such as incompatible data types or a misspelled function name. The class will not compile until these errors are fixed. In addition to compiler errors, you may have errors (such as dividing by zero) that will stop execution of the application or logical errors that may not stop the script from running, but will produce incorrect results. A debugger helps you find these errors. Debug allows you to suspend the application at selected points in a J2EE class (stops) and review the contents of variables used in the application.

Selecting the Code to Breakpoint

In debug mode, you select the script you want to debug, insert stops in the Java code, and then run or single-step through the code. When a GUI development encounters a stop, it suspends execution of the application and displays the debug page.

In the debug page, you can usually do the following:

- Display the objects and user-defined functions in the application, the current values of the objects, the instance variables, and the attributes of the objects.
- Display the current values of the global, shared, and local variables.
- Edit (add or modify) existing stops.
- Select another script to debug.
- Modify variable values.
- Select the variables you want to watch during the debugging session.
- Continue executing the application until the next stop or step until the next executable statement.

Refining Your Code

At some point in the application development, key developers will see that certain patterns are being repeated frequently within the application. This may mean that certain application functions are being repeated, certain database accesses are being repeated, and certain user tendencies are emerging. The developers must respond and refine those parts of the application so that they perform optimally. This is the point in the development cycle that will make or break the new application's acceptance and use.

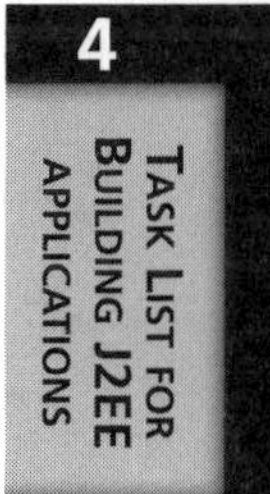

You should strive to accomplish the following:

- Code reusability (this reduces development time)
- Code modularity
- Reduced maintenance costs
- Improved consistency (visual look and feel, nonvisual standards)
- Improved performance

You will accomplish these objectives by carrying out the following tasks:

- Optimize data access paths (use good SQL).
- Remove redundant classes.
- Minimize the use of large bitmaps.
- Minimize or isolate commonly used server processing outside of page processing.
- Optimize libraries and classes.

Creating an Executable

J2EE components are packaged and bundled into a J2EE application for deployment. Each component, its related files such as images and HTML files or server-side classes, and a deployment descriptor are assembled and added to the J2EE application. A J2EE application consists of one or more enterprise bean, Web, or application client component modules. The final enterprise solution can use one or more J2EE applications depending on design requirements.

A J2EE application and each of its modules has its own deployment descriptor. A deployment descriptor is an eXtensible Markup Language (XML) text-based file with an extension that describes a component's deployment settings. An enterprise bean module deployment descriptor declares transaction attributes and security authorizations for an enterprise bean. Because deployment descriptor information is declarative, it can be changed without modifying the bean source code. At runtime, the J2EE server reads the deployment descriptor and acts on the component accordingly.

Preparing to Create the Executable

A J2EE application is delivered in an Enterprise Archive (EAR) file. An EAR file is a JAR file with a .ear extension. In the GUI version of the J2EE application deployment tool, you create an EAR file and then add JAR and WAR files to the EAR. Each EJB JAR file includes its deployment descriptor, related files, and the class files for the enterprise bean. Each application client JAR file includes its deployment descriptor, related files, and the class files for the application client. Each WAR file includes its deployment descriptor, related files, and the class files for the servlet or JSP files for a JSP page. Using EAR files makes it possible to assemble a number of different J2EE applications using some of the same components. No extra code is needed. It is just a matter of assembling J2EE modules into J2EE EAR files.

To create a .ear file, you perform a series of steps that we mentioned in the last paragraph not for the sake of procedure but because each of these items must be fashioned properly long before you reach this point in the development cycle. Make sure that you have considered the placement of the executable library components.

Creating the Deployable Application Executable

Usually the GUI tool creates the executable, stores it in the specified directory, and closes the Create Executable page. Consider its size and the following questions:

- How many libraries must be packaged?
- If the application is large, can it be broken up into smaller deliverables?
- Is the security in place?
- Has the production database been defined with the proper sizing and partitioning?
- Is it available for use?
- Are the user identifiers in place with the proper permissions?
- Do the users have connectivity?
- Has the user-acceptance team been put in place?
- Are the database support people ready?

These are the types of issues that must be addressed before deploying a production J2EE application. We will expand upon each of these issues and options throughout the remainder of this book. We hope that this iterative style will minimize the amount of time and effort required to understand how to develop applications in the Web world.

Summary

This chapter has covered the steps required to plan an application development effort for J2EE, as well as the programming standards that need to be addressed when establishing a development environment. In the next sequence of chapters, we will elaborate on each of the plan components mentioned in this chapter. You are now ready to start designing and constructing the application.

CHAPTER

Build Resource Access: JNDI and LDAP

IN THIS CHAPTER

- Naming and Directory Services 124
- What is JNDI? 124
- Finding Sample Application Resources 124
- JNDI Architecture 128
- JNDI Operations 131
- Lightweight Directory Access Protocol 132
- JNDI/LDAP Practical Examples 133

In this chapter we will describe naming services in general and Java Naming and Directory Interface (JNDI) in particular. We will explain the architecture and interfaces of JNDI, providing explanations and examples that demonstrate how a distributed application's components can locate one another using the JNDI. Additionally, we will introduce directory services, discussing the Lightweight Directory Access Protocol (LDAP) in detail.

Naming and Directory Services

Naming services map names to objects. The Domain Name Service (DNS) is an example of a naming service that maps Internet Protocol (IP) addresses to names. Directory services extend naming services by providing the ability to add attributes to names. Directory services usually define namespaces in a hierarchical way and include attributes that provide additional information about named objects. Later in this chapter, we'll discuss these services in more detail.

What is JNDI?

The Java Naming and Directory Interface (JNDI) is an application programming interface (API) that provides a common, uniform way for developers to find and access a variety of naming and directory services. It is built on an abstraction layer similar to JDBC.

JNDI is designed to provide a common interface for accessing existing services such as:

- Domain Name Service (DNS)
- Novell Directory Services (NDS)
- Lightweight Directory Access Protocol (LDAP)
- Common Object Request Broker Architecture (CORBA)
- Remote Method Invocation (RMI)

JNDI is also independent of any specific naming or directory service implementation. It allows for easy navigation across directory servers, file systems, naming services (such as DNS), and so on.

Finding Sample Application Resources

When building enterprise systems, in which components of one application may depend on components developed by other groups in different departments, finding resources is very important.

Today, there are millions of servers available on the Internet. There is no way to remember the physical addresses of all the servers. In order to connect to the particular services available on the server, you need a way to associate names with the locations of services and with specific information. Directory and naming services organize information hierarchically to map names and directory objects for human understanding.

DNS is an example of a naming service; it maps IP addresses to names. For example, DNS servers know that the plain-English EJDean.com is mapped to the IP address 109.89.198.34, a precise numerical reference to a computer's location on the Internet.

Benefits of JNDI

JNDI API is used to manage distributed applications, providing many benefits including the following:

- Encompasses a broad range of naming and directory services and is used to access any naming or directory service using the same API calls
- Can connect to multiple naming and directory services simultaneously
- Allows association of a name with a Java object or resource, eliminating the need to know the physical ID of that object or resource
- Is able to access heterogeneous directory services using a common interface
- Enables application developers to focus on using and implementing one type of naming or directory service client API instead of several

JNDI and J2EE

JNDI plays an important role in Java technologies including Enterprise JavaBeans (EJB), Java Database Connectivity (JDBC), and the Java Message Service (JMS).

JNDI and Enterprise JavaBeans

The Enterprise JavaBeans architecture is a standard component architecture for developing distributed applications using Java. In future chapters, we will describe the process of developing and building such components in detail.

When developing Enterprise JavaBeans, JNDI is used to obtain references to an EJB home interface. The home interface is a factory interface for creating, finding, and removing EJB. In addition, JNDI can be used to gain access to EJB environmental entries, which are used to customize EJB behavior.

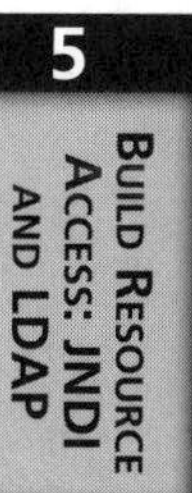

JNDI and JDBC

The Java Database Connectivity (JDBC) API 2.0 introduced the DataSource interface. The JNDI can be used in addition to the JDBC driver manager to manage data sources and connections. DataSource objects provide the preferred way to achieve a connection. They offer advantages over using driver managers, such as easier code maintenance, improved performance due to the use of connection pooling, and support for distributed transactions through XADataSource.

JNDI provides a uniform way to find and access services on a network. To create a database connection with JNDI, you specify a resource name, which corresponds to an entry in a database or naming service. The information necessary to establish a connection with your database is then returned.

DataSource objects can be created and managed separately from JDBC applications. In the following example, JNDI is used to look up a data source object and create a connection:

```
try{
Context cntxt = new InitialContext();
DataSource ds = (DataSource) cntxt.lookup("jdbc/dpt");
}
catch(NamingException ne) {
    // Handle your exception
}
Connection conn = ds.getConnection();
...
```

JNDI and JMS

Messaging is a method of communication used by software components or applications. The Java Message Service (JMS) is the Java technology that allows applications to create, send, receive, and read messages.

The JNDI naming context is used to look up JMS API resources. Additionally, JNDI is used to locate objects and resources within and/or from the various J2EE containers. When the J2EE server starts up, it will bind the JNDI names established in the deployment descriptors or deployment plans to the objects or resources on the server.

In the following example, JNDI is used to look up a JMS connection factory:

```
try {
// Populate the JNDI connection:
    Properties env = new Properties();
    // define JNDI properties based on the vendor specification
    InitialContext inictxt = new InitialContext(env);
    // Look up a JMS connection factory:
    TopicConnectionFactory connFactory = (TopicConnectionFactory)
                inictxt.lookup("TopicConnectionFactory");
```

```
...
}
catch(Exception e){
    // Handle Exceptions
}
```

JNDI Service Providers

JNDI's goal is to allow plug and play of naming and directory services. The JNDI Service Provider Interface (SPI) provides the means by which naming and directory services are integrated into the JNDI framework. Vendors who are developing service providers for JNDI can use the JNDI SPI. The SPI enables a variety of naming and directory services to be used, allowing an application to transparently access such naming and directory services. It provides the classes and interfaces that a directory service must implement to be available to a JNDI client. These service provider implementations can be easily plugged into the JNDI architecture, thus enabling the application layer to access their services using the JNDI.

In client/server terminology, the JNDI acts as the client and the naming or directory server is the server.

The JNDI Software Development Kit (SDK), which is available at `http://java.sun.com/products/jndi`, contains a number of service providers including

- File system
- CORBA Object Service (COS)—the naming service for CORBA that allows applications to handle access to CORBA objects
- Lightweight Directory Access Protocol (LDAP)—a means of ordering a file system that was developed by the University of Michigan (the LDAP will be discussed in more detail in this chapter)
- Java Remote Method Invocation (RMI)—a service that allows you to write distributed objects using Java

As a programmer, you have access to a very flexible way to switch from one service to another. The simplest way is coded as follows:

```
Hashtable env = new Hashtable();
// Define the class:
env.put(Context.INITIAL_CONTEXT_FACTORY,"oldservice");
// Define the New Class:
env.put(Context.INITIAL_CONTEXT_FACTORY,"newservice");
```

JNDI Architecture

The JNDI architecture consists of three main layers, as illustrated in Figure 5.1:

- The application layer, which uses the JNDI API
- The JNDI API layer, which defines a set of classes and interfaces for supporting common naming and directory service functionality
- The implementation layer

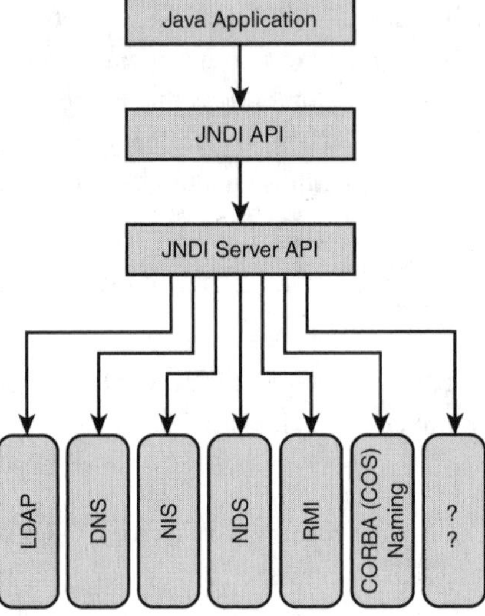

FIGURE 5.1
JNDI architecture layers.

JNDI Packages

The JNDI class libraries are included with the Java 2 SDK. The JNDI API is used to access any naming or directory service using the same API calls.

The API consists of these packages:

- `javax.naming` for naming operations
- `javax.naming.directory` for directory operations
- `javax.naming.event` for requesting event notification in naming and directory services
- `javax.naming.ldap` for LDAP support
- `javax.naming.spi`, which allows different implementations to be plugged in dynamically

For more information about API documentation of the Java Naming and Directory Interface, please visit Sun's J2EE documentation page at `http://java.sun.com/j2ee/`.

Naming

JNDI naming services map objects to names. This mapping provides a way to obtain references and invoke methods on remote objects without knowing the object's physical address in the network.

JNDI provides the namespace for storing object references including JDBC databases and JMS providers.

The Internet's Domain Name Service (DNS) is perhaps the largest and best-known naming service. It allows Internet users to refer to host computers through easily recognizable names. Other examples of naming services are CORBA and RMI. CORBA and RMI are examples of distributed object systems that employ naming services. In these types of systems, the naming service associates names with live objects, allowing an application on one computer to access live objects from a different computer.

JNDI naming services are accessed through the `javax.naming` package. This package includes naming methods that enable you to obtain an initial context, bind objects to names, look up objects, and so on.

Contexts

Contexts are objects that can contain from zero to many bindings. They are used as a starting point to look for objects in a naming system. On a file system, each directory can be considered a context.

The JNDI API defines the Context interface that plays the main role in JNDI. JNDI also defines an `InitialContext` class that assists in the process of finding a place to start. The JNDI API defines an initial context factory interface containing a method that returns the initial context. This method accepts a single parameter, which is a hashtable of property value pairs. This table of property-value pairs represents the environment in which the naming service is accessed, including requirements for security and level of service.

To perform any operation you must establish an `InitialContext`. `InitialContext` is the starting point for name resolution. You'll use the JNDI API methods to create a reference to an initial context of a naming service.

To create a handle to a specific naming service, you'll use the `javax.naming.InitialContext` class methods. The Context interface defines static public properties that can be set and used during the initialization.

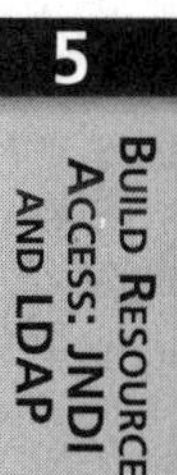

Table 5.1 lists Context properties.

TABLE 5.1 Context Properties

Property	*Description*
INITIAL_CONTEXT_FACTORY	The fully qualified class name of the service provider.
PROVIDER_URL	Contains the protocol, hostname, and port number of the service. (Note the default port number of LDAP is 389).
SECURITY_AUTHENTICATION	Defines the level of security to be used for this context. Can be set to "non", "simple", or "strong".
SECURITY_PRINCIPAL	Defines the principal's name, such as the username.
SECURITY_CREDENTIALS	Defines the principal's credentials, such as a password.
SECURITY_PROTOCOL	Specifies the security protocol to be used, such as SASL or SSL.
OBJECT_FACTORIES	Defines the name of the environment property for specifying the list of object factories to use (a colon-separated list).
STATE_FACTORIES	Defines the name of the environment property for specifying the list of state factories to use (a colon-separated list).
AUTHORITATIVE	Specifies the name of the environment property for specifying the authoritativeness of the service requested. A value of "true" indicates that the service access provides the most authoritative source.
URL_PKG_PREFIXES	Defines the name of the environment property for specifying the list of package prefixes when loading context factories (a colon-separated list).
DNS_URL	Defines the URL that holds the DNS host.
BATCHSIZE	The batch size of data returned from a service protocol.
REFERRAL	Specifies the name of the environment property for indicating how referrals encountered by the service provider are to be processed.
LANGUAGE	Specifies the name of the environment property for indicating the preferred language to use with the service.
APPLET	Specifies an applet for the initial context constructor to use when searching for other properties.

Namespaces

A naming system is a set of contexts of the same type that provide a common set of operations. In other words, a naming system is a collection of connected contexts. The contents of a hard drive or LDAP directory are examples of naming systems. A namespace consists of all the names contained within a naming system. JNDI allows you place all the namespaces under one logical namespace. A directory is a connected set of context objects.

A directory service provides operations for adding and updating the attributes associated with objects in a master directory. The service is accessed through its interface.

Directory services provide extended functionality by supporting attributes, which define additional information about the objects. Clients using directory services can search for an object by its name or by its attributes.

You can access directory-specific services through the `javax.naming.directory` package.

In order to use a directory service, create an `InitialDirContext` as follows:

```
Hashtable env = new Hashtable();
env.put(Context.INITIAL_CONTEXT_FACTORY,"com.sun.jndi.ldap.LdapCtxFactory");
env.put(Context.PROVIDER_URL, "ldap://localhost:389/o=JNDIChapter");
DirContext ctx = new InitialDirContext(env);
```

You'll use the `getAttributes()` method to retrieve all of the attributes associated with the object bound to the name `"cn=Person, ou=General"`:

```
Attributes attrs = ctx.getAttributes("cn = Person, ou=General");
```

JNDI Operations

The JNDI API package contains a set of classes as well as a handful of operations. Table 5.2 lists the most commonly used JNDI operations.

TABLE 5.2 Commonly Used JNDI Operations

Operation	*Description*	*Syntax*
bind	The process of associating a name with an object	`void bind(String sName, Object object);`
rebind	Used to rebind an object to an existing name	`void rebind(String sName, Object object);`
unbind	Used to unbind the object from the directory	`void unbind(String sName);`

TABLE 5.2 continued

Operation	*Description*	*Syntax*
lookup	Returns an object in the directory	`void lookup(String sName, Object object);`
rename	Used for changing the name an object is bound to	`void rename(String sOldName, String sNewName);`
list	Returns a list of the objects bound for a particular context	`NamingEnumeration listBinding(String sName);` `NamingEnumeration list(String sName);`

The next example retrieves names, class names, and bound objects:

```
NamingEnumeration namEnumList = ctxt.listBindings("cntxtName");
...
while(namEnumList.hasMore() ) {
Binding bnd = (Binding) namEnumList.next();
String sObjName = bnd.getName(); // Get the Binding Name
String sClassName = bnd.getClassName(); // Class Name
SomeObject objLocal = (SomeObject) bnd.getObject(); // Object
}
```

Lightweight Directory Access Protocol

LDAP is a set of protocols for accessing information directories. Directories that contain information such as names, phone numbers, and addresses are often stored on a variety of incompatible systems.

LDAP enables developers to locate resources such as files and devices in a network, whether on the Internet or on a corporate intranet. LDAP was originally conceived of as a way to simplify access to a directory service that was modeled according to the X.500 standards.

LDAP defines a set of operations that an LDAP client can perform on an LDAP server. These operations include add, delete, modify, and search.

The LDAP service provider implements the DirContext interface. You can use this provider with JNDI in order to access LDAP directories.

Developers using JNDI can produce queries that use LDAP or other access protocols to retrieve results; however, they are not limited to LDAP nor do they have to develop their applications wired to LDAP.

JNDI/LDAP Practical Examples

This section demonstrates different types of simple code in order to further illustrate use of JNDI API methods.

When working with JNDI, the first step is to obtain an initial context. The following example provides the code that defines how to use the JNDI/LDAP naming service provider to connect to `LDAPNameService`. You may specify any extra information required by the service provider such as the login information (the username and password).

```
String sInitialContext = "com.sun.jndi.ldap.LdapCtxFactory";
String sUrl = "ldap://localhost:389/";
String sUserName = "userid";
String sPassword = "userpassword";
Hashtable env = new Hashtable();
env.put(Context.INITIAL_CONTEXT_FACTORY, sInitialContext);
env.put(Context.PROVIDER_URL, sUrl);
env.put(Context.SECURITY_PRINCIPAL, sUserName);
env.put(Context.SECURITY_CREDENTIALS, sPassword);

try {
Context ctx = new InitialContext(env);
}
catch (NamingException e) {
// Process Naming Exception
}
```

The next example uses JNDI to get a listing of a directory in a local file system.

```
Hashtable env = new Hashtable();
env.put(Context.INITIAL_CONTEXT_FACTORY,
"com.sun.jndi.fscontext.RefFSContextFactory");
env.put(Context.PROVIDER_URL, directoryURL);
try {
        Context context = new InitialContext(env);
        NamingEnumeration bindingList = context.listBindings("");

        while (bindingList.hasMore()) {
                Binding binding = (Binding) bindingList.next();
                String sDirName = binding.getName()
                // At this point, we have the DirName.
        }
}
```

```
catch (NamingException ex) {
        // Process Exceptions
}
```

As mentioned previously, once a context has been obtained, you can use it to look up and retrieve named objects.

The following code will retrieve an EJB named `shoppingBean`:

```
try {
        shoppingBean beanShopping =
                        (shoppingBean)ctx.lookup("ejb.shoppingBean");
}
catch (NameNotFoundException e) {
        // Handle your Exception
}
catch (NamingException e) {
        // Failure occurred, handle the NamingException
}
```

The following example processes attributes associated with an entry. The `Attributes` class represents a whole collection of attributes that contain instances of the `Attribute` class:

```
Hashtable env = new Hashtable();
env.put(Context.INITIAL_CONTEXT_FACTORY,"com.sun.jndi.ldap.LdapCtxFactory");
env.put(Context.PROVIDER_URL,"ldap://localhost:398/o=JNDI_Chapter");
try {
        // Create the initial directory context
        DirContext dctx = new InitialDirContext(env);

        // Create the attribute set;
        Attributes attrs = new BasicAttributes(true);
        attrs.put(new BasicAttribute("firstAttr"));
        attrs.put(new BasicAttribute("secondAttr","simple"));

        NamingEnumeration result =dctx.search("ou=People", attrs);

        // Process search result
        while (result.hasMore())  {
                SearchResult sr = (SearchResult)result.next();
                String sName =  sr.getName());
                Attributes srchAttrs = sr.getAttributes();

                NamingEnumeration attributes = srchAttrs.getAll();
                ...
                // Process the attributes:
                while(attributes.hasMore()) {
                        Attribute attr = (Attribute)attributes.next();
                        NamingEnumeration values = attr.getAll();
                        ...
```

```
                    // Process values:
                    while(values.hasMore()) {
                            Object objValue = values.next();
                            ...
                    }
            }
        }
}
catch(Exception e){
        // Handle your Exception
}
```

The next example describes how to obtain a connection from a JDBC client using a JDNI lookup to locate the `DataSource` object:

```
Context ctx = null;
Hashtable env = new Hashtable();
env.put(Context.INITIAL_CONTEXT_FACTORY,"Specfy Initial Context Factory");
env.put(Context.PROVIDER_URL,"Specify Port");

try {
        ctx = new InitialContext(env);
        DataSource ds = (DataSource) ctx.lookup
                        ("Specify your DataSource");
        Connection conn = ds.getConnection();
            // Now the conn object is available for you to create
                // Statements
        ...
}
catch (NamingException e) {
        // Handle Naming Exception Errors  }
finally {
        try {
                ctx.close();
        }
        catch (Exception e) {
                // Exception
        }
}
```

Summary

JNDI is an enterprise Java API that provides naming and directory functionality using a common set of classes and interfaces that are independent of a specific naming and directory service implementation. This chapter discussed methods of using JNDI to reach these services as well as how to use JNDI to access resources on J2EE servers.

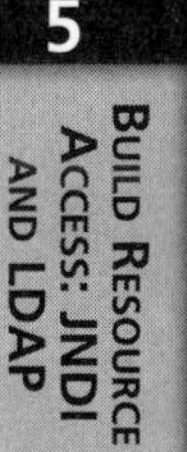

CHAPTER 6

Build Data Access: JDBC

In This Chapter

- Introduction *138*
- JDBC Architecture: API and Drivers *139*
- The JDBC API *143*
- Retrieving and Updating Data *148*
- SQL-to-Java Data Types *153*
- JDBC Exception Types *157*
- Metadata *158*
- Scrollable Resultsets *159*
- Updating Rows *162*
- Transaction Support *163*
- Batch Statements *164*
- JDBC 2.1 New Data Types *166*
- JDBC 2.0 Optional Package API: `javax.sql` *168*
- Case Study: The SilverStream Application Server *171*

Introduction

In this chapter, we will examine Java Database Connectivity (JDBC) technology, which is an integral part of the Java platform. We'll discuss JDBC in three parts:

- JDBC 2.1 Core API: the `java.sql` package
- JDBC 2.0 Optional Package API: the `javax.sql` package
- Case Study: JDBC in a SilverStream Application Server

We'll present short examples to illustrate the usage of the common JDBC 2.0 API.

In the first part of this chapter, we will discuss the JDBC 2.1 Core API. The topics will include

- JDBC architecture
- JDBC driver types
- Database connections via JDBC
- Performing various SQL statements using JDBC API
- Processing query results in JDBC
- Mapping SQL types in Java language
- Getting information about databases via JDBC
- New feature of JDBC 2.1 Core API: scrollable resultsets

In the second part of this chapter, we will discuss JDBC 2.0 Optional Package API. The topics will include

- Database Naming via JNDI
- Connection Pools
- Distributed Transactions
- Row Sets
- Advanced Data Types

In the last part of this chapter, we will introduce code examples using JDBC within a SilverStream Application Server. The topics for discussion include

- JDBC in a SilverStream Application Server
- SilverStream connection pooling
- Accessing JDBC from a session bean in a SilverStream Application Server

What Is JDBC?

An Application Programming Interface (API) is a set of classes, methods, and resources that programs can use to do their work. APIs exist for windowing systems, file systems, database systems, networking systems, and others. JDBC is a Java API for database connectivity that is part of the Java API developed by Sun Microsystems.

Sun claims that JDBC is not an abbreviation, though people often think it stands for "Java DataBase Connectivity."

JDBC provides Java developers with an industry standard API for database-independent connectivity between your Java Applications (Applets, Servlets, JSP, EJB, and so on) and a wide range of relational database management systems such as Oracle, Informix, Microsoft SQL Server, and Sybase. The API provides a call level interface to the database.

In its simplest form, JDBC makes it possible to do these basic things:

- Connect to a database
- Execute SQL statements to query your database
- Generate query results
- Perform updates, inserts, and deletions
- Execute stored procedures

Benefits of JDBC

The benefits of using JDBC include the following:

- A developer only needs to know one API to access any relational database.
- There is no need to rewrite code for different databases.
- There is no need to know the database vendor's specific APIs.
- It provides a standard API and is vendor independent.
- Almost every database vendor has some sort of JDBC driver.
- JDBC is part of the standard Java 2 platform.

JDBC Architecture: API and Drivers

The JDBC architecture consists of two layers: first, the JDBC API, which supports Java application–to–JDBC Driver Manager communications; and, second, the JDBC Driver API, which supports JDBC Driver Manager–to–ODBC Driver communications. Open

Database Connectivity (ODBC) is an open standard Application Programming Interface (API) for accessing a database. By using ODBC statements in your program, you can access files in a number of different databases, including Access, Oracle, Sybase, Excel, and Text. In addition to the ODBC software, a separate module or driver is needed for each database to be accessed. ODBC is based on and closely aligned with The Open Group standard Structured Query Language (SQL) Call-Level Interface. It allows programs to use SQL requests that will access databases without having to know the proprietary interfaces to the databases. ODBC handles the SQL request and converts it into a request the individual database system understands. The JDBC Driver Manager is designed to handle communication with multiple drivers of different types. Most database vendors provide built-in distributed JDBC drivers to support the many SQL-based DBMSs.

The JDBC API provides support for both two-tier and three-tier models for database access.

In the two-tier database access model, your application communicates directly with the database, as shown in Figure 6.1.

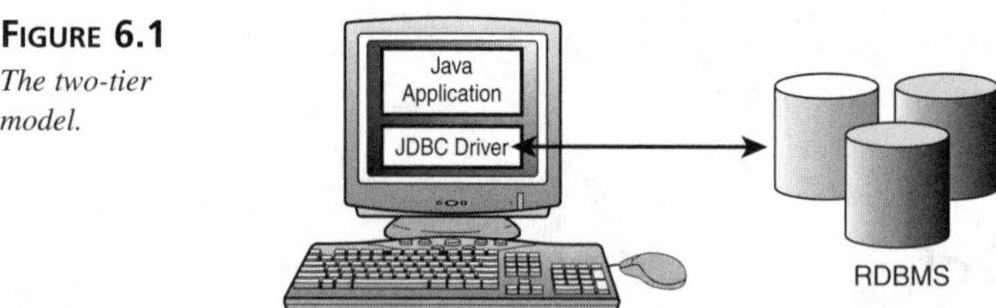

FIGURE 6.1
The two-tier model.

The two-tier model requires a JDBC Driver, which delivers users' SQL statements directly to the database. The results of these statements are sent back to the application.

In the three-tier database access model, the JDBC Driver sends your commands to a middle tier application service, which then sends the commands to the database. The database processes these commands and sends the results back to the middle tier, which then sends them to the application.

The three-tier model is based on the capability to build partitioned applications. Partitioning an application breaks up your code into logical components. The three-tier architecture offers advantages in scalability, usability, maintenance, and performance.

Figure 6.2 illustrates this process.

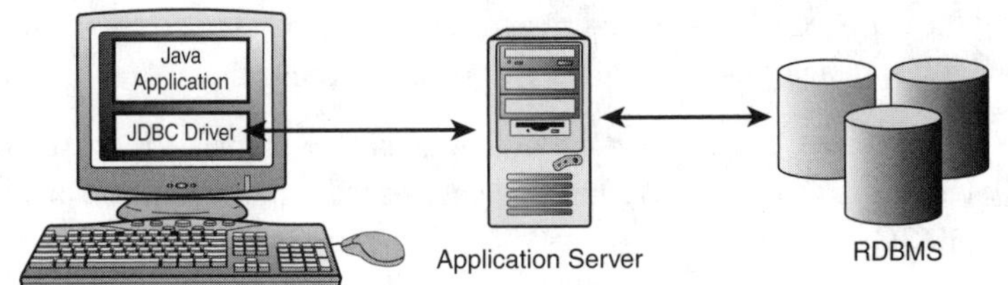

FIGURE 6.2
The three-tier model.

For the application developer, JDBC API allows you to

- Connect to a data source
- Send SQL statements
- Process results by providing methods to navigate, inspect, and modify data
- Access metadata that describe the database and the results of queries, allowing for dynamic SQL

Database Drivers

As Java and JDBC provide an established map for accessing SQL DBMS data, JDBC drivers are available for most popular databases.

There are four types of JDBC database drivers: the JDBC-ODBC Bridge, partial Java, middleware, and pure Java.

Type 1: JDBC-ODBC Bridge Driver

This is the most basic driver. In this case, JDBC connects to ODBC, which connects to the vendor's client library (for example, sqlnet). The JDBC-ODBC Bridge converts the JDBC methods in your Java programs to ODBC functions. Figure 6.3 illustrates this process.

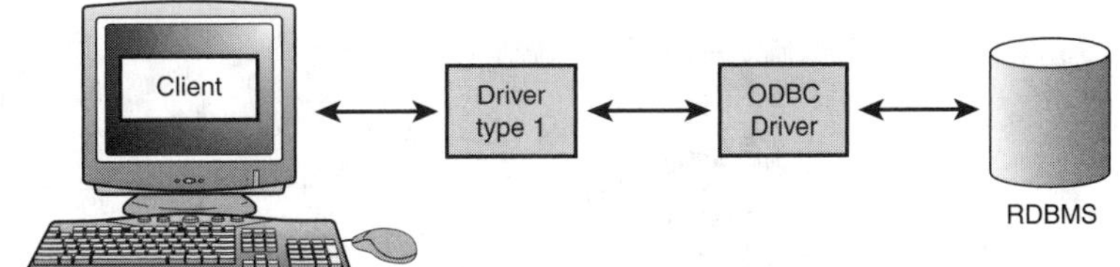

FIGURE 6.3
JDBC-ODBC Bridge driver.

Using the JDBC-ODBC Bridge driver, you can access almost any database. But there are a few disadvantages of using this driver in large applications:

- Performance of a JDBC/ODBC Bridge is slower than a JDBC driver alone would be, due to the added overhead. A database call must be translated from JDBC to ODBC to a native API.
- Because an ODBC driver must be installed on each client machine, type 1 drivers cannot be used for the Internet.

Type 2: Partial Java

In this type of database driver, JDBC connects to a vendor's client library. Only Java programs with full security access to the computer can use this type of driver (applets cannot use it). Figure 6.4 illustrates a partial Java driver.

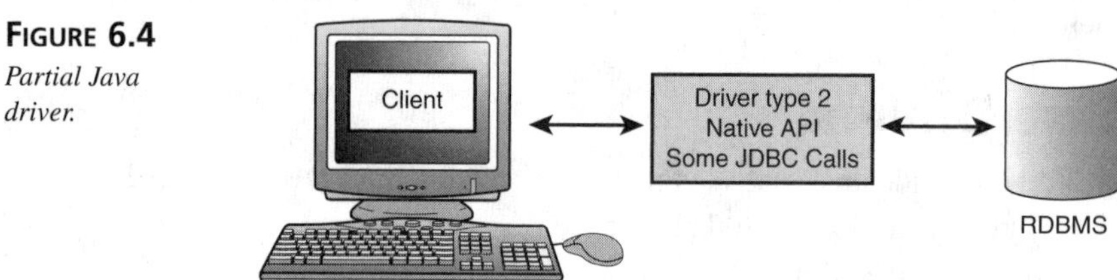

FIGURE 6.4
Partial Java driver.

This type of driver offers better performance than the JDBC-ODBC Bridge driver. However, because a database library needs to be loaded on each client machine, type 2 drivers cannot be used for the Internet.

Type 3: Middleware

In the third driver type, JDBC connects to middleware, which connects to a database (see Figure 6.5).

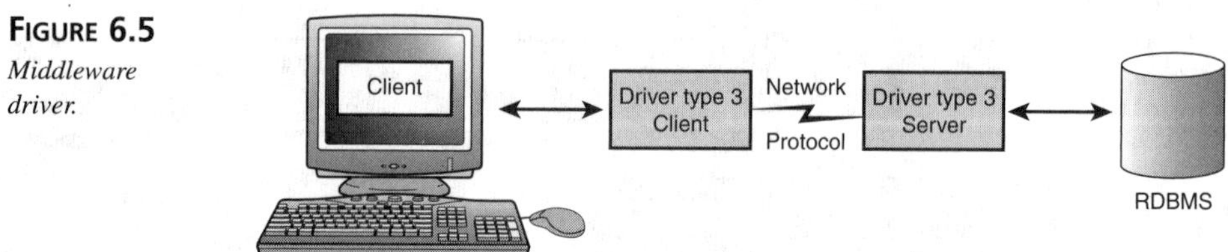

FIGURE 6.5
Middleware driver.

Type 4: Pure Java

This type converts JDBC calls into the network protocol used directly by the DBMS, allowing for direct calls from the client machine to the DBMS server. This direct call capability has a significant effect on performance; Type 4 JDBC drivers are markedly faster than Type 3 JDBC drivers.

Figure 6.6 shows the structure of a pure Java driver.

FIGURE 6.6
Pure Java driver.

This driver is recommended for server-side Java developments. It is referred to as a "thin" driver.

Type 3 and Type 4 drivers are used for Internet-related applications.

The JDBC API

The JDBC API is broken into two packages:

- `java.sql` Core API—This is part of the Java 2 Standard Edition (J2SE). This API adds a few classes to the previous versions, such as scrollable resultsets, batch updates, transaction isolation, and the new SQL3 data types such as Binary Large Object (BLOB) and Character Large Object (CLOB).
- `javax.sql` Optional Extensions API—This is part of the Java 2 Enterprise Edition (J2EE). The extensions are not included when you download the JDK; you must download them separately. This API includes classes for Java Naming and Directory Interface (JNDI)–based resources and classes for managing connection pooling, distributed transactions, and rowsets.

JDBC 2.1 Core API: The `java.sql` Package

The JDBC 2.1 API is the latest update of the JDBC API. It includes many new features and enhancements to the core JDBC API, including scrollable resultsets and the new SQL: 1999 (formerly SQL 3) data types.

All visible classes are placed in the `java.sql` package.

Connecting to the Sample Application

A Connection object is the representation of a connection to a data source through a JDBC driver. Generally, the data source is your database, but it can also be a legacy file system or some other source of data with a corresponding JDBC driver.

There are two mechanisms that allow you to connect to a data source. One way is by using the `DriverManager` class, and the other way is by using the `DataSource` interface, which is part of the JDBC 2.0 Optional Package and will be discussed in the second part of this chapter.

JDBC uses the `java.sql.DriverManager` class and the `java.sql.Driver` and `java.sql.Connection` interfaces for connecting to a database.

`java.sql.Driver`

Database access is achieved through drivers, which are specific to a particular implementation. As we mentioned, a program connecting to a database requires a driver for that database.

DBMS vendors usually provide drivers. Any driver must implement the Driver interface.

This driver processes the JDBC statements in your applications and routes the SQL arguments they contain to your database engines.

`java.sql.DriverManager`

The uppermost class in the `java.sql` hierarchy is the `DriverManager`. The `DriverManager` keeps track of driver information. The `DriverManager` class maintains a list of driver implementations and presents an application with one that matches a requested URL.

`java.sql.Connection`

The Connection interface is used for sending a series of SQL statements to the database and managing the committing or aborting of those statements.

In order to open a connection with your DBMS, the first thing you have to do is establish a connection. This involves the following steps:

- Loading the database driver
- Defining the Uniform Resource Locator (URL)
- Establishing the connection

Loading the Database Driver

Loading a driver is very simple and requires just one line of code. You may refer to this process as bringing the Java class representing the JDBC driver into the Java Virtual Machine.

To load the driver you must know the complete package path to the driver.

Use the `Class.forName()` method to load the driver into memory.

When the driver is loaded it is automatically registered with the `DriverManager`.

For example, to load the SilverStream JDBC driver `com.sssw.jdbc.mss.odbc.AgOdbcDriver`, use the following:

```
String sDriverName =
"com.sssw.jdbc.mss.odbc.AgOdbcDriver";
    try {
        Class.forName(sDriverName);
    }
    catch( ClassNotFoundException cnfe ) {
        System.err.print("ClassNotFoundException: );
        System.err.println(cnfe.getMessage());
    }
```

Once you have loaded a driver, it is available for making a connection with your DBMS.

Defining the URL

A URL is used to locate a JDBC Data Source. JDBC borrows the URL syntax for globally unique database addressing. You need to consult each JDBC driver's documentation for the correct format for the URL.

The syntax of a JDBC URL is

```
jdbc:<subprotocol><subname>
```

This URL has three parts:

- `jdbc`—this indicates the protocol (JDBC)
- `<subprotocol>`—the driver of the database connectivity mechanism
- `<subname>`—the database

Suppose we have the following JDBC URL:

```
jdbc:odbc://host.domain.com:500/db-file
```

This structure includes a subprotocol for ODBC, which indicates how the JDBC Manager will access the database. The rest indicates the hostname, the port the database is listening on, and the database location and name.

If the database resides on the same machine where your Java applications are located, then you may omit the hostname and slashes. An Oracle database called "demo" using a driver provided by SilverStream would look like this:

```
jdbc:sssw:oracle:demo
```

And an ODBC datasource called "demo" might look like this:

```
jdbc:sssw:odbc:demo
```

Establishing the Connection

Once a JDBC driver has been loaded and registered with the `DriverManager`, it is available for establishing a connection with a database. Simply use the `getConnection()` method on the `DriverManager` class.

The `DriverManager` contains three different methods of `getConnection()` to establish connections:

```
public static Connection getConnection(String url)
throws SQLException
```

This returns a connection to a given database that was specified in the form

```
jdbc:<subprotocol><subname>
```

The preceding method can be used if your database accepts connection requests without authentication.

The second connection method looks like this:

```
public static Connection getConnection(String url,
String user, String password) throws SQLException
```

In addition to the given database URL, this method takes two more arguments: a database username and the database user's password.

For example:

```
String sDBUrl = "jdbc:sssw:odbc:demo";
String sDBUserID = "admin";
String sDBPassword = "password";
Connection con = DriverManager.getConnection( sDBUrl ,
sDBUserID, sDBPassword);
```

The third connection method looks like this:

```
public static Connection getConnection(String url,
java.util.Properties info) throws SQLException
```

In addition to the given database URL, this method takes another argument: a set of properties.

The `Properties` object may contain required parameters for the specified database. Sometimes the database's username and password are passed in along with other properties via this Properties object.

For example, we can use a property file named "DemoPro.txt" to set and read properties with different values:

```
DemoPro.txt:
# Database URL:
DB_URL=jdbc:sssw:odbc:demo
# Database username:
DB_USER_ID =DEMO_USER
# Database user's password:
DB_PASSWORD=DEMO_PASSWORD
# Database Connection Properties:
USER=DEMO_USER
PASSWORD=DEMO_PASSWORD
```

The following code illustrates using the `Properties` object to get a connection:

```
Properties dbProp = new Properties();
String sPropFile = "DemoProp.txt";
try {
FileInputStream propFileStream = new
FileInputStream(sPropFile);
dbProp.load(propFileStream);
}
catch(FileNotFoundException fnfe) {
// Process FileNotFoundException Exception...
}
catch(IOException ioe) {
// Process IOException Exception...
}
// Establish the connection:
Connection con = DriverManager.getConnection(
sDBUrl,dbProp );
...
```

The following code illustrates using the `Properties` object that is populated during runtime:

```
java.util.Properties prop = new java.util.Properties();
info.addProperty ("user", "scott");
info.addProperty ("password","tiger");
getConnection ("jdbc:oracle:oci8:",prop);
```

Sometimes, you may invoke the following `DriverManager` methods to get and set the maximum timeout in seconds that a driver will wait while attempting to connect to a database:

```
public static void DriverManager.setLoginTimeout(int seconds)
public static int DriverManager.getLoginTimeout()
```

Connection Example

The following code demonstrates the process of connecting to a database:

```
try{
// Load SilverStream jdbc-odbc Driver:
String driverName = "com.sssw.jdbc.mss.odbc.AgOdbcDriver";
Class.forName(driverName);
        // Connect to the Data Source:
String url = "jdbc:sssw:odbc:demo";
Connection con =
DriverManager.getConnection(url,"dba","sql");
    ...
}
catch (ClassNotFoundException cnfe) {
// Driver Not Found (if the driver is not
// installed on the Client Machine):
System.err.println ("Unable to load SilverStream database
driver");
System.err.println ("ClassNotFoundException: " + cnfe.getMessage());
// (Do not continue) Handle your Exception:
...
}
catch(SQLException sqle) {
System.err.println("SQLException: " + sqle.getMessage());
// (Do not continue) Handle your Exception:
...
}
```

Retrieving and Updating Data

After you are connected to your database, you may start processing updates (`INSERT`, `UPDATE`, or `DELETE`) and queries (`SELECT`). In the following paragraphs, we will discuss more database access that allows you to execute SQL statements.

Statements

Statements are used to perform both data/schema modifications and queries.

JDBC supports three types of statements:

- `Statement`: used for executing an SQL statement immediately
- `PreparedStatement`: used for executing a compiled SQL statement
- `CallableStatement`: used for executing Stored Procedures

The Statement Object

A Statement object is used for executing a static SQL statement and obtaining the results produced by it.

A Statement object is created using the createStatement method in the Connection object. You simply create it and then execute by calling the appropriate execute method.

For a SELECT statement, the method to use is executeQuery().

For statements such as UPDATE, DELETE, or DDL the method to use is executeUpdate().

The executeQuery() method returns only one ResultSet object. If your SQL statement needs to return more than one ResultSet object, you should use the execute() method, in which case your SQL statement may return either a ResultSet object or the total number of updated rows. If the execute() method returns true then the result is a ResultSet object; otherwise, the result is an update count.

The executeUpdate() method returns an integer indicating how many rows are affected by your SQL statement.

You may create multiple Statement objects from a single connection.

The following is an example of using executeQuery:

```
try {
...
String sSQL = "SELECT FIRST_NM,LAST_NM FROM EMPLOYEE";
Statement stmt = con.createStatement();
ResultSet rs = stmt.executeQuery(sSQL);
While( rs.next() )
{
// Process the resultset
...
}
}
catch(SQLException sqle) {
System.err.println("SQLException: " +
sqle.getMessage());
}
```

Here is an example of executeUpdate:

```
String sSQL = "UPDATE EMPLOYEE SET OVERTIME='Y' WHERE
STATUS='Y'";
Statement stmt = con.createStatement();
int iTotalUpdated = stmt.executeUpdate(sSQL);
stmt.close();
...
```

When you finish processing the statement, it's recommended that you use the close() method on the statement to close it. When you close a connection, all statements will automatically be closed. Closing a Statement object will also close any instances of ResultSet produced by that Statement object. It's a good practice to explicitly close ResultSet objects; otherwise, all resources held in storage by that ResultSet object might not be released until garbage collection runs again.

The PreparedStatement Object

The PreparedStatement object is used for precompiling an SQL statement. Your SQL statement can be precompiled and stored in a PreparedStatement object. This object can then be used to efficiently execute your SQL statement multiple times.

The PreparedStatement interface extends Statement. PreparedStatement provides support for IN parameters. An IN parameter is a parameter whose value is not specified when the SQL statement is created. Parameter markers, represented by ?, are used to specify input values.

PreparedStatement introduces a series of set*XXX*() methods to set the value of a specific parameter. The *XXX* represents the data types.

To execute a PreparedStatement, as with Statement objects, you call the appropriate execute method depending on the type of SQL statement being executed.

For a SELECT statement that returns a ResultSet object, the method to use is executeQuery().

For statements such as UPDATE, DELETE, or DDL the method to use is executeUpdate().

If the return type of your SQL statement is unknown, you should use the execute() method.

Using PreparedStatement for data retrieval offers better performance than queries executed with Statement class methods.

For example:

```
try
{
...
String sSQL = "INSERT INO EMPLOYEE(FIRST_NM,LAST_NM)"+
" VALUES(?,?)";
PreparedStatement pstmt = con.prepareStatement(sSQL);
    pstmt.setString(1, "JOE");
    pstmt.setString(2, "BROWN");
...
}
```

```
}
catch(SQLException sqle) {
    System.err.println("SQLException: " + sqle.getMessage());
}
```

To set any parameter to `JDBC NULL`, you use the `setNull()` method. For instance, in our previous example, if you need to set the first name to `NULL`, use the following:

```
pstmt.setNull(1, java.sql.Types.VARCHAR);
```

The following is an example of returning a `ResultSet` object using `executeQuery`:

```
try {
...
String sSQL = "SELECT FIRST_NM,LAST_NM FROM EMPLOYEE "+
" WHERE DEPT  = ? ";
PreparedStatement pstmt = con.prepareStatement(sSQL);
pstmt.setString(1, "MIS");

ResultSet rs = pstmt.executeQuery();
While( rs.next() ) {
    // Process the resultset record
    ...
}
rs.close();
pstmt.close();
}
catch(SQLException sqle) {
    System.err.println("SQLException: " + sqle.getMessage());
}
```

Here is an example of returning a Row Count using `executeUpdate`:

```
    try {
...
String sSQL = "UPDATE EMPLOYEE SET STATUS='N'  "+
" WHERE DEPT  = ? ";
PreparedStatement pstmt = con.prepareStatement(sSQL);
    pstmt.setString(1, "WEB");
int iTotalUpdated  = pstmt.executeUpdate();
...
rs.close(;)
pstmt.close();
}
catch(SQLException sqle) {
    System.err.println("SQLException: " + sqle.getMessage());
```

CallableStatement

The `CallableStatement` interface extends `PreparedStatement` for use with stored procedures. It includes methods for executing and getting results from stored procedures.

CallableStatement objects are created by the Connection object. To obtain a CallableStatement, call prepareCall() on the Connection object.

You may supply up to three types of parameters: IN, OUT, and INOUT.

Any input parameters must be specified with the set*XXX*() methods.

Any output parameters must register their data type with registerOutParameter().

Once all the parameters have been set up, call the execute() method on the CallableStatement.

After the stored procedure executes, you can use the get*XXX*() methods to get values from the output parameters.

Here is an example of executing a stored procedure:

```
//Connection is assumed
String sSQL = "{ call spDeptInfo (?)}";
CallableStatement stmt =  conn.prepareCall(sSQL);
stmt.registerOutParameter(1,Types.VARCHAR);
stmt.execute();
String sDeptDescription = stmt.getString(1);
```

ResultSet

JDBC returns results in a ResultSet object. A ResultSet is the retrieved data from a currently executed SQL statement.

The java.sql.ResultSet interface encapsulates an object that represents retrieved data from a database query.

Driver vendors implement this interface by writing drivers to produce the API specification.

Navigating the ResultSet

The executeQuery() method on the Statement interface and its subinterfaces returns a ResultSet object. The execute() method also can return multiple results. In such cases, the getMoreResults() method on the Statement interface may be invoked when you move to the next ResultSet.

After you obtain a handle to a ResultSet object, the pointer is initially positioned before the first row. At any given point while parsing through a ResultSet object, you are pointing to one particular row in the ResultSet object. Using the next() method of the ResultSet object, you can loop through all rows retrieved from the database. The next() method returns a Boolean value indicating whether there is a next row. If there is, the pointer is positioned on that row. The `next()` method returns false if no more rows are available in the `ResultSet`.

Navigating the `ResultSet` Object Example

When using `executeQuery()`, a `ResultSet` object containing one or more rows may be returned. The `ResultSet` object is used to process the data that was returned by the SQL statement.

As for `Cursor` objects, `ResultSet` objects have a current row, which is simply the row being pointed to in the resultset. Initially, the pointer is positioned before the first row of the resultset. To see the values in the rows of the resultset, you use the `next()` method to move the pointer through the rows in the resultset, as shown in the following example:

```
try {
    Statement stmt = con.createStatement();
String sSQL = "SELECT FIRST_NM,LAST_NM, SSN
FROM EMPLOYEE";
    ResultSet rs = stmt.executeQuery(sSQL);
    while( rs.next() )    {
        // Process the resultset
        ....
    }
}
catch(SQLException sqle) {
        // Process SQLException
}
```

Getting Data from the `ResultSet` Object

Based on the table columns' data types, you use the matching `datatype()` method of the `ResultSet` to retrieve the data. The `getXXX()` methods retrieve column values for the current row. You can retrieve values using either the index number of the column or the name of the column. Column names used as input to `getXXX()` methods are not case sensitive. If you're using the index number, you should remember that columns are numbered starting from 1, not zero.

SQL-to-Java Data Types

JDBC SQL types are specified in the `java.sql.Types` interface.

Tables 6.1 and 6.2 provide reference for Java and SQL object type mappings.

TABLE 6.1 Converting SQL Types to Java

SQL type	*Java type*	*Notes*
CHAR	String	Fixed length string of characters
VARCHAR	String	Variable length string of characters
LONGVARCHAR	String java.io.InputStream	Any length (multibyte) strings
NUMERIC	Java.math.BigDecimal	Absolute precision decimal value
DECIMAL	Java.math.BigDecimal	Absolute precision decimal value
BIT	Boolean	Single bit/binary value (on or off)
TINYINT	Byte	8-bit integer
SMALLINT	Short	16-bit integer
INTEGER	Integer	Signed 32-bit integer
BIGINT	Long	Signed 64-bit integer
REAL	Float	Floating-point value
FLOAT	Float	Floating-point value
DOUBLE	Double	Large floating-point value
BINARY	Byte[]	Array of binary values
VARBINARY	Byte[]	Variable length array of binary values
LONGVARBINARY	Byte[]	Any length (multi-megabyte) array of binary values
DATE	Java.sql.Date	Date value
TIME	Java.sql.Time	Time value
TIMESTAMP	Java.sql.Timestamp	Time value with additional nanosecond field

TABLE 6.2 Converting Java Object Types to SQL Types

Java type	*SQL type*
`String`	`VARCHAR LONGVARCHAR`
`Java.math.BigDecimal`	`NUMERIC`
`Boolean`	`BIT`
`Integer`	`INTEGER`
`Long`	`BIGINT`
`Float`	`FLOAT`
`Double`	`DOUBLE`
`Byte[ ]`	`VARBINARY LONGVARBINARY`
`Byte`	`TINYINT`
`Short`	`SMALLINT`
`Java.sql.Date`	`DATE`
`Java.sql.Time`	`TIME`
`Java.sql.Timestamp`	`TIMESTAMP`

Handling Nulls

Since some `get`*`XXX`*`()` methods return objects and some return primitives, you have to be aware of what nulls mean for each case:

- `object = null`—a Java "null" value for those `get`*`XXX`* methods that return Java objects
- `primitive = 0`—a zero value for `getByte`, `getShort`, `getInt`, `getLong`, `getFloat`, and `getDouble`
- `boolean = false`—a false value for `getBoolean`

The resultset provides the method `wasNull()` to check if the last column read has a value of `SQL NULL`. To use this method, first you have to call a `get`*`XXX`*`()` method, and after that call `wasNull()`.

Stored Procedures

Stored procedures are programs written in SQL that are stored as part of the database. Stored procedures can be called by client applications or by other stored procedures. Unfortunately, they are not standard. Each DBMS vendor has a different implementation for these procedures. There are many advantages of using stored procedures such as faster execution, reduced network traffic, modular programming, and enforced consistency. Stored procedures can take parameters, and return values.

Fortunately, JDBC supports the ability to call stored procedures. Your JDBC programs can execute stored procedures by using the `java.sql.CallableStatement` class.

Database stored procedures may be declared with or without parameters. If they are declared with any input parameters, you have to specify these input parameters with the `setXXX()` methods. Procedure calls can return values for `OUT` parameters or `INOUT` parameters.

Any output parameters must register their data type with `registerOutParameter()`.

After the stored procedure executes, you can use any of the `getXXX()` methods to get values from the output parameters.

If the procedure returns a resultset you call the `executeQuery()` method on the `CallableStatement`; otherwise, you should call the `execute()` method.

Examples of Stored Procedures

Here's an example of a stored procedure with an `INOUT` parameter. Suppose you have the following stored procedure:

```
SPEmpl(IN EMP_ID NUMBER,INOUT DEPT_ID INTEGER)
```

Here, `SPEmpl` provides an integer employee ID that is set to the value 100 in the following code. The second parameter, the department ID, serves as input and, once the stored procedure executes, as an output to be used in another process.

```
//Connection "conn" is assumed
CallableStatement cs = con.prepareCall(" CALL SPEmpl(?,?) ");
// Register Input Parameters:
cs.setInt(1, 100);      // Employee ID: 100
cs.setInt(2, 500);    // Department ID: 500

// Register Output Parameter:
cs.registerOutParameter(2, Types.INTEGER);
// Execute:
cs.execute();
int iMatchingDeptID = cs.getInt(2);
cs.close();
```

JDBC Exception Types

As a matter of course, you should try to handle everything that may go wrong at execution time so that the user experiences a soft and user-friendly failure rather than a hard failure. JDBC provides many exception objects to facilitate a soft failure.

JDBC provides these types of exceptions:

- `SQLException`
- `SQLWarning`
- `DataTruncation`

SQLException

Most of the methods in the `java.sql` package throw `SQLException` to indicate failure, which requires a try/catch block.

The `SQLException` has methods to provide developers with more detailed information about the errors. To track many problems that occur, you may use `getNextException()`. This method will either retrieve the next `SQLException` or return null if there are no more exceptions.

The following example illustrates the use of this method:

```
try {
    ....
}
catch(SQLException sqle) {
    while(sqle != null )
    {
        System.err.print("SQLException: " ) ;
        System.println(sqle.toString());
        sqle = sqle.getNextException();
    }
}
```

Additionally, to get the vendor-specific exception error code, you may use the `getErrorCode()` method on `SQLException`.

SQLWarning

`SQLWarning` is a subclass of `SQLException`. You can get a list of all the warnings using the `getWarning()` method on the connection:

```
SQLWarning sqlw = con.getWarnings();
while( sqlw != null ) {
```

```
    System.err.print("SQL Warning: " );
    System.println(con.getWarnings());
    sqlw = sqlw.getNextWarning();
}
```

DataTruncation Warnings

The `DataTruncation` exception indicates that a data value was truncated, resulting in a loss of data.

Metadata

Metadata is commonly used for object introspection. It is data about the data. JDBC provides several objects and methods that support DBMS metadata. For example, JDBC can be used to get information about the structure of your database. You can retrieve a list of tables and the column names for any table. This information is useful when programming for any database. There are a lot of metadata methods available in JDBC.

Two types of metadata can be obtained using JDBC. The first type describes a resultset and the second type describes the database.

The ResultSetMetaData Object

A `ResultSetMetaData` object is used to get information about a specific resultset.

```
ResultSetMetaData rsmd = rs.getMetaData();
```

Using the `ResultSetMetaData` object, you can obtain resultset information such as the number of columns returned, column names, and column types.

In the following example, we will print the names and data types of all resultset columns:

```
Statement stmt = con.createStatement();
String sSQL = "SELECT * FROM EMPLOYEE";
ResultSet rs = stmt.executeQuery(sSQL);
ResultSetMetaData rsmd = rs.getMetaData();
int iTotColumns = rsmd.getColumnCount();
for ( int iLoop = 1; iLoop < iTotColumn + 1 ; iLoop++)
{
        System.out.println("Column " + iLoop + ":") ;
System.out.println("Name: " + rsmd.getColumnName(iLoop));
System.out.println("Type: " +  rsmd.getColumnType(iLoop));
}
```

The DatabaseMetaData Interface

The `DatabaseMetaData` interface provides a great deal of information about the database that you're accessing. You may use its methods to retrieve any type of database structures, such as listing tables, columns, indexes, and procedures.

```
DatabaseMetaData dbmd = con.getMetaData();
System.out.println("Database: " +
dbmd.getDatabaseProductName());
System.out.println("User Name: " + dbmd.getUserName());
System.out.println("URL of the Database: " +
dbmd.getURL());
```

A common method is the `getTables()` method:

```
DatabaseMetaData dbmd = con.getMetaData();
ResultSet rs = dbmd.getTables( null, null, null,
new String[] {"TABLE"} );
```

Some other helpful methods that provide information about the SQL objects are `getSchemas()`, `getPrimaryKeys()`, `getProcedures()`, and `getProcedureColumns()`.

Scrollable Resultsets

One of the new features of JDBC 2.1 API is a scrollable resultset. Scrollable resultsets have the ability to scroll a pointer backwards or position it at a particular row in the resultset.

The `ResultSet` interface has three types of resultsets:

- `TYPE_FORWARD_ONLY`—supports forward scrolling only
- `TYPE_SCROLL_INSENSITIVE`—supports scrolling in both directions
- `TYPE_SCROLL_SENSITIVE`—scrollable and generally sensitive to changes made by others

It should be mentioned that not all drivers support these features. You may use the following methods to find out whether your driver supports scrollable resultsets.

To find out whether your driver supports forward scrolling only, use the following method:

```
public boolean IsTypeForwardOnly(Connection con)
{
        DataBaseMetaData dbmd = con.getMetaData();
        return(dbmd.supportsResultSetType(ResultSet.TYPE_FORWARD_ONLY));
}
```

To check whether your driver supports scrolling in both directions, use this method:

```
public boolean IsTypeScrollInsensitive(Connection con)
{
        DataBaseMetaData dbmd = con.getMetaData();
        return(dbmd.supportsResultSetType(ResultSet.TYPE_SCROLL_INSENSITIVE));
}
```

Use the following method to find out whether your driver supports sensitive scrolling:

```
public boolean IsTypeScrollSensitive(Connection con)
{
        DataBaseMetaData dbmd = con.getMetaData();
        return(dbmd.supportsResultSetType(ResultSet.TYPE_SCROLL_SENSITIVE));
}
```

Besides specifying a scroll direction, JDBC 2.1 programs can specify how many rows to fetch using the `setFetchSize()` method, and you can also control in which direction the rows are processed.

The next example shows how to restrict `ResultSet` object records to 100 rows and process the rows from the bottom up:

```
Statement stmt = con.CreateStatement();
stmt.setFetchSize(100);
stmt.setFetchDirection(ResultSet.FETCH_REVERSE);
ResultSet rs = stmt.executeQuery("SELECT * FROM
EMPLOYEE");
...
```

Scrollable `ResultSet` Methods

Methods available to scrollable `ResultSets` include the following:

- `boolean previous() throws SQLException`—moves the pointer to the previous row in the resultset from the current position
- `boolean first() throws SQLException`—positions the pointer on the first row of the resultset
- `boolean last() throws SQLException`—positions the pointer on the last row in the resultset
- `boolean absolute(int row)`—positions the pointer on the given row number

Scrollable ResultSet Example

The following code creates a scrollable ResultSet object:

```
String sSQL = "SELECT LNAME,FNAME FROM EMPLOYEE";
Statement stmt = con.createStatement(
        ResultSet.TYPE_SCROLL_INSENSITIVE,
        ResultSet.CONCUR_READ_ONLY);
ResultSet rs = stmt.executeQuery(sSQL);
While (rs.next()) {
        // Process resultset
}
// The Employee Table has 200 rows:
// Move the cursor to sixth row:
rs.relative(6);
// Process sixth row
// Move cursor to fifth row:
rs.previous();
// Process fifth row:
// Move the cursor to second row:
rs.relative(-3)
// Get the Current Row:
int iRowNo = rs.getRow();
```

Updateable Resultsets

JDBC 2.0 introduced a new feature that allows one to insert, update, and delete rows in a resultset. The java.sql.ResultSet interface has two new constants to indicate whether the resultset is read-only or updateable.

- CONCUR_READ_ONLY—This is a read-only resultset.
- CONCUR_UPDATABLE—You may insert, update, or delete rows in the resultset.

To find out the concurrency type, you may use the getConcurrency() method on the resultset.

Creating Updateable Resultsets

When you declare ResultSet objects with the CONCUR_UPDATABLE identifier, you may use methods defined in the ResultSet interface to update, insert, or delete rows in the resultset.

The following is an example of creating an updateable resultset:

```
String sSQL = "SELECT * FROM EMPLOYEE WHERE EMPL_ID=1200";
Statement stmt = con.createStatement(ResultSet.TYPE_FORWARD_ONLY,
                ResultSet.CONCUR_UPDATABLE);
ResultSet rs = stmt.executeQuery(sSQL);
```

In this example, after calling the `executeQuery()` method, the `ResultSet` object `rs` is updateable.

Updating Rows

To update individual columns associated with a row in the resultset, you use a series of methods that take the form `updateXXX()`.

The `updateXXX()` methods are used to update column values in the current row. They do not directly update the underlying database; instead, the methods are called as a hint to update the database. Some of the update methods are listed here:

```
updateAsciiStream()
updateBigDecimal()
updateBinaryStream()
updateBoolean()
updateByte()
```

For each JDBC type, you may use one of two update methods of the ResultSet interface: One requires the column name and the other requires the column index. The second argument of each `updateXXX()` method is an object of type *XXX*.

For instance, to update a column with a string value, you may use one of these methods:

- `public void updateString( int columnIndex, String x) throws SQLException`
- `public void updateString(String columnName, String x) throws SQLException`
- The `updateNull()` method is used to update a nullable column to a null value. The `updateNull()` method takes only one argument of type `int`: the column index.

As an example:

```
...
String sSQL = "SELECT FIRST_NM,LAST_NM,CITY,STATE,ZIP_CODE FROM EMLOYEE WHERE
EMPL_ID = 500";
Statement stmt = con.createStatement(ResultSet.TYPE_FORWARD_ONLY,
                    ResultSet.CONCUR_UPDATABLE);
ResultSet rs = stmt.executeQuery(sSQL);
rs.next();
rs.updateString("CITY","EAST BRUNSWICK");
rs.updateString("ZIP_CODE","08816");
rs.updateRow();
...
```

Deleting Rows

You may delete the current row from a ResultSet as well as from the database using the method deleteRow().

For example:

```
...
rs.absolute(2);
rs.deleteRow(0);
...
```

Inserting Rows

To insert a row using the ResultSet interface, first move the pointer to the insert row at the end of the table by calling the moveToInsertRow() method. Next, set the values for the columns using update methods. Finally, insert the new row into the ResultSet object and eventually the underlying database using the insertRow() method.

For example:

```
...
// Select Required Columns from the Table PROJECT:
String sSQL = "SELECT PROJ_ID,PROJ_NAME, PROJ_TITLE FROM
PROJECT";
ResultSet rs = stmt.executeQuery(sSQL);
rs.moveToInsertRow();
// Set value to each required column:
rs.updateInt(1, 100);
rs.updateString(2,"Customer Master");
rs.updateString(3,"Security Master");
rs.insertRow();
...
```

Transaction Support

If you're executing a series of update statements in a single transaction, it's important to ensure that all succeed or all fail.

By default, when a new Connection object is created, it is set to auto commit mode, which means that every time you execute a statement, it is committed to the database. However, the Connection object provides methods to explicitly control a transaction and commit or roll back at will:

```
void setAutoCommit( boolean autoCommit) throws SQLException
void commit() throws SQLException
void rollback() throws SQLException
```

At the beginning of a transaction, we call `setAutoCommit(false)`. Then, if the group of update operations is successful, we call the `commit()` method. If any error occurs, we call the `rollback()` method to undo any changes.

For example:

```
String sEmplSQL = ...;
String sDeptSQL=...;
try {
con.setAutoCommit(false);
Statement stmtEmpl = con.createStatement();
Statement stmtDept = con.createStatement();
stmtEmpl.executeUpdate(sEmplSQL);
stmtDept.executeUpdate(sDeptSQL);
con.commit();
stmtEmpl.close();
sDeptSQL.close();
}
catch( SQLException sqle) {
try {
con.rollback();
}
catch(SQLException sqle){
{
// Process SQLException
...
}
}
```

Batch Statements

One of the new features of JDBC 2.0 is the ability to submit multiple update statements to the database as a single transaction.

Not all database drivers support batch updates. To find out whether your driver supports batch updates, you can use the `DatabaseMetaData.supportsBatchUpdates()` method, which returns true if the driver supports batch updates and false otherwise.

Major methods such as `addBatch()`, `clearBatch()`, and `executeBatch()` are provided to manipulate and execute the SQL statement list.

The return value of the `executeBatch()` method, used to submit a batch of commands to the database for execution, is an array of ints that provide completion or error information for each SQL statement executed.

Make sure you disable autocommit by calling the `setAutoCommit(false)` method, which turns off the implicit commit. If any of the updates fail to execute within the database, a `BatchUpdateException` is thrown.

The following code provides an example of using batch statements:

```
try {
...
String sSQL1 = "INSERT INTO EMPLOYEE VALUES...";
String sSQL2 = "INSERT INTO EMPLOYEE VALUES...";
String sSQL3 = "INSERT INTO DEPARTMENT VALUES...";
con.setAutoCommit(false);
stmt.clearBatch();
// Your batch statements:
stmt.addBatch(sSQL1);
stmt.addBatch(sSQL2);
stmt.addBatch(sSQL3);
int [] aiTotalUpdated = stmt.executeBatch();
con.commit();
...
}
catch(BatchUpdateException bue) {
        System.out.println("** Batch Update Exception **");
        System.out.println("SQL State:  " + bue.getSQLState());
        System.out.println("Message:  " + bue.getMessage());
        System.out.println("Vendor:  " + bue.getErrorCode());
        System.out.print("Total Updated:");
        int[] aiTotalUpdated = bue.getUpdateCount();
        int iTotal = aiTotalUpdated.length();
        for (int i = 0; i < iTotal; i++) {
                System.out.print (aiTotalUpdated[i]);
        }
        SQLException sqle = bue;
        while(sqle != null )
        {
                // Handle Exception
                ...
                sqle = sqle.getNextException();
        }
        stmt.clearBatch();
}
catch(Exception e) {
        // Handle general Exception:
        System.out.println("** SQL Exception **");
        System.out.println("SQL State:  " + e.getSQLState());
        System.out.println("Message:  " + e.getMessage());
        System.out.println("Vendor:  " + e.getErrorCode());
}
```

JDBC 2.1 New Data Types

The next version of the ANSI/ISO SQL standard defines some new data types, commonly referred to as the SQL3 types. The new SQL3 data types give a relational database more flexibility in determining what can be used as a type for each table column.

The primary new SQL3 types are

- `BLOB`—Binary Large Objects. Mapped to the `java.sql.Blob` type.
- `CLOB`—Character Large Objects. Mapped to the `java.sql.Clob` type.
- `ARRAY`—Can store values of a specified type. Mapped to the `java.sql.Array` type.
- `STRUCT`—This is the default mapping for any SQL structured type, and is mapped to the `java.sql.Struct` type.
- `REF`—Serves as a reference to SQL data within the database. Can be passed as a parameter to an SQL statement. Mapped to the `java.sql.Ref` type.

BLOB and CLOB

The `java.sql.Blob` and `java.sql.Clob` interfaces give you the ability to load only a portion of the column's value into memory. Methods in the interfaces `ResultSet`, `PreparedStatement`, and `CallableStatement`, such as `getBlob()` and `setBlob()`, allow a programmer to access the SQL `BLOB`. The `BLOB` contains a logical pointer to the SQL `BLOB` data rather than the data itself. Methods such as `getBlob()` and `setBlob()` return a pointer to the value. Using such a pointer, your application can read some or all of the data as needed.

For instance, assume that we have a table called `APPLICANT` that contains a column of type `VARCHAR` called `RESUME`. If we execute the following statement, it's straightforward to get the data stored in `RESUME` by calling the `getString()` method:

```
try {
...
String sResume = null;
String sSQL = "SELECT RESUME FROM APPLICANT "+
" WHERE APPLICANT_ID  = ? ";
PreparedStatement pstmt = con.prepareStatement(sSQL);
pstmt.setInt(1, 100); // Assume the APPLICANT_ID = 100
ResultSet rs = pstmt.executeQuery();
if( rs.next() ) {
        // Process the resultset record
        sResume = rs.getString("RESUME");
}
rs.close();
pstmt.close();
```

```
}
catch(SQLException sqle) {
        System.err.println("SQLException: " + sqle.getMessage());
}
```

After executing this code, the entire column value is loaded into memory.

Let's modify the code to load a portion of the column's value into memory by using the `java.sql.Clob` class. This will be useful for searching the `RESUME` column for `CLOB`s. It can also be used to search any other column for a binary sequence of `BLOB`s.

```
try {
...
String sResume = null;
String sSQL = "SELECT RESUME FROM APPLICANT "+
" WHERE APPLICANT_ID  = ? ";
PreparedStatement pstmt = con.prepareStatement(sSQL);
pstmt.setInt(1, 100); // Assume the APPLICANT_ID = 100
ResultSet rs = pstmt.executeQuery();
if( rs.next() ) {
        // Process the resultset record
        Clob clbResume = rs.getClob();
        long lResumeLen = clbResume.length();
        // Loop through the clbResume and process 50 characters:
        for ( long lLoop = 0 ; lLoop < lResumeLenl; lLoop +=50)
        {
                sResume = clbResume.getSubString(lLoop,50);
        // Do your search: if found, break the loop:
        ...
        }
}
rs.close();
pstmt.close();
}
catch(SQLException sqle) {
        System.err.println("SQLException: " + sqle.getMessage());
}
```

ARRAY

The new SQL data type `ARRAY` allows an array to be used as a column value in a database table.

Using an `Array` object is as easy as using a basic data type. An SQL `ARRAY` value is retrieved with the method `getArray()`.

For instance, assume we have a table called `APPLICANT` that contains a column called `LANGUAGE` and that it stores SQL `ARRAY` values.

```
String sSQL = "SELECT LANGUAGE FROM APPLICANT WHERE " +
" APPLICANT_ID=100";
ResultSet rs = stmt.executeQuery(sSQL);
rs.next();
Array arrLanguages = rs.getArray("LANGUAGE");
```

The variable `arrLanguages` now is a logical pointer to the `LANGUAGE` field for `APPLICANT_ID 100` that resides on the server. This means that you can operate on `arrLanguages` just as if you were operating on the SQL `ARRAY` object itself but without incurring the overhead of bringing all the data in the array over to the client.

STRUCT

The `STRUCT` interface is the standard mapping for an SQL structured type.

SQL structured types are similar to Java classes that contain public member variables only. They can be retrieved from `ResultSet` objects using the `getObject()` method.

REF

`REF` serves as a reference to SQL data within the database. Because the SQL `REF` value is a pointer and does not contain actual data, the `REF` object also is a pointer. An SQL `REF` can be retrieved by calling the `getRef()` method of the `ResultSet`.

For example:

```
...
String sSQL = "SELECT EMP_HIST FROM EMPLOYEE WHERE EMPL_ID = 300";
ResultSet rs = stmt.executeQuery(sSQL);
rs.next();
Ref ref = rs.getRef("EMP_HIST");
Experience exp = (Experience) ref.getObject();
...
```

JDBC 2.0 Optional Package API: `javax.sql`

The JDBC 2.0 Optional Package API adds new functionality:

- The `DataSource` interface—Used for working with JNDI, allowing a connection to be made using a `DataSource` object registered with a JNDI naming service.
- Connection Pooling—New layer for implementing connection pooling to reuse connections instead of creating new ones.

- Distributed transactions—Transactions that may be distributed across multiple database instances. They are usually managed using a technique called a two-phase commit. The first phase involves preparing each database involved in the transaction to make the appropriate changes and allows the database to indicate whether the changes would result in an error. If committing the changes would cause an error, the proposed changes are rolled back. Otherwise, in the second phase, the changes are committed in all of the participating databases.
- `RowSets`—JavaBeans-compliant objects that encapsulate database resultsets and the accessible information.

Database Access with JNDI

JDBC 2.0 introduced the `DataSource` interface and the JNDI technology for naming and location services.

JNDI can be used in addition to the JDBC driver manager to manage data sources and connections.

As mentioned before, you may obtain a connection using the `DriverManager` object; however, using a `DataSource` object is the preferred way because it has many advantages such as easier code maintenance, increased performance due to the use of connection pooling, and support for distributed transactions through `XADataSource`.

To create a database connection with JNDI, you specify a resource name, which corresponds to an entry in a database or naming service, and then receive back the information necessary to establish a connection with your database. JNDI provides a uniform way to find and access services on a network.

`DataSource` objects can be created and managed separately from the JDBC applications.

JDBC data sources are registered in the `jdbc` subcontext. For example:

```
Context ctx = new InitialContext();
DataSource ds = (DataSource) ctx.lookup("jdbc/demo");
Connection con = ds.getConnection("username", "password");
```

Connection Pooling

Connection pooling is defined as part of the JDBC 2.1 Standard Extension API. A connection pool is a set of database connections that are loaded into memory so that they can be reused. This allows sharing of database connections, instead of requiring a separate connection for each client.

Connecting to a database can be an expensive operation. Each time your application attempts to access a database, it must connect to that database. However, connecting to a database is a time-consuming activity since the database connection requires resources (communication, memory, authentication, and so on) to create each connection, maintain it, and then release it when it is no longer required. The overhead is particularly high for Web-based applications because Web users connect and disconnect more frequently. Usually, usage volumes can be large and difficult to predict. Establishing a connection once and then reusing it for subsequent requests can dramatically improve performance and response times of Web-based applications.

Most good Application Servers establish a pool of database connections that is shared by all the applications, as in Figure 6.7.

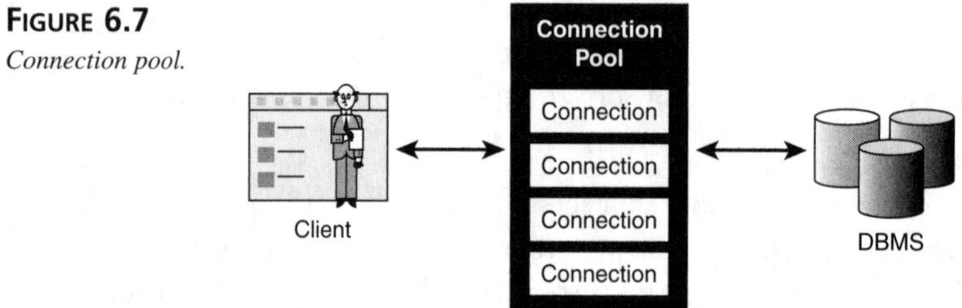

FIGURE 6.7
Connection pool.

The following is a JDBC Connection Pooling example:

```
//Get a handle to the JNDI context
Context ctx = new InitialContext();
//Get a reference to the connection pool
String dsName = "java:comp/env/jdbc/poolname";
DataSource ds = (DataSource) ctx.lookup(dsName);
//Get a connection
Connection con = ds.getConnection();
// Handle single transaction (optional)
con.setAutoCommit(false);
// Your Code goes here: Standard JDBC code SELECT/UPDATE/...)
...
// Commit or rollback the transaction:
con.commit();
// Close the connection (return the connection object
// back to the pool)
con.close();
```

Distributed Transactions

The JDBC 2.0 Specification provides the capability for handling distributed transactions. A distributed transaction is a single transaction that applies to multiple, heterogeneous databases that may reside on separate server machines.

For supporting distributed transactions, JDBC 2.0 provides two new interfaces: `javax.sql.XADataSource` and `javax.sql.XAConnection`.

JDBC RowSets

`RowSets` exist to provide the flexibility of a disconnected operation. JavaBean is a portable platform-independent component model written in Java and follows the JavaBean specification. It enables you to write reusable components. JDBC `RowSet` objects are JavaBeans capable of operating without an active database connection. This is useful for sending data across a network to thin clients, such as Web browsers, laptops, and PDAs.

Because a `RowSet` is a JavaBean, you can implement events for the `RowSet`, and you can set properties on the `RowSet`.

Here are some possible `RowSet` implementations:

- `CachedRowSet`: a `RowSet` that can be used to pass a set of rows across a network or to add scrollability and updateability to resultset data.
- `JDBCRowSet`: a `RowSet` that can be used to encapsulate a JDBC driver as a JavaBeans component.
- `WebRowSet`: a set of rows that are being cached outside of a data source. `WebRowSet` is an extension of `CachedRowSet`.

Case Study: The SilverStream Application Server

The SilverStream Application Server is a comprehensive, J2EE-certified platform for building and deploying enterprise-class Web applications. It offers customers a proven, scalable, and reliable platform with comprehensive support for the J2EE standard. The SilverStream Application Server includes support for popular Java Integrated Development Environments (IDEs), EJB development tools, and JavaServer Pages (JSP) design tools from third parties. This development flexibility, combined with other new features and integration with popular Web servers, provides customers with a powerful, open platform for efficiently building, deploying, and managing powerful e-business applications.

Database Connectivity in SilverStream

The SilverStream Application Server handles all connections between a SilverStream client and a database. The server allocates database connections as needed and releases them as quickly as possible, depending on the type of processing being done.

SilverStream can access databases through a native Java Database Connectivity (JDBC) driver or through a JDBC-ODBC Bridge driver.

For performance reasons, SilverStream has written its own JDBC drivers for the major databases.

Some sample SilverStream JDBC drivers are listed here:

- ODBC: `com.sssw.jdbc.mss.odbc.AgOdbcDriver`
- Oracle 8i: `com.sssw.jdbc.oracle8.Driver`

The SilverStream client does not pass SQL statements to the SilverStream server for execution. Instead, the client passes row selection and ordering information to the SilverStream server as SilverStream expressions. The server combines this information with other information built by a SilverStream designer and dynamically constructs the SQL, which it then passes to the database through JDBC for execution. This process is illustrated in Figure 6.8.

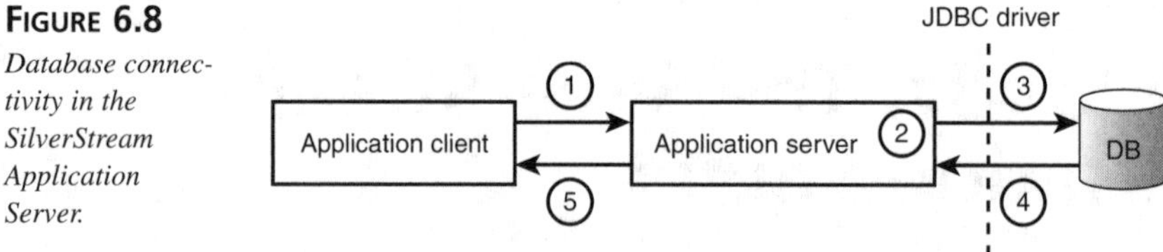
JDBC driver
Application client
Application server
DB
1
2
3
4
5
1. Client sends row selection and ordering information to Server.
2. Server generates SQL query.
3. Query passes through JDBC layer.
4. Results are passed back from database through JDBC to the server.
5. Server passes data to client.

FIGURE 6.8
Database connectivity in the SilverStream Application Server.

JDBC Within SilverStream

JDBC allows you to pass query strings to an underlying database. The target database must be JDBC compliant. This means that the database must at least have the functionality of ANSI SQL92 Entry Level. All the databases supported by SilverStream meet this minimum requirement.

SilverStream has its own expression engine (parser and evaluator) that is used on top of the JDBC driver (a Java SQL API). This engine is used to help translate SilverStream expression statements back into database statements (mainly SQL). These expressions do a computation on a column, perform a validation, or act as a `WHERE` and `ORDER BY` clause.

The SilverStream parser handles some parts of the database expression, while other parts are passed through to the database for processing. The server evaluates any non-database-supported expressions in `WHERE` clauses as each row is retrieved. The processing for non-database-supported `ORDER BY` clauses, on the other hand, is deferred until all the rows have been retrieved.

The SilverStream Application Server connects to databases using the standard JDBC connection object. It creates and maintains a pool of connections. The number of connections in the pool is configurable through the SilverStream Management Console. Only the SilverStream server accesses the database. Clients communicate through the SilverStream server for database access. This process is illustrated in Figure 6.9.

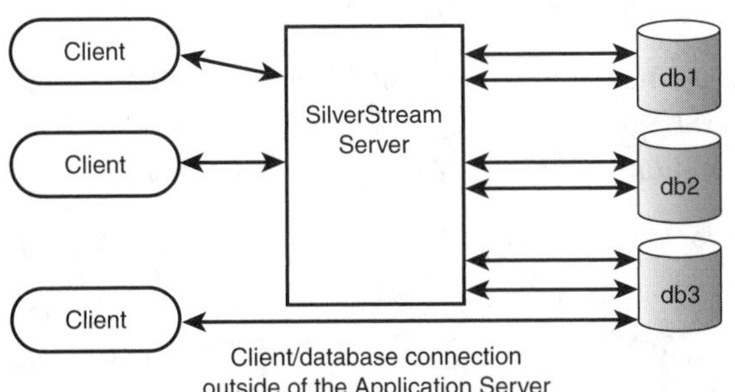

FIGURE 6.9
SilverStream server/database connections.

The `AgiDatabase` interface provides access to the internal connection pool to allocate raw JDBC connection objects. You can obtain an `AgiDatabase` object using `evt.getServer().getDatabase(`*`dbName`*`)` or `evt.getDatabase()`.

You gain access to the database connection pool through the `AgiDatabase.getConnection()` method. The `getConnection()` method obtains the next available JDBC (database) connection object. You can specify the action to take when no connections are currently available. The `getConnection()` method has the declaration

```
Connection getConnection(boolean doWait)
```

where `doWait` specifies the action to take when no connection is available. When set to true, `getConnection()` suspends until a connection is available. When set to false, `getConnection()` returns with or without a connection. It returns null if no connection is available.

The Connection Pool Manager manages the connection object. Once the Connection Pool Manager allocates a connection, it cannot be reused until the manager releases it back to the pool. The system will deadlock due to lack of connection resources if connections are allocated and not released. Always return the connection object to the pool with the `releaseConnection()` method.

You release a connection object by calling the `AgiDatabase.releaseConnection()` method. Many databases require that you close the `Statements` and `ResultSets` as soon as possible. Before you return a connection to the pool, it is a good idea to do the following:

- Close all open `ResultSets`
- Close all open `Statements`
- Commit or abort any uncommitted transactions

Accessing JDBC from a Session Bean in a SilverStream Database

In this part we'll discuss how to write a session bean that gets stock quotes using a JDBC connection to a SilverStream database. In order to build and execute this example, you need to install and configure the SilverStream Application Server.

Please visit `www.silverstream.com` for the latest information regarding the Server.

We'll build a simple page, `pgSymbolTrade.html`, where the user may enter a stock quote and hit a submit button to get the latest trade. The page will appear as in Figure 6.10.

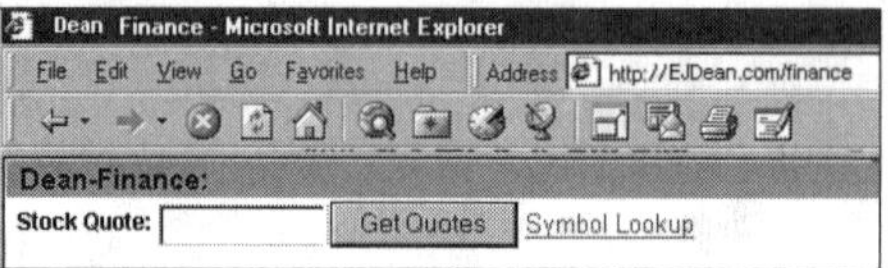

FIGURE 6.10
Symbol trade page.

When the user presses the Get Quotes button, the page accesses the `SBSymbolTradeJDBC` session bean, which makes JDBC calls to get the latest trade for the symbol entered by the user.

In this example we'll build the components that appear in Table 6.3.

Table 6.3 Brief Summary of the Application Components

Component	*Description*
`SBSymbolTradeJDBCBean`	The Symbol Trade Session Bean. This bean includes all of the JDBC code
`SBSymbolTradeHome`	The `SBSymbolTradeJDBCBean`'s home interface
`SBSymbolTradeRemote`	The `SBSymbolTradeJDBCBean`'s remote interface
`SBSymbolTradeJDBC.jar`	The EJB JAR
`SBSymbolTradeJDBCDeplPlan`	The EJB Deployment Plan
`SBSymbolTradeJDBCRemote.jar`	The `SBSymbolTradeJDBCBean`'s remote JAR
`SBSymbolTradeJDBCDeployed`	The deployed object
`pgSymbolTrade.html`	The user interface for accessing the EJB components

Accessing JDBC from a Session Bean

To access JDBC from a session bean, we need to follow these steps:

- Import the `java.sql.*` and `javax.sql.DataSource` packages.
- Define a resource reference lookup in the session bean.
- Construct the JDBC calls that access the data. The JDBC calls should

    Get a database connection from SilverStream's connection pool.

    Construct, compile, and run the SQL statement that returns the required data.

    Close the database connection when done.

- Create an environment entry in the deployment descriptor for the session bean when adding it to the EJB JAR. The environment entry for the session bean must be a resource reference. By convention, DataSource references are named `jdbc/xxx`. This name must exactly match the name on which the session bean does the environment context lookup.
- Map the resource reference to a SilverStream database when creating a deployment plan for the session bean.

Defining a Resource Reference Lookup in the Session Bean

Your session bean can obtain a `javax.sql.DataSource` object by doing a JNDI lookup in the `java:comp/env` context. In our example, the resource reference in the deployment descriptor is

```
/jdbc/SymbolTradeDataSource
```

So a lookup for this entry in the `java:comp/env` context looks like this:

```
  String dataSourceName =
     "java:comp/env/jdbc/SymbolTradeDataSource";
m_jdbcSource = (DataSource)ctx.lookup(dataSourceName);
```

where `m_jdbcSource` is defined as

```
  private DataSource m_jdbcSource = null;
```

Constructing the JDBC Calls

The JDBC calls in our example are

- Get a `java.sql.Connection` from the SilverStream connection pool.
- Construct, compile, and execute an SQL `Select` statement.
- Manipulate the query's `ResultSet` object.

Getting a Connection

We use the `javax.sql.DataSource` object `m_jdbcSource` to get a connection as follows

```
connection = m_jdbcSource.getConnection();
```

where `connection` is a `java.sql.Connection` object initialized earlier to `null`:

```
Connection connection = null;
```

Constructing, Compiling, and Executing an SQL Select Statement

This example needs to obtain the last trade (`current_trade`) for the stock quote (`stock_id`) that was passed to the session bean from the calling page (the `psStockID` parameter). The Select statement looks like this:

```
String stmt = "SELECT current_trade " +
"FROM trade WHERE stock_id = '" + psStockID + "'";
```

To precompile the statement, you call the `connection.prepareStatement()` method passing in a string representing the SQL you constructed:

```
PreparedStatement preparedStatement =
connection.prepareStatement(stmt);
```

Once you have a compiled SQL query (a `javax.sql.PreparedStatement`), you can execute the SQL using the `executeQuery()` method, manipulating the query's `ResultSet` object and returning it to the caller:

```
resultSet = preparedStatement.executeQuery();
```

The `ResultSet` object is defined earlier as a `java.sql.ResultSet` object like this:

```
ResultSet resultSet = null;
```

The `current_trade` is returned as the first column. To get it, we use the `getObject(index)` method like this:

```
Object objCurrentTrade = resultSet.getObject(1);
```

Cast the `current_trade` to a `BigDecimal` variable (the `resultSet.getObject()` method returns the `BigDecimal` value as an `Object`):

```
BigDecimal bdCurrentTrade = (BigDecimal) objCurrentTrade;
return bdCurrentTrade;
```

Finally, close the `preparedStatement`, the `ResultSet`, and the `Connection` objects:

```
  try {
       if (preparedStatement != null)
         preparedStatement.close();
       if (resultSet != null)
         resultSet.close();
       if (connection != null)
         connection.close();
  }
    catch (Exception e) {
    // Handle you Exception...
  }
```

Creating an Environment Entry

So that the session bean's environment context lookup actually finds a `javax.sql.DataSource` object, the deployment descriptor for the session bean must include a resource reference entry. A resource reference is considered an environment entry like a role reference or a bean reference. Such references will be discussed in greater detail in future chapters.

The resource reference entry in the deployment descriptor must exactly match the session bean's lookup. For this example, the name must match `/jdbc/SymbolTradeDataSource`. Since it is defined as a resource reference, the SilverStream container will store it in the `java:comp/env` context.

The SilverStream entry for this example appears as in Figure 6.11.

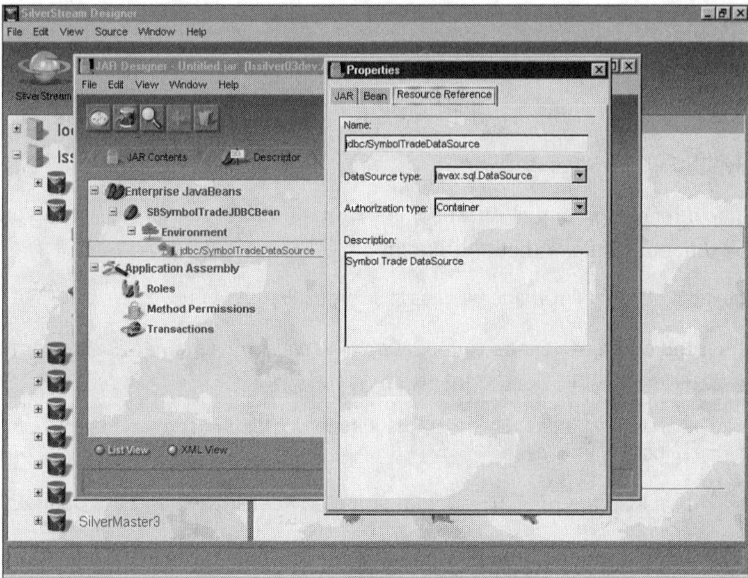

FIGURE 6.11
Creating an environment entry.

Mapping the Resource Reference to a SilverStream Database

For the container to be able to resolve a resource reference to a database at runtime, the resource reference must be mapped in the deployment plan.

The database must be a SilverStream database and must already be added to the server before you can map it.

The mapping of a resource reference screen is shown in Figure 6.12.

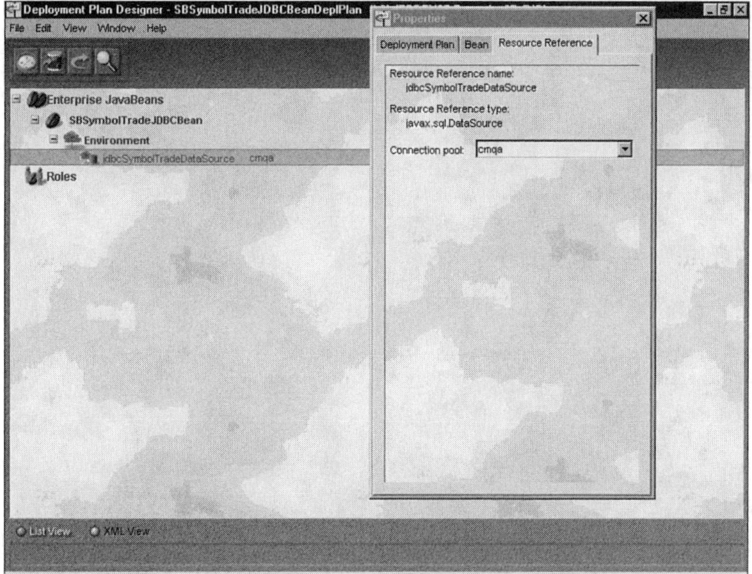

FIGURE 6.12
Mapping the resource reference to a SilverStream database.

Summary

In this chapter, we examined most new features in the `java.sql` package, including support for SQL3 data types, scrollable resultsets, programmatic updates, and batch updates. We covered the new JDBC Standard Extension API, the `javax.sql` package, which is an integral part of the Enterprise JavaBeans (EJB) technology that allows you to write distributed transactions that use connection pooling. Finally, we provided a detailed example of accessing JDBC from a session bean in a SilverStream Application Server.

CHAPTER 7

Build Control Flow: Servlets

IN THIS CHAPTER

- What Are Servlets? *182*
- Benefits of Servlets *184*
- Use as Controller in MVC and the Sample Application *184*
- Basic HTTP *185*
- Servlet Container *188*
- Servlet API *188*
- Service Method Detail *189*
- HTML Clients *192*
- Servlet Life Cycle *195*
- `ServletContext` *196*
- HTTP Request Header *197*
- HTTP Response Header *203*
- Session Management *205*
- Dispatching Requests *209*
- Servlets with JDBC *211*
- Web Applications *213*
- Using Servlets in the SilverStream Application Server *218*
- Servlet 2.3 API *223*

Servlet technology is a part of the Java Enterprise Edition (J2EE) platform. Servlets are currently a popular choice for the construction of interactive Web applications. In this chapter, we will introduce Java Servlets and see how they fit in with the J2EE framework for enterprise Web application development and deployment.

In this chapter we will be looking at aspects of the servlets in API 2.2. We'll focus on writing Java Servlets that generate responses to HTTP requests.

What Are Servlets?

Servlets are part of the Java 2 Platform, Enterprise Edition specification. Java Servlets are modules that run on the server, enabling you to extend the server's functionality. Servlets work within a Web server environment, and they are a key component of server-side Java development. Servlets are an effective replacement for CGI (Common Gateway Interface) scripts.

Before introducing servlets, we'll take a quick look at Common Gateway Interface (CGI), Internet Server Application Programming Interface/Netscape Server Application Programming Interface (ISAPI/NSAPI), and Netscape's Web Application Interface (WAI).

First Generation—CGI

The Common Gateway Interface (CGI) is the traditional way of adding functionality to a Web server. CGI is a standard for external gateway programs to interface with information servers such as HTTP servers; it handles the communication between HTML forms and your programs.

A CGI script can be written in any programming language. Perl is the most popular, but C and C++ are also used. The original CGI programs were written in Unix shell scripts.

The following is the typical sequence of steps that a CGI script follows:

- Get the user's form input through environment variables, the command line, and its standard input stream (stdin).
- Process the user's request.
- Write the HTML response to its standard output stream (stdout).

Figure 7.1 diagrams this process.

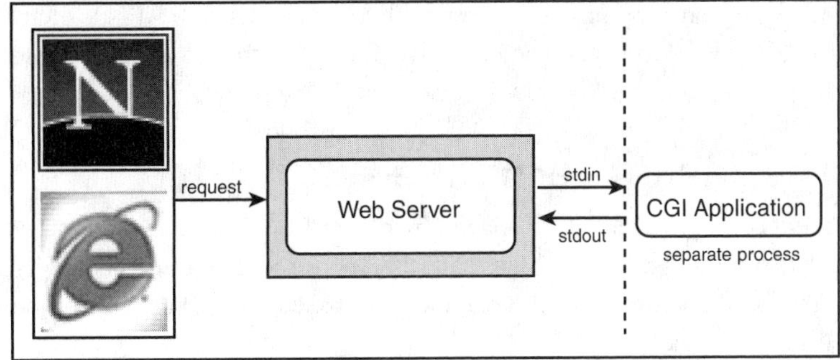

FIGURE 7.1
CGI process.

CGI is not without its drawbacks. Performance and scalability are big problems because each request to the server, which executes a CGI script, is answered in a separate process by a separate instance of the CGI program. This type of execution has high overhead and requires significant server resources.

Second Generation—ISAPI/NSAPI

Internet Server API, normally referred to as ISAPI, is the standard Internet Server API that was initially created as the Microsoft Information Server API, but was subsequently offered as the open standard. NSAPI is the standard Netscape Server API that was used for interaction with the Netscape Web server.

Because ISAPI/NSAPI are server-specific extensions and do not require process creation, they run much faster than CGI programs. However, although they dramatically increase the speed of Web server applications, these APIs introduce new problems that CGI doesn't have. Because applications written in ISAPI/NSAPI run on the same process as the Web server, any buggy code might crash the Web server. To write good applications using ISAPI/NSAPI, a programmer must master the internal operations and functions of the specific Web server.

The Netscape Web Application Interface (WAI) is one of the programming interfaces enabling extended functionality of Netscape Web servers. WAI is a CORBA-based programming interface used to define object interfaces to the HTTP request-response data and server information.

Using WAI, a Web application can be written in C, C++, or Java that accepts an HTTP request from a client, processes it, and returns a response to the client. A WAI process is started when the Web server is started and doesn't exit after a request is processed; instead, it goes back and waits for more requests.

Adversely, any application written with Server Extension APIs is attached to one particular server vendor. If you need to move the application to another server from a different vendor, you will be required to start from the beginning.

The Java Alternative—Servlets

Servlets are Java classes, managed by containers, that generate dynamic content. Servlets interact with Web clients by a request-response model implemented by the Servlet Container. This request-response model is based on the behavior of the Hypertext Transfer Protocol (HTTP).

The Servlet API was developed to leverage the advantages of the Java platform to solve the issues of CGI and Server Extension APIs. The Servlet API is supported by virtually all Web servers, including load-balancing, fault-tolerant Application Servers.

Benefits of Servlets

Java Servlets provide many benefits and features that enable you to build powerful Web-based server-side applications.

These benefits include the following:

- Servlets can be deployed into distributed server environments.
- Servlets are platform- and server-independent.
- Servlets are easy to develop and follow a standard API.
- Servlets are extensible. JavaServer Pages (JSP) build on top of the Servlet API.
- A servlet is a server resource, providing access to other server resources, such as other servlets, EJBs, JSPs, JDBC, and so on.

Use as Controller in MVC and the Sample Application

Web applications consist of requests made from Web browsers to Web application servers using the HTTP protocol. The architecture and components that handle these interactions between a Web client and a Web application server can be employed using a Model-View-Controller (MVC) pattern.

The Model-View-Controller pattern is a paradigm that specifies how you create user interfaces in programming languages. The main advantage of the MVC paradigm is that it effectively limits and defines the interaction between the interface components and the underlying problem-domain classes.

- The Model is the data representation of the real-world class that you want to create an interface on. For Web applications, the Model is the component that exposes the business logic for a particular Web application or service.
- The View implements the visual view of a model. It is the class that receives input from the user and displays output to the user. In terms of a Web definition, the View represents the component that constructs HTML pages that are returned to a user by a Web application in response to HTTP requests.
- The Controller receives all input events from the user. It is the class that deals with the physical input devices and translates those signals into messages to the appropriate view. In another words, the Controller is the component or service that drives the Model and View components.

The servlet/JavaServer Pages (JSP) interaction closely follows the Model-View-Controller design for Web applications. The idea of such a design is to use servlets to process HTTP requests and interact with JavaBeans or EJB, where the business logic of the request is encapsulated. Finally, JSP is invoked to compose the presentation layer of the application.

This kind of interaction between servlets and JSP would fit into the MVC framework as follows:

- Model: JavaBeans or EJB—business logic.
- View: JSP—used to compose the user interface.
- Controller: Servlet—used to process the HTTP request and manage the application's workflow.

One of the Model-View-Controller implementations is the Struts Framework. The Struts Framework is an open source initiative from the Jakarta Project, which is sponsored by the Apache Software Foundation. The goal of the Struts Framework is to provide an open source framework useful in building Web applications with Java using JSP and servlets.

For the latest information about the Struts Framework, please visit `http://jakarta.apache.org/struts/`.

Basic HTTP

As mentioned earlier, servlets interact with Web clients by a request-response model that is implemented by the Servlet Container. The request-response model in use is based on the behavior of HTTP.

In order to use servlets effectively, you need to understand HTTP, and how this protocol that drives the Web actually works. Additionally, you have to be familiar with the contents of the HTTP request and response headers.

HTTP operates over TCP/IP connections. The browser sends a request to the Web server in the form of a request method, uniform resource identifier (URI), and protocol version. This will be followed by a message containing request modifiers, client information, and possible body content.

An example of an HTTP version 1.1 request:

```
GET /locate?keywords=SilverStream+J2EE HTTP/1.1
Date: Sun, 24 Jun 2001 19:18:37 GMT
Accept: image/gif, image/jpg, */*
Accept-Encoding: gzip
Accept-Charset: iso-8859-1,*,utf-8
Accept-Language: en
Connection: keep-Alive
Cookie: userID=id89111123
Host: www.EJDean.com
Referrer: http://www.EJDean.com/EJBVendors.html
User-Agent: Mozilla/4.7 [en] (Win98; u)
```

In this example, the `GET` defines the HTTP method, followed by the resource name and the protocol version. Table 7.1 lists and describes several methods that are used frequently in HTTP 1.1.

TABLE 7.1 Commonly Used HTTP 1.1 Methods

Method	*Description*
`GET`	The client requests information from the given URL
`HEAD`	Similar to `GET`, except the body is not retrieved
`POST`	Client adds info to URI (HTML forms)
`PUT`	Used to place documents on the Server
`DELETE`	Client deletes resource of URI
Others…	

The Web server responds with a status line, one or more response headers, a blank line, and, optionally, the document or other data.

As mentioned earlier, the status line, which is also referred to as the response line, consists of the server protocol and a status code. The status code indicates the success or failure of the client request (see Table 7.2).

TABLE 7.2 Status Codes Divided into Different Categories

Status Code	*Category*
100s	Informational
200s	Successful
300s	Redirection
400s	Request Error
500s	Server Error

Commonly used status codes include the following:

- 200—OK
- 400—Bad request
- 401—Request requires HTTP authentication
- 403—Forbidden
- 404—Requested resource not available
- 500—HTTP server error

One of the server header fields will be `Content-Type`, which specifies a MIME (Multipurpose Internet Mail Extension) type to describe how the document should be interpreted.

An example of an HTTP response:

```
HTTP/1.0 200 OK
Content-Length: 2109
Content-Type: text/html
Expires: 0
Last-Modified: Thu, 08 Feb 2001 16:43:41 GMT
Cache-Control: no-cache
Connection: Keep-Alive
Date: Fri, 27 Apr 2001 10:12:01 GMT
Pragma: no-cache
Server: Apache/1.3.12
<HTML
<HEAD><TITLE>Welcome to Servlet Chapter</TITLE></HEAD>
<BODY>
...
</BODY>
</HTML>
```

Notice the line stating `Content-Type: text/html`. This tells the browser that the data that follows should be interpreted as HTML or "Web text."

The HTTP protocol is connectionless. After the server responds to the client's request, the connection between client and server is dropped. In addition, it is also stateless. The client makes a request, the Web server responds, and the transaction is done. The HTTP server implementation treats every request as if it was a new request, that is, without context.

Servlet Container

As already mentioned, a servlet is a Web component, managed by a container, that generates dynamic content. Based on the Java Servlet API 2.2 specification, the term *Servlet Engine* has been replaced by *Servlet Container*. Servlets interact with Web clients via a request-response model that is implemented by the Servlet Container.

The Servlet Container, in conjunction with a Web server or application server, provides the network services over which HTTP requests and responses are implemented. A Servlet Container contains and manages servlets throughout their life cycle. Figure 7.2 shows a graphic representation of a Servlet Container.

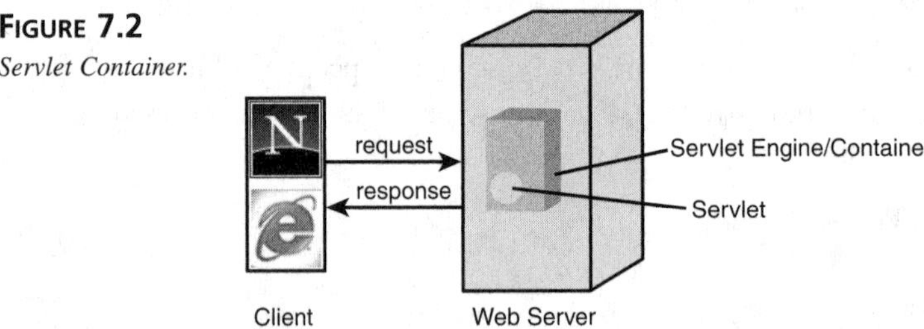

FIGURE 7.2
Servlet Container.

Servlet Containers must support HTTP protocol for requests and responses, but might also support additional request-response-based protocols such as HTTPS (HTTP over SSL).

A Servlet Container can be run as a standalone, or embedded into a full Web Server.

Servlet API

The Servlet API defines a standard interface for handling request and response between the browser and the Web server.

The Servlet API is composed of two packages:

- `javax.servlet`
- `javax.servlet.http`

All servlet classes and interfaces are defined in these two packages.

The `javax.servlet` package contains classes that support generic, protocol-independent servlets. It is the standard base class for HTTP servlets, including specific support for HTTP protocol.

This interface must be implemented by every servlet. There are two options to implement the servlet interface: either directly, or by extending a class that implements the interface.

There are two main types of classes that implement the servlet interface:

- `javax.servlet.GenericServlet`—Servlets that extend this class are protocol-independent. They do not contain any support for HTTP or other protocols.
- `javax.servlet.HttpServlet`—Servlets that extend the `HttpServlet` class have built-in support for HTTP protocol. For most purposes, you'll extend this class.

Servlet Exceptions

The `javax.servlet` package specifies two exception classes:

- `javax.servlet.ServletException`
- `javax.servlet.UnavailableException`

The `javax.servlet.ServletException` is a general exception to indicate exceptions in a servlet.

The `javax.servlet.UnavailableException` indicates that a servlet is unavailable.

Service Method Detail

The Servlet Container invokes the servlet `service()` method, passing the `HttpServletRequest` and `HttpServletResponse` objects. These are Java classes from the Java Servlet API, which developers use to interact with HTTP requests and responses.

The `service()` method gets necessary information from the request object, processes the request, and uses methods of the response object to create the client response. Depending on the HTTP transfer method, the `service()` method routes the request to another method. HTTP `GET` requests are routed to the `doGet()` method, HTTP `POST` requests are routed to the `doPost()` method, and so on. Refer to the Basic HTTP section of this chapter for other methods.

Sometimes you might want to handle a `POST` request the same way as a `GET` request. In this case, you simply call `doGet` from `doPost`:

```
protected void doPost(HttpServletRequest req,
HttpServletResponse res)
    throws ServletException, IOException {
  doGet(req, res);
}
```

Streaming Data to the Client

Within a servlet, you can generate the HTML page by writing directly to the output stream.

You might use the `ServletOutputStream` or `PrintWriter` to send data back to the client. First, you should get a reference to the stream from the Response parameter:

```
ServletOutputStream out =
response.getOutputStream();
```

After that, you get a reference to the writer from the `Response` parameter:

```
PrintWriter out = response.getWriter();
```

Using this pointer, you write the output to the stream:

```
out.println("<HTML>Inside HTML</HTML>");
```

Finally, close the writer:

```
out.close();
```

Setting MIME Type

You must always specify the output MIME type using the `setContentType()` method before any other output commences, as in this example:

```
response.setContentType("text/html");
```

For textual output, such as plain HTML, create a `PrintWriter` object and then write to it using `println`. For example:

```
PrintWriter out = response.getWriter();
out.println("This is the Servlet output!");
```

The following example demonstrates an HTTP servlet that generates an HTML page, which just displays “This is just a Servlet!” every time you access it from a browser.

```
package j2eeunleashed.chapter07;

import java.io.*;
import javax.servlet.*;
import javax.servlet.http.*;
```

```
public class srvltJust extends HttpServlet {

protected void doGet(HttpServletRequest req,
HttpServletResponse res)
              throws ServletException, IOException  {

    // Set the MIME content type:
    res.setContentType("text/html");
    // Get a print writer which used to send data back
    // to the client:
    PrintWriter out = res.getWriter();
    // Now print (display) the data to the client:
    out.println("<HTML>");
    out.println("<HEAD><TITLE>Servlet</TITLE></HEAD>");
    out.println("<BODY>");
    out.println("<H1>This is a just a Servlet!</H1>");
    out.println("</BODY></HTML>");
    // Close the PrintWriter:
    out.close();
    }

}
```


Now, let's discuss each component of this example individually.

In the first line of this example

```
package j2eeunleashed.chapter07;
```

we defined the servlet `srvltJust` to be a part of the `j2eeunleashed.chapter07` package, which will be used for all other servlets in this chapter.

The next three lines of this example

```
import java.io.*;
import javax.servlet.*;
import javax.servlet.http.*;
```

import packages that contain many classes that are used by the servlet (almost every servlet needs classes from these packages).

The `srvltJust` servlet extends `HttpServlet`, the standard base class for HTTP servlets. You extend this class for servlets that use HTTP in order to communicate with a Web browser.

In this example we override `HttpServlet`'s `doGet()` method. The `doGet()` method accepts two arguments. The first parameter is an `HttpServletRequest` object that provides an input stream enabling servlets to read client requests. The second parameter is an `HttpServletResponse` object that provides an output stream enabling servlets to write a response back to the client.

We use the `setContentType()` method to set the MIME type of the servlet's output to `text/html`.

After that, we call the `getWriter()` method, which returns a `PrintWriter` object. The `PrintWriter` object enables servlets to return text to the browser. Then, we call the `out.println()` method to specify the HTML formatting and text being sent to the browser.

Finally, you have to compile the preceding code to produce your servlet class file. Depending on which server you're using, copy the `srvltJust.class` to the appropriate directory as defined by your server. Figure 7.3 shows the servlet's output.

FIGURE 7.3
The output of the preceding servlet.

HTML Clients

This section provides you with an overview of the general HTML elements.

Forms

HTML forms are a means of collecting information by providing a way to prompt the user for information, and then carry out actions based on the input.

To create a form, you use the `<FORM>` element to enclose HTML controls and other elements.

The `<FORM>` element specifies which action to take when the user provides the information.

As is typical in HTML, a structure starts with an opening tag and ends with a closing tag. Form tags begin with `<FORM>` and end with `</FORM>`. Forms can be everywhere inside the body of an HTML document.

Commonly Used `<FORM>` Tag Attributes

Most of the interaction between the user and the server is mediated through HTML forms. All elements located between `<FORM>` and `</FORM>` tags are part of a form.

METHOD

There are two methods available to the form to send information to the server: GET and POST. This attribute specifies how the information will be sent. The difference between the two has to do with the way the information is sent to the server. The GET method is used if you want to send information via a browser URL. With POST, the information is not sent by the URL. The sending is invisible to the site visitor. In most cases you'll use GET when you're requesting a small amount of data and POST for large amounts.

ACTION

This tells the form what program the server should execute when the form's data is submitted. To execute a servlet, you specify the servlet's class name path in the action.

```
<FORM METHOD="POST" ACTION="/Servlets/myServletClass">
...
</FORM>
```

HTML Controls

Data entry elements within the form are as follows:

<INPUT>, <TEXTAREA>, and <SELECT>

New in HTML 4.0:

<OPTGROUP>, <BUTTON>, <LABEL>, <FIELDSET>, and <LEGEND>

An example of posting data (see Figure 7.4 for the output of this code):

```
<HTML>
<HEAD>
    <TITLE>Servlet Chapter</TITLE>
</HEAD>

<BODY>
<FORM ACTION="/servlet/srvltDisplayParms"  METHOD="POST">
<TABLE BGCOLOR="#fcf8ad">

<TR>
        <TD>First Name: </TD>
        <TD><INPUT TYPE="TEXT" NAME="firstname"></TD>
</TR>
<TR>
        <TD>Last Name:</TD>
        <TD><INPUT TYPE="TEXT" NAME="lastname"></TD>
</TR>
<TR>
<TD>Address:</TD>
<TD><TEXTAREA NAME="address" ROWS=4 COLS=30></TEXTAREA>
```

```
</TD></TR>
<TR>
       <TD>E-mail:</ TD>
       <TD><INPUT TYPE="TEXT" NAME="email"></TD>
</TR>
<TR>
<TD>Add to Mailing List:</ TD>
<TD><INPUT TYPE="RADIO" NAME="addtolist" VALUE="Y">Yes
<INPUT TYPE="RADIO" NAME="addtolist" VALUE="N">No</TD>
</TR>
<TR>

       <TD></TD>
       <TD><INPUT TYPE="SUBMIT" VALUE="Submit"></TD>
</TR>
</TABLE>
</FORM>
</BODY>
</HTML>
```

FIGURE 7.4
The output of this HTML file.

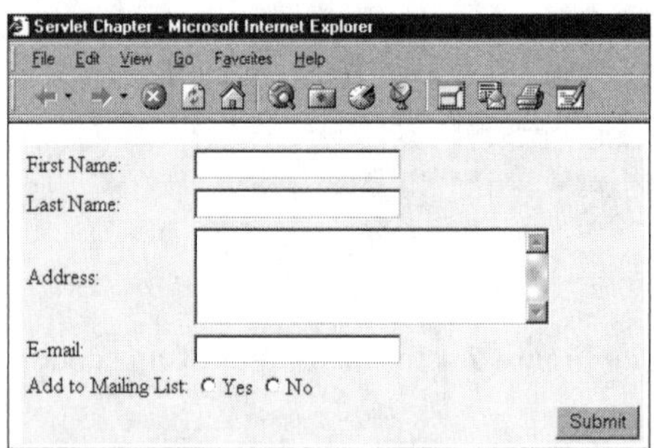

To access the form data we'll use the `HttpServletRequest` method:

```
public String getParameter(String name)
```

The preceding example has the HTML form fragment

```
<INPUT TYPE="TEXT" NAME="firstname">
```

Inside your servlet's `doPost()` method, you'll write the following code:

```
String sFirstName = request.getParameter("firstname");
```

Instead of hard-coding HTML inside your servlets using the `println()` method, it would be much better to use an object-oriented approach. This makes your servlets expandable, and makes it easier to make global changes to HTML templates. The idea is to implement HTML classes that encapsulate HTML. You may create your own classes for this purpose or use an existing one.

If you're using the WebLogic Application server, you may use the `htmlKona` package. These classes facilitate the programmatic generation of complex HTML documents. WebLogic's documentation provides more information about this package.

Another package is the Element Construction Set (ECS). ECS is a Java API for generating elements for different markup languages. It directly supports HTML 4.0 and XML and can easily be extended to create tags for any markup language. ECS is available at `http://java.apache.org/ecs/index.html`.

Servlet Life Cycle

Servlets have a well-defined life cycle. A servlet goes through a three-stage life cycle: initialization, service, and destruction. The servlet interface defines life cycle methods. The life cycle of a servlet begins when it is loaded into the server memory and ends when the servlet is terminated or reloaded.

The life cycle is shown in Figure 7.5.

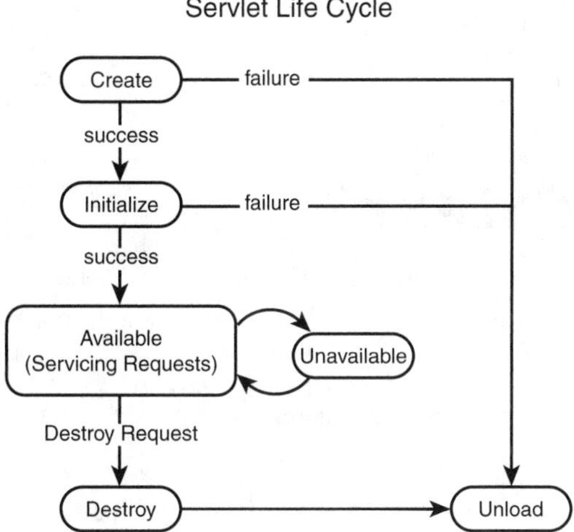

FIGURE 7.5
Servlet's life cycle.

Initialization

The Servlet Container loads servlets either at server startup (pre-loading) or when they are accessed (dynamically). Many of the application servers contain a way of specifying which servlets are loaded at startup. After a servlet class is instantiated, the container creates the servlet configuration `ServletConfig` object that can be optionally passed as a parameter to the `init()` method.

You can override the no-argument `init()` method if you need to perform startup tasks such as opening database connections, creating session objects, finding naming services, and so on.

If the initialization is successful, the servlet is available for service; otherwise, the process will throw `ServletException` or `UnavailableException`.

Service

After initialization, the container invokes the `service()` method, passing a request and response object. The main purpose of the `service()` method is to get information from the HTTP request, perform the tasks needed to answer this request, collate the needed information, and finally post the response based on that information.

Destruction

The Servlet Container stops a servlet by invoking the `destroy()` method of the servlet interface. The `destroy()` method is invoked when the container determines that the servlet should be removed from the service; for example, if the container is being shut down or more memory is required.

Typically, you override the `destroy()` method to release any resources previously allocated in the `init()`.

ServletContext

The `ServletContext` object permits multiple servlets within a Web application to have access to shared information and resources. There is one instance per Web application per Java Virtual Machine (JVM).

Using the `ServletContext` object, a servlet can log events, set and get attributes, and obtain URLs.

The `ServletContext` object is rooted at a specified path. The path can be obtained during runtime using the `getContextPath()` method of the `HttpServletRequest` object.

`ServletContext` provides methods to retrieve initialization parameters:

```
public String getInitParameter(String name)
public Enumeration getInitParameterNames()
```

Later in this chapter, we'll describe how to define initialization parameters using `<context-param>` tags.

HTTP Request Header

The `HttpServletRequest` object encapsulates all information from the client. When the Servlet Container receives a request, an object of this type is constructed and passed on to a servlet.

Parameters

The `HttpServletRequest` object provides methods to extract servlet parameter names and values. The request parameters are always of type `String`. To access request parameters, you might use one of these methods:

```
public String getParameter(String name)
public Enumeration getParameterNames()
public String[] getParameterValues(String name)
```

These methods help you access the HTTP parameters whether the servlet was requested with the `GET` or the `POST` method.

Content

```
public int getContentLength()
```

returns the length, in bytes. `-1` is returned if the length is not known. This is the same as CGI variable `CONTENT_LENGTH`.

```
getContentType():
```

returns the request's MIME type of the content (`null` if it's not known). This is the same as CGI variable `CONTENT_TYPE`.

```
getCharacterEncoding():
```

returns the name character encoding style of the request.

For example, you can execute this servlet:

```
package com.EJDean.servlets;
import javax.servlet.*;
import javax.servlet.http.*;
import java.io.*;

public class srvltContents HttpServlet {
        public void service( HttpServletRequest req,
                             HttpServletResponse res)
throws ServletException, java.io.IOException  {
     // Specify the content type of the response
     res.setContentType("text/html");
```

```
        // Create a PrintWriter
        PrintWriter out = res.getWriter();

        // Print the HTML header
        out.println("<HTML>");
        out.println("<HEAD>");
        out.println("<TITLE>Content Information</TITLE>");
        out.println("</HEAD>");
        out.println("<BODY>");
        // Display the Content:
           out.println (getContentInfo(req) );

       out.println("</BODY>");
        out.println("</HTML>");
        out.close();
       }
public String getContentInfo(HttpServletRequest
req) {
    StringBuffer sbHTML = new StringBuffer(2048);

sbHTML.append("<B>Content Info.:</B>");
    sbHTML.append("<BR>getContentLength : " +
    req.getContentLength() );
    sbHTML.append("<BR>getContentType : " +
req.getContentType() );
    sbHTML.append("<BR>getCharacterEncoding : " +
req.getCharacterEncoding() );

    return sbHTML.toString();
        }
    }
```

The result of calling this method from your servlet will be

```
Content Info.:
getContentLength : 76
getContentType : application/x-www-form-
urlencoded
getCharacterEncoding : null
```

Connection

In the next example, we'll illustrate the usage of connection methods:

```
package com.EJDean.servlets;
import javax.servlet.*;
import javax.servlet.http.*;
import java.io.*;
```

```
public class srvltConnection HttpServlet {
        public void service( HttpServletRequest req,
                             HttpServletResponse res)
throws ServletException, java.io.IOException  {
     // Specify the content type of the response
     res.setContentType("text/html");

     // Create a PrintWriter
     PrintWriter out = res.getWriter();

     // Print the HTML header
     out.println("<HTML>");
     out.println("<HEAD>");
     out.println("<TITLE>Connection Information</TITLE>");
     out.println("</HEAD>");
     out.println("<BODY>");
    // Display the Content:
        out.println (getConnectionInfo(req) );

    out.println("</BODY>");
     out.println("</HTML>");
     out.close();
    }
public String getConnectionInfo(HttpServletRequest
req) {
        StringBuffer sbHTML = new StringBuffer(2048);

    sbHTML.append("<B>Connection Info.:</B>");
sbHTML.append("<BR>Protocol  " +
"(protocol/majorVersion.minorVersion): " +
    req.getProtocol() );
    sbHTML.append("<BR>Internet Protocol (IP)"+
"address: " +
    req.getRemoteAddr() );
    sbHTML.append("<BR>Remote Host(name):" +
     req.getRemoteHost() );
    sbHTML.append("<BR>Remote User: " +
    req.getRemoteUser() );
        sbHTML.append("<BR>Name of the Scheme: " +
    req.getScheme() );
    sbHTML.append("<BR>Server Name: " +
    req.getServerName() );
        sbHTML.append("<BR>Port Number: " +
    req.getServerPort() );

    return sbHTML.toString();
        }
    }
```

Depending on the setup of your Web server, the output of calling this servlet will look similar to this:

```
Connection Info.:
Protocol (protocol/majorVersion.minorVersion): HTTP/1.1
Internet Protocol (IP) address : 122.40.18.09
Remote Host (name): 122.40.18.09
Remote User: null
Name of the Scheme: http
Server Name: localhost
Port Number: 80
```

One very important note regarding the Internet protocol (IP) address: As you know, the IP address is a unique string of numbers that identifies a computer on the Internet. These numbers are usually shown in groups that are separated by periods such as: 122.40.18.09. Frequently, the IP address of a computer is always the same. On some networks, however, the IP address is randomly assigned each time a computer connects to the network.

In addition, there are situations in which people might want to visit a site without leaving a trace of the visit. There are many different tools that help to hide your IP address. There are even cases where a dummy IP address might be used. As a result, when developing servlets, you cannot rely on IP address to identify your visitors.

Cookies

The request object provides methods for accessing cookies. A *cookie* is a piece of information generated by a Web server and stored in the user's computer, ready for future access. The following code will display all available cookies:

```
Cookie[] cookies = request.getCookies();
    int cookiesLen = cookies.length;
    if ( cookiesLen > 0 ) {
        for ( int i= 0 ; i < cookiesLen ; i++) {
            // Get cookie's name:
            String sName = cookies[i].getName();
            // Get cookie's value:
            String sValue = cookies[i].getValue();
        }
    }
```

Header

The method `getHeader()` enables you to access useful information about the client request. For instance, the next example illustrates how to get information about the client's browser:

```
String sUserAgent = request.getHeader("User-Agent");
out.println(sUserAgent);
```

The result will look like the following:

```
Mozilla/4.0 (compatible; MSIE 5.01; Windows NT 5.0)
```

The following code will list all Header information:

```
String sName = "";
String sValue = "";

Enumeration enumHdrs = request.getHeaderNames();
while (enumHdrs.hasMoreElements()) {
    sName = (String) enumHdrs.nextElement();
    sValue = request.getHeader(sName);
    out.println( sName+ ": "  + sValue + "<BR>");
}
```

Depending on the request, simple output will look like this:

```
connection: Keep-Alive
cookie: JSESSIONID=@3e1bc8:e673982542
accept: */*
accept-encoding: gzip, deflate
accept-language: en-us
host: localhost
user-agent: Mozilla/4.0 (compatible; MSIE 5.01; Windows NT 5.0)
```

For detailed descriptions of these methods, please see the Java Servlet API Reference, v2.2.

In the following example, we'll build a utility servlet that provides methods to list information about a user's request. We'll use most of the methods in `HttpServletRequest` that provide information about the request.

```
package j2eeunleashed.chapter07;
import javax.servlet.http.HttpServletRequest ;
import java.util.Enumeration;

public class utilServlet
{

  public String getRequestInfo(HttpServletRequest req)
  {
    StringBuffer sbHTML = new StringBuffer(2048);

    sbHTML.append("<B>Request Information:</B>");
    sbHTML.append("<BR>Authentication Scheme: " +
req.getAuthType() );
    sbHTML.append("<BR>HTTP Method: " +
    req.getMethod());
    sbHTML.append("<BR>Path information: " +
```

```
    req.getPathInfo() );
    sbHTML.append("<BR>Real Path(translated): " +
    req.getPathTranslated() );
    sbHTML.append("<BR>Request Query String: " +
    req.getQueryString() );
    sbHTML.append("<BR>User's making this request: " +
    req.getRemoteUser() );
    sbHTML.append("<BR>Request URI: " +
    req.getRequestURI() );
    sbHTML.append("<BR>Servlet Path: " +
    req.getServletPath() );
    sbHTML.append("<BR>Content Length (in bytes): " +
    req.getContentLength() );
    sbHTML.append("<BR>Content MIME Type: " +
    req.getContentType() );
    sbHTML.append("<BR>Protocol: " +
req.getProtocol() );
    sbHTML.append("<BR>IP Address: " +
    req.getRemoteAddr() );
    sbHTML.append("<BR>Remote Host(qualified name): " +
    req.getRemoteHost() );
    sbHTML.append("<BR>Remote User: " +
    req.getRemoteUser() );
    sbHTML.append("<BR>Name of the Scheme: " +
    req.getScheme() );
    sbHTML.append("<BR>Server Name: " +
    req.getServerName() );
    sbHTML.append("<BR>Port Number: " +
req.getServerPort() );

    sbHTML.append("<HR>");
    return sbHTML.toString();
}


public String getRequestHeader(HttpServletRequest req)
{
    StringBuffer     sbHTML = new StringBuffer(2048);
    String         sName  = "";
    String         sValue = "";

    sbHTML.append("<B>Request Header information:</B>" );

    Enumeration enNames = req.getHeaderNames();
    for (     boolean bMoreElements =
enNames.hasMoreElements() ;
            bMoreElements;
            bMoreElements = enNames.hasMoreElements() )
    {
        sName = (String) enNames.nextElement();
        sValue = req.getHeader(sName);
```

```
        sbHTML.append("<BR>" + sName +": " + sValue);
    }
    sbHTML.append("<HR>");
    return sbHTML.toString();

}

public String getRequestAttributes(HttpServletRequest req)
{
    StringBuffer sbHTML = new StringBuffer(2048);
    String    sName     = "";
    String    sValue    = "";

    sbHTML.append("<B>Request Attributes:</B>" );

    Enumeration enNames = req.getAttributeNames();
    for (boolean bMoreElements =
        enNames.hasMoreElements() ;
            bMoreElements;
            bMoreElements = enNames.hasMoreElements() )
    {
        sName     =    (String) enNames.nextElement();
        sValue    =    (String) req.getAttribute(sName);
        sbHTML.append("<BR>" + sName +": " + sValue);
    }
    sbHTML.append("<HR>");
    return sbHTML.toString();
}

}
```

In this example, `utilServlet` defines three methods:

- `String getRequestInfo(HttpServletRequest req)`—This method accepts a request and returns an HTML string that lists most commonly used request methods.
- `String getRequestHeader(HttpServletRequest req)`—This method processes request header names.
- `String getRequestAttributes(HttpServletRequest req)`—This method processes request attribute information.

HTTP Response Header

The `HttpServletResponse` object encapsulates all communications to the client and provides a variety of methods for accessing and manipulating HTTP headers, attributes, and so on.

The most general way to define any header you specify is to use the `setHeader()` method of `HttpServletResponse`:

```
public void setHeader(String name, String value)
```

The `HttpServletResponse` also supports different specialized methods to set headers, including

- `setDateHeader()`
- `setIntHeader()`
- `setContentType()`
- `setContentLength()`
- `addCookie()`
- `sendError()`

Setting Response Status

As mentioned earlier, the status line, also referred to as the response line, consists of the server protocol and a status code. The status code indicates the success or failure of the client request.

When processing the `doXXX()` methods discussed in previous sections, the server will specify the status code. By default the status code is 200. However, the `HttpServletResponse` interface provides the method `setStatus()` that enables you to explicitly specify the status code. The argument of this method is an integer:

```
public void setStatus(int sc)
```

The `HttpServletResponse` interface defines constants to be used as arguments to this method. Table 7.3 lists the most common status constants.

TABLE 7.3 Common Status Constants

Name	*Status code*	*Description*
`SC_OK`	200	Request succeeded normally
`SC_ACCEPTED`	202	Request was accepted for processing, but it was not completed
`SC_BAD_REQUEST`	400	Request sent by the client was incorrect syntax
`SC_UNAUTHORIZED`	401	The request requires HTTP authentication
`SC_FORBIDDEN`	403	The server understood the request but will not fulfill it
`SC_NOT_FOUND`	404	The requested resource is not available

For complete details about the status code in HTTP response, please see the Java documentation.

Session Management

Because HTTP is a stateless protocol, there is no way for a server to recognize that sequences of requests are all from the same client. There needs to be a way to identify a user across more than one page request or visit to a Web site.

A session is a series of requests that originate from the same user at the same browser. There are different ways to remember state information.

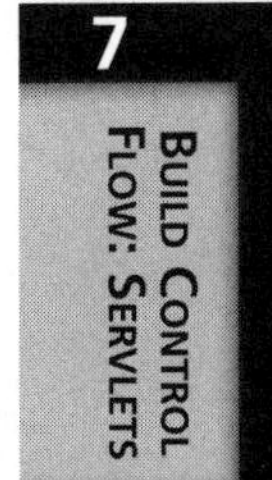

In the following section, we'll discuss these techniques:

- Hidden form fields
- URL rewriting
- Persistent cookies
- Session tracking API

Hidden Form Fields

If you want to pass information to your servlet that you don't want users to see, the HTML form can contain fields that are declared to be *type hidden*:

```
<input name="pageid" type="hidden" value="5">
```

The servlet can access these fields like regular fields. There is no difference between hidden fields and other fields in a submitted form.

One of the disadvantages of using hidden fields is that the user might view the page's source and see the data assigned to the hidden fields.

URL Rewriting

A common technique for sending additional information to the servlet is by using an URL-encoded query string. This is implemented by appending information to the URL.

The additional information begins with a `?`, followed by the name of a parameter and the value you want to assign to that parameter. The pairs are separated by an ampersand (`&`). For example, to pass the employee ID "1009" and department ID "200", you would specify

```
http://myServer/servlets/srvltEmp?EMPID=1009&DEPID=200
```

These attributes can also be posted as form data. The `ServletRequest` interface provides methods such as the following to access these parameters:

```
public String getParameter(String name)
public Enumeration getParameterNames()
public String[] getParameterValues(String name)
```

For instance, to get the Employee ID from the preceding URL, you use the following:

```
String sEmplID = req.getParameter("EMPID");
```

The URL rewriting technique has some limitations. For instance, the URL must be in strings, some browsers limit the length of the URL, and the user can see the URL.

Persistent Cookies

One of the most common ways to implement session tracking is by using persistent cookies. A persistent cookie is a cookie that is intended to maintain information over more than one browser session.

For example, many Web sites will store a user's login ID or password as a cookie, so that the user won't need to retype these every time she visits the site.

The `HttpServletRequest` interface provides a method `getCookies()` that returns an array of cookies included in the current request.

The next example demonstrates the usage of the `getCookies()` method:

```
package com.EJDean.servlets;
import javax.servlet.*;
import javax.servlet.http.*;
import java.io.*;

public class srvltCookies extends HttpServlet
{

    public void service(HttpServletRequest req,
                     HttpServletResponse res)
throws ServletException, java.io.IOException
    {
     // Specify the content type of the response
     res.setContentType("text/html");

     // Create a PrintWriter
     PrintWriter out = res.getWriter();

     // Print the HTML header
     out.println("<HTML>");
```

```
        out.println("<HEAD>");
        out.println("<TITLE>Cookie Information</TITLE>");
        out.println("</HEAD>");
        out.println("<BODY>");
        // Display the Request Cookie:
        out.println ( getRequestCookies(req) );

           out.println("</BODY>");
        out.println("</HTML>");
        out.close();
       }

public String getRequestCookies(HttpServletRequest req){
    StringBuffer sbHTML = new StringBuffer(2048);
    String    sName     = "";
    String    sValue    = "";

    sbHTML.append("<B>Request Cookies:</B>" );

    Cookie[] reqCookies = req.getCookies();
    if ( reqCookies != null ) {
        for ( int i=0; i < reqCookies.length; i++) {
            sName     = reqCookies[i].getName();
            sValue    = reqCookies[i].getValue();
            sbHTML.append("<BR>" + sName +": " +
sValue);
        }
    }

    sbHTML.append("<HR>");
    return sbHTML.toString();
}
}
```

After executing this servlet, the result will be an HTML page listing all the requests' cookies.

As an example, let's describe how to establish a cookie. Suppose that when a user logs into the system we want to create a cookie that holds the login time. The servlet will have code that looks like this:

```
Date dtLogin = new Date();
Cookie cooLoginTime = new Cookie("loginTime",
dtLogin.toString());
```

We have to include this cookie in the response that will be sent to the client using the `HttpServletResponse` object's method `addCookie()`:

```
response.addCookie(cooLoginTime);
```

If the user then returns to the servlet another time, your servlet can access the cookie through the `HttpServletRequest` object's `getCookies()` method and will know the last time the user has logged in:

```
Cookie[] allCookies = request.getCookies();
String sCookieName="";
String sCookieValue="";

for(int i=0; i<allCookies.length; i++) {
sCookieName = allCookies[i].getName());
        if (sCookieName != null &&
            sCookieName.equalsIgnoreCase("loginTime"))
        sCookieName= allCookies[i].getValue();
        break;
    }
}
```

The Session Tracking API

In the Java Servlet 2.2 API, the `HttpSession` interface provides session management functionality. Each client browser that accesses a Web server results in the generation of a session object. Sessions are useful if you want to share a user's information between various servlets.

In order to create a new session, you use the `HttpServletRequest` object's `getSession()` method:

```
// Create a new session:
HttpSession session = request.getSession();
```

To associate an attribute with a session and access it later you'll use `HttpSession` methods `setAttribute()` and `getAttribute()`.

In the following example, we'll define two servlets. The first servlet will be called by a user when he logs into a system. This servlet will keep an application identification code (`APPID`) to be used later:

```
import java.io.*;
import java.net.*;
import java.util.*;
import javax.servlet.*;
import javax.servlet.http.*;

public class srvltHoldAppID extends HttpServlet
{
   public void service(HttpServletRequest req,
        HttpServletResponse res)
                throws IOException, ServletException {
        resp.setContentType("text/html");
```

```
        PrintWriter out = res.getWriter();
        String sAPPID = "undefined";
        String[] sAPPID = req.getParameter("APPID");
        if(sAPPID != null && sAPPID.length > 0) {
        // Create session:
        HttpSession session = req.getSession();
        session.setAttribute("APPID", sAPPID);
      }
    }
}
```

Later, when you need to access the APPID in your application, you'll obtain a reference to the session object and use the getAttribute() method. Here is an example:

```
import java.io.*;
import java.net.*;
import java.util.*;
import javax.servlet.*;
import javax.servlet.http.*;

    public class srvltGeneral extends HttpServlet {

public void service(HttpServletRequest req,
HttpServletResponse res)
  throws IOException, ServletException {

res.setContentType("text/html");
PrintWriter out = resp.getWriter();
// Get the Application ID user from session
// object:
HttpSession session = req.getSession();
String sAppID = (String)
session.getAttribute("APPID");
if(sAPPID != null) {
           // Process...
}
}
    }
```

Dispatching Requests

The RequestDispatcher interface provides methods that enable you to forward a request to another servlet to fill out the whole response or include some output from another servlet.

You obtain a reference to the RequestDispatcher object through the getRequestDispatcher() method.

The getRequestDispatcher() method is available in both the ServletContext object and the ServletRequest object. The difference between the ServletRequest.getRequestDispatcher() and ServletContext.getRequestDispatcher() methods is that the first can take a relative path.

Let's say we are writing a srvltTest servlet:

```
public class srvltTest extends HttpServlet {
    public void doGet(HttpServletRequest req,
                        HttpServletResponse res)
            throws ServletException, IOException {
```

And later, after some processing is done, we'll forward the request to another servlet:

```
ServletContext sc = this.getServletContext();
RequestDispatcher rd =
sc.getRequestDispatcher("/srvltComplete");
    if (rd !=null) {
try {
rd.forward(req, res);
}
catch (Exception e) {
// Handle Exception
}
}
```

You can also use the RequestDispatcher object to pass control to a JSP page.

```
ServletContext sc = this.getServletContext();
RequestDispatcher rd =
sc.getRequestDispatcher("/jspFile.jsp");
    if (rd != null) {
try {
rd.forward(req, res);
}
catch (Exception e) {
// Handle Exception
}
}
```

RequestDispatcher defines another very useful method: include(). This method enables you to include the content of a resource (servlet, JSP page, HTML file) in the response.

The following example demonstrates how to include JavaScript from external files in servlets:

```
ServletContext sc = this.getServletContext(); RequestDispatcher rd =
sc.getRequestDispatcher("/javascriptFile.js");
```

```
if (rd != null) {
try {
rd.include(req, res); }
catch (Exception e) {
System.out.println("Exception: " +
e.getMessage());
}
}
```

Servlets with JDBC

Using JDBC in servlets is quite straightforward. In the next example, we'll demonstrate a servlet that connects to a database, queries the table "EMPLOYEE", and generates an HTML page that displays last names, first names, phone numbers, and extensions. In our example we'll illustrate how to use the JNDI to obtain a handle to a JDBC `DataSource` object and subsequently obtain a JDBC Connection handle. Here is an example:

```
package com.EJDean.servlets;
import java.io.*;
import javax.servlet.*;
import javax.servlet.http.*;
import java.sql.*;
import javax.naming.*;

/**
 * srvltEmplPhoneList Servlet
 *
 * The srvltEmplPhoneList Servlet demonstrates how to
 * access employee table and generate HTML that will
 * be display names and phones.
*/
public class srvltEmplPhoneList extends HttpServlet {

public void doGet(HttpServletRequest req,
HttpServletResponse res)
throws ServletException, IOException {
    res.setContentType("text/html");
    PrintWriter out = res.getWriter();

    Connection conn = null;
    Statement stmt = null;
    ResultSet rs = null;
    String sSQL =      " SELECT EMP_LNM, EMP_FNM, "      +
                   " EMP_PHONE, EMP_PHONE_EXT "      +
                   " FROM EMPLOYEE " +
                   " ORDER BY EMP_LNM ";

    out.println("<HTML><HEAD>");
    out.println("<TITLE>Employee List</TITLE>");
```

```
    out.println("</HEAD>");
    out.println("<BODY>");
    out.println("<H1 ALIGN=\"CENTER\">");
    out.println("Employee Listing</H1>");
    out.println("<TABLE WIDTH=\"100%\" ");
    out.println("BORDER=\"1\" ALIGN=\"CENTER\">");
    out.println("<TR>");
        out.println("    <TD ALIGN=\"CENTER\">");
out.println("Last Name</TD>");
    out.println("    <TD ALIGN=\"CENTER\">");
out.println("First Name</TD>");
    out.println("    <TD ALIGN=\"CENTER\">");
out.println("Phone No</TD>");
    out.println("    <TD ALIGN=\"CENTER\">");
out.println("Ext.</TD>");
    out.println("</TR>");
        try {
        //Get handle to the JNDI context:
    InitialContext ic = new InitialContext();

        //Get a reference to the datasource:
        String dsName = "java:comp/env/jdbc/emplphone";
        DataSource ds = (DataSource) ic.lookup(dsName);

        // Get a Connection:
        conn = ds.getConnection();

        // Create the Statement:
        stmt = conn.createStatement();

        // Execute the SQL Statement:
        rs = stmt.executeQuery(sSQL);

        // Display the Result Set inside the HTML table:
        while( rs.next() )    {
            out.println("<TR>");
            out.println("<TD>" + rs.getString(1) +
"</TD>");
            out.println("    <TD>" + rs.getString(2) +
"</TD>");
            out.println("    <TD>" + rs.getString(3) +
"</TD>");
            out.println("    <TD>" + rs.getString(4) +
"</TD>");
            out.println("</TR>");
        }
    }
    catch(Exception e) {
        out.println("<FONT COLOR=\"#ff0066\">");
        out.println("<B>Servlet Exception:" +
e.toString() );
```

```
        out.println("</B></FONT>");
        e.printStackTrace();
    }

    finally {
        // Close the Database Connection:
        try {
            stmt.close();
            conn.close();
        catch( Exception e1) {
            out.println("<FONT COLOR=\"#ff0066\">");
            out.println("<B>Servlet Close Exception:" +
e1.toString() );
            out.println("</B></FONT>");
        }
    }

    out.println("</TABLE></BODY></HTML>");
    out.close();
    }
}
```

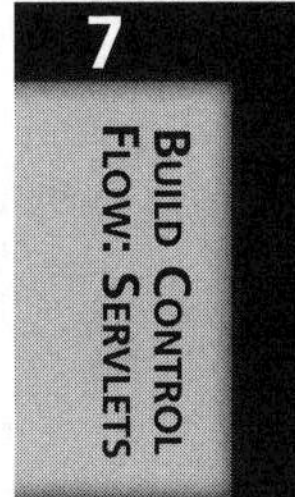

Web Applications

As defined by the Java Servlet API 2.2 specification, a Web application is a collection of servlets, JSP pages, static content such as HTML pages, and any additional resources required by the Web application.

Web Archive (WAR)

Web Archive files have the extension .WAR. A WAR file defines and represents a single Web application. A WAR file contains all the elements that make up the Web application, such as images, HTML pages, JSP pages, servlets, and any other relevant documents. WAR files are actually Java Archive (JAR) files created using the JAR utility and saved with an alternative extension.

The different extensions of these two files are chosen to let people treat them differently.

Directory Structure

As we stated before, the WAR file packages all the Web application elements: JSPs, servlets, HTML pages, images, audio files, and so on into a single JAR file for deployment to a server's JSP container. The application server will unbundle the WAR into a specific directory hierarchy. The root of this directory hierarchy serves as a document root of the application for serving files that are part of this context. Figure 7.6 illustrates the structure of the directory.

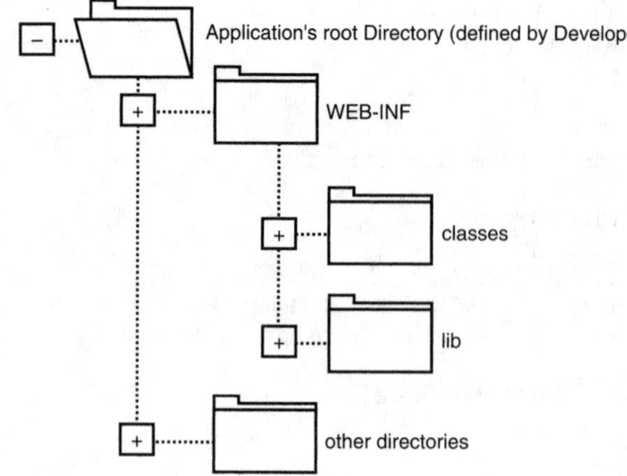

FIGURE 7.6
Web application directory structure.

The document root contains a subdirectory called WEB-INF. The WEB-INF subdirectory contains the following files and directories:

- WEB-INF/classes—contains the application's Java Servlets' .class files, utility classes, and JavaBeans components
- WEB-INF/lib—contains .JAR and/or .ZIP library files (tag libraries and any utility libraries called by server-side classes)
- web.xml file—the Web application deployment descriptor
- Tag Library Descriptor files (.tld)—used by a Web container to validate the tags and also by JSP page development tools

Today, most Web application servers provide visual tools to create WAR files; however, you may switch to a root directory containing your Web service objects and use a Java command as in the following:

```
jar -cf EJDeanApp.war *
```

This command will create an archive file named EJDeanApp.war and will archive all contents under the directory EJDeanApp including subdirectories.

To list the table of contents for this archive you can use this command:

```
jar -tvf EJDeanApp.war
```

Deployment Descriptor/Mapping Requests to Servlets

A deployment descriptor is an XML text-based file with an .XML extension. As mentioned previously, for Web containers, the WEB-INF/web.xml file must be included in the Web application to describe the component's deployment settings.

Some of the purposes for the deployment descriptor are to define the following properties:

- Servlets/JSP definitions
- Mapping requests to servlets/JSP
- Initialization parameters
- MIME types
- Welcome and error pages
- Security authorization and authentication

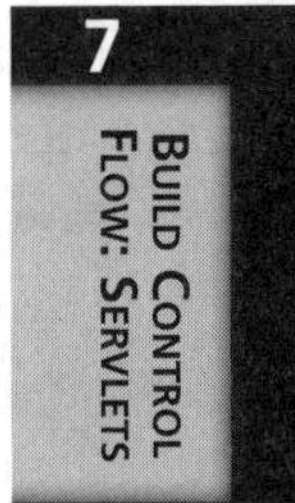

The header of the deployment descriptor web.xml file must be as follows:

```
<!DOCTYPE web-app PUBLIC
"-//Sun Microsystems, Inc.//DTD Web Application 2.2//EN"
"http://java.sun.com/j2ee/dtds/web-app_2_2.dtd">
```

This header specifies the version/location of the document type definition (DTD) for the deployment descriptor.

After the header, the main body starts with `<web-app>` and ends with `</web-app>`:

```
<web-app>
...
</web-app>
```

Inside the body you'll declare servlets and map them to a URL pattern. When you declare the servlet, you give it a name and specify the class file used to implement the servlet's behavior. After the declaration, you map the servlet's name to one or more URL-patterns.

Additional information such as initialization parameters might be included.

To declare each servlet in your Web application, you use the opening and closing tags:

```
<servlet>...</servlet>
```

The body of the `<servlet>` tag consists of the following:

```
<servlet-name>ServletName</servlet-name>
<servlet-class>srvltServletClass</servlet-class>
```

Optionally, you might declare the initialization parameters:

```
<init-param>
     <param-name>servletParamName</param-name>
     <param-value>servletParamValue</param-value>
     <description>servletParamDescription</description>
</init-param>
```

Here is an example using these tags:

```
<servlet>
<servlet-name>ShoppingCart</servlet-name>
<description>
This servlet lists the items currently in the Shopping Cart.
</description>
<servlet-class>com.EJDean.Servlets.srvltShoppingCart</servlet-class>
<init-param>
<param-name>listOrders</paramName>
<param-value>com.EJDean.Act.ItemsAction
</param-value>
</init-param>
</servlet>
```

After you define the name and class of the servlet, you'll define mappings that are used by the Servlet Container to translate a particular request URL to a particular servlet.

```
<servlet-mapping>
<servlet-name>ShoppingCart</servlet-name>
<url-pattern>ShoppingCart</url-pattern>
</servlet-mapping>
```

The `ServletContext` provides methods to retrieve initialization parameters:

```
public String getInitParameter(String name)
public Enumeration getInitParameterNames()
```

If you use the `getInitParameter(String name)` method, the argument "name" matches the `<param-name>` element of one of these initialization parameters.

In order to define parameters that will be shared constants (`Strings`) used within your application, you use the `<context-param>` tag. Here is an example:

```
<context-param>
<param-name>contactus</param-name>
<param-value>mail@EJDean.com</param-value>
<description>
The main E-mail address of the company.</description>
</context-param>
```

Multi-MIME Types

Multipurpose Internet Mail Extension (MIME) protocol is used by the Internet community to send multipart, multimedia, and binary data over the Internet. Web browsers use MIME types to identify non-HTML files such as Microsoft Word, Excel, and Adobe PDF, as well as to determine how to present the data contained in them.

A MIME type is often written as two strings with a slash between them. For instance, "text/plain" is the MIME type for generic text and "text/html" is the type for an HTML Web document.

The MIME type for a Microsoft Word document is "application/msword". So, to open a Microsoft Word document in a servlet, you set the content type in the response header to "application/msword":

```
res.setContentType( "application/msword" );
```

To open a PDF file, you set the response object's content type to "application/pdf" instead of "application/msword":

```
res.setContentType( "application/pdf" );
```

A few of these MIME types are listed in Table 7.4.

Table 7.4 MIME Types

Description	*Type*
HTML text	text/html
Usual mail or news message	text/plain
Common image format	text/gif
Adobe PDF	Application/pdf
Microsoft Word	Application/msword
Excel document	Application/vnd.ms-excel
	(vnd: application vendor)
General MIDI music files	audio/midi
RealAudio files	audio/x-pn-realaudio
	(for files with extension .ra, .ram)
	audio/x-pn-realaudio-plugin
	(for files with extension .rpm)
Unknown type, any kind of data as bytes	Application/octet-stream

Using Servlets in the SilverStream Application Server

The SilverStream Application Server is an industry leading, J2EE certified application server that permits corporations to easily build and deploy complex J2EE-compliant applications with rich HTML and Java interfaces and broad access to enterprise data sources.

The current version 3.7 of SilverStream Application Server is compatible with Java 2 platform, Enterprise Edition 1.2 (J2EE 1.2). It includes support for Enterprise JavaBeans (EJB 1.1), JSP 1.1, servlets that conform to the Java Servlet 2.2, JDBC 2.0, XML, Java Transaction API(JTA 1.0), JNDI 1.0, and the standard J2EE mail API (JavaMail 1.1). Additionally, the SilverStream Application Server provides an integrated architecture for building real-world J2EE products.

For more information about the SilverStream Application Server, please visit `www.silverstream.com`.

There are different ways to build servlets and deploy them on a SilverStream server:

- Using the SilverStream Business Object Designer to create a non-triggered business object
- Using an external IDE to write the servlet classes
- Using the SilverStream servlet-triggered business object

In the following section, we'll describe in detail how to develop servlets and deploy them on a SilverStream server.

Developing Standard Servlets

You can develop standard servlets using the SilverStream Object Designer by creating a non-triggered business object. The SilverStream Business Object Designer gives you an object-oriented, visual environment for creating SilverStream business objects. You can create packages to contain your business objects, Java interfaces, Common Object Request Broker Architecture (CORBA), Interface Definition Language (IDL), and Enterprise JavaBeans.

By creating non-triggered business objects, you'll get the full support of the Servlet and JSP specifications. Later in this chapter we'll explain what servlet-triggered business objects are.

SilverStream recommends that you use WARs to deploy servlets and JSP pages.

To create a non-triggered business object in the Main Designer, choose the Business Object Designer icon. Click the New button at the bottom of the right pane, then choose New Object from the menu.

The Business Object Designer starts the Business Object Wizard, which is shown in Figure 7.7.

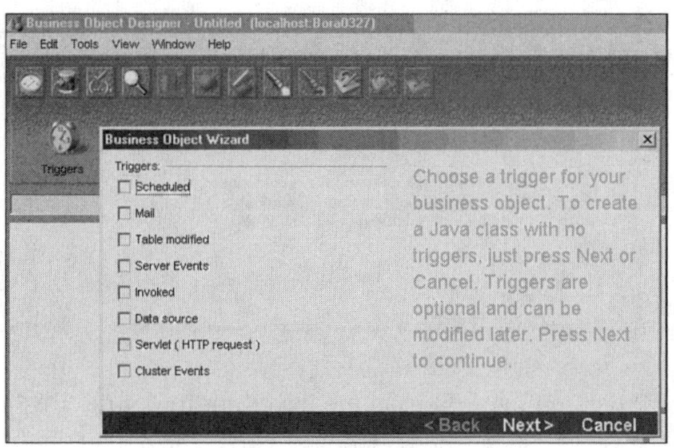

FIGURE 7.7
Business Object Wizard.

To create a non-triggered business object, just press Next.

The next wizard form will prompt you to enter the Object Name. In our case the Object Name will be `srvltShoppingCart`, and it will extend `javax.servlet.http.HttpServlet` (see Figure 7.8).

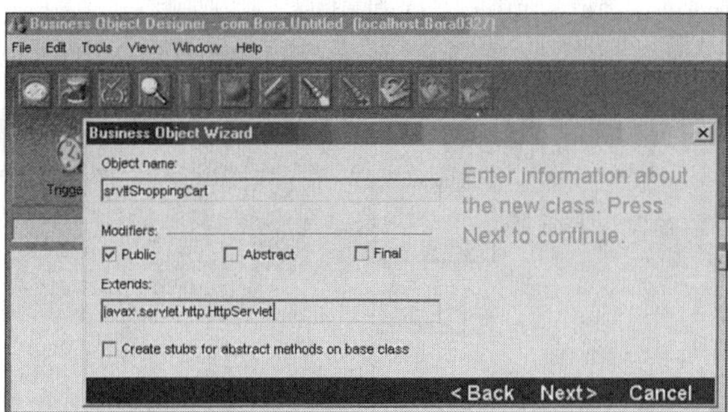

FIGURE 7.8
Business Object Wizard—defining the servlet.

After you press next, the Business Object Designer appears (see Figure 7.9).

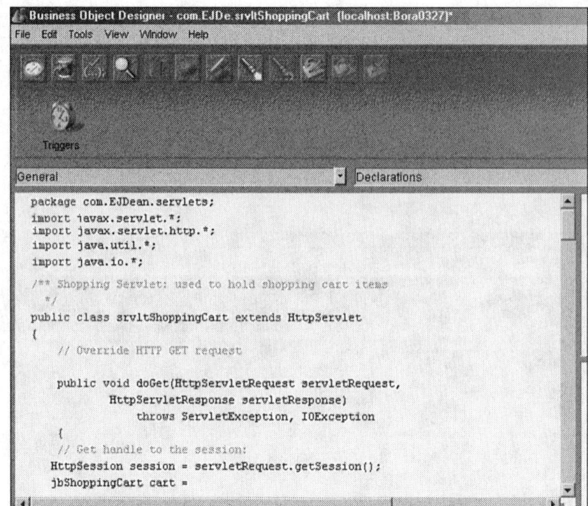

FIGURE 7.9
Business Object Designer.

Now you use the Programming Editor, in the lower portion of the Designer, to write the servlet code for the `servltShoppingCart` object you created. Note here that you can specify an external code editor.

Select File|Save Object or click the Save icon. If the object does not compile cleanly, SilverStream saves the source code only and displays the compilation errors. Before you can run the object, you must fix the compilation errors.

If the object compiles without error, the source code and compiled code are saved. Figure 7.10 shows the location of our sample servlet class.

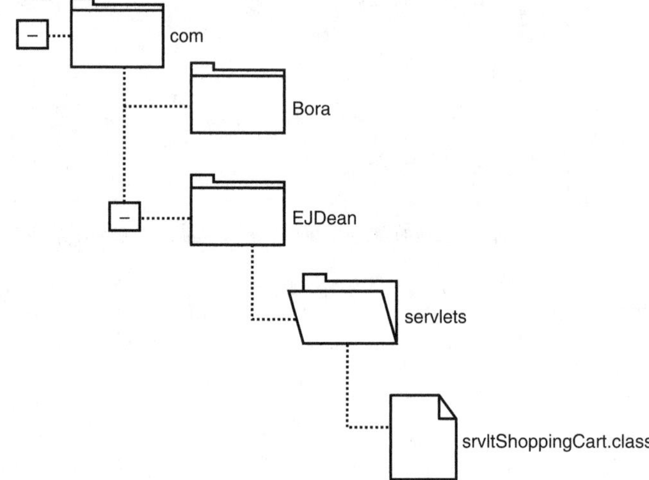

FIGURE 7.10
Servlet class.

Please note that you may also use any external IDE to write the servlet classes.

Now, your servlet class is ready to be packaged in a J2EE-compatible WAR file and deployed on the SilverStream server.

SilverStream provides the `SilverCmd BuildWAR` command for packaging the servlet, or you can use any other appropriate tool. For deploying the WAR file to a SilverStream server, you will use the `SilverCmd DeployWAR` command.

The syntax of `SilverCmd BuildWAR` is

```
SilverCmd BuildWar server[:port] database rootDir [options]
```

The valid arguments are shown in Table 7.5.

TABLE 7.5 `SilverCmd BuildWar` Arguments

Argument	*Description*
`Server[:port]`	Specifies the name of the target SilverStream server and the design-time port
	This value is optional unless `-d` is specified
`Database`	Specifies the name of the targeted database
`RootDir`	Specifies the directory of files to be placed in the JAR

To deploy a J2EE-compatible Web archive (WAR) to a SilverStream server, you'll use the next command:

```
SilverCmd DeployWAR server[:port] database [WARFile]
      -f deploymentPlan [options]
```

The valid arguments are listed and described in Table 7.6.

TABLE 7.6 `SilverCmd DeployWAR` Arguments

Argument	*Description*
`Server[:port]`	Specifies the name of the target SilverStream server and the design-time port.
`Database`	Specifies the name of the targeted database.
`WARFile`	Specifies the name of the WAR file to deploy.
	This value can be specified either at the command line or in the deployment plan. Values specified at the command line override input file settings.
`-f deploymentPlan`	An XML-based file that specifies the SilverStream-specific deployment information.

Please review SilverStream Help for more details about using `SilverCmd`. SilverStream Help is available online at `http://devcenter.silverstream.com`.

Servlet-Triggered Business Objects

A triggered business object is a specific type of Java class that resides on the SilverStream server. It has a set of properties that the server stores as metadata, and it implements one or more predefined SilverStream event listener interfaces.

SilverStream provides a servlet-triggered business object. Although these servlets are not pure J2EE and are not portable to non-SilverStream J2EE servers, they do support much of the Java Servlet Specification, v2.2.

In the SilverStream server, servlets are associated with a URL or multiple URLs. When a SilverStream application performs an operation on that URL, (like HTTP `GET` and `POST`), the SilverStream server finds the associated servlet (HTTP listener), instantiates it (if it is an event-lifetime object), and fires the service event. The service event is passed two parameters, one representing the request (and providing access to the server environment) and another representing the response.

To create a servlet-triggered business object, in the Main Designer, choose the Business Object Designer icon. Click the New button at the bottom of the right pane, then choose New Object from the menu.

The Business Object Designer starts the Business Object Wizard as illustrated in Figure 7.11.

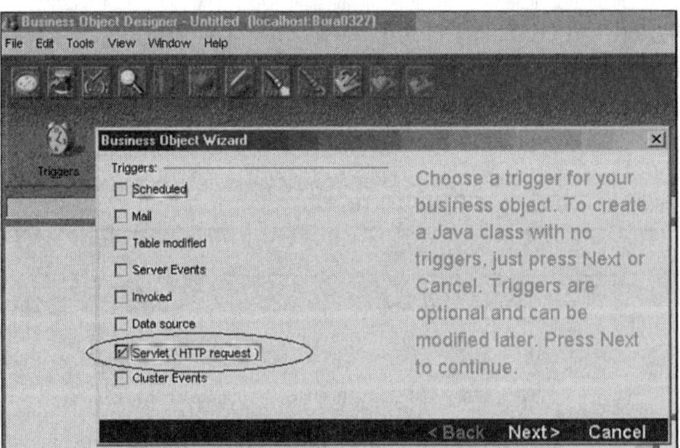

FIGURE 7.11
Choose the servlet trigger in the Business Object Wizard.

Select Servlet (HTTP request) and press Next. The wizard provides the panel seen in Figure 7.12 to supply the URLs.

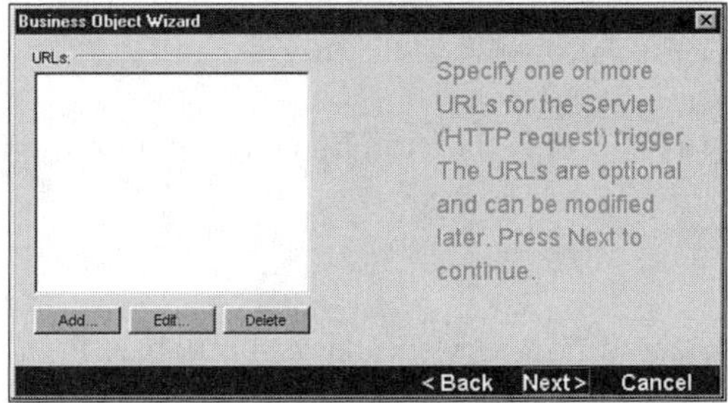

FIGURE 7.12
Specifying the URL for the Business Object.

You can specify the URLs at design time, or programmatically using the `createServletResource()` method.

SilverStream provides some interfaces that extend the standard `javax.servlet.http.HttpServletRequest` interface with additional functionality.

The SilverStream `com.sssw.shr.http` package defines classes and interfaces that help provide support for the HTTP protocol. It specifies two main interfaces:

- `AgiHttpServletRequest`—This interface extends the standard `javax.servlet.http.HttpServletRequest` interface with additional SilverStream functionality.
- `AgiHttpServletResponse`—This interface extends the standard `javax.servlet.http.HttpServletResponse` interface with additional SilverStream functionality.

These objects provide access to SilverStream standard business object methods such as `getAgaData()`, `getDatabase()`, `getUser()`, and others through `AgoBusinessObjectEvent`.

For more information about these interfaces, please see the SilverStream help system.

Servlet 2.3 API

At the time of this book's writing, the Servlet API 2.3 is under development. Several new classes, interfaces, and API methods have been added into the Servlet 2.3 specification.

One of the changes made in the Servlet 2.3 proposed final draft specification is the addition of application life cycle events and filtering.

Application life cycle events give you greater interaction with the `ServletContext` object and the `HttpSession` objects. A *filter* is defined as a reusable piece of code that can inspect or transform the content of an HTTP request or response. You may write the filters by implementing the `javax.servlet.Filter` interface and packaging it within the WAR file for the application.

The Servlet API 2.3 is a part of Java 2 Platform, Enterprise Edition 1.3 (J2EE 1.3).

Summary

In this chapter, we've introduced Java Servlets and seen how they fit in the J2EE framework for enterprise Web application development and deployment.

We've looked at servlet life cycles, major Servlet API 2.2 specifications, development, and deployment.

CHAPTER 8

JavaServer Pages: Introduction

In This Chapter

- Features of JSP Pages *229*
- The Components of a JSP Page *231*
- Developing and Deploying JSP Pages *233*
- JSP Architectures *240*
- Conclusion: JSP Pages Are a Big Part of the Enterprise Java Solution *254*

The ability to deliver dynamic content on the Web has been a primary factor in its astronomical growth. The static Web page now connotes an unsophisticated organization. Tools and proprietary components that facilitate dynamic content, generating different HTML for different occasions, were the featured parts of tools such as SilverStream and Cold Fusion. Unfortunately, the word "proprietary" has become undesirable and we are now in a time when "standards" are considered better.

One of the most popular standards for viewing dynamic content is JavaServer Pages (JSP) technology. This technology allows Web developers and designers to develop and maintain platform-independent, information-rich, dynamic Web pages that leverage existing business systems. JSP pages help to achieve the design objective of separating view and content. JavaServer Pages technology separates the user interface from content generation, enabling designers to change the overall page layout without altering the underlying dynamic content.

In a simple implementation, the browser directly invokes a JSP page, which then generates the requested content (perhaps invoking JDBC to get information directly from a database). The JSP page can call JDBC components to generate results, and creates standard HTML that it sends back to the browser as a result.

This model basically replaced the proprietary servlet designers like Cold Fusion and SilverStream with a JSP page. The advantage of this method is that it is simple to program and the page author can easily generate dynamic content based on the request and state of the resources.

JavaServer Pages technology makes use of XML-like tags and scriptlets written in the Java programming language to encapsulate the logic that generates the content for the page. This small footprint, which can include common logic, promotes ease of maintenance and portability. This is achievable because the application logic resides on server-based resources that the page accesses with these tags and scriptlets. Any and all formatting (HTML or XML) is passed directly back to the response page. By separating the page logic from its design and display while supporting a reusable component-based design, JSP technology facilitates the construction of Web-based applications.

JavaServer Pages technology is an evolutionary and natural extension of the Java Servlet technology. Servlets are platform-independent server-side modules that fit into a Web server framework, extending the capabilities of a Web server with minimal overhead, maintenance, and support. Unlike other scripting languages, servlets do not involve any platform-specific consideration or modifications. They are Java components that listen for and are activated by a particular request, that is to say a specific URL. They are then activated and can perform almost any server-side task, responding with the desired result.

JSP technology and servlets provide an alternative to other types of dynamic Web scripting/programming, while also offering platform independence and separation of logic from display. Early servlet models were proprietary and therefore vendor dependent.

A JSP page is executed by a JSP engine, which is installed in a Web server or a JSP-enabled application server such as WebLogic or SilverStream. The JSP engine receives requests made by a client to a JSP page, then generates responses from the JSP page back to the client. Normally, JSP pages are compiled into Java Servlets, a standard Java extension, see Figure 8.1. If the servlet does not exist when it is initially called, the JSP page will be compiled into a Java Servlet class and stored in the server cache. This increases the speed of response to ensuing calls to that page. This quick response is possible because the page, when still valid, is instantly retrieved for viewing.

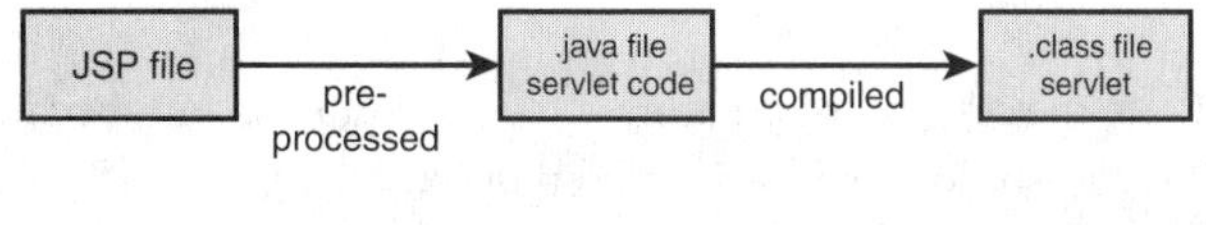

FIGURE 8.1
JSP translated to Java Servlet before being compiled.

The JSP specification is the product of industry-wide collaboration with the enterprise software and tools markets, obviously led by Sun Microsystems. JSP pages share the "Write Once, Run Anywhere" characteristic of Java technology. JSP technology is the "view" component in the Java 2 Platform, Enterprise Edition.

Sun's J2EE platform promotes the use of JSP pages to provide the core of the user interface (UI) of an application, usually in Web-based J2EE applications. Today's typical Web applications include JSP pages, servlets, JavaBeans, utility classes, images, and so on packaged and combined with an XML descriptor file in a Web Application Archive (WAR) file. These applications are uploaded into a vendor application server (BEA, SilverStream) and accessed by browser-based clients. The diagram in Figure 8.2 shows how JSP pages and servlets are part of J2EE's middle tier, sometimes called the Web tier.

The Web tier responds to client requests by using a Web container within the J2EE application server to support the generation of pages that will be presented to the user. The pages call servlets that can generate content and control which page is used to respond to the user request. The servlets may invoke EJB components to build the content. These EJB components access data throughout the enterprise.

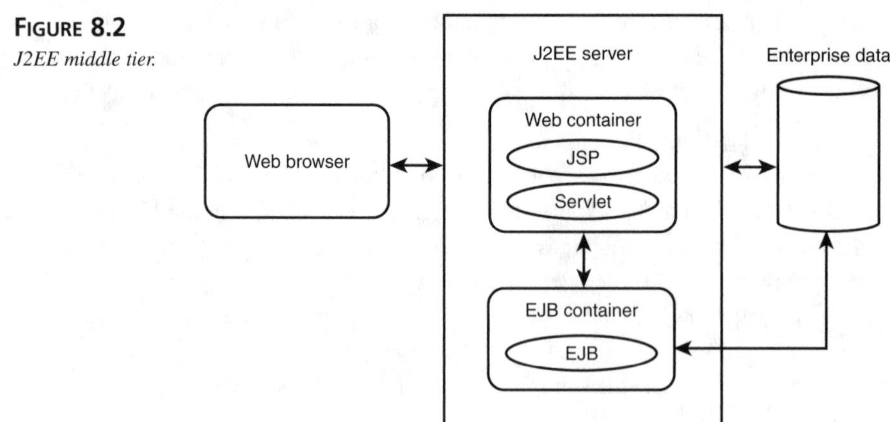

FIGURE 8.2
J2EE middle tier.

JSP pages facilitate the process of creating dynamic Web content, because they combine code that invokes Java-based logic with a Web markup language. JSP pages

- Describe how to process and respond to HTTP requests
- Are text-based documents that include a combination of HTML and JSP tags, Java code, and other information
- Separate the presentation tier (expressed in HTML) from the application logic, coded in Java
- Allow extension of the capabilities of a JSP page by including calls to JavaBeans components as well as embedded Java code fragments
- Can contain custom tags, helping to separate presentation from implementation
- Can act as a front end to Enterprise JavaBeans components running on an application server such as SilverStream

Tags, in the JSP context, are bean-like components that encapsulate logic to provide content generation. If none of the standard JSP tags provide the functionality needed for an application, developers can write their own application-specific tag library and use custom tags defined by this library in their pages. Alternatively, a tag library provided by a third party, such as the Jakarta server project, can be used. This is an area where third party software vendors can utilize the broad functionality of JSP technology to provide tools/painters that can generate code to standardize the look, feel, and flow of the user interface. See the Jakarta site (`http://jakarta.apache.org/`) for an example of providing commercial-quality server solutions.

As most application server vendors support JSP pages with their products, you can use the application server and tools of your choice with some minor adjustments, changing tools or servers without affecting current applications.

As integrated development environments (IDEs) evolve, the process of J2EE development will become easier. When integrated with the Java 2 Platform, Enterprise Edition (J2EE) and Enterprise JavaBeans technology, JSP pages provide enterprise-class scalability and performance necessary for deploying Web-based applications across the virtual enterprise.

Features of JSP Pages

JSP pages are feature rich and make for efficient use of server-side Java. Their development can be shared among various developers while still promoting consistency and standards for development. We will review these qualities in the following sections.

The Efficient Use of Server-Side Java

Many features of Java make it a desirable platform for writing server applications. Server applications benefit from Java's development features such as type safety, virtual absence of memory leaks and multithreading support. The Java platform makes the enterprise extensible. JSP technology is a key component of the Java 2 Platform, Enterprise Edition. Using JSP technology provides the ability to leverage existing Java platform expertise and create highly scalable enterprise applications.

Web Development, Deployment, and Maintenance

JSP pages facilitate the development process for programmers and page authors alike. Instead of writing a Java program, page authors simply write a page using HTML, then add the XML-like tags. Then, if necessary, an integration developer can add scriptlets to tie everything together. By supporting component-based development and customized tag libraries, JSP pages not only simplify page authoring but also provide a strong foundation for a wide range of page authoring tools. This provides opportunities for IDE vendors to create Rapid Application Development (RAD) JSP authoring tools. See Appendix B, "Related Tools," for review and contact information on such tools. Separation of application logic (typically residing within customized tag libraries or beans) and the page design/content makes JSP pages easily maintainable.

Components That Are Reusable

Most JSP pages rely on reusable, cross-platform components (JavaBeans or Enterprise JavaBeans components) to perform the processing required of the application. Developers are able to share and exchange components that perform common operations, including making them available to larger user or customer communities. The component-based approach speeds overall development while allowing organizations to leverage their existing expertise and development efforts for optimal results. It promotes reuse, which in turn promotes consistency.

Separating Business Logic and Presentation

Using JSP technology, Web page developers construct HTML and/or XML tags to design and format the Web page. JSP tags or scriptlets are used to generate the dynamic content on the page—the content that changes according to the request, such as the price of a specific product. The logic that generates the content is brought together in tags and JavaBeans components and bound together in scriptlets, which are ultimately executed on the server side. If the core logic is encapsulated in tags and beans, other individuals (for example, page designers) can edit and work with the JSP page without affecting the generation of the content. This helps authors protect their own proprietary code while ensuring complete portability for any HTML-based Web browser.

Large Development Community and Widespread Support

As of the date of this publication, nearly all software development vendors except Microsoft have merged to form the "Java Community." The JSP specification is developed under the Java Community Process, ensuring that the specification has a broad spectrum of industry input and support. The reference implementation is developed openly under the Apache process. By working through the open process of the Apache Software Foundation, developers will be able to offer a world-class implementation of the latest JSP technology as soon as possible.

Platform Independence

JavaServer Pages technology provides a component-based, platform-independent process for building Web-based applications. Most developers of Web and application servers are currently delivering or are about to deliver products that support this technology. This widespread, multi-platform support allows Web developers to write their JavaServer Pages code once and run it anywhere.

Next Generation Page Development with Tags

Web page authors are not always programmers familiar with scripting languages. The JavaServer Pages technology encapsulates much of the functionality required for dynamic content generation in easy-to-use, JSP-specific XML-like tags, allowing Web page developers to work with familiar tools and constructs to perform sophisticated functions. Standard JSP tags can perform functions that are difficult and time-consuming to code such as accessing and instantiating JavaBeans components, setting or retrieving bean attributes, and downloading applets. JSP technology is extensible through development of custom tag libraries. Over time, third-party developers will undoubtedly create tag libraries for common functions.

The Components of a JSP Page

At first glance, the JSP page looks busy with all sorts of tagged text including but not limited to HTML, Java scriptlets, JSP directives, tag-like directives, and JavaScript. Not to worry. In this chapter and Chapter 9, "JavaServer Pages: Practical Development with Tag Libraries," we will discuss all of these JSP components in detail.

JSP Directives

JSP directives are used to pass instructions to the JSP engine. These directives include the following:

- Page directives—These directives communicate page-specific information, such as buffer and thread information or error handling.
- Language directives—These specify the scripting language, along with any extensions.
- The `include` directive—This directive can be used to include an external document in the page. A good example of this would be a copyright file or company information file. If an element is to be used many times throughout a site, it is easier to maintain common files in one central location and include them in several pages than to update them in each JSP page. The included file could be another JSP file, as well.
- A `taglib` directive—This indicates a library of custom tags that the page can invoke. This is powerful and relatively unobtrusive. It avoids adding scriptlet or embedded code, which is hard to maintain.

JSP Tags

Most JSP processing is implemented through JSP-specific XML-based tags. JSP 1.1 includes a number of standard tags, referred to as the core tags. These include

- `jsp:useBean`—This tag declares the usage of an instance of a JavaBeans component. The JavaBeans component instantiates and registers the tag if the bean does not already exist.
- `jsp:setProperty`—This sets the value of a property in a bean.
- `jsp:getProperty`—This tag gets the value of a bean instance property, converts it to a string, and puts it in the implicit object "out".
- `jsp:include`—This tag will cause the specified file to be included in the current JSP page.
- `jsp:forward`—This tag will forward or redirect control to another JSP page.

The 1.2 release, which was a proposed final draft at publication, will include additional standard tags.

Tags are advantageous because they are easy to use and share between applications. The real power of a tag-based syntax comes with the creation of custom tag libraries, which allow tool vendors or other parties to create and distribute tags for specific functions. This facilitates rapid development as well as consistency in look and feel. We will cover tag libraries in detail in Chapter 9.

Here is an example of code that contains taglib directives. See Figure 8.5 for the generated results of the page's execution.

```
<%@ page import="java.sql.*" errorPage="error.jsp" %>
<jsp:useBean id="customer" class="CustNameBean" scope="page"/>

<html>
<head>
<title>Customer Listing</title>
</head>

<body>
<h1 align="center">Customer Listing </h1>
<hr>
  <table width="75%" border="1" align="center">
    <tr>
      <td><b>First Name</b></td>
      <td><b>Last Name</b></td>
      <td><b>EMail</b></td>
    </tr>
<% customer.query();
```

```
    while(customer.next()) {
%>
    <tr>
      <td><jsp:getProperty name="customer"
  property="firstName" /></td>
      <td><jsp:getProperty name="customer"
  property="lastName" /></td>
      <td><jsp:getProperty name="customer"
  property="email" /></td>
    </tr>
<%
    } //end while
%>
</table>
</body>
</html>
```

Scripting Elements

JSP pages can include small scripts called scriptlets. A scriptlet is a code fragment that is executed at request time processing. Scriptlets may be combined with static elements on the page (as in the preceding example), thus creating a dynamically generated page.

Scripts are delineated within `<%` and `%>` markers. Anything within those markers will be evaluated by the scripting language engine. In our example it would be evaluated by the Java virtual machine on the host.

The JSP specification supports all of the customary script elements such as expressions and declarations.

Developing and Deploying JSP Pages

To develop and deploy JSP pages (Web applications):

- Write your JSP pages, Java servlets, JavaBeans components, and other supporting Java classes.
- Package the JSP pages and supporting classes in the appropriate archive format.
- Deploy the archive to a J2EE-compliant server (for example, WebLogic, SilverStream).

Writing JSP Pages

With early Web tools such as SilverStream, visual page designers allowed developers to select and drop controls onto a designer canvas to build HTML, fostering rapid application development (RAD). RAD tools for JSP pages are also emerging. Developers may choose from a variety of JSP editors to author JSP files. Figures 8.3 and 8.4 depict the WebGain tools for constructing JSP pages. In Figure 8.3, VisualCafé is used to enter scriptlet code and tag directives. In Figure 8.4, Dreamweaver is used to design WSIWYG HTML headers, tables, controls, and other visual components. In Figure 8.5, the JSP page `CustomerListing` is executed under the aegis of a SilverStream J2EE-certified server.

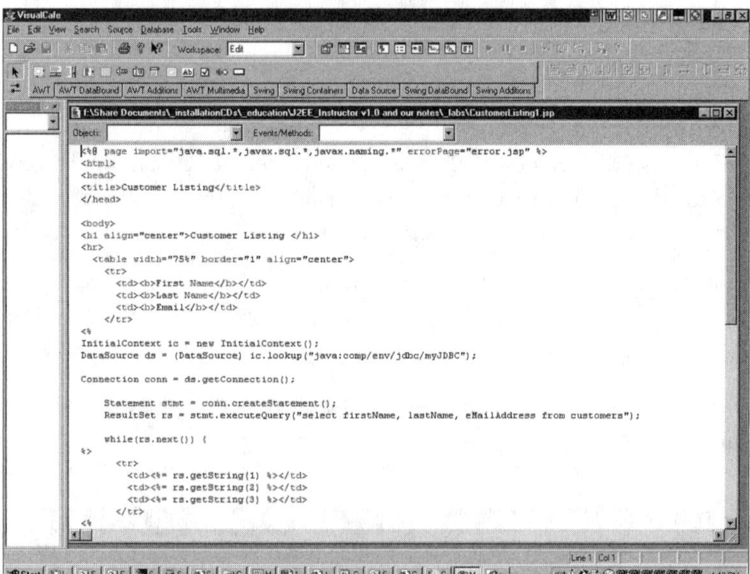

FIGURE 8.3
VisualCafé editor with JSP code.

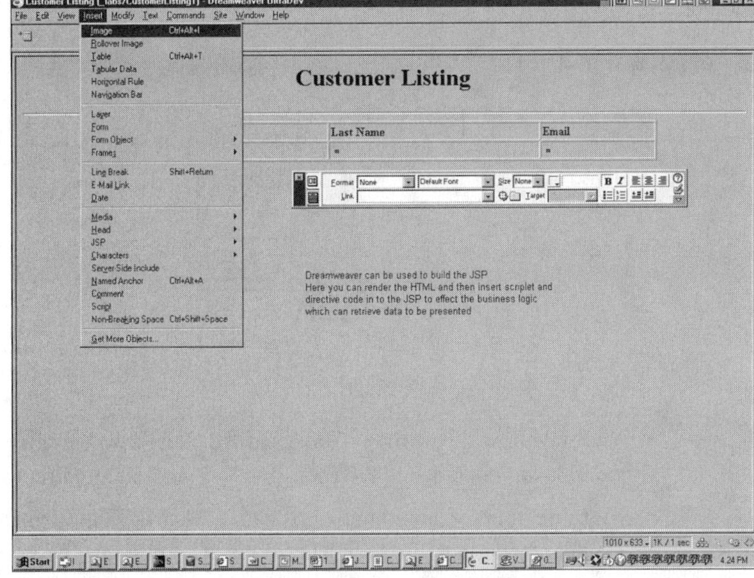

FIGURE 8.4
Dreamweaver editor with WYSIWYG view of a JSP page.

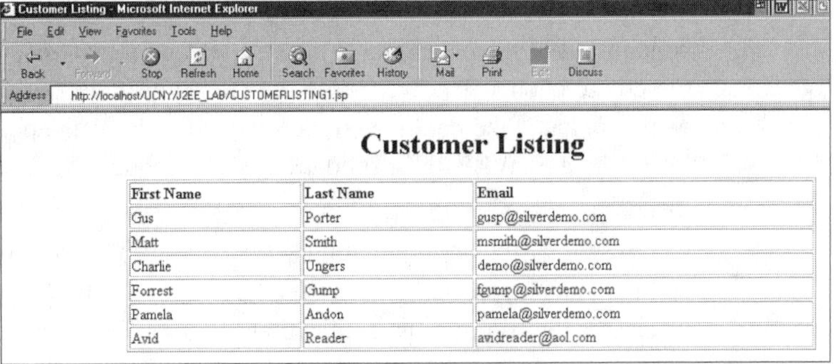

FIGURE 8.5
SilverStream execution of the `CustomerListing` *JSP page.*

To create a Web application that contains one or more JSP pages

1. Create a directory structure for the application that conforms to the format required for the Web application. The directory structure should look somewhat like Figure 8.6.

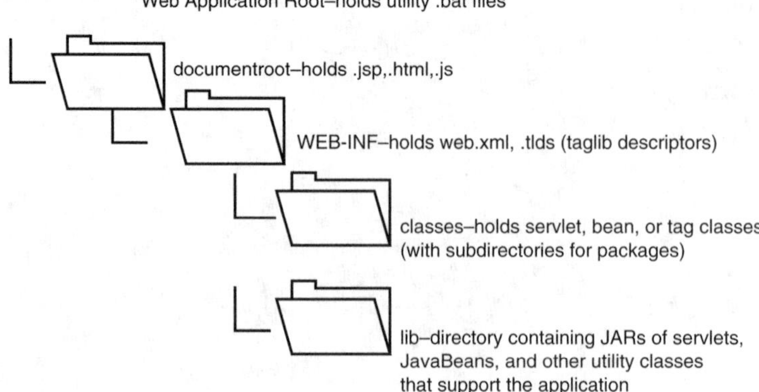

FIGURE 8.6
Directory structure for the application.

- WAR (Web Archive) file—Container for Web-based application. A zip file contains the contents of the root directory and all subdirectories.
- Root directory—Can contain JSP pages, HTML documents, and any other contents for the application. These objects could also be in subdirectories of the root.
- WEB-INF—A required subdirectory for descriptive deployment files that contains all of the components of the application that should not be available directly to clients. The WEB-INF directory must contain a file called web.xml that is the deployment descriptor for the Web application. The Web infrastructure (WEB-INF) subdirectory can contain the following subdirectories:

  classes—Directory containing servlet and utility classes

  lib—Directory containing JARs of servlets, JavaBeans, and other utility classes that support the application

In addition to the classes and lib subdirectories, the WEB-INF subdirectory can have other subdirectories. You can give these subdirectories any names you like. For example, you might include a subdirectory that contains Tag Library Definitions and give it the name tlds or a subdirectory containing images called img.

2. Write your JSP pages and save them in the root directory of the Web application.
3. Create any Java servlets, JavaBeans components, or other supporting Java classes required by the application and compile these classes. If you do not want these files to be exposed in the URL space for the application, save them under the WEB-INF\classes directory or package them into JAR files and save the JAR files in the WEB-INF\lib directory. The package root for any package you create under WEB-INF\classes is WEB-INF\classes.

Samples of JSP 1.1 Pages

This first example shows the source for a basic JSP page. It looks like HTML but contains what looks like embedded Java code. Then there is more HTML and more Java code. It is somewhat busy looking at first glance, but after a while developers become familiar with the structure and can modify the code with ease and comfort.

```
<html>
<body>
<P> The following is a JSP declaration<P>
<%!
    int x = 5;
    private int aMethod(int y) {
        return x * y;
    }
%>
<P> The following is a JSP expression, notice the lack of semi-colon<P>
<P> This is a basic jsp<P>
<%= new java.util.Date() %>
<P> The following is a JSP scriptlet<P>
<UL>
<%
    for (int i = 0; i < 3; i++) {
%>
    <LI><%= aMethod(i) %>
<%
    }
%>
</UL>
<body>
```

Figure 8.7 illustrates the results of running the basic JSP page.

Here we have embedded some Java scriptlet code that defines a method to multiply 5 times a value passed by the method call. The method is then invoked within a `for` loop three times.

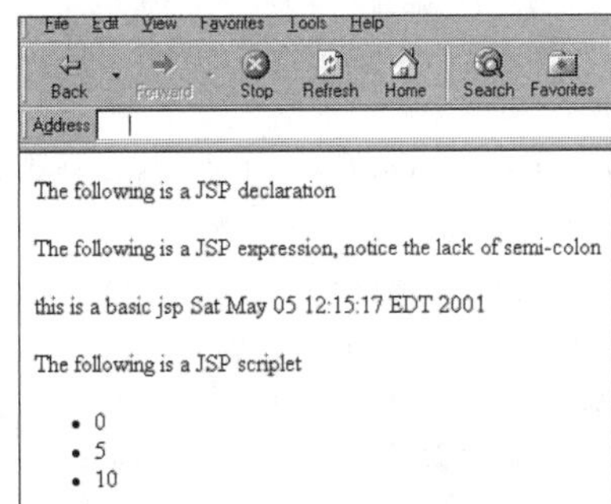

FIGURE 8.7
Results of running a basic JSP page.

The next sample page demonstrates many of the features of JSP pages. Don't be concerned that it looks foreboding. All of these features will be presented in this and the following chapter.

The components of this page include

- A custom tag called `Hello` to print out a greeting.

```
<mytags:Hello/>
```

- A `taglib` directive on the page that specifies a uniform resource identifier (URI) and a prefix for the tag library that contains the custom tag. A URI is either a uniform resource locator (URL) or a uniform resource name (URN) that uses a name to address directory service to resolve a link.

```
<%@ taglib uri="/mytaglib" prefix="mytags" %>
```

- The prefix, which specifies an identifier that is prepended to all tags in the library that are used on the page. The URI maps to a tag library descriptor (TLD) file, which is named in the web.xml file for the Web application.

```
<web-app>
...
<taglib>
<taglib-uri>/mytaglib</taglib-uri>
<taglib-location>/WEB-INF/tlds/mytaglib.tld</taglib-location>
</taglib>
...
</web-app>
```

- The tag library descriptor (TLD) file, which provides a mapping between the tags in the library and the Java classes that implement those tags.
- Two JavaBeans to perform processing. The page uses a standard action (`<jsp:useBean>`) to associate each bean with an ID. Once this association has been made, the page uses the `<jsp:getProperty>` action or an expression (`<%= ... %>`) to get data back from the beans.
- Implicit objects that are accessed through implicit variables.
- The implicit request variable to call several methods associated with the servlet request that triggered this page.
- A declaration (`<%! ... %>`) to define a function on the page. The declaration uses an expression to call the function.
- A scriptlet (`<% ... %>`) to execute some conditional logic on the page. Depending on the result of the test, the scriptlet writes the embedded text Good Morning or Good Afternoon directly to the output stream.

- The <jsp:include> action to include the contents of another JSP page in the current page. The <jsp:include> action includes content at runtime. JSP technology also provides a compile-time include mechanism. To include content that should be evaluated at compile time, use the <%@ include > directive.

Here's the source for the date.jsp sample page:

```
  <html>
  <jsp:useBean id='clock' scope='page' class='util.JspCalendar'
type="util.JspCalendar"/>
  <jsp:useBean id='sql' scope='request' class='util.JspSQL'/>

  <%@ taglib uri="/mytaglib" prefix="mytags" %>

  <mytags:Hello/>

  <h1> Use the implicit Request object </h1>
  <ul>
  <li>Query string: <%= request.getQueryString() %>
  <li>Server name: <%= request.getServerName() %>
  <li>Server port: <%= request.getServerPort() %>
  <li>Remote address: <%= request.getRemoteAddr() %>
  </ul>

  <h1> Use a Bean to access date information</h1>
  <ul>
  <li>Day of month: is  <jsp:getProperty name="clock" property="dayOfMonth"/>
  <li>Another form of Day of month: is  <%=clock.getDayOfMonth() %>
  <li>Year: is  <jsp:getProperty name="clock" property="year"/>
  <li>Month: is  <jsp:getProperty name="clock" property="month"/>
  <li>Time: is  <jsp:getProperty name="clock" property="time"/>
  <li>Date: is  <jsp:getProperty name="clock" property="date"/>
  </ul>

  <h1> Call a function declared on the JSP page </h1>
  <%-- Function declaration --%>
  <%!
     public String getAString(String x)
     {
     return x + " was passed in";
     }
  %>

  <ul>
  <li>  call getAString: <%= getAString("Hello") %>
  </ul>

  <h1> Use a bean to access a database </h1>
  <%= sql.getSQL(request, "Select employeeid as ID, lastname
   as Name from employees") %>
```

```
<h1> Execute a scriptlet that has embedded text </h1>
<% if (java.util.Calendar.getInstance().get(java.util.Calendar.AM_PM)
  == java.util.Calendar.AM) {%>
Good Morning
<% } else { %>
Good Afternoon
<% } %>

<h1>Include the output of another JSP page</h1>
<jsp:include page="include.jsp"/>
</html>
```

As you can see from this example, JSP pages can contain HTML, JSP and tag library directives, and Java code. Interspersing HTML and Java in the same file works in this example because it is very simple; however, it is not desirable in larger applications. Most Web page designers don't know Java, and most Java programmers don't write HTML as well as page designers. Furthermore, maintaining HTML and Java in the same place blurs the distinction between static content and dynamic content. For these reasons, not to mention the benefits of separating view from control and business logic, it is best to keep Java code separate from JSP pages. This is accomplished by maintaining the Java code in JavaBeans components and making calls to these components from the JSP pages. An alternative approach is to encapsulate your Java code in custom tag libraries and use custom tags to perform actions implemented in these libraries.

JSP Architectures

As previously mentioned, JSP technology is a natural evolution from various vendor tools that facilitate servlets for generating dynamic views. JSP technology provides a standard for a declarative, presentation-centric method of developing servlets. As noted before, the JSP specification itself is defined as a standard extension on top of the Servlet API. Consequently, servlets and JSP pages have much in common.

As their purpose is to build dynamic views, JSP pages are subject to a translation phase and a request-processing phase. The translation phase is carried out only once, unless the JSP page changes, in which case it is repeated. As long as there are no syntax errors within the page, the result is a JSP page implementation class file that implements the Servlet interface.

Typically, the translation phase is carried out by the JSP engine when the first incoming request for the JSP page is received. Note that the JSP 1.1 specification also allows for JSP pages to be precompiled into class files. Precompilation may be especially useful in removing the startup delay that occurs when a JSP page delivered in source form receives the first request from a client. Many details of the translation phase, including the storage location of the source and class files, are implementation dependent.

The JSP page implementation class file extends HttpJspBase, which implements the Servlet interface. The service method of this class, `_jspService()`, essentially sends the contents of the JSP page to the method. The `_jspService()` method can describe initialization and destroy events by providing implementations for the `jspInit()` and `jspDestroy()` methods within their JSP pages.

Once this class file is loaded within the servlet container, the `_jspService()` method replies to a client's request. By default, the `_jspService()` method is dispatched on a separate thread by the servlet container in processing concurrent client requests.

As in any new development, there are at least two approaches to building and applying JSP technology. These approaches differ essentially in terms of where the request processing is performed. They offer a useful paradigm for building applications using JSP technology.

Loosely described, one approach allows for business logic and presentation code to be intermixed with the presentation itself (HTML). This, as anyone experienced in maintaining applications knows, can be costly. Maintaining hundreds of JSP pages could be expensive, especially if the corporate look and feel changes often. The more mature approach prescribes that all code, business logic, and such be excluded from the presentation to the extent that this is possible.

Simple Application

The primary advantage of the first approach is that there is only one file per view to maintain for changes to your application. The major disadvantage is readability and the difficulty of maintaining the JSP pages. Unless you are very careful, HTML and Java code can become so intermingled that it is difficult to debug and maintain the application.

In the basic architecture, just like the servlet, the incoming request from a Web browser is sent directly to the JSP page, which is responsible for processing it and replying to the client. There is still separation of presentation from content, because all data access is performed using beans (see Figure 8.8).

FIGURE 8.8
Basic architecture.

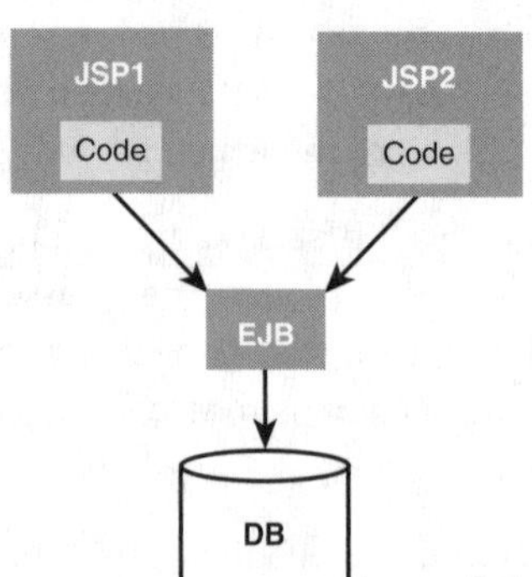

- Direct data access from JSPs makes it hard to
  - change the application
  - tune its performance
- Instead, encapsulate data access in EJBs or JavaBeans
- Better yet, use taglibs and MVC

For this example, we are going to review a JSP page called the customer listing. We will find the database, make a connection, and then execute an SQL query to select all of our customer table rows. The JSP page will then navigate through all of the customer rows embedding the resultset in an HTML table.

```
<%@ page import="java.sql.*,javax.sql.*,javax.naming.*" %>
<html>
<head>
<title>Customer Listing</title>
</head>
<body>
<h1 align="center">Customer Listing </h1>
<hr>
  <table width="75%" border="1" align="center">
    <tr>
      <td><b>First Name</b></td>
      <td><b>Last Name</b></td>
      <td><b>Email</b></td>
    </tr>
<%
InitialContext ic = new InitialContext();
DataSource ds = (DataSource) ic.lookup("java:comp/env/jdbc/myJDBC");
Connection conn = ds.getConnection();

Statement stmt = conn.createStatement();
ResultSet rs = stmt.executeQuery("select firstName,
lastName, eMailAddress from customers");
while(rs.next())
{
%>
  <tr>
  <td><%= rs.getString(1) %></td>
  <td><%= rs.getString(2) %></td>
  <td><%= rs.getString(3) %></td>
  </tr>
```

```
<%
} //close while loop
     stmt.close();
     conn.close();
%>
</table>
</body>
</html>
```

Similarly, the resultset data to be displayed could have been retrieved using a JavaBean. In the next example, we are going to revisit the customer listing JSP page. However, we will use a JavaBean to make the database connection and then execute an SQL query to select all of our customer table rows. The JSP page will then use directives to get bean properties containing the resultset and navigate through all of the customer rows embedding the resultset in an HTML table.

```
<%@ page errorPage="error.jsp" %>
<jsp:useBean id="customer" class="com.sssw.demo.silverbooks.CustNameBean"
scope="page"/>
<html>
<head>
<title>Customer Listing</title>
</head>
<body>
<h1 align="center">Customer Listing </h1>
<hr>
<table width="75%" border="1" align="center">
    <tr>
      <td><b>First Name</b></td>
      <td><b>Last Name</b></td>
      <td><b>Email</b></td>
    </tr>
<% customer.query();
    while(customer.next()) {
%>
<tr>
  <td><jsp:getProperty name="customer"
          property="firstName" /></td>
  <td><jsp:getProperty name="customer"
          property="lastName" /></td>
  <td><jsp:getProperty name="customer"
          property="email" /></td>
</tr>
<%
    } //end while
%>
</table>
</body>
</html>
```

Here is the code for CustNameBean:

```
package com.sssw.demo.silverbooks;
import java.sql.*;
import javax.sql.*;
import javax.naming.*;
public class CustNameBean {
    public String firstName;
    public String lastName;
    public String email;

    Connection conn = null;
    Statement stmt = null;
    ResultSet rs = null;

    public String getFirstName() { return this.firstName; }
    public String getLastName() { return this.lastName; }
    public String getEmail() { return this.email; }

    public void setFirstName(String name) { this.firstName = name; }
    public void setLastName(String name) { this.lastName = name; }
    public void setEmail(String email) { this.email = email; }

    public void query() throws Exception{
        InitialContext ic = new InitialContext();
        DataSource ds = (DataSource) ic.lookup("java:comp/env/jdbc/myJDBC");
        conn = ds.getConnection();
            stmt = conn.createStatement();
            rs = stmt.executeQuery("select firstName, lastName,
                 eMailAddress from customers");
        }

        public boolean next() throws Exception {
            boolean moreRows = rs.next();
            if (moreRows){
                  firstName = rs.getString(1);
                  lastName = rs.getString(2);
                  email = rs.getString(3);
            } else
            {
                  stmt.close();
                  conn.close();
            }
```

Mature Architecture: Redirecting Requests

Once organizations become experienced with JSP page development, utilizing tag libraries and utility classes for completing most user interface coding in a standard fashion, they begin to employ a mature approach to developing JSP pages. The mature architecture, shown in Figure 8.9, is a server-side implementation of the popular Model-View-Controller design pattern. Here, the processing is divided between view/presentation and processing control components. View components are JSP pages that generate the HTML/XML response depending upon the user interface when rendered by the browser. Control components process the HTTP requests. They are responsible for creating any beans or objects used by the presentation components, as well as determining which View component to forward the request to, based upon the user's actions. Front end components can be implemented as either servlets or JSP pages.

FIGURE 8.9
Mature architecture.

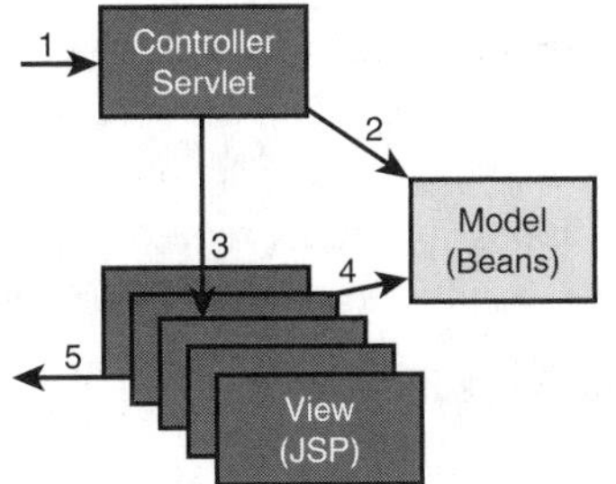

- Use a servlet to dispatch requests
  - (1) Client request accepted by the controller servlet
  - (2) Data validated against the Model and updates are made
  - (3) Control is passed to the View (JSP)
  - (4) JSP retrieves the relevant data from the Model
  - (5) A fully formed response is sent back to the client

This architecture, sometimes referred to as Model-View-Controller (MVC), has been advocated for years. The advantage is that there is no processing logic within the View component itself. The view JSP page is responsible for retrieving any objects or beans created by the controller, and extracting the dynamic content within for insertion within its static templates. This separation of view from business logic leads to delineation of the roles and responsibilities of the developers and page designers.

Another benefit of this approach is that the View components present a single point of entry into the application, thus making the management of application state, security, and presentation uniform and easier to maintain. This approach was implemented as early as the 1980s in systems developed using IBM's CICS DB2 and Basic Mapping Support (BMS) as the View component with COBOL programs as Controllers.

In a team environment that includes both HTML designers and Java programmers, this approach can be particularly strong. The Java programmers are able to concentrate on creating reusable code.

Now we'll take the same desired behavior from the basic example and present it using the mature methodology, following the Model-View-Controller (MVC) paradigm. For this example, we'll have one class (or page or servlet) process the request (Controller), get the action, set all the required variables for presentation, and pass control off to a presentation page (View).

The controller can be a servlet or a JSP file. The action servlet is the cornerstone of the Controller component of the MVC design paradigm. In one of our example applications, SilverBooks, the action servlet performs three key functions:

- Receives requests from the client (in this case, a user interacting with the SilverBooks application in a Web browser)
- Determines the action to perform
- Delegates to an appropriate View component the responsibility for producing the next part of the user interface

Two XML specifications are used to configure the action servlet. The specification in web.xml associates the URL pattern `*.do` with the action servlet. This association means that any URL request or post ending in `.do` will go to the action servlet for processing. The specification in action.xml maps each possible client request to an action class that performs the appropriate business logic or handles the possible exceptions.

For example, here is one of the URL mappings in action.xml:

```
<action path="/bookDetail"
    actionClass="com.sssw.demo.silverbooks.action.DetailAction">
<forward name="success" path="/bookdetail.jsp" />
</action>
```

This mapping means that when the URL `bookDetail.do` is requested, the action servlet instantiates the `DetailAction` class (or uses one that has already been instantiated) to display the detail data about a book selected by the user. The book identifier is passed as a parameter on the URL. This action class has access to a forward-mapping address called `success`, which is mapped to the relative URL `bookdetail.jsp`.

The `DetailAction` class services the client request as follows:

- Gets a reference to the book in the EJB data source, based on the book identifier. Each book is represented by a book bean.
- Retrieves the book data and places the book in the session.
- If no exceptions occur, passes control to the JSP page `bookdetail.jsp`, which calls properties on the book bean to determine how to display the page.

Here is an excerpt from `bookdetail.jsp`.

```
<%@ page import="java.text.NumberFormat" language="java"
errorPage="errorPage.jsp" %>
<%@ taglib uri="/WEB-INF/struts.tld" prefix="struts" %>
<jsp:useBean id="book" scope="session"
```

```
 class="com.sssw.demo.silverbooks.BookBean"/>
<HTML>
<HEAD>
<TITLE><struts:message key="page.title"/></TITLE>

</HEAD>

<BODY marginheight="0" BACKGROUND="Images/bookBack.jpg"
leftmargin="0" topmargin="0" marginwidth="0">
<%@ include file="topnav.jsp" %>
  <P ALIGN=LEFT>
  <TABLE BORDER=0 BORDERCOLOR="#808080" CELLPADDING=0 CELLSPACING=0>
    <TR>
     <P><B><FONT SIZE=4 FACE="Verdana"><SPAN STYLE="font-size:20;">
       <struts:property name="book" property="title"/> </SPAN></FONT></B>
     .....
     <P><FONT FACE="Verdana"><struts:message key="book.by"/>
           <A HREF="searchAction.do?aid=<%= book.getAuthorId() %>">
       <struts:property name="book" property="authorName"/></A> </FONT>
     ......
     <P><BIG><B><FONT SIZE=3 COLOR="#2C2C94" FACE="Verdana">
      <SPAN STYLE="font-size:14;">
     <struts:message key="book.listprice"/>:</SPAN></FONT></B></BIG>
     .........
     <P ALIGN=CENTER><FONT SIZE=2 FACE="Verdana"><SPAN STYLE="font-size:12;"><A
HREF="cart.do?action=add&bid=<%= book.getBookId()%>">
     <IMG BORDER="0" NAME="addtocart" SRC="Images/AddToCart.jpg"
         HEIGHT="27" WIDTH="174"></a>
  </TABLE>

<%@ include file="bottomnav.sub" %>
</BODY>
</HTML>
```

The controller uses the Request values to obtain the required data, putting that data into the Request object. The difference in this case is that the View page will call the Controller using RequestDispatcher.include(). As a result, the client is never redirected, and Requests are not "chained"; rather, the class/jsp called asks another component to do some work for it, then continues. This is explained in greater detail in Chapter 10, "Building the User Interface to the Application."

In the SilverBooks sample application, this method is used to create chains of classes, each responsible for its own processing. By identifying common presentation formats, we've created View objects that can be reused in higher level JSP pages. The goal is to create pages that are designed for reuse, and to reduce the number of presentation classes.

Model-View-Controller (MVC) Design

To reiterate, in the MVC design pattern, a central Controller mediates application flow. This design technique dates back to the 1980s, when large corporations developed IBM CICS-based transaction systems. Here, one COBOL program "controlled" the next screen (or map, as they were called). The Controller delegates requests to an appropriate handler. The handlers are tied to a Model and act as adapters between the request and the Model. The Model represents, or encapsulates, an application's business logic or state. Control is usually then forwarded back through the Controller to the appropriate View. The forwarding can be established by consulting a set of mappings that are typically loaded from a database or configuration file. This provides a loose coupling between the View and Model, making an application significantly easier to create and maintain.

Struts Framework Overview

Let's drill down a little further into MVC. This time we will use the Struts framework. Struts is a popular framework for application development using MVC. Struts is part of the Jakarta Project, sponsored by the Apache Software Foundation. The official Struts home page is at `http://jakarta.apache.org/struts`.

See Figure 8.10 for a depiction of how the MVC design construct can be implemented using a Struts-based framework.

Struts applications have three major components: a servlet controller (Action.Class in Figure 8.10), JSP pages (the "view"), and the application's business logic (or the "model").

The servlet controller bundles and routes HTTP requests to other objects within the framework, including JSP pages. When initialized, the controller parses a configuration resource file (action.xml in Figure 8.10). Like a large IF/ELSEIF statement, the configuration resource defines the action mappings for the application. Using these mappings, the controller turns HTTP requests into application actions.

Usually, a variable directing the request is passed to the action servlet controller. This maps to code in the controller. A mapping must specify (1)a request path and (2)the object type in order to act upon the request.

For example, the `searchAction.do` reference in the `bookdetail.jsp` is passed to one controller:

```
<P><FONT FACE="Verdana"><struts:message key="book.by"/>
<A HREF="searchAction.do?aid=<%= book.getAuthorId() %>">
<struts:property name="book" property="authorName"/></A> </FONT>
```

FIGURE 8.10
MVC and Struts implementation.

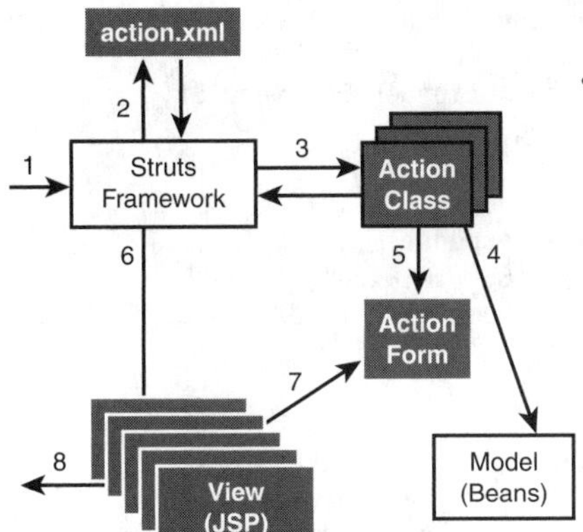

- Struts is MVC plus the following steps
  - (2) Look up URL to Action mapping in Action.xml
  - (3) Run selected Action class, get a name of a JSP to use
  - (5) Action stores params in ActionForm
  - (7) JSP retrieves request params out of ActionForm

The controller maps this request to `searchAction` in the Struts configuration resource file action.xml:

```
<action  path="/searchAction"
    actionClass="com.sssw.demo.silverbooks.action.SearchAction">
    <forward name="failure"    path="/errorPage.jsp"/>
    <forward name="booklist"   path="/searchresults.jsp"/>
    <forward name="bookdetail" path="/bookDetail.do"/>
  </action>
```

The action object that the actionClass parameter points to is a Java class named SearchAction. This object can handle the request and respond to the client (usually a Web browser), or indicate that control should be forwarded to another action. Here we have passed an author ID (AID) variable.

```
public final class SearchAction extends ActionBase {

    // ------------------------------------------------------- Public Methods
    /**
     *  Process the specified HTTP request, and create the corresponding HTTP
     *  response (or forward to another web component that will create it).
     *  Return an <code>ActionForward</code> instance describing where and how
     *  control should be forwarded, or <code>null</code> if the response has
     *  already been completed.
     *
     *@param  servlet      The ActionServlet making this request
     *@param  mapping      The ActionMapping used to select this instance
     *@param  request               The HTTP request we are processing
     *@param  response              The HTTP response we are creating
     *@param  form                  Description of Parameter
     *@return                       Description of the Returned Value
     *@exception  IOException       if an input/output error occurs
```

```
    *@exception  ServletException  if a servlet exception occurs
    */
   public ActionForward perform(ActionServlet servlet,
           ActionMapping mapping,
           ActionForm form,
           HttpServletRequest request,
           HttpServletResponse response)
            throws IOException, ServletException {
       ActionForward forwardURL = mapping.findForward("failure");

       try {

           HttpSession session = request.getSession();
           String title = request.getParameter("title");
           String authorId = request.getParameter("aid");
       ................................
           Collection books = null;
           StringBuffer sbuffer = new StringBuffer();
                       //build title search
           ...........................................
                 ...........................................
//   perform some JDBC lookups and then decide on the what
// should be set as the forward URL

           if (books.size() == 0) {
               session.removeAttribute(SilverBooksConstants.KEY_SEARCHRESULTS);
               forwardURL = mapping.findForward("booklist");
           }
           else if (books.size() == 1) {
               Iterator itBooks = books.iterator();
               BookBean singleBook = (BookBean) itBooks.next();
               session.setAttribute(SilverBooksConstants.KEY_BOOKDETAIL,
                singleBook);
               forwardURL = mapping.findForward("bookdetail");
           }
           else {
               session.setAttribute(SilverBooksConstants.
                 KEY_SEARCHRESULTS, books);
               forwardURL = mapping.findForward("booklist");
           }

       }
       catch (Exception e) {
           System.out.println("searchAction exception:" + e);

       }

       return forwardURL;
   }

}
```

For example, if a search succeeds and finds only one book associated with this AID, it will return "bookdetail" and then forward control via bookDetail.do back to the configuration file action.xml. If multiple books are found then the return will be "booklist", which will forward control to `searchresults.jsp`.

Action objects are linked to the application's controller and therefore have access to that servlet's methods. When forwarding control, an object can indirectly forward one or more shared objects, including JavaBeans, by placing them in one of the standard collections shared by Java servlets.

Action objects carry out the tasks required at each state of a business transition. They can create a shopping cart bean, add an item to the cart, place the bean in the session collection, and then forward control to another action that may use a JSP page to display the contents of the user's cart. All clients have their own session; subsequently, they will each have their own shopping cart. In a Struts-designed application, most of the business logic can be represented using JavaBeans.

JavaBeans can also be used for managing input forms. An important requirement in designing Web applications is retaining and validating what a user has entered while keeping the information persistent between requests. With the Struts design style, you can easily store the data for an input form in a form bean. The bean is saved in a standard, shared context collection. In this form, other objects, especially the action object, can use the same bean data.

A JSP page can utilize the form bean to collect data from the user. It is passed to an action object to validate the user-entered data and then by the JSP page again to repopulate the form fields. In the case of validation errors, Struts has a built-in mechanism for raising and displaying error messages.

A Struts form bean is defined in the configuration resource file. It is linked to an action mapping using a common property name. When a request calls for an action that uses a form bean, the controller servlet either retrieves the form bean or creates it, passing it to the action object. Transaction processing systems based on IBM CICS have been employing this for over 20 years. The action object can then check the contents of the form bean before its input form is displayed, and can queue messages to be handled by the form. When ready, the action object can return control with a forwarding to its input form, which is usually a JSP page. The controller can then respond to the HTTP request and direct the client to the JSP page.

The Struts framework includes custom tags that are able to automatically populate fields from a form bean. JSP pages need to know about the proper field names and where to submit the form. Common systems components such as the messages set by the action object can be output using a single custom tag. Other application-specific tags can also be used to hide implementation details from the JSP pages.

The custom tags in the Struts framework are designed to use the internationalization features that have been built into the Java platform. All the field labels and messages are retrieved from a message resource. Java automatically provides the correct resource for a client's country and language. To add messages for another language, one only needs to add another resource file.

Internationalization aside, another benefit to this approach is consistency of look and feel. For the developer and user, it provides the ability to review all labels and messages from a central location.

For simple applications, an action object can manage the business logic associated with a request. This object would be large and hard to maintain in a larger application. Typically, an action object passes the request to another object, usually a JavaBean. To enable reuse on other platforms, these business-logic JavaBeans should not refer to any Web application objects. Instead, the action object should translate required details from the HTTP request, passing those along to the business-logic beans as regular Java variables.

In database applications, the business-logic beans might connect to the database to query it, returning the resultset back to the action's servlet. It is then stored in a form bean and displayed by the JSP page. It is not necessary for the action's servlet or the JSP page to know where the resultset comes from.

The rest of this chapter introduces various Struts MVC implementation components in greater detail. The Struts release also includes several Developer Guides covering various aspects of the frameworks, along with sample applications, the standard JavaDoc API, and the source code.

Struts is distributed under the Apache Software Foundation license. The code is copyrighted, but is free to use in any application.

The Model: System State and Business Logic

We have discussed view and control extensively, but the heart of a system is the model. The Model portion of an MVC-based system can be subdivided into two concepts: the internal state of the system, and the actions that can be taken to change that state. In one way, state information can be thought of as nouns, while actions can be thought of as verbs. After performing the requested action, if a "success" is received in the current state, the application is moved forward to the next state as determined by the model.

Here it is wise to review and build application state flow diagrams to determine the components needed to fulfill the model. Generally, your application represents the internal state of the system as a set of one or more JavaBeans, with properties that represent the details of the state. These beans may be self-contained (and know how to save their state information persistently somehow), or they may be objects that know how to retrieve information from external sources (such as a database) when it is requested. Entity Enterprise JavaBeans (EJB) are used to represent internal state. Another technique uses session EJB with JDBC calls to build resultset objects containing multiple rows of database data.

Large applications will often represent the business logic actions as methods that can be called on the beans maintaining the state information.

In small applications, usually pilots or prototypes, the available actions are sometimes embedded within the Action classes that are part of the Controller role. This is appropriate when the logic is very simple, or where reuse of the business logic in other environments is not intended. As previously mentioned, the Struts MVC framework supports any of these approaches, but recommends separating the business logic from the role that controller Action classes play.

The View: JSP Pages and Presentation

The View portion of a Struts-based application is usually constructed utilizing JavaServer Pages (JSP) technology. JSP pages can contain static text, written in HTML or XML, referred to as "template text." Dynamic content can also be inserted based on the interpretation (at page request time) of special action tags. The JSP environment includes a set of standard action tags such as `<jsp:useBean>`, whose purposes are described in detail within the JavaServer Pages Specification. In addition, the environment offers the standard facility to define your own tags, which are organized into custom tag libraries.

Struts includes a custom tag library that facilitates creating user interfaces that are fully internationalized, and that interact gracefully with `ActionForm` beans that are part of the Model portion of the system.

In addition to JSP pages, with the action and custom tags they contain, it is frequently necessary for business objects to be able to render themselves in HTML (or XML), based on their current state at the time of the request. The rendered output from such objects can easily be included in a resulting JSP page by using the `<jsp:include>` standard action tag.

The Controller: `ActionServlet` and `ActionMapping`

The center of the application flow is, predictably, the Controller. The Controller focuses on receiving requests from the client, deciding what business logic is to be performed, and then delegating responsibility for moving to the next state of the user interface to an appropriate View component. In Struts, the key component of the Controller is a servlet of class `ActionServlet`. You configure this servlet and make it useful by defining a set of mappings. Basically, the mappings pair each request with an action—for example, if the response in state 1 is "success", go to state 2. Each mapping defines a path that is matched against the request URI of the incoming request and the fully qualified class name of an Action class (that is, a Java class extending the Action class). This Action class is responsible for performing the matching business logic and then dispatching control to the appropriate View component, which creates the response.

Struts supports the use of `ActionMapping` classes that have additional properties beyond the standard ones required to operate the framework. This allows storage of additional information specific to your application, while still utilizing the remaining features of the framework. In addition, Struts lets you define logical "names" to which control should be forwarded so that an action method can ask for the "Main Menu" page without knowing what the actual name of the corresponding JSP page is. These features greatly assist you in separating the control logic (What do I do next?) from the view logic (What is the name of the corresponding page?).

Conclusion: JSP Pages Are a Big Part of the Enterprise Java Solution

JSP and Java Servlet technologies offer advantages provided by the Java language. They are a mature yet simplified solution applicable to both large and small applications. They offer

- Portability across platforms and servers
- Robust exception management and memory management
- Access to the wide range of Java APIs (JDBC, JavaMail, and so on)

JSP and Java Servlet technologies are part of the Java 2 Platform, Enterprise Edition (J2EE), and provide a highly flexible and scalable solution for building multitier applications in the enterprise environment. They can use Enterprise JavaBeans and other J2EE components and containers that include a wide range of application capability. They also provide multithreaded processing and multiple concurrent requests, supporting applications with large numbers of concurrent users.

In conclusion, using JSP and Java Servlet technologies helps give all the benefits of Java technology for rapid application deployment and application maintenance. Servlets and JSP pages can support large-scale interactive Web applications in the enterprise environment with a distributed development model. Web developers can create cross-platform application components as JavaBeans, Enterprise JavaBeans, or customized tag libraries. Page authors can employ a simplified interface to integrate this logic into their page designs.

JSP Pages: Advantages Over Servlets Alone

Although JSP pages can jumpstart servlet development, they are only part of the story. Even if you're comfortable writing servlets, there are several convincing reasons to consider using JSP technology to complement your existing work:

- JSP technology is built on servlets. It is an extension of the servlet technology created to support authoring of HTML and XML pages. It simplifies the combination of fixed or static template data with dynamic content. With JSP technology, pages are dynamically compiled into servlets; therefore, they have all of the benefits of servlets in addition to having access to Java APIs.
- JSP technology is easier to use for interactive pages. Although you can certainly create dynamic, interactive pages with servlets alone, using JSP technology makes the process easier.
- With JSP pages, you can combine static templates, including HTML or XML fragments, with the code to generate dynamic content.
- JSP pages compile dynamically into servlets when requested. They can also be precompiled into servlets.
- The JSP page structure facilitates the manual page authoring process.
- The JSP tags for invoking JavaBeans components manage these components completely. This allows the page author to concentrate on presentation.
- The JSP page structure also supports authoring tools like SilverStream's JSP designer; such tools are now becoming more readily available.
- Most importantly, JSP technology provides developers with a way to distribute application functionality to a wide range of page authors. As mentioned, these authors do not have to know the Java language or even be able to write servlets.

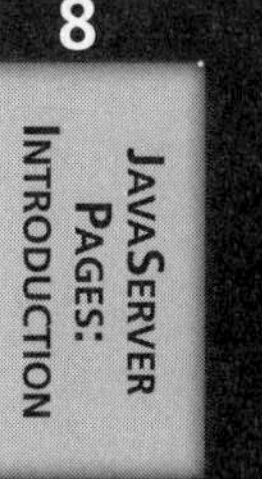

Working with Your Existing Servlets

Because JSP technology is an extension of the servlet technology, JSP pages and servlets work well together. JSP pages compile into servlets and they can include/forward servlets. Servlets can include/forward JSP pages.

If servlets are already utilized in your Web-based applications, JSP technology can provide even faster deployment, easier maintenance, and better page authoring support. By separating logic from the page design, JSP pages allow maintenance of individual pages to occur at different times than maintenance of the core application logic components. Through use of customized tag libraries, application functionality can be easily distributed to a wide range of page authors. This provides more time to focus on application architecture and create new applications. In short, while servlets may serve the current need for dynamic content, JSP technology will bring significant long-term benefits to organizations deploying dynamic, Web-based applications.

CHAPTER 9

JavaServer Pages: Practical Development with Tag Libraries

IN THIS CHAPTER

- JSP Syntax *258*
- Tag Libraries *282*

The purpose of this chapter is to help you to understand JavaServer Pages. You will learn the main concepts of developing programs using JSP.

JSP Syntax

In this section we'll explore JSP syntax, providing examples that illustrate its use.

JSP Comments

Two types of comments can be used within JSP blocks: HTML comments that are sent back to the client and hidden comments that are part of JSP itself.

Note that you can also place standard Java comments in JSP with the scripting language used in the page. For instance, comments can be added as follows:

```
<% /* this is a Java Comment */ %>
```

```
<% // this is also a Java Comment %>
```

HTML Comments

A typical HTML comment generates a comment that is sent to the client. HTML comments within JSP files operate very similarly to any other HTML comments. They document the file and are viewable in the page source from the Web browser.

Expressions can be used in an HTML comment in a JSP file. These expressions are dynamic and are evaluated when the page is loaded or reloaded in the Web browser. Any expression that is valid in the page scripting language can be used.

Syntax

The syntax of an HTML comment is as follows:

```
<!--  comment -->
```

Examples

The following are examples of HTML comments that are output to the client.

Example 1:

```
<!-- Simple Comments -->
```

displays in the page source as

```
<!-- Simple Comments -->
```

Example 2:

```
<!-- If it's important to know, this page was loaded on
    <%= (new java.util.Date()).toLocaleString() %> -->
```

displays in the page source as

```
<!-- If it's important to know, this page was loaded on June 28, 2001 -->
```

Hidden Comments

Hidden comments aren't sent to the client; they mark text or lines that the JSP container should ignore. The JSP container doesn't process anything within the `<%--` and `--%>` characters. This is useful for hiding blocks of code for testing purposes.

You can use any characters in the body of the comment except the closing `--%>` combination. If you need to use `--%>` in your comment, you can escape it by typing **`--%\>`**.

Syntax

Hidden comments are written as follows:

```
<%-- This comment is not visible to the client --%>
```

Example

Here is an example of hidden comments:

```
<%@ page language="java" %>
<html>
<head><title>A Comment Test</title></head>
<body>
<h2>A Test of Comments</h2>
<%-- This comment will not be visible in the page source --%>
</body>
</html>
```

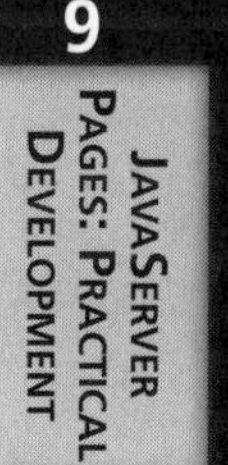

JSP Directives

JSP directives are used to define and set attributes that apply to the entire JSP page and the resulting servlet. A directive affects the overall structure of the servlet class.

The syntax of a directive is

```
<%@directive attr_name=value %>
```

You can also combine multiple attribute settings as follows:

```
<%@ directive attrone="valueOne"
attrtwo="valueTwo"
```

```
...
attrN="valueN" %>
```

Three types of JSP directives are as follows:

- include
- page
- taglib

include Directive

The include directive is used to instruct the JSP container to insert text into a JSP page at translation time. Later in this chapter, we'll introduce the include action used to insert text at runtime.

The included file can be an HTML file, a JSP file, a text file, or a code file written in the Java programming language.

Syntax

The syntax for an include directive is as follows:

```
<%@ include file="fileName" %>
```

Attributes

```
file="fileName"
```

The attribute "fileName" can be an HTML file, a JSP file, a text file, or a code file written in the Java programming language.

You might also specify the pathname to the included file, which is always a relative URL. A relative URL is the path segment of a URL, without the inclusion of a protocol, port, or domain name, like this:

```
"header.jsp"
"/templates/search.html"
"/beans/calendar.jsp"
```

It is important to know that if the relative URL starts with /, the path is relative to the JSP application's context, which is a javax.servlet.ServletContext object stored in the application object. Conversely, if the relative URL begins with a directory or filename, the path is relative to the current JSP file.

Examples: JSP Date Time

Listing 9.1 is the JSP page that will be included in another page.

LISTING 9.1 jspDateTime.jsp

```
<%@ page import="java.util.*" %>
<P><FONT SIZE=2 COLOR="#2C547C" FACE="Helvetica">
<SPAN STYLE="font-size:11;">
The current date and time:
<%= (new java.util.Date() ).toLocaleString() %>
</SPAN></FONT>
```

The output of the jspDateTime.jsp file is shown in Figure 9.1.

FIGURE 9.1
Output of jspDateTime.jsp.

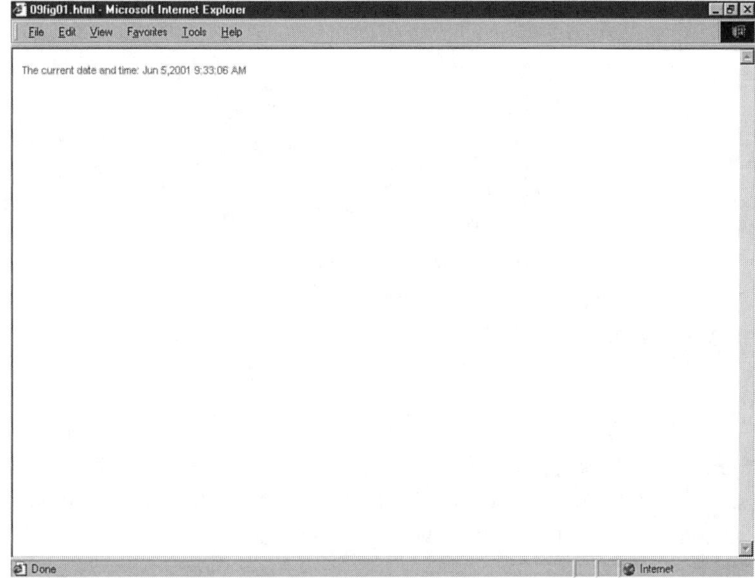

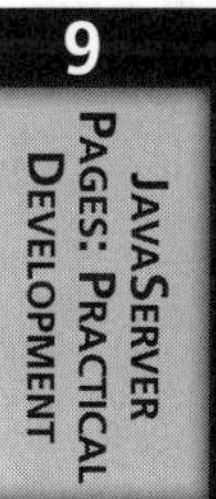

Listing 9.2 is the JSP main page that uses the `include` tag.

LISTING 9.2 jspIncludeDirective.jsp

```
<HTML>
<HEAD>
<TITLE>JSP Include Directive</TITLE>
</HEAD>
<BODY BGCOLOR="#EDF1C8">
This is the Main Page.
<BR>
<%@ include file="jspDateTime.jsp" %>
</BODY>
</HTML>
```

The output of the jspIncludeDirective.jsp file is shown in Figure 9.2.

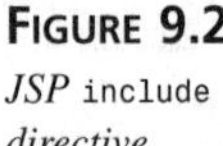

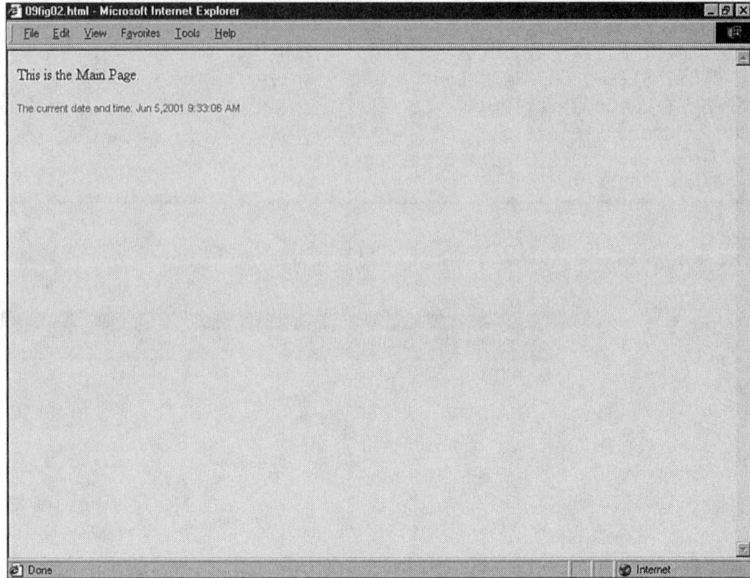

FIGURE 9.2
JSP `include` *directive.*

page Directive

A JSP page has attributes that describe its runtime behavior. The `page` directive is used to define one or more attributes for the whole JSP page.

You can use the `<%@ page %>` directive more than once in a translation unit, but you can use each attribute only once, except for the `import` attribute. The `import` attribute is similar to the `import` statement in the Java programming language.

No matter where you position the `<%@ page %>` directive in a JSP file or included file, it applies to the entire translation unit.

Syntax

The syntax of the `page` directive is

```
<%@ page attributes %>
```

Attributes

The syntax in Listing 9.3 lists all `page` directive attributes.

LISTING 9.3 Attributes of page Directives

```
<%@ page
    [ language="Scripting Language" ]
    [ extends="ClassName" ]
    [ import="{package.class | package.*}, ..." ]
    [ session="true|false" ]
    [ buffer="none|8kb|sizekb" ]
    [ autoFlush="true|false" ]
    [ isThreadSafe="true|false" ]
    [ info="text" ]
    [ errorPage="relativeURL" ]
    [ contentType="mimeType [ ;charset=characterSet ]" |
        "text/html ; charset=ISO-8859-1" ]
    [ isErrorPage="true|false" ]
%>
```

In the following list, we will describe each attribute separately:

- `language="Scripting Language"`—This attribute defines the scripting language used in scriptlets, declarations, and expressions in the JSP file and any included files. The default value is `java`.
- `extends="ClassName"`—The fully qualified name of the superclass of the Java class file this JSP file will be compiled to.
- `import="{package.class | package.*}, ..."`—A comma-separated list of Java packages that the JSP file should import. More than one package can be imported by specifying a comma-separated list after import. `import` can also be used more than once in a JSP file.

  The following packages are implicitly imported:

  ```
  java.lang.*
  javax.servlet.*
  javax.servlet.jsp.*
  javax.servlet.http.*
  ```

  Any `import` attribute must be placed before the element that calls the imported class.
- `session="true|false"`—The session attribute can be set to `true` if the client must join a session in order to use the JSP page. If the value is `false`, the `session` variable isn't available to scripting elements in your page. The default value is `true`.
- `buffer="none|8KB|sizeKB"`—Defines the buffer size in kilobytes for the page. The default value is 8KB. If you specify a buffer size, the output is buffered with at least the size you specified. You can disable buffering by specifying `none`.

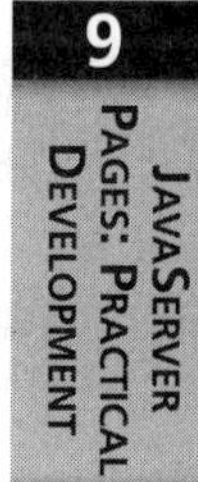

- `autoFlush="true|false"`—The value of this attribute specifies whether the buffered output should be flushed automatically when the page buffer is full. The default value is `true`.
- `IsThreadSafe="true|false"`—Specifies whether thread safety is implemented in the JSP file. The default value is `true`, meaning that the JSP container is able to send multiple, concurrent client requests to the JSP page. You must write code in the JSP page to synchronize the multiple client threads. If `false` is used, the JSP container will send client requests one at a time to the JSP page.
- `info="text"`—Specifies an informative text string that is incorporated verbatim into the compiled JSP page. The container can later retrieve the text for administrative purposes.
- `errorPage="relativeURL"`—Defines the pathname to a JSP file that your JSP page forwards any exceptions.
- `isErrorPage="true|false"`—Determines whether the JSP file is used as an error page. The default value is `false`.
- `contentType="mimeType [; charset=characterSet ]" |"text/html;charset=ISO-8859-1"`—Defines the MIME type for the response. You can use any MIME type or character sets that are valid for the JSP container. The default MIME type is `text/html` and the default character set is `ISO-8859-1`.

Examples

Here is an example of the `page` directive:

```
<%@ page import="java.util.*, java.sql.*" %>

<%@ page import="java.text.*" %>

<%@ page errorPage="jspError.jsp" %>
```

`taglib` Directive

The popular design of Web applications strives for separation of view from business logic. Tag libraries facilitate this separation. Basically, a tag library is an encapsulation of a behavior that makes it possible to use the behavior on many JSP pages.

The `<%@ taglib %>` directive declares that the JSP file uses custom tags, names the tag library that defines them, and specifies their tag prefix. The `taglib` directive introduces an additional library of tags.

Later in this chapter we'll describe how to write custom tag libraries in more detail.

Syntax

The syntax for `taglib` directives is as follows:

```
<%@ taglib uri="URIToTagLibrary"  prefix="tagPrefix" %>
```

Attributes

The following list describes attributes of `taglib` directives:

- `uri="URIToTagLibrary"`—This attribute is the *Uniform Resource Identifier (URI)* that uniquely names the set of custom tags associated with the named tag prefix. It specifies where to find the tag library description.
- `prefix="tagPrefix"`—This attribute defines the prefix, which is unique for the tag library. Empty prefixes are illegal.

Example

Here is an example of a `taglib` directive:

```
<%@ taglib uri="/emplTags" prefix="empl" %>
```

JSP Scripting Elements

JSP scripting elements allow Java code to be inserted into the servlet that will be generated from the defined JSP page.

Three types of JSP scripting elements are as follows:

- Declarations
- Scriptlets
- Expressions

Declarations

A JSP declaration allows you to define methods or variables that get inserted into the main body of the servlet class.

Such methods or variables are valid in the scripting language used in the JSP page. You must declare the variables or methods before you use them in your JSP file.

Much like hidden comments, if you need to use the characters `%>`, you can escape them by typing `%\>`.

Syntax

The syntax for a declaration is as follows:

```
<%! declaration; [ declaration; ]+   ... %>
```

An XML equivalent can also be used:

```
<jsp:declaration>
declaration;
</jsp:declaration>
```

Example

The following is a simple example of a JSP declaration:

```
<%! int iStart = 500; %>
<%! int a, b, c; %>
<%! String sMessage = "HPD Users"; %>
```

Scriptlets

JSP scriptlets give you the ability to insert arbitrary code into the servlet method that will be built to generate the page. A scriptlet can include any quantity of language statements, variable or method declarations, or expressions that are valid in the page scripting language. Text, HTML tags, and JSP elements must exist outside the scriptlet.

Syntax

Scriptlet syntax is as follows:

```
<% java_code %>
```

The XML equivalent can also be used:

```
<jsp:scriptlet>
java_code
</jsp:scriptlet>
```

Example

Here is an example of a JSP scriptlet:

```
<%
    String sLoginID = null;
    if (request.getParameter("LOGINID") == null) {
%>
<%@ include file="jspError.html" %>
<%
} else {
beanUserInfo.setName(request.getParameter("LOGINID"));
}
%>
```

Expressions

An expression element contains an expression that is valid in the scripting language used in the JSP page. Expressions are used to insert values directly into the output. The value is evaluated, converted to a string, and inserted where the expression appears in your JSP file.

Syntax

The syntax of an expression is as follows:

```
<%= expression %>
```

The XML equivalent can also be used:

```
<jsp:expression>
expression
</expression>
```

Example

A JSP expression looks like this:

```
The current time is: <%= new java.util.Date() %>
```

JSP Actions

When a request is sent to a JSP page from a client, the JSP actions within the page are executed. These JSP actions are constructed inside the JSP page using XML syntax.

JSP actions include dynamically inserting a file, implementing user-input validation by using JavaBeans components, forwarding the user to another page, or handling database access.

In the next sections, we will discuss the following actions:

- `<jsp:useBean>`
- `<jsp:getProperty>`
- `<jsp:setProperty>`
- `<jsp:include>`
- `<jsp:forward>`
- `<jsp:plugin>`

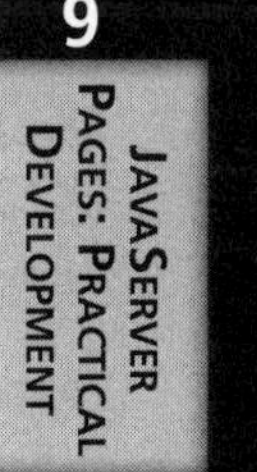

<jsp:useBean>

A JavaBean is a special type of class that has a number of methods. The JSP specification includes standard tags for using and manipulating beans. The `accessor` method is a public method defined in a bean that reads or writes the value of a property. A `getter` method is an accessor method that reads, or gets, the value of a property. A `setter` method is an `accessor` method that writes, or sets, the value of a property.

The <jsp:useBean> action is used to locate or instantiate a JavaBeans component that will be used in the JSP page. This is very useful because it facilitates the reuse of Java classes without sacrificing the convenience that JSP adds over servlets alone.

When using this action, the Web container will first attempt to locate an instance of the bean using the `id` and the `scope` attributes. If the bean isn't found, the container will instantiate it from a class or serialized template.

It is important to note that the <jsp:useBean> doesn't support Enterprise JavaBeans. In order to use Enterprise JavaBeans, a <jsp:useBean> element can be written to calls a standard JavaBean that will in turn call the enterprise bean. A custom tag that calls an enterprise bean directly can also be written.

Syntax

Listing 9.4 defines an instance of a JavaBean.

LISTING 9.4 useBean syntax

```
<jsp: useBean id="name"
scope=" page| request| session| application"
typeSpec >
body
</jsp: useBean>
```

Attributes and Usage

The <jsp:useBean> attributes are listed and described here:

- `id="Name"`—A variable that identifies the case-sensitive name. This variable name is used in expressions or scriptlets in the JSP file. The name must conform to the naming conventions of the scripting language used in the JSP page. If the bean has already been created by another <jsp:useBean> element, the value of `id` must match the value of `id` that was used in the original <jsp:useBean> element.
- `scope="page|request|session|application"`—The scope in which the bean exists and the variable named in `id` is available. The default value is `page`.

  Table 9.1 provides a reference for the meanings of the different JSP page scopes.

TABLE 9.1 JSP Page Scope

Scope	*Description*
`page`	Object is accessible only by a single client from the page on which it is created. This is the default scope for a JavaBean, which stores the object in the `javax.servlet.jsp.PageContext` of the current page.

TABLE 9.1 continued

Scope	*Description*
`request`	Object is accessible by a single client for the lifetime of a single client request. It is stored in the current `ServletRequest`, and it is available to other included JSP pages that are passed the same request object. The object is discarded when the current request is completed.
`session`	Object is accessible by a single client from anywhere in the application for the lifetime of an entire user session. The reference to the JavaBean is stored in the page's `HttpSession` object.
`application`	Object is accessible by any client from any page within the application for the lifetime of the application. Your JavaBean object is stored in the Web application.

- `class="package.class"`—Instantiates a bean from a class using the new keyword and the class constructor. The class cannot be abstract. Additionally, it must have a public, no-argument constructor. Both the package and class name are case sensitive.
- `type="package.class"`—If the bean already exists in the scope, this will give the bean a data type other than the class from which it was instantiated. The value of `type` must be either a superclass of `class` or an interface implemented by `class`. If `type` is used without either `class` or `beanName`, no bean will be instantiated. Both package and class name are case sensitive.
- `class="package.class" type="package.class"`—Instantiates a bean from the class named in `class` and assigns the bean the data type specified in `type`. The value of `type` can be equal to that of `class`, a superclass of `class`, or an interface implemented by `class`. The class specified in `class` cannot be abstract. Additionally, it must have a public, no-argument constructor. The package and classnames used with both `class` and `type` are case sensitive.
- `beanName="{package.class | <%= expression %>}" type="package.class"`—Instantiates a bean from a class, a serialized template, or an expression that evaluates to a class or serialized template. When `beanName` is used, the bean is instantiated by the `java.beans.Beans.instantiate` method. The `Beans.instantiate` method checks whether the package and class you specify represents a class or a serialized template. If it represents a serialized template, `Beans.instantiate` reads the serialized form (which has a name similar to `package.class.ser`) using a class loader. The value of `type` can be equal to that of `beanName`, a superclass of `beanName`, or an interface implemented by `beanName`. The package and classnames used with both `beanName` and `type` are case sensitive.

Examples

In these examples, we'll create a JavaBean called `userInfo` and a JSP page that uses our JavaBean.

The `userInfo` bean resembles the code in Listing 9.5.

LISTING 9.5 `userInfo`

```
package chapter09.beans;
public class userInfo implements java.io.Serializable {
  private String last_name;
  private String first_name;
  private String phone;
  private String email;
  public userInfo() {}
  public String getLastName() {
    return last_name;
  }
  public void setLastName(String lastName) {
    last_name = lastName;
  }
  public String getFirstName() {
    return first_name;
  }
  public void setFirstName(String firstName) {
    first_name= firstName;
  }
  public String getPhone() {
    return phone;
  }
  public void setPhone(String p) {
    phone = p;
  }
  public String getEmail() {
    return email;
  }
  public void setEmail(String e) {
    email = e;
  }
}
```

Listing 9.6 is a JSP page that calls `userInfo`.

LISTING 9.6 JSP Page to Call `userInfo`

```
<%@ page import="chapter09.beans.userInfo" %>
<%@ page import="java.util.*" %>
<jsp:useBean id="user"
```

LISTING 9.6 continued

```
            class="userInfo"
            scope="page" />
<HTML>
<HEAD>
    <TITLE>User Information</TITLE>
</HEAD>
<BODY>
<TABLE BORDER=1 CELLSPACING=2 CELLPADDING=2>
<TR VALIGN="top">
    <TD ALIGN="right"><B>Last Name:</BR></TD>
    <TD><INPUT TYPE="Text" NAME="lname" VALUE="<%= user.getLastName() %>"
MAXLENGTH="30" SIZE="20">
    </TD>
</TR>
<TR VALIGN="top">
    <TD ALIGN="right"><B>First Name:</BR></TD>
    <TD><INPUT TYPE="Text" NAME="fname" VALUE="<%= user.getFirstName() %>"
MAXLENGTH="30" SIZE="20">
    </TD>
</TR>
<TR VALIGN="top">
    <TD ALIGN="right"><B>Phone:</BR></TD>
    <TD><INPUT TYPE="Text" NAME="phone" VALUE="<%= user.getPhone() %>"
MAXLENGTH="30" SIZE="20">
    </TD>
</TR>
<TR VALIGN="top">
    <TD ALIGN="right"><B>Email:</BR></TD>
    <TD><INPUT TYPE="Text" NAME="email" VALUE="<%= user.getEmail() %>"
MAXLENGTH="30" SIZE="20">
    </TD>
</TR>
</TABLE>
</BODY>
</HTML>
```

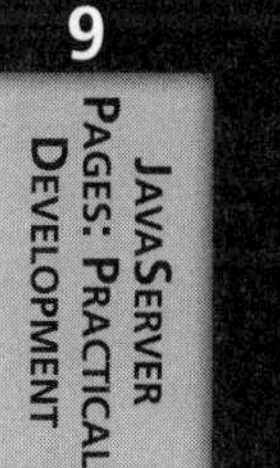

<jsp:getProperty>

Bean classes have `set` and `get` methods, which enable JSP pages to access properties. Beans can be instantiated, and the properties can then be called from within the JSP.

The `<jsp:getProperty>` element gets a bean property value using the property's `get` methods and displays the property value in a JSP page. A bean must be created or located with `<jsp:useBean>` before `<jsp:getProperty>` can be used.

Syntax

The syntax for this method is as follows:

```
<jsp:getProperty name="examplebean"  property="propertyName" />
```

Attributes

The `<jsp:getProperty>` attributes are listed and described here:

- `name="examplebean"`—The name of an object as declared in a `<jsp:useBean>` element.
- `property="propertyName"`—The name of the bean property whose value you want to display. The property is declared as a variable in a bean and must have a corresponding `get` method.

Example

Here is an example of `<jsp:getProperty>`:

```
<jsp:useBean id="saletax" scope="page" class="beans.tax" />
<H2>
State Tax: <jsp:getProperty name="saletax" property="curr_tax" />
</H2>
```

<jsp:setProperty>

Using the bean's `setter` methods, the `<jsp:setProperty>` element is used to set the value of one or more properties in a bean. The bean must be declared with `<jsp:useBean>` before a property value can be set with `<jsp:setProperty>`. Because `<jsp:useBean>` and `<jsp:setProperty>` work jointly, the bean instance names used in each must match. In other words, the value of `name` in `<jsp:setProperty>` must be the same as the value of `id` in `<jsp:useBean>`.

Syntax

The `<jsp:setProperty>` syntax looks like this:

```
<jsp:setProperty
        name="beanInstanceName"
    {    property="*" |
        property="propertyName" [ param="parameterName" ] |
        property="propertyName" value="{string | <%= expression %>}"
    }
/>
```

Attributes and Usage

- `name="beanInstanceName"`—The name of a bean instance that has already been created or located using a `<jsp:useBean>` element. The value of `name` must be the same as the value of `id` in `<jsp:useBean>`. The `<jsp:useBean>` element must appear before `<jsp:setProperty>` in the JSP file.

- `property="*"`—Stores all the values the user enters in the viewable JSP page (called *request parameters*) in matching bean properties. The names of the properties in the bean must be the same as the names of the request parameters. These parameters are often the elements of an HTML form.

  The values of the request parameters that are sent from the client to the server are always of type `String`. The `String` values are converted to other types of data in order to be stored in bean properties. The bean property types that are allowed, along with their conversion methods, are shown in Table 9.2.

  `<jsp:setProperty>` can also be used to set the value of an indexed property in a bean. The indexed property must be an array of one of the data types displayed in Table 9.2. These array elements are converted using the conversion methods that are also shown in the table.

  If a request parameter has an empty or null value, the corresponding bean property isn't set. Similarly, if the bean has a property that is without a matching request parameter, the property value isn't set.

TABLE 9.2 Converting Strings to Other Values with `<jsp:setProperty>`

Property Type	*String Is Converted Using*
`boolean` or `Boolean`	`java.lang.Boolean.valueOf(String)`
`byte` or `Byte`	`java.lang.Byte.valueOf(String)`
`char` or `Character`	`java.lang.Character.valueOf(String)`
`double` or `Double`	`java.lang.Double.valueOf(String)`
`integer` or `Integer`	`java.lang.Integer.valueOf(String)`
`float` or `Float`	`java.lang.Float.valueOf(String)`
`long` or `Long`	`java.lang.Long.valueOf(String)`

- `property="propertyName" [ param="parameterName" ]`—Sets one bean property to the value of one request parameter. In the syntax, `property` specifies the name of the bean property and `param` specifies the name of the request parameter by which data is being sent from the client to the server. If the bean property and the request parameter have different names, both `property` and `param` must be specified. If the names are the same, you can specify `property` and omit `param`. The corresponding bean property won't be set if a parameter has an empty or null value.

- `property="propertyName" value="{string | <%= expression %>}"`—Sets one bean property to a specific value. The value can be a string or an expression that is evaluated at runtime. If the value is a string, it is converted to the bean property's data type according to the conversion rules shown in Table 9.2. If it is an expression, its value must have a data type that matches the data type or the value of the expression must match the data type of the bean property.

  The corresponding bean property won't be set if a parameter has an empty or null value. It isn't possible to use both the `param` and `value` attributes in a `<jsp:setProperty>` element.

Example

Here is an example of `<setProperty>`:

```
<jsp:setProperty name="testbean" property="*" />
<jsp:setProperty name="testbean" property="loginid" />
<jsp:setProperty name="testbean" property="loginid" value="admin" />
```

<jsp:include>

To promote object reuse and consistency, a `<jsp:include>` can be used to include a static file or send a request to a dynamic file. In the case of a static file, the content is included in calling the JSP file. With a dynamic file, a request is acted upon, sending back a result that is included in the JSP page. When the include action is finished, the JSP container continues processing the remainder of the JSP file. A `<jsp:param>` clause can be used if the included file is dynamic, passing the name and value of a parameter to the dynamic file. As an example, you could pass the string `username` and a user's name to a login form that is coded in a JSP file.

Syntax

The syntax for these elements is as follows:

```
<jsp:include page="{relativeURL | <%= expression %>}" flush="true" />
```

or:

```
<jsp:include page="{relativeURL | <%= expression %>}" flush="true" >
      <jsp:param name="parameterName"
        value="{parameterValue | <%= expression %>}" />
</jsp:include>
```

Attributes

The `<jsp:include>` attributes are listed and described here:

- `page="{relativeURL | <%= expression %>}"`—As you have seen in other JSP directives, this is the relative URL that locates the file to be included or an expression that evaluates to a string equivalent to the relative URL.
- `flush="true"`—You must include `flush="true"` because it isn't a default value. The value cannot be `false`. The `flush` attribute should be used exactly as it is given here.
- `<jsp:param name="parameterName" value="{parameterValue | <%= expression %>}" />`—The `<jsp:param>` clause allows you to pass one or more name/value pairs as parameters to an included file. This included file should be dynamic, such as a JSP file, servlet, or any other file that can process the parameter.

  More than one `<jsp:param>` clause can be used if you want to send more than one parameter to the included file. The `name` attribute specifies the parameter name, taking a case-sensitive literal string. The `value` attribute specifies the parameter value, taking either a case-sensitive literal string or an expression that is evaluated at request time.

Example

Here is an example of `<jsp:include>`:

```
<jsp:include page="/header.html" />
<jsp:include page="/loginPage.jsp">
    <jsp:param name="loginid" value="zd" />
</jsp:include>
```

`<jsp:forward>`

A `<jsp:forward>` tag forwards or passes control of a client request to an HTML file, JSP file, or servlet for processing. The `<jsp:forward>` element forwards the request object including request data from one JSP to another. The target file can be HTML, another JSP, or a servlet.

You can send parameters (names and values) to the target by using a `<jsp:param>` clause. An example of this would be passing the parameter name `username` (with `name="username"`) and the value `michael` (with `value="michael"`) to a servlet login file as part of the request. Obviously, if you use `<jsp:param>`, the target should be able to handle the parameters.

Syntax

The syntax for these tags is as follows:

```
<jsp:forward page="{relativeURL | <%= expression %>}" />
```

or

```
<jsp:forward page="{relativeURL | <%= expression %>}" >
    <jsp:param name="parameterName"
        value="{parameterValue | <%= expression %>}" />
</jsp:forward>
```

Attributes

The `<jsp:forward>` attributes are listed and described here:

- `page="{relativeURL | <%= expression %>}"`—This demonstrates a string or an expression representing the relative URL of the file to which you are forwarding the request. The file can be another JSP, a servlet, or any other dynamic file that can handle a request object.

  The relative URL looks like a path file, meaning it doesn't contain an IP protocol, port number, or domain name. The URL can be absolute or relative to the current JSP file. If it is absolute, thus beginning with a `/`, the path is resolved by the Web or application server. For example, in SilverStream that might be c:/silverstream4/bin.

- `<jsp:param name="parameterName" value="{parameterValue | <%= expression %>}" />`—This sends one or more name/value pairs as parameters to a dynamic file. The `name` attribute specifies the parameter name, taking a case-sensitive literal string as a value. The `value` attribute specifies the parameter value, taking either a case-sensitive literal string or an expression that will be evaluated at request time.

Example

A `<jsp:forward>` example:

```
<jsp:forward page="/servlet/login" />
<jsp:forward page="/servlet/login">
    <jsp:param name="loginid" value="admin" />
</jsp:forward>
```

<jsp:plugin>

This element executes an applet or bean and, if necessary, downloads a Java plug-in to execute it.

When the JSP file has been translated and compiled, sending an HTML response back to the client, the `<jsp:plugin>` element is replaced by either an `<object>` or `<embed>` element, according to the browser version. The `<object>` element is defined in HTML 4.0 and `<embed>` is defined in HTML 3.2.

In general, the attributes to the `<jsp:plugin>` element specify whether the object is a bean or an applet, locate the code that will be run, position the object in the browser window, specify an URL from which to download the plug-in software, and pass parameter names and values to the object.

Syntax

Listing 9.7 shows the syntax of `<jsp:plugin>`.

LISTING 9.7 The `plugin` Syntax

```
<jsp:plugin
    type="bean|applet"
    code="classFileName"
    codebase="classFileDirectoryName"
    [ name="instanceName" ]
    [ archive="URIToArchive, ..." ]
    [ align="bottom|top|middle|left|right" ]
    [ height="displayPixels" ]
    [ width="displayPixels" ]
    [ hspace="leftRightPixels" ]
    [ vspace="topBottomPixels" ]
    [ jreversion="JREVersionNumber | 1.1" ]
    [ nspluginurl="URLToPlugin" ]
    [ iepluginurl="URLToPlugin" ] >
    [ <jsp:params>
        [ <jsp:param name="parameterName"
            value="{parameterValue | <%= expression %>}" /> ]+
    </jsp:params> ]
    [ <jsp:fallback> text message for user </jsp:fallback> ]
</jsp:plugin>
```

Attributes

The `<jsp:plugin>` attributes are listed and described below:

- `type="bean|applet"`—Defines the type of the component. You must specify either bean or applet because this attribute has no default value.
- `code="classFileName"`—Demonstrates the method of signifying the name of the Java class file the plug-in will execute. The .class extension must be included in the name. The specified file should be in the directory named in the `codebase` attribute.

- `codebase="classFileDirectoryName"`—Defines the directory (or path to the directory) that contains the Java class file the plug-in will execute. If a value is not supplied, the path of the JSP file that calls `<jsp:plugin>` is used.
- `name="instanceName"`—The name for the instance of the bean or applet that makes it possible for applets or beans called by the same JSP file to communicate with each other.
- `archive="URIToArchive, ..."`—Shows a comma-separated list of pathnames that locate archive files that will be preloaded with a class loader located in the directory named in codebase. These archive files are loaded securely over a network, improving the applet's performance.
- `align="bottom|top|middle|left|right"`—The position of the image, object, or applet. In the following position descriptions , the term text line means the line in the viewable JSP page that corresponds to the line in the JSP file where the `<jsp:plugin>` element appears. The values accepted for `align` are
    - `bottom`—Aligns the bottom of the image with the baseline of the text line.
    - `top`—Aligns the top of the image with the top of the text line.
    - `middle`—Aligns the vertical center of the image with the baseline of the text line.
    - `left`—Floats the image to the left margin and flows text along the image's right side.
    - `right`—Floats the image to the right margin and flows text along the image's left side.
- `height="displayPixels"` and `width="displayPixels"`—The initial height and width, in pixels, of the image the applet or bean displays, not counting any windows or dialog boxes the applet or bean brings up.
- `hspace=leftRightPixels"` and `vspace="topBottomPixels"`—The amount of space, in pixels, to the left and right (or top and bottom) of the image the applet or bean displays. The value must be a nonzero number. The `hspace` attribute creates space to both the left and right, while `vspace` creates space to both the top and bottom.
- `jreversion="JREVersionNumber|1.1"`—The version of the *Java Runtime Environment (JRE)* the applet or bean requires. The default value is 1.1.
- `nspluginurl="URLToPlugin"`—The URL where the user can download the JRE plug-in for Netscape Navigator. The value is a full URL, complete with protocol name, optional port number, and domain name.

- `iepluginurl= "URLToPlugin"`—The URL where the user can download the JRE plug-in for Internet Explorer. The value is a full URL, with a protocol name, optional port number, and domain name.
- `<jsp:params> [ <jsp:param name="parameterName" value="{parameterValue | <%= expression %>}" /> ]+</jsp:params>`—The parameters and values that you want to pass to the applet or bean. To specify more than one parameter value, more than one `<jsp:param>` element can be used within the `<jsp:params>` element.

  The `name` attribute indicates the parameter name, taking a case-sensitive literal string. The `value` attribute indicates the parameter value, taking either a case-sensitive literal string or an expression that will be evaluated at runtime.

  If the dynamic file to which the parameter is being passed is an applet, it will read the parameter with the `java.applet.Applet.getParameter` method.
- `<jsp:fallback> text message for user </jsp:fallback>`—A text message displays to the user if the plug-in cannot be started. If the plug-in begins but the applet or bean doesn't, the plug-in will normally display a pop-up window to explain the error to the user.

Example

Here is an example of `<jsp:plugin>`:

```
<jsp:plugin type=applet code="Molecule.class" codebase="/html">
    <jsp:params>
        <jsp:param name="molecule" value="molecules/benzene.mol" />
    </jsp:params>
    <jsp:fallback>
        <p>Unable to load applet</p>
    </jsp:fallback>
</jsp:plugin>
```

How the JSP Page Is Compiled

It is very important to understand how a JSP page is compiled after a user has loaded it into a Web browser. The first time a user makes a request to a JSP page, the JSP container will handle the request. The requested JSP page is translated into a Java class, which is then compiled into a Servlet. From then on, each additional request to this JSP page will execute much faster as long as the JSP page isn't modified because the Servlet has already loaded into the Web server memory. If the JSP page is modified, the JSP container will recompile and reload it the next time the page is requested.

The source code of a compiled JSP page contains three methods, which are generated by the JSP container. Two methods are defined in `javax.servlet.jsp.JspPage`:

```
public void jspInit()
```

and

```
public void jspDestroy()
```

The third method is defined in `javax.servlet.jsp.HttpJspPage`:

```
public void _jspService( HttpServletRequest request,
HttpServletResponse response)
throws ServletException, IOException
```

The life cycle of a JSP is as follows:

1. `jspInit()` is called.
2. `jspService()` is called.
3. When the page is no longer needed, `jspDestroy()` is called.

Object Scope

When learning a new technology such as JSP, it is important that we become familiar with syntax and semantics. It is perhaps more important, especially from a design standpoint, to understand the scope or visibility of Java objects within JSP pages that are processing a request. Objects might be created implicitly using JSP directives, explicitly through actions, or, in rare cases, directly using scripting code. The instantiated objects can be associated with a scope attribute defining where there is a reference to the object and when that reference is removed.

Implicit Objects

As a convenience feature, the JSP container makes available implicit objects that can be used within scriptlets and expressions without the page author first having to create them. These objects act as wrappers around underlying Java classes or interfaces typically defined within the Servlet API (see Table 9.3).

TABLE 9.3 Nine Implicit Objects

Implicit Object	*Type*	*Scope*	*Some Useful Methods (see class or interface for others)*
`Request`	Subclass of `javax.servlet.ServletRequest`	request	`getParameter`, `getParameterNames`, `getParameterValues`

TABLE 9.3 continued

Implicit Object	*Type*	*Scope*	*Some Useful Methods (see class or interface for others)*
`Response`	Subclass of `javax.servlet.ServletResponse`	page	Normally not used by JSP page authors
`PageContext`	`javax.servlet.jsp.PageContext`	page	`findAttribute`, `getAttribute`, `getAttributesScope`, `getAttributeNamesInScope`
`Session`	`javax.servlet.http.HttpSession`	session	`getId`, `getValue`, `getValueNames`, `putValue`
`Application`	`javax.servlet.ServletContext`	application	`getMimeType`, `getRealPath`
`Out`	`javax.servlet.jsp.JspWriter`	page	`clear`, `clearBuffer`, `flush`, `getBufferSize`, `getRemaining`
`Config`	`javax.servlet.ServletConfig`	page	`getInitParameter`, `getInitParameterNames`
`Page`	`java.lang.Object`	page	Normally not used by JSP page authors
`Exception`	`java.lang.Throwable`	page	`getMessage`, `getLocalizedMessage`, `printStackTrace`

These implicit objects are only visible within the system-generated `jspService()` method. They aren't visible within methods you define yourself in declarations.

Error Handling

As we mentioned before, some of the page directive attributes are `errorPage` and `isErrorPage`. If there is any exception in the JSP page, the client request is forward to the `errorPage`. The attribute `isErrorPage` must be set to `true` for the error page, which means that the implicit variable `exception` is available and refers to the instance of the `java.long.Throwable`.

The following code is a simple error page, `jspError.jsp`, which will be referenced by our JSP pages:

```
<@page isErrorPage="true" %>
<HTML>
<HEAD>
    <TITLE>Error</TITLE>
</HEAD>
</BODY>
    The following error has occurred: <%= exception.toString() %>
</BODY>
</HTML>
```

The location of the error page file must be placed in the root directory of the application.

To reference our error page in other JSP pages, the attribute `errorPage` must be pointed to the error page. For example:

```
<%page errorPage="/jspError.jsp" %>
```

The second type of error is a translation-time error. This error can occur when the JSP container translates JSP code into a servlet.

Another type of error is a runtime error, which occurs after the JSP has been translated. Usually, runtime errors occur when a problem exists in the JSP page itself.

Tag Libraries

In this section, we will describe tag libraries along with how to build them. *Tag libraries* give you the ability to build libraries of reusable JSP tags where you encapsulate most common behavior and use them across your JSP pages in one or many Web applications.

Declaring Tag Libraries

The `taglib` directive is used to declare that your JSP page will use tags defined in a tag library.

The syntax is as follows:

```
<%@ taglib uri="..." prefix="..." %>
```

The `uri` attribute refers to a URI that uniquely identifies the tag library. There are different ways to define the `uri`, such as

- Placing a reference to a tag library from the Web-application descriptor web.xml file. For example:

  ```
  <%@ taglib uri="deptTag" prefix="dept" %>
  ```

  The reference in web.xml will be defined as

  ```
  <taglib>
  <taglib-uri>deptTag</taglib-uri>
  ```

```
<taglib-location>/WEB-INF/deptTags.tld</taglib-location>
</taglib>
```

- Directly reference an unpacked tag library:

```
<%@ taglib uri="deptTags.tld" prefix="dept" %>
```

- Referencing a jar file that contains the tag library:

```
<%@ taglib uri="/WEB-INF/deptTags.jar" prefix="dept" %>
```

Tag Handler

A *tag handler* is a Java class in which the custom tag's logic is defined. The tag handler must implement one of two interfaces defined in the `javax.servlet.jsp.tagext` package, `Tag` or `BodyTag`.

The `javax.servlet.jsp.tagext.Tag` interface handles the communication between the Web container and the tag handler. This communication passes different phases such as initializing, setting properties, and executing tag handler's methods. The main methods we'll discuss are `doStartTag()` and `doEndTag()`.

The `doStartTag()` is called when the JSP container is about to open the tag during runtime.

The signature is

```
int doStartTag() throws JspException
```

The return value of this method is one of two constants: `EVAL_BODY_INCLUDE` or `SKIP_BODY`.

The second method is `doEndTag()`, which is called when the JSP container is about to close the tag. Its signature is

```
int doEndTag() throws JspException
```

The return value could be the `EVAL_PAGE` constant, which instructs the JSP container to continue evaluating the rest of the page. Or, it could be `SKIP_PAGE`, which instructs the JSP container to terminate the page execution.

The `javax.servlet.jsp.tagext.BodyTag` interface extends `javax.servlet.jsp.tagext.Tag`. It defines new methods to work with the content of the tag.

New steps of the communication between the JSP container and the tag handler are executing `doInitBody()` and `doAfterBody()` methods. The `doAfterBody()` can be called multiple times.

The javax.servlet.jsp.tagext package defines TagSupport and BodyTagSupport classes that implement Tag and BodyTag.

Listing 9.8 illustrates writing a tag handler.

LISTING 9.8 Writing a Tag Handler

```
package chapter09;
import javax.servlet.jsp.*;
import javax.servlet.jsp.tagext.*;
import java.io.*;
public class CorpTag extends TagSupport {
    public int doStartTag() throws JspTagException {
        return EVAL_BODY_INCLUDE;
    }
    public int doEndTag() throws JspTagException {
        try {
        pageContext.getOut().write("Simple Corp. Tag");
        }
        catch(IOException ioe) {
            throw new JspTagException("Exception...");
        }
        return EVAL_PAGE;
    }
}
```

Tag library Descripters (TLD)

Tag Library Descripters (TLD) are simple XML documents that have a .tld extension and define tag extensions. The root element is <taglib>.

The root element is defined in the *Document Type Definition (DTD)* as the following:

```
<!ELEMENT taglib (tlibversion, jspversion, shortname, uri, info, tag)>
```

The following lists and describes taglib attributes:

- tlibversion—Defines the version number of the library. Specified by the developer.
- jspversion—Optionally defines the version of the JSP specification.
- shortname—The tag library's short name.
- uri—Optional Uniform Resource Identifier (URI), usually a URL that defines the library's location.
- info—Optional information about the tag library.

And the <tag> element is defined in DTD as

```
<!ELEMENT tag (name, tagclass, teiclass, bodycontent, info, attribute)>
```

The following lists and describes tag attributes:

- name—The tag's name defined by the developer.
- tagclass—The tag handler class that implements this tag.
- teiclass—Optional subclass TagExtraInfo.
- bodycontent—Optional attribute that defines the body content of the tag.
- info—Information about the tag.
- attribute—Defines the name (required). The rtexprvalue specifies whether the value is a fixed value or is a result of a JSP expression. The rtexprvalue is optional and it defines if the nesting attribute can have scriptlet expressions as a value.

Listing 9.9 shows an example of a tag library descriptor (.tld).

LISTING 9.9 Tag Library Descriptor (.tld)

```
<?xml version="1.0" encoding="ISO-8859-1" ?>
<!DOCTYPE taglib
        PUBLIC "-//Sun Microsystems, Inc.//DTD JSP Tag Library 1.1//EN"
    "http://java.sun.com/j2ee/dtds/web-jsptaglibrary_1_1.dtd">
<taglib>
    <tlibversion>1.0</tlibversion>
    <jspversion>1.1</jspversion>
    <shortname>projectShortName</shortname>
    <uri>http://www.EJDean.com</uri>
    <info>
        Define Information on the tag library
    </info>

    <tag>
        <name>Define the tag Name</name>
        <tagclass>Define the tag Class</tagclass>
        <teiclass>Define tag extra info Class</teiclass>
        <bodycontent>empty|JSP|tagdependent</bodycontent>
        <info>
            Define Information about the tag
        </info>

        <attribute>
            <name>Define the attribute name</name>
            <required>true|false</required>
            <rtexprvalue>true|false</rtexprvalue>
```

LISTING 9.9 continued

```
        </attribute>
    </tag>
</taglib>
```

Creating a Corporation Banner Custom Tag

In the following example, we'll develop a simple custom tag library, a handler class, and a JSP page.

First, we'll create a tag library descriptor named CorpTagLib.tld. This is just a text file with the extension .tld, and it will be located in the WEB-INF directory of the Web Application containing your JSP(s).

Listing 9.10 shows our CorpTagLib.tld file.

LISTING 9.10 CorpTagLib.tld

```
<!DOCTYPE taglib PUBLIC "-//Sun Microsystems, Inc.
//DTD JSP Tag Library 1.1//EN" "web-jsptaglib_1_1.dtd">

<taglib>
    <tlibversion>1.0</tlibversion>
    <jspversion>1.1</jspversion>
    <shortname>corp</shortname>
    <info>Corporate Info</info>

    <tag>
        <name>CorpBannerTag</name>
        <tagclass>chapter09.CorpBannerTag</tagclass>
        <info>Used to display Corporate Banner</info>
       </tag>
</taglib>
```

Next, we'll develop the tag handler, which will define the custom tag's logic. As we mentioned earlier, the handler class must implement the `javax.servlet.jsp.tagext.Tag` interface. The Java file will be CorpBannerTag.java, and its contents are shown in Listing 9.11.

LISTING 9.11 CorpBannerTag.java

```
package chapter09;
import javax.servlet.jsp.*;
import javax.servlet.jsp.tagext.*;
import java.io.*;
```

LISTING 9.11 continued

```
public class CorpBannerTag extends BodyTagSupport {
    private String mCorpName = "My Corp";
    private String mCorpEmail = "HelpDesk@MyCorp.com";

    public int doAfterBody() throws JspTagException {
        BodyContent bc = getBodyContent();
        String body = bc.getString();
        bc.clearBody();
        StringBuffer output = new StringBuffer();

        try {
                      output.append("<font color=\"navy\">");
                      output.append(mCorpName );
                      output.append(" E-mail:" + mCorpEmail);
                      output.append("</font>");
                      getPreviousOut().print(output.toString());
        }
        catch( IPException ioe) {
            throw new JspTagException("CorpBannerTag:"+
                + ioe.getMessage());
        }
        return SKIP_BODY;
    }
}
```

Now, in our final step, we'll create a JSP page that uses the `CorpBanner` tag in our library. The page's name will be CorpBanner.jsp, and it's shown in Listing 9.12.

LISTING 9.12 CorpBanner.jsp

```
<%@ taglib uri="/WEB-INF/CorpTagLib.tld" prefix "corpLib" %>
<HTML>
    <HEADER>
               <TITLE>Corporate Tag Library</TITLE>
    </HEADER>
    <BODY>
    This is a Tag Library Example <BR>
    <corpLib:CorpBannerTag></corpLib:CorpBannerTag>
    </BODY>
</HTML>
```

Summary

In this chapter, we covered JSP, the latest Java technology for the development of Web applications. We introduced JSP elements that give you the ability to embed Java code directly in your JSP pages. We explored JSP syntax, as well as handling JSP errors and exceptions. We explained how to use elements for accessing JavaBeans components and how they integrate with JSP. Finally, we explained creating custom tag libraries and provided examples for writing such tags.

CHAPTER 10

Building the User Interface to the Application

In This Chapter

- The Model-View-Controller Paradigm *290*
- The Struts Framework *293*

The Model-View-Controller Paradigm

A common method for designing applications is to organize them around an event-driven user interface. In this design pattern, the developer creates the interface and subsequently writes code that will execute the desired application actions in response to user gestures. This structure can be successful for small, single-user systems that will require little alteration to the functionality over time. It is not suitable for most larger, distributed projects for the following reasons:

- More sophisticated applications may require data to be viewed and manipulated in several different ways. When business logic is implemented in the display code, display inconsistencies can result because the logic can be copied and modified in one object and not another. In addition, any change to the data display requires updates in several places.
- When data manipulation logic, format and display code, and user event handling are entangled, application maintenance can be very difficult, especially over a long span of time.
- User interfaces cannot be reused if the application logic has been combined with the code for an existing interface.
- Added functionality may require several changes to existent code, which may be difficult to locate.
- Business logic code may access a vendor-specific product (a database, for example), thus making the application much less portable.
- Changes to a single piece of code may have far-reaching side effects.
- Development cannot occur on a modular basis, as everything is dependent on everything else. This problem is amplified on large-scale development projects because it is difficult for a large team of developers to split tasks.
- Code is less reusable, because components are dependent on one another; therefore, they are less usable in other contexts.

Utilizing the Model-View-Controller (MVC) design pattern results in a separation of the application data from the ways that the data can be accessed or viewed as well as from the mapping between system events (such as user interface events) and application behaviors.

The MVC pattern consists of three component types. The Model represents the application data along with methods that operate on that data. The View component displays that data to the user. The Controller translates user actions such as mouse movement and keyboard input and dispatches operations on the Model. As a result, the Model will update the View to reflect changes to the data. Figure 10.1 illustrates the functions of each of these component types as well as the relationships between them.

FIGURE 10.1
Relationships between components.

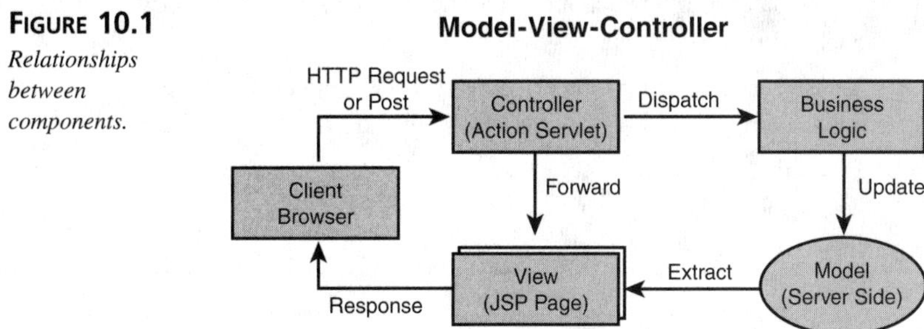

When this paradigm is used properly, the Model should have no involvement in translating the format of input data. This translation should be performed by the Controller. In addition, the Model should not carry any responsibility for determining how the results should be displayed. Table 10.1 displays the participants and collaborations involved with the three components.

TABLE 10.1 MVC: Participants and Collaborations

Component	*Participants*	*Collaborations*
Model	Extrapolates the business logic of the application	
	Maintains the application state	Informs the View when it makes changes to the application data
	Provides access to functions of the application	Can be queried by the View
	Manages persistence	Gives the Controller access to application functionality
	Extracts data for the View component	
	Informs interested parties of changes to data	
View	Extrapolates data presentation	Provides Model data for the user
	Responds to users with data	Refreshes display when informed of data changes by the Model

TABLE 10.1 continued

Component	*Participants*	*Collaborations*
	Maintains consistency with Model data	Transfers user input to the Controller
Controller	Extrapolates user interaction/ application semantic map	Transforms user inputs and dispatches class logic or application actions on the Model
	Transforms user actions into application actions	Selects the View to present based on user input and Model action outcomes
	Determines the appropriate data display based on user input and context	

The Model-View-Controller model should be used

- For distributed applications
- For larger applications
- For applications with a long lifetime
- Where interface and back-end portability are important
- Where data must be viewed and manipulated in multiple ways
- To facilitate maintenance
- To support simultaneous, modular development by multiple developers
- To allow division of labor by skill set
- To facilitate unit testing
- When employing enterprise beans that are reusable across applications

Advantages

MVC offers the following benefits:

- Clarifies application design through separation of data modeling issues from data display and user interaction
- Allows the same data to be viewed in many ways
- Allows the same data to be viewed by many users
- Simplifies impact analysis, thereby improving extensibility
- Facilitates maintenance by encapsulating application functions behind trusted APIs
- Enhances reusability by separating application functionality from presentation

- Facilitates distribution of the application, as MVC boundaries are natural distribution interface points
- Can be used to divide deployment as well as make incremental updates possible
- Forces clear designation of responsibilities and functional consistency, thereby facilitating testability
- Increases flexibility, because data model, user interaction, and data display can be made "pluggable"

Disadvantages

MVC designs may encounter the following problems:

- Components aren't able to take advantage of knowledge of other components' implementation details. This may have a negative effect on application performance. Skillful API design that optimizes the length of the code path (number of machine cycles) for each API function can assist in avoiding this problem to some extent.
- Communication volume and other latency issues must be carefully addressed; otherwise, MVC may not scale well in distributed systems.
- Maintenance of an MVC application may be difficult if the Model's API is unstable, because the Controller is written in terms of the Model API. API drift can be minimized by implementing Controller/Model communication as a command pattern. A command pattern is an object behavioral pattern that attempts to achieve a decoupling between the sender and the receiver. A sender is an object that invokes an operation, and a receiver is an object that receives the request to execute a certain operation. The term *request* here refers to the command that is to be executed. The command pattern also allows us to vary when and how a request is fulfilled. Therefore, a command pattern provides us with flexibility as well as extensibility. The command pattern turns the request itself into an object. This object can be stored and passed around in the same way as other objects. This provides a hook for Controller extensions to handle new Model functions. In addition, an adapter can often provide backward API compatibility.

The Struts Framework

The Struts framework has been developed by the Jakarta Project, which is sponsored by the Apache Software Foundation, to provide an open source framework for building Web applications with Java Servlet and JavaServer Pages (JSP) technology. Struts supports application architectures based on the MVC design paradigm. The official Struts home page can be found at `http://jakarta.apache.org/struts`.

The primary areas of functionality included in Struts are

- A controller servlet—Dispatches requests to appropriate Action classes provided by the application developer
- JSP custom tag libraries—Facilitate creation of interactive, form-based applications
- Utility classes—Provide support for XML parsing, automatic population of JavaBeans properties, and internationalizing prompts and messages

Installing Struts

The final version of Struts 1.0 is available at `http://jakarta.apache.org/builds/jakarta-struts/release/v1.0`. Source code can be downloaded from `http://jakarta.apache.org/builds/jakarta-struts/release/v1.0/src`.

The basic steps involved in obtaining and setting up Struts are

1. Download from `http://jakarta.apache.org/struts`.
2. Start with a basic Web application (typical directories beneath a Web server's root include docroot, web-inf, lib, and classes).
3. Place Struts.jar in the web-inf\lib directory.
4. Place struts.tld, struts-logic.tld, struts-bean.tld, and struts-template.tld into web-inf.
5. Modify docroot\web-inf\web.xml to use the action servlet and the taglibs.
6. Build a simple JSP page that uses one of the Struts custom tags.
7. Build the Web Application Archive (WAR).
8. Deploy the WAR.
9. Test the application. In addition to the Struts distribution, prerequisite software applications (see the list in the following section) must be installed. Detailed instructions for building Struts from the source distribution are located at `http://jakarta.apache.org/struts/installation.html#Building`. Instructions for installation and use of a Struts binary distribution in your Web application can be found at `http://jakarta.apache.org/struts/installation.html#Installing`.

Prerequisite Software

The following software must be installed in order to utilize Struts:

- Java Development Kit—You'll need version 1.2 or later.
- Servlet container—This container must be compatible with the Servlet API Specification, version 2.2 or later, and the JavaServer Pages (JSP) Specification,

version 1.1 or later. A popular choice is Apache's Tomcat (version 3.2 or later recommended).

- Ant build system (see `http://jakarta.apache.org/ant/index.html`)—When building Struts from the source distribution, version 1.3 must be installed.
- Servlet API classes—A servlet.jar file containing the Servlet and JSP API classes is required to compile Struts or the applications that use Struts.
- JDBC 2.0 optional package classes—Struts supports an optional implementation of javax.sql.DataSource; therefore, it requires the API classes to be compiled. They can be downloaded from `http://java.sun.com/products/jdbc/download.html`.
- XML parser—You'll need an XML parser that is compatible with the Java API for XML Parsing (JAXP) specification, 1.0 or later.
- Xalan XSLT processor—When building Struts from the source distribution, this processor is used to convert the Struts documentation from its internal XML-based format into the HTML that is presented in the Struts documentation application.

Struts Framework Overview

Struts applications adhere to the Model-View-Controller design pattern. The three major components are the servlet Controller, JavaServer pages (the View), and the application's business logic (the Model), as shown in Figure 10.2.

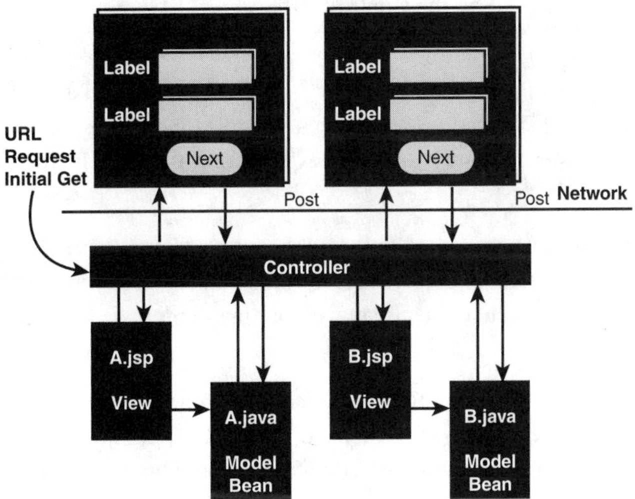

FIGURE 10.2
Simple MVC/ Struts example flow.

The following text describes the process illustrated in Figure 10.2:

First, the user request goes to a Controller that initializes the context/session for the overall transaction and alerts Page A's Model. The Controller then forwards execution to Page A's View (JSP).

Page A posts back to the Controller, which calls Model A to validate the posted form data. If the input is invalid, Model A returns a result that the Controller uses to forward/redisplay Page A. The entire `HttpServletRequest` might be made available to the Model A bean, or the Controller might be clever enough to call setters for each posted form field via introspection.

The Controller determines who is next in the chain through use of a multitude of options: straight if-else (or switch-case) code, an XML document, database records, or a rules engine.

The Controller is the centralized "traffic cop" that knows when all required steps in a transaction are complete. The Model preserves the "state" (posted form fields) and holds validation logic. If the user action is invalid, the Controller is alerted to redisplay the same View/JSP.

The Controller bundles and directs HTTP requests to other objects in the framework, including JavaServer Pages. After it has been initialized, the Controller parses a configuration resource file. This resource file defines the action mappings for the application. These mappings are used by the Controller, turning HTTP requests into application actions.

At the very least, a mapping must specify a request path as well as what object type is to act upon the request. The action object either handles the request and responds to the client (usually a Web browser), or indicates that control should be forwarded to another action.

Because action objects are linked to the application's Controller, they have access to that servlet's methods. When an object is forwarding control, it can indirectly forward one or more shared objects, such as JavaBeans, by putting them in a standard collection shared by Java Servlets.

Most of the business logic in a Struts application can be represented using JavaBeans. In addition, JavaBeans can be used to manage input forms, eliminating the common problem with retaining and validating user input between requests. Using Struts, data can be stored in a form bean. The bean can then be saved in a shared context collection, making it accessible to other objects, especially action objects. It could be used by a JSP to collect data, by an action object to validate user input, and then by the JSP again to repopulate the form fields.

In the case of validation errors, Struts has a shared mechanism for raising and displaying error messages.

Struts form beans are defined in the configuration resource, then linked to an action mapping via a common property name. When a request calls for an action that utilizes a form bean, the controller servlet will either retrieve the form bean or create one. That form bean is passed to the action object. The action object checks the contents of the form bean before its input form is displayed, queuing messages that are to be handled by the form. When the action object is ready, it can return control by forwarding to its input form, which is usually a JSP. The controller is then able to respond to the HTTP request, directing the client to the JavaServer Page.

Custom tags are included within the Struts framework. They have the ability to automatically populate fields from a form bean. Most JavaServer Pages must only know the proper field names and where to submit the form. Components such as messages set by the action object can be output using a single custom tag. Application-specific tags can be defined to hide implementation details from the JSP pages.

These custom tags are designed to use the Java platform internationalization features. All field labels and messages can be retrieved from a message resource, with Java automatically providing correct resources for the client's country and language. Providing messages for another language requires only the addition of another resource file.

Other benefits of custom tags are consistent labeling between forms and the ability to review all labels and messages from a central location.

In most applications, action objects should pass requests to other objects, primarily JavaBeans. In order to enable reuse on other platforms, business logic JavaBeans should not refer to any Web application objects. Action objects should translate required details from the HTTP request, passing those along to business-logic beans as regular Java variables.

In database applications, business-logic beans may connect to and query the database, returning the resultset to the action's servlet, where it is stored in a form bean and then displayed by the JSP.

The Model

The Model in an MVC-based application can be divided two parts: the internal state of the system, and the actions that can be taken to alter that state.

An application typically represents the internal state of the system as a set of one or more JavaBeans with properties that represent the details of that state. These beans may be self-contained, able to persistently save their state information. Additionally, they may be facades, knowing how to retrieve information from external sources such as databases when that information is requested. Entity EJB (Enterprise JavaBeans) can also be used to represent internal state.

Larger applications often represent possible business logic actions for a system as methods. Other systems may represent possible actions separately, often as Session EJB. Smaller scale applications may embed the available actions within the Action classes that are part of the Controller role. This is effective only when the logic is simple and reuse is not an issue. It is a good idea to always separate the business logic from the roles of the Action classes.

The View

Struts-based applications generally utilize JavaServer Pages to construct the View component. The JSP environment includes a set of standard action tags such as `<jsp:useBean>` as well as the ability to define custom tags and organized custom tag libraries.

In addition, it is sometimes necessary for business objects to render themselves in HTML or XML, based on their state at request time. It is easy to include the output from these objects in a resulting JSP page by using the `<jsp:include>` standard action tag.

The Controller

The Controller portion of the application focuses on receiving requests from the client (most often a user running a Web browser), deciding what business logic function is to be performed, and delegating responsibility for producing the next phase of the user interface to an appropriate View component. Struts utilizes a servlet of class `ActionServlet` as the main component of the Controller. This servlet is configured through definition of a set of mappings that are described by a Java class `ActionMapping`. Each mapping defines a path, matched against the request URI of the incoming request as well as the fully qualified class name of an Action class. The Action class is responsible for performing the desired business logic and subsequently dispatching control to the appropriate View component to create the response.

In addition, Struts supports the ability to use `ActionMapping` classes with additional properties beyond the standard ones needed to operate the framework. This enables storage of additional application-specific information while utilizing the remaining features of the framework. Furthermore, Struts allows definition of logical names for the forwarding of the control. The method can ask for the logical name of the page without knowing the actual name of the corresponding JSP page.

Here is a quick example using some sample application code and a figure to illustrate a Struts implementation of the MVC. Here we will be choosing to view details about a book that is displayed in a list.

In Figure 10.3, you can see a list of books. When you hover the mouse pointer over one of the featured books, you see the URL that can provide a display of book details.

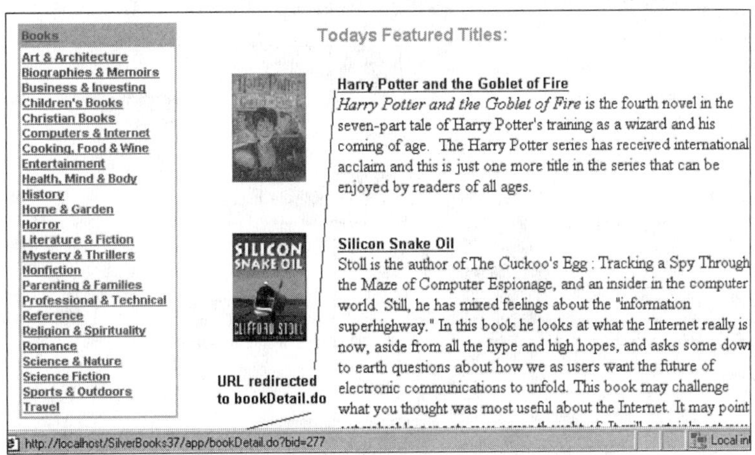

FIGURE 10.3
Choosing a book with Struts-based URL redirect.

In Figure 10.4, you can see the display of book details.

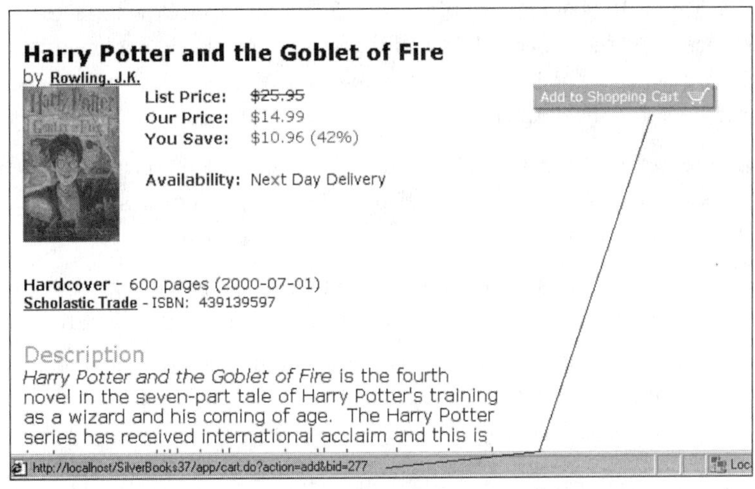

FIGURE 10.4
Displaying book details with Struts-based components.

The example shown in Figure 10.5 will step through the high-level view of the components, which come into play to accomplish the task. The task is simply to pass parameters to a Controller, which communicates with the Model session bean (database lookup), obtains detailed data about the book, and passes the resultset to a View component (a JSP) to make it visible to the user.

FIGURE 10.5
Struts implementation of MVC.

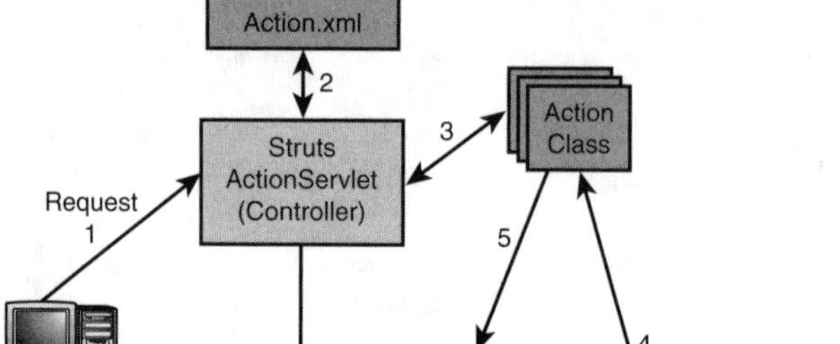

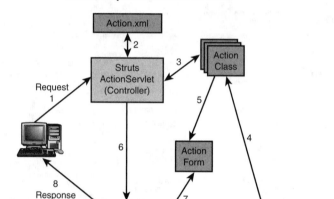

See Figure 10.5 and review Figures 10.3 and 10.4 to follow the screen shots and code snippets and see the actual flow of the application. The components and their roles in the bigger picture, which is the Struts implementation of MVC, will be explained in more detail later in the chapter.

The objective of Figure 10.5 is to depict the Struts component flow used to choose a book in our sample application. Follow the numbered code snippets to see what happens behind the scenes.

1. By clicking on a link in the current view, the user invokes the URL
   http://<server>/SilverBooks37/app/bookDetail.do?bid=277.

   The J2EE application uses web.xml and the pattern *.do to determine where to route the request:

   ```
   <servlet-mapping>
     <servlet-name>action</servlet-name>
     <url-pattern>*.do</url-pattern>
   </servlet-mapping>
   ...
   ```

```
<servlet>
  <servlet-name>action</servlet-name>
  <servlet-class>org.apache.struts.action.ActionServlet</servlet-class>
  ...
</servlet>
```

2. The `ActionServlet` uses Action.xml to determine what to do next. In this case it routes the request to the Action class `DetailAction`, a Java class that will access the database to retrieve book details:

```
<action path="/bookDetail"
  actionClass="com.sssw.demo.silverbooks.action.DetailAction">
  <forward name="success"    path="/bookDetail.jsp"/>
</action>
```

3. `ActionServlet` calls the `perform()` method of `DetailAction`:

```
   HttpSession session = request.getSession();
  String bid = request.getParameter("bid");

  JDBCSessionMgr sessMgr = JDBCSessionMgr.getInstance();
  JDBCSource jdbcSource = sessMgr.getTheSessionBean();
  int bookId = Integer.parseInt(bid);

  //Load book details into BookBean JavaBean
  BookBean book = jdbcSource.getBook(bookId);
  //Save BookBean to the session
  session.setAttribute(SilverBooksConstants.KEY_BOOKDETAIL, book);
  return (mapping.findForward("success"));
```

4. The Model session bean method `getBook` is passed the `bookId` and executes the following statement:

```
SQL SELECT * FROM BOOKS, AUTHORS, PUBLISHERS  WHERE bookId=? AND BOOKS.
AUTHORID = AUTHORS.AUTHORID AND BOOKS.PUBLISHERID=PUBLISHERS.PUBLISHERID
```

5. The Action class returns the book detail to the `ActionForm` bean.
6. `ActionServlet` forwards to bookDetail.jsp if "success" `ActionForward` is returned; the requested results are now collected and added to a View component for presentation to the user.
7. bookDetail.jsp displays book details from `BookBean` via the Struts tag library, which will include the Struts `taglib` directive

```
<%@ taglib uri="/WEB-INF/struts.tld" prefix="struts" %>
```

   and the `BookBean` JavaBean

```
<jsp:useBean id="book" scope="session"
class="com.sssw.demo.silverbooks.BookBean"/>
```

8. The completed bookDetail.jsp is returned to the user/requestor.

JavaBeans and Scope

JavaBeans can be stored in and accessed from different collections of attributes. Each of these collections has different rules for its lifetime and for the visibility of beans stored there. These rules are referred to as the *scope* of those beans. Table 10.2 displays the definitions of scope choices per the JSP Specification.

TABLE 10.2 JSP Scope Choices

Scope Choice	*Definition*	*Servlet API Concept*
page	Beans visible within a single JSP page for the lifetime of the current request	Local variants of the `service()` method
request	Beans visible within a single JSP page and any page or servlet that is included in or forwarded to by that page	Request attributes
session	Beans visible to all JSP pages and servlets participating in a particular user session across one or more requests	Session attributes
application	Beans visible to all JSP pages and servlets that are part of a Web application	Servlet context attributes

JSP pages and servlets in the same application share the same sets of bean collections. A bean stored as an attribute in a servlet is immediately visible to a JSP page, which that servlet forwards to using a standard action tag.

Building Model Components

The developer of the Model components generally focuses on the creation of JavaBeans classes to support the functional requirements of the application. The beans required by the application vary widely according to the desired functionality, but they can be classified into several categories.

`ActionForm` Beans

The Struts framework generally presupposes that an `ActionForm` bean has been created for each input form required in the application. If those beans are defined in the `ActionMapping` configuration file, the Struts controller servlet will automatically perform the following services, even before the appropriate Action method is invoked:

- Search the user's session for an instance of a bean of the appropriate class, under the appropriate key.
- If no such session scope bean is available, a new one is created and added to the user's session automatically.
- A corresponding setter method will be called for every request parameter with a name corresponding to the name of a property in the bean.
- The updated `ActionForm` bean is passed to the Action class `perform()` method when it is called, with the resulting values becoming available immediately.

When coding `ActionForm` beans, the following principles are important:

- The `ActionForm` class is used to identify the role these particular beans play in the overall architecture, requiring no specific methods to be implemented.
- The `ActionForm` object offers a standard validation mechanism, which can also be ignored if a more customized mechanism is desired.
- A property with associated `getXxx()` and `setXxx()` methods must be defined for each field present in the form. The field name and property name must match according to the JavaBeans standards.
- A bean instance with nested property references can be placed on a form.

A form in this sense does not necessarily correspond to a single JSP page in the user interface. Struts encourages defining a single `ActionForm` bean that contains properties for all of the fields, regardless of which page the field is displayed on. The various pages of the same form should all be submitted to the same Action class. This allows page designers to rearrange the fields among the various pages without requiring changes to the processing logic.

System State Beans

The actual state of a system is usually represented as a set of one or more JavaBeans classes whose properties define the current state. When creating small scale systems or those where state information only needs to be kept for a short period of time, a set of system state beans may contain all the knowledge that the system ever has of these particular details. Alternately, system state beans can represent information that is stored permanently in some external database that is created or removed from the server's memory as needed. In large-scale applications, entity beans serve this purpose.

Business Logic Beans

The functional logic of an application should be encapsulated as method calls on JavaBeans that are designed for this purpose. These methods can be part of the same classes used for the system state beans. They may also be in separate classes dedicated to performing that logic, but in that case, the system state beans to be manipulated will need to be passed to these methods as arguments.

To facilitate maximum code reuse, business logic beans should be designed and implemented so that they do not know they are being executed in a Web application environment. Action classes should translate all required information from the HTTP request being processed into property setter calls on the business logic beans. Subsequently, a call to an `execute()` method can be made. As a result, the business logic class can be reused in environments other than the one in which it was constructed.

Business logic beans can be ordinary JavaBeans that interact with system state beans passed as arguments. They may also be ordinary JavaBeans that access a database using JDBC calls. In larger applications, they are often stateful or stateless EJBs.

Building View Components

As previously mentioned, the View components of the application are primarily created using JSP technology. The Struts framework provides support for building internationalized applications, as well as for interacting with input forms. Several other topics related to the View components are briefly discussed.

Internationalized Messages

The drastic increase in application development based on Web technologies and the deployment of those applications on the Internet and other broadly accessible networks have created the necessity for applications to support internationalization and localization. Struts builds upon the Java platform to assist in the creation of applications. Classes essential to internationalization include

- `Locale (java.util.Locale)`—This is the fundamental Java class for supporting internationalization. Each `Locale` represents a particular country and language (with an optional language variant) plus a set of formatting assumptions for things such as numbers and dates.
- `ResourceBundle (java.util.ResourceBundle)`—This provides the basic tools for supporting messages in multiple languages.
- `PropertyResourceBundle (java.util.PropertyResourceBundle)` —This is a standard implementation of `ResourceBundle` that allows resources to be defined using the same `name=value` syntax used to initialize properties files.
- `MessageFormat (java.text.MessageFormat)`—This allows portions of a message string (such as one retrieved from a resource bundle) to be replaced with arguments specified at runtime.

- `MessageResources` (`org.apache.struts.util.MessageResources`)—This is the Struts class that allows a set of resource bundles to be treated like a database and allows a particular message string to be requested for a particular `Locale`.

Forms and FormBean Interactions

Users tend to expect interactive applications to have certain behaviors when dealing with forms. An important interaction relates to error handling. In the event of a user error, the application should allow users to correct just that mistake without requiring reentry of any other information on the form.

Fulfilling this expectation when coding exclusively with HTML and JSP pages can be difficult and time-consuming. The Struts framework facilitates form handling by providing tags that offer common user interface functionality.

The following code snippet, in conjunction with Figure 10.6, will illustrate how Struts handles form processing.

```
<%@ page language="java" import="com.sssw.demo.silverbooks.data.*,
com.sssw.demo.silverbooks.*" errorPage = "errorPage.jsp" %>
<%@ taglib uri="/WEB-INF/struts.tld" prefix="struts" %>
<!DOCTYPE HTML PUBLIC "-//W3C//DTD HTML 4.0 Transitional//EN">
<SCRIPT>
<!--
function Shandle_btnDefaults_onClick()
{
    document.CustomerLogin.username.value = "demo@silverdemo.com";
    document.CustomerLogin.password.value = "demo";
}
//-->
</SCRIPT>
<HTML>
<HEAD><TITLE><struts:message key="page.title"/></TITLE>
<META http-equiv=Content-Type content="text/html; charset=utf-8">
</HEAD>
<BODY leftMargin=0 background="Images/bookBack.jpg" topMargin=0
marginheight="0" marginwidth="0">
<%@ include file="topnav.jsp" %>
<struts:errors/>
<struts:form action="customerLogin.do" name="CustomerLogin"
type="com.sssw.demo.silverbooks.form.CustomerLogin">
 ... ... ... ... ... ... ... ... ... ...
<struts:message key="login.heading"/>
<struts:message key="login.newheading"/>
<struts:message key="login.retheading"/></FONT></B></P>
<struts:message key="login.newinfo"/>
<struts:button property="" onClick="window.location=
\'createaccount.jsp?action=create\'" >
        <struts:message key="button.createaccount"/>
```

```
</struts:button>
<struts:message key="login.retinfo"/></SPAN></FONT></P>
<struts:message key="login.email"/></SPAN></FONT></P>
<struts:text  size="25"  property="username"/>
<struts:message key="login.password"/></SPAN></FONT></P>
<struts:password size="25"  property="password"/>
<struts:submit>
        <struts:message key="button.continue"/>
</struts:submit>
<struts:button property="" onClick="Shandle_btnDefaults_onClick();" >
        <struts:message key="button.defaults"/>
</struts:button>
</struts:form>
<p></P>
</BODY></HTML>
```

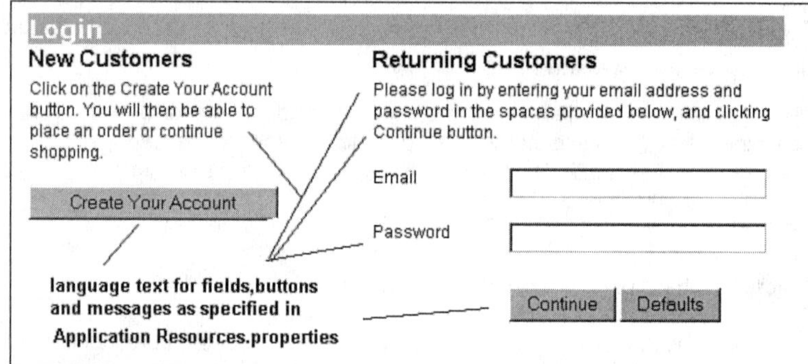

FIGURE 10.6
Example form: CustomerLogin.jsp.

The following items extrapolated from customerLogin.jsp illustrate the key features of form handling in Struts:

- The `taglib` directive (`<%@ taglib uri="/WEB-INF/struts.tld" prefix="struts" %>`) tells the JSP page compiler where to find the tag library descriptor for the Struts tag library. In this case, `struts` is used as the prefix identifying tags from the struts-bean library. Any desired prefix can be used.
- This page uses several occurrences of the message tag (for example, `<struts:message key="login.heading"/>`) to look up internationalized message strings from a `MessageResources` object (`ApplicationResources.properties`) containing all the resources for this application. For this page to work, the following message keys must be defined in these resources:
  - `login.heading`—Title of the logon page
  - `login.password`—A "Password:" prompt string
  - `button.createaccount`—"Create *x*" for the button label
  - `button.defaults`—"Defaults" for the button label

- Once a user is logged on, the application can store a `Locale` object in the user's session. This `Locale` is used to select messages in the proper language. This makes it easy to implement giving the user an option to switch languages; simply change the stored `Locale` object, and all messages are switched automatically.
- The `errors` tag displays any error messages that have been stored by a business logic component, or nothing if no errors have been stored.
- The `form` tag renders an HTML `<form>` element based on the attributes that have been specified. It also associates all of the fields within this form with a session scoped bean (for example, `<struts:form action="customerLogin.do" name="CustomerLogin">`).

  This form bean provides initial values for all of the input fields that have names that match the property names of the bean. If an appropriate bean is not found, a new one will be created automatically using the specified Java class name.
- The form bean can be specified in the Struts configuration file, as well. In that case, the `Name` and `Type` can be omitted here.
- The `text` tag renders an HTML `<input>` element of type `text`. In this case, the number of character positions to occupy on the browser's screen has also been specified. When this page is executed, the current value is the `username` property of the corresponding bean—in other words, the value returned by `getUsername()`.
- The `password` tag is used in a similar fashion. The difference is that the browser will echo asterisk characters, instead of the input value, as users type their password.
- The `submit` and `reset` tags generate the corresponding buttons at the bottom of the form. The text labels for each button, as well as any prompts, are created using `message` tags; therefore, those values are internationalized.

Handling multipart forms is relatively easy. When creating a multipart form, the first step is to utilize the struts-html taglib to create the presentation page (see the example booklist.jsp code below, which corresponds to Figure 10.3):

```
<%@ page language="java" import="com.sssw.demo.silverbooks.data.*,
com.sssw.demo.silverbooks.*" errorPage = "errorPage.jsp" %>
<%@ taglib uri="/WEB-INF/struts.tld" prefix="struts" %>
<jsp:useBean id="featuredBooks"
class="com.sssw.demo.silverbooks.data.FeaturedBooks" scope="application"/>
<HTML>
<HEAD>
<TITLE><struts:message key="page.title"/></TITLE>
</HEAD>
<BODY marginheight="0" background="Images/bookBack.jpg" leftmargin="0"
topmargin="0" marginwidth="0">
```

```
<%@ include file="topnav.jsp" %>
<struts:errors/>
<struts:form action="" name="bookList"
type="com.sssw.demo.silverbooks.form.BookList">
<struts:message key="button.search"/>:
<struts:select property="searchType" size="1">
<struts:options property="searchChoiceValues" labelProperty="searchChoices"/>
</struts:select></SPAN></FONT>
<struts:text property="searchfor" size="14"/>
<A href="javascript:doSearch()" onClick="doSearch()">
        <img src="Images/goButton.JPG" border="0" width="19" height="19">
</A>
<struts:iterate id="featuredBook" name="featuredBooks" property="books">
        <A href="bookDetail.do?bid=<%=((BookBean)featuredBook).getBookId()%>">
                <IMG src="imagesdb/<%= ((BookBean)featuredBook).getImageURL()%>"
width="70" height="100" border="0">
        </A>
        <A href="bookDetail.do?bid=<jsp:getProperty name="featuredBook"
property="bookId"/>">
                <struts:htmlProperty name="featuredBook" property="title"/>
    </A>
        <jsp:getProperty name="featuredBook" property="descHTML"/>
</struts:iterate>
</struts:form>

<SCRIPT>
function doSearch()
{
var searchMode = document.forms['bookList'].elements['searchType'].options
[document.forms['bookList'].elements['searchType'].selectedIndex].value;
var searchTerm = document.forms['bookList'].elements['searchfor'].value;
    /* JavaScript validation. */
    if (searchTerm == "") {
        alert("Please enter a search term.");
        return;
    }
    if ((navigator.appName).indexOf("Netscape") >= 0) {
        if (searchTerm != "") {
            searchTerm = escape(searchTerm);
        }
    }

    var finalQuery = "searchAction.do?";
    finalQuery += searchMode;
    finalQuery += "=";
    finalQuery += searchTerm;

    window.location = finalQuery;
}
<jsp:include page="/categorylist.jsp" flush="true"/>
<struts:message key="booklist.welcomeimg"/>" width="286" height="101"
```

```
 border="0" hspace="15">
<struts:iterate id="featuredBook" name="featuredBooks" property="books">
        <A href="bookDetail.do?bid=<%=((BookBean)featuredBook).getBookId()%>">
                <IMG src="imagesdb/<%= ((BookBean)featuredBook).getImageURL()%>"
width="70" height="100" border="0">
        </A>
</struts:iterate>
<!------------------------------------------------------------->
<%@ include file="bottomnav.sub" %>
</BODY>
</HTML>
```

You create your `ValidatingActionForm` bean to check the user input, in this case search criteria such as title and author name:

```
import java.util.*;
import org.apache.struts.action.ValidatingActionForm;
import java.lang.Integer;
import org.apache.struts.util.ErrorMessages;
import java.io.*;
import java.beans.*;

public final class BookList implements ValidatingActionForm {
    private String searchFor = "";
    private String searchType = "";
    private Vector vFeaturedBooks = new Vector();
    private Collection featuredBooks;

    // Instance Variables
    private final static String[] searchChoices = {"Title", "Last Name",
"Publisher"};
    private final static String[] searchChoiceValues = {"title", "lname",
"pub"};

    public void setSearchfor(String newSearchFor) {
        searchFor = newSearchFor;
    }

    public void setSearchType(String newSearchType) {
        searchType = newSearchType;
    }

    public String[] getSearchChoices() {
        return (searchChoices);
    }
    public String getSearchfor() {
        return searchFor;
    }
    public String getSearchType() {
        return searchType;
    }
```

```
    public String[] getSearchChoiceValues() {
        return searchChoiceValues;
    }
    public String[] validate() {

        ErrorMessages errors = new ErrorMessages();

        if (errors.getSize() > 0) {
            return errors.getErrors();
        }

        return errors.getErrors();
    }

}
```

The next step is to create your `ActionForm` bean, which will access the database to get the list of books that meet the search criteria:

```
import java.io.IOException;
import java.util.*;
import javax.servlet.RequestDispatcher;
import javax.servlet.ServletException;
import javax.servlet.http.HttpServletRequest;
import javax.servlet.http.HttpSession;
import javax.servlet.http.HttpServletResponse;
import org.apache.struts.action.ActionBase;
import org.apache.struts.action.ActionForm;
import org.apache.struts.action.ActionForward;
import org.apache.struts.action.ActionMapping;
import org.apache.struts.action.ActionServlet;
import org.apache.struts.util.ErrorMessages;
import org.apache.struts.util.MessageResources;

public final class SearchAction extends ActionBase {

public ActionForward perform(ActionServlet servlet,
            ActionMapping mapping,
            ActionForm form,
            HttpServletRequest request,
            HttpServletResponse response)
            throws IOException, ServletException {
        ActionForward forwardURL = mapping.findForward("failure");
        try {
                HttpSession session = request.getSession();
        String title = request.getParameter("title");
            String authorId = request.getParameter("aid");
            String pub = request.getParameter("pub");
                  String pubId = request.getParameter("pid");
            String catId = request.getParameter("cid");
            String cat1 = request.getParameter("cat1");
```

```
            String cat2 = request.getParameter("cat2");
            String cat3 = request.getParameter("cat3");
            String lastName = request.getParameter("lname");
            String firstName = request.getParameter("fname");
            Collection books = null;
            StringBuffer sbuffer = new StringBuffer();
            if (title != null) {
                  title = this.checkForQuote(title);
            sbuffer.append("BOOKTITLE like '%");
            sbuffer.append(title);
            sbuffer.append("%'");
            }
        else if (authorId != null) {
            if (sbuffer.length() > 0) {
                      sbuffer.append(" AND ");
              }
            sbuffer.append("BOOKS.AUTHORID=");
            sbuffer.append(authorId);
            JDBCSessionMgr sessMgr = JDBCSessionMgr.getInstance();
            JDBCSource jdbcSource = sessMgr.getTheSessionBean();
            books = jdbcSource.getSearchedBooks(sbuffer.toString());
            if (books.size() == 0) {
                session.removeAttribute(SilverBooksConstants.KEY_SEARCHRESULTS);
                forwardURL = mapping.findForward("booklist");
            }
            else if (books.size() == 1) {
                Iterator itBooks = books.iterator();
                BookBean singleBook = (BookBean) itBooks.next();
                session.setAttribute(SilverBooksConstants.KEY_BOOKDETAIL,
singleBook);
                forwardURL = mapping.findForward("bookdetail");
            }
            else {
                session.setAttribute(SilverBooksConstants.KEY_SEARCHRESULTS,
books);
                forwardURL = mapping.findForward("booklist");
            }
        }
    catch (Exception e) {
        System.out.println("searchAction exception:" + e);
    }
    return forwardURL;
}
```

Input Field Types Supported

Struts defines HTML tags for the following types of input fields:

- check boxes
- hidden fields

- password input fields
- radio buttons
- reset buttons
- select lists with embedded options
- submit buttons
- text input fields
- text areas

A `field` tag must always be nested within a `form` tag, informing the field which bean to use for initializing displayed values.

Other Useful Presentation Tags

There are several tags that are useful for creating presentations:

- `iterate`—This repeats its tag body once for each element of a specified collection. See the code snippet for booklist.jsp.
- `present`—This tag checks the current request, evaluating the nested body content of this tag only if the specified value is present. Only one attribute may be used in one occurrence of this tag, unless the `property` attribute is used. In that case, the `name` attribute is also required. Attributes include `cookie`, `header`, `name`, `parameter`, `property`, `role`, `scope`, and `user`.
- `notPresent`—`notPresent` provides the same functionality as `present` in cases where the specified attribute is not present.
- `link`—This tag generates an HTML <a> element as an anchor definition or a hyperlink to the specified URL. It also automatically applies URL encoding to maintain session state when cookie support is absent.
- `img`—This generates an HTML `<img>` element with the ability to dynamically modify the URLs specified by the `src` and `lowsrc` attributes.
- `parameter`—The `parameter` tag retrieves the value of the specified request parameter, defining the result as a page scope attribute of type `String` or `String[]`.

Automatic Form Validation

Struts offers the ability to validate the input fields of a form upon receipt. The following method in the `ActionForm` class must first be overridden:

```
public ActionErrors
  validate(ActionMapping mapping,
    HttpServletRequest request);
```

The default implementation of the `validate()` method returns `null`. The controller servlet will then assume that any required validation is done by the Action class.

The `validate()` method is called by the controller servlet after the bean properties have been populated, but before the corresponding Action class's `perform()` method has been invoked. The `validate()` method has the following possible outcomes:

- Perform the appropriate validations and find no problems: Either a null or a zero-length `ActionErrors` instance is returned, then the controller servlet will call the `perform()` method of the appropriate Action class.
- Perform the appropriate validations and find problems: An `ActionErrors` instance containing `ActionErrors` is returned. These are classes containing the error message keys that should be displayed. The controller servlet stores this array as a request attribute suitable for use by the `<html:errors>` tag, forwarding control back to the input form as identified by the input property for this `ActionMapping`.

Building Controller Components

When working with the Struts framework, the responsibilities related to the Controller are

- Writing an Action class such as `DetailAction` for each logical request that may be received. Optionally, an `ActionMapping` class that defines the class names and other information associated with each possible mapping can be written.

  For example:

  ```
  <action path="/bookDetail" actionClass="com.sssw.demo.silverbooks.
  action.DetailAction">  <forward name="success" path="/bookdetail.jsp"/>
  </action>
  ```
- Writing the action mapping configuration file (in ACTION.XML). This file is used to configure the controller servlet. For example:

  ```
  <forward name="booklist"  path="/booklist.jsp"/>
  ```
- Updating the Web application deployment descriptor file (in WEB.XML) for the application, in order to include the necessary Struts components. For example:

  ```
  <!-- Struts Tag Library Descriptor -->
  <taglib>
      <taglib-uri>/WEB-INF/struts.tld</taglib-uri>
          <taglib-location>/WEB-INF/struts.tld</taglib-location>
  </taglib>
  ```
- Adding the appropriate Struts components to the application.

Action Classes

The Action class defines two methods that can be executed depending on the servlet environment. The `HttpServletRequest` version is the most frequently utilized.

```
public ActionForward perform(ActionMapping mapping,
                             ActionForm form,
                             ServletRequest request,
                             ServletResponse response)
  throws IOException, ServletException;
```

The Action class processes the request, returning an `ActionForward` object that identifies the JSP page (if any) to which control should be forwarded in order to generate the corresponding response. A typical Action class implements the following logic in its `perform()` method:

- It validates the current state of the user's session, confirming that he or she is properly logged on. If it determines that the user is not logged on, the request should be forwarded to the JSP page displaying the username and password fields.
- If validation has not yet taken place, the Action class validates the form bean properties as necessary. If a problem is located, it stores the appropriate error message keys as a `request` attribute, forwarding control back to the input form for error correction.
- It performs the processing necessary to handle the request. This can be achieved by code within the Action class itself; however, it is typically performed by calling an appropriate method of a business logic bean.
- The Action class updates the server-side objects that will create the next page of the user interface. This is typically achieved via request scope or session scope beans, depending on the duration that the items must remain available.
- It returns an appropriate `ActionForward` object to identify the JSP page used to generate the response, based on the recently updated beans. Normally, a reference to such an object will be acquired by calling `findForward()` on either the `ActionMapping` object that was received or on the controller servlet itself. This varies depending on whether a logical name local to this mapping or one global to the application is used.

The following design issues are essential when coding Action classes:

- The controller servlet generates only one instance of the Action class, which is used for all requests. Therefore, the Action class must be coded so it will operate correctly in a multithreaded environment, just as a servlet's `service()` method must be coded safely.

- Local variables should be used instead of instance variables in Action classes to aid in thread-safe coding. Local variables are created on a stack and assigned by the JVM to each request thread, hence they need not be shared.
- Beans representing the Model of the system may throw exceptions due to problems accessing databases or other resources. These exceptions should be trapped in the logic of the `perform()` method and logged to the application logfile with the corresponding stack trace by calling

```
servlet.log("Error message text", exception);
```

- Resources such as database connections should be released prior to forwarding control to the appropriate View component, even if a bean method that was called throws an exception. This will help eliminate scalability problems.
- Very large Action classes should be avoided. This is easily achieved by coding functional logic in separate business logic beans rather than embedding it in the Action class itself. This approach will also increase the reusability of the business logic code as well as make the Action class itself easy to understand and maintain.

The `ActionMapping` Implementation

The Struts controller servlet requires several pieces of information about how each request URI should be mapped to an appropriate Action class. This information is encapsulated in a Java interface named `ActionMapping`. The most important properties of this interface are

- `type`—This is the Java class name of the Action implementation class that is used by this mapping.
- `name`—This is the name of the form bean as defined in the config file that the action will use.
- `path`—This is the request URI path that is matched in order to select this mapping.
- `unknown`—This is set to `true` if the action should be configured as the default for the application, handling all requests not handled by another action. A single application may have only one action that is defined as a default.
- `validate`—This is set to `true` if the `validate()` method of the action that is associated with this mapping should be called.

The Action Mappings Configuration File

The controller servlet must somehow find out about the desired mappings. To facilitate this, Struts includes a Digester module that is capable of reading XML-based descriptions of the desired mappings. In addition, it creates the appropriate objects along the way.

The developer must create the XML file named struts-config.xml, placing it in the WEB-INF directory of the application. The format of this document is constrained by the definition provided in struts-config_1_0.dtd.

The outmost XML element is required to be `<struts-config>`. Two important elements used to describe actions are located inside the `<struts-config>` element. These are

- `<form-bean>`—This contains the form bean definitions. A `<form-bean>` element is used for each form bean, having the following important attributes:

  `name`—the name of the request or session level attribute that the form bean will be stored as

  `type`—the fully qualified Java classname of the form bean

- `<action-mappings>`—This contains the action definitions. An `<action>` element is used for each of the actions you want to define. Each `<action>` element requires that the following attributes be defined:

  `path`—the application path to the action

  `type`—the fully qualified Java classname of the Action class

  `name`—the name of the `<form-bean>` element that should be used with this action

The struts-config.xml file from the example SilverBooks application includes the following mapping entry for the `login` function, which we will use to illustrate the requirements:

```
<struts-config>
  <action-mappings>

  <!-- Global Forward Declarations -->
  <forward name="booklist" path="/booklist.jsp"/>
  <forward name="login" path="/customerLogin.jsp"/>

  <!-- Process database properties-->
  <action path="/bookDetail"
    actionClass="com.sssw.demo.silverbooks.action.DetailAction">
    <forward name="success" path="/bookdetail.jsp"/>
  </action>

   ... ... ... ....

  <action path="/customerLogin"
    inputForm="/customerLogin.jsp"
    formAttribute="customerLogin"
    formClass="com.sssw.demo.silverbooks.form.CustomerLogin"
    actionClass="com.sssw.demo.silverbooks.action.CustomerLoginAction">
    <forward name="success" path="/checkout.jsp"/>
  </action>
```

```
  <action path="/searchAction"
    actionClass="com.sssw.demo.silverbooks.action.SearchAction">
    <forward name="failure" path="/errorPage.jsp"/>
    <forward name="booklist" path="/searchresults.jsp"/>
    <forward name="bookdetail" path="/bookDetail.do"/>
  </action>

  </action-mappings>

</struts-config>
```

The `Global Forward` section is utilized for creating logical name mappings between commonly used JSP pages. Each of these forwards is available through a call to the action mapping instance, for example `actionMappingInstance.findForward("logicalName")`.

As you can see, this mapping matches the path `/customerLogin` (actually, because the example application uses extension mapping, the request URI you specify in a JSP page would end in `/customerLogin.do`). When a request that matches this path is received, an instance of the `customerLoginAction` class will be created (the first time only) and used. The controller servlet will look for a session-scoped bean under key `customerLogin`, creating and saving a bean of the specified class if needed.

An optional but very useful section is the `Local Forward`. In the example application, many actions include a local `"success"` and/or `"failure"` forward as part of an action mapping:

```
<action path="/searchAction"
    actionClass="com.sssw.demo.silverbooks.action.SearchAction">
    <forward name="failure" path="/errorPage.jsp"/>
    <forward name="booklist" path="/searchresults.jsp"/>
    <forward name="bookdetail" path="/bookDetail.do"/>
  </action>
```

Using just these two extra properties, the Action classes in the example application are almost totally independent of the actual names of the JSP pages that are used by the page designers. The pages can be renamed (for example, during a redesign) with negligible impact on the Action classes themselves. If the names of the "next" JSP pages were hard-coded into the Action classes, all of these classes would also need to be modified. It is possible to define local forward properties that will make sense for your own application.

Note that when you call `the findForward()`, method it searches through the local forwards for the specified name. If no local forwards are defined, it searches through the global forwards collection, if it is present.

Another useful section is the <data-sources> section, specifying data sources that can be used by your application. This is how you would specify a basic data source for your application inside of struts-config.xml:

```
<struts-config>
  <data-sources>
    <data-source
      autoCommit="false"
     description="Example Data Source Description"
     driverClass="org.postgresql.Driver"
        maxCount="4"
        minCount="2"
        password="mypassword"
        url="jdbc:postgresql://localhost/mydatabase"
        user="myusername"/>
  </data-sources>
</struts-config>
```

The Web Application Deployment Descriptor

The last step in setting up the application is configuring the application deployment descriptor, stored in WEB-INF/web.xml. It should include all of the requisite Struts components. Using the deployment descriptor of the example application for reference, it is necessary to create or modify the entries discussed in the following subsections.

The Action Servlet Instance

An entry defining the action servlet itself must be added, along with the appropriate initialization parameters. The entry might look like this:

```
<servlet>
    <servlet-name>action</servlet-name>
    <servlet-class>org.apache.struts.action.ActionServlet</servlet-class>
    <init-param>
      <param-name>application</param-name>
      <param-value>com.sssw.demo.silverbooks.res.
ApplicationResources</param-value>
    </init-param>
    <init-param>
      <param-name>config</param-name>
      <param-value>/WEB-INF/action.xml</param-value>
    </init-param>
    <init-param>
      <param-name>debug</param-name>
      <param-value>2</param-value>
    </init-param>
    <init-param>
      <param-name>detail</param-name>
      <param-value>2</param-value>
```

```
    </init-param>
    <load-on-startup>2</load-on-startup>
</servlet>
```

The initialization parameters that are supported by the controller servlet are described in Table 10.3. (You can also find these details in the Javadocs for the `ActionServlet` class.) The default value is assumed if a value for an initialization parameter has not been provided.

TABLE 10.3 Initialization Parameters

Parameter	*Description*	*Default Value*
`application`	Java class name for the base class of the application resources bundle	`---`
`bufferSize`	The size of the input buffer used while processing file uploads	`4096`
`config`	Context-relative path to the XML resource containing the configuration information	`/WEB-INF/struts-config. xml`
`content`	Default content type and character encoding; may be overridden by a forward to servlet or JSP page	`text/html`
`debug`	The debugging detail level for this servlet, which controls how much information is logged	`0`
`detail`	The debugging detail level, which logs to System. out instead of the servlet log	`0`
`factory`	The Java class name for the `MessageResourcesFactory` used to create the application `MessageResources` object	`---`
`FormBean`	The Java class name for the `ActionFormBean` implementation to use	`org.apache.struts.action.ActionFormBean`
`forward`	The Java class name for the `ActionForward` implementation to use	`org.apache.struts.action.ForwardingActionForward` (subclass of `org.apache.struts.action.ActionForward` that defaults the redirect property to `false`)

TABLE 10.3 continued

Parameter	*Description*	*Default Value*
		or org.apache.struts.action.RedirectingActionForward (subclass of org.apache.struts.action.ActionForward that defaults the redirect property to true)
locale	If this is set to true, and there is a user session, identify and store an appropriate java.util.Locale object in the user's session if there is not a Locale object there already	---
mapping	The Java class name for the ActionMapping implementation to use	org.apache.struts.action.RequestActionMapping (subclass of org.apache.struts.action.ActionMapping that defaults the scope property to request) or org.apache.struts.action.SessionActionMapping (subclass of org.apache.struts.action.ActionMapping that defaults the scope property to session)
maxFileSize	The maximum size of a file to be accepted as a file upload (in bytes)	250M

Table 10.3 continued

Parameter	*Description*	*Default Value*
`multipartClass`	The fully qualified name of the `MultipartRequestHandler` implementation class used for processing file uploads	`org.apache.struts.upload.DiskMultipartRequestHandler`
`nocache`	If set to `true`, HTTP headers should be added to every response; this is intended to defeat browser caching of any response that is generated or forwarded to	`false`
`null`	If set to `true`, application resources should be set to return `null` if an unknown message key is used. Otherwise, an error message including the offending message key will be returned	`true`
`tempDir`	The working directory to use while processing file uploads	The working directory provided to this Web application as a servlet context attribute
`validate`	Tells whether the new configuration file format is being used	`true`

The Action Servlet Mapping

Two different approaches, prefix matching and extension matching, are commonly used to define the URLs that will be processed by the controller servlet.

In prefix matching, all URLs that have a particular value immediately after the context path will be passed to this servlet. An entry might look like this:

```
<servlet-mapping>
   <servlet-name>action</servlet-name>
   <url-pattern>/execute/*</url-pattern>
</servlet-mapping>
```

This means that a request URI to match the `/logon` path might look like this: `http://www.ucny.com/serverapp/execute/logon`, where `/serverapp` is the context path under which the application is deployed.

With extension mapping, the request URI is matched to the action servlet based on the criterion that the URI ends with a period followed by a defined set of characters. For example, to use the *.do extension, implying "do something," the mapping entry would look like this:

```
<servlet-mapping>
     <servlet-name>action</servlet-name>
     <url-pattern>*.do</url-pattern>
 </servlet-mapping>
```

The Struts Tag Library

Next, An entry defining the Struts tag library must be added. Struts is currently packaged with four taglibs:

- The struts-bean taglib contains tags useful for accessing beans and their properties, in addition to defining new beans that are accessible to the remainder of the page through scripting variables and page scope attributes. It also provides convenient mechanisms for creating new beans based on the value of request cookies, headers, and parameters.
- The struts-html taglib contains tags used to create Struts input forms and HTML-based user interfaces.
- The struts-logic taglib contains tags that are useful for managing conditional generation of output text, looping over object collections for repetitive generation of output text, and application flow management.
- The template taglib contains tags defining a template mechanism.

The following example demonstrates the method for defining all taglibs to be used within the application:

```
<taglib>
  <taglib-uri>
    /WEB-INF/struts-bean.tld
  </taglib-uri>
  <taglib-location>
    /WEB-INF/struts-bean.tld
  </taglib-location>
</taglib>
<taglib>
  <taglib-uri>
    /WEB-INF/struts-html.tld
  </taglib-uri>
  <taglib-location>
    /WEB-INF/struts-html.tld
  </taglib-location>
</taglib>
<taglib>
  <taglib-uri>
    /WEB-INF/struts-logic.tld
```

```
    </taglib-uri>
    <taglib-location>
      /WEB-INF/struts-logic.tld
    </taglib-location>
  </taglib>
  <taglib>
    <taglib-uri>
      /WEB-INF/struts-template.tld
    </taglib-uri>
    <taglib-location>
      /WEB-INF/struts-template.tld
    </taglib-location>
  </taglib>
```

The JSP system is instructed as to where the tag library descriptor for this library can be found (for example, in the WEB-INF directory).

Adding Struts Components to the Application

To utilize Struts, the requisite .tld files must be copied into the WEB-INF directory, and the struts.jar must be copied into the WEB-INF/lib directory.

Accessing Relational Databases

When using Struts, the data sources for an application can be defined from within the standard configuration file. A simple JDBC connection pool is also provided. The following is an example of establishing a connection from within an Action perform method after the data source has been defined:

```
// JAVA SESSION BEAN

import java.sql.ResultSet;
import java.util.*;
import java.io.*;
import java.rmi.RemoteException;
import javax.sql.DataSource;
import javax.naming.InitialContext;
import javax.rmi.PortableRemoteObject;
import java.math.BigDecimal;
.............
import java.text.SimpleDateFormat;
import javax.ejb.*;
import java.sql.*;

public class JDBCSourceBean implements javax.ejb.SessionBean {
   // for our initialContext
   /**
    *  Description of the Field
    */
```

```
   protected SessionContext m_context;
   // name of this object
   private DataSource m_jdbcSource = null;
   private final String getImage = "SELECT * FROM IMAGES WHERE URL=?";
   private final String getBook = "SELECT * FROM BOOKS, AUTHORS, PUBLISHERS
WHERE bookId=? AND BOOKS.AUTHORID = AUTHORS.AUTHORID
AND BOOKS.PUBLISHERID=PUBLISHERS.PUBLISHERID";
   final static String THIS = "JDBCSourceBean";

   /**
    *  Sets the SessionContext attribute of the JDBCSourceBean object
    *
    *@param  psessionContext               The new SessionContext value
    *@exception  javax.ejb.EJBException    Description of Exception
    *@exception  java.rmi.RemoteException  Description of Exception
    */
    public void setSessionContext(javax.ejb.SessionContext psessionContext)
throws javax.ejb.EJBException, java.rmi.RemoteException {
        System.out.println(THIS + ".setSessionContext()");
      m_context = psessionContext;
   }

   /**
    *  Gets the Image attribute of the JDBCSourceBean object
    *
    *@param  url                       Description of Parameter
    *@return                           The Image value
    *@exception  RemoteException       Description of Exception
    *@exception  SilverBooksException  Description of Exception
    */

  /**
    *  Gets the Book attribute of the SqlBooks object
    *
    *@param  id                        Description of Parameter
    *@return                           The Book value
    *@exception  RemoteException       Description of Exception
    *@exception  SilverBooksException  Description of Exception
    */
    public BookBean getBook(int id) throws RemoteException,
    SilverBooksException {

      // Initialize our database object
      if (m_jdbcSource == null) {
         initializeSessionBean();
      }
      Connection connection = null;
      PreparedStatement preparedStatement = null;
      ResultSet results = null;
      try {
```

```
         do {
            connection = m_jdbcSource.getConnection();
         } while (connection == null);
         preparedStatement = connection.prepareStatement(getBook);

         synchronized (preparedStatement) {
            preparedStatement.clearParameters();
            preparedStatement.setInt(1, id);
            results = preparedStatement.executeQuery();
         }
         if (results.next()) {
            return makeBook(results);
         }
         else {
            throw new SilverBooksException("Could not find Book# " + id);
         }
      }
      catch (Exception e) {
         System.out.println;
         throw new SilverBooksException(e.getMessage());
      }
      finally {
         try {
            if (preparedStatement != null) {
               preparedStatement.close();
            }
            if (results != null) {
               results.close();
            }
            if (connection != null) {
               connection.close();
            }
         }
         catch (Exception e) {
            // ignore
         }
      }
   }

   public void ejbCreate() throws CreateException, RemoteException {
   }

   public void ejbRemove() throws javax.ejb.EJBException,
java.rmi.RemoteException {
   }

   public void ejbActivate() throws javax.ejb.EJBException,
java.rmi.RemoteException {
   }
```

```
  public void ejbPassivate() throws javax.ejb.EJBException,
java.rmi.RemoteException {
  }

  private void initializeSessionBean()
         throws RemoteException, SilverBooksException {
     //************************************************************
     // *******************
     // Initialize this bean.
     //**********************************************
     //*********************************
     try {
        InitialContext ctx = new InitialContext();
        synchronized (ctx) {
           String dataSourceName = "java:comp/env/jdbc/SilverBooksDataSource";
           m_jdbcSource = (DataSource) ctx.lookup(dataSourceName);
        }
     }
     catch (Exception e) {
         e.printStackTrace();
        }
        String sErrorMessage = e.toString();
        throw new EJBException(sErrorMessage);
     }
  }
```

Summary

Things change every month in the business of software development. In 25 years, I have seen things go from card decks to handheld network browsers. Never in that span of time has the curve been steeper than it is now. With respect to Web delivery, we have moved from CGI/Perl scripts to Microsoft's ASP with VB, and now Java and J2EE. We in the Java community have been working hard to adapt changes to the JSP/servlet architecture, just as Java aficionados have in the past with the Java language and API.

Struts uses tags and MVC to encourage code reusability and flexibility. Separating the problem into smaller components is the way to reuse the technology. Additionally, Struts enables page designers and Java developers to focus on what they do best. The tradeoff in increased robustness implies an increase in complexity. Struts is very complex if you're just creating a simple single JSP page, but for larger systems Struts helps to manage the complexity. Just as actual struts are essential to keeping an airplane wing intact, Apache Struts might become an essential part of your next Web project.

Enterprise JavaBeans: Introduction

IN THIS CHAPTER

- Enterprise JavaBeans Overview *328*
- Distributed Programming Overview *330*
- EJB Framework *330*
- Session and Entity Beans *333*
- Attributes of a Bean *335*
- Parts of a Bean *336*
- CMP and BMP *338*
- The Life Cycle of Enterprise JavaBeans *340*
- JMS and MDB *341*
- Distributed Programming Services *346*
- CORBA and RMI *347*
- Transactions and Transaction Management *349*
- Security *352*
- Deployment *352*
- Personal Roles for EJB Development *353*
- Corporate Roles *355*

Enterprise JavaBeans Overview

The Enterprise JavaBeans (EJB) specification is an industry initiative led and driven by Sun Microsystems with participation from many supporting vendors in the industry. Sun owns the process of defining, creating, and publishing the specification while ensuring the incorporation of input and feedback from the industry and the general public.

The EJB initiative was announced at JavaOne '97. A specification draft was posted in December '97. EJB 1.1 specification Final Release was provided as part of the first J2EE platform Final Release in December 1999. On October 25, 2000, Sun released the EJB 2.0 specification Final Proposed Draft for public review. This draft was developed through the Java Community Process (JCP). The JCP is the program created by Sun used to manage changes to the Java platform. The site `www.jcp.org` has been created to enable members of the Java community to be involved with the evolution of the Java platform and related technologies.

The EJB 2.0 public draft specification includes requirements on EJB container/server providers, which allow interoperability for invocations on enterprise beans. These requirements enable communication with J2EE clients including JavaServer Pages, Servlets, and Application Clients as well as with EJBs in other EJB containers. The goal of these features is to allow EJB invocations to work even when client components and EJBs are deployed in J2EE products from different vendors. Support for interoperability between components includes transaction propagation, naming services, and security services. Other major enhancements have been made in the following areas:

- JMS (Java Message Service) integration
- Improved support for container-managed persistence (CMP)
- Support for RMI/IIOP protocol for network interoperability
- Management of beans relationships
- Structured Query Language (SQL) support

The term *Enterprise* implies that the application will be scalable, available, reliable, secure, transactional, and distributed. In order to provide these types of features, an Enterprise application requires access to a variety of infrastructure services, such as distributed communication services, naming and directory services, transaction services, messaging services, data access and persistence services, and resource-sharing services.

These infrastructure services are often implemented on different platforms using a variety of products and technologies, thus, building portable enterprise-class application systems can be very difficult. The J2EE APIs provide a common interface that supply easy access to these underlying infrastructure services, regardless of their actual implementation. Although Java code runs in a Java virtual machine (JVM), allowing the Java application to run on any operating system with Write Once, Run Anywhere (WORA) portability, server components often require additional services that are not supplied directly by the JVM, such as database access, transaction support, security enforcement, caching, and concurrency.

These services can be supplied either by a proprietary application server or by a distributed object infrastructure, such as Common Object Request Broker Architecture (CORBA). Traditionally, application servers supply sets of proprietary programming interfaces that allow access to the services. This is a pretty good solution, however, since there is no standard, the developer can only take advantage of one vendor's resources and tools at a time.

With J2EE, the minimum requirements that a programmer needs from the application server have been standardized. This standardization enhances the benefits that the proprietary application server gives by making both the developer's code and the third party vendor's code more useful. The developer's code becomes more useful because it can run on multiple systems as well as multiple platforms. Third party vendor's code becomes more useful because there is a larger selection of vendors to choose *plug-in* objects from. The following benefits are gained by adhering to the J2EE standard:

- Reusable application components—The productivity benefits of writing components in the Java programming language include component reuse and outsourcing, declarative customization (not programmatic), and the ability for the developer to focus on business logic only.
- Portability—The portability characteristics of EJB components are made possible by J2EE. This platform consists of several standard Java application programming interfaces (APIs) that provide access to a core set of enterprise-class infrastructure services. It is these standardized APIs that ensure that Java code can be run on any vendor's application server.
- Broad industry adoption—Wider selection of vendor tools and components allowing choice and flexibility in server selection.
- Application portability—Code is more than just platform independent; it is also middleware independent.
- No vendor lock-in—Architecture decisions are made at deployment, not at development; Inter-server portability allows code to be deployed on any EJB server; Inter-server scalability allows Servers to be transparently replaced to accommodate changing needs for service-level, performance, or security.

- Protection of IT investment—Wraps and integrates with the existing infrastructure, application, and data stores; Is portable across multiple servers and databases; Serves multi-lingual clients (such as Browsers, Java technology, ActiveX, or CORBA clients); EJB framework simplifies and enhances CORBA, a registered trademark of the Object Management Group (OMG), and Distributed Component Object Model (DCOM), a registered trademark of Microsoft Corporation; Existing middleware solutions are being adapted by the well-established vendors to support the EJB framework via a thin portability layer.

Distributed Programming Overview

When a distributed framework is used, a client makes a call to what appears to be the interface of a business object. What it actually calls is a *stub* that mimics the interface of that business object. This layer between clients and business objects is added because it is more practical to place stubs in the remote and *distributed* locations of clients than it is to place complete copies in the location of business objects.

In a distributed framework, the client calls a business method on a stub as if it were the real object. The stub then communicates this request to a *tie*. The tie calls the method on the real business object. A result is returned to the stub and the client (see Figure 11.1).

A stub is also known as a proxy or a surrogate, and a tie is also known as a skeleton.

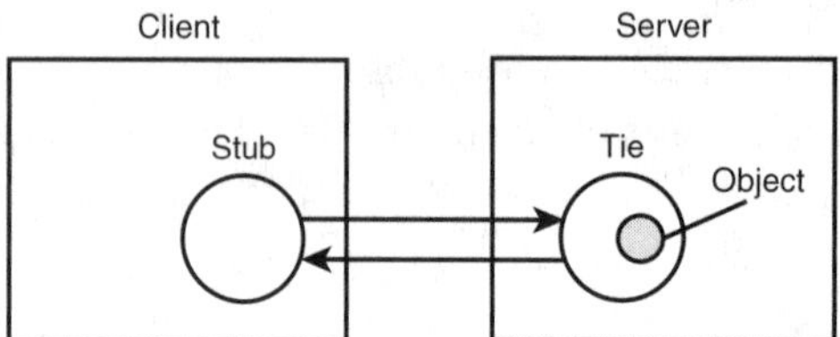

FIGURE 11.1
Distributed programming overview.

EJB Framework

Some of the primary benefits of the EJB framework are as follows:

- EJB components are server-side components written entirely with the Java programming language; therefore, applications based on EJB components are not only platform independent but also middleware independent. They can run on any operating system and on any middleware that supports EJB.

- EJB components contain business logic only, giving developers freedom from maintaining system-level code that would be integrated with their business logic. The EJB server automatically manages system-level services such as transactions, security, life cycle, threading, and persistence for the EJB component.
- EJB architecture is inherently transactional, distributed, portable, multitier, scalable, and secure.
- Components are declaratively customized. Customizable traits include transactional behavior, security features, life cycle, state management, and persistence.

Figure 11.2 demonstrates how the `Home` interface, `Remote` interface, `EJBHome` object, and `EJBObject` of the EJB framework fit into the generic distributed programming model. These components will be discussed in more detail throughout this chapter.

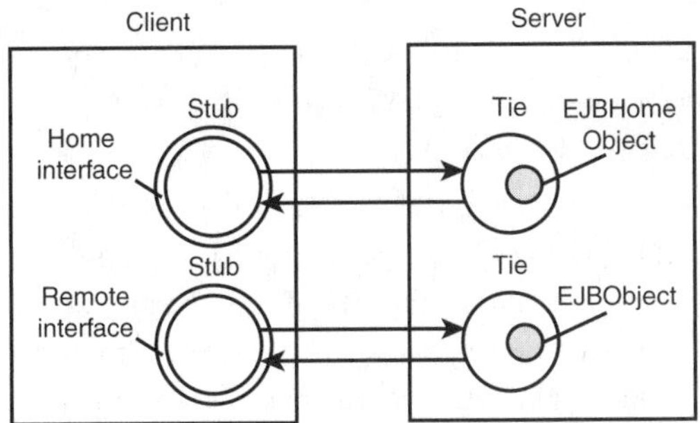

FIGURE 11.2
Distributed programming with EJB.

Containers

The application server provides a container that supports services for components. A container is an entity that provides life cycle management, security, deployment, and runtime services to components. Each container type (including EJB, Web, JSP, Servlet, Applet, and Application Client) provides component-specific services as well.

After a client invokes a server component, the container will automatically allocate a process thread and initiate the component. The container manages all resources on behalf of the component and interactions between the component and the external systems. A container provides Enterprise JavaBeans components with services such as

- Bean life cycle management and instance pooling—These services include creation, activation, passivity, and destruction. Individual EJBs do not need to explicitly manage process allocation, thread management, object activation, or object destruction. The EJB container automatically manages the object life cycle on behalf of the EJB.

- State management—Individual EJBs do not need to explicitly save or restore the conversational object state between method calls. The EJB container automatically manages the object state on behalf of the EJB.
- Bean transaction management—This service intercedes between client calls on the `Remote` interface and the corresponding methods in a bean to enforce transaction and security constraints. It can provide notification at both the beginning and the ending of each transaction that involves a bean instance. Individual EJBs do not need to explicitly specify the transaction demarcation code to participate in distributed transactions. The EJB container can automatically manage the start, the enrollment, the commitment, and the rollback of transactions on behalf of the EJB.
- Security constraint enforcement—EJBs do not need to explicitly authenticate users or check authorization levels. The EJB container automatically performs all security checking on behalf of the EJB.
- Distributed remote access—EJBs use technologies and protocols that are commonly used in distributed programming, such as Remote Method Invocation (RMI) and Internet InterORB Protocol (IIOP).
- Container-managed persistence (CMP)—EJBs do not need to explicitly retrieve or store persistent object data from a database. The EJB container can automatically manage persistent data on behalf of the EJB. Entity beans can either manage their own persistence or delegate those persistence services to their container. If persistence is delegated to the container, that container will also perform all data retrieval and storage operations automatically on behalf of the bean.

  The majority of the changes made between EJB 1.1 and EJB 2.0 are found in the definition of a new CMP component model. The new CMP model is extremely different from the previous CMP model because it introduces an entirely new entity, the persistence manager, and a completely new way of defining container-managed fields, as well as relationships with other beans and dependent objects.
- Generated remote stubs—The container will create remote stubs for wrappers such as RMI and CORBA.

Additional Functionality

The EJB server provides an environment that supports the execution of applications developed using EJB architecture, managing and coordinating allocation of resources to the applications. The EJB server must provide one or more EJB containers, which provide homes for the EJBs. EJB containers manage the EJBs contained within them. For each EJB, the container is responsible for registering the object, providing a `Remote` interface for the object, creating and destroying object instances, checking security for the object, managing the active state for the object, and coordinating distributed transactions. In addition, the container has the ability to manage all persistent data within the object.

Vendor-Specific Containers

The exact natures of process management, thread pooling, concurrency control, and resource management are not defined within the scope of the EJB specification. Individual vendors can differentiate their products based on the simplicity or sophistication of the services provided by proprietary containers. A software vendor might elect to develop a new application server specifically to support EJB components. It is more likely, however, that vendors will simply adapt their existing systems. A number of application servers are currently available, and any of these systems could be extended to support a container for EJB components. An impressive number of vendors are extending a wide variety of products, which can be found in Appendix B, "Related Tools."

Container Location

Any number of EJB classes can be installed in a single EJB container. A particular class of EJB is assigned to one and only one EJB container, but a container may not necessarily represent a physical location. The physical manifestation of an EJB container is not defined in the EJB specification. An EJB container could be implemented as a physical entity, such as a single multithreaded process within an EJB server, or it could be implemented as a logical entity that can be replicated and distributed across any number of systems and processes.

Session and Entity Beans

The EJB specification supports both transient and persistent objects. A transient object is referred to as a *session bean*, and a persistent object is known as an *entity bean*.

Session Beans

A session bean is an EJB that is created by a client and usually exists only for the duration of a single client-server session. A session bean usually performs operations such as calculations or database access on behalf of the client. While a session bean may be transactional, it is not recoverable if a system crash occurs. Session bean objects can be either stateless or they can maintain a conversational state across methods and transactions. If a session bean maintains a state, then the EJB container manages this state if the object must be removed from memory. However, persistent data must be managed by the session bean object itself.

The tools for a container generate additional classes for a session bean at deployment time. These tools obtain information from the EJB architecture by examining its classes and interfaces. This information is utilized to dynamically generate two classes that implement the `Home` and the `Remote` interfaces of the bean. These classes enable the container to intercede in all client calls on the session bean. The container generates a serializable `Handle` class as well, which provides a way to identify a session bean instance within a specific life cycle. These classes can be implemented to perform customized operations and functionality when mixed in with container-specific code.

In addition to these custom classes, each container provides a class that provides metadata to the client and implements the `SessionContext` interface. This provides access to information about the environment in which a bean is invoked.

Entity Beans

An entity bean is an object representation of persistent data maintained in a permanent data store such as a database. A primary key identifies each instance of an entity bean. Entity beans can be created in two ways. Entity beans are transactional and are recoverable in the event of a system crash.

Entity beans represent specific data or collections of data, such as a row in a relational database. Entity bean methods provide operations for acting on the data represented by the bean. An entity bean is persistent and survives as long as its data remains in the database.

An entity bean can be created in two ways: first, by direct action of the client in which a create method is called on the bean's `Home` interface, or second, by some other action that adds data to the database that the bean type represents. In fact, in an environment with legacy data, entity objects may exist before an EJB is even deployed.

An entity bean can implement either bean-managed or container-managed persistence. In the case of bean-managed persistence, the implementer of an entity bean stores and retrieves the information managed by the bean through direct database calls. The bean may utilize either JDBC or SQLJ for this method. A disadvantage to this approach is that it makes it harder to adapt bean-managed persistence to alternate data sources.

In the case of container-managed persistence, the container provider may implement access to the database using standard APIs. The container provider can offer tools to map instance variables of an entity bean to calls to an underlying database. This approach makes it easier to use Entity Beans with different databases.

Session beans may also access the data they manage using JDBC or SQLJ.

Encapsulating Entity Beans with Session Beans

Encapsulating an entity bean inside a session bean is usually a good design choice for several reasons: First, it will prevent a remote client from starting a transaction. Second, it will eliminate direct exposure of the entity beans to remote clients. Finally, it allows entity beans to be more reusable (see Figure 11.3).

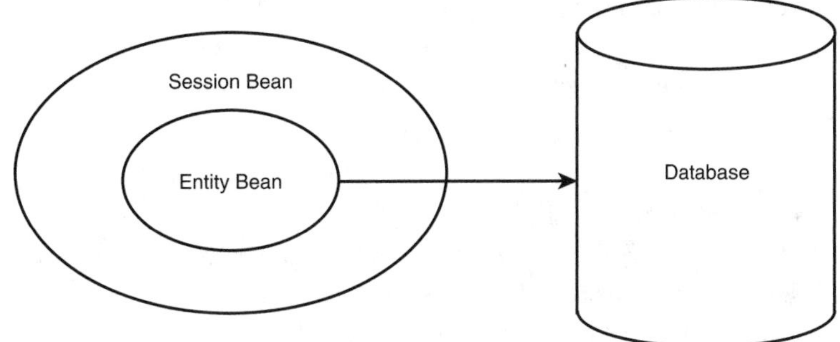

FIGURE 11.3
Entity bean encapsulation.

Bean Relativity

Even though session beans have the ability to implement the complex functionality of an object database, they still retain the ability to function as simple wrappers around tables in a relational database. To support this ability to wrap tables, session beans support the relational concepts of one-to-one, one-to-many, or many-to-many.

One-to-One, One-to-Many

Entity beans may also have one-to-one, one-to-many, or many-to-many relationships with other entity beans. One-to-many relationships with other beans should be represented as `java.util.Collection` or `java.util.Set` types. One-to-one relationships use the bean's `Remote` interface type.

Attributes of a Bean

There are two choices that can be made for a "state" attribute of a bean. Beans can either be stateful or stateless. With stateful beans, the EJB container saves internal bean data during and in between method calls on the client's behalf. With stateless beans, the clients may call any available instance of an instantiated bean for as long as the EJB container has the ability to pool stateless beans. This enables the number of instantiations of a bean to be reduced, thereby reducing required resources.

Stateless Beans

A session bean represents work performed by a single client. That work can be performed within a single method invocation, or it may span across multiple method invocations. If the work spans multiple methods, the object must maintain the user's object state between method calls. The state management options for session beans are defined in the `StateManagementType` attribute in the `DeploymentDescriptor` object.

Generally, stateless beans are intended to perform individual operations automatically and don't maintain state across method invocations. They're also amorphous, in that any client can use any instance of a stateless bean at any time at the container's discretion. They are the lightest weight and easiest to manage of the various EJB component configurations.

Stateful Beans

Stateful session beans maintain state both within and between transactions. Each stateful session bean is associated with a specific client. Containers are able to save and retrieve a bean's state automatically while managing instance pools of stateful session beans.

Stateful session beans maintain data consistency by updating their fields each time a transaction is committed. To keep informed of changes in transaction status, a stateful session bean implements the `SessionSynchronization` interface. The container calls methods of this interface while it initiates and completes transactions involving the bean.

Session beans, whether stateful or stateless, are not designed to be persistent. The data maintained by stateful session beans is intended to be transitional. It is used solely for a particular session with a particular client. A stateful session bean instance typically can't survive system failures and other destructive events. While a session bean has a container-provided identity (called its handle), that identity passes when the client removes the session bean at the end of a session. If a client needs to revive a stateful session bean that has disappeared, it must provide its own means to reconstruct the bean's state.

Parts of a Bean

Some of the components used to create, access, describe, and work alongside business logic contained in bean classes are described in this section. These components give developers the control of their business logic that is normally required by an enterprise system.

Home Interface

The EJBHome object is an object that provides the life cycle operations (create, remove, find) for an EJB. The container's deployment tools generate the class for the EJBHome object. The EJBHome object implements the EJB's Home interface. The client references an EJBHome object in order to perform life cycle operations on an EJBObject. JNDI is used by the client to locate an EJBHome object.

The EJBHome interface provides access to the bean's life cycle services and can be utilized by a client to create or destroy bean instances. For entity beans, it provides finder methods that allow a client to locate an existing bean instance and retrieve it from its persistent data store.

EJBObject Interface

The EJBObject interface provides access to the business methods within the EJB. An EJBObject represents a client view of the EJB. The EJBObject exposes all of the application-related interfaces for the object, but not the interfaces that allow the EJB container to manage and control the object. The EJBObject wrapper allows the EJB container to intercept all operations made on the EJB. Each time a client invokes a method on the EJBObject, the request goes through the EJB container before being delegated to the EJB. The EJB container implements state management, transaction control, security, and persistence services transparently to both the client and the EJB.

Deployment Descriptor

The deployment descriptor is an XML file provided with each module and application that describes how the parts of a J2EE application should be deployed. The deployment descriptor configures specific container options in your deployment tool of choice.

The rules associated with the EJB governing life cycle, transactions, security, and persistence are defined in an associated XML deployment descriptor object. These rules are defined declaratively at the time of deployment rather than programmatically at the time of development. At runtime, the EJB container automatically performs the services according to the values specified in the deployment descriptor object associated with the EJB.

SessionContext and EntityContext Objects

For each active EJB instance, the EJB container generates an instance context object to maintain information about the management rules and the current state of the instance. A session bean uses a SessionContext object, while an entity bean uses an EntityContext object. Both the EJB and the EJB container use the context object to coordinate transactions, security, persistence, and other system services. A properties table called the `Environment` object is also associated with each EJB. The `Environment` object contains the customized property values set during the application assembly process or the EJB deployment process.

Dependent and Fine-Grained Objects

There is a natural conflict between a large *many* in a *one-to-many* object relationship and a distributed framework. The EJB framework is not adapted to fine-grained objects, which may be associated with a large number of related objects. Many of these related objects will have methods that are called frequently. The overhead for supporting the distributed nature of the EJB framework is demonstrated in the next two chapters where the code required for communication between client and server components is presented. It is this overhead that makes calling fine-grained objects impractical as data will be returned one bean at a time. For this type of object, the EJB specification recommends using a more lightweight model.

In order to ensure performance when passing fine-grained objects over a distributed framework, the local interface was created. This interface allows intracontainer objects to be passed by reference instead of by value. Passing objects by reference eliminates most of the overhead that would be created by sending the entire copies of objects across a distributed framework.

Container-Managed Persistence (CMP) and Bean-Managed Persistence (BMP)

There are two ways that bean persistence can be managed. The first method is to let the container manage the persistence of the bean. This method is called container-managed persistence (CMP). The second method for managing persistence is called bean-managed persistence (BMP). This method requires that the developer implement the interaction code between the EJB and the persistence engine. This is a complex and intricate task. Thus, this mode must not be seen as a general development model, but more as a means to implement a low-level persistence mechanism if necessary. In other words, only when the limits of the automatic persistence mode have been exceeded should BMP mode be used. It is not realistic to consider using this model for all EJBs due to the complexity of development. The container-managed mode should be considered as the general persistence model for most application development.

Container-Managed Persistence (CMP)

In container-managed persistence, entity bean data is maintained automatically by the container that uses the mechanism of its choosing. For example, a container implemented on top of a Relational Database Management System (RDBMS) may manage persistence by storing each bean's data as a row in a table. The container may also use the Java programming language serialization functionality for persistence. When a programmer chooses to utilize CMP beans, the programmer specifies which fields are to be retained.

Persistence Manager

A persistence manager is used to separate the management of bean relationships from the container. With this separation, a container has the responsibility for managing security, transactions, and so on, while the persistence manager is able to manage different databases via different containers. Using this architecture allows entity beans to become more portable across EJB vendors.

Entity beans are mapped to the database using a bean-persistence manager contract called the abstract persistence schema. The persistence manager is responsible for implementing and executing find methods based on Enterprise JavaBeans Query Language (EJB *QL)*.

The persistence manager generates a mapping of CMP objects to a persistent data store's objects based on the information provided by the deployment descriptor, the bean's abstract persistence schema, and settings set by the deployer. Persistent data stores may include relational databases, flat files, Enterprise Resource Planning (ERP) systems, and so on.

The Contract

A contract between the CMP entity bean and persistence manager allows for defining complex and portable bean-to-bean, bean-to-dependent, and even dependent-to-dependent object relationships within an entity bean. In order for the persistence manager to be separated from the container, a contract between the bean and the persistence manager is defined.

Persistence Management Tools

When EJB is deployed, the persistence manager is used to generate an instantiated implementation of the EJB class and its dependent object classes. It does this based on its XML deployment descriptor and the bean class. The instantiated implementation will include the data access code that will read and write the state of the EJB to the database at runtime. When this happens, the container uses the subclasses generated by the persistence manager instead of the EJBs abstract classes defined by the bean provider.

Bean-Managed Persistence (BMP)

When using bean-managed persistence (BMP), it is the bean that is responsible for storing and retrieving its persisted data. The entity bean interface provides methods for the container to notify an instance when it needs to store or retrieve data.

In BMP mode, the EJB must implement persistence. To do this, methods such as `ejbStore` and `ejbLoad` must be created and used, and communication with SQL databases must be implemented manually using JDBC.

The Life Cycle of Enterprise JavaBeans

Detailed documentation describing the life cycle of an EJB can be found in the EJB specifications on the Sun Web site. The following list provides a general description of the life cycle states of an EJB:

1. The client locates the bean's home using the JNDI services in the application server.
2. The JNDI service returns a reference to the client's `Home` interface.
3. The client uses its `Home` interface to call `home.create()`. In response to this call, the `Home` object creates an `EJBObject`. A new instance of the code in the bean class is also instantiated by the `newInstance()` method.
4. The new instance of the bean class is given a session context. This instantiation is now called a Session Bean.
5. The `Home` object gives the client's Remote interface a reference to the `EJBObject` in the container.
6. The client's Remote interface can now invoke methods on the `EJBObject` in the container. This `EJBObject` then passes these method calls to the Session Bean.
7. The session bean returns a resultset to the `EJBObject`, which in turn returns it to the client's `Remote` interface.

Figure 11.4 illustrates this life cycle.

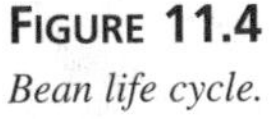
FIGURE 11.4
Bean life cycle.

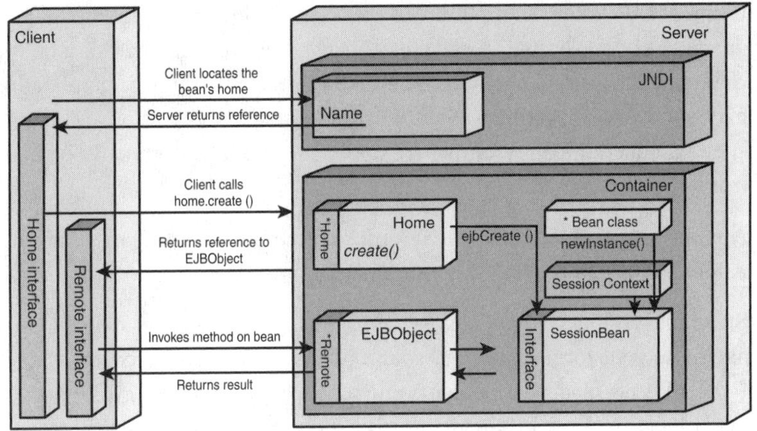

Java Message Service (JMS) and Message-Driven Beans (MDB)

Because message-driven beans (MDBs) use part of the standard JMS API, it will help you to have some knowledge of the JMS messaging system before creating a message-driven bean.

Java Message Service (JMS)

Session and entity beans are Remote Procedure Call (RPC)–based objects. Because synchronous communications used in an RPC is not always preferred over asynchronous communications in a distributed system, access to the JMS API was included as an EJB resource. Using the JNDI environment-naming context, an `EJBObject` can obtain access to a JMS factory and deliver an asynchronous message to a topic without having to wait for a reply from the servicing object.

JMS is a vendor-independent API used to access messaging systems. It is similar to Java Database Connectivity (JDBC), an API used to access different relational databases. JMS provides vendor-independent access to messaging services.

JMS allows messages to be sent from one JMS client to another via a messaging service called a message broker or a router.

Using JMS lets the bean publish a message without blocking thread processing. A bean does not know who will receive a message, because messages are delivered to a virtual channel called a topic as opposed to being sent directly to an application. Applications may choose to subscribe to that topic and receive notifications. This makes it possible to create an uncoupled system where applications can dynamically be added or removed from virtual channels.

Applications that subscribe to an order topic receive notification of new orders. Applications can process these orders at appropriate times.

Since messaging systems are asynchronous, the JMS client may send a message without having to wait for a reply. That is the opposite of the RPC-based systems used in EJB, CORBA, and Java RMI. When using an RPC client, after invoking a method on a distributed object on a server, the client is blocked until the invoked method returns a response to the client. With RPC, the client must wait for the method invocation to end before it can execute the next instruction. While using JMS, a client may deliver a message to a topic that many JMS clients are subscribing to. After a JMS client sends a message, it does not wait for a reply. JMS is discussed in greater detail in Chapter 15, "Messaging with Applications: Java Message Service (JMS)."

Message-Driven Beans (MDB)

The message-driven bean (MDB) is a stateless component that is invoked by a container as a result of the arrival of a JMS message. MDBs were created in order to have an EJB that can be asynchronously invoked to process incoming JMS messages in a similar manner to that of a JMS `MessageListener`, while getting the same services from the EJB container that session and entity beans are provided. A MDB acts as a message consumer, and like standard JMS message consumers, it receives messages from a JMS Topic and performs business logic based on the message contents. MDBs receive JMS messages from clients in the same manner as any other JMS servicing object.

To receive JMS messages, MDBs implement the `javax.jms.MessageListener` interface, which defines a single `onMessage()` method.

```
public void onMessage(javax.jms.Message message)
{
    //Your code here.
}
```

When a message is sent to a topic, the topic's container ensures that the MDB corresponding to the topic does exist. If the MDB needs to be instantiated, the container will do this. The `onMessage()` method of the bean is called and the client's message is passed as an argument. The MDBs implementation of the `onMessage()` method initiates the business logic that processes the message.

The EJB deployer is the person responsible for having MDBs assigned to a Topic at deployment time. The container provides the service of creating and removing MDB instances as they are needed.

MDBs and stateless session EJBs are similar in the sense that they are dynamically created and their instances only exist for the duration of a particular method call. MDBs differ from stateless session beans and entity beans because MDBs have no `Home` or `Remote` interface and hence cannot be directly accessed by internal or external clients. Clients may interact with message-driven beans only indirectly by sending a message to a JMS Topic.

MDBs implement the `javax.jms.MessageListener` interface. A client that writes to a topic has no knowledge of the fact that an MDB is acting as a message consumer. This type of architecture leads to loosely coupled systems that allow for a flexibly distributed computing environment.

In an MDB, the `onMessage()` method has a singular argument of type `javax.jms.Message` which can accept any valid JMS message type. The `onMessage()` method does not include a throws clause, so no application exceptions may be thrown.

Containers and Message-Driven Beans

The EJB container or application server provides many services for MDBs so the developer can concentrate on implementing business logic. Some of the services that the container provides are listed here:

- The container handles communications for JMS messages.
- The container checks its pool of available instances in order to see which MDB should be used.
- The container enables the propagation of a security context by associating the role designated in the deployment descriptor to the appropriate thread of execution.
- The container creates an association with a transactional context if one is required by the deployment descriptor.
- The container passes the JMS message to the `onMessage()` method of the appropriate MDB instance.
- The container re-allocates MDB resources to a pool of available instances.

Message-Driven Beans and Concurrent Processing

In the EJB framework, a deployed message bean represents a single message consumer, but the bean itself is serviced by one or more bean instances. Each bean instance may consume messages received by the message bean. This means that a message bean does not have to consume messages in a serial fashion. A message bean can consume its messages in a concurrent fashion, making it possible to have a larger scale enterprise system.

Message-Driven Bean Container Services

The EJB container provides the following services based on the entries in the declarative deployment descriptor file contained in the EJB jar file:

- MDB life cycle management—The life cycle of an MDB corresponds to the life span of the EJB container in which it is deployed. Since MDBs are stateless, bean instances are usually pooled by the EJB container and retrieved by the container when a message becomes available on the topic for which it is acting as a message consumer. The container creates a bean instance by invoking the `newInstance()` method of the bean instance class object. After the instance is created, the container creates an instance of `javax.ejb.MessageDrivenContext` and passes it to the bean instance via the `setMessageDrivenContext()` method. The bean instance is then placed in the pool and is available to process messages.
- Exception handling—MDBs may not throw application exceptions while processing messages. This means that the only exceptions that may be thrown by a MDB are runtime exceptions indicating a system-level error. The container should handle this exception by removing the bean instance and rolling back any transaction started by the bean instance or by the container.
- Threading and concurrency—An MDB instance is assumed to execute in a single thread of control, which simplifies the developer's task. The EJB container will guarantee this behavior. In addition, the EJB container may provide a mode of operation that allows multiple messages to be handled concurrently by separate bean instances. This deployment option utilizes expert level classes that are defined in the JMS specification. The JMS provider is not required to provide implementations for these classes, so the EJB container may not be able to take advantage of them with every JMS implementation. Using these classes involves a tradeoff between performance and serialization of messages delivered to the server.
- Message acknowledgment—The container always handles message acknowledgment for MDBs; it is illegal for the bean to use the client message acknowledgment methods defined in the JMS specification. The message acknowledgment can be set to `DUPS_OK_ACKNOWLEDGE` or `AUTO_ACKNOWLEDGE`. The former allows the delivery of duplicate messages after a failure, while the latter provides a strict guarantee that the message will be delivered only once. As noted, a bean with the `Required` transaction attribute assigned to the `onMessage()` method will involve the message delivery in a transaction.

- Security—Because the MDB has no client, no security principal is propagated to the container on receipt of a message. The EJB framework provides facilities for a bean method to execute in a declaratively specified role. As a result, the MDB can be configured to execute in a security context that can be propagated to other EJBs used during message processing. This allows method-level security to be maintained for MDBs.

Java Message Service and Standard Protocols

The MDB portion of the EJB framework allows messages received via a JMS implementation to be handled by a simple but enterprise quality component model. MDBs have such a high degree of practicality that it is possible they will evolve to be the standard component model for handling any kind of programmatic message, not just messages delivered by a JMS server. If an application server has the facility to convert protocols such as HTTP, FTP, and e-mail into a JMS message, an MDB can process messages sent by any of these protocols as if they were sent as a JMS message. This allows for a standard and portable component model that can process any message delivered by any protocol.

Message-Driven Beans (MDBs) Versus Session and Entity Beans

There are several differences between MDBs and EJB session and entity beans. A message bean has neither a `Remote` nor a `Home` interface. This is because the message bean is not an RPC component. MDBs do not have business methods that are synchronously invoked by EJB clients. An MDB listens to a virtual message channel topic and consumes messages delivered by other JMS clients to that channel.

In addition to MDBs being similar to stateless session beans because both beans maintain no state between requests, they both also contain instance variables that are maintained throughout the bean instances' life.

MDBs can consume messages from any topic provided by a JMS-compliant vendor. Messages consumed by MDBs may have come from other beans such as session, entity, or message beans; non-EJB Java applications; or non-Java applications that use a JMS-compliant vendor.

Distributed Programming Services

The EJB container and application server are also responsible for maintaining the distributed object environment. This means that they must manage the logistics of the distributed objects as well as the communications between them.

Naming and Registration

For each class installed in a container, the container automatically registers an `EJBHome` interface in a directory using the Java Naming and Directory Interface (JNDI) API. Using JNDI, any client can locate the `EJBHome` interface to create a new bean instance or to find an existing entity bean instance. When a client creates or finds a bean, the container returns its `EJBObject` interface.

Remote Method Invocation (RMI)

RMI is a high-level programming interface that makes the location of the server transparent to the client. The RMI compiler creates a stub object for each `Remote` interface. The stub object is either installed on the client system or it can be downloaded at runtime, providing a local proxy object for the client. The stub implements all the `Remote` interfaces and transparently delegates all method calls across the network to the remote object.

The EJB framework uses the Java Remote Method Invocation API to provide access to EJBs. Both the `EJBHome` and `EJBObject` interfaces, which are both required when creating EJBs, are extended from the `java.rmi.Remote` interface.

When a client object invokes methods on either a session bean or an entity bean, the client is using RMI in a synchronous fashion. This is different from a message-driven bean, which has its methods invoked by messages in an asynchronous fashion.

Protocols

The EJB specification asserts no requirements for a specific distributed object protocol. RMI is able to support multiple communication protocols. The Java Remote Method Protocol is the RMI native protocol, supporting all functions within RMI. The next release of RMI plans to add support for communications using the CORBA standard communications protocol, Internet InterORB Protocol (IIOP). IIOP supports almost all functions within RMI. EJBs that rely only on the RMI/IIOP subset of RMI are portable across both protocols. Third-party implementations of RMI support additional protocols such as Secure Sockets Layer (SSL).

Common Object Request Broker Architecture (CORBA) and Remote Method Invocation (RMI)

The EJB specification is intended to support compliance with the range of CORBA standards, current and proposed. The two technologies can function in a complementary manner. CORBA provides a great Standards-based infrastructure on which to build EJB containers. EJB framework makes it easier to build an application on top of a CORBA infrastructure. Additionally, the recently released CORBA components specification refers to EJB as the architecture when building CORBA components in Java.

CORBA

The Common Object Request Broker Architecture is a language-independent, distributed object model specified by the Object Management Group (OMG), which is a consortium, founded April 1989, of eleven companies. This architecture was created in order to support the development of object-oriented applications across heterogeneous computing environments that might contain different hardware platforms and operating systems.

CORBA relies on the protocol Internet InterORB Protocol (IIOP) for communications between objects. The center of the CORBA architecture lies in the Object Request Broker (ORB). The ORB is a distributed programming service that enables CORBA objects to locate and communicate with one another. CORBA objects have interfaces that expose sets of methods to clients. To request access to an objects method, a CORBA client acquires an object reference to a CORBA server object. Then the client makes method calls on the object reference as if the CORBA object were local to the client. The ORB finds the CORBA object and prepares it to receive requests, to communicate requests to it, and then to communicate replies back to the client. A CORBA object interacts with ORBs either through an ORB interface or through an Object Adapter.

Java/RMI

Since a Bean's `Remote` and `Home` interfaces are RMI compliant, they can interact with CORBA objects via RMI/IIOP, Sun, and IBM's forthcoming adaptation of RMI that conforms to the CORBA-standard IIOP protocol.

The Java Transaction API (JTA), which is the transaction API prescribed by the EJB specification for bean-managed transactions, was designed to be well integrated with the OMG Object Transaction Service (OTS) standard.

Security Issues with IIOP

As of the time of this publishing, there are no security standards for interoperability between ORBs. Without this security feature, a client ORB will be unable to authenticate with a server ORB unless they are from the same vendor.

Native Language Integration

By using IIOP, EJBs can interoperate with native language clients and servers. IIOP facilitates integration between CORBA and EJB systems. EJBs can access CORBA servers, and CORBA clients can access EJBs. Also, if a COM/CORBA Internetworking service is used, ActiveX clients can access EJBs, and EJBs can access COM servers. Eventually there may also be a DCOM implementation of the EJB framework.

Bean-Managed Persistence (BMP)

If the entity object manages its own persistence, then the EJB must implement persistence operations (for example, JDBC or embedded SQL calls) directly in the EJB class methods.

Container-Managed Persistence (CMP)

If the entity object delegates persistence services, the EJB container transparently and implicitly manages the persistent state. The EJB does not need to code any database access functions within the EJB class methods. The first release of the EJB specification does not define how the EJB container must manage object persistence. A vendor may implement a basic persistence service in the EJB container that simply serializes the EJB's state and stores it in some persistent storage. As an alternative, they may implement a more sophisticated persistence service with increased functionality. As an example, the persistence service may transparently map the object's persistent fields to columns in an underlying relational database. An embedded object database could also be used by a vendor to implement persistence.

Session Object Persistence

The problem of persistence is very complex. One of the important points to remember is that at runtime, objects (including EJBs) are not isolated entities but referenced mutually. Therefore, the problem of persistence does not concern isolated objects, but complex object graphs. Session objects, by definition, are not persistent, although they may contain information that needs to be persisted. As with bean-managed entity objects, session objects can implement persistence operations directly in the methods in the EJB. Often, Session objects will maintain a cache of database information that must be synchronized with the database when a transaction is started, committed, or aborted. An EJB can implement transaction synchronization methods directly in the EJB class using the optional `SessionSynchronization` interface. Transaction demarcation points are signaled by the `afterBegin`, `beforeCompletion`, and `afterCompletion` notifications. These allow the object to read or write data to the database as is required.

Transactions and Transaction Management

A transaction is one or more tasks that execute as a single atomic operation or unit of work. If all tasks involved in a transaction do not proceed successfully then an inverse task or rollback procedure for all tasks is performed, setting all resources back to their original state. Transactions are characterized by the acronym ACID that stands for Atomic, Consistent, Isolated, and Durable.

The EJB container provides the services and management functions required to support transaction demarcation, transactional resource management, synchronization, and transaction context propagation.

Since JDBC operates at the level of an individual database connection, it does not support transactions that span across multiple data sources. To compensate for this, the Java Transaction API (JTA) provides access to the services offered by a transaction manager. If an EJB requires control of global transaction, it can get access to JTA via the container.

Distributed Transactions

Although the EJB framework can be used to implement non-transactional systems, the model was designed to support distributed transactions. EJB framework requires the use of a distributed transaction management system that supports two-phase commit protocols for flat transactions.

In addition to container-managed transactions, an EJB may participate in client-managed and bean-managed transactions.

The EJB architecture provides automatic support for distributed transactions in component-based applications. Such distributed transactions can automatically update data in multiple databases or even data distributed across multiple sites. The EJB model shifts the complexities of managing these transactions from the application developer to the container provider.

J2EE-compliant containers support the following transaction attributes of EJBs:

- `NotSupported`—The bean runs outside the context of a transaction. Existing transactions are suspended during method calls. The bean cannot be invoked within a transaction. An existing transaction is suspended until the method called in this bean completes.
- `Required`—Method calls require a transaction context. If one already exists, it will be used; if one does not exist, it will be created. The container starts a new transaction if no transaction exists. If a transaction exists, the bean uses that transaction.
- `Supports`—Method calls use the current transaction context if one exists but don't create one if none exists. The container will not start a new transaction. If a transaction already exists, the bean will be included in that transaction. Note that with this attribute the bean can run without a transaction.
- `RequiresNew`—Containers create new transactions before each method call on the bean and commit transactions before returning. A new transaction is always started when the bean method is called. If a transaction already exists, that transaction is suspended until the new transaction completes.
- `Mandatory`—Method calls require a transaction context. If one does not exist, an exception is thrown. An active transaction must already exist. If no transaction exists, the `javax.ejb.TransactionRequired` exception is thrown.
- `Never`—Method calls require that no transaction context be present. If one exists, an exception is thrown. The bean must never run with a transaction. If a transaction exists, the `java.rmi.RemoteException` exception is thrown.

Multiple Transactions

A container can manage multiple transactions in two different ways. The container could instantiate multiple instances of the bean, allowing the transaction management of the DBMS to handle any transaction processing issues. Conversely, the container could acquire an exclusive lock on the instance's state in the database, serializing access from multiple transactions to this instance.

Java Transaction Service (JTS)

The Java Transaction Service specifies the implementation of a transaction manager supporting the Java Transaction API (JTA). JTS also implements the Java mapping of the OMG Object Transaction Service (OTS). The EJB specification suggests but does not require transactions based on the JTS API. JTS supports distributed transactions, which have the ability to span multiple databases on multiple systems coordinated by multiple transaction managers. By using JTS, an EJB container ensures that its transactions can span multiple EJB containers.

Java Transaction API (JTA)

EJB applications communicate with a transaction service using the Java Transaction API (JTA). JTA provides a programming interface to start transactions, to join existing transactions, to commit transactions, and to roll back transactions.

When a bean with bean-managed transactions is invoked, the container suspends any current transaction in the client's context. In its method implementation, the bean will initiate the transaction through the JTA `UserTransaction` interface. In stateful beans, the container will associate the bean instance with the same transaction context across consequent method calls until the transaction is explicitly completed by the bean. However, stateless beans aren't allowed to maintain transaction context across method calls. Each method invocation is required to complete any transaction it initiates.

Entity Bean Methods and Transaction Attributes

All developer-defined methods in the `Remote` interface as well as all methods defined in the `Home` interface (such as create, remove, and finder methods) require transaction attributes.

Session Bean Methods and Transaction Attributes

All developer-defined methods in the `Remote` interface require transaction attributes. Note that transaction attributes are not needed for the methods in the `Home` interface.

Methods in the `Remote` interface run with the `NotSupported` attribute by default.

Transaction Services for Message-Driven Beans

MDBs, like other EJBs, can demarcate transaction boundaries. They are capable of maintaining their own transactions using bean-managed transactions (BMT). They are also able to have the application server or container manage transactions on their behalf using container-managed transactions (CMT). In either case, a message-driven bean does not receive a transaction context from the client that sends a message. It is the server that calls a bean's `onMessage()` method using the transaction context defined in the bean's deployment descriptor.

Because there are no client transactions in MDBs, attributes may only be set for the message-driven bean's `onMessage()`. Only `Required` and `NotSupported` transaction attributes are supported for CMT MDBs. When creating an MDB using a CMP demarcation that implements the `onMessage()` method, using the `NotSupported` transaction attribute is relatively simple, because the container will not create transactions and the EJB is prohibited from accessing the `UserTransaction` object. When using the `Required` transaction attribute, the container will create a global transaction that enlists any referenced resources and will be propagated to any other EJBs that are used during message processing. This is the only case where the JMS topic interface is involved in an EJB transaction.

Security

In order to simplify the development process for the Bean Writer, the implementation of the security infrastructure is left to the EJB Container provider and the task of defining security policies is left to the Bean Deployer. By avoiding putting hard-coded security policies inside bean code, EJB applications gain flexibility when configuring and reconfiguring security policies for complex enterprise applications. Applications also gain portability across different EJB servers that may use different security mechanisms.

The EJB framework specifies flexibility with regards to security management allowing it to be declarative (container-managed) or programmatic (bean-managed).

Security Not Covered by the EJB Specification

As opposed to Access Control, authentication and communication security are not specified in the EJB security guidelines. These aspects of security are left to the proprietary application server or the container.

Deployment

When an EJB application is ready to be deployed to an EJB container, the desired beans and deployment information must be placed in an ejb-jar file. The deployment information to be placed in this JAR file is contained in an XML file called a deployment descriptor.

Deployment Descriptors

The deployment descriptor is an XML file containing elements that specify how to create and maintain EJB components and how to establish runtime service settings. The deployment descriptor contains settings that are not to be hard-coded inside EJB components. These settings tell the EJB container how to manage and control EJB components. These settings can be set at application assembly time or at application deployment time. There are two basic types of elements contained inside the deployment descriptor file that can be categorized as follows:

- Bean elements—These elements declare the internal structure and external dependencies of EJB components. The descriptor defines, among other things, the EJB class names, the JNDI namespace that represents the container, `Home` interface names, and `Remote` interface names.
- Application assembly elements—These elements describe how EJB components are to be integrated into larger applications. Some of the application assembly elements describe environment values, security roles, and transaction attributes.

Packaging Hierarchies

An important attribute of the EJB specifications is that it not only provides the programming interfaces, but also defines how the component/application has to be packaged. The deployment descriptor that has to go into the packaging is the standard way of customizing parameters of a specific installation.

EJB components can be packaged as individual EJBs, as a collection of EJBs, or as a complete application system. EJB components are distributed in a Java Archive (JAR) file called an ejb-jar file. The ejb-jar file contains Java class files, as well as `Home` and `Remote` interfaces for EJBs. It also contains the XML deployment descriptor for the EJB.

`Home` and `Remote` Interfaces

The client view is provided through the `Home` interface and the `Remote` interfaces. Classes constructed by the container when a bean is deployed, based on information provided by the bean, provide these interfaces. The `Home` interface provides methods for creating a bean instance, while the `Remote` interface provides the business logic methods for the component. By implementing these interfaces, the container can intercede in client operations of an EJB. This offers the client a simplified view of the component.

Personal Roles for EJB Development

The J2EE standard describes roles for developers who must perform the different types of tasks necessary to create and deploy a J2EE/EJB application. Some of these roles are illustrated in Figure 11.5 and described in the following sections.

FIGURE 11.5
Main development roles.

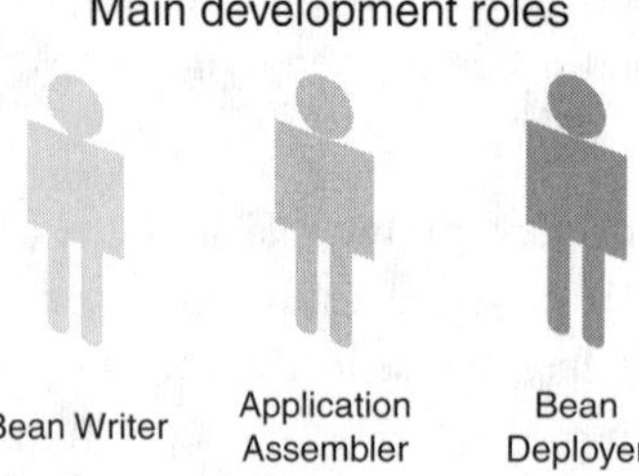

Entity Bean Developer

The entity bean developer defines both the `Home` and `Remote` interfaces representing the client view of the bean. They also create classes that implement the `EntityBean` interface, as well as methods corresponding to those classes in the bean's `Home` and `Remote` interfaces.

In addition to defining create methods in the `EJBHome` interface, the entity bean developer must also implement finder methods, providing a way to access an entity bean. Finder methods are designed to be introspected and displayed by deployment and development tools. This enables a user to manipulate entity beans with a graphical interface while developing applications.

The primary finder method that must be implemented by all entity beans is `findByPrimaryKey`. In addition to this method, the developer must also implement a `PrimaryKey` class to provide each entity bean with a unique and serializable identity.

Bean Writer

The bean writer, sometimes known as the *bean provider*, has the following responsibilities:

- To write Java code reflecting business logic.
- To provide interfaces and implementations.
- To make course references to data and security access. There is no need to code for security when controlling access at the method level. The bean writer can also use generic security references such as Accounting.
- To integrate code with third-party objects.
- To set transaction attributes.
- To control access programmatically within a method.

- To allow the application assembler to add roles and associate these roles with methods.
- To create a `Home` interface that is used to create and find beans.
- To create a `Remote` interface for business logic methods.
- To create an implementation of the bean class itself and utility classes if needed.
- To create a deployment descriptor giving security and transaction descriptions for the EJB's methods.

Application Assembler

The application assembler combines components and modules into deployable application units. An application assembler may be a higher-level business analyst that designs overall applications on the component level. The responsibilities include

- Building applications using EJBs. This usually includes the presentation layer.
- Specifying transaction management requirements.
- Setting transaction attributes for either all of the bean's methods or none of them.
- Defining security roles.
- Associating roles with methods by adding permissions.
- Specifying which roles belong to particular methods or using a wildcard (*) to apply to all methods.

Bean Deployer

The bean deployer adapts applications for a specific server's environment as well as making final customizations. The skills required would be those of a DBA and an application administrator. Their responsibilities include

- Managing persistence by mapping fields to actual database columns
- Managing security by defining roles, users, and user/groups
- Using deployment tools to create wrapper classes
- Making sure that all methods of the deployed bean have been assigned a transaction attribute
- Mapping roles of users and user groups for specific environments

Corporate Roles

Third party software companies can play several roles in the EJB framework, such as component provider, application server provider, and EJB container provider.

Component Provider

The responsibilities of the component provider lie in the business domain such as business process, software object modeling, Java programming, EJB architecture, and XML. They implement business functions with portable components.

Application Server Provider

The application server provider provides the platform on which distributed applications can be developed and provides runtime environment. The application server provider will usually contain an EJB container.

EJB Container Provider

The EJB container provider provides the runtime environment for EJB and binds it to the server. It may also generate standard code to transact with data resources. The application server provider is often the container provider as well.

Summary

Now that you've seen the services and benefits that an EJB container and application server can provide for your Java code, you may be interested in implementing some EJBs. The next two chapters will show you how to integrate your Java code into the EJB framework, while giving you some useful examples that you can use in your own applications.

CHAPTER

Enterprise JavaBeans: Building Session Beans

In This Chapter

- Creating Session Beans *358*
- Packaging and Deploying a Session Bean *400*
- Changes to Bean Code *402*
- Finding Session Beans from a Client *402*
- Calling Session Beans from a Client *405*

Building a session bean can be quite simple once a few basic steps have been mastered. In this chapter, these steps have been broken down and explained through the example of a session bean that provides validation for fields passed to it in a hash table.

Creating Session Beans

Before the session bean is created, it should be decided whether the session bean should be stateless or stateful. With stateful beans, the server saves information on the client's behalf. With stateless beans, the EJB specification allows vendors to call any bean so that fewer beans will be needed as long as the EJB container has the ability to pool stateless beans.

Stateful Versus Stateless Session Beans

As previously mentioned, the state attribute must be defined when creating the session bean. In order to help with that choice, a re-cap of the properties of stateless and stateful session beans is given below, along with some useful guidelines for deciding between the two states.

Stateful Session Beans

A stateful session bean is one that contains a conversational state with a client. The state of the stateful session is maintained for the duration of the conversation between the client and the session bean. When the session bean is removed by the client, its session ends and the state is destroyed. The transient nature of the state of the stateful session bean should not be problematic for either the client or the bean, because once the conversation between the client and the stateful session bean ends, neither the client nor the stateful session bean should have any use for the state.

Stateless Session Beans

Stateless session beans do not maintain conversational states for specific clients longer than the period of an individual method invocation. Instance variables used by a method of a stateless bean may have a state, but only for the duration of the method invocation. After a method has finished running either successfully or unsuccessfully, the states of all its instance variables are dropped. The transient nature of this state gives the stateless session bean beneficial attributes, such as

- Method Pooling—Any stateless session bean method instance that is not currently invoked is equally available to be called by an EJB container or application server in order to service the request of a client. This allows the EJB container to pool stateless method instances and increase performance.

- Scalability—Because stateless session beans are able to service multiple clients, they tend to be more scaleable when applications have a large number of clients. When compared to stateful session beans, stateless session beans usually require fewer instantiations.
- Performance—An EJB container will never move a stateless session bean from RAM out to a secondary storage, which it may do with a stateful session bean; therefore, stateless session beans may offer greater performance than stateful session beans.

Since there is no explicit mapping between multiple clients and stateless bean instances, the EJB container is free to service any client's request with any available instance. Even though the client calls the `create()` and `remove()` methods of the stateless session bean making it appear that the client is controlling the lifecycle of an EJB, it is actually the EJB container that is handling the `create()` and `remove()` methods without necessarily instantiating or destroying an EJB instance.

Guidelines: Use of Stateful Versus Stateless Session Beans

Stateful session beans should be considered when any of the following conditions are true:

- The session bean needs to maintain data in its member variables across method invocations.
- The state of the session bean must be initialized when the session bean is instantiated.
- The session bean needs to maintain information about the client across multiple method invocations.
- The session bean is servicing an interactive client whose individual presence needs to be known to the EJB container or applications server.

Stateless session beans may be considered when either of the following conditions are true:

- The session bean does *not* need to maintain any data in its member variables across method invocations.
- The session bean provides a service that is not client specific.

Defining the Session Bean Class

The session bean class must be declared with the attribute `public`. This attribute enables the container to obtain access to the session bean.

Session Beans and Inheritance

Java gives a developer the ability to extend a base class and inherit its properties. This ability pertains to session beans as well, allowing developers to take full advantage of any object oriented legacy code that they may wish to reuse. The following is an example of a session bean extending a base class:

```
public class fieldValidationBean implements SessionBean
                                 extends    validationBaseClass
{ ... }
```

Session Bean Interface

Session beans are held to the J2EE EJB specification by requiring all session beans to implement the `javax.ejb.SessionBean` interface. This requirement forces session beans to contain the following methods:

- `ejbActivate()`
- `ejbPassivate()`
- `ejbRemove()`
- `setSessionContext(SessionContext)`

A minimum sample of how a bean class must look is as follows:

```
public class fieldValidationBean implements SessionBean
{
public void ejbActivate  () throws RemoteException {..}
public void ejbPassivate () throws RemoteException {..}
public void ejbRemove    () throws RemoteException {..}

public void setSessionContext (SessionContext scContext)
                  throws RemoteException
{
sessionContext = scContext;
        ..
      }
 }
```

Clients of a session bean may either be remote or local depending on what interfaces are implemented.

Remote clients access a session bean via their *remote* and *remote home* interfaces (`javax.ejb.EJBObject` and `javax.ejb.EJBHome`, respectively). Remote clients have the advantage of being location independent. They have the ability to access a session bean in an EJB container from any RMI/IIOP-compliant application including non-Java programs such as CORBA-based applications. Because remote objects are accessed through standard Java RMI APIs, objects that are passed as method arguments are passed by value. This means that a copy of the object being passed is created and sent between the client and the session bean.

Local clients access a session bean via their *local* and *local home* interfaces (`javax.ejb.EJBLocalObject` and `javax.ejb.EJBLocalHome`, respectively). Using a local client gives the ability to have objects passed as arguments to methods by reference. Doing this avoids the overhead of creating copies of objects sent between clients and session beans. Certain applications will perform considerably better without this overhead. The bean writer should be aware that both the client and the session bean have the ability to change common objects. A local client is location dependent. It must reside inside the same Java Virtual Machine (JVM) as the session bean it interfaces with.

Both local and remote home interfaces (`javax.ejb.LocalHome` and `javax.ejb.EJBHome`, respectively) provide an interface to the client, allowing the client to create and remove session objects.

Neither local nor remote clients access session beans directly. In order to gain access to session bean methods, they use a component interface to the session bean. Instances of a session bean's remote interface are called session `EJBObjects` while instances of a session bean's local interface are called session `EJBLocalObjects`.

Both local and remote interfaces provide the following services to a client:

- Delegate business method invocations on a session bean instance.
- Return the session object's home interface.
- Test to see whether a session object is identical to another session object.
- Remove a session object.

Any method on a session bean class that is to be made visible to a client must be added to the bean's remote interface. This makes it possible to hide session bean methods from clients as well as to make different methods of a session bean available using different interfaces. Figure 12.1 illustrates how the client views the session bean interfaces.

When the application is deployed, the container or application server will use the interfaces defined by the bean writer and create `EJBHome`, `EJBObject`, stub, and tie classes:

- The `EJBHome` class is used to create instances of the session bean class and the `EJBObject` class.
- The `EJBObject` class provides access to the desired methods of the session bean.
- The stub classes act as proxies to the remote `EJBObjects`.
- The tie classes provide the call and dispatch mechanisms that bind the proxy to the `EJBObject`.

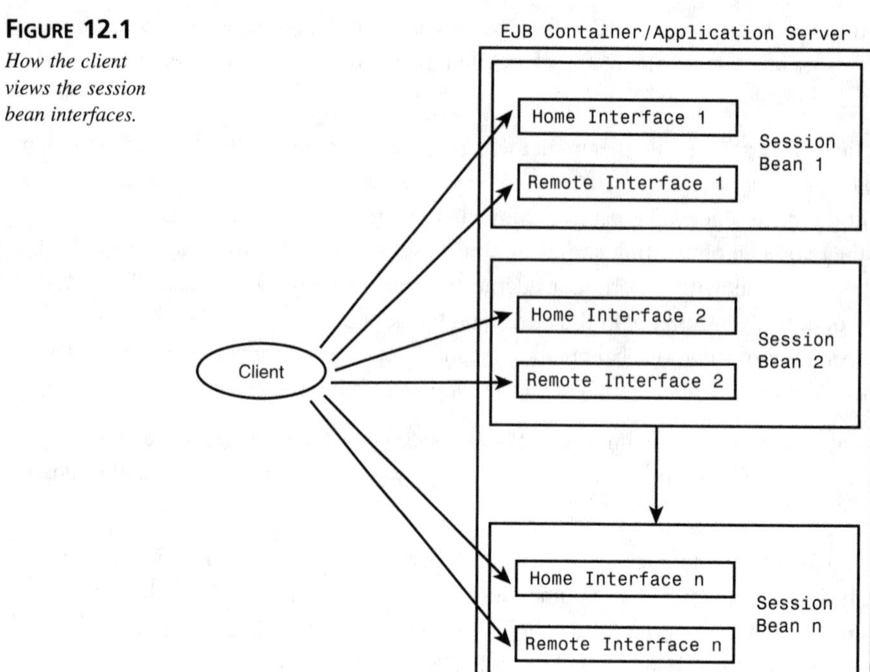

FIGURE 12.1
How the client views the session bean interfaces.

Creating a Remote Interface

All remote interfaces must extend the class `javax.ejb.EJBObject`. The following is an example:

```
public interface fieldValidationBean extends EJBObject { .. }
```

Methods in Remote Interfaces

The bean writer provides the session bean's remote interface, which extends `javax.ejb.EJBObject`, and the EJB container implements this interface. An enterprise bean's remote interface provides the client's view of a session object and defines the business methods that are callable by the client.

All business methods declared in the remote interface must have the same parameters and same return value types as the bean class. It is not necessary for all bean class methods to be exposed to the remote client.

All business methods declared in the remote interface must also throw at least the same exceptions as those in the bean class. They must also throw the `java.rmi.RemoteException` exception, because EJBs are dependent on the RMI package, specifically the `java.rmi.Remote` package, for distributed processing.

Normally the container or application server being used will generate the necessary remote interface code. The container should also update this code when changes are made to the bean class.

The method names and the signatures in the remote interface must be identical to the method names and signatures of the business methods defined by the enterprise bean. This is different from the home interface, where method signatures must match, but method names can be different.

In addition to business methods that may be defined in the remote interface, the methods listed here and shown in Figure 12.2 must be contained inside the remote interface:

- `getEJBHome()`—This method returns a reference to the session bean's home interface.
- `getHandle()`—This method returns a handle for the EJB object. This handle can be used at a later time to re-obtain a reference to the EJB object. A session object handle can be serialized to a persistent data store to enable the retrieval of a session object even beyond the lifetime of a client process. This is assuming that the EJB container does not crash or time out the session object, thereby destroying it.
- `getPrimaryKey()`—This method is not to be used for session beans. It returns the session bean object's primary key, but since individual session objects are to be used only by the specific client that creates them, they are intended to appear anonymous. If `getPrimaryKey()` is called looking for the identity of a session object, the method will throw an exception. This is different from entity objects (covered in Chapter 13, "Enterprise JavaBeans: Building Entity Beans"), which expose their identity as primary keys.
- `isIdentical()`—This method is used to test whether the EJB object passed is identical to the invoked EJB object.
- `remove()`—This method is used to remove a session bean object.

A typical remote interface definition for a session bean looks something like this:

```
import javax.ejb.*;
import java.rmi.* ;
import   java.util.*  ;
public interface fieldValidationBean extends EJBObject
{
     void isInt (double amount) throws RemoteException;
     void isNum (double amount) throws RemoteException;
}
```

FIGURE 12.2
Session bean remote interface.

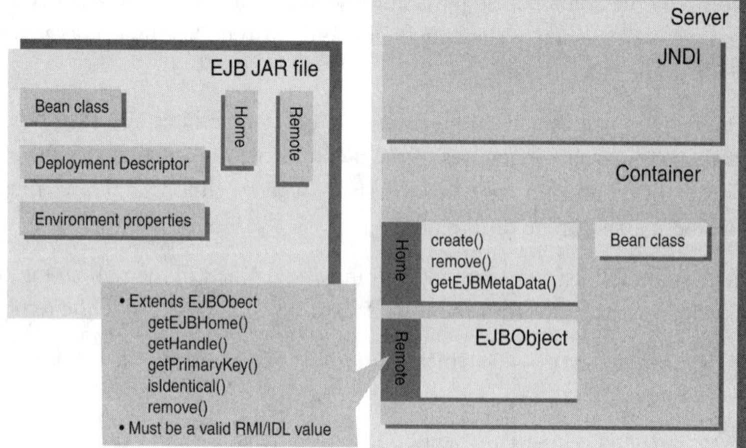

Creating a Home Interface

Session beans are instantiated when a client makes a call to one of the `create()` methods defined in the home interface. The home interface contains a `create()` method for every corresponding `ejbCreate()` method in the bean class.

The home interface is implemented in a container through an object called the `Home` object. The container makes an instance of the `Home` object visible to clients that want to instantiate a session bean.

In addition to `create` methods that are to be defined in the home interface, the methods listed here and shown in Figure 12.3 are to be contained in the home interface:

- `getEJBMetaData()`—This method is used to obtain the `EJBMetaData` interface of an EJB. EJB deployment tools are responsible for implementing classes that provide metadata to the remote client. The `EJBMetaData` interface enables the client to get information about the enterprise bean. This metadata may be used to give access to the enterprise bean clients that use a scripting language to access these enterprise beans. Development tools may also use this metadata. The `EJBMetaData` interface is not a remote interface, so its class must be serializable.
- `getHomeHandle()`—This method is used to obtain a handle of a `Home` object. The EJB specification allows a client to obtain a handle for the remote home interface. The client can use the home handle to store a reference to an entity bean's remote home interface in stable storage, and re-create the reference later. This handle functionality may be useful to a client that needs to use the remote home interface in the future, but does not know the JNDI name of the remote home interface.

- `remove(Handle h)`—This method is used to remove EJB objects that are identified by their handles. A handle may be retrieved by the `getHomeHandle()` method.
- `remove(Object primaryKey)`—This method should not be used for session beans. It is used to remove EJB objects that are identified by their primary key. Because session objects do not have primary keys that are accessible to clients, invoking this method on a session bean will result in a `RemoveException`. A container may also remove the session object automatically when the session object's lifetime expires.

Since all session objects keep their identity anonymous, `finder()` methods for session beans should not be defined. Finder methods are covered in Chapter 13, which considers entity beans.

Here is an example of a home interface definition for an EJB:

```
import javax.ejb.*;
import java.rmi.* ;
public interface fieldValidationBeanHome extends EJBHome
{
 Account create ()
  throws CreateException,
         RemoteException;
}
```

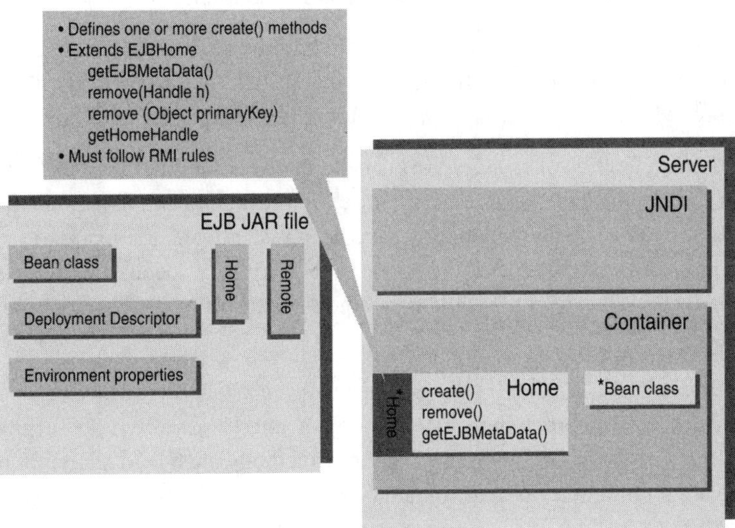

FIGURE 12.3
Session bean home interface.

Session Bean Class Methods

Session bean classes are used as the "molds" for instantiating session bean instances. These instances are indirectly called as local and remote clients via home and remote interfaces. `EJBCreate()` methods correspond with the `create()` methods of the session bean's home interface and are used for initializing the session bean's instance. The business methods created in a session bean class are a superset of those defined for the session bean's local or remote interface. It is these business methods that implement the core business logic for session beans.

`create()` Methods

The EJB specification requires the session bean class to contain one or more `ejbCreate()` methods. These `ejbCreate()` methods are normally used to initialize the bean.

As many `ejbCreate()` methods as necessary may be added to the bean, as long as their signatures meet the following requirements:

- They must have a `public` access control modifier.
- They must have a return type of `void`.
- They must have RMI-compliant arguments.
- They must not have a `static` or `void` modifier.

Several exceptions may be thrown including the `javax.ejb.CreateException` and other application-specific exceptions. The `ejbCreate()` method will usually throw a `CreateException` if an input parameter is not valid.

When a client invokes a `create()` method of a home interface, the `ejbCreate()` method of the session bean is called and the session bean and `EJBObject` are instantiated. After the session bean and `EJBObject` have been instantiated, the `create()` method returns a remote object reference of the `EJBObject` instance associated with the session bean instance to the client. The client can then invoke all of the business methods of this reference.

Because the `ejbCreate()` method is able to throw both `javax.ejb.CreateException` when there is a problem creating an object and the `java.rmi.RemoteException` when there is a system problem, the `create()` methods must be declared in order to throw both of these exceptions as well. In addition to the two aforementioned exceptions, the `create()` method must also throw any programmer-defined applications exception that may be thrown in the `ejbCreate()` method.

Business Methods

The primary purpose of a session bean is to execute business methods that implement business logic for use by a client. `create` methods return object references from which clients may invoke business methods. To the client, these business methods appear to be running locally; however, they actually run remotely in the session bean container.

Session bean business methods, like any other Java method, are defined with the following procedures:

- Adding a method to the bean
- Writing and saving the code
- Debugging your code
- Finishing the bean

It is important to note that the bean class should NOT implement the remote interface. The bean class code is where all of the actual business code exists. This code is not meant to be called without a proxy; therefore, it cannot be viewed directly by the client.

Sample Session Bean Component Code

The following sections give a sample of the source code and interfaces that the bean writer is responsible for creating. This is the core of the session bean that is surrounded by the EJB container and all of its services.

Session Bean Class Source Code

The following example session bean code implements business logic that can be used to validate text entered into a field of an application. In order to use this validation function's primary method, `fieldLevelValidationBean(...)`, a Hashtable needs to be passed into this method as an argument. This Hashtable, of type `java.util.Hashtable`, may contain multiple fields or values that need to be validated. If a hash element added to the Hashtable has a hash key that matches a `String` that is being looked for in `fieldLevelValidationBean(...)`, its corresponding hash value will be tested. If a field name is not contained within the Hashtable, its validation method is not executed. This "field-level" validation session bean is useful for checking all of the fields on any screen in an application. It is used to check the validity of fields individually. For example, let's say you were building an screen with all of the necessary input fields that would allow a user to buy and sell stocks. If the user were to enter a value of *S* for *sell* into the *side* field on the screen, the field-level validation method might check to see whether *S* is a valid input for this field.

After performing field-level validation of all fields on a screen, the next logical validation method that might be invoked on the same session bean would be a "cross-product" validation method. This validation method would check to see whether combinations of fields are legal. For example, a client may not be allowed to sell option orders; if this is the case, the combination of *order* = *O* and *side* = *S* would not be valid. It is good practice to break validation logic into at least two parts like this so that potentially complicated cross-product validation logic is not executed due to trivial errors such as typos.

The following example is a small part of a validation function that might be found in a financial application where stock or option orders are entered into an HTML-based order entry screen. Some of the fields that can be checked are `side`, with legal values of `Buy`, `Sell`, or `Hold`; `quantity`, which must be a valid number not less than or equal to zero; `duration`, with legal values of `Day`, `Month`, or `Year`; and `order`, with legal values of `Option` or `Stock`.

```
import javax.ejb.*         ;
import java.util.*         ;
import java.math.BigDecimal;

//////////////////////////////////////////////////////////////////////
//
//  Fields to check.
//
//sideKey
//quantityKey
//durationKey
//order_typeKey
//////////////////////////////////////////////////////////////////////

public class fieldLevelValidationBean implements javax.ejb.SessionBean
{
     protected   SessionContext m_context;

    public void setSessionContext(javax.ejb.SessionContext sessionContext)
    {
        m_context = sessionContext;
    }
    public void ejbCreate   () throws CreateException {}
    public void ejbRemove   () {}
    public void ejbActivate () {}
    public void ejbPassivate() {}

    public Hashtable isValid(Hashtable hParms)
    {
        System.out.println(this+" Inside  isValid"); System.out.flush();

        Hashtable hValidationReturn = new Hashtable ();
```

```
        System.out.println(this+" hParms = [" + hParms + "]");
        System.out.flush();

        hValidationReturn.put ( "returnCode", "0" );

        for ( Enumeration enumHParms = hParms.keys();
              enumHParms.hasMoreElements(); )
        {
            String sHashKey = (String) enumHParms.nextElement ();

            System.out.println(this+" hParms            = ["
                                    + hParms             + "]");
            System.out.flush();
            System.out.println(this+" hValidationReturn = ["
                                    + hValidationReturn  + "]");
            System.out.flush();
            System.out.println(this+" sHashKey          = ["
                                    + sHashKey           + "]");
            System.out.flush();

            ///////////////////////////////////////////////////////////////
//  Check for sideKey
            ///////////////////////////////////////////////////////////////
            if ( sHashKey.equals("sideKey") )
            {
                System.out.println(this+" inside if ( sHashKey ) " );
                System.out.println(this
                                    +" (String) hParms.get (sHashKey) = ["
                                    + (String) hParms.get (sHashKey) +"]" );

                if ( !(   ((String) hParms.get (sHashKey)).equals("B") //Buy
                       || ((String) hParms.get (sHashKey)).equals("S") //Sell
                       || ((String) hParms.get (sHashKey)).equals("H") //Hold
                     )
                   )
                   {
                   hValidationReturn.put ( "returnCode"   , "-1" );
                   hValidationReturn.put ( "returnString",
                        "Please choose a side (B=Buy, S=Sell, H=Hold for "
                        +(String) hParms.get ("symbolKey")+".");
                   System.out.println(this+" hValidationReturn = ["
                        + hValidationReturn + "]");
                   System.out.flush();
                   System.out.println(this
                        +" Leaving  isValid - false sideKey");
                   System.out.flush();
                   return hValidationReturn;
                   }
            }
```

```
////////////////////////////////////////////////////////////////////////////
//                         Checking for quantityKey
////////////////////////////////////////////////////////////////////////////
            else if ( sHashKey.equals("quantityKey") )
                {
                if (    (String) hParms.get (sHashKey) == null
                    || ((String) hParms.get (sHashKey)).equals ("")
                   )
                    {
                    hValidationReturn.put ( "returnCode"   , "-1" );
                    hValidationReturn.put ( "return String",
                       "Error: No Quantity entered for "
                       +(String) hParms.get ("symbolKey")+".");
                    System.out.println(this
                       +" Leaving isValid - false quantityKey 1");
                    System.out.flush();
                    return hValidationReturn;
                    }
                Double dbQuantity =
                       new Double ((String) hParms.get (sHashKey));
                if (   dbQuantity.intValue() <= 0 )
                    {
                    hValidationReturn.put ( "returnCode"   , "-1" );
                    hValidationReturn.put ( "returnString",
                       "Error: invalid Quantity, "
                       +dbQuantity.intValue()
                       +", for "
                       +(String) hParms.get ("symbolKey")
                       +"");
                    System.out.println(this
                       +" Leaving  isValid - false Key 2");
                    System.out.flush();
                    return hValidationReturn;
                    }
                }
             /////////////////////////////////////////////////////////////
             //                          checking account_typeKey
             /////////////////////////////////////////////////////////////
            else if ( sHashKey.equals("account_typeKey" ) )
                {
                String    AccountType  = (String) hParms.get (sHashKey);
                if ( !(   AccountType.equals("10")  // Preferred
                       || AccountType.equals("20")  // Expert
                       || AccountType.equals("30")  // Super Expert
                      )
                   )
                    {
                    hValidationReturn.put ( "returnCode"   , "-1" );
                    hValidationReturn.put ( "returnString",
                        "Error, Account Type "
                        + AccountType
```

```
            + " must be Cash, Margin or Short for "
            + (String) hParms.get ("symbolKey")
            + ".");
        System.out.println(this
            +" Leaving  isValid - false account_typeKey");
        System.out.flush();
        return hValidationReturn;
        }
    }

////////////////////////////////////////////////////////////
//                          checking durationKey
////////////////////////////////////////////////////////////
else if ( sHashKey.equals("durationKey" ) )
    {
    String Duration = (String) hParms.get (sHashKey);

    if ( ! (   Duration.equals("Day")
            || Duration.equals("Month")
            || Duration.equals("Year")
           )
       )
        {
        hValidationReturn.put ( "returnCode"  , "-1" );
        hValidationReturn.put ( "returnString",
            "Error, Invalid Duration "
            + Duration
            + " for "
            +(String) hParms.get ("symbolKey")
            +".");
        System.out.println(this
            +" Leaving  isValid - false durationKey");
        System.out.flush();
        return hValidationReturn;
        }
    }

////////////////////////////////////////////////////////////
//                          checking order_typeKey
////////////////////////////////////////////////////////////
else if ( sHashKey.equals("order_typeKey" ) )
    {
    String orderType = (String) hParms.get (sHashKey);

    if ( ! (   orderType.equals("O")     // Option
            || orderType.equals("S")      // Stock
           )
       )
        {
        hValidationReturn.put ( "returnCode"  , "-1" );
        hValidationReturn.put ( "returnString",
```

```
                        "Error, Invalid Order Type "
                        + orderType
                        + " for "
                        +(String) hParms.get ("symbolKey")
                        +".");
                    System.out.println(this
                        +" Leaving  isValid - false order_typeKey");
                    System.out.flush();
                    return hValidationReturn;
                    }
                }

            } // for ( Enumeration enumHParms = hParms.keys();...

        System.out.println(this
           +" Leaving  isValid - true"); System.out.flush();
        return hValidationReturn;
    } // public Hashtable isValid(Hashtable hParms)

    public void businessMethod2 (String sInput)
    {
System.out.println(this+" Inside  businessMethod2. sInput = ["+sInput+"]");
System.out.flush();
}

}
```

Session Bean Home Interface

The following code is a sample of a session bean home interface. Note that it has a `create` method that corresponds to the `ejbCreate()` method in the `javax.ejb.SessionBean` class `fieldLevelValidationBean`.

```
import javax.ejb.*;
import java.rmi.*;

public interface fieldLevelValidationHome
      extends   javax.ejb.EJBHome
{
    public fieldLevelValidation create()
        throws CreateException, RemoteException;
}
```

Session Bean Remote Interface

The following code is a sample of a session bean remote interface. Note that only one method, `isValid()`, is exposed to the client. The method `businessMethod2()` was left in as a comment in order to make it clear that one or all of the methods in the EJB class may be exposed to a client. It is not necessary to have unused methods commented out inside the remote interface. Figure 12.4 illustrates that the client views the `fieldLevelValidation` home and remote interfaces and that these interfaces interact with the session bean class.

```
import javax.ejb.*;
import java.rmi.*;
import java.util.Hashtable;

public interface fieldLevelValidation
      extends javax.ejb.EJBObject
{
    public Hashtable isValid(Hashtable hInput)
        throws RemoteException;

//    public void businessMethod2(String sInput)
//        throws RemoteException;
}
```


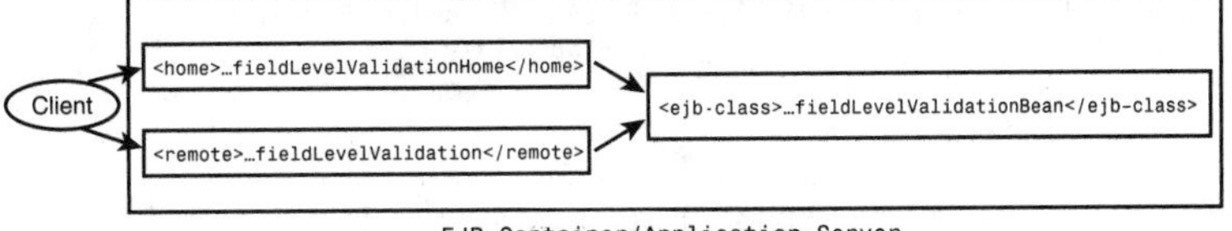

FIGURE 12.4
How the client views the `fieldLevelValidation` *interfaces.*

Stub, Tie, and Object Sample Code

In the previous section, the sample code is similar to what an EJB developer might be responsible for maintaining. This section presents code that the EJB container or application server is required to produce in order to support the distributed aspect of the EJB architecture.

The following code segments have been chosen to help clarify what is happening among the EJB components whether they are created by the developer or the container. It is also important to get a good look at what is going on under the hood in order to see what overhead is generated supporting this distributed architecture for both the client and the server. The following code was created using the J2EE certified SilverStream application server version 3.71; thus, these samples contain server-specific code. Once again, even though the development of the following code is not the responsibility of the developer, it is highly recommended that the programmer familiarize themselves with these pieces of the EJB framework in order to have a comprehensive understanding about how it works.

Home Stub Class

A reference to the home stub class in this example can be found by the client application using the JNDI naming service. This class is extended from the `javax.rmi.CORBA.Stub` class and it uses the RMI-IIOP services in order to communicate with the `javax.rmi.CORBA.Tie` interface that is mentioned in the next section. It also implements the session bean home interface `fieldLevelValidationHome` ensuring that the `create()` methods defined in the home interface are implemented. The following code consists primarily of calls to methods that are contained in the `javax.rmi.CORBA` and `org.omg.CORBA` packages:

```
public class _fieldLevelValidationHome_Stub extends javax.rmi.CORBA.Stub
            implements tgtg.fieldLevelValidationHome
{

...

    public javax.ejb.EJBMetaData getEJBMetaData()
          throws java.rmi.RemoteException
    {
        _local_stub:

        if (javax.rmi.CORBA.Util.isLocal(this)) {

            // get the Servant Object
            org.omg.CORBA.portable.ServantObject servObj =
                 servant_preinvoke("_get_EJBMetaData",
                 tgtg.fieldLevelValidationHome.class);
            if (_servObj == null) break _local_stub;

            try {
                // invoke on the servant
                return (javax.ejb.EJBMetaData)
                    javax.rmi.CORBA.Util.copyObject
                (
                 ((tgtg.fieldLevelValidationHome) _
                       servObj.servant).getEJBMetaData(), _orb()
                );

            } catch (Throwable ex) {
                // copy the exception
                ex = (Throwable) javax.rmi.CORBA.Util.copyObject(ex, _orb());

                throw javax.rmi.CORBA.Util.wrapException(ex);

            } finally {
                _servant_postinvoke(_servObj);
            }
        }
```

```
        org.omg.CORBA_2_3.portable.InputStream in = null;

        try {
            try {
                // create an output stream
                org.omg.CORBA_2_3.portable.OutputStream out =
                    (org.omg.CORBA_2_3.portable.OutputStream)
                     _request("_get_EJBMetaData", true);

                // do the invocation
                in = (org.omg.CORBA_2_3.portable.InputStream) _invoke(out);
                return (javax.ejb.EJBMetaData) in.read_abstract_interface
                (
                javax.ejb.EJBMetaData.class
                );

            } catch (org.omg.CORBA.portable.ApplicationException ex) {

                // get the input stream
                in = (org.omg.CORBA_2_3.portable.InputStream)
                    ex.getInputStream();

                // read the exception id
                String id = ex.getId();
                in.read_string();

                // unexpected exception
                throw new java.rmi.UnexpectedException(id);

            } catch (org.omg.CORBA.portable.RemarshalException rex) {
                return getEJBMetaData();

            } finally {
                _releaseReply(in);
            }

        } catch (org.omg.CORBA.SystemException ex) {
            throw javax.rmi.CORBA.Util.mapSystemException(ex);
        }
    }

////////////////////////////////////////////////////
//   Here is the create() function
////////////////////////////////////////////////////
    public tgtg.fieldLevelValidation create()
        throws javax.ejb.CreateException, java.rmi.RemoteException
    {
        _local_stub:

        if (javax.rmi.CORBA.Util.isLocal(this)) {
```

```
            // get the Servant Object
            org.omg.CORBA.portable.ServantObject _servObj =
            servant_preinvoke("create", tgtg.fieldLevelValidationHome.class);
            if (_servObj == null) break _local_stub;

            try {
                // invoke on the servant
                return (tgtg.fieldLevelValidation)
                javax.rmi.CORBA.Util.copyObject
                (
                  ((tgtg.fieldLevelValidationHome) _
                        servObj.servant).create(), _orb()
                );

            } catch (Throwable ex) {
                // copy the exception
                ex = (Throwable) javax.rmi.CORBA.Util.copyObject(ex, _orb());

                if (ex instanceof javax.ejb.CreateException)
                    throw (javax.ejb.CreateException) ex;

                throw javax.rmi.CORBA.Util.wrapException(ex);

            } finally {
                _servant_postinvoke(_servObj);
            }
        }

...


public javax.ejb.HomeHandle getHomeHandle()
        throws java.rmi.RemoteException
    {
        _local_stub:

        if (javax.rmi.CORBA.Util.isLocal(this)) {

            // get the Servant Object
            org.omg.CORBA.portable.ServantObject _servObj =
                _servant_preinvoke("_get_homeHandle",
                       tgtg.fieldLevelValidationHome.class);
            if (_servObj == null) break _local_stub;

            try {
                // invoke on the servant
                return (javax.ejb.HomeHandle) javax.rmi.CORBA.Util.copyObject
               (
                 ((tgtg.fieldLevelValidationHome) _
                      servObj.servant).getHomeHandle(), _orb()
               );
```

```
        } catch (Throwable ex) {
            // copy the exception
            ex = (Throwable) javax.rmi.CORBA.Util.copyObject(ex, _orb());

            throw javax.rmi.CORBA.Util.wrapException(ex);

        } finally {
            _servant_postinvoke(_servObj);
        }
    }

    org.omg.CORBA_2_3.portable.InputStream in = null;

    try {
        try {
            // create an output stream
            org.omg.CORBA_2_3.portable.OutputStream out =
                (org.omg.CORBA_2_3.portable.OutputStream)
                 _request("_get_homeHandle", true);

            // do the invocation
            in = (org.omg.CORBA_2_3.portable.InputStream) _invoke(out);
            return (javax.ejb.HomeHandle) in.read_value
           (
             javax.ejb.HomeHandle.class
           );

        } catch (org.omg.CORBA.portable.ApplicationException ex) {

            // get the input stream
            in = (org.omg.CORBA_2_3.portable.InputStream)
                ex.getInputStream();

            // read the exception id
            String id = ex.getId();
            in.read_string();

            // unexpected exception
            throw new java.rmi.UnexpectedException(id);

        } catch (org.omg.CORBA.portable.RemarshalException rex) {
            return getHomeHandle();

        } finally {
            _releaseReply(in);
        }

    } catch (org.omg.CORBA.SystemException ex) {
        throw javax.rmi.CORBA.Util.mapSystemException(ex);
    }
  }
}
```

One of the most interesting points about the previous code, without looking at it in depth, is the amount of code involved in the `stub` class. By looking at what is involved in implementing this `stub`, you can get a pretty good idea of what kind of overhead is involved in this framework. This will be important to keep in mind while considering certain optimization techniques when you are designing your system.

Home Tie Class

The home tie class acts as the interface between the previous home stub class and the container-generated `Home` object. It is extended from the `org.omg.PortableServer.Servant` class and it implements the `javax.rmi.CORBA.Tie` interface.

The bulk of the server-specific content of this tie class code is omitted. Much like the stub class, this class primarily consists of calls to methods that are contained in the `javax.rmi.CORBA` and `org.omg.CORBA` packages.

```
public class sbFieldLevelValidationHomePOATie
    extends org.omg.PortableServer.Servant
    implements javax.rmi.CORBA.Tie, tgtg.fieldLevelValidationHome
{
    public sbFieldLevelValidationHomePOATie() {}

    public sbFieldLevelValidationHomePOATie(java.rmi.Remote target)
    {
        setTarget(target);
    }

    public org.omg.CORBA.Object thisObject()
    {
        return _this_object();
    }

    public org.omg.CORBA.ORB orb()
    {
        return _orb();
    }

    public void orb(org.omg.CORBA.ORB orb)
    {
        _orb(orb);
    }

    public synchronized void deactivate() {}

    private
       tgtgUtilitiesDeployed.com.tgtg.sbFieldLevelValidationHome  target;
```

```
public void setTarget(java.rmi.Remote target)
{
    target=
     (tgtgUtilitiesDeployed.com.tgtg.sbFieldLevelValidationHome) target;
}

public java.rmi.Remote getTarget()
{
    return _target;
}

private static java.util.Dictionary _mtable = new java.util.Hashtable();
static {
    _mtable.put("_get_EJBMetaData", new java.lang.Integer(0));
    _mtable.put("create", new java.lang.Integer(1));
    _mtable.put("remove__javax_ejb_Handle", new java.lang.Integer(2));
    _mtable.put("remove__java_lang_Object", new java.lang.Integer(3));
    _mtable.put("_get_homeHandle", new java.lang.Integer(4));
}

public org.omg.CORBA.portable.OutputStream _invoke(String method,
    org.omg.CORBA.portable.InputStream in1,
    org.omg.CORBA.portable.ResponseHandler rh)
{
    org.omg.CORBA_2_3.portable.InputStream in =
        (org.omg.CORBA_2_3.portable.InputStream) in1;
    org.omg.CORBA_2_3.portable.OutputStream out = null;

    try {
        java.lang.Integer _m = (java.lang.Integer) _mtable.get(method);
        if (_m == null) throw new org.omg.CORBA.BAD_OPERATION(method);

        switch(_m.intValue()) {

            // getEJBMetaData ( _get_EJBMetaData )
            case 0: {
                javax.ejb.EJBMetaData result = _target.getEJBMetaData();
                out = (org.omg.CORBA_2_3.portable.OutputStream)
                    rh.createReply();
                javax.rmi.CORBA.Util.writeAbstractObject(out, result);
                break;
            }

            // create
            case 1: {
                try {
                    tgtg.fieldLevelValidation result = _target.create();
                    out = (org.omg.CORBA_2_3.portable.OutputStream)
                        rh.createReply();
                    javax.rmi.CORBA.Util.writeRemoteObject(out, result);
                } catch (javax.ejb.CreateException ex) {
```

```
            out = (org.omg.CORBA_2_3.portable.OutputStream)
                rh.createExceptionReply();
            out.write_string("IDL:javax/ejb/CreateEx:1.0");
            out.write_value(ex);
        }
        break;
    }

    // remove ( remove__javax_ejb_Handle )
    case 2: {
        try {
            javax.ejb.Handle _arg0 =
                 (javax.ejb.Handle) in.read_value
            (
              javax.ejb.Handle.class
             );
            _target.remove(_arg0);
            out = (org.omg.CORBA_2_3.portable.OutputStream)
                rh.createReply();
        } catch (javax.ejb.RemoveException ex) {
            out = (org.omg.CORBA_2_3.portable.OutputStream)
                rh.createExceptionReply();
            out.write_string("IDL:javax/ejb/RemoveEx:1.0");
            out.write_value(ex);
        }
        break;
    }

    // remove ( remove__java_lang_Object )
    case 3: {
        try {
            java.lang.Object arg0 =
                javax.rmi.CORBA.Util.readAny(in);
          _target.remove(_arg0);
            out = (org.omg.CORBA_2_3.portable.OutputStream)
                rh.createReply();
        } catch (javax.ejb.RemoveException ex) {
            out = (org.omg.CORBA_2_3.portable.OutputStream)
                rh.createExceptionReply();
            out.write_string("IDL:javax/ejb/RemoveEx:1.0");
            out.write_value(ex);
        }
        break;
    }

    // getHomeHandle ( _get_homeHandle )
    case 4: {
        javax.ejb.HomeHandle result = _target.getHomeHandle();
        out = (org.omg.CORBA_2_3.portable.OutputStream)
            rh.createReply();
        out.write_value(result);
```

```
                    break;
                }
            }

        } catch (org.omg.CORBA.SystemException ex) {
            throw ex;

        } catch (java.lang.Throwable ex) {
            throw new org.omg.CORBA.portable.UnknownException(ex);
        }

        return out;
    }

    public javax.ejb.EJBMetaData getEJBMetaData()
           throws java.rmi.RemoteException
    {
        // delegate the invocation to target
        return _target.getEJBMetaData();
    }

    public tgtg.fieldLevelValidation create()
    throws javax.ejb.CreateException, java.rmi.RemoteException
    {
        // delegate the invocation to target
        return _target.create();

    }

    public void remove(javax.ejb.Handle _arg0)
    throws java.rmi.RemoteException, javax.ejb.RemoveException
    {
        // delegate the invocation to target
        _target.remove(_arg0);

    }

    public void remove(java.lang.Object _arg0)
    throws java.rmi.RemoteException, javax.ejb.RemoveException
    {
        // delegate the invocation to target
        _target.remove(_arg0);

    }

    public javax.ejb.HomeHandle getHomeHandle()
           throws java.rmi.RemoteException
    {
        // delegate the invocation to target
        return _target.getHomeHandle();
```

```
    }
    private static final String[] __ids = {
        "RMI:tgtg.fieldLevelValidationHome:0000000000000000",
        "RMI:javax.ejb.EJBHome:0000000000000000"
    };

    public String[] _all_interfaces(org.omg.PortableServer.POA poa,
           byte[] oid)
    {
        return __ids;
    }
}
```

Home Object Class

In a prior section, "Creating a Home Interface," an example of a simple home interface that is to be maintained by a developer is shown. In this section, a portion of the `Home` object code that is produced by an EJB container is shown. This `Home` object is used to connect the home tie class to the developer-written home life cycle methods. Since this object implements the previous `fieldLevelValidationHome` interface, it is guaranteed to support the required `create()` methods.`sbFieldLevelValidationHome.java`.

```
import java.awt.*;
import java.util.*;
import java.math.*;

// SilverStream imports
//----- Java imports -----
import javax.ejb.*;
import java.rmi.*;
import java.security.*;
import java.security.*;

public class sbFieldLevelValidationHome
extends AgoEJBSessionHome
implements fieldLevelValidationHome
{

    // ------ Method constant declarations ------

    static final public int METHOD_getEJBMetaData_void = 0;
    static final public int METHOD_getHomeHandle_void = 1;
    static final public int METHOD_remove_javaLangObject = 3;
    static final public int METHOD_create_void = 2;
    static final public int METHOD_isValid_javaUtilHashtable = 5;
    static final public int METHOD_remove_void = 4;
    static final public int METHOD_remove_javaxEjbHandle = 6;
```

```
public sbFieldLevelValidationHome() throws java.rmi.RemoteException
{
}

// ------ Create methods ------

public fieldLevelValidation create()
throws javax.ejb.CreateException,
       java.rmi.RemoteException
{
    AgoEJBCompletionAction action = null;
    try
    {
        // this check encompasses removed/discarded, reentrancy,
        // security checking
        // 1st arg is index into depl info, 2nd is txType
        action = checkEJBBegin(METHOD_create_void, 2);
        AgoEJBSessionContext ctxt = super.newContext();
        fieldLevelValidationBean b =
             (fieldLevelValidationBean) super.createBean
                                   (
                                      action, ctxt
                                   );
        EJBObject e = super.create(b);
        e = export(e, b, ctxt);
        b.ejbCreate();
        return (fieldLevelValidation)e;
    }
    catch (javax.ejb.CreateException ex0)
    {
        throw ex0;
    }
    catch (Throwable ex)
    {
        throw handleSystemExceptions(ex, action);
    }
    finally
    {
        checkEJBEnd(action);
    }
}


// ------ remove methods ------

public void remove(Handle handle)
throws RemoveException,
       java.rmi.RemoteException
{
    AgoEJBCompletionAction action = null;
    try
```

```
        {
            // this check encompasses removed/discarded, reentrancy,
            // security checking
            // 1st arg is index into depl info, 2nd is txType

            action = checkEJBBegin(METHOD_remove_javaxEjbHandle, 2);
            super.remove(handle);
        }
        catch (RemoveException ex0)
        {
            throw ex0;
        }
        catch (Throwable ex)
        {
            throw handleSystemExceptions(ex, action);
        }
        finally
        {
            checkEJBEnd(action);
        }
    }
    public void remove(java.lang.Object primaryKey)
    throws RemoveException,
           java.rmi.RemoteException
    {
        AgoEJBCompletionAction action = null;
        try
        {
            // this check encompasses removed/discarded, reentrancy,
            // security checking
            // 1st arg is index into depl info, 2nd is txType

            action = checkEJBBegin(METHOD_remove_javaLangObject, 2);
            super.remove(primaryKey);
        }
        catch (RemoveException ex0)
        {
            throw ex0;
        }
        catch (Throwable ex)
        {
            throw handleSystemExceptions(ex, action);
        }
        finally
        {
            checkEJBEnd(action);
        }
    }
}
```

Remote Stub Class

As mentioned previously, a reference to the `Remote` object is returned to the client when the client calls the `home.create()` method. To the client, it appears that they are accessing the business methods of the EJB class. It is actually calling methods on the remote stub class, which eventually returns the results of the business method to the client. Like the home stub class, the container-generated remote stub class is extended from the `javax.rmi.CORBA.Stub` class. This stub also uses RMI-IIOP services in order to communicate with its corresponding remote `javax.rmi.CORBA.Tie` interface. This remote stub class implements the session bean remote interface `fieldLevelValidation`, ensuring that all of the developer-defined methods in the remote interface are implemented. Like the home stub class, the functionality in this class primarily consists of calls to methods that are contained in the `javax.rmi.CORBA` and `org.omg.CORBA` packages.


```
public class _TGTGfieldLevelValidation_Stub extends javax.rmi.CORBA.Stub
    implements fieldLevelValidation
{
    private static final String[] __ids = {
        "RMI:fieldLevelValidation:0000000000000000",
        "RMI:javax.ejb.EJBObject:0000000000000000"
    };

    public String[] _ids() { return __ids; }

    public javax.ejb.EJBHome getEJBHome()
        throws java.rmi.RemoteException
    {
        _local_stub:

        if (javax.rmi.CORBA.Util.isLocal(this)) {

            // get the Servant Object
            org.omg.CORBA.portable.ServantObject _servObj =
                _servant_preinvoke("_get_EJBHome",
                      fieldLevelValidation.class);
            if (_servObj == null) break _local_stub;

            try {
                // invoke on the servant
                return (javax.ejb.EJBHome) javax.rmi.CORBA.Util.copyObject
               (
               ((fieldLevelValidation) _servObj.servant).getEJBHome(), _orb()
               );

            } catch (Throwable ex) {
                // copy the exception
                ex = (Throwable) javax.rmi.CORBA.Util.copyObject(ex, _orb());
```

```
            throw javax.rmi.CORBA.Util.wrapException(ex);

        } finally {
            _servant_postinvoke(_servObj);
        }
    }

    org.omg.CORBA_2_3.portable.InputStream in = null;

    try {
        try {
            // create an output stream
            org.omg.CORBA_2_3.portable.OutputStream out =
                (org.omg.CORBA_2_3.portable.OutputStream)
                 _request("_get_EJBHome", true);

            // do the invocation
            in = (org.omg.CORBA_2_3.portable.InputStream) _invoke(out);
            return (javax.ejb.EJBHome) in.read_Object
                   (javax.ejb.EJBHome.class);

        } catch (org.omg.CORBA.portable.ApplicationException ex) {

            // get the input stream
            in = (org.omg.CORBA_2_3.portable.InputStream)
                ex.getInputStream();

            // read the exception id
            String id = ex.getId();
            in.read_string();

            // unexpected exception
            throw new java.rmi.UnexpectedException(id);

        } catch (org.omg.CORBA.portable.RemarshalException rex) {
            return getEJBHome();

        } finally {
            _releaseReply(in);
        }

    } catch (org.omg.CORBA.SystemException ex) {
        throw javax.rmi.CORBA.Util.mapSystemException(ex);
    }
}

public java.lang.Object getPrimaryKey()
    throws java.rmi.RemoteException
{
    _local_stub:
```

```
if (javax.rmi.CORBA.Util.isLocal(this)) {

    // get the Servant Object
    org.omg.CORBA.portable.ServantObject _servObj =
    servant_preinvoke("_get_primaryKey", fieldLevelValidation.class);
    if (_servObj == null) break _local_stub;

    try {
        // invoke on the servant
        return javax.rmi.CORBA.Util.copyObject
       (
         ((fieldLevelValidation) _
               servObj.servant).getPrimaryKey(), _orb()
       );

    } catch (Throwable ex) {
        // copy the exception
        ex = (Throwable) javax.rmi.CORBA.Util.copyObject(ex, _orb());

        throw javax.rmi.CORBA.Util.wrapException(ex);

    } finally {
        _servant_postinvoke(_servObj);
    }
}

org.omg.CORBA_2_3.portable.InputStream in = null;

try {
    try {
        // create an output stream
        org.omg.CORBA_2_3.portable.OutputStream out =
            (org.omg.CORBA_2_3.portable.OutputStream)
             _request("_get_primaryKey", true);

        // do the invocation
        in = (org.omg.CORBA_2_3.portable.InputStream) _invoke(out);
        return javax.rmi.CORBA.Util.readAny(in);

    } catch (org.omg.CORBA.portable.ApplicationException ex) {

        // get the input stream
        in = (org.omg.CORBA_2_3.portable.InputStream)
            ex.getInputStream();

        // read the exception id
        String id = ex.getId();
        in.read_string();

        // unexpected exception
        throw new java.rmi.UnexpectedException(id);
```

```
            } catch (org.omg.CORBA.portable.RemarshalException rex) {
                return getPrimaryKey();

            } finally {
                _releaseReply(in);
            }

        } catch (org.omg.CORBA.SystemException ex) {
            throw javax.rmi.CORBA.Util.mapSystemException(ex);
        }
    }

    public boolean isIdentical(javax.ejb.EJBObject _arg0)
        throws java.rmi.RemoteException
    {
        _local_stub:

        if (javax.rmi.CORBA.Util.isLocal(this)) {

            // get the Servant Object
            org.omg.CORBA.portable.ServantObject _servObj =
                _servant_preinvoke("isIdentical", fieldLevelValidation.class);
            if (_servObj == null) break _local_stub;

            try {
                // invoke on the servant
                return ((fieldLevelValidation) _servObj.servant).isIdentical
               (
                 (javax.ejb.EJBObject)
                       javax.rmi.CORBA.Util.copyObject(_arg0, _orb())
               );

            } catch (Throwable ex) {
                // copy the exception
                ex = (Throwable) javax.rmi.CORBA.Util.copyObject(ex, _orb());

                throw javax.rmi.CORBA.Util.wrapException(ex);

            } finally {
                _servant_postinvoke(_servObj);
            }
        }

        org.omg.CORBA_2_3.portable.InputStream in = null;

        try {
            try {
                // create an output stream
                org.omg.CORBA_2_3.portable.OutputStream out =
                    (org.omg.CORBA_2_3.portable.OutputStream)
                     _request("isIdentical", true);
```

```
            // marshal the parameters
            javax.rmi.CORBA.Util.writeRemoteObject(out, _arg0);

            // do the invocation
            in = (org.omg.CORBA_2_3.portable.InputStream) _invoke(out);
            return in.read_boolean();

        } catch (org.omg.CORBA.portable.ApplicationException ex) {

            // get the input stream
            in = (org.omg.CORBA_2_3.portable.InputStream)
                ex.getInputStream();

            // read the exception id
            String id = ex.getId();
            in.read_string();

            // unexpected exception
            throw new java.rmi.UnexpectedException(id);

        } catch (org.omg.CORBA.portable.RemarshalException rex) {
            return isIdentical(_arg0);

        } finally {
            _releaseReply(in);
        }

    } catch (org.omg.CORBA.SystemException ex) {
        throw javax.rmi.CORBA.Util.mapSystemException(ex);
    }
}

public java.util.Hashtable isValid(java.util.Hashtable _arg0)
    throws java.rmi.RemoteException
{
    _local_stub:

    if (javax.rmi.CORBA.Util.isLocal(this)) {

        // get the Servant Object
        org.omg.CORBA.portable.ServantObject _servObj =
            _servant_preinvoke("isValid", fieldLevelValidation.class);
        if (_servObj == null) break _local_stub;

        try {
            // invoke on the servant
            return (java.util.Hashtable) javax.rmi.CORBA.Util.copyObject
           (
             ((fieldLevelValidation) _
                    servObj.servant).isValid((java.util.Hashtable)
             javax.rmi.CORBA.Util.copyObject(_arg0, _orb())), _orb()
```

```
            );

        } catch (Throwable ex) {
            // copy the exception
            ex = (Throwable) javax.rmi.CORBA.Util.copyObject(ex, _orb());

            throw javax.rmi.CORBA.Util.wrapException(ex);

        } finally {
            _servant_postinvoke(_servObj);
        }
    }

    org.omg.CORBA_2_3.portable.InputStream in = null;

    try {
        try {
            // create an output stream
            org.omg.CORBA_2_3.portable.OutputStream out =
                (org.omg.CORBA_2_3.portable.OutputStream)
                 _request("isValid", true);

            // marshal the parameters
            out.write_value(_arg0);

            // do the invocation
            in = (org.omg.CORBA_2_3.portable.InputStream) _invoke(out);
            return (java.util.Hashtable) in.read_value
                   (java.util.Hashtable.class);

        } catch (org.omg.CORBA.portable.ApplicationException ex) {

            // get the input stream
            in = (org.omg.CORBA_2_3.portable.InputStream)
                ex.getInputStream();

            // read the exception id
            String id = ex.getId();
            in.read_string();

            // unexpected exception
            throw new java.rmi.UnexpectedException(id);

        } catch (org.omg.CORBA.portable.RemarshalException rex) {
            return isValid(_arg0);

        } finally {
            _releaseReply(in);
        }
```

```
    } catch (org.omg.CORBA.SystemException ex) {
        throw javax.rmi.CORBA.Util.mapSystemException(ex);
    }
}

public javax.ejb.Handle getHandle()
    throws java.rmi.RemoteException
{
    _local_stub:

    if (javax.rmi.CORBA.Util.isLocal(this)) {

        // get the Servant Object
        org.omg.CORBA.portable.ServantObject _servObj =
            _servant_preinvoke("_get_handle",
                    fieldLevelValidation.class);
        if (_servObj == null) break _local_stub;

        try {
            // invoke on the servant
            return (javax.ejb.Handle) javax.rmi.CORBA.Util.copyObject
           (
              ((fieldLevelValidation) _
                    servObj.servant).getHandle(), _orb()
           );

        } catch (Throwable ex) {
            // copy the exception
            ex = (Throwable) javax.rmi.CORBA.Util.copyObject(ex, _orb());

            throw javax.rmi.CORBA.Util.wrapException(ex);

        } finally {
            _servant_postinvoke(_servObj);
        }
    }

    org.omg.CORBA_2_3.portable.InputStream in = null;

    try {
        try {
            // create an output stream
            org.omg.CORBA_2_3.portable.OutputStream out =
                (org.omg.CORBA_2_3.portable.OutputStream)
                 _request("_get_handle", true);

            // do the invocation
            in = (org.omg.CORBA_2_3.portable.InputStream) _invoke(out);
            return (javax.ejb.Handle)
                    in.read_value(javax.ejb.Handle.class);
```

```
            } catch (org.omg.CORBA.portable.ApplicationException ex) {

                // get the input stream
                in = (org.omg.CORBA_2_3.portable.InputStream)
                    ex.getInputStream();

                // read the exception id
                String id = ex.getId();
                in.read_string();

                // unexpected exception
                throw new java.rmi.UnexpectedException(id);

            } catch (org.omg.CORBA.portable.RemarshalException rex) {
                return getHandle();

            } finally {
                _releaseReply(in);
            }

        } catch (org.omg.CORBA.SystemException ex) {
            throw javax.rmi.CORBA.Util.mapSystemException(ex);
        }
    }

    public void remove()
        throws java.rmi.RemoteException, javax.ejb.RemoveException
    {
        _local_stub:

        if (javax.rmi.CORBA.Util.isLocal(this)) {

            // get the Servant Object
            org.omg.CORBA.portable.ServantObject _servObj =
                _servant_preinvoke("remove", fieldLevelValidation.class);
            if (_servObj == null) break _local_stub;

            try {
                // invoke on the servant
                ((fieldLevelValidation) _servObj.servant).remove();
                return;

            } catch (Throwable ex) {
                // copy the exception
                ex = (Throwable) javax.rmi.CORBA.Util.copyObject(ex, _orb());

                if (ex instanceof javax.ejb.RemoveException)
                    throw (javax.ejb.RemoveException) ex;

                throw javax.rmi.CORBA.Util.wrapException(ex);
```

```
            } finally {
                _servant_postinvoke(_servObj);
            }
        }

        org.omg.CORBA_2_3.portable.InputStream in = null;

        try {
            try {
                // create an output stream
                org.omg.CORBA_2_3.portable.OutputStream out =
                    (org.omg.CORBA_2_3.portable.OutputStream)
                     _request("remove", true);

                // do the invocation
                in = (org.omg.CORBA_2_3.portable.InputStream) _invoke(out);

            } catch (org.omg.CORBA.portable.ApplicationException ex) {

                // get the input stream
                in = (org.omg.CORBA_2_3.portable.InputStream)
                    ex.getInputStream();

                // read the exception id
                String id = ex.getId();
                in.read_string();

                // handle user exceptions
                if (id.equals("IDL:javax/ejb/RemoveEx:1.0")) {
                    throw (javax.ejb.RemoveException) in.read_value
                          (javax.ejb.RemoveException.class);
                }

                // unexpected exception
                throw new java.rmi.UnexpectedException(id);

            } catch (org.omg.CORBA.portable.RemarshalException rex) {
                remove();

            } finally {
                _releaseReply(in);
            }

        } catch (org.omg.CORBA.SystemException ex) {
            throw javax.rmi.CORBA.Util.mapSystemException(ex);
        }
    }
}
```

Remote Tie Class

Similar to the home tie class, the remote tie class acts as an interface between the previous remote stub class and the container-generated `Remote` object. This tie class communicates with the stub class via RMI-IIOP in order to get the business object method invocations of the client to the remote bean object class and then get the business object responses back to the client. In order to do this, the remote tie class extends the `org.omg.PortableServer.Servant` class and implements the `javax.rmi.CORBA.Tie` interface. As with the stub class, this tie class primarily consists of calls to methods that are contained in the `javax.rmi.CORBA` and `org.omg.CORBA` packages.

```
public class sbFieldLevelValidationObjectPOATie
    extends org.omg.PortableServer.Servant
    implements javax.rmi.CORBA.Tie, fieldLevelValidation
{
    public sbFieldLevelValidationObjectPOATie() {}

    public sbFieldLevelValidationObjectPOATie(java.rmi.Remote target)
    {
        setTarget(target);
    }

    public org.omg.CORBA.Object thisObject()
    {
        return _this_object();
    }

    public org.omg.CORBA.ORB orb()
    {
        return _orb();
    }

    public void orb(org.omg.CORBA.ORB orb)
    {
        _orb(orb);
    }

    public synchronized void deactivate() {}

    private
      tgtg.gen.ejb.TGTGUtilitiesDeployed.com.tgtg.sbFieldLevelValidationObject
      target;

    public void setTarget(java.rmi.Remote target)
    {
   _target =
    (tgtg.gen.ejb.TGTGUtilitiesDeployed.com.tgtg.sbFieldLevelValidationObject)
     target;
    }
```

```
public java.rmi.Remote getTarget()
{
    return _target;
}

private static java.util.Dictionary _mtable = new java.util.Hashtable();
static {
    _mtable.put("_get_EJBHome", new java.lang.Integer(0));
    _mtable.put("_get_primaryKey", new java.lang.Integer(1));
    _mtable.put("isIdentical", new java.lang.Integer(2));
    _mtable.put("isValid", new java.lang.Integer(3));
    _mtable.put("_get_handle", new java.lang.Integer(4));
    _mtable.put("remove", new java.lang.Integer(5));
}

public org.omg.CORBA.portable.OutputStream _invoke(String method,
    org.omg.CORBA.portable.InputStream in1,
    org.omg.CORBA.portable.ResponseHandler rh)
{
    org.omg.CORBA_2_3.portable.InputStream in =
        (org.omg.CORBA_2_3.portable.InputStream) in1;
    org.omg.CORBA_2_3.portable.OutputStream out = null;

    try {
        java.lang.Integer _m = (java.lang.Integer) _mtable.get(method);
        if (_m == null) throw new org.omg.CORBA.BAD_OPERATION(method);

        switch(_m.intValue()) {

            // getEJBHome ( _get_EJBHome )
            case 0: {
                javax.ejb.EJBHome result = _target.getEJBHome();
                out = (org.omg.CORBA_2_3.portable.OutputStream)
                    rh.createReply();
                javax.rmi.CORBA.Util.writeRemoteObject(out, result);
                break;
            }

            // getPrimaryKey ( _get_primaryKey )
            case 1: {
                java.lang.Object result = _target.getPrimaryKey();
                out = (org.omg.CORBA_2_3.portable.OutputStream)
                    rh.createReply();
                javax.rmi.CORBA.Util.writeAny(out, result);
                break;
            }

            // isIdentical
            case 2: {
                javax.ejb.EJBObject _arg0 = (javax.ejb.EJBObject)
                        in.read_Object(javax.ejb.EJBObject.class);
```

```
                boolean result = _target.isIdentical(_arg0);
                out = (org.omg.CORBA_2_3.portable.OutputStream)
                    rh.createReply();
                out.write_boolean(result);
                break;
            }

            // isValid
            case 3: {
                java.util.Hashtable _arg0 = (java.util.Hashtable)
                                in.read_value(java.util.Hashtable.class);
                java.util.Hashtable result = _target.isValid(_arg0);
                out = (org.omg.CORBA_2_3.portable.OutputStream)
                    rh.createReply();
                out.write_value(result);
                break;
            }

            // getHandle ( _get_handle )
            case 4: {
                javax.ejb.Handle result = _target.getHandle();
                out = (org.omg.CORBA_2_3.portable.OutputStream)
                    rh.createReply();
                out.write_value(result);
                break;
            }

            // remove
            case 5: {
                try {
                    _target.remove();
                    out = (org.omg.CORBA_2_3.portable.OutputStream)
                        rh.createReply();
                } catch (javax.ejb.RemoveException ex) {
                    out = (org.omg.CORBA_2_3.portable.OutputStream)
                        rh.createExceptionReply();
                    out.write_string("IDL:javax/ejb/RemoveEx:1.0");
                    out.write_value(ex);
                }
                break;
            }
        }

    } catch (org.omg.CORBA.SystemException ex) {
        throw ex;

    } catch (java.lang.Throwable ex) {
        throw new org.omg.CORBA.portable.UnknownException(ex);
    }
```

```
    return out;
}

public javax.ejb.EJBHome getEJBHome() throws java.rmi.RemoteException
{
    // delegate the invocation to target
    return _target.getEJBHome();

}

public java.lang.Object getPrimaryKey() throws java.rmi.RemoteException
{
    // delegate the invocation to target
    return _target.getPrimaryKey();

}

public boolean isIdentical(javax.ejb.EJBObject_arg0)
       throws java.rmi.RemoteException
{
    // delegate the invocation to target
    return _target.isIdentical(_arg0);
}

public java.util.Hashtable isValid(java.util.Hashtable _arg0)
       throws java.rmi.RemoteException
{
    // delegate the invocation to target
    return _target.isValid(_arg0);

}

public javax.ejb.Handle getHandle() throws java.rmi.RemoteException
{
    // delegate the invocation to target
    return _target.getHandle();

}

public void remove() throws java.rmi.RemoteException,
                            javax.ejb.RemoveException
{
    // delegate the invocation to target
    _target.remove();

}
private static final String[] __ids = {
    "RMI:fieldLevelValidation:0000000000000000",
    "RMI:javax.ejb.EJBObject:0000000000000000"
};
```

```
    public String[] _all_interfaces(org.omg.PortableServer.POA poa,
        byte[] oid)
    {
        return __ids;
    }
}
```

Remote Object Class

This container-generated remote object class connects the remote tie class to the developer-maintained business class code. At the request of the `Tie` object, specific business methods are invoked. Since this object implements the previous `fieldLevelValidation` interface, it is guaranteed to support all of the business methods contained in the developer-created remote class.

```
import java.awt.*;
import java.util.*;
import java.math.*;

// SilverStream imports
//----- Java imports -----
import javax.ejb.*;
import java.rmi.*;
import java.security.*;
import java.security.*;
//----- SilverStream imports -----
import com.sssw.srv.ejb.*;
import com.sssw.srv.api.*;
import com.sssw.srv.ambry.*;
import com.sssw.rt.util.*;
import com.sssw.rt.ejb.*;

public class sbFieldLevelValidationObject
extends AgoEJBSessionObject
implements fieldLevelValidation
{

    // ------ Method constant declarations ------

    static final public int METHOD_getEJBMetaData_void = 0;
    static final public int METHOD_getHomeHandle_void = 1;
    static final public int METHOD_remove_javaLangObject = 3;
    static final public int METHOD_create_void = 2;
    static final public int METHOD_isValid_javaUtilHashtable = 5;
    static final public int METHOD_remove_void = 4;
    static final public int METHOD_remove_javaxEjbHandle = 6;

    protected int m_callCount;
    public sbFieldLevelValidationObject() throws java.rmi.RemoteException
    {
```

```
        m_callCount = 0;
    }

    // ------ Remote Interface methods ------

    public java.util.Hashtable isValid(java.util.Hashtable javaUtilHashtable0)
    throws java.rmi.RemoteException
    {
        AgoEJBCompletionAction action = null;
        try
        {
            // this check encompasses removed/discarded, reentrancy,
            // security checking
            // 1st arg is index into depl info, 2nd is txType
            action = checkEJBBegin(METHOD_isValid_javaUtilHashtable, 2);
            fieldLevelValidationBean b =
           (com.tgtg.TGTGfieldLevelValidationBean) getBean(action);
            java.util.Hashtable r = b.isValid(javaUtilHashtable0);
            return r;
        }
        catch (Throwable ex)
        {
            throw handleSystemExceptions(ex, action);
        }
        finally
        {
            checkEJBEnd(action);
        }
    }

    public void remove() throws RemoveException, java.rmi.RemoteException
    {
        AgoEJBCompletionAction action = null;
        try
        {
            // this check encompasses removed/discarded, reentrancy,
            // security checking
            // 1st arg is index into depl info, 2nd is txType
            action = checkEJBBegin(METHOD_remove_void, 2);
            super.remove();
        }
        catch (RemoveException ex0)
        {
            throw ex0;
        }
        catch (Throwable ex)
        {
            throw handleSystemExceptions(ex, action);
        }
        finally
```

```
            {
                checkEJBEnd(action);
            }
        }
}
```

Packaging and Deploying a Session Bean

After all of the components of the session bean have been created and compiled, for example the home interface, remote interface, bean code, and helper classes, they must be placed in a Java Archive (JAR) file along with a deployment descriptor file. This JAR file, with the extension .jar, is used for encapsulating the EJB components when deploying them to an EJB container. When using the deployment tools of a popular application server or EJB container such as SilverStream or I-Planet, EJBs can be packaged and deployed easily through a GUI. Hence, many of the steps mentioned next may be obsolete to the developer or deployer.

JAR Contents

As previously mentioned, EJB components are placed in a file that ends with the extension .jar. This JAR file must follow the format specified by the *zip* compression standard. This means that if a developer needs to see the contents of a JAR file, the extension of the JAR file may be re-named to .zip, enabling the files' contents to be viewed with any readily available zip utility.

Deployment Descriptor

A deployment descriptor, located within a JAR file, allows the properties of an EJB to be maintained outside of Java code. It allows the bean developer to make information about the bean available to the application assembler and the bean deployer. A deployment descriptor also provides run time information used by the EJB container. The EJB specification is very specific with regards to the content and format of deployment descriptors.

The deployment descriptor, written in XML, contains the structural information about the EJB such as the relative path and name of the bean class file, remote interface, and home interface, as well as the state management type and the transaction management type.

The deployment descriptor file may also contain optional information pertaining to multiple role names, environment entries, and data-source references. Note that all of the attributes of the bean are contained within XML tags.

```
<?xml version="1.0" encoding="UTF-8"?>
<!DOCTYPE ejb-jar PUBLIC
"-//Sun Microsystems, Inc.//DTD Enterprise JavaBeans 1.1//EN"
"http://java.sun.com/j2ee/dtds/ejb-jar_1_1.dtd">
<ejb-jar>
    <description>Jar Description</description>
    <enterprise-beans>
        <session>
            <description>Description for fieldLevelValidation</description>
            <ejb-name>fieldLevelValidation</ejb-name>
            <home>tgtg.utilities.fieldLevelValidationHome</home>
            <remote>tgtg.utilities.fieldLevelValidation</remote>
            <ejb-class>tgtg.utilities.fieldLevelValidationBean</ejb-class>
            <session-type>Stateful</session-type>
            <transaction-type>Container</transaction-type>
        </session>
    </enterprise-beans>
</ejb-jar>
```


Some of the elements in the preceding deployment descriptor sample are described as follows:

- `ejb-jar`—The root element of the EJB deployment descriptor
- `enterprise-beans`—Declares the session, entity, and/or message-driven beans
- `session`—Defines the enterprise bean to be a session bean as opposed to an entity or message-driven bean
- `ejb-name`—A unique name of a session, entity, or message driven-bean in an ejb-jar file; this element is used to tie ejbs together and for constructing a URL (note that there is no relationship between the element `ejb-name` and the JNDI name that is assigned to an enterprise bean's home)
- `home`—The fully-qualified name of an enterprise bean's home interface
- `remote`—The fully-qualified name of enterprise bean's remote interface
- `ejb-class`—The fully-qualified name of the enterprise bean's class
- `session-type`—The `session-type` element is either `Stateful` or `Stateless`
- `transaction-type`—Declares whether transaction demarcation is performed by the enterprise bean or the EJB Container

Types of JAR Files

There are several types of JAR files, including

- Distribution JARs—A JAR file that contains the basic components of a compliant EJB. It does not contain any server-specific information. Distribution JARs are portable and ready to be deployed across EJB-compliant containers and servers from different vendors.

- Deployment JARs—A JAR file that contains everything a distribution JAR does but also contains server-specific deployment information. Deployment JAR files are server specific; therefore, they are not portable across different containers or servers. The person serving as deployer is charged with the task of ensuring that the content of the deployment descriptor is complete and accurate. This deployer is also responsible for providing installation-specific information.
- Server JARs—A Server JAR, also known as a deployed JAR, is the file that contains all of the EJB components and descriptors that are to be run on the server side, for example in the container or application server.
- Client JARs—A Client JAR is the file that contains all of the EJB components necessary for inclusion in a client application in order to get access to the session bean business logic.

Deployment

As mentioned before, when the application is deployed, the container or application server will take the interfaces defined by the bean writer and create `EJBHome`, `EJBObject`, stub and tie classes. The `EJBHome` class is used to create instances of the session beans while the `EJBObject` class provides access to business methods and the stub and tie classes communicate requests and results between the clients and the session bean objects.

Changes to Bean Code

After session bean code has been modified, some or all of the other dependent EJB components may need to be updated. The container or application server may do this automatically or the programmer may be required to make these updates as necessary. If the constant rebuilding of EJB components becomes inconvenient, batch files may be written that can be either executed by the developer or integrated to work with the container for automatic execution.

Finding Session Beans from a Client

When a client calls an EJB, the ultimate goal is to gain the benefits derived from executing the business methods on a bean class. Before the EJB can get access to these methods, it must first find the `EJBHome` interface necessary to make an instance of the EJB Class. The first step in the process of finding the `EJBHome` starts with creating an `InitialContext`.

InitialContext

The `InitialContext` class acts as the client's interface to the JNDI interface. The `InitialContext` may contain information that will allow a client to bind to many naming services such as JNDI, CORBA COS, and DNS. Using the `InitialContext` class allows a client to only have to maintain a single interface to any naming service in the client's environment that supports JNDI.

Code that creates an `InitialContext` object and then calls its lookup method for the purpose of locating an `EJBHome` object may look something like this:

```
try
{
InititalContext iContext = new InitialContext();

fieldValidationBeanHome fvh =
(fieldValidationBeanHome) iContext.lookup("validate");
catch (javax.naming.NamingException error)
{
    System.out.println ("Initial Context Error:" + error);
}
```

If there are any problems with the creation of the `InitialContext` object or with calling one of its methods, the `javax.naming.NamingException` will be thrown so it is necessary to encapsulate this code in a try/catch block that handles this exception.

If you are trying to debug a naming service error, or any other error for that matter, you may find that your application server may generate more details about an exception if you comment out the following line from the catch statement above:

```
System.out.println ("Initial Context Error:" + error);
```

Type-Narrowing

In a standalone Java application, if a Java object such as `Object` is returned from a Hashtable, the return type of the method `get()` will be the supertype `Object` instead of the derived type `String`. For example:

```
Hashtable hash = ..;
..;
hash.get("keyToAStringElement");
```

It is left to the developer to cast, or narrow, the return value of the method `get()` to the proper object type. For example:

```
String aString = (String) hash.get("keyToAStringElement");
```

In the EJB application, once an object reference is obtained by a client, the method `javax.rmi.PortableRemoteObject.narrow(...)` must be used to perform type-narrowing for its client-side representation of its home and remote interfaces. The `javax.rmi.PortableRemoteObject` class is part of the RMI-IIOP standard extension. Type-narrowing ensures that the client programs are interoperable with different EJB containers.

Once the `InitialContext` has been used as the starting point for looking up a specific JNDI registered object, the `javax.rmi.PortableRemoteObject.narrow()` method should be called in order to perform type-narrowing of the client-side representations of the home interface.

Finding Objects and Interfaces: The Java Naming and Directory Interface (JNDI)

Clients that have access to the JNDI API may use this API to look up enterprise beans, resources such as databases, and data in environment variables. For example, a client application may locate an EJB with a call, something like

```
Object oReference = iContext.lookup
("java:server/directory/fieldValidationHome");
```

The name that a J2EE client uses to refer to an EJB does not necessarily have to be identical to the JNDI name of the EJB deployed in the EJB container or application server. For example, the EJB's JNDI name may be *validate* but the client refers to the EJB by *directory/fieldValdiationHome*. In this case, the naming services would need to have a mapping from the client reference *directory/fieldValdiationHome* to the EJB reference *validate*.

The level of indirection provided by the ability to map J2EE client names to JNDI registered EJBs gives great flexibility to distributed applications by allowing the client to use names that reference EJBs that make logical sense to the client. The client even has the ability to reference a single EJB with different names, when it makes sense to do so. This flexibility comes in handy when either the client code or the server code changes dynamically. The name that a standalone Java client uses to refer to an EJB using a JNDI lookup method must be identical to the EJBs JNDI name in the EJB container or application server. Hence the flexibility that the J2EE client has with calling EJBs does not pertain to standalone Java clients.

Creating an Instance Using EJBHome

Finally, after the home reference has been found, narrowed, and called, the home reference's `create()` method can be called returning the remote reference upon which the desired business methods can be invoked. The syntax for the calling of the `create()` method may be somewhat like this:

```
FieldValidation sbfieldValidation = fieldValidationHome.create();
```

Note

Remember that `create()` returns a reference to a remote interface, not the bean object itself. This means that certain programming practices that may be taken for granted in Java may not be used with EJBs. For example, objects are passed to EJBs via the arguments of the method calls and results are passed back to the client via the EJBs return object. It is not possible to maintain a reference to an input argument of an EJB, change that argument's values inside of the EJB, and then have access to those changes at the client.

Calling Session Beans from a Client

After all the components of a session bean have been created and a remote reference to the EJB is made available to a client, the exposed business methods of the `EJBObject` and the lifecycle methods of the EJBHome are available to the client as if the EJB were local to that client.

Coding Clients to Call EJBs

After the session bean reference has been made available to a client, it is up to the client to instantiate the bean components through the beans home interface. Only then can the business logic methods of the bean class be accessed via the exposed methods of the `EJBObject`. In order for J2EE applications to run in an efficient and stable fashion, both client and server developers should adhere to standard programming policy practices and procedures, two of which are mentioned next.

Session Beans, Reentrance, and Loop-back Calls

If a bean is allowed to invoke methods on itself or another bean that invokes methods on the initial bean, then the initial bean is said to be reentrant. This type of self-accessing call is referred to as a loop-back call. As opposed to an entity bean, a session bean is never allowed to be reentrant. If a session bean attempts to make a loop-back the EJB container should throw a `java.rmi.RemoteException` exception.

Remove the Bean When Done

When a client no longer has use for a session bean, it should remove the session object using the `javax.ejb.EJBObject.remove()` method or the `javax.ejb.EJBHome.remove(Handle handle)` method. If the `javax.ejb.EJBHome.remove(Object primaryKey)` method is called on a session by mistake, the `javax.ejb.RemoveException` will be thrown because session beans, unlike entity beans, do not have a primary key.

Different Types of Clients

The EJB framework allows many different types of clients to instantiate EJBs and takes advantage of the business logic that they implement. For the rest of this chapter, examples of different types of clients calling a session bean will be given along with some of the necessary tasks that need to be completed in order to support these different clients. More detailed reference can be found elsewhere in this book. This section concentrates on how clients can be integrated with EJBs.

Servlets Calling Session Beans

A servlet is a Java program that runs within a Web or application server and implements the `javax.servlet.Servlet` interface. Servlets are designed to receive and respond to requests from Internet clients or browsers. The standard protocols used for communication between a browser and a servlet are usually HyperText Transfer Protocol (HTTP) or secure hypertext transfer protocol (HTTPS). Servlets receive and respond to requests from Internet clients using methods defined by the `javax.servlet.Servlet` interface. After the Web or application server constructs the servlet, the servlet gets initialized by the life-cycle method `init()`. This example demonstrates how the servlet performs a lookup on the session bean and then narrows its data type:

```
private fieldLevelValidation m_sbFieldLevelValidation;

public void init() throws ServletException
{
    javax.naming.InitialContext initialContext =
    new javax.naming.InitialContext ();

    // JNDI Bean name
    Object obj = initialContext.lookup ("RMI/sbFieldLevelValidation");
    fieldLevelValidationHome sbFieldLevelValidationHome =
    (fieldLevelValidationHome) javax.rmi.PortableRemoteObject.narrow
```

```
    (obj, tgtg.fieldLevelValidationHome.class);
    m_sbFieldLevelValidation = sbFieldLevelValidationHome.create();
}
```

The second part of this example shows how the validation business method is called from the reference obtained from the home methods in the first part of the example:

```
private void actionPerformed ()
{
    Hashtable hField            = new Hashtable ();
    Hashtable hValidationReturn = new Hashtable ();

    // put the field name and value in the input Hash Table
    hField.put( (String)fieldName.trim(), (String)fieldValue.trim() );

    ////////////////////////////////////////////////////////////////
    // This is what its all about, the EJB business method call!!!
    ////////////////////////////////////////////////////////////////
    hValidationReturn  = m_sbFieldLevelValidation.isValid ( hField );
    ////////////////////////////////////////////////////////////////

    String sReturnCode = (String)hValidationReturn.get ("returnCode");

    if ( sReturnCode.equals ("0") )
    {
        lblSuccessMessage.setText( "Nice Value" );
        lblSuccessMessage.setEnableHTMLGeneration(true);
1234567890
        lblErrorMessage   .setEnableHTMLGeneration(false);
    }
    else
    {
        lblErrorMessage.setText(
                        (String)hValidationReturn.get ("returnString") );
        lblErrorMessage.setEnableHTMLGeneration(true);
        lblSuccessMessage.setEnableHTMLGeneration(false);
    }

}
```

The `java.util.Hashtable` `hField` is passed to the session bean business method by value, not by reference as it might naturally be assumed. So it is not possible for the client to pass `hField` in to a session business method, change the `Hashtable` inside of the session bean and then see the resultant changes inside of `hField`. All results are given to the client by the return object of the session bean.

Other Clients That Can Call Session Beans

Because they are Java based, EJBs are easily integrated with many other types of clients other than servlets. Some of the clients that work with EJBs are

- JavaServer Pages (JSP)—JSP pages are the primary client for J2EE applications and discussed in detail in the J2EE chapter of this book. The home interface of an enterprise bean can be found by defining an action that will call the lookup and narrowing methods. This action method can then be defined in a tag library for the JSP page.
- Standalone Java Applications—Standalone Java applications can make calls to EJBs if the application contains the appropriate stub classes. These stub classes can be placed in a jar file that is the classpath of the system that is to run the standalone application. Here are some examples of setting the class path for an application.

  For Unix:

  ```
  CPATH=$J2EE_HOME/tgtg/lib/j2ee.jar:validation.jar:.
  java -classpath "$CPATH" standAloneValidation
  ```

  For Windows:

  ```
  set CPATH=.;%J2EE_HOME%\tgtg\lib\j2ee.jar;validation.jar
  java -classpath "%CPATH%" standAloneValidation
  ```

  The previous commands will work for standalone applications that are running on the same server as the J2EE server. For standalone applications to be able to run a server other than the J2EE server, the stub .jar file must be placed on the remote server, and the Java run time switch `Dorg.omg.CORBA.ORBInitialHost` should be used when running the standalone application.
- Standalone Non-Java Applications—Standalone non-Java applications can make calls to EJBs (for example, CORBA applications can use the COS naming service to locate and call EJBs).
- J2EE Application Clients—One J2EE application may be run as a client to other J2EE applications. What is necessary to do this is to configure the JNDI naming service to find the EJB on the hosting J2EE server.
- Enterprise Beans—It is common for both session and entity beans to call each other from within a J2EE application.

Summary

The basics of creating a session bean that have been presented here are primarily container, application server, and IDE independent. In addition to giving an overview of what is necessary while building a session bean, this chapter should also be useful for the developer as they are actually going through the process of creating a session bean with a vendor-specific container or application server.

CHAPTER 13

Enterprise JavaBeans: Building Entity Beans

In This Chapter

- Defining Entity Beans *412*
- Container- and Bean-Managed Persistence *415*
- The Anatomy of a CMP Entity Bean *416*
- Developing Entity Beans *421*
- A Closer Look at Developing Entity Beans *428*
- EJB Clients *437*
- Using a GUI Tool to Configure, Package, and Deploy Entity Beans *439*

Defining Entity Beans

An entity bean is an EJB that models data which is typically stored in a relational database. Usually, it exists for as long as the data associated with it exists.

An entity bean is an object representation of data. An object is generally considered to be any entity with two specific attributes:

- An object has state.
- An object has functionality.

Entity beans implement the preceding criteria and are therefore considered objects. An entity bean contains a copy of persisted data; therefore, it has a state. It also contains business logic; therefore, it has functionality. With these properties, entity beans have the capability to give the same types of benefits as those of object databases.

Entity beans allow data to be persisted as Java objects as opposed to existing as rows in a table. They enable the Bean Writer to abstractly associate Java objects with relational database components (see Figure 13.1). Subsequently, the EJB Deployer is able to map these abstract relational components to existing persistence devices.

FIGURE 13.1
Entity beans as object representations of SQL data.

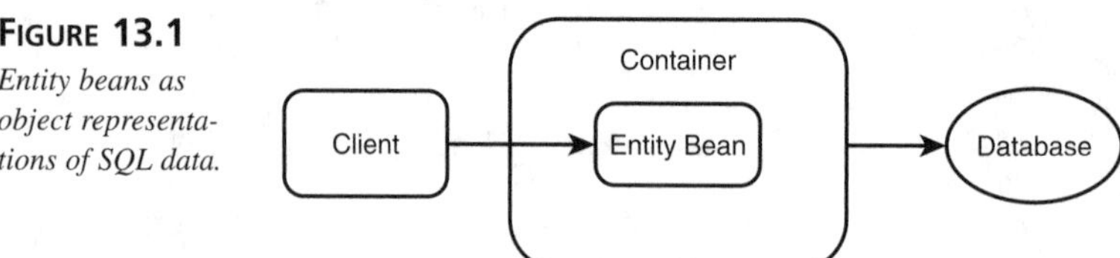

Entity beans access relational databases as well as enterprise systems or applications used to persist data (see Figure 13.2). Entity beans are able to be written in a robust and object oriented fashion so that they can be used with a variety of data sources or data streams.

FIGURE 13.2
Entity beans as object representations of data interfaced by a legacy application.

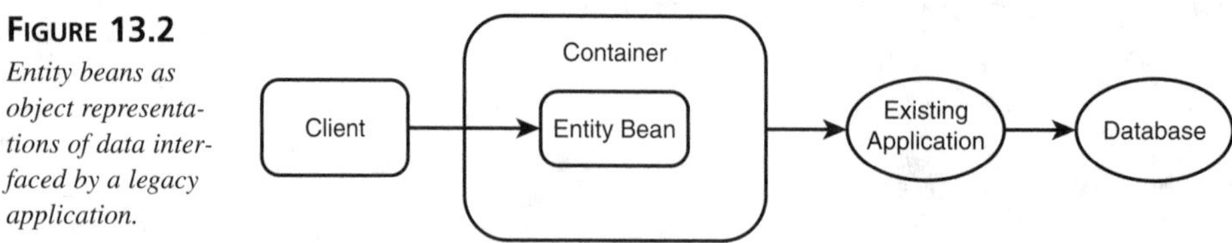

Entity beans are most often used for representing a set of data, such as the columns in a database table, with each entity bean instance containing one element of that data set, such as a row from a database table.

Methods of the entity bean's home interface, as defined in the EJB specification, allow clients to read, insert, update, and delete entities in a database.

Entity bean instances hold a copy of persisted data. If multiple clients execute the same find operation, all of them will get handles to the same entity bean instance. If there is contention between entity bean calls, it is handled by regarding each call as a separate transaction. The entity bean's transactional mode determines what will happen if multiple clients do insert or update operations on the same instance.

Uses of Entity Beans

The following are common uses of entity beans:

- Entity beans can be used to enforce the integrity of data that will be persisted as well as data that might potentially be persisted.
- Entity beans can be reused in order to cache data, therefore saving trips to the database.
- Entity beans can be used to model domain objects with unique identities that might be shared by multiple clients
- Unlike session beans, entity beans are intended to model records in a data set, not to maintain conversations with clients.
- Entity beans can be used for wrapping JDBC code, hence giving the application an object-oriented interface for the data set.
- Entity beans can be wrapped by session beans, giving the developer more control in determining how clients can control data.
- Entity beans can be used in either bean-managed persistence (BMP) or container-managed persistence (CMP) mode. CMP mode should be used if at all possible, allowing the Bean Writer to concentrate on writing business logic instead of JDBC logic.

Entity Bean Life Cycle States

As they execute the bean methods described later in this section, entity bean instances can be in one of three states (see Figure 13.3):

- The Null state—When the bean instance doesn't exist
- The Pooled state—When the bean exists, but isn't associated with any specific entity object
- The Ready state—When the bean instance has been assigned an entity object identity

FIGURE 13.3
Entity bean states.

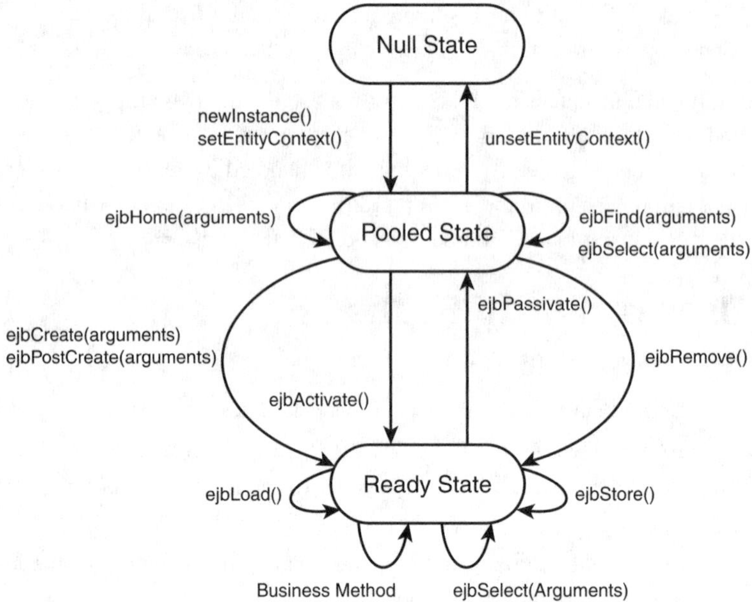

The EJB container invokes the following `EntityBean` interface methods when life cycle events occur. The Bean Writer is responsible for placing business logic in this container to handle the events of the application. The container invokes the following methods:

- `ejbActivate()`—An entity bean instance is chosen, removed from the available pool, and assigned to a specific EJB object.
- `ejbLoad()`—The container synchronizes its state by loading data from the underlying data source.
- `ejbPassivate()`—An entity bean instance is about to be disassociated with a specific EJB object and put back in the available pool.
- `ejbRemove()`—An EJB object that is associated with an entity bean instance is removed by a client-invoked remove operation on the entity bean's home or remote interface.
- `ejbStore()`—The container needs to synchronize the underlying data source, or persistent state, with the entity bean instance by storing data to the underlying data source.

More detailed information about these methods is available in Chapter 9, "JavaServer Pages: Practical Development with Tag Libraries."

Container- and Bean-Managed Persistence

As discussed in Chapter 11, "Enterprise JavaBeans: Introduction," entity beans can have their persistence managed in one of two ways, bean-managed persistence (BMP) or container-managed persistence (CMP). When the container handles the overhead necessary to support a bean in a manner that is satisfactory to the Bean Writer, more of the Bean Writer's development efforts might be focused on writing business logic. Throughout this chapter, we will focus primarily on creating beans that are container managed.

Bean-Managed Persistence

Bean-managed persistence (BMP) works well when data is being persisted to something other than a relational database, such as file system or a legacy enterprise application. When a bean manages its own persistence, it must also define its own JDBC calls. In this case, the entity bean is directly responsible for saving its own state. On the other hand, the container isn't required to make any database calls. Some benefits and drawbacks of BMP are detailed next.

BMP Pros

Benefits of bean-managed persistence include

- Container-Independent—Entity bean code written for one EJB container should be easily portable to any other certified EJB container.
- Standards-based—The standard EJB and JDBC APIs can be used for data access calls.
- Data-types—The ability to access non-standard data types and legacy applications is supported.
- Maximum Flexibility—Data validation logic of any complexity is supported.
- Database-specific features—The application is able to take advantage of nonstandard SQL features of different SQL servers.

BMP Cons

Drawbacks to bean-managed persistence include

- Entity bean code is database-specific—If access to multiple databases is required, the Bean Writer will have to account for this in their data access methods.
- The Bean Writer must have knowledge of SQL.

Container-Managed Persistence

When *container-managed persistence (CMP)* is used, the Persistence Manager of the EJB container is used to manage the persistence of the bean state or data. As previously mentioned, the Bean Writer in this scenario is able to concentrate on implementing business logic with Java code. A bean using CMP is simpler than one that uses BMP; however, it is also dependent on a container for database access.

Using CMP, the EJB container is responsible for saving the bean's state. Because the persistence process is container managed, the Java code used to retrieve and store data is independent of the data source. On the other hand, the container-managed fields do need to be specified in the Deployment Descriptor file so the EJB container's Persistence Manager can automatically handle the persistence process. This will be discussed in more detail later in this chapter.

CMP Pros

Benefits of using container-managed persistence include

- Database-Independence—The container, not the Bean Writer, maintains database access code to most popular databases.
- Container-specific features—Features such as full text search are available for use by the Bean Writer.

CMP Cons

Drawbacks to use of container-managed persistence include

- Only container-supported algorithms persistence can be used.
- Portability to other EJB containers can be lost.
- The developer has no access to the view and cannot modify the actual code.

The Anatomy of a CMP Entity Bean

There are many components to EJB entity beans. These components must interact with each other and with their container. The following is a summary of the `javax.ejb` package entity bean components and the methods they use. The Bean Writer creates some of these components. The EJB container, building on what the Bean Writer created, generates the remainder of the required components.

Bean Writer–Created Components

The Bean Writer is responsible for the creation of classes and interfaces. Business logic is placed in classes. Interfaces are used to define how the EJB container should build supporting objects as well as to define what business methods are to be visible to clients. The following sections describe varieties of these components in further detail.

The Abstract Entity Bean Class—Interface `EntityBean`

The abstract entity bean class is where the Bean Writer places the bulk of the business logic. The primary methods used toward this goal are the `EJBLoad()` and `EJBStore()` methods. The Bean Writer can put logic in these methods in order to get and set data to the underlying database. Other methods on bean instances are called by the container as life cycle events occur include: `ejbActivate()`, `ejbPassivate()`, `setEntityContext()`, `unsetEntityContext()`, and `ejbRemove()` as well as the `EJBLoad()` and `EJBStore()` methods.

The Primary Key Class

A primary key is a unique identifier of a Java object that doesn't necessarily have to relate directly (or at all) to a primary key of a database table. It isn't always necessary to write a primary key class because it is possible to use Java objects defined in the entity bean class such as `Strings` or `Integers` as primary keys. Primitive data types such as `int` can be used only if properly wrapped by Java objects.

A primary key class is defined inside of the deployment descriptor. Although an entity bean class can define a unique class as its primary key, it is possible for multiple entity beans to use the same primary key class. If two entity objects have the same home instance and the same primary key, they are considered to be identical.

The Remote Home Interface—Interface `EJBHome`

The Bean writer creates the remote home interface so that the EJB container can create an `EJBHome` object. The `EJBHome` object can be used to create, destroy, and find entity bean objects inside a home domain. When the EJB container implements the remote home interface, it enables clients to

- Create new entity objects within a home domain
- Find existing entity objects within a home domain
- Remove an entity object from a home domain
- Execute a home instance business method
- Obtain a handle for the home interface
- Get metadata information allowing for loose client/server binding and scripting

Zero or more `create()` methods, with the prefix name `create`, can be defined in the `EJBHome` Interface. Each entity object should have one or more `create()` methods. Each method's argument should be used to initialize the state of the entity object.

One `finder()` method should be defined for each different way of finding an entity object or a collection of entity objects within a home domain. The name of a `finder()` method should begin with the prefix `find`. The arguments of the method are used to locate desired entity objects. The return type must be either the entity bean's remote interface or a type that is a collection of objects implementing the entity bean's remote interface.

`Remove()` methods can also be defined to remove entity objects that are qualified by either a handle or a primary key. `Home()` methods are static methods provided by the Bean Writer for global business logic that isn't specific to any bean instance. `Home()` methods can have any name that doesn't begin with `create`, `find`, or `remove`.

The Home Handle—Interface `HomeHandle`

A client can use the home handle after it loses the Java Naming and Directory Interface (JNDI) name of a remote home interface. If a home handle is returned as the result of a `getEJBHome()` method, the client will be required to narrow the results in order to get the remote home interface.

The Handle—Interface `Handle`

The handle object created according to this interface is an abstraction on top of a network reference to an EJB object. It can be used as a persistent reference to that object.

The Remote Interface—Interface `EJBObject`

An entity bean's remote interface is used to define which methods in the abstract entity bean class will be visible to the client. Other required methods of the remote interface allow the client to

- Obtain the handle of an entity object
- Obtain the home interface of an entity object
- Remove an entity object

The Local Home Interface—Interface `EJBLocalHome`

The local home interface is similar to the remote home interface; however, it is faster because the local objects and the clients that call them are inside the same EJB container. As a result, these local objects don't need to support the overhead associated with distributed applications.

The Local Interface—Interface `EJBLocalObject`

Local interfaces are similar to the remote interface, having the benefit of speed like that of the local home interface.

The Remote Client

A remote client accesses an entity bean via methods defined in both the remote and remote home interfaces of the entity bean. The EJB container provides remote Java objects that implement those interfaces. These objects are accessible from a client through the standard Java APIs for remote object invocation. A remote client of an entity object can be another enterprise bean deployed in either the same or in a different container. A client can also be an arbitrary Java program, such as an application, applet, or servlet. In addition, the remote client view of an entity bean can be mapped to non-Java client environments such as CORBA.

The Local Client

A local client is one residing in the both the same JVM and EJB container as the entity bean it uses. In the interest of speed, a local client should access an entity bean through that entity bean's local and local home interfaces. Processing speed is gained because arguments of the methods of the local interface and local home interface are passed by reference instead of by value.

The `EntityContext`

The EJB container provides entity bean instances with an `EntityContext`. This `EntityContext` gives an instance access to the references of any objects associated with the instance (including `EJBLocalObjects`, `EJBObjects`, and primary key objects). This access is provided by the `getEJBLocalObject()`, `getEJBObject()`, and `getPrimaryKey()` methods, respectively.

The instance is also given access to information returned by the following methods, which are inherited from the `EJBContext` object:

- `getEJBHome()`—Returns the remote home interface of the entity bean.
- `getEJBLocalHome()`—Returns the local home interface of the entity bean.
- `getCallerPrincipal()`—Returns the `java.security.Principal`, identifying the invoker of the bean instance's EJB object.
- `isCallerInRole()`—Tests whether the caller of the entity bean instance has a particular role.
- `setRollbackOnly()`—Marks the current transaction so that a rollback is the only outcome of that transaction.

- `getRollbackOnly()`—Tests to see whether the current transaction of an instance has been marked for rollback.
- `getUserTransaction()`—Entity bean instances must not call this method, which returns the `javax.transaction.UserTransaction` interface.

The XML Deployment Descriptor

The deployment descriptor is used to declare entity bean persistent fields (cmp-fields) as well as field relationships (cmr-fields). It contains information about entity beans persistence and container managed relationships in the form of XML elements. This information, known as the *abstract persistence schema*, includes

- The `ejb-name` for each entity bean, which must be unique within an ejb-jar file.
- The `abstract-schema-name` for each entity bean, which must be unique within an ejb-jar file. This name can be used when specifying EJB QL queries.
- The ejb-relation set, containing a pair of `ejb-relationship-role` elements.
- The `ejb-relationship-role`, which describes a relationship role including its name, its multiplicity within a relation, and its navigability. The name of the cmr-field is specified from the perspective of the relationship participant. Each relationship role refers to an entity bean via an `ejb-name` element contained in the `relationship-role-source` element.

Container-Created Objects

After all the required interfaces and abstract classes are designed and developed by the Bean Writer, they are introspected by the EJB container. It examines the entity bean's deployment descriptor in order to create concrete objects that have the additional functionality required to integrate the business logic with the requirements of the EJB distributed object framework. These classes include

- Bean class—Extends the abstract entity bean `Class`, which implements the `EntityBean` interface.
- EJBHome class—Implements the remote home interface `EJBHome`. The EJB container makes these instances accessible to the clients through JNDI.
- EJBObject class—Implements the remote interface `EJBObject`.
- EJBLocalHome class—Implements the local home interface `EJBLocalHome`.
- EJBLocalObject class—Implements the local interface `EJBLocalObject`.

Figure 13.4 illustrates EJB objects provided by beans and containers. Entity bean objects are considered to be *persistent objects*; their lifetime isn't limited by the lifetime of the

Java Virtual Machine (JVM) process in which the entity bean instance executes. To illustrate, a JVM crash might result in a rollback of a transaction, but it will neither destroy previously created entity objects nor invalidate references interfaces held by clients.

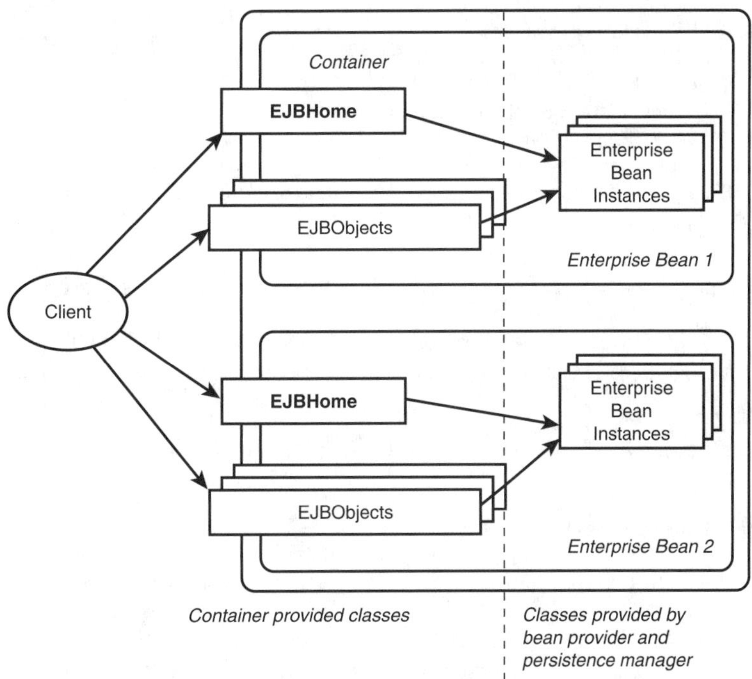

FIGURE 13.4
Bean and container provided EJB objects.

Developing Entity Beans

Throughout this chapter, we have presented most of the components of an entity bean. The following sections complete a checklist of tasks, annotated with helpful hints. These steps should be completed in order to develop an entity bean. Often, a development tool will be provided with the particular application or EJB server in use, such as SilverStream, Web Logic, or WebSphere. When using development tools, many of these tasks will be wrapped in a GUI IDE for creating interfaces and deployment descriptor files.

Step 1—Set Up A Data Source to a Database

A sample script used for creating a database table is shown next. Tables map to entity bean objects through use of the `abstract-schema-name` and the `sql-table-name` element tags in the deployment descriptor. Database columns are mapped to accessor methods in the entity bean. The item_number field maps to the `getItemNumber()` method. The description column maps to the `getInstructor()` and `setInstructor()` methods. The following sample script creates a table (note that this SQL is valid for Microsoft SQL Server or Sybase Adaptive Server Anywhere):

```
CREATE TABLE item_master
(
  item_number      VARCHAR(25) NOT NULL,
  item_description VARCHAR(25),
  PRIMARY KEY(item_number)
);
INSERT INTO item_master VALUES('27018301820A', 'TEA CHINA BLACK');
INSERT INTO item_master VALUES('70734070112A', 'BLK TEA EARL GREY');
```

Step 2—Develop a Primary Key Class

The following example shows how a primary key class implements the `java.io.Serializable` interface. This class could also have been extended from any base class.

```
public class ItemPK implements java.io.Serializable
{
    public int number;
    public ItemPK()
    {
        System.out.println( this + " Starting  ItemPK::ItemPK()");
    }
    public ItemPK(int itemNo)
    {
        System.out.println( this + " Starting ItemPK::ItemPK(itemNo)");
        number = itemNo;
    }
}
```

Step 3—Develop the Entity Bean Class

The entity bean `get()`, `set()`, `init()`, `create()`, and `postCreate()` methods are displayed in the following code example. Included in these methods is some standard debugging code that can or should be used in all methods.

```
import java.rmi.*;
import javax.ejb.*;
import java.util.*;

public class ItemMasterBean implements EntityBean
{

  protected EntityContext entityContext;
```

```
  public    String        number;        //item_number
  public    String        description;   //item_description
  //Accessor Methods
  public String getNumber ()
  {
    System.out.println ( this
              + " ItemMasterBean::getNumber() = [" + number + "]""]");
    return number;
  }
  public void setNumber (String itemNo)
  {
   number = itemNo;
   System.out.println ( this
             + " ItemMasterBean::setNumber() = [" +number+ "]");
  }
  public String getDescription ()
  {
    System.out.println ( this
              + " ItemMasterBean::getDescription() = [" +description+ "]""]");
    return description;
  }
  public void setDescription (String desc)
  {
   description = desc;
   System.out.println ( this
             + " ItemMasterBean::setDescription() = [" +description+ "]""]");
}
public ItemMasterBean ()
  {
    System.out.println ( this + " ItemMasterBean::ItemMasterBean ");
    try
    {
      tgtgInit ();
    }
    catch (Exception e)
    {
      e.printStackTrace ();
      System.out.println ( this
                + " ItemMasterBean::ItemMasterBean - tgtgInit() failed");
    }
  }
  private void tgtgInit () throws Exception
  {
    System.out.println ( this + " ItemMasterBean::tgtgInit()");
  }
  public void ejbCreate ( String itemNo)
    throws RemoteException, CreateException
  {
    System.out.println (this + " ItemMasterBean::ejbCreate(itemNo)");
    number      = itemNo;
```

```
    description = "";
    System.out.println (">>>>>>>>>>>>>>>>>>>>>>");
    System.out.println ( this + " number      = [" + number      + "]");
    System.out.println ( this + " description = [" + description + "]");
    System.out.println ("<<<<<<<<<<<<<<<<<<<<<<");
   }
  public void ejbCreate ( String itemNo, itemDesc)
    throws RemoteException, CreateException
  {
    System.out.println (this + " ItemMasterBean::
    ejbCreate(itemNo, itemDesc)");
    number      = itemNo;
    description = itemDesc;
    System.out.println (">>>>>>>>>>>>>>>>>>>>>>");
    System.out.println ( this + " number      = [" + number      + "]""]");
    System.out.println ( this + " description = [" + description + "]");
    System.out.println ("<<<<<<<<<<<<<<<<<<<<<<");
  }
  public void ejbPostCreate ( String itemNo)
    throws RemoteException, CreateException
  {
    System.out.println (this + " ItemMasterBean::ejbPostCreate(itemNo)");
    System.out.println (">>>>>>>>>>>>>>>>>>>>>>");
    System.out.println ( this + " number      = [" + number      + "]");
    System.out.println ( this + " description = [" + description + "]");
    System.out.println ("<<<<<<<<<<<<<<<<<<<<<<");
   }
  public void ejbPostCreate ( String itemNo, itemDesc)
    throws RemoteException, CreateException
  {
    System.out.println (this + " ItemMasterBean::
    ejbPostCreate(itemNo, itemDesc)");
    System.out.println (">>>>>>>>>>>>>>>>>>>>>>");
    System.out.println ( this + " number      = [" + number      + "]");
    System.out.println ( this + " description = [" + description + "]");
    System.out.println ("<<<<<<<<<<<<<<<<<<<<<<");
  }
  public void ejbActivate () throws RemoteException
  {
    System.out.println (this + " ItemMasterBean::ejbActivate()");
  }
  public void ejbLoad () throws RemoteException
  {
    System.out.println (this + " ItemMasterBean::ejbLoad()");
  }
  public void ejbPassivate () throws RemoteException
  {
    System.out.println (this + " ItemMasterBean::ejbPassivate()");
  }
  public void ejbRemove () throws RemoteException, RemoveException
  {
```

```
    System.out.println (this + " ItemMasterBean::ejbRemove()");
  }
  public void ejbStore () throws RemoteException
  {
    System.out.println (this + " ItemMasterBean::ejbStore()");
  }
  public void setEntityContext (EntityContext context) throws RemoteException
  {
    System.out.println (this + " ItemMasterBean::setEntityContext()");
    entityContext = context;
  }
  public void unsetEntityContext () throws RemoteException
  {
    System.out.println (this + " ItemMasterBean::unsetEntityContext()");
    entityContext = null;
  }
}
```

Step 4—Define the Home or Local Home Interface

The `home` interface should extend the `EJBLocalHome` interface in cases where the client will be calling the entity bean from inside the same EJB container, such as servlet-based database applications. If the client will be calling the entity bean from outside the EJB container, the `home` interface should extend the `EJBHome` interface.

The `home` interface is responsible for both finding existing objects and creating new objects. Each `home` interface enables the entity bean's primary key to find an entity bean object. A `findByPrimaryKey` method exists for any entity bean. `Finder` methods return the local interface for a bean or a collection of local interfaces. To clarify, the variable names `itemNo` and `itemDesc` match the arguments found in the `create` methods of the `EntityBean`. The `itemNo` and `itemDesc` fields are arbitrarily named local variables used to pass information into the `ejbCreate` method of the `EntityBean`.

```
Package tgtg.chadf.store;
import javax.ejb.*;

public interface ItemLocalHome extends EJBLocalHome
{
Item create (String itemNo)             throws CreateException;
Item create (String itemNo, itemDesc)   throws CreateException;

Item findByPrimaryKey(ItemPK pk)       throws FinderException;
}

public interface ItemRemoteHome extends EJBHome
{
```

```
  Item create (String itemNo)          throws CreateException, RemoteException;
  Item create (String itemNo, itemDesc) throws CreateException, RemoteException;
  Item findByPrimaryKey(ItemPK pk)     throws FinderException, RemoteException;
}
```

Step 5—Define the Local or Remote Interface

Methods of choice are exposed to clients in either the local or remote interface. The local interface extends the `EJBLocalObject` Interface, whereas the remote interface extends the `EJBObject` Interface.

```
package tgtg.chadf;

import javax.ejb.*;

public interface LocalItem extends EJBLocalObject
{
  String getNumber();
  void   setNumber (String itemNo);
  String getDescription();
  void   setDescription(String desc);
}

public interface RemoteItem extends EJBObject
{
  String getNumber();
  void   setNumber (String itemNo);
  String getDescription();
  void   setDescription(String desc);
}
```

Step 6—Define a Deployment Descriptor

The primary key class can be extended from any base class. In order to be a valid RMI/IIOP type, the primary key must implement the `Serializable` interface. A `hashCode()` method and an `equals()` method must be implemented in order for the EJB container to manage primary keys. These methods are necessary for the container to determine whether particular instances are the same.

```
<ejb-jar>
<enterprise-beans>
  <entity>
    <ejb-name>ItemMasterBean</ejb-name>
    <local-home>tgtg.chadf.ItemLocalHome</local-home>
    <local>tgtg.chadf.Item</local>
    <ejb-class>tgtg.chadf.Item </ejb-class>

    <prim-key-class>ItemPK</prim-key-class>
    <primkey-field>number</primkey-field>
```

```
    <persistence-type>Container</persistence-type>
    <reentrant>True</reentrant>

    <abstract-schema-name>item</abstract-schema-name>
    <sql-table-name>item_master</sql-table-name>

    <cmp-field><field-name>number</field-name></cmp-field>

    <cmp-field>
      <field-name>description</field-name>
      <sql-name>item_description</sql-name>
    </cmp-field>
  </entity>
</enterprise-beans>
</ejb-jar>
```

Some of the elements in the preceding deployment descriptor sample are described as follows:

- `ejb-jar`—The root element of the EJB deployment descriptor.
- `enterprise-beans`—Declares the session, entity, or message-driven beans.
- `entity`—Defines a session, entity, or message-driven bean.
- `ejb-name`—A unique name of a session, entity, or message-driven bean in an ejb-jar file. This element is used to tie EJBs together and to construct a URL. Note that there is no relationship between the element `ejb-name` and the JNDI name that is assigned to an enterprise bean's home.
- `local-home`—The fully-qualified name of an enterprise bean's local home interface.
- `local`—The fully-qualified name of enterprise bean's local interface.
- `ejb-class`—The fully-qualified name of the enterprise bean's class.
- `prim-key-class`—The fully-qualified name of the entity bean's primary key class. If the primary key class definition is deferred until the time of deployment, the `prim-key-class` element should specify `java.lang.Object`. Examples are as follows:

  ```
  <prim-key-class>tgtg.chadf.ItemPK</prim-key-class>
  <prim-key-class>java.lang.Object</prim-key-class>
  ```
- `primkey-field`—The name of the primary key field. This element must be one of the elements declared as a cmp-field field, and its type must be the same as that of the primary key type. Note that this field is not used for compound keys.
- `persistence-type`—Either `Bean` for BMP or `Container` for CMP.
- `reentrant`—Determines whether the bean can call itself. `True` if it can and `False` if it cannot.

- `abstract-schema-name`—Abstract name of a bean to be used in EJB QL queries.
- `sql-table-name`—The physical SQL table name for the bean.
- `sql-name`—The SQL table name for the field.
- `cmp-field`—Contains the `field-name` element and optionally the description element.
- `field-name`—A CMP bean's field name. This field must be a public field of a bean class or a bean class's super class. The first character of the field name must begin with a lowercase letter and is accessed by a method whose name is that of the field name with the first character made uppercase and with `get` or `set` added as a prefix.

Step 7—Deploy Using Container-Provided Tools

The tools provided for building and deploying EJB components vary from provider to provider. In the section of this chapter entitled "Using a GUI Tool to Configure, Package, and Deploy Entity Beans," the GUI provided by the SilverStream application server is shown, demonstrating what kind of tools are available to help the Bean Writer create EJBs.

Step 8—Creating a Client Application

A client application can be either remote or local. A remote client can be another bean either in the same or different EJB container, a Java program, or a non-Java program. A local client must run inside of the same JVM as the entity bean.

A Closer Look at Developing Entity Beans

This section provides a more in-depth look at the issues that need to be addressed when developing EJB component methods and configuration files.

Primary Keys

As mentioned previously, primary key classes can map to either a single field or multiple fields of an entity bean.

Mapping to a Single Field

Single field mappings are the simpler of the two cases. In this scenario, the `primkey-field` element in the deployment descriptor is used to specify which field specified by the container-managed element is to be used as the primary key. The `primkey-field` and the container-managed elements are required to be the same type.

Primary Keys that Map to Multiple Fields

In this situation, the fields of the primary key class must be a subset of the container-managed fields. The primary key class, its parameter-less constructor, and all primary key class fields are required to be declared as public.

The Unknown Primary Key Class

If the choice of the primary key field or fields is to be delayed until deployment time, the `findByPrimaryKey()` method, always a single-object finder, must be declared as `java.lang.Object`. The `prim-key-class` element in the deployment descriptor must also be `java.lang.Object`.

The `isIdentical()` Method

Client applications can test to see whether different object references are pointing to the same entity object by using the `isIdentitcal()` method.

The following example uses this method:

```
// Get Home references
ItemsItemRemoteHome itemHome1 = (ItemsItemRemoteHome)
                                javax.rmi.PortableRemoteObject.narrow(
                                initialContext.lookup("java:tgtg/chadf/items"),
                                ItemsItemRemoteHome.class);

ItemsItemRemoteHome itemHome2 = (ItemsItemRemoteHome)
                                javax.rmi.PortableRemoteObject.narrow(
                                initialContext.lookup("java:tgtg/chadf/items"),
                                ItemsItemRemoteHome.class);

if (itemHome1.isIdentical(itemHome2))
{
  System.out.println ( this + " The home objects are identical.");
}
else
{
  System.out.println ( this + " The home objects are not identical.");
}
```

Object Equality

The EJB framework doesn't specify *object equality*: that is, the use of the == operator. Instead, the `isIdentical()` method should be used to support this functionality.

The equals() Method

The java.lang.Object equals() method relies heavily on memory addresses. For this reason, the Bean Writer should either override this method or simply not use it. It is recommended to use the isIdentitcal() method when possible.

The hashCode() Method

The EJB framework doesn't specify the behavior of the Object.hashCode() method on object references pointing to entity objects. Instead, the isIdentical()method should be used to determine whether two entity object references refer to the same entity object. If the Bean Writer desires to use the hashCode() method, the following condition must be enforced:

```
if a.equals(b)
{
   if (a.hashCode() == b.hashCode())
      System.out.println(this + " is implemented correctly");
   else
      System.out.println(this + " is NOT implemented correctly");
}
```

The EntityBean Class and Life Cycle Event Methods

Much like the primary key class, the bean class can be extended from any Java class. If the Bean Writer extends an EntityBean class from another Java class, the methods of the base class will be available to the client through the defining of these base class methods in the stub for the EntityBean.

The Public Constructor

In order to control the initial state of all objects, the Bean Writer creates a public constructor. This constructor enables the container to create stable instances of the entity bean class. It is specified that this constructor should take no arguments. The container calls the public constructor in order to create a bean instance. The ejbCreate() and ejbPostCreate() methods are invoked to initialize that bean instance.

Declaring Member Variables

A public member variable should be defined in the declaration section of the entity bean class for each database field managed by the entity bean. Because they are never directly accessible to the client, these member variables can be made public without sacrificing good programming practice.

Accessor Methods

When using CMP, the Bean Writer doesn't make direct read and write calls to persistent storage devices. Instead, relational data is accessed via `get` and `set` accessor methods. These accessor methods, as well as the persistent fields and relationships, are declared in the abstract persistence schema of the XML deployment descriptor file.

The `cmr-field-name` element in the abstract persistence schema corresponds to the name used for the `get` and `set` accessor methods used for the relationship. The `cmr-field-type` element is used only for collection-valued cmr-fields. Accessor methods that start with `get` and `set` can be seen in the prior `ItemMasterBean` example.

The `ejbCreate()` Method

When using the `create()` and `remove()` methods, it is important to note the difference between session beans and entity beans. When these methods are used with session beans, bean objects are being created and destroyed. When these methods are used with entity beans, records in a database are being created and destroyed.

An entity bean can have zero or more `ejbCreate()` methods. However, the signature of each one should map to the `create()` methods in the entity bean home interface. When a client invokes a `create()` method to create an entity object, the container invokes the appropriate `ejbCreate()` method.

After the `ejbCreate()` method is completed, the EJB container performs a database insert. It is the container's responsibility to ensure that the container-managed fields have been set to their appropriate Java defaults (that is, `0` for Integers) before the `ejbCreate()` is invoked.

The `ejbPostCreate()` Method

For each `ejbCreate()` method declared, a matching `ejbPostCreate()` method with a void return type should be declared. Immediately after the EJB container invokes the `ejbCreate()` method on an `EntityBean` instance, it will call the corresponding `ejbPostCreate()` method on that same instance. The `ejbPostCreate()` method can be used to refine the instance created by the `ejbCreate()` method before this instance becomes available to the client.

To illustrate, it might be desirable to return a value of either the string `"You have won!"` or `"Please play again."` when a database value contains a Boolean value of either `0` or `1`. The `ejbPostCreate()` method can be used to make these types of modifications.

The `ejbCreate` method can be used to initialize persistent data, whereas the `ejbPostCreate()` method might do initialization involving the entity's context. Context information isn't available while the ejbCreate() method is being invoked, but is available when the ejbPostCreate() is being invoked.

After the ejbPostCreate() method is invoked, the instance can discover the primary key by calling the getPrimaryKey() method on its entity context object.

The ejbRemove() Method

When a container invokes the ejbRemove() method on a bean instance or a client calls the corresponding remove() method in its remote home or remote interface, it not only removes the entity bean instance, but it also destroys physical data that is related to the bean instance.

Another way to destroy an entity object and its corresponding physical data is by use of the deployment descriptor's cascade-delete deployment descriptor element, contained in the ejb-relationship-role element.

The ejbFind() Method

An ejbFind() method is defined for each of the find() methods in the home interface. This includes at least an ejbFindByPrimaryKey() method, which returns the primary key to the container.

The setEntityContext() Method

In order for an entity bean instance to use its EntityContext information during the instances lifetime, the bean instance must save the state of the EntityContext internally. The following code example accomplishes this:

```
EntityContext myContext;
public void setEntityContext(EntityContext ctx)
{
 myContext = ctx;
}
```

The unsetEntityContext() Method

The container invokes this method before terminating the entity bean instance.

```
public void unsetEntityContext()
{
 myContext = null;
}
```

The ejbLoad() Method

When in ready state in the bean pool, an entity bean must keep its state synchronized with underlying data. During the call to the ejbLoad() method, the data is read from the database and the instance variables are updated accordingly. Similarly, calling the `ejbStore()` method results in its writing the entity bean state to the database.

The container invokes the `ejbLoad()` method right after a bean is instantiated or a transaction begins.

The `ejbStore()` Method

When data is to be persisted to a permanent storage medium, the EJB container invokes the `ejbStore()` method.

The `ejbPassivate()` Method

This method is a counterpart of `ejbActivate()`. The EJB container invokes this API on the entity bean instance when the EJB container decides to return that instance to the bean pool. This method allows the entity bean instance to release any resources that shouldn't be held while in the bean pool. If resources are created during the execution of the `ejbActivate()` method, they should be freed in the `ejbPassivate()` method.

The `ejbActivate()` Method

The `ejbActivate()` method is invoked by the EJB container when an entity bean instance is chosen from the bean pool and is assigned a specific *object identity (OID)*. This method lets the entity bean acquire any necessary resources while the bean is in the ready state.

Some databases don't support activation and passivation. In these cases, empty `ejbActivate()` and `ejbPassivate()` methods should be supplied as demonstrated in the following:

```
public void ejbActivate (){}
public void ejbPassivate(){}
```

Home Interfaces and `create()` Methods

There are two types of home interfaces. The first is the remote home interface, which implements the `EJBHome` Interface. The second is the local home interface, which implements the `EJBLocalHome` Interface. The remote interface creates entity beans that can be accessed from outside of the EJB container by clients. The local interface creates entity beans that are accessed inside the EJB container by clients. The performance gained by using local entity beans is significant because clients get access to entity bean objects by reference as opposed to getting access to them by value. This saves considerable time while communicating with RMI and IIOP.

Much like that of session beans, the entity bean's home interface must contain a `create()` method. The client invokes this method in order to create an entity bean object. The name of each `create()` method starts with the prefix `create`. Unique signatures for `create()` methods are made using different method names, as long as the prefix starts with `create`, as well as by overloading `create()` methods with different arguments.

When an entity bean is first created, the `ejbCreate()` method creates a primary key that uniquely identifies that entity object. For the life of the entity bean object, the entity bean is associated with this primary key. As a result, the entity bean object can be retrieved by providing this primary key object to the `findByPrimaryKey()` method.

A bean's home interface can declare zero or more `create()` methods. A `create()` method exists for each different way of creating an entity object. Each of these `create()` methods must have corresponding `ejbCreate()` and `ejbPostCreate()` methods in the bean class. These creation methods are linked at runtime; when a `create()` method is invoked on the home interface, the container delegates the invocation to the corresponding `ejbCreate()` and `ejbPostCreate()` methods on the bean class. For example:

```
public interface ShoppingCartHome extends javax.ejb.EJBHome
{
  public ShoppingCart create(String firstName, String lastName,
  int itemNumber)
  throws RemoteException, CreateException;

  public ShoppingCart create(Integer customerNumber, int itemNumber)
  throws RemoteException, CreateException;

  public ShoppingCart createWholesaleCart(int firmNumber)
  throws RemoteException, CreateException;
...
}
```

A client can create a new entity object with code similar to

```
ShoppingCartHome cartHome = ...
Account account = cartHome.create("Bruce", "Pops", 5921);
```

Home Interfaces and `finder()` Methods

When an entity bean is first created, the `ejbCreate()` method creates a primary key that uniquely identifies that entity object. For the life of the entity bean object, the entity bean is associated with this primary key; therefore, the entity bean object can be retrieved by providing the `findByPrimaryKey()` method of the home interface with a unique primary key object. This primary key is defined by the developer and can be of any type as long as it is unique.

One or more `finder()` methods can be defined in the home interface. One method should exist for every way it is required to find an entity bean object or collection of entity bean objects. `finder()` methods start with a prefix `find`. The arguments of a `finder()` method are used to locate the desired entity objects. The return type of a `finder()` method is an instance of an entity bean or a collection of entity bean instances.

The following example shows the `findByPrimaryKey` method:

```
public interface ItemHome extends javax.ejb.EJBLocalHome
{
  //...
  public Item findByPrimaryKey(String number)
  throws FinderException;
  public Item findItemByDescription(String description)
  throws FinderException;
  public Collection findAllItems()
  throws FinderException;
}
```

The following example demonstrates how a client uses the `findByPrimaryKey` method:

```
ItemRemoteHome itemHome = (ItemRemoteHome)
                          javax.rmi.PortableRemoteObject.narrow(
                          initialContext.lookup("java:tgtg/chadf/items"),
                          ItemRemoteHome.class);
Item item = itemHome.findByPrimaryKey("27018301820A");
```


The entity bean provider doesn't write the corresponding `ejbFind()` method of `finder()` methods. `finder()` methods are configured by the development tools provided by the EJB container and then created when the entity bean is deployed.

Home Interfaces and `remove()` Methods

The `remove()` method of `EJBHome` interface supports the destruction of entity bean objects using either a handle object or a primary key object.

The `remove()` method of `EJBLocalHome` interface supports the destruction of entity bean objects using only the primary key object. The following code demonstrates how local home and home interface can be declared:

```
public interface EJBHome extends Remote
{
  void remove(Handle handle) throws RemoteException,
  RemoveException;
  void remove(Object primaryKey) throws RemoteException,
  RemoveException;
}
```

```
public interface EJBLocalHome
{
  void remove(Object primaryKey) throws RemoveException,
  EJBException;
}
```

When a `remove()` method is invoked on an entity object, the container invokes the entity bean instance's `ejbRemove()` method. After the `ejbRemove()` method returns from its invocation but before the `remove()` method acknowledges its completion to the client, the EJB container removes the entity object from all relationships in which it participates and then removes its persistent representation.

Home Interfaces and `getEJBMetaData()` Methods

The `getEJBMetaData()` method returns a reference to an object that implements the `EJBMetaData` interface. The `EJBMetaData` Interface allows application assembly tools to discover metadata information about an entity bean. This metadata information allows for loose client/server binding.

Remote Interfaces

Remote interfaces extend the `EJBObject` interface. They specify what methods of an entity object, created by the Bean Writer while implementing the `EntityBean` interface, can be accessed by a client. The client can exist either inside or outside of the EJB container. If the client exists inside of the EJB container, such as the case of a servlet application, the local interface should be used instead. Remote interfaces allow clients to

- Obtain the remote home interface for the entity object
- Remove the entity object
- Obtain the entity object's handle
- Obtain the entity object's primary key

Local Interfaces

Local interfaces extend the `EJBLocalObject` interface. These interfaces specify which methods of an entity object, created by the Bean Writer while implementing the `EntityBean` interface, can be accessed by a client that is local to the EJB container. The `EJBLocalObject` interface defines methods that allow the local client to

- Obtain the local home interface for the entity object
- Remove the entity object
- Obtain the entity object's primary key

Local interfaces can be used as a replacement for JDBC—supporting fast calls to a database while the client runs inside of the same JVM as the entity bean.

Use of local interfaces enhances performance because method arguments are passed by reference whereas requests never go across a protocol such as RMI or CORBA/IIOP. Because the EJB transaction support enables aggressive database caching, the performance of the application should be better than one using raw JDBC calls.

EJB Clients

There are two types of EJB clients: remote clients that exist outside of an EJB container and local clients that exist inside of an EJB container.

Multiple clients can access an entity object simultaneously while the EJB container synchronizes access to the entity objects via a transaction manager.

EJB containers make home interfaces available in a JNDI name space; therefore making these home interfaces available to clients. The home interfaces of entity beans allow clients to create, find, and remove entity objects within the enterprise bean's home domain. These interfaces also allow clients to execute static home business methods that aren't specific to a particular entity bean object.

Remote Clients

Remote clients can be enterprise beans deployed in the same or different EJB containers, standalone Java applications or applets via Java APIs for remote object invocation, or non-Java clients such as CORBA clients.

A remote client can get a reference to an existing entity object's remote interface in any of the following ways:

- Receive the reference as a parameter in a method call as an input parameter or result
- Find the entity object using a `finder()` method defined in the entity bean's remote home interface
- Obtain the reference from the entity object's handle

A client that has a reference to an entity object's remote interface can do the following:

- Invoke business methods on the entity object through the remote interface
- Obtain a reference to the enterprise bean's remote home interface
- Pass the reference as a parameter or return value of a method call

- Obtain the entity object's primary key
- Obtain the entity object's handle
- Remove the entity object

Locating a Remote Home Interface

The physical location of the EJB container is usually transparent to the client. A client locates an entity bean's home interface by using the *Java Naming and Directory Interface (JNDI)*. JNDI enables applications to access multiple naming and directory services using a single interface. A client's JNDI name space can be configured to contain the home interfaces of enterprise beans located on multiple EJB containers on multiple machines on a network.

A client that is to be interoperable with compliant EJB containers must use the `javax.rmi.PortableRemoteObject.narrow()` method in order to perform type-narrowing of the client-side representations of the remote home and remote interfaces.

The remote home interface `ItemRemoteHome` for the `ItemMasterBean` entity bean can be located using the following code segment:

```
Context  initialContext = new InitialContext();
ItemRemoteHome itemHome = (ItemRemoteHome)
 javax.rmi.PortableRemoteObject.narrow(
initialContext.lookup("java:tgtg/chadf/items"), ItemRemoteHome.class);
```

Locating an entity bean's local home interface using JNDI is done in a similar manner. It doesn't, however, involve the APIs for remote access. For example, if the `Item` entity bean provided a local home interface rather than a remote home interface, a local client might use the following code segment:

```
Context initialContext  = new InitialContext();
ItemRemoteHome itemHome = (ItemRemoteHome)
initialContext.lookup("java:tgtg/chadf/items");
```

Local Clients

Local clients access entity beans through local and local home interfaces with the arguments of the local and local home methods being passed by reference. The Bean Writer should be aware that argument objects shared between local clients and entity beans can be modified by either the local clients or the entity beans.

A local client can get a reference to an existing entity object's local interface in either of the following ways:

- Receive the reference as a result of a method call
- Find the entity object using a `finder()` method defined in the entity bean's local home interface

A local client that has a reference to an entity object's local interface can invoke business methods on the entity object through the local interface.

Using a GUI Tool to Configure, Package, and Deploy Entity Beans

EJB components were designed to encapsulate business logic in a container; therefore, the Bean Writer need not worry about developing code for tasks such as database access, transaction support, security, caching, and concurrency. Primarily, this logic is located in the entity bean class residing inside an EJB container.

Although the Bean Writer isn't required to develop code to handle all the tasks mentioned previously, the application assembler and the deployer, who is often the same person as the Bean Writer, will be required to configure the EJB container, defining the manor in which all these tasks are to behave. In and of itself, this is no small task. The tools provided by the EJB container greatly simplify these tasks. In addition, they might make some of the corresponding components, such as the deployment descriptor, transparent to the Bean Writer, application assembler, and deployer. Instead of flat files, they are left with an intuitive GUI interface to work with.

In this section, the interface provided by the SilverStream Application server is demonstrated in order to show how a GUI tool can be used to aid the application assembler and deployer when configuring and deploying the entity beans created by the Bean Writer. Note that the same type of GUI tools might also have been used earlier in the development process by the Bean Writer, such as during creation of components such as the local, remote, and home interfaces.

Assembling, Configuring, and Packaging Entity Beans

The ejb-jar file is the medium used for packaging an enterprise bean. This file, produced by the Bean Writer, can contain one or more enterprise beans. Normally, the enterprise beans don't contain application assembly instructions.

Creating a Jar File and Adding an Entity Bean to It

Once an entity bean has been specified, Application Assembly information can be added or modified. The GUI designer of choice can organize assembly information by category rather than by specific entity bean name. This will help keep groups of entity beans together inside common categories.

Figures 13.5 and 13.6 demonstrate the initial process of creating a jar file and adding an entity bean to that jar file.

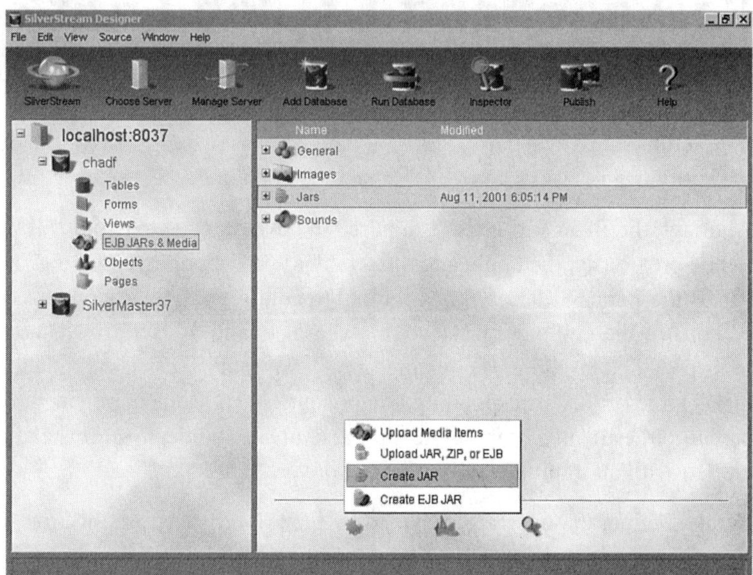

FIGURE 13.5
Creating a jar file for deployment.

Using a Property Inspector to Configure an Entity Bean

A property inspector provides an easy-to-use interface for configuring the entity bean. This relieves both the Application Assembler and Deployer from having to work directly with the XML Deployment Descriptor.

The bean name appears in the JAR Designer, identifying the bean. This name will also be used to fill in EJB reference links from other beans during application assembly.

Persistence type and primary key classes and fields can be configured easily.

Figure 13.7 shows the page where Roles, Method Permissions, and Transactions can be configured using a GUI tool instead of coding in XML.

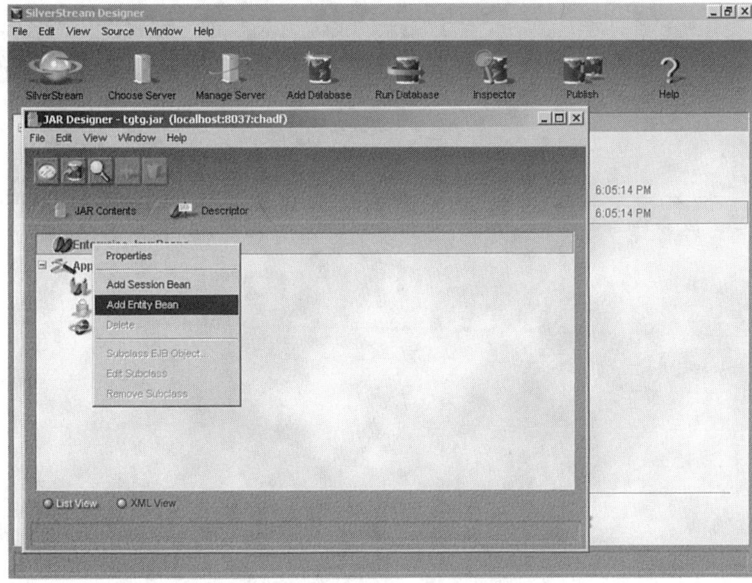

FIGURE 13.6
Adding an entity bean to a jar file.

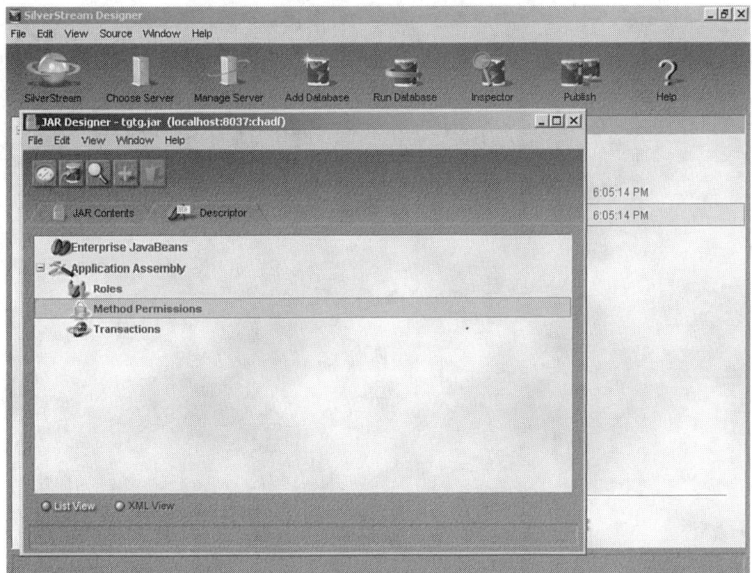

FIGURE 13.7
GUI page for configuring Roles, Method Permissions, and Transactions.

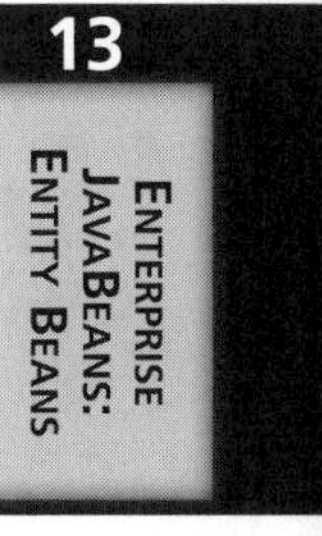

The role of admin has been added using the property inspector. This change is reflected in both the GUI property inspector and in the XML file that the property inspector updates. This is demonstrated in Figures 13.8 and 13.9.

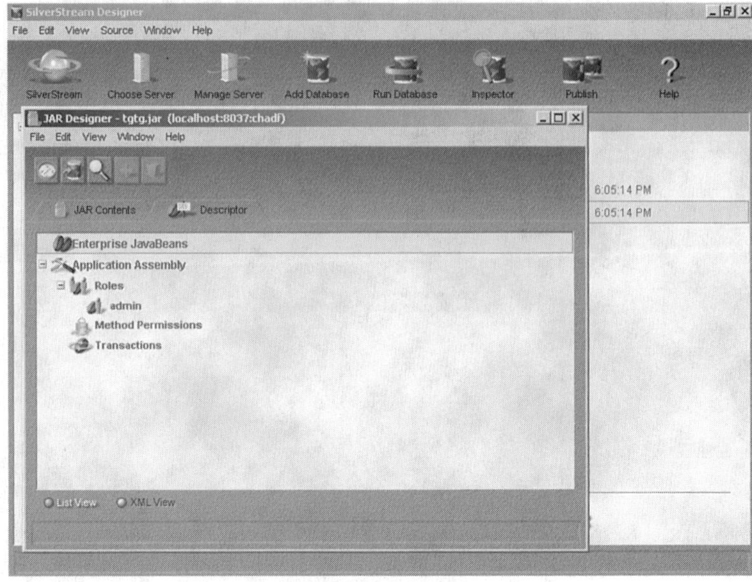

FIGURE 13.8
GUI configuring of the admin role.

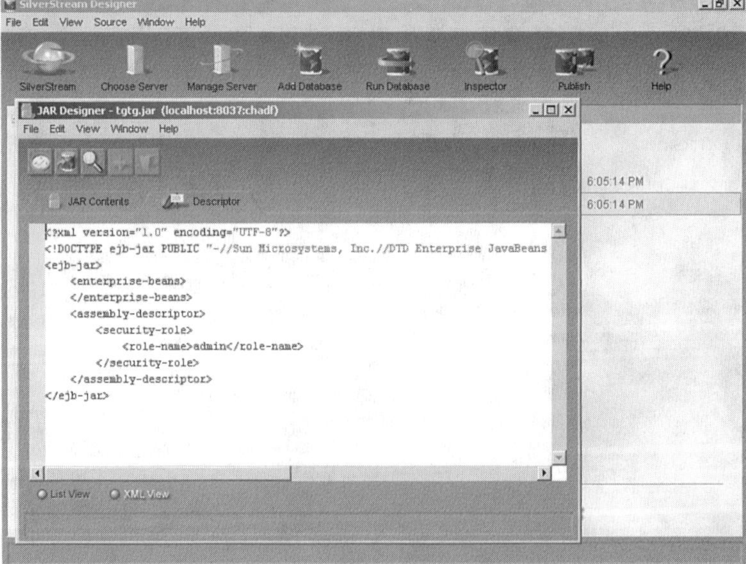

FIGURE 13.9
XML view of the configuring of the admin role.

Using a GUI to Add Persistent Fields

EJB containers make use of schema information derived from SQL databases. Persistent fields suggestions assist choosing persistent fields for the entity bean. Figure 13.10

demonstrates how persistent fields to be used in an entity bean can be chosen from a database table.

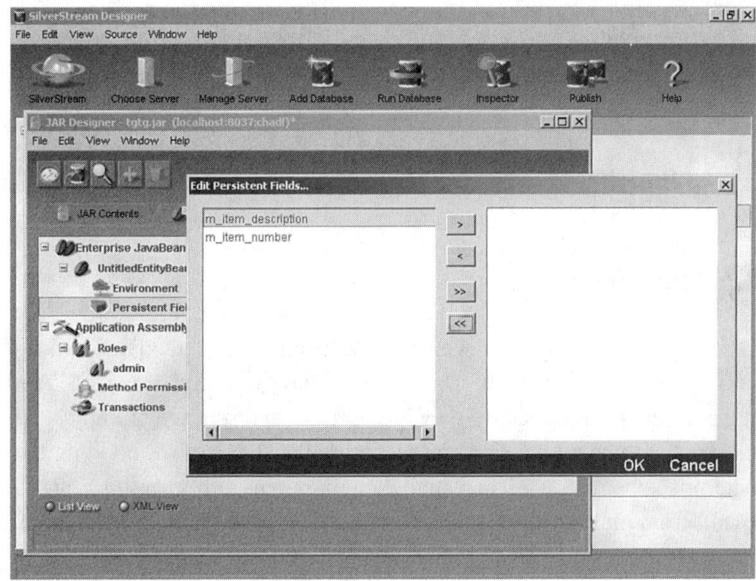

FIGURE 13.10
Choose persistent fields for entity beans.

Deploying Entity Bean Jar Files

The jar file is now ready to be deployed to any J2EE compliant EJB container. Besides packaging the entity bean, the ejb-jar file is used to package one or more enterprise beans as well as application assembly information produced by the Application Assembler. This information describes how the enterprise beans are integrated with an application.

The ejb-jar file must contain the following class files:

- The entity bean class
- The entity bean home and component interfaces
- The primary key class of the entity beans

The ejb-jar file must also contain the class files for all the classes and interfaces that each enterprise bean class, plus the home and component interfaces, depend on. These include super classes and super interfaces, dependent classes, and the classes and interfaces used as method parameters, results, and exceptions.

Deploying the jar file can be achieved using either a GUI tool or by using command line arguments. Some of the final tasks needed to be completed before deploying a jar file are as follows:

- Specify primary tables for the entity beans
- Map Finder Methods to entity bean fields
- Create JNDI names in order to make the entity beans accessible to clients

The jar file should now be ready to be deployed to the specific application server for which it was configured.

Summary

Using Java technologies as well as other open system standards builds on the promise of cross-platform deployment. This is particularly true in the case of Web-based applications. Entity beans, because they are used to represent the omnipresent relational database rows, show all the signs of becoming the standard for building the middle tier of enterprise applications. Their main benefit is reusability; entity bean components can be used across multiple applications using different relational DBMSes. An example is a shopping cart component of the sample SilverBooks application, which you can use in any J2EE application without having to recode its functionality. EJB entity beans components can also be deployed to different J2EE-compliant application servers and operating systems without modification of the components.

CHAPTER 14

Messaging with E-mail: JavaMail

In This Chapter

- E-mail Messaging in General *446*
- What Does JavaMail Do? *447*
- The Provider Registry *448*
- JavaMail Architecture and Primary Classes *450*
- Sending and Receiving Messages *466*
- Using JavaMail in JavaServer Pages *474*

This chapter gives an overview of messaging in general and covers in detail the major capabilities of the JavaMail API. This chapter also discusses the JavaMail architecture and the main classes involved with sending and receiving mail. Specifically, the chapter covers service providers, the Java Activation Framework (JAF), and the `Message` and `MimeMessage` objects.

E-mail Messaging in General

Most computer users are familiar with e-mail, which is by far the most popular service on the Internet. An e-mail message is made up of two components. The first component is the header, which contains information about the message, including the sender and the recipient(s). The second component is the content itself, which may contain multiple parts (for example, a text portion and one or more attachments). Here is an example of an e-mail message:

```
Received: from f45.law15.hotmail.com (64.4.23.45)
by mail01b.rapidsite.net (RS ver 1.0.60s) with SMTP id 032409761
for <reader@hotmail.com>; Thu, 19 Jul 2001 05:07:14 -0400 (EDT)
Received: from mail pickup service by hotmail.com with Microsoft SMTPSVC;
Thu, 19 Jul 2001 02:07:05 -0700
Received: from 193.250.45.34 by lw15fd.law15.hotmail.msn.com with HTTP;
Thu, 19 Jul 2001 09:07:04 GMT
X-Originating-IP: [193.250.45.34]
From: sender@hotmail.com
To: reader@hotmail.com
Bcc:
Subject: Something you should know
Date: Thu, 19 Jul 2001 09:07:04
Mime-Version: 1.0
Content-Type: text/plain; format=flowed
Message-ID: <F45ifWoqFXfyY0QUUBP0000040b@hotmail.com>
X-OriginalArrivalTime: 19 Jul 2001 09:07:05.0117 (UTC)
FILETIME=[2E1D5CD0:01C11032]
X-Loop-Detect: 1
X-UIDL: cbae30a3b2b484793e76dbbae1863ead.9c

PA:
sounds good 2 me.
JB
```

In this e-mail message, the header and the content are separated by an empty line. Each header attribute is on its own line and contains a header attribute name followed by a colon and the attribute value.

When you use an e-mail client application, it knows how to send and receive messages because it can deal with the various mail protocols. These protocols are Simple Mail

Transfer Protocol (SMTP), which is used when sending e-mail, and Post Office Protocol 3 (POP3) or Internet Message Access Protocol 4 (IMAP4), which are used for receiving e-mail. IMAP4 is considered more advanced than POP3; for example, it supports folders and status flags. Another protocol is Multipurpose Internet Mail Extensions (MIME), which is a standard e-mail message format for the Internet.

What Does JavaMail Do?

The JavaMail API is a set of abstract APIs that sits on top of the electronic mail vendor's system. The JavaMail API, like other J2EE APIs, provides a standard and independent framework for Java client applications to use electronic mail, allowing a J2EE developer to create applications that can do the following:

- Compose messages, including multi-part messages with attachments
- Send messages to particular servers
- Retrieve and store messages in folders

The J2EE developer does not need to understand the underlying protocols. The service providers actually handle the electronic mail by implementing handlers for these protocols (for example, POP3, IMAP4, SMTP). Sun's reference JavaMail implementation includes providers for most of the commonly used protocols (SMTP, IMAP4, MIME). Sun has also implemented a separate provider for POP3. There are other third-party providers available for applications such as Microsoft Exchange and Lotus Notes, or you may choose to implement your own providers.

The JavaMail API is constructed with an open architecture, so it will be able to support future protocols and standards. Figure 14.1 shows the interaction between a Java client application and the provider's protocol handler. There are two different types of protocols that providers can implement. The first is a `Transport`, which is the service that can send messages to the destination. The most commonly used `Transport` is SMTP. The second is a `Store`, which is the service that provides access to messages that have been delivered to a mailbox. The most commonly used `Store` is POP3, but IMAP4 `Stores` are becoming more popular.

When a Java client application uses the JavaMail API packages, the client application needs network access to a POP3 or IMAP4 server to read mail. When sending mail, the client application needs network access to an SMTP mail server. These mail server services are either provided on a local network (as in the case of corporations and organizations) or by an Internet Service Provider (ISP) (for dial-up/cable/DSL users).

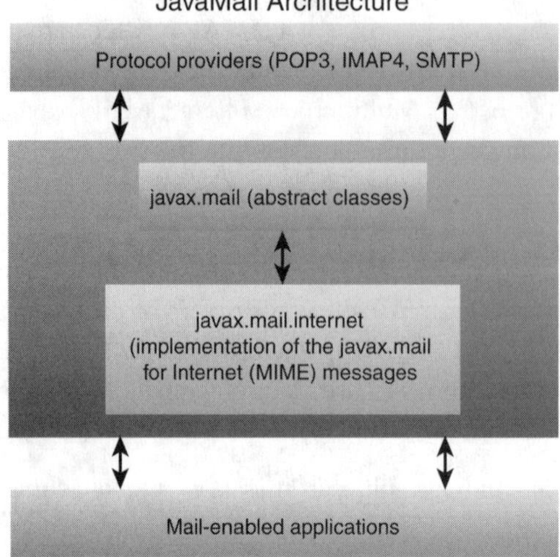

FIGURE 14.1 *JavaMail architecture.*

The Provider Registry

As mentioned earlier, JavaMail is extensible. This means that if new mail protocols are developed, pre-existing JavaMail-enabled applications will be able to use these new protocols when they are loaded into the Provider Registry. The Provider Registry is a list of providers that are available and can be detected by JavaMail-based applications.

The providers that come with the JavaMail reference implementation are listed in javamail.default.providers. When you add a package containing a new provider, it should include a javamail.providers file in its META-INF directory.

To list the available providers on the system at your location, compile and run the following code:

```
import javax.mail.*;
class ListProviders
{
   public static void main(String[] args)
   {
      java.util.Properties props = System.getProperties();
      Session sess = Session.getInstance(props, null);
      Provider[] provs = sess.getProviders();
      for (int i = 0; i < provs.length; ++i)
      {
         System.out.println(provs[i]);
      }
   }
}
```

The output will look something like this:

```
javax.mail.Provider[STORE,pop3,
com.sun.mail.pop3.POP3Store,Sun Microsystems, Inc]
javax.mail.Provider[STORE,imap,
com.sun.mail.imap.IMAPStore,Sun Microsystems, Inc]
javax.mail.Provider[TRANSPORT,smtp,
com.sun.mail.smtp.SMTPTransport,Sun Microsystems, Inc]
```

As the service provider, you implement abstract classes in terms of your specific protocol or system. For example, an IMAP provider implements the JavaMail API using the IMAP4. Client applications can then be constructed to use the implementation to manipulate an electronic mail that supports folders.

The provider software must be packaged in order for it to be used by a JavaMail client application. The steps involved in doing this are as follows:

1. Choose a name for your package. Convention dictates that you reverse your corporate domain name (for example, UCNY Inc.'s POP3 provider is named `com.ucny.mail.pop3`).
2. Define the classes as public. This allows JavaMail to instantiate your classes.
3. Load the provider classes into a JAR file. This JAR file must be added to the client application's classpath.
4. Create a provider registry entry for the protocol. This entry is a simple set of attributes that describe the implementation. There are five name-value pairs separated by semicolons that describe a protocol implementation. See Table 14.1 for a description of these attribute values.
5. Create any mapping from an address type to your protocol. If you are providing an implementation that allows applications to send mail, you must create a mapping between the types of addresses that your implementation can deliver and your protocol. The mapping has the format *`addressType=protocol`*, where
    - *`addressType`* is the string returned by the `Address` subclass's `getType()` method
    - *`protocol`* is the value of the protocol attribute that you defined in step 4

For example, the entry for the POP3 provider from UCNY, Inc. looks like this:

```
protocol=pop3;type=store;class=com.ucny.pop3.POP3Store;
vendor=UCNY, Inc.;version=1.3
```

TABLE 14.1 Provider Registry Protocol Attributes

Attribute	*Description*
`protocol`	Protocol name, such as `pop3`, `imap`, or `smtp`
`type`	Protocol type (specify `store` or `transport`)
`class`	The package and name of the class that implements the protocol
`vendor`	Vendor's name (optional)
`vendor`	Version number (optional)

The users or administrators of a JavaMail application must place the registry entry into a registry, either manually or using a configuration tool. This installs your provider into the client's JavaMail system. The registry is a set of resource files and the name of the file for JavaMail providers is javamail.providers. When required, JavaMail searches for provider resource files in the following order:

1. java.home/lib/javamail.providers
2. META-INF/javamail.providers

Provider developers should provide the registry entry and request that it be placed in one of these two files.

The users or administrators of a JavaMail application must also place the mapping into the address.map registry, either manually or using a configuration tool. The name of the file that holds your mapping is called javamail.address.map. JavaMail searches for address.map resource files in the following order:

1. java.home/lib/javamail.address.map
2. META-INF/javamail.address.map

Provider developers should provide the mapping and request that it be placed in one of these two files.

JavaMail Architecture and Primary Classes

Although there are many classes and packages contained in the JavaMail API, after studying the core classes, you will find that this API is a simple yet powerful means for implementing electronic mail functionality in your Java applications.

The next section will discuss some of the core classes in the JavaMail API (see Figure 14.2). Not all of the classes are discussed in this chapter. For more information, go to `http://java.sun.com/products/javamail/index.html`.

FIGURE 14.2
Core JavaMail classes.

Core JavaMail Classes

javax.mail.Session	- Connection point to a mail server
javax.mail.Store	- Models a mailbox
javax.mail.Folder	- Holds messages and subfolders
javax.mail.Search	- Package for searching through messages in folders
javax.mail.Address & javax.mail.internet.InternetAddress	- Represents an e-mail and Internet address
javax.mail.Message & javax.mail.internet.MimeMessage	- The e-mail message and Internet e-mail message
javax.mail.Transport	- Mechanism to send messages

Java Activation Framework

JavaMail relies heavily on the Java Activation Framework (JAF) API. JAF is designed to work, in a standard way, with different data types (for example, images, audio, video). When an application needs to work with a particular data type, these JAF objects can be "activated" and used to process the data. JavaMail uses JAF when dealing with attachments. When a JavaMail client receives a mail message, the client can use the JAF technologies to instantiate JavaBean components that provide all the commands the client needs to read, display, print, and otherwise interact with the message's content.

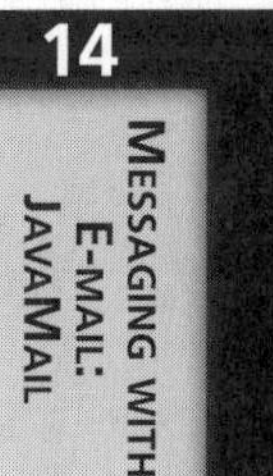

The JAF provides the following services to an application:

- It determines the content type of the message.
- It exposes the set of commands, or operations, that can be performed on the content of a mail message.
- It instantiates and calls a JavaBean that will provide access to the data. In other words, the component can effect the commands, or operations, that were "exposed."

javax.mail.Session

The javax.mail.Session class is the starting point of the JavaMail API. This class allows the application to specify properties such as the transport mechanism and mail server. This class provides the ability to control and load the classes that represent the service provider implementations for various mail protocols. The remainder of this section shows and describes some commonly used methods.

```
Static Session getDefaultInstance(Properties props, Authenticator authenticator)
```

The getDefaultInstance() method returns a reference to the shared Session instance based on the specified properties and authenticator. The first time that this method is called in the JVM, the Session will be created and a reference to it returned. Subsequent calls to this method will return a reference to the Session only if the Authenticator is the same as the one sent on the call that first constructed the Session. If the Authenticator is different, a SecurityException is thrown.

```
Session getInstance(Properties props, Authenticator authenticator)
```

The getInstance() method creates and returns a new Session instance based on the specified Properties and Authenticator.

```
Store getStore(java.lang.String protocol) throws NoSuchProviderException
```

The getStore() method returns an instance of the Store for the specified protocol (for example, getStore("POP3") for POP3's INBOX).

Session Properties

The Properties object that is used for obtaining a Session instance can be created in the following way:

```
java.util.Properties props = System.getProperties();
props.put("mail.store.protocol", "pop3");
props.put("mail.pop3.host", "mail.mydomain.com");
Session sess = Session.getInstance(props, null);
```

Table 14.2 describes the properties that can be set for the Session.

TABLE 14.2 JavaMail Session Properties

Property	*Description*	*Example*	*Default*
mail.transport.protocol	The default Transport protocol returned by Session.getTransport()	mail.transport.protocol=smtp	The first configured Transport protocol

TABLE 14.2 continued

Property	*Description*	*Example*	*Default*
`mail.store.protocol`	The default `Store` protocol returned by `Session.getStore()`	`mail.store.protocol=pop3` or `mail.store.protocol=imap`	The first configured `Store` protocol
`mail.host`	Default host for protocols without their own host property	`mail.host=ucny.com`	The local machine
`mail.user`	Default user for protocols without their own user property	`mail.user=pallen`	`user.name`
`mail.from`	Return e-mail address	`mail.from=pallen@ucny.com`	`Userid@machine-name`
`mail.protocol.host`	Host for specified protocol	`mail.pop3.host=ucny.com`	`mail.host`
`mail.protocol.user`	User for specified protocol	`mail.pop3.user=jbambara`	`mail.user`
`mail.debug`	Default debug setting—override programmatically using `Session.setDebug(boolean)`	`mail.debug=true`	`false`

javax.mail.Store

The `javax.mail.Store` class is implemented by the provider and typically represents the user's inbox. The main purpose of this class is to be a container for `Folder` objects. Note that POP3 supports only one folder. This class allows a client application to read, write, monitor, and search through a particular mail protocol. Some commonly used methods are shown and described here:

```
Folder getDefaultFolder() throws MessagingException
```

The `getDefaultFolder()` method returns a `Folder` instance that represents the root of the `Store`. Note that this is not used for POP3.

```
Folder getFolder(java.lang.String name) throws MessagingException
```

The `getFolder()` method returns a `Folder` instance for the specified name (for instance, `getFolder("INBOX")` for POP3).

javax.mail.Folder

The service provider implements the `javax.mail.Folder` class. This class holds messages and subfolders in a hierarchical format similar to Explorer in the Windows operating system. Note that POP3 only supports a single folder `INBOX`. The `INBOX` folder is a reserved folder name, indicating the primary folder. A folder, closed by default, can be opened in either `READ_ONLY` or `READ_WRITE` mode. Some commonly used methods are shown and described here:

```
boolean create(int type) throws MessagingException
```

The `create()` method creates a folder of the specified type on the store. The method returns `true` if successful, `false` in the event of a failure. See Table 14.3 for a list of the types of folders that can be created.

TABLE 14.3 Types of Folders

Type	*Description*
`Folder.HOLDS_MESSAGES`	This folder can hold messages only
`Folder.HOLDS_FOLDERS`	This folder can hold folders only
`Folder.HOLDS_MESSAGES + Folder.HOLDS_FOLDERS`	This folder can hold both messages and folders

```
boolean delete(boolean recurse) throws MessagingException
```

The `delete()` method deletes an unopened folder from the `Store`. This method will return `true` if the delete succeeds and `false` if the delete fails. If `true` is specified for the `recurse` argument, all subfolders and messages will be removed. If `false` is specified and the folder contains other subfolders then those subfolders will not be deleted, but any messages found within the folders may or may not be deleted depending on the implementation.

```
Message[] expunge() throws MessagingException
```

The `expunge()` method permanently removes messages marked `deleted` and returns an array containing the expunged `Message` objects.

```
Message[] getMessages() throws MessagingException
```

The `getMessages()` method retrieves all `Message` objects from this `Folder`. It returns an empty message array if the `Folder` has no messages.

```
void open(int mode) throws MessagingException
```

The `open()` method opens the folder in the specified mode. The mode can be `Folder.READ_ONLY` or `Folder.READ_WRITE`. This method can only be used for folders that are of the type that can contain `Messages` (that is, folders whose type is `Folder.HOLDS_MESSAGES`).

```
boolean renameTo(Folder f) throws MessagingException
```

The `renameTo()` method renames the folder and will only succeed on a closed folder. The argument to this method is a `Folder` object representing the new name for this folder.

```
Message[] search(SearchTerm term) throws MessagingException
```

This `search()` method searches the folder for messages matching the specified search criterion. This method returns an array containing the matching messages, or an empty array if no matches were found. This method invokes `search(term, getMessages())` to search all of the messages in the folder.

```
Message[] search(SearchTerm term, Message[] msgs) throws MessagingException
```

This form of the `search()` method searches the specified array of messages for those that match the specified search criteria. This method returns an array containing the matching messages, or an empty array if no matches were found. This method loops through the message array and calls its `match()` method with the given term. The messages that match the search term are returned.

```
void setFlags(Message[] msgs, Flags flag, boolean value)
throws MessagingException
```

The `setFlags()` method sets flags to the specified value for the array of messages (there are overloaded versions of this method that allow you to identify the messages in a different way). The specified `Message` objects must belong to this folder. See Table 14.4 for a list of flags that can be set.

TABLE 14.4 Types of Flags

Type	*Description*
`Flags.Flag.ANSWERED`	This message has been answered.
`Flags.Flag.DELETED`	This message is marked `deleted`.
`Flags.Flag.DRAFT`	This message is a draft.
`Flags.Flag.FLAGGED`	This message is flagged
`Flags.Flag.RECENT`	This message is recent.
`Flags.Flag.SEEN`	This message has been seen.
`Flags.Flag.USER`	This folder supports user-defined flags.

javax.mail.search

Search criteria in JavaMail are expressed as a tree of search terms, forming a parse-tree for the search expression. Table 14.5 shows the classes in the `search` package.

TABLE 14.5 Classes in the `javax.mail.search` Package

Class	*Description and Constructor Method*
`AddressStringTerm`	Matches `Message` addresses. This differs from the `AddressTerm` class in that this does comparisons on address strings rather than `Address` objects.
`AddressTerm`	Matches `Message` addresses.
`AndTerm`	The logical `AND` operator on `SearchTerm` objects.
	`AndTerm(SearchTerm[] t)`
	Constructor that takes an array of `SearchTerm` objects. Matches when all terms match.
	`AndTerm(SearchTerm t1, SearchTerm t2)`
	Constructor that takes two `SearchTerm` objects. Matches when both terms match.
`BodyTerm`	Matches `Message` body.
	`BodyTerm(java.lang.String pattern)`
	Body searches are only done on single part `Text` messages or on multipart/mixed messages whose first body part is `Text`.

TABLE 14.5 continued

Class	*Description and Constructor Method*
`ComparisonTerm`	Models the comparison operator. Used by `DateTerm`, `IntegerComparisonTerm`, `ReceivedDateTerm`, `SentDateTerm`, and `SizeTerm` to implement comparisons for appropriate datatypes. Defines the following constants: `EQ` (equal to), `GE` (greater than or equal to), `GT` (greater than), `LE` (less than or equal to), `LT` (less than), and `NE` (not equal to).
`DateTerm`	Matches dates using the `ComparisonTerm` constants (`EQ`, `GE`, `GT`, `LE`, `LT`, and `NE`). `DateTerm(int comparison, java.util.Date date)`
`FlagTerm`	Matches `Message Flags`. `FlagTerm(Flags flags, boolean setting)` Matches if a message's flags are on when `true` is the specified `setting`, or off when `false` is the specified `setting`.
`FromStringTerm`	Matches `Address` header. `FromStringTerm(java.lang.String pattern)` This differs from the `FromTerm` class in that this does comparisons on address strings rather than `Address` objects. The string comparisons are not case sensitive.
`FromTerm`	Matches the `Address` header. `FromTerm(Address address)`
`HeaderTerm`	Matches `Message` headers with comparison string (not case sensitive). `HeaderTerm(java.lang.String headerName, java.lang.String pattern)`
`IntegerComparisonTerm`	Matches integers using the `ComparisonTerm` constants (`EQ`, `GE`, `GT`, `LE`, `LT`, and `NE`). `IntegerComparisonTerm(int comparison, int number)`
`MessageIDTerm`	Matches the `MessageId` on Internet messages. `MessageIDTerm(java.lang.String msgid)`
`MessageNumberTerm`	Matches `Message` numbers. `MessageNumberTerm(int number)`

TABLE 14.5 continued

Class	*Description and Constructor Method*
`NotTerm`	The logical `NEGATION` operator. Results in a match when the item does not match and vice versa. `NotTerm(SearchTerm t)`

`OrTerm`	The logical `OR` operator on `SearchTerm` objects.
	`OrTerm(SearchTerm[] t)`
	Constructor that takes an array of `SearchTerm` objects. Matches if any term matches.
	`OrTerm(SearchTerm t1, SearchTerm t2)`
	Constructor that takes two `SearchTerm` objects. Matches if either term matches.

`ReceivedDateTerm`	Matches `Message` received date. `ReceivedDateTerm(int comparison, java.util.Date date)`
`RecipientStringTerm`	Matches recipient `Address` header. `RecipientStringTerm(Message.RecipientType type, java.lang.String pattern)` This differs from the `RecipientTerm` class in that this does comparisons on address strings rather than `Address` objects. The string comparisons are not case sensitive.
`RecipientTerm`	Matches recipient `Address` header. `RecipientTerm(Message.RecipientType type, Address address)`
`SearchTerm`	Root class for all search items.
`SentDateTerm`	Matches `Message` sent date using the `ComparisonTerm` constants (`EQ`, `GE`, `GT`, `LE`, `LT`, and `NE`). `SentDateTerm(int comparison, java.util.Date date)`
`SizeTerm`	Matches `Message` sizes using the `ComparisonTerm` constants (`EQ`, `GE`, `GT`, `LE`, `LT`, and `NE`). `SizeTerm(int comparison, int size)`

TABLE 14.5 continued

Class	*Description and Constructor Method*

`StringTerm`	Implements the `match()` method for `Strings`.
	`StringTerm(java.lang.String pattern)`
	`StringTerm(java.lang.String pattern, boolean ignoreCase)`

`SubjectTerm`	Matches `Message` subject header (not case sensitive). `boolean match(Message msg)`

Here is some example code that uses the `javax.mail.search` package:

```
if (msg-in.match(new AndTerm(
            new SubjectTerm("development standards"),
            new BodyTerm("send")
        )
    )
)
{
    Message msg-out = msg-in.reply();
    msg-out.setText("Development standards request received.");
    Transport.send(msg-out);
}
```

javax.mail.Address

The `javax.mail.Address` is an abstract class that models a mail address for a message. For the most part, you will deal with implementations of this class such as `javax.mail.internet.InternetAddress`, which we will cover next.

javax.mail.internet.InternetAddress

The `javax.mail.internet.InternetAddress` is an implementation of the `javax.mail.Address` class and it represents an Internet e-mail address. This class is used to specify the recipients of a message. There are two ways to construct an `InternetAddress`:

- `InternetAddress("e-mail@domain")`, using the constructor method.
- `InternetAddress.parse("e-mail1@domain, e-mail2@domain, e-mail3@domain,...")`, which takes a `String` and returns an array of `InternetAddress`. The comma is used as a separator for each e-mail address within the `String`.

javax.mail.Message

The `javax.mail.Message` class models an electronic mail message. It is an abstract class that implements the `javax.mail.Part` interface. As such, the `Message` object contains attributes, such as the subject line, sender, recipient(s), and sent date. The attributes, which are name-value pairs, specify addressing information and define the structure of the message's content (its content type). The `Message` also contains content and flags indicating state within the folder (see the `setFlags()` method on the `Folder` class described earlier). Messages contain either a single content object or multiple content objects. In both cases, the content is held by a `DataHandler` object.

javax.mail.internet.MimeMessage

The `javax.mail.internet.MimeMessage` class is the most commonly used implementation of `javax.mail.Message` and it represents a MIME (Multi-purpose Internet Mail Extensions) message. A MIME message can contain text, image, audio, video, or other data. Figure 14.3 is a diagram showing the components of a `MimeMessage` object.

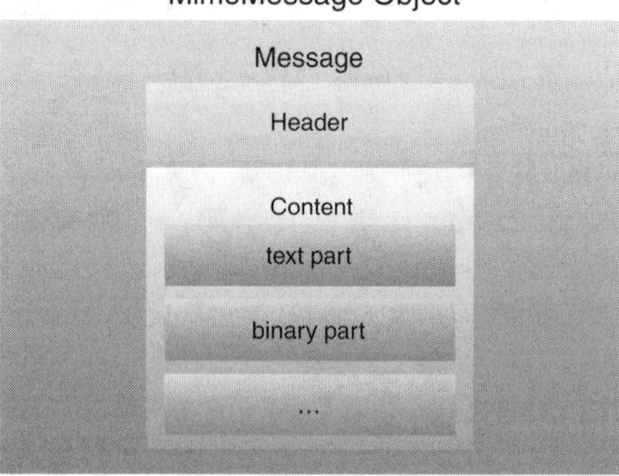

FIGURE 14.3
Components of the `MimeMessage` *object.*

A `MimeMessage` also supports messages that have multiple parts. This provides the ability to attach files to a message. Here are most of the methods that you will use when dealing with `MimeMessage`:

```
MimeMessage(Session session)
```

The `MimeMessage()` method is the default constructor and it creates an instance of an empty message object for the given `Session`. The header and flags fields are set to an empty `InternetHeaders` object and `Flags` object, respectively.

```
void addFrom(Address[] addresses) throws MessagingException
```

The `addFrom()` method adds the specified addresses to the existing `From` field. If the `From` field does not exist, it will be created.

```
void addRecipients(Message.RecipientType type,
Address[] addresses) throws MessagingException
```

The `addRecipients()` method adds the given addresses of the specified recipient type to the message. See Table 14.6 for a description of the various recipient types.

TABLE 14.6 Recipient Types

Recipient type	*Description*
`Message.RecipientType.TO`	For primary recipients
`Message.RecipientType.CC`	For carbon copy recipients
`Message.RecipientType.BCC`	For blind carbon copy recipients
`MimeMessage.RecipientType.NEWSGROUPS`	For MimeMessages posted to a newsgroup

```
java.util.Enumeration getAllHeaders() throws MessagingException
```

The `getAllHeaders()` method returns all the headers as an enumeration of `Header` objects. These headers are encoded if they contain non-US-ASCII characters and these should be decoded.

```
java.util.Enumeration getAllHeaderLines() throws MessagingException
```

The `getAllHeaderLines()` method returns all header lines as an enumeration of `String` objects. A header line contains both the `name` and `value` fields.

```
Address[] getAllRecipients() throws MessagingException
```

The `getAllRecipients()` method gets all the recipient addresses for the message.

```
java.lang.Object getContent() throws java.io.IOException, MessagingException
```

The `getContent()` method returns the content as a Java object. The data type of this object is dependent on the content (for example, a `String` will be returned for "text/plain" content and a `MimeMultipart` object will be returned for a "multipart" message. An `InputStream` is returned if the content type is unknown to the `DataHandler` system. This method obtains the content by invoking `getDataHandler().getContent()`.

```
DataHandler getDataHandler() throws MessagingException
```

The `getDataHandler()` method returns a `DataHandler` to handle the message content.

```
Flags getFlags() throws MessagingException
```

The `getFlags()` method returns a `Flags` object that contains the flags for this message. The `Flags` object returned is actually a clone of the internal `Flags`, so any modifications will not actually affect the flags of the message.

```
Folder getFolder()
```

The `getFolder()` method (inherited from `Message`) gets a reference to the folder from which this message was obtained. If this is a new message, this method returns `null`.

```
Address[] getFrom() throws MessagingException
```

The `getFrom()` method returns the value of the `From` header field. If this header field is absent, the `Sender` header field is used, and if the `Sender` header field is also absent, `null` is returned.

```
java.io.InputStream getInputStream()
throws java.io.IOException, MessagingException
```

The `getInputStream()` returns a decoded input stream for the content of the message. This method obtains the input stream from the `DataHandler`; that is, it invokes `getDataHandler().getInputStream()`.

```
java.lang.String getMessageID() throws MessagingException
```

The `getMessageID()` method returns the value of the `Message-ID` header field. If this field is unavailable or its value is absent, you will get a `null` value.

```
int getMessageNumber()
```

The `getMessageNumber()` method (inherited from `Message`) gets the message number. The message number is the relative position of the message in the folder. Newly composed or derived messages have `0` (zero) as their message number; other valid message numbers start at 1. The message number can change during a `Session` if other messages in the folder are deleted and expunged.

```
java.util.Date getReceivedDate() throws MessagingException
```

The `getReceivedDate()` method returns the date that the message was received. For `MimeMessage` this currently returns `null`; however, other implementations of `Message` may provide the value.

```
Address[] getRecipients(Message.RecipientType type) throws MessagingException
```

The `getRecipients()` method returns the recipients for the specified type. See Table 14.6 for a description of the various recipient types.

`Address[] getReplyTo() throws MessagingException`

The `getReplyTo()` method returns the value of the `Reply-To` header field. If this header is unavailable or its value is absent, the `getFrom()` method is called and its value is returned.

`java.util.Date getSentDate() throws MessagingException`

The `getSentDate()` method returns the value of the `Date` header field. This is the date on which this message was sent. If this field is unavailable or its value is absent you will get a `null` value.

`int getSize() throws MessagingException`

The `getSize()` method returns the size of the content of this message in bytes. It will return `-1` if the size cannot be determined. Note, however, that the number returned may not be an accurate measure of the content size and also may or may not take into account the encoding of the content.

`java.lang.String getSubject() throws MessagingException`

The `getSubject()` method returns the decoded value of the `Subject` header field. If this field is unavailable or its value is absent you will get a `null` value.

`boolean isExpunged()`

The `isExpunged()` method (inherited from `Message`) checks whether this message is expunged. No other methods except `getMessageNumber()` are valid on an expunged `Message`.

`boolean isSet(Flags.Flag flag) throws MessagingException`

The `isSet()` method checks to see whether the flag specified in the `Flag` argument is set to `true` in the message. If the specified flag is `true`, the method returns `true`; otherwise, it returns false.

`boolean match(SearchTerm term) throws MessagingException`

The `match()` method (inherited from `Message`) returns `true` if the message matches the specified searchTerm criteria for this message; otherwise, it returns `false`.

`Message reply(boolean replyToAll) throws MessagingException`

The `reply()` method creates a `Message` object with its attributes and headers set up appropriately for a reply. The new message will not have any content; this must be suitably filled in by the caller. The `Subject` field will be filled in with the original subject prefixed with `Re:`. If this prefix already exists, a new one will not be added.

The `In-Reply-To` header is set in the new message if this message has a `Message-Id` header. The `ANSWERED` flag is also set to `true` for the original message. If `replyToAll` is set to `true`, the new `Message` will be addressed to all recipients of this message. Otherwise, the reply will be addressed to only the sender of this message (obtained by calling the `getReplyTo()` method).

```
void saveChanges() throws MessagingException
```

The `saveChanges()` method updates the appropriate header fields of this message to be consistent with the message's contents. This includes the creation of the message ID for new messages. If this message is contained in a folder, any changes made to the message are saved in the containing folder.

If any part of a message (header or content) is changed, `saveChanges()` must be called to ensure that the changes are saved. Otherwise, any such modifications may or may not be saved, depending on the folder implementation.

Messages obtained from folders opened `READ_ONLY` should not be modified and `saveChanges()` should not be called on such messages.

```
void setContent(java.lang.Object o,
java.lang.String type) throws MessagingException
```

The form of the `setContent()` method sets the content and content MIME type of the message (for example, `setContent("my content", "text/html")`). The content is wrapped in a `DataHandler` object. The `DataContentHandler` class for the specified type should be installed and available to the JavaMail implementation in order for this to work correctly. For example, to attach an Acrobat PDF file using `setContent(mypdf, "application/pdf")`, a `DataContentHandler` for `"application/pdf"` must be available.

```
void setContent(Multipart mp) throws MessagingException
```

The form of the `setContent()` method sets the `Message`'s content to that of a `Multipart` object.

```
void setExpunged(boolean expunged)
```

The `setExpunged()` method (inherited from `Message`) sets the expunged flag for this `Message` to the value specified.

```
void setFlags(Flags flag, boolean set) throws MessagingException
```

The `setFlags()` method sets the flags for this message to the value specified.

```
void setFrom() throws MessagingException
```

This form of the `setFrom()` method sets the `From` header field using the value returned by the `InternetAddress.getLocalAddress()` method, replacing any existing values.

```
void setFrom(Address address) throws MessagingException
```

This form of the `setFrom()` method sets the `From` header field to the given address, replacing the existing values. If the address array is `null`, the `From` header field is removed.

```
void setRecipients(Message.RecipientType type,
Address[] addresses) throws MessagingException
```

The `setRecipients()` method sets the recipient addresses for the specified recipient type. See Table 14.6 for a description of the various recipient types.

```
void setReplyTo(Address[] addresses) throws MessagingException
```

The `setReplyTo()` method sets the `Reply-To` header field. If the address parameter supplied is `null`, this header will be removed.

```
void setSentDate(java.util.Date date) throws MessagingException
```

The `setSentDate()` method sets the `Date` header field. This is the date that the message was completed and ready for delivery. If the date parameter supplied is `null`, the existing `Date` field will be removed.

```
void setSubject(java.lang.String subject) throws MessagingException
void setSubject(java.lang.String subject,
java.lang.String charset) throws MessagingException
```

The `setSubject()` methods set the subject header field. If the subject contains only US-ASCII characters, do not specify the charset. If the subject contains non-US-ASCII characters, specify the charset and the subject will then be encoded accordingly. If the subject is `null`, the `Subject` header field is removed.

```
void setText(java.lang.String text) throws MessagingException
```

This form of the `setText()` method sets the content to the given `String`, with a MIME type of `text/plain`. There may be a performance penalty if a large amount of text is supplied, because this method may need to scan all the characters to determine which charset to use.

```
void setText(java.lang.String text,
java.lang.String charset) throws MessagingException
```

This form of the `setText()` method sets the content to the given `String`, with a MIME type of `text/plain`. The `String` is also encoded with the specified charset.

javax.mail.Transport

The `javax.mail.Transport` class is another class that is implemented by the provider. It has only one use, the actual sending of messages over a specific protocol. To send a message you call the static `send()` method (for example, `send(Message msg, Address[] addresses)`). The most frequently used methods are shown and described here:

`void send(Message msg) throws MessagingException`

The form of the `send()` method sends a message to all recipient addresses specified in the message (as returned from the `getAllRecipients()` method on the `Message`), using message transports appropriate to each address. This method calls the `saveChanges()` method on the message before sending it. If any of the recipient addresses are invalid, a `SendFailedException` is thrown. Whether or not the message is still sent successfully to any valid addresses depends on the `Transport` implementation. The `SendFailedException` has the following methods to help determine the state of the transmission for each recipient:

> `getInvalidAddresses()` returns an `Address[]` containing invalid addresses.
>
> `getValidSentAddresses()` returns an `Address[]` containing addresses for which transmission was successful.
>
> `getValidUnsentAddresses()` returns an `Address[]` containing addresses for which transmission was not successful.

`void send(Message msg, Address[] addresses) throws MessagingException`

This form of the `send()` method sends the message to the specified addresses, ignoring any recipients specified in the message itself. This method also calls the `saveChanges()` method on the message prior to sending it.

`void sendMessage(Message msg, Address[] addresses) throws MessagingException`

The `sendMessage()` method sends the message to the specified list of addresses. If any of the addresses is invalid, a `SendFailedException` is thrown but the message is still sent to the valid addresses. This method does not call the `saveChanges()` method; the caller should do so.

Sending and Receiving Messages

We will now take a look at the steps involved in sending and receiving `MimeMessages`. We will first take a look at what it takes to construct and send a message, and then discuss the steps involved in receiving (reading) a message.

Sending Internet Messages

The following is a summary list of how to send an Internet message:

- Get a `Session` instance by passing it parameters on how to connect to the mail server.
- Create a `MimeMessage` instance, set the necessary attributes (`from`, `to`, and `subject`) and content.
- Deliver the message using the `Transport` class.

Now we'll expand this summary list by showing working code for each of the steps:

- Get a `Session` instance (note that some of the keys for the `Properties` object are specific to the protocol being used; refer to the documentation provided by the implementer of the protocol):

```
Properties props = new Properties();
// Add the protocol (SMTP)
props.put("mail.transport.protocol","smtp");
// Add the mail server name
props.put("mail.smtp.host","smtp.mydomain.com");
// Get a new Session instance
Session sess = Session.getDefaultInstance(props,null);
```

- Create a `MimeMessage` instance:

```
// Create a new MimeMessage instance
MimeMessage msg = new MimeMessage(sess);

// Set the FROM address
msg.setFrom(new InternetAddress("j2ee@mydomain.com"));

// Set the TO address list
msg.setRecipients(Message.RecipientType.TO,
    InternetAddress.parse ("user@mydomain.com",false));

// Set the subject
msg.setSubject("This is the subject line");

// Add the content to the message
msg.setContent("Here is some content","text/plain");

// Above line could also have been coded as follows
// msg.setText("Here is some content");
```

- Deliver the message:

```
// Send the message using the Transport
Transport.send(msg);
```

Receiving Internet Messages

The following list is a summary of how to receive an Internet message:

- Get a Session instance by passing it parameters on how to connect to the mail server.
- Get a handle to the Store/Mailbox.
- Open the folder.
- Get the messages and contents.
- Close the folder.

Now we'll expand this summary list by showing working code for each of the steps:

- Get a Session instance (note that some of the keys for the Properties object are specific to the protocol being used; refer to the documentation provided by the implementer of the protocol):

```
Properties props = new Properties();
// Add the protocol (SMTP)
props.put("mail.store.protocol","pop3");
// Add the mail server name
props.put("mail.pop3.host","mydomain.com");
// Get a new Session instance
Session sess = Session.getInstance(props,null);
```

- Get a handle to the Store/Mailbox:

```
Store store = sess.getStore("pop3");
store.connect("mailserver", "userid", "password");
```

- Open the folder (note that the default folder is named INBOX. POP3 only has one folder. Folders can be opened in read-only or read-write mode):

```
Folder inbox = store.getFolder("INBOX");
inbox.open(Folder.READ_ONLY);
```

- Get the messages and contents (note that at this point the messages are still on the server. getContent() will return a Multipart message if the message is made up of multiple parts):

```
Message[] msgs = inbox.getMessages();
for(int i=0;i<msgs.length;i++)
  System.out.println(msgs[i].getContent());
```

- Close the folder:

```
inbox.close(false);
// calling inbox.close(true) will expunge all deleted messages in folder
store.close();
```

Working with Multipart Messages

In addition to the simple message structure shown earlier, messages can also contain multiple parts. An example of this would be when you attach one or more files to an e-mail message. In this case the `DataHandler` object contains a `Multipart` object, which is a container for `BodyPart` objects. The structure of a `BodyPart` object is similar to the structure of a `Message` object, because they both implement the `Part` interface.

Each `BodyPart` object contains attributes and content, but the attributes of a `BodyPart` object are limited to those defined by the `Part` interface. An important attribute is the content-type of this part of the message content. The content of a `BodyPart` object is a `DataHandler` that contains either data or another `Multipart` object.

Sending `MimeMultipart` Messages

Here is the code required to send `MimeMultipart` messages:

```
java.util.Properties props = System.getProperties();
props.put("mail.transport.protocol", "smtp");
props.put("mail.smtp.host", "mydomain.com");
Session sess = Session.getInstance(props, null);

// Create a new MimeMessage instance
MimeMessage msg = new MimeMessage(sess);

// Set the FROM address
msg.setFrom(new InternetAddress("joe.bambara@mydomain.com"));

// Set the TO address list
msg.setRecipients(Message.RecipientType.TO,
    InternetAddress.parse("paul.allen@mydomain.com", false));

// Set the subject
msg.setSubject("Here is a message of two parts");

// Now add the content to each part
// Build the first part
MimeBodyPart part1 = new MimeBodyPart();

// Set first part's content
part1.setContent("here's the first part of my message", "text/plain");

// Build the second part
MimeBodyPart part2 = new MimeBodyPart();

// Set second part's content
part2.setText("here's the second part of my message!");
```

```
// Build a part container for the parts
MimeMultipart mult = new MimeMultipart();

// Add the first part to the part container
mult.addBodyPart(part1);

// Add the second part to the part container
mult.addBodyPart(part2);

// Add the content to the message
msg.setContent(mult);

// Display the message on the console
msg.writeTo(System.out);

// Send the message using the Transport
Transport.send(msg);
```

Receiving `MimeMultipart` Messages

Here is the code required to receive single and `MimeMultipart` messages:

```
java.util.Properties props = System.getProperties();
props.put("mail.store.protocol", "pop3");
props.put("mail.pop3.host", "mydomain.com");
Session sess = Session.getInstance(props, null);

Store store = sess.getStore("pop3");
store.connect("mydomain.com", "paul.allen", "prada7");
Folder inbox = store.getFolder("INBOX");
inbox.open(Folder.READ_ONLY);

Message[] msgs = inbox.getMessages();
for(int i=0;i<msgs.length;i++)
{
    Object o = msgs[i].getContent();
    if(o instanceof MimeMultipart)
    {
        // It has multiple parts,
        // so cast it to a part container
        MimeMultipart mp = (MimeMultipart) o;

        // Loop through the container
        for(int j=0,count=mp.getCount();j<count;j++)
        {
            // Get the individual part
            Part p = mp.getBodyPart(j);

            // Print it's contents
            System.out.println(p.getContent());
```

```
            }
        }
        else
        {
            // Otherwise it's a single message
            // Print it's contents
            System.out.println(msgs[i].getContent());
        }
    }
    // Close the folder and store
    inbox.close(false);
    store.close();
```

Sending Binary Data in a Message

The prior example had simple text-based parts that were sent and received. To deal with non-text-based, or binary, parts you need to make some additional calls to the Java Activation Framework and let it deal with the binary data. `FileDataSource` and `URLDataSource` are examples of the `javax.activation.DataSource` object that represents binary data.

A `DataHandler` object is responsible for transferring the data from the `DataSource` into the message.

Here is the code for sending a binary attachment along with some text:

```
java.util.Properties props = System.getProperties();
props.put("mail.transport.protocol", "smtp");
props.put("mail.host", "mydomain.com");
Session sess = Session.getInstance(props, null);

// Create a new MimeMessage instance
MimeMessage msg = new MimeMessage(sess);

// Set the FROM address
msg.setFrom(new InternetAddress("joe.bambara@mydomain.com"));

// Set the TO address list
msg.setRecipients(Message.RecipientType.TO,
    InternetAddress.parse("paul.allen@mydomain.com", false));

// Set the subject
msg.setSubject("Some text and a spreadsheet");

// Now add the content to each part
// Build the first part
MimeBodyPart part1 = new MimeBodyPart();
```

```
// Set first part's content
part1.setContent("here's the spreadsheet that we discussed.", "text/plain");

// Build the second part
MimeBodyPart part2 = new MimeBodyPart();

// Set second part's content
FileDataSource fds = new FileDataSource("c:\\j2ee.xls");
part2.setDataHandler(new DataHandler(fds));
part2.setFileName(fds.getName());

// Build a part container for the parts
MimeMultipart mult = new MimeMultipart();

// Add the first part to the part container
mult.addBodyPart(part1);

// Add the second part to the part container
mult.addBodyPart(part2);

// Add the content to the message
msg.setContent(mult);

// Display the message on the console
msg.writeTo(System.out);

// Send the message using the Transport
Transport.send(msg);
```

Receiving Binary Data in a Message

To receive non-text-based, or binary, data you need to use the same process that you use to get content out of any `Multipart` message. The `Part` object has a `getInputStream()` method that will return to the caller the binary data as an `InputStream`. This `InputStream` can then be used to save that data to disk.

Here is the code for saving binary attachments:

```
java.util.Properties props = System.getProperties();
props.put("mail.store.protocol", "pop3");
props.put("mail.pop3.host", "mydomain.com");
Session sess = Session.getInstance(props, null);

Store store = sess.getStore("pop3");
store.connect("mydomain.com", "paul.allen", "mypass");
Folder inbox = store.getFolder("INBOX");
inbox.open(Folder.READ_ONLY);
```

```
Message[] msgs = inbox.getMessages();
for(int i=0;i<msgs.length;i++)
{
    Object o = Msg.getContent();
    if(o instanceof MimeMultipart)
    {
        // It has multiple parts,
        // so cast it to a part container
        MimeMultipart mp = (MimeMultipart) o;

        // Loop through the container
        for(int i=0,count=mp.getCount();i<count;i++)
        {
            // Get the individual part
            Part p = mp.getBodyPart(i);

            if (!p.getContentType().equals("text/plain"))
            {
                // If not plain text,
                // get the decoded InputStream
                InputStream is = p.getInputStream();

                // Try to get the file name for the part
                String filename = p.getFileName();
                if (filename == null) filename = "content"+i;

                // Create the OutputStream
                OutputStream os = new FileOutputStream(filename);

                int b;
                byte buffer[] = new byte[1024];

                // Read the file block and write it out
                while ((b = is.read(buffer)) > 0)
                {
                    os.write(buffer, 0, b);
                }
                // Tell them about the attachment
                System.out.println(filename+" saved to disk");

                // Flush and close the OutputStream
                os.flush();
                os.close();
            }
            else
            {
                // Print its contents
                System.out.println(p.getContent());
            }
        }
    }
```

```
        else
        {
            // Otherwise it's a single message
            // Print it's contents
            System.out.println(msgs[i].getContent());
        }
    }
    // Close the folder and store
    inbox.close(false);
    store.close();
```

Using JavaMail in JavaServer Pages

In this section, we will take a look at calling JavaMail code from a J2EE application. We will show you mostly JavaServer Pages (JSP) code and the associated J2EE packaging. The purpose of this section is to take you through building two JavaMail-enabled functions that send and receive mail. The directory structure for this exercise is as follows:

```
JavaMail
JavaMail\src
JavaMail\src\app
JavaMail\src\app\docroot
JavaMail\src\app\docroot\web-inf
JavaMail\src\earroot
JavaMail\src\earroot\Meta-inf
```

Summary Instructions

These are the summary instructions for building a J2EE JavaMail application. If you prefer detailed, step-by-step instructions, skip to the "Detailed Instructions" section later in the chapter.

Create the HTML Form

1. Using Notepad, create an HTML form and save it as sendmail.html in the JavaMail\src\app\docroot directory.
2. The form should have the following characteristics:
    - A text field named `from`.
    - A text field named `to`.
    - A text field named `subject`.
    - A textarea field named `msgpart1`.

- A textarea field named msgpart2.
- A Submit button.
- The action attribute of the form tag should be set to http://localhost/JavaMail/app/sendmail.jsp (replace localhost/JavaMail with your server/directory combination).
- The method attribute of the form tag should be post.

Create the Sending JSP File

1. Using Notepad, create a new text file called sendmail.jsp in the JavaMail\src\app\docroot directory.
2. Add a JSP page directive to import the following packages:
   - javax.naming.*
   - javax.mail.*
   - javax.mail.internet.*
   - java.util.*
3. Get a handle to a JavaMail Session object via JNDI using the JNDI name java:comp/env/mail/mymail.
4. Create a multipart e-mail, the first part containing the data from the msgpart1 form field and the second part containing the data from the msgpart2 form field.
5. Send the e-mail to the address specified in the to form field.

Create the Receiving JSP File

1. Using Notepad, create a new text file called readmail.jsp in the JavaMail\src\app\docroot directory.
2. Add a JSP page directive to import the following packages:
   - javax.naming.*
   - javax.mail.*
   - javax.mail.internet.*
   - java.util.*
3. Retrieve the user ID, password, and server of the user's e-mail account from the query string, using the keys userid, password, and server.
4. Get a handle to a JavaMail Session object via JNDI using the JNDI name java:comp/env/mail/mymail.
5. Loop through all of the user's e-mail messages and display them to the user's browser.

Create the J2EE Application File

Using Notepad, create a new text file called application.xml in the JavaMail\src\earroot\Meta-inf directory. The file must map the context root, named app, to the Web Archive, javamail.war:

```
<web-uri>javamail.war</web-uri>
<context-root>app</context-root>
```

Create the J2EE Deployment Descriptor

Using Notepad, create a new text file called web.xml in the JavaMail\src\app\docroot\web-inf directory. This file must define the initial page, sendmail.html, for the application:

```
<welcome-file-list>
  <welcome-file>sendmail.html</welcome-file>
</welcome-file-list>
```

You also need to add a JNDI resource reference for the `Session` object:

```
<resource-ref>
 <description></description>
 <res-ref-name>mail/mymail</res-ref-name>
 <res-type>javax.mail.Session</res-type>
 <res-auth>Container</res-auth>
</resource-ref>
```

Create the J2EE Deployment Plan

Using Notepad, create a new text file called javamail.plan.xml in the JavaMail root directory. Within the `<warJar>` tag you must add entries to support the ability to get a handle to the `Session` object via JNDI.

Create the Web Archive and Enterprise Archive

From the JavaMail\src\app directory, using the `jar` utility, create the Web Archive (WAR) and name it javamail.war. Then from the JavaMail root directory, create the Enterprise Archive (EAR) and name it javamail.ear.

Deploy the Enterprise Archive

Using the appropriate tool for your J2EE application server, deploy the Enterprise Archive (EAR) file.

Test the Pages

With the coding completed, test the send and receive pages by taking the following steps:

1. Run the sendmail.html page `http://localhost/JavaMail/app/sendmail.html` (replace `localhost/JavaMail` with your server/directory combination), fill out the HTML form and press Send. Figure 14.4 shows the HTML form filled out.

2. Run the readmail.jsp page http://localhost/JavaMail/app/readmail.jsp?userid=<userid>&password=<pass>&server=<srvr> (replace localhost/JavaMail with your server/directory combination and also substitute userid, pass, and srvr values). Figure 14.5 shows the JSP output.

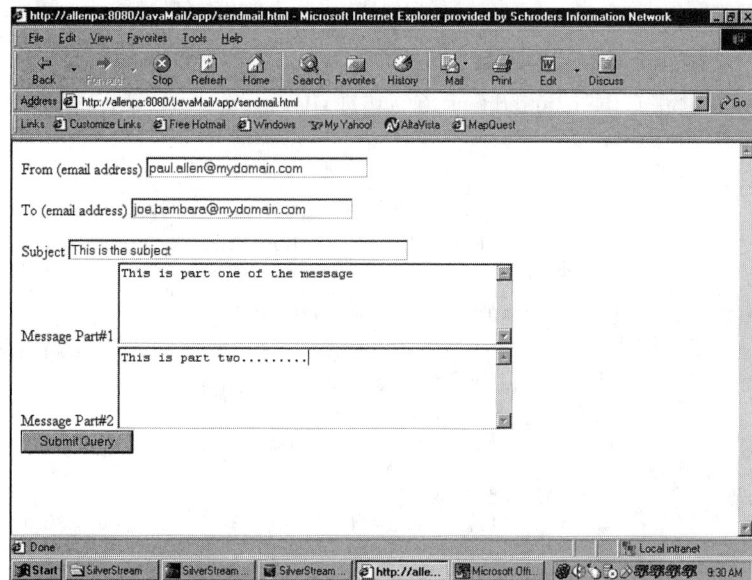

FIGURE 14.4
HTML form for sending Internet e-mail.

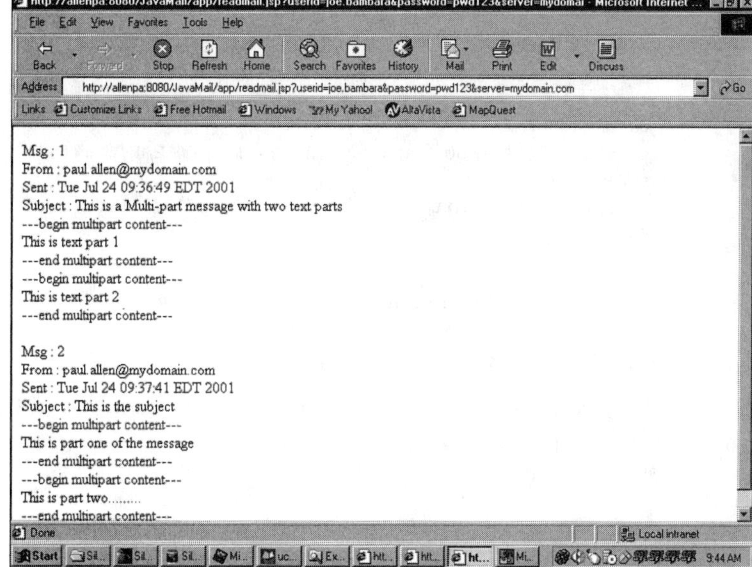

FIGURE 14.5
JSP output after receiving Internet e-mail.

Detailed Instructions

These are the detailed step-by-step instructions for building a J2EE JavaMail application.

Create the HTML Form

The first step is to create a new file that contains the HTML for the fill-in form:

1. Create a new text file using a text editor.
2. Define the required tags for an HTML page.

   ```
   <html>
   </html>
   ```

3. Add a `form` tag within the `<html>` tag created in step 2. The `action` attribute should be `/sendmail.jsp` and the `method` attribute should be `post`. (Substitute the current database for `JavaMail`.)

   ```
   <form action="sendmail.jsp" method="post">
   </form>
   ```

4. Add the input fields within the `<form>` tag created in step 3.

   ```
   <p>From (e-mail address)
     <input type="text" name="from" size="32" maxlength="32">
   </p>
   <p>To (e-mail address)
     <input type="text" name="to" size="32" maxlength="32">
   </p>
   <p></p>
   <p>Subject
     <input type="text" name="subject" size="50" maxlength="50">
     <br>
     Message Part#1
     <textarea cols="50" rows="5" name="msgpart1"></textarea>
     <br>
     Message Part#2
     <textarea cols="50" rows="5" name="msgpart2"></textarea>
     <br>
     <input type="submit">
     <br>
   </p>
   ```

5. Save the file as sendmail.html in the JavaMail\src\app\docroot directory.

Create the Sending JSP File

The next step is to create a new file that contains the JSP code that will send the e-mail message to the recipient:

1. Create a new text file.
2. Add a JSP page directive to import the following packages:
   - `javax.naming.*`
   - `javax.mail.*`
   - `javax.mail.internet.*`
   - `java.util.*`

```
<%@ page import=
 "javax.naming.*,javax.mail.*,javax.mail.internet.*,java.util.*" %>
```

3. Using JNDI, get a handle to the `Session` object via the JNDI name `java:comp/env/mail/mymail`:

```
<%
InitialContext ic = new InitialContext();
Session sess = (Session) ic.lookup("java:comp/env/mail/mymail");
```

4. Create an e-mail message with two parts, the first part coming from the `msgpart1` field and the second part coming from the `msgpart2` form field:

```
MimeMessage m = new MimeMessage(sess);
MimeBodyPart part1 = new MimeBodyPart();
part1.setContent(request.getParameter("msgpart1"),"text/plain");
MimeBodyPart part2 = new MimeBodyPart();
part2.setContent(request.getParameter("msgpart2"),"text/plain");
MimeMultipart mp = new MimeMultipart();
mp.addBodyPart(part1);
mp.addBodyPart(part2);
m.setContent(mp);
```

5. Identify to whom the message will be sent and create a subject line:

```
m.setFrom(new InternetAddress(request.getParameter("from")));
m.setRecipients(Message.RecipientType.TO,
   InternetAddress.parse(request.getParameter("to"),false));
m.setSubject(request.getParameter("subject"));
```

6. Send the message:

```
Transport.send(m);
out.println("Message sent.");
%>
```

7. Save the file in the JavaMail\src\app\docroot directory as sendmail.jsp.

Create the Receiving JSP File

In this step, create a new file that contains the JSP code that is used to retrieve the e-mail messages from the recipient's e-mail inbox:

1. Create a new text file.
2. Add a JSP page directive to import the following packages:
   - `javax.naming.*`
   - `javax.mail.*`
   - `javax.mail.internet.*`
   - `java.util.*`

   ```
   <%@ page import=
    "javax.naming.*,javax.mail.*,javax.mail.internet.*,java.util.*" %>
   ```
3. Using JNDI, get a handle to the `Session` object via the JNDI name `java:comp/env/mail/mymail`:

   ```
   <% InitialContext ic = new InitialContext();
   Session sess = (Session) ic.lookup("java:comp/env/mail/mymail");
   ```
4. Get the `userid` and `password` query parameters from the URL's query string:

   ```
   String userid = request.getParameter("userid");
   String password = request.getParameter("password");
   String server = request.getParameter("server");
   ```
5. Connect to the `Store` using the `userid` and `password` you got from the query string in step 4:

   ```
   Store store = sess.getStore();
   store.connect(server,userid,password);
   ```
6. Open the folder:

   ```
   Folder folder = store.getFolder("INBOX");
   folder.open(Folder.READ_WRITE);
   ```
7. Loop through all the messages and send them to the browser:

   ```
   Message[] msg = folder.getMessages();
   for(int i=0;i<msg.length;i++)
   {
       out.println("<p>Msg     : "+msg[i].getMessageNumber()+"<br>");
       out.println("From    : "+msg[i].getFrom()[0]+"<br>");
       out.println("Sent    : "+msg[i].getSentDate()+"<br>");
       out.println("Subject : "+msg[i].getSubject()+"<br>");
       if(msg[i].getContent() instanceof MimeMultipart)
       {
           MimeMultipart mp = (MimeMultipart) msg[i].getContent();
           for(int j=0,count=mp.getCount();j<count;j++)
           {
               Part p = mp.getBodyPart(j);
               out.println("---begin multipart content---<br>");
               out.println(p.getContent()+"<br>");
               out.println("---end multipart content---<br>");
           }
       }
   ```

```
            else
        {
            out.println("---begin content---<br>");
                 out.println(msg[i].getContent()+"<br>");
            out.println("---end content---<br>");
        }
        out.println("</p>");
    }
    folder.close(false);
    store.close();
    %>
```

8. Save the file in the JavaMail\src\app\docroot directory as readmail.jsp.

Create the J2EE Application File

Using Notepad, create a new text file called application.xml in the JavaMail\src\earroot\Meta-inf directory. Here is the complete file:

```
<?xml version="1.0" encoding="ISO8859_1"?>
<!DOCTYPE application PUBLIC '-//Sun Microsystems, Inc.
//DTD J2EE Application 1.2//EN'
'http://java.sun.com/j2ee/dtds/application_1_2.dtd'>
<application>
  <display-name>JavaMail</display-name>
  <description>Application description</description>
  <module>
   <web>
    <web-uri>javamail.war</web-uri>
    <context-root>app</context-root>
   </web>
  </module>
</application>
```

Create the J2EE Deployment Descriptor

Using Notepad, create a new text file called web.xml in the JavaMail\src\app\docroot\web-inf directory. This file must define the initial page, sendmail.html, for the application and also add a JNDI resource reference for the `Session` object. Here is the complete file:

```
<?xml version="1.0" encoding="ISO-8859-1"?>
<!DOCTYPE web-app
  PUBLIC "-//Sun Microsystems, Inc.//DTD Web Application 2.2//EN"
  "http://java.sun.com/j2ee/dtds/web-app_2_2.dtd">
<web-app>
  <!-- The Welcome File List -->
  <welcome-file-list>
    <welcome-file>sendmail.html</welcome-file>
  </welcome-file-list>
  <resource-ref>
```

```
    <description></description>
    <res-ref-name>mail/mymail</res-ref-name>
    <res-type>javax.mail.Session</res-type>
    <res-auth>Container</res-auth>
  </resource-ref>
</web-app>
```

Create the J2EE Deployment Plan

Using Notepad, create a new text file called javamail.plan.xml in the JavaMail root directory. Within the `<warJar>` tag you must add entries to support the ability to get a handle to the `Session` object via JNDI. Here is the complete file for the SilverStream Application Server environment (see Chapter 19, "Deploying the Application," for more information regarding the contents of this file for other J2EE-compliant application servers):

```
<?xml version="1.0" encoding="UTF-8" standalone="yes"?>
<?AgMetaXML 1.0?>
<earJarOptions isObject="true">
 <earJar isObject="true">
  <earJarName>javamail.ear</earJarName>
  <moduleList isObject="true">
   <module isObject="true">
    <warJar isObject="true">
     <warJarName>javamail.war</warJarName>
     <isEnabled type="Boolean">true</isEnabled>
     <URL>javamail</URL>
     <resourceReferenceList isObject="true">
      <resourceReference isObject="true">
       <name>mail/mymail</name>
       <mailRefProperties type="StringArray">
        <el>mail.transport.protocol</el>
        <el>smtp</el>
        <el>mail.host</el>
        <el>ucny.com</el>
        <el>mail.store.protocol</el>
        <el>pop3</el>
       </mailRefProperties>
      </resourceReference>
     </resourceReferenceList>
    </warJar>
   </module>
  </moduleList>
 </earJar>
</earJarOptions>
```

Create the Web Archive and Enterprise Archive

Now package the necessary files into a Web Archive (WAR) and then insert the Web Archive into the Enterprise Archive (EAR). The Enterprise Archive is then ready to be deployed to the J2EE server.

1. From the JavaMail\src\app directory, execute the following:

   ```
   jar cfv javamail.war -C docroot\ .
   ```

2. From the JavaMail root directory, execute the following:

   ```
   jar cfv javamail.ear -C src\javamail javamail.war
   jar ufv javamail.ear -C src\earroot .
   ```

Deploy the Enterprise Archive

From a command prompt, deploy the J2EE EAR file:

```
silvercmd deployear localhost JavaMail javamail.ear
-f javamail.plan.xml -o -i +verbose:vmopts +Xmx256m -v 5
```

Test the Pages

With the coding completed, test the send and receive pages by taking the following steps:

1. Run the sendmail.html page `http://localhost/JavaMail/app/sendmail.html` (replace `localhost/JavaMail` with your server/directory combination), fill out the HTML form and press Send. Figure 14.4 shows the HTML form filled out. (You'll find this figure at the end of the "Summary Instructions" section earlier in the chapter.)
2. Run the readmail.jsp page `http://localhost/JavaMail/app/readmail.jsp?userid=<userid>&password=<pass>&server=<srvr>` (replace `localhost/JavaMail` with your server/directory combination and also substitute `userid`, `pass`, and `srvr` values). Figure 14.5 shows the JSP output (see the "Summary Instructions" section).

Code Solution

The following subsections contain the complete code for the HTML file and the two JSP files described in the "Summary Instructions" and "Detailed Instructions" sections.

sendmail.html

Here is the code for the HTML file containing the fill-in form:

```
<html><form action="sendmail.jsp" method="post">
  <p>From (e-mail address)
    <input type="text" name="from" size="32" maxlength="32">
  </p>
  <p>To (e-mail address)
    <input type="text" name="to" size="32" maxlength="32">
  </p>
  <p></p>
```

```
  <p>Subject
    <input type="text" name="subject" size="50" maxlength="50">
    <br>
    Message Part#1
    <textarea cols="50" rows="5" name="msgpart1"></textarea>
    <br>
    Message Part#2
    <textarea cols="50" rows="5" name="msgpart2"></textarea>
    <br>
    <input type="submit">
    <br>
  </p>
  </form>
</html>
```

sendmail.jsp

Here is the code for the JSP file that sends the e-mail message to the recipient:

```
<%@ page import="javax.naming.*,javax.mail.*,
javax.mail.internet.*,java.util.*" %>
<%
    InitialContext ic = new InitialContext();
    Session sess = (Session) ic.lookup("java:comp/env/mail/mymail");

    MimeMessage m = new MimeMessage(sess);
    MimeBodyPart part1 = new MimeBodyPart();
    part1.setContent(request.getParameter("msgpart1"),"text/plain");
    MimeBodyPart part2 = new MimeBodyPart();
    part2.setContent(request.getParameter("msgpart2"),"text/plain");
    MimeMultipart mp = new MimeMultipart();
    mp.addBodyPart(part1);
    mp.addBodyPart(part2);
    m.setContent(mp);

    m.setFrom(new InternetAddress(request.getParameter("from")));
    m.setRecipients(Message.RecipientType.TO,
       InternetAddress.parse(request.getParameter("to"),false));
    m.setSubject(request.getParameter("subject"));

    Transport.send(m);
    out.println("Message sent.");
%>
```

readmail.jsp

Here is the code for the JSP file that retrieves messages from the recipient's e-mail inbox:

```
<%@ page import="javax.naming.*,javax.mail.*,
javax.mail.internet.*,java.util.*" %>
<%
    InitialContext ic = new InitialContext();
    Session sess = (Session) ic.lookup("java:comp/env/mail/mymail");

    String userid = request.getParameter("userid");
    String password = request.getParameter("password");
    String server = request.getParameter("server");

    Store store = sess.getStore();
    store.connect(server,userid,password);

    Folder folder = store.getFolder("INBOX");

    folder.open(Folder.READ_WRITE);

    Message[] msg = folder.getMessages();
    for(int i=0;i<msg.length;i++)
    {
        out.println("<p>Msg  : "+msg[i].getMessageNumber()+"<br>");
        out.println("From    : "+msg[i].getFrom()[0]+"<br>");
        out.println("Sent    : "+msg[i].getSentDate()+"<br>");
        out.println("Subject : "+msg[i].getSubject()+"<br>");
        if(msg[i].getContent() instanceof MimeMultipart)
        {
            MimeMultipart mp = (MimeMultipart) msg[i].getContent();
            for(int j=0,count=mp.getCount();j<count;j++)
            {
                Part p = mp.getBodyPart(j);
                out.println("---begin multipart content---<br>");
                out.println(p.getContent()+"<br>");
                out.println("---end multipart content---<br>");
            }
          }
          else
        {
            out.println("---begin content---<br>");
                 out.println(msg[i].getContent()+"<br>");
            out.println("---end content---<br>");
        }
        out.println("</p>");
        }
        folder.close(false);
        store.close();
%>
```

Summary

JavaMail, as part of the Java 2 Platform, Enterprise Edition (J2EE), provides a convenient layer between Java applications and e-mail services. It allows developers to add send and receive e-mail capability to any Java-based application. The addition of the Java Activation Framework greatly simplifies the processing of e-mail items including text, images, video and audio. The addition of JavaMail makes Java a very strong and robust platform for developing a wide range of application types for the Enterprise.

CHAPTER 15

Messaging with Applications: Java Message Service (JMS)

IN THIS CHAPTER

- Messaging Basics *488*
- Where Does JMS Fit In? *490*
- JMS Components *498*
- Producing and Consuming Messages *500*
- JMS Examples *501*
- JMS Implementation and Deployment Issues *522*

Messaging Basics

The Java Message Service (JMS) is an API developed by Sun Microsystems as part of the Java 2 Platform, Enterprise Edition (J2EE). It provides a common way for Java programmers to create, send, receive, and read an enterprise messaging system's messages.

Messages

A message is a unit of data that is sent from a process running on one computer to other processes running on the same or a different computer. The message can be simple text or a much more complex data structure, such as a Java `Hashtable` object. However, the object must be Serializable. An object that is Serializable can be transformed into a sequence of bytes, transmitted across a network and then re-created into a copy of the original object. This is commonly used to pass objects from one computer to another via the network.

Middleware

Many companies that have created successful e-commerce solutions to serve either their customers (Business to Consumer or B2C) or their suppliers (Business to Business or B2B) become acutely aware of the fact that these legacy database-to-client systems will be unable to keep pace with the ever-increasing transaction volume. They also realize that adding new hardware to the mix will still not solve the problem.

These types of applications are now being created using three tiers instead of two. The lower and upper tiers are carried over from the two-tier approach, with the lower tier containing the client interface and the upper tier containing the legacy applications and data. The additional middle layer contains server-side applications, known as middleware. Figure 15.1 depicts the three application layers.

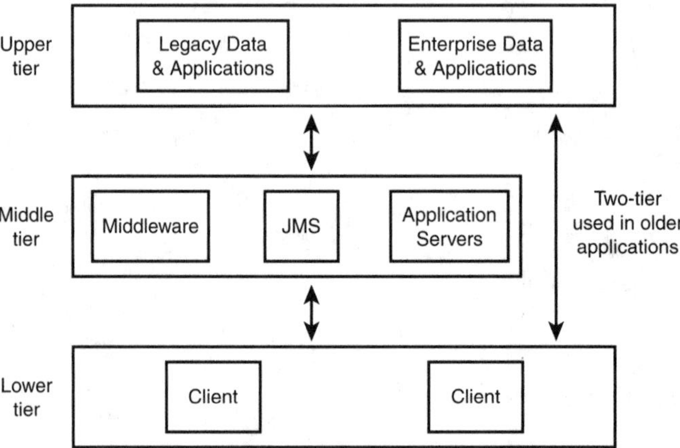

FIGURE 15.1
Application layers.

The middle tier, or middleware, provides business solutions and services, such as

- Database management—the ability to access a database server such as DB/2, Oracle, or SQL Server
- Messaging—the ability to send and receive data between applications
- Naming—the ability to find a resource by name instead of location
- Security—the ability to authenticate and authorize a user

The J2EE APIs extend standard Java and provide access to these services. The middleware is loosely coupled with applications running in the first and third tiers. The loose coupling improves the reliability of middleware by isolating it from failures that may occur on either of the other tiers.

Message-Oriented Middleware

Message-oriented middleware, or MOM, is a specialized type of middleware that coordinates the sending and receiving of messages. MOM is the infrastructure that connects heterogeneous applications. It provides dependable mechanisms that enable applications to create, send, and receive messages asynchronously within an enterprise environment.

The advantage of MOM-based applications is that they are event driven. They exchange messages in a wide variety of formats and deliver messages quickly and reliably.

Examples of MOM:

- IBM MQ Series
- Fiorano Message Server
- Progress SonicMQ
- SilverStream JBrokerMQ

(See Appendix C, "Quick Reference Material," for a more complete list of messaging products.)

Communication Modes

Most applications use synchronous communication. When using this type of communication, the requester is blocked from processing any further commands until the response (or a timeout) is received. These days, some Internet-based applications use asynchronous communication to facilitate certain types of transactions.

Synchronous Communication

Synchronous communication is conducted between two parties. Both parties must be active to participate, and must acknowledge receipt of a message, also known as a blocking call, before proceeding. As the volume of traffic increases, more bandwidth is required, and the need for additional hardware becomes critical. Such implementations are easily affected by failures at the hardware, software, and network levels, resulting in delayed messages and traffic backups. When capacities are exceeded, information is usually lost.

Asynchronous Communication

In asynchronous communication the parties are peers, and can send and receive messages at will. Asynchronous communication does not require real-time acknowledgment of a message; the requester can continue with other processing once it sends the message, also known as a non-blocking call.

A practical example of asynchronous communication is e-mail. The e-mail client may not be running on your PC, but other people can still send e-mail messages to you. When you start your e-mail client, you will be able to receive the e-mail messages that have accumulated.

Where Does JMS Fit In?

Message-oriented middleware (MOM) products allow a developer to loosely couple applications together. However, MOMs are proprietary and quite often complex and expensive products. With Java becoming a standard platform, JMS provides a standard Java interface to these MOM products. JMS frees developers from having to write low-level infrastructure code, also known as "plumbing," allowing them to build solutions quickly and more easily.

JMS integrates with other components of J2EE including J2EE APIs such as Java Database Connectivity (JDBC), Java Naming and Directory Interface (JNDI) and Enterprise JavaBeans (EJB).

JMS applications use databases to provide the message persistence necessary for guaranteeing delivery and order of messages. JMS-based applications can use JNDI to name, look up, and retrieve administered objects. With the arrival of the EJB 2.0 specification, EJB is now more easily integrated into JMS-based applications. The new EJB message-driven bean can asynchronously receive and process asynchronous messages within the container. These message-driven beans can be instantiated multiple times to provide concurrent processing of a message Queue.

JMS in Applications

JMS provides an interface from Java applications to MOM products. JMS enables clients (or peers) to exchange data in the form of messages.

The major advantages of using messaging for this exchange are

- Easy integration of incompatible systems
- Asynchronous communications
- One-to-many communications
- Guaranteed messaging
- Transactional messaging

Table 15.1 shows the various composite parts of a JMS messaging application.

TABLE 15.1 Components of a JMS Messaging Application

Component	*Function*
JMS provider	The host application on which the JMS application runs. The JMS provider converses with JMS applications and supplies the underlying mechanisms required for a messaging application.
Administered objects	JMS objects that are created and maintained by an administrator to be used by JMS clients.
Clients	Applications that can send and/or receive messages.
Messages	Bundles of information that are passed between applications. Each application defines the types of information a message can contain.

Message Models in JMS

JMS supports two message models known as Publish/Subscribe (Pub/Sub) and Point-to-Point (PTP). Depending on the implementation, either model can deliver messages synchronously or asynchronously. The JMS specification requires that the MOM product support at least one of these models to be compliant.

The Point-to-Point Message Model

The Point-to-Point model sends messages to a receiver on a one-to-one basis. Figure 15.2 is a diagram showing the Point-to-Point model. Examples of its implementation include

- Instant messaging
- Receiving a transaction from another system
- Sending an order to another system
- Supply-chain processing

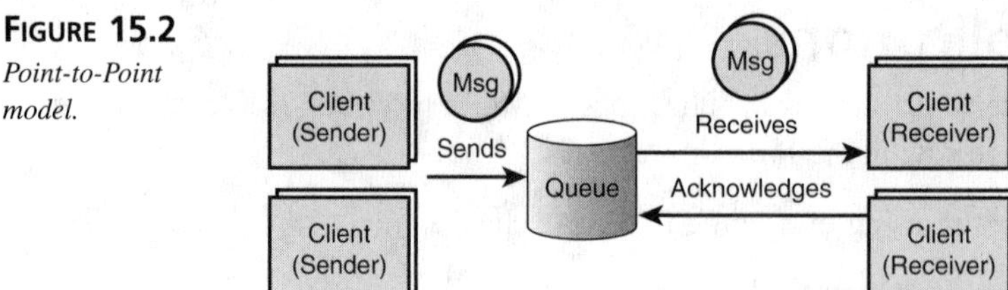

FIGURE 15.2
Point-to-Point model.

A message is delivered to a particular Queue. Messages in a Queue are processed on a first-in, first-out (FIFO) basis. In other words, the subscriber is guaranteed to get each message in the order in which it was sent. Only one receiver can process each message, regardless of the number of receivers that exist for the Queue. This differs from the Publish/Subscribe model, in which a single message can be published to one or more subscribers. In addition to processing the next message in a Queue, the receiver can also look through the messages in a Queue (for example, to count them). However, the receiver is unable to process the messages in any other order than FIFO.

The following is a list of the steps and interface classes required for the Point-to-Point model of communication:

1. Obtain the `Queue` via a JNDI lookup (the lookup name will vary depending on the MOM vendor).
2. Obtain the `QueueConnectionFactory` object via another JNDI lookup (the lookup name will vary depending on the MOM vendor).
3. Obtain a `QueueConnection` to the provider via the `QueueConnectionFactory` (if security is enabled, pass a user id and password to the `createQueueConnection` method).
4. Obtain a `QueueSession` with the provider via the `QueueConnection`.
5. Create either a `QueueSender` or a `QueueReceiver` via the `QueueSession` for the required `Queue`.
6. Send and/or receive messages.
7. Close the `QueueConnection` (this will also close the `QueueSender` or `QueueReceiver`, and the `QueueSession`).

The Publish/Subscribe Model

The Publish/Subscribe model allows an application to publish messages on either a one-to-many or a many-to-many basis. Figure 15.3 is a diagram showing the Publish/Subscribe model. Examples of its implementation include

- Sending news stories to interested parties
- Sending sales forecasts to various people in an organization
- Sending stock prices to traders on the trading floor

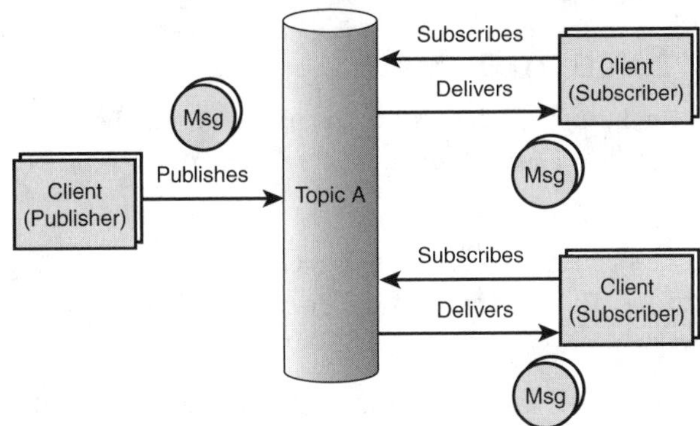

FIGURE 15.3
Publish/Subscribe model.

Messages are published to a Topic (or subject). One or more publishers can publish messages to the Topic. Any client application that wants to receive messages on this Topic must first subscribe to the Topic. Multiple clients can subscribe to the Topic and subsequently receive a copy of the message. Typically, the subscriber must be connected at the time a message is published in order to receive that message. If no subscribers to a Topic are online to receive messages, the messages are destroyed. This is known as a non-durable subscription to the Topic. The subscriber can also request a durable subscription, in which case the messages will be received when the subscriber is reconnected to the Topic. Durable subscriptions require greater overhead because the messages need to be persistently stored until they can be delivered to the subscriber.

The following is a list of the steps and interface classes required for the Publish/Subscribe model of communication:

1. Obtain the `Topic` via a JNDI lookup (the lookup name will vary depending on the MOM vendor).
2. Obtain the `TopicConnectionFactory` object via another JNDI lookup (the lookup name will vary depending on the MOM vendor).
3. Obtain a `TopicConnection` to the provider via the `TopicConnectionFactory` (if security is enabled, pass a user id and password to the `createTopicConnection` method).
4. Obtain a `TopicSession` with the provider via the `TopicConnection`.

5. Create either a `TopicPublisher` or a `TopicSubscriber` via the `TopicSession` for the required `Topic`.
6. Publish and/or receive messages.
7. Close the `TopicPublisher` or `TopicSubscriber`, the `Session`, and the `Connection`.

Handling Exceptions

If there is a problem during a JMS session, an application can be notified of the problem. These error notifications are asynchronous and are achieved via the `ExceptionListener` interface.

The `ExceptionListener` is an interface used to communicate the JMS provider problem details to a JMS client. This interface is used primarily to report connection problems in asynchronous communication.

To handle exceptions, the developer needs to create a listener object that implements the `ExceptionListener` interface. This listener object must implement the `onException(JMSException exception)` method. The JMS provider should then be instructed to call this listener object by calling the `setExceptionListener(listener)` method on the Session.

Session Management

Table 15.2 describes the details of the JMS session. Unless noted otherwise, this information applies to both the Publish/Subscribe and Point-to-Point models.

TABLE 15.2 JMS Session Details

Session Detail	*Description*
Transacted session	A transacted session is a related group of consumed and produced messages that are treated as a single work unit. A transaction can be either committed or rolled back. When a transaction's `commit` method is called, the consumed messages are acknowledged, and the associated produced messages are sent. When a transaction's `rollback` method is called, the produced messages are destroyed, and the consumed messages are recovered.
Duplicate messages	Clients must be able to send messages knowing that JMS will deliver them only once. Therefore, the JMS provider must never deliver a message more than once, or deliver a copy of a message that has already been acknowledged.

TABLE 15.2 continued

Session Detail	*Description*
	The message header contains a redelivery flag field. When this flag is set, it tells the client that this message may have been received before but that, for whatever reason, the JMS server did not receive the client's acknowledgment of receipt. The redelivery flag is set by the JMS provider application, usually as the result of a recovery operation.
Message acknowledgment	If a JMS session is transacted, messages are acknowledged automatically by the commit mechanism and recovered by the rollback mechanism. If a session is not transacted, recovery must be handled manually, and messages are acknowledged in one of three ways: • `AUTO_ACKNOWLEDGE`—For each message, the session automatically acknowledges that a client has received a message when the client returns from a call to receive a message or the `MessageListener` called by the session to process the message returns successfully. • `CLIENT_ACKNOWLEDGE`—Client acknowledges the message by calling the `acknowledge` method on the message. This also acknowledges all messages that were processed during the session. • `DUPS_OK_ACKNOWLEDGE`—If JMS fails, some duplication of messages may result, but this option uses fewer resources during the session.

Messages

JMS messages have a basic but flexible format that allows the sender to create messages that match layouts used by non-JMS applications on varied platforms. JMS messages are typically formatted data (such as a request, an event, or a status) that is passed between applications. The message can contain simple or complex data types. JMS applications can also pass serializable Java objects to other Java-based applications.

A JMS message is made up of one required component and two optional components:

- A header (required)
- Properties (optional)
- A body (optional)

Figure 15.4 illustrates the structure of a JMS message.

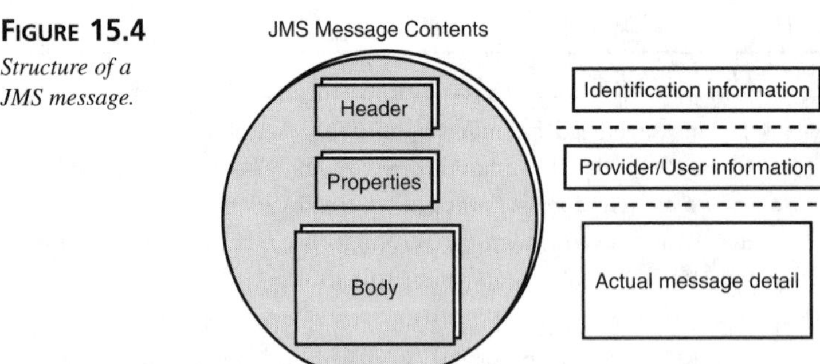

FIGURE 15.4
Structure of a JMS message.

Header Fields

The JMS message header contains a number of fields that contain information that can be used to identify and route messages. Each of these header fields has the appropriate get/set methods. Most of the values are automatically set by the `send()` or `publish()` methods, but some of them can be set by the client.

Table 15.3 describes a few header fields. For a complete list, refer to the JMS specification at `http://java.sun.com/products/jms/docs.html`.

TABLE 15.3 JMS Message Headers

Header Field	*Description*
`JMSMessageID`	Unique identifier for every message.
`JMSDeliveryMode`	`PERSISTENT` means that delivery of a message is guaranteed. It will continue to exist until all subscribers who requested it receive it. The message is delivered only once. `NON-PERSISTENT` delivery means that every reasonable attempt is made to deliver the message. But in the event of some kind of system failure, the message may be lost. These messages are delivered at most once.
`JMSExpiration`	The length of time, in milliseconds, that a message will exist before it is removed. Setting the `JMSExpiration` to zero will prevent the message from being removed.
`JMSPriority`	Although it is not guaranteed, messages with a higher priority are generally delivered before messages with a lower priority. Priority 0 is the lowest and 9 is the highest. Priority 4 is the default. Priorities of 0–4 are grades of normal priority and priorities of 5–9 are grades of higher priority.

TABLE 15.3 continued

Header Field	*Description*
`JMSRedelivered`	Notifies the client that the client probably received this message at least once before, but for whatever reason, the client did not acknowledge its receipt. The JMS provider sets this flag, typically during a recovery operation after a failure.
`JMSReplyTo`	Contains a Destination provided by the client indicating where a reply to this message should be sent. When this field is filled, a response is generally expected but is optional; it is up to the client to decide.

Properties

Properties are values that can add to the information contained in header fields. The JMS API provides some predefined property names that the JMS provider can support (these properties have a `JMS_` prefix).

The use of properties is optional. If you decide to use them, they can be of the type `boolean`, `byte`, `short`, `int`, `long`, `float`, `double`, or `string`. They can be set when a message is sent, or by consumers upon receipt of the message. These properties, along with the header field, can be used in conjunction with a `MessageSelector` to filter and route messages based on the criteria specified.

Body

There are five different message body formats or types, which allow a JMS client to send and receive data in many different forms, and which provide compatibility with existing messaging formats. Table 15.4 describes these message body formats.

TABLE 15.4 JMS Message Body Formats

Form	*Content*
`ByteMessage`	A stream of uninterpreted bytes. This is the type of message body that should be used to match most legacy messages.
`MapMessage`	A set of name/value pairs, similar to a `HashMap`. The name part is a `String` object and the value is a Java primitive type.
`ObjectMessage`	A single serializable Java object or a collection of objects.
`StreamMessage`	A stream of Java primitive values that are entered and read sequentially.
`TextMessage`	Text formatted as a `java.lang.String`. This form is well suited to exchanging XML data.

JMS Components

There are several components that are required by an application that uses JMS. See Table 15.5 for the components used by a JMS messaging application.

TABLE 15.5 Components Used by a JMS Messaging Application

Component	*Function*
`Destination`	Topic for Publish/Subscribe model and Queue for Point-to-Point model
`ConnectionFactory`	Gets a handle, containing the IP address, to a connection on a JMS server
`Connection`	Physical connection to the JMS Server
`Session`	Responsible for sending/receiving messages, managing transactions, and handling acknowledgments

Administered Objects

An administered object is one that is created by the administrator of the JMS provider application. Administered objects are placed in a Java Naming and Directory Interface (JNDI) namespace, and can be administered from a common management console.

JMS has two types of administered objects: `Destination` and `ConnectionFactory`. See Table 15.6 for descriptions of these two types of objects.

TABLE 15.6 JMS Administered Objects

Administered Object	*Description*
`Destination`	The `Destination` object contains configuration information supplied by the JMS provider. The client uses this object to specify a destination for messages that it wishes to send and/or a location from which to receive messages. There are two types of `Destination` interfaces, a Queue for the Point-to-Point model and a Topic for the Publish/Subscribe model.
`ConnectionFactory`	The `ConnectionFactory` is obtained via a JNDI lookup. It contains connection configuration information enabling a JMS client application to create a connection with the JMS server.

Even though JMS clients can look up and access these objects via JNDI, the actual management of the administered objects varies from provider to provider. The JMS provider supplies a tool that will let the administrator create and destroy these administered objects.

Interface Classes

JMS defines interface classes that create and manage connections to MOM products. The set of interfaces required depends on the message model that the developer uses. Table 15.7 shows all of the interface classes that can be used in a JMS application and Figure 15.5 shows the relationships between these objects and the sequence in which they should be created.

TABLE 15.7 JMS Interface Classes

Base Interfaces	*Point-to-Point Interfaces*	*Publish/Subscribe Interfaces*
`Destination`	`Queue`	`Topic`
`ConnectionFactory`	`QueueConnectionFactory`	`TopicConnectionFactory`
`Connection`	`QueueConnection`	`TopicConnection`
`Session`	`QueueSession`	`TopicSession`
`MessageProducer`	`QueueSender`	`TopicPublisher`
`MessageConsumer`	`QueueReceiver` and `QueueBrowser`	`TopicSubscriber`

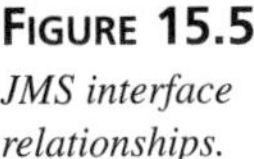

FIGURE 15.5
JMS interface relationships.

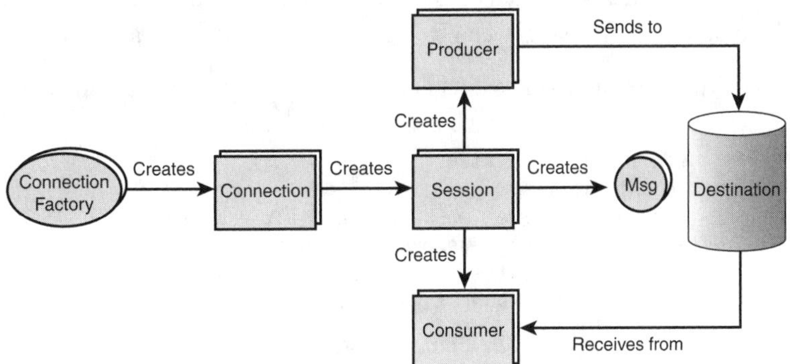

Producing and Consuming Messages

There are four objects that are used to create and receive messages in a JMS client application: `MessageProducer`, `MessageConsumer`, `MessageListener`, and `MessageSelector`.

MessageProducer

A `MessageProducer` is created by a session and used to send messages to a Destination. In the Point-to-Point model, the Destination is called a Queue. For the Publish/Subscribe model the Destination is called a Topic. When creating a `MessageProducer`, you can also specify the

- Default delivery mode (`setDeliveryMode`)—This can be either `NON-PERSISTENT`, which has a lower overhead because the message is not logged, or `PERSISTENT`, which requires the message to be logged, typically to a database.
- Priority of the message (`setPriority`)—0 is the lowest priority and 9 is the highest priority. 4 is the default. Priorities of 0–4 are grades of normal priority and priorities of 5–9 are grades of higher priority.
- Expiration time (`setTimeToLive`)—The amount of time, in milliseconds, that a message should be available. Specify 0 for unlimited time.

MessageConsumer

A `MessageConsumer` is created by a session and used to receive messages sent to the Destination. The messages can be received in one of two ways:

- Synchronously—The client calls one of the receive methods (`receive` or `receiveNoWait`) after the consumer is started.

```
// start the connection
queueConn.start();
// receive the first message (wait for a message)
Message message = queueReceiver.receive();
// receive the next message (wait for a minute only)
Message message = queueReceiver.receive(60000);
```

- Asynchronously—The client registers a `MessageListener` and then starts the consumer (see the following section for more details on the `MessageListener`).

MessageListener

A `MessageListener` is an interface that needs to be implemented in order to receive messages asynchronously. To receive an asynchronous message, you must

- Create an object that implements the `MessageListener` interface. This includes coding the `onMessage()` method.
- Tell the `QueueReceiver` which object messages should be sent to via the `setMessageListener()` method.
- Call the `Start()` method on the `Connection` object to begin receiving messages.

MessageSelector

A `MessageSelector` is an object specified by the client to filter out messages that meet the criteria specified. The `MessageSelectors` will look at the message header and properties fields and compare them to an expression contained in a string. The syntax of this expression is based on a subset of SQL92 conditional expression syntax. Table 15.8 shows some examples of these expressions.

TABLE 15.8 JMS Message Selector Filter Examples

Value	*Example*
Literals	`'string literal', 64, FALSE`
Identifiers	`$name, JMSPriority, JMSXId, JMS_timeout`
Logical operators	`AND, OR, NOT`
Comparison operators	`<, >, <=, >=, IS NULL, IS NOT NULL, BETWEEN`
Arithmetic operators	`+, -, *, /`
Expressions	`(Qty * Price) >= 50000`
	`Day = 'Monday'`
	`Month IN ('March', 'April', 'May')`
	`Day NOT IN ('Saturday', 'Sunday')`
	`Description LIKE 'SILVER%'`

JMS Examples

This section provides examples of JMS clients that demonstrate the Point-to-Point model, Publish/Subscribe model, browsing a Point-to-Point Queue, using a `MessageSelector`, using a `MessageListener`, and creating and destroying Queue and Topic Destinations.

A Simple Point-to-Point Example

In this example, the sending client (see Listing 15.1) sends simple Messages to a Queue. The receiving client (see Listing 15.2) retrieves the simple Messages from the Queue. Note that for this example we are supplying "queue/queue0" for the JNDI lookup. This name will differ per the MOM vendor and site naming convention.

LISTING 15.1 The Sending Client

```
package ptp;

import javax.jms.Queue;

import javax.naming.Context;
import javax.naming.InitialContext;

import javax.jms.Queue;
import javax.jms.Session;
import javax.jms.Message;
import javax.jms.QueueSender;
import javax.jms.DeliveryMode;
import javax.jms.QueueSession;
import javax.jms.QueueReceiver;
import javax.jms.QueueConnection;
import javax.jms.QueueConnectionFactory;

public class SimpleSender
{
    public static void main(String[] args) throws Exception
    {
    // get the initial context
    InitialContext ctx = new InitialContext();

    // lookup the queue object
    Queue queue = (Queue) ctx.lookup("queue/queue0");

    // lookup the queue connection factory
    QueueConnectionFactory connFactory = (QueueConnectionFactory)
        ctx.lookup("queue/connectionFactory");

    // create a queue connection
    QueueConnection queueConn = connFactory.createQueueConnection();

    // create a queue session
    QueueSession queueSession = queueConn.createQueueSession(false,
        Session.DUPS_OK_ACKNOWLEDGE);

    // create a queue sender
    QueueSender queueSender = queueSession.createSender(queue);
    queueSender.setDeliveryMode(DeliveryMode.NON_PERSISTENT);
```

Listing 15.1 continued

```
    // get the number of messages to send
    int numMsgs = (args.length > 0) ? new Integer(args[0]).intValue() : 500;

    // send the messages
    for (int i=0; i < numMsgs; i++) {
        // construct a simple message
        Message message = queueSession.createMessage();

        queueSender.send(message);
        System.out.println("Sent msg#"+(i+1));
    }

    // close the queue connection
    queueConn.close();
    }
}
```

Listing 15.2 The Receiving Client

```
package ptp;

import javax.jms.Queue;

import javax.naming.Context;
import javax.naming.InitialContext;

import javax.jms.Queue;
import javax.jms.Session;
import javax.jms.Message;
import javax.jms.QueueSender;
import javax.jms.QueueSession;
import javax.jms.QueueReceiver;
import javax.jms.QueueConnection;
import javax.jms.QueueConnectionFactory;

public class SimpleReceiver
{
    public static void main(String[] args) throws Exception
    {
    // get the initial context
    InitialContext ctx = new InitialContext();

    // lookup the queue object
    Queue queue = (Queue) ctx.lookup("queue/queue0");

    // lookup the queue connection factory
    QueueConnectionFactory connFactory = (QueueConnectionFactory)
```

LISTING 15.2 continued

```
        ctx.lookup("queue/connectionFactory");
    // create a queue connection
    QueueConnection queueConn = connFactory.createQueueConnection();

    // create a queue session
    QueueSession queueSession = queueConn.createQueueSession(false,
        Session.DUPS_OK_ACKNOWLEDGE);

    // create a queue receiver
    QueueReceiver queueReceiver = queueSession.createReceiver(queue);

    // start the connection
    queueConn.start();

    // get the number of messages to receive
    int numMsgs = (args.length > 0) ? new Integer(args[0]).intValue() : 500;

    // receive the messages
    for (int i=0; i < numMsgs; i++) {
        Message message = queueReceiver.receive();
        System.out.println("Received msg#"+(i+1));
    }

    // close the queue connection
    queueConn.close();
    }
}
```

A Simple Publish/Subscribe Example

In this example, the publishing client (see Listing 15.3) publishes simple Messages to a Topic. The subscribing client (see Listing 15.4) receives the simple Messages from the Topic. Note that for this example we are supplying `"topic/topic0"` for the JNDI lookup. This name will differ per the MOM vendor and site naming convention.

LISTING 15.3 The Publishing Client

```
package pubsub;

import javax.jms.Topic;

import javax.naming.Context;
import javax.naming.InitialContext;

import javax.jms.Topic;
import javax.jms.Session;
import javax.jms.Message;
```

LISTING 15.3 continued

```
import javax.jms.TopicPublisher;
import javax.jms.DeliveryMode;
import javax.jms.TopicSession;
import javax.jms.TopicConnection;
import javax.jms.TopicConnectionFactory;

public class SimplePublisher
{
    public static void main(String[] args) throws Exception
    {
    // get the initial context
    InitialContext ctx = new InitialContext();

    // lookup the topic object
    Topic topic = (Topic) ctx.lookup("topic/topic0");

    // lookup the topic connection factory
    TopicConnectionFactory connFactory = (TopicConnectionFactory)
        ctx.lookup("topic/connectionFactory");

    // create a topic connection
    TopicConnection topicConn = connFactory.createTopicConnection();

    // create a topic session
    TopicSession topicSession = topicConn.createTopicSession(false,
        Session.AUTO_ACKNOWLEDGE);

    // create a topic publisher
    TopicPublisher topicPublisher = topicSession.createPublisher(topic);
    topicPublisher.setDeliveryMode(DeliveryMode.NON_PERSISTENT);

    // create a simple message
    Message message = topicSession.createMessage();

    // get the number of messages to publish
    int numMsgs = (args.length > 0) ? new Integer(args[0]).intValue() : 500;

    // publish the messages
    for (int i=0; i < numMsgs; i++) {
        topicPublisher.publish(message);
        System.out.println("Published msg#"+(i+1));
    }

    // close the topic connection
    topicConn.close();
    }
}
```

LISTING 15.4 The Subscribing Client

```
package pubsub;

import javax.jms.Topic;

import javax.naming.Context;
import javax.naming.InitialContext;

import javax.jms.Topic;
import javax.jms.Session;
import javax.jms.Message;
import javax.jms.TopicSession;
import javax.jms.TopicSubscriber;
import javax.jms.TopicConnection;
import javax.jms.TopicConnectionFactory;

public class SimpleSubscriber
{
    public static void main(String[] args) throws Exception
    {
    // get the initial context
    InitialContext ctx = new InitialContext();

    // lookup the topic object
    Topic topic = (Topic) ctx.lookup("topic/topic0");

    // lookup the topic connection factory
    TopicConnectionFactory connFactory = (TopicConnectionFactory)
        ctx.lookup("topic/connectionFactory");

    // create a topic connection
    TopicConnection topicConn = connFactory.createTopicConnection();

    // create a topic session
    TopicSession topicSession = topicConn.createTopicSession(false,
        Session.DUPS_OK_ACKNOWLEDGE);

    // create a topic subsscriber
    TopicSubscriber topicSubscriber = topicSession.createSubscriber(topic);

    // start the connection
    topicConn.start();

    // get the number of messages to receive
    int numMsgs = (args.length > 0) ? new Integer(args[0]).intValue() : 500;

    // receive the messages
    for (int i=0; i < numMsgs; i++) {
```

LISTING 15.4 continued

```
            Message message = topicSubscriber.receive();
            System.out.println("Received msg#"+(i+1));
        }

        // close the topic connection
        topicConn.close();
        }
}
```

A Point-to-Point Browsing Example

In this example, the sending client (see Listing 15.5) sends Messages, which also include properties, to a Queue. The receiving client (see Listing 15.6) first browses the queue to look at all messages and then reads (processes) the Messages in the Queue. Note that for this example we are supplying `"queue/queue0"` for the JNDI lookup. This name will differ per the MOM vendor and site naming convention.

LISTING 15.5 The Sending Browse Client

```
package browser;

import javax.jms.Queue;

import javax.naming.Context;
import javax.naming.InitialContext;

import javax.jms.Queue;
import javax.jms.Session;
import javax.jms.Message;
import javax.jms.QueueSender;
import javax.jms.DeliveryMode;
import javax.jms.QueueSession;
import javax.jms.QueueReceiver;
import javax.jms.QueueConnection;
import javax.jms.QueueConnectionFactory;

public class Sender
{
    public static void main(String[] args) throws Exception
    {
        // get the initial context
        InitialContext ctx = new InitialContext();

        // lookup the queue object
        Queue queue = (Queue) ctx.lookup("queue/queue0");
```

LISTING 15.5 continued

```
        // lookup the queue connection factory
        QueueConnectionFactory connFactory = (QueueConnectionFactory)
            ctx.lookup("queue/connectionFactory");

        // create a queue connection
        QueueConnection queueConn = connFactory.createQueueConnection();

        // create a queue session
        QueueSession queueSession = queueConn.createQueueSession(false,
            Session.DUPS_OK_ACKNOWLEDGE);

        // create a queue sender
        QueueSender queueSender = queueSession.createSender(queue);
        queueSender.setDeliveryMode(DeliveryMode.NON_PERSISTENT);

        // get the number of messages to send
        int numMsgs = (args.length > 0) ? new Integer(args[0]).intValue() : 5;

        // send the messages
        for (int i=0; i < numMsgs; i++) {
            Message message = queueSession.createMessage();
            message.setIntProperty("MsgNumber", (i+1));
            if (i == (numMsgs-1))
                message.setBooleanProperty("EndMessage", true);
            queueSender.send(message);
            System.out.println("Sent msg#"+(i+1));
        }

        // close the queue connection
        queueConn.close();
    }
}
```

LISTING 15.6 The Receiving Browse Client

```
package browser;

import java.util.Enumeration;

import javax.jms.Queue;

import javax.naming.Context;
import javax.naming.InitialContext;

import javax.jms.Queue;
import javax.jms.Session;
import javax.jms.Message;
import javax.jms.QueueSender;
```

LISTING 15.6 continued

```
import javax.jms.QueueSession;
import javax.jms.QueueBrowser;
import javax.jms.QueueReceiver;
import javax.jms.QueueConnection;
import javax.jms.QueueConnectionFactory;

public class Receiver
{
    public static void main(String[] args) throws Exception
    {
        // get the initial context
        InitialContext ctx = new InitialContext();

        // lookup the queue object
        Queue queue = (Queue) ctx.lookup("queue/queue0");

        // lookup the queue connection factory
        QueueConnectionFactory connFactory = (QueueConnectionFactory)
            ctx.lookup("queue/connectionFactory");

        // create a queue connection
        QueueConnection queueConn = connFactory.createQueueConnection();

        // create a queue session
        QueueSession queueSession = queueConn.createQueueSession(false,
            Session.DUPS_OK_ACKNOWLEDGE);

        // create a queue browser
        QueueBrowser queueBrowser = queueSession.createBrowser(queue);

        // start the connection
        queueConn.start();

        System.out.println("\nBrowse all messages first...");

        // Enumerate all the messages on the queue
        Enumeration enum = queueBrowser.getEnumeration();

        // Loop through enumeration
        while (enum.hasMoreElements()) {
            Message message = (Message) enum.nextElement();
            System.out.println("Browse message#: "+
                message.getStringProperty("MsgNumber"));
        }
        // close the browsing queue connection
        queueBrowser.close();
```

LISTING 15.6 continued

```
        System.out.println("\nNow read (process) all of the messages...");
        // create a queue receiver
        QueueReceiver queueReceiver = queueSession.createReceiver(queue);
        while (true) {
            Message message = queueReceiver.receiveNoWait();
            if (message == null) break;
            System.out.println("Received message#: "+
                message.getStringProperty("MsgNumber"));
        }
        // close the reading queue connection
        queueConn.close();
    }
}
```

A MessageListener Example

In this example, the receiving client (see Listing 15.8) implements the `MessageListener` interface (see Listing 15.9) in order to receive messages from the Queue. Note that the sending client (see Listing 15.7) sends two types of messages: first an object message containing a `Hashtable` and then a text message.

LISTING 15.7 The Sending `MessageListener` Client

```
import javax.jms.Queue;

import javax.naming.Context;
import javax.naming.InitialContext;

import javax.jms.Queue;
import javax.jms.Session;
import javax.jms.Message;
import javax.jms.TextMessage;
import javax.jms.ObjectMessage;
import javax.jms.QueueSender;
import javax.jms.DeliveryMode;
import javax.jms.QueueSession;
import javax.jms.QueueReceiver;
import javax.jms.QueueConnection;
import javax.jms.QueueConnectionFactory;

import java.util.Hashtable;

public class SenderListener
{
    public static void main(String[] args) throws Exception
    {
```

LISTING 15.7 continued

```
    // get the initial context
    InitialContext ctx = new InitialContext();

    // lookup the queue object
    Queue queue = (Queue) ctx.lookup("queue/queue0");

    // lookup the queue connection factory
    QueueConnectionFactory connFactory = (QueueConnectionFactory)
        ctx.lookup("queue/connectionFactory");

    // create a queue connection
    QueueConnection queueConn = connFactory.createQueueConnection();

    // create a queue session
    QueueSession queueSession = queueConn.createQueueSession(false,
        Session.DUPS_OK_ACKNOWLEDGE);

    // create a queue sender
    QueueSender queueSender = queueSession.createSender(queue);
    queueSender.setDeliveryMode(DeliveryMode.PERSISTENT);

    // create an Object message
         ObjectMessage objectmsg = queueSession.createObjectMessage();
         Hashtable hTable = new Hashtable();
         hTable.put("color","red");
         hTable.put("item","sauce");
         objectmsg.setObject(hTable);

      System.out.println("Message sent. "+objectmsg.getObject());
         queueSender.send(objectmsg);

    // create a Text message
         TextMessage textmsg= queueSession.createTextMessage();
         textmsg.setText("hello world");

      System.out.println("Message sent. "+textmsg.getText());
      queueSender.send(textmsg);

    // create a finish Text message
         textmsg.setText("finish");

      System.out.println("Message sent. "+textmsg.getText());
      queueSender.send(textmsg);

    // close the queue connection
    queueConn.close();
    }
}
```

LISTING 15.8 The Receiving `MessageListener` Client

```
import MsgListener;

public class ReceiverListener
{
    public static void main(String[] args) throws Exception
    {
        try {
            MsgListener msgLis = new MsgListener();
            msgLis.init();
            while (true) {
                synchronized(msgLis) {
                    try {
                        msgLis.wait();
                        if (msgLis.finish) {
                            msgLis.close();
                            break;
                        }
                    }
                    catch (Exception e)
                    {
                        System.out.println(e);
                    }
                }
            }
        }
        catch (Exception e)
        {
            System.out.println(e);
        }
    }
}
```

LISTING 15.9 The `MessageListener` Class for the Client

```
import javax.jms.*;
import javax.naming.*;
import java.rmi.RemoteException;

public class MsgListener implements javax.jms.MessageListener
{
    protected QueueConnectionFactory    connFactory = null;
    protected QueueConnection            queueConn = null;
    protected QueueSession            queueSession = null;
    protected Queue                  queue = null;
    protected QueueReceiver             queueReceiver = null;
    public boolean finish = false;
```

Listing 15.9 continued

```
public void init() throws NamingException, JMSException, RemoteException
{
    // get the initial context
    InitialContext ctx = new InitialContext();

    // lookup the queue object
    queue = (Queue) ctx.lookup("queue/queue0");

    // lookup the queue connection factory
    connFactory = (QueueConnectionFactory)
          ctx.lookup("queue/connectionFactory");

    // create a queue connection
    queueConn = connFactory.createQueueConnection();

    // create a queue session
    queueSession = queueConn.createQueueSession(
         false, Session.DUPS_OK_ACKNOWLEDGE);

    // create a queue receiver
    queueReceiver = queueSession.createReceiver(queue);

    // set the message listener
    queueReceiver.setMessageListener (this);

    // start the connection
    queueConn.start();

    System.out.println("JMS MsgListener started.");
}

public void close () throws JMSException
{
    queueReceiver.close();
    queueSession.close();
    queueConn.close();
    System.out.println("JMS MsgListener stopped.");
}

public void onMessage (Message msg)
{
    String text = "";
    System.out.println("onMessage() called.");
    try
    {
        if(msg instanceof ObjectMessage) {
            ObjectMessage objmsg = (ObjectMessage)msg;
            System.out.println("Received object: " + objmsg.getObject() );
        }
```

LISTING 15.9 continued

```
            else if(msg instanceof TextMessage) {
                  TextMessage textmsg = (TextMessage) msg;
                  text = textmsg.getText();
                  if (text == null) text = "";
                  if (text.equalsIgnoreCase("finish")) {
                      synchronized(this) {
                          System.out.println(
                              "***Received finish indicator in text***");
                          finish = true;
                      }
                  }
                  else System.out.println("Received text: "
                      + textmsg.getText() );
        }
        else System.out.println("message type not supported");
        }
        catch (JMSException e)
        {
            e.printStackTrace ();
        }
        synchronized(this) {
            this.notifyAll();
        }
    }
}
```

A `MessageSelector` Example

In this example, the sending client (see Listing 15.10) sends a variety of `TextMessages` and `ObjectMessages` to a Queue. Some of these messages are marked with an `Interesting=true` property. The sending client then finishes up by sending a simple Message containing a `MarketStatus=closed` property.

The receiving client (see Listing 15.11) first reads the queue via a `MessageSelector(filter)` looking for messages with an `Interesting=true` property. It then reads all remaining messages in the Queue. The receiving client stops looking for messages if it reads a message containing a `MarketStatus=closed` property.

LISTING 15.10 Sending `MessageSelector` Client

```
package selector;

import javax.jms.Queue;

import javax.naming.Context;
import javax.naming.InitialContext;
```

LISTING 15.10 continued

```
import javax.jms.Queue;
import javax.jms.Session;
import javax.jms.Message;
import javax.jms.TextMessage;
import javax.jms.ObjectMessage;
import javax.jms.QueueSender;
import javax.jms.DeliveryMode;
import javax.jms.QueueSession;
import javax.jms.QueueReceiver;
import javax.jms.QueueConnection;
import javax.jms.QueueConnectionFactory;

import java.util.Hashtable;

public class Sender
{
    public static void main(String[] args) throws Exception
    {
        // get the initial context
        InitialContext ctx = new InitialContext();

        // lookup the queue object
        Queue queue = (Queue) ctx.lookup("queue/queue0");

        // lookup the queue connection factory
        QueueConnectionFactory connFactory = (QueueConnectionFactory)
            ctx.lookup("queue/connectionFactory");

        // create a queue connection
        QueueConnection queueConn = connFactory.createQueueConnection();

        // create a queue session
        QueueSession queueSession = queueConn.createQueueSession(false,
            Session.DUPS_OK_ACKNOWLEDGE);

        // create a queue sender
        QueueSender queueSender = queueSession.createSender(queue);
        queueSender.setDeliveryMode(DeliveryMode.PERSISTENT);

        // get the number of messages to send
        int numMsgs = (args.length > 0) ? new Integer(args[0]).intValue() : 20;

        // send the messages
        for (int i=0,j=0,k=0; i < numMsgs; i++) {
            j++;k++;    //Increment counters
            if (i == (numMsgs-1)) {
                Message message = queueSession.createMessage();
                message.setStringProperty("MarketStatus", "closed");
                System.out.println("Sending MarketStatus=closed message.");
                queueSender.send(message);
```

LISTING 15.10 continued

```
            }
            else if (k == 1) {
                TextMessage message = queueSession.createTextMessage();
                message.setText("News item #"+i);
                if (j == 3) message.setBooleanProperty("Interesting", true);
                System.out.println("Sending Text message. News item #"
                    +i+((j==3)?"(Interesting)":""));
                queueSender.send(message);
            }
            else {
                ObjectMessage message = queueSession.createObjectMessage();
                Hashtable hTable = new Hashtable();
                hTable.put("symbol","sunw");
                hTable.put("bid",new String(""+(100+i)));
                hTable.put("ask",new String(""+(100+i+1)));
                message.setObject(hTable);
                if (j == 3) message.setBooleanProperty("Interesting", true);
                System.out.println("Sending Object message. "
                    +hTable+((j==3)?"(Interesting)":""));
                queueSender.send(message);
                k=0; //reset counter
            }
            if (j == 3) j=0;
        }

        // close the queue connection
        queueConn.close();
    }
}
```

LISTING 15.11 The Receiving `MessageSelector` Client

```
package selector;

import javax.jms.Queue;

import javax.naming.Context;
import javax.naming.InitialContext;

import javax.jms.Queue;
import javax.jms.Session;
import javax.jms.Message;
import javax.jms.TextMessage;
import javax.jms.ObjectMessage;
import javax.jms.QueueSender;
import javax.jms.QueueSession;
import javax.jms.QueueReceiver;
import javax.jms.QueueConnection;
import javax.jms.QueueConnectionFactory;
```

LISTING 15.11 continued

```
public class Receiver
{
    public static void main(String[] args) throws Exception
    {
        // get the initial context
        InitialContext ctx = new InitialContext();

        // lookup the queue object
        Queue queue = (Queue) ctx.lookup("queue/queue0");

        // lookup the queue connection factory
        QueueConnectionFactory connFactory = (QueueConnectionFactory)
            ctx.lookup("queue/connectionFactory");

        // create a queue connection
        QueueConnection queueConn = connFactory.createQueueConnection();

        // create a queue session
        QueueSession queueSession = queueConn.createQueueSession(false,
            Session.DUPS_OK_ACKNOWLEDGE);

        // create a queue receiver for the filtered (interesting) messages
        QueueReceiver filteredQueueReceiver =
        queueSession.createReceiver(queue,"Interesting=true");

        // create a queue receiver for all types of messages
        QueueReceiver queueReceiver = queueSession.createReceiver(queue);

        // start the connection
        queueConn.start();

        // get the filtered messages first...
        System.out.println("================================");
        System.out.println("Looking for interesting messages first...");
        System.out.println("================================");
        receiveMsgs(filteredQueueReceiver);

        // get the all other messages next...
        System.out.println("================================");
        System.out.println("Looking for all remaining messages...");
        System.out.println("================================");
        receiveMsgs(queueReceiver);

        // close the queue connection
        queueConn.close();
    }

    private static void receiveMsgs(QueueReceiver qr) throws Exception
    {
```

LISTING 15.11 continued

```
        while (true) {
            Message message = qr.receive(1000);     // timeout every second
            if (message != null) {
                String marketStatus = message.getStringProperty("MarketStatus");
                if (marketStatus == null) marketStatus = "";
                if (marketStatus.equalsIgnoreCase("closed")) {
                    System.out.println(
                        "Received Market Closed message, closing up shop.");
                    break;
                }
                if (message instanceof TextMessage) {
                    System.out.println(
                        "Received text message: "
                        +((TextMessage) message).getText()); }
                else if (message instanceof ObjectMessage) {
                    System.out.println(
                        "Received object message: "
                        +((ObjectMessage) message).getObject()); }
                else {
                    System.out.println(
                        "Ignored message type: "
                        +message.getClass().getName()); }
            }
            else break;    // stop receive if we do not get a message
        }
    }
}
```

Queue and Topic Destination Maintenance Examples

The examples in Listings 15.12–15.15 show how you can programmatically create and destroy JMS Destination Queues and Topics. Although this function will typically be carried out in an administrative tool supplied by the JMS provider, you may find these examples useful anyway.

LISTING 15.12 Creating the Queue Destination

```
package destination;

import javax.jms.Queue;
import javax.jms.QueueConnectionFactory;

import javax.naming.Context;
import javax.naming.InitialContext;
```

LISTING 15.12 continued

```
import com.sssw.jms.api.JMQQueue;
import com.sssw.jms.api.JMQDestination;
import com.sssw.jms.api.JMQQueueConnection;
import com.sssw.jms.api.JMQQueueConnectionFactory;

import com.sssw.jms.api.admin.JMQDestinationAdmin;

public class CreateQueue
{
    public static void main(String[] args) throws Exception
    {
    // get the initial context
    InitialContext ctx = new InitialContext();

    // create a JMS Queue Connection
    QueueConnectionFactory qconFactory = (QueueConnectionFactory)
        ctx.lookup("queue/connectionFactory");
    JMQQueueConnection queueConn = (JMQQueueConnection)
        qconFactory.createQueueConnection();

    // create a queue
    String queueName = (args.length > 0) ? args[0] : "myQueue";
    JMQDestinationAdmin destAdmin = queueConn.getDestinationAdmin();
    Queue queue = (Queue) destAdmin.createDestination(queueName,
        JMQDestination.QUEUE, null);
    System.out.println("Created queue: "+queueName);

    // close the queue connection
    queueConn.close();
    }
}
```

LISTING 15.13 Destroying the Queue Destination

```
package destination;

import javax.jms.Queue;
import javax.jms.QueueConnectionFactory;

import javax.naming.Context;
import javax.naming.InitialContext;

import com.sssw.jms.api.JMQQueue;
import com.sssw.jms.api.JMQDestination;
import com.sssw.jms.api.JMQQueueConnection;

import com.sssw.jms.api.admin.JMQDestinationAdmin;
```

LISTING 15.13 continued

```
// Note: destination deletion requires private APIs

public class DestroyQueue
{
    public static void main(String[] args) throws Exception
    {
    // get the initial context
    InitialContext ctx = new InitialContext();

    // create a JMS Queue Connection
    QueueConnectionFactory qconFactory = (QueueConnectionFactory)
        ctx.lookup("queue/connectionFactory");
    JMQQueueConnection queueConn = (JMQQueueConnection)
        qconFactory.createQueueConnection();

    // destroy the queue
    String queueName = (args.length > 0) ? args[0] : "myQueue";
    queueConn.getDestinationAdmin().deleteDestination(queueName,
        JMQDestination.QUEUE);
    System.out.println("Destroyed queue: " + queueName);

    // close the queue connection
    queueConn.close();
    }
}
```

LISTING 15.14 Creating the Topic Destination

```
package destination;

import javax.jms.Topic;
import javax.jms.TopicConnectionFactory;

import javax.naming.Context;
import javax.naming.InitialContext;

import com.sssw.jms.api.JMQTopic;
import com.sssw.jms.api.JMQDestination;
import com.sssw.jms.api.JMQTopicConnection;
import com.sssw.jms.api.JMQTopicConnectionFactory;

import com.sssw.jms.api.admin.JMQDestinationAdmin;

public class CreateTopic
{
    public static void main(String[] args) throws Exception
    {
```

Listing 15.14 continued

```
    // get the initial context
    InitialContext ctx = new InitialContext();

    // create a JMS Topic Connection
    TopicConnectionFactory tconFactory = (TopicConnectionFactory)
        ctx.lookup("topic/connectionFactory");
    JMQTopicConnection topicConn = (JMQTopicConnection)
        tconFactory.createTopicConnection();

    // create a topic
    String topicName = (args.length > 0) ? args[0] : "myTopic";
    JMQDestinationAdmin destAdmin = topicConn.getDestinationAdmin();
    Topic topic = (Topic) destAdmin.createDestination(topicName,
        JMQDestination.TOPIC, null);
    System.out.println("Created topic: "+topicName);

    // close the topic connection
    topicConn.close();
    }
}
```

Listing 15.15 Destroying the Topic Destination

```
package destination;

import javax.jms.Topic;
import javax.jms.TopicConnectionFactory;

import javax.naming.Context;
import javax.naming.InitialContext;

import com.sssw.jms.api.JMQTopic;
import com.sssw.jms.api.JMQDestination;
import com.sssw.jms.api.JMQTopicConnection;

import com.sssw.jms.api.admin.JMQDestinationAdmin;

// Note: destination deletion requires private APIs

public class DestroyTopic
{
    public static void main(String[] args) throws Exception
    {
    // get the initial context
    InitialContext ctx = new InitialContext();

    // create a JMS Topic Connection
    TopicConnectionFactory tconFactory = (TopicConnectionFactory)
```

LISTING 15.15 continued

```
        ctx.lookup("topic/connectionFactory");
    JMQTopicConnection topicConn = (JMQTopicConnection)
        tconFactory.createTopicConnection();

    // destroy the topic
    String topicName = (args.length > 0) ? args[0] : "myTopic";
    topicConn.getDestinationAdmin().deleteDestination(topicName,
        JMQDestination.TOPIC);
    System.out.println("Destroyed topic: " + topicName);

    // close the topic connection
    topicConn.close();
    }
}
```

JMS Implementation and Deployment Issues

As with almost any API, there are aspects of a complete application that are not directly catered to. This section will present some of the issues surrounding implementation and deployment.

What Else Needs to Be Implemented?

The JMS specification does not describe how to include certain functions in a JMS application. Implementing these functions (which are listed and described in Table 15.9) is left to the application developer.

TABLE 15.9 JMS Functional Limitations

Function	*Description*
Administration	The administrative aspects of the messaging application.
Load balancing	The distribution of system services among servers to provide balance, redundancy, and scalability.
Message repository	The location where messages are stored when durability and guaranteed delivery are required. The repository is typically a relational database.
Security	Message integrity, confidentiality, and user access.

TABLE 15.9 continued

Function	*Description*
System messages	Error conditions or status information that is asynchronously conveyed to a client. Using messages can compromise application portability, so the JMS specification provides guidelines on how to avoid problems.
Wire protocol	The communication protocol over which the JMS application is deployed. TCP/IP and HTTP are often used.

Deployment

Here are some things to consider when deploying JMS client applications:

- JNDI can be used to aid deployment.
- `QueueConnectionFactory` and `TopicConnectionFactory` are typically stored in the JNDI directory.
- EJB and Web applications can reference the connection factories via resource references.
- The `Queue` (or `Topic`) name can also be stored inside the JNDI directory, making it possible to set the `Queue` (or `Topic`) dynamically.

Summary

JMS is part of the Java 2 Platform, Enterprise Edition (J2EE), and it provides a highly flexible and scalable solution for building loosely coupled applications in the enterprise environment.

Java Messaging Service brings all of the advantages of a messaging-based application into the Java language. JMS now links messaging systems with all the benefits of Java technology for rapid application deployment and application maintenance. JMS adds to Java, making it a very strong and robust platform for developing a wide range of applications with the capability to service large numbers of concurrent users across an entire enterprise.

CHAPTER 16

Data Exchange with XML

IN THIS CHAPTER

- What Is XML? *526*
- Structure of an XML Document *527*
- Unparsed Data *533*
- Processing Instructions *534*
- Document Type Definitions (DTDs) *535*
- XML Schema *540*
- XML Parsers *549*
- Document Object Model (DOM) *549*
- Simple API for XML (SAX) *553*
- XML Output *556*
- XSL *557*
- Style Sheet Structure *560*
- Applying Style Sheets *564*
- XML Linking Language (XLink) *564*
- XML Security *566*

What Is XML?

This chapter discusses the fundamentals of the eXtensible Markup Language (XML). XML is a key technology in J2EE, facilitating many different tasks, such as transporting information, viewing existing legacy applications, and managing data. XML enables data to contain the metadata, or the data that describes the organization and traits of other data, in the same file.

Brief History of XML

Standard Generalized Markup Language (SGML) is an early attempt to combine the metadata with the data. This text-based language can be used to mark-up or add metadata to a file so it is self-describing. SGML was used primarily in large document management systems.

Because SGML is a very complex language, it has limited mass appeal. The most recognized application of SGML is Hypertext Markup Language (HTML), devised to allow any Web browser or application that understands HTML to display information in a consistent form. HTML has been highly successful at displaying information over the Internet; however, it does not lend itself to the exchange of information from one computer to another. For example, an HTML document is great when it comes to laying out and displaying data, but it is not a very portable data solution. Unlike HTML, XML is created with tags that help to describe the data, not how to display it. HTML is a fixed set of tags, and it does not have the flexibility to describe different document and data types. HTML, in conjunction with Cascading Style Sheets (CSS), is reasonably good at displaying data, but it is not as good as XML at transporting data that is meant to be viewed or parsed in dozens of different ways by a variety of devices (for example, a Web browser, a Web-enabled phone or PDA, or another remote application program performing some form of information exchange or lookup).

The need to extract data and put structure around information led to the creation of XML. Since it was released in 1997, XML use has been growing rapidly. One can only guess in what ways XML will be used in the future.

Key features of XML include the following:

- Information can be shared between programs without prior coordination.
- Information can be shared between other users, regardless of the platform in use.
- Descriptive tags are interspersed with the data, making XML self-describing and therefore extending its flexibility.

- Legacy applications can be integrated to new intranet applications.
- Printed and electronic documents are supported.

It is important to realize that XML is not a language, but a standard made up of a set of criteria. For example, a text document containing book information would look like this:

```
Book Title: J2EE Unleashed
Author: Paul Allen, Joseph Bambara,
Mark Ashnault, Tom Garben, Sherry Smith, Ziyad Dean
```

The XML document would look something like this:

```
<?xml version="1.0"?>
<?xml version="1.0" standalone="yes"?>
<?xm-well_formed path = ""?>
 <Book>
 <Title>J2EE Unleashed</Title>
 <Category>Programming</Category>
 <ISBN>0-672-32180-7</ISBN>
 <Author>Paul Allen</Author>
 <Author>Joseph Bambara</Author>
 <Author>Tom Garben</Author>
 <Author>Mark Ashnault</Author>
 <Author>Sherry Smith</Author>
 <Author>Ziyad Dean</Author>
</Book>
```

Utilizing tags, such as `<Book>` and `<Title>`, this simple example clearly demonstrates why XML is called self-describing.

Much like HTML, XML utilizes style sheets to format data, but how they are used is very different. HTML is not strict with the creation of style sheets and allows data to be formatted in many ways. Conversely, XML requires precise styles for formatted and enhanced output. XML goes beyond HTML for document creation with the use of XML Path Language (XPath), eXtensible Stylesheet Language (XSL), and XSL Transformations (XSLT). The eXtensible Hypertext Markup Language (XHTML), the successor of HTML, also recommends the use of cascading style sheets to format output. Style sheets will be discussed in greater detail later in this chapter.

Structure of an XML Document

XML documents are intended to store data, not necessarily to be viewed. They follow a layout very similar to that of HTML documents. In HTML, the `<HTML>` tag is at the top, with the `<Head>` and `<Body>` tags signifying the two main sections of the document. An XML document contains two sections: the document prolog at the head of the document and the instance, or the body.

Prolog

The document prolog must be the first thing in an XML document. The prolog may contain comments and processing instructions that tell the XML parser how to handle the preceding statements in the document. A Document Type Definition (DTD), which sets all the rules for the document regarding elements, attributes, and other components may be specified in the prolog. This DTD may be either an external DTD or Internal DTD.

An internal DTD document is contained completely within the XML document. An example of an internal DTD:

```
  <?xml version="1.0"?>
<!Doctype Book [
<!Element Title (#PCDATA)>]>
```

An external DTD document is a separate document, referenced from the XML document. The same DTD document may be used in many different XML documents. An example of an external DTD:

```
  <?xml version="1.0"?>
<!Doctype Book [ System "Book.dtd">]>
```

DTDs will be discussed in greater detail later in this chapter.

XML documents consist of markup and character data. The markup data tells the browser and/or the parser how to process the document. The character data is the information displayed on the browser or printed page.

Instance Section

The instance contains the remaining parts of the XML document, including the actual contents of the document, such as characters, paragraphs, pages, and graphics.

Elements

Elements are the most important part of an XML document. An element consists of content enclosed in an opening tag and a closing tag. An element can contain several different types of content:

- Element content—Contains only other elements
- Mixed content—Contains both text and other elements
- Simple content—Contains only text
- Empty content—Does not contain information

Default values for elements can be defined in the DTD. In addition, Elements can also have attributes and can be nested. For example:

```
<Book><Title><Author></Author></Title></Book>
```

Since an XML document requires both a begin and an end tag, end tags must be added to the elements when converting an HTML document to XML, otherwise an error will occur. For example, this is not valid XML:

```
<Book>J2EE Unleashed
```

Whereas the above is a valid statement in HTML, XML will return an error and stop processing the document. A valid tag would be

```
<Book>J2EE Unleashed </Book>
```

Tags

XML tags operate in the same manner as HTML tags. Several rules apply to tag names. They must start with an alphabetic character, an underscore, or a colon. Punctuation can be used, except colons, which are only used to define namespace. Whitespace, including tabs and carriage returns, is not allowed. In addition, tag names are case sensitive. Tags may not be overlapped in XML. For example, the following is invalid and will cause an error in an XML parser:

```
<Book><Author><Title></Author></Title></Book>
```

XML tags are case sensitive; therefore, opening and closing tags must be written in the same case.

Empty Elements

Tags that contain no content, known as empty elements, are allowed in XML. An empty element can be specified as

```
<image src="Book.jpeg" />
```

or

```
<image src="book.gif"></image>
```

Attributes

XML attributes are identical to HTML attributes. They help to explain the element tag. Consider the following HTML declaration:

```
<P ALIGN=LEFT> ... </P>
```

The paragraph tag shown here has a single attribute name called ALIGN with an assigned value of LEFT. Attributes in HTML provide additional information or instructions to the browser. They are essential when using the document object model when the ID attribute is used to identify HTML elements.

Similarly, attributes may be used inside the opening tags of XML documents, but they do not carry more specific processing information than the tags themselves. Instead, they provide an additional means to associate data or information with the element. Each attribute inside the tag has an attribute name that allows this specific piece of data to be accessed. The naming of attributes follows the same rules as that of elements. All attribute values must be contained in quotes. For example:

```
<Book currency = "USD" in-stock = "yes">
    <price>45.99</price>
...
</Book>
```

There are three XML attribute types:

- String types—May take any literal string as a value.
- Tokenized types—Follow a fixed set of keyword types with special meanings. Varieties of tokenized attributes include ID Attribute Default, IDREF, Entity Name, and Name Token.
- Enumerated types—Contain a set of specific text strings. Varieties include Enumeration and Notation types.

Entities

XML documents are made up of units of storage called entities. The entire XML document is considered the document entity that serves as the entry point for XML parsers. The two main categories of entities are general entities, which are useable within an XML document, and parameter entities, which are only used in DTDs. General entities may be either external or internal, in other words contained within the XML or placed within an external file. There are two types of general entities: parsed entities, which can be either external or internal, and unparsed entities, which are always external. Parameter entities are always parsed entities. Entities help to give structure to the XML document. Names can be assigned to commonly used text, hence allowing that name to refer to that content. An entity enables the abbreviation to be entered with information including the description value. The description value is called the replacement text.

XML provides several types of entities (see Figure 16.1).

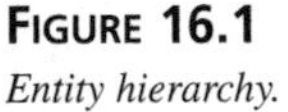

FIGURE 16.1
Entity hierarchy.

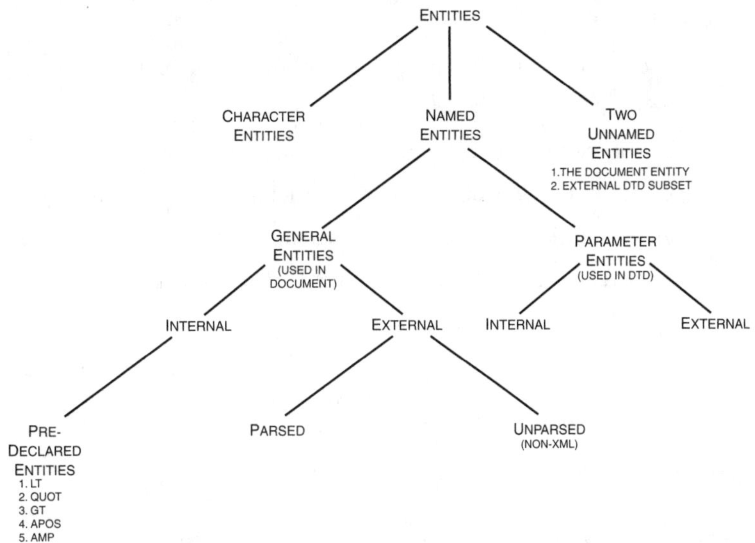

Parsed entities are always referenced by name using either a general or parameter entity reference:

```
<!ENTITY Name "replacement text">
```

To insert the entity into a document, the format is as follows:

```
&Name
```

Here is an example of a parsed entity:

```
<!ENTITY thePublisher "SAMS">
<Publisher> &thePublisher <Publisher>
```

Unparsed entities may or may not have text. These general entities are always given a name and might only be used as a value of an attribute having the `ENTITIES` or `ENTITY` type. All unparsed entities must have an associated notation, which is identified by name. Here is an example of an unparsed entity:

```
<!NOTATION copyright SYSTEM "http:/booklist/images/copyright.jpg">
<!ENTITY Header SYSTEM "header.png" NDATA copyright>
<header img="Header"/>
```

Here are a couple of examples of predeclared entities:

```
&amp = &<solicitors>Cassio &amp; Biazzo</solicitors>
```

Here are the different types of entities:

- Parsed—Only parsed if used in the current document
- Unparsed—Will never be parsed
- Internal entity—Declared in the document being used
- External entity—Declared in an external document referred to by a URL
- General entities—Named within the character data in an XML document
- Parameter entities—Named within a DTD document

The following restrictions apply to declaring entities:

- No circular references
- No substitution of document text with a general reference

Here are some examples of illegal entities:

```
!entitya; "&entityb; is neat"
!entityb; "&entitya; is neat"
```

Escape Characters

Some characters such as < and &, called illegal characters, are reserved for use in XML syntax. If a character such as < is placed inside an XML element, an error will be generated, because the parser interprets the < as the start of a new tag. The following example would return an error:

```
<bookprice>if price < 60 then</bookprice>
```

To avoid this, the < character must be replaced with an entity reference. This is referred to as escaping the characters. For example:

```
<bookprice>if price &lt; 60 then</bookprice>
```

XML includes several predefined entities, as listed in Table 16.1.

TABLE 16.1 Predefined Entity References in XML

Predefined Entity	*Value*	*Description*
`<`	<	Less than
`>`	>	Greater than
`&`	&	Ampersand
`'`	'	Apostrophe
`"`	"	Quotation mark

Entity references always begin with the & character and end with the ; character.

Note

While the characters < and & are strictly illegal, other characters such as apostrophes, quotation marks, and greater than signs are legal, but it is a good coding habit to replace them with entity references.

Unparsed Data

In XML, there are three kinds of data that will be ignored by the parser: comments, processing instructions (PIs), and character data (CDATA). When the parser encounters one of these, normal operation is suspended while the parser looks for the end marker. They differ in the intent of the unparsed data.

Comments

XML comments are exactly like comments in HTML. Comments may appear anywhere in a document outside other markup; in addition, they may appear within the document type declaration at places allowed by the grammar. They are not part of character data in the document. Most XML parsers ignore the comments in the XML document. An XML processor may make it possible for an application to retrieve the text of comments, but it is not necessary.

```
<!--  this is an example of a comment -->
```

Two hyphens in a row may not be used as part of the comment text. Instead, use an equal sign, or an underscore, or some other symbol. This comment will cause problems:

```
<!--NOT--Allowed -->
```

Here is the syntax of a comment:

```
'<!--' ((Char - '-') | ('-' (Char - '-')))* '-->'
```

CDATA

Character Data (CDATA) sections allow you to put information that might be recognized as markup anywhere character may occur. CDATA sections begin with `<![CDATA[` and end with `]]>`. The parser will ignore everything within the CDATA section.

Here is the syntax of a CDATA section:

```
<![CDATA[ Character Data ]]>
```

Within a CDATA section, only the CDEnd string is recognized as markup, so that left angle brackets and ampersands may occur in their literal form; they need not (and cannot) be escaped using < and &. CDATA sections cannot nest. As shown in the following code, CDATA can contain reserved characters without the parser becoming involved:

```
<![CDATA[p = &q;
b = (i <= 3);]]>
```

The text between the start and end tag of an element is referred to as the element content or PCDATA (Parsed Character Data).

Processing Instructions

Processing Instructions (PIs) allow XML documents to contain instructions for applications. Like comments, they are not part of the document's character data, so they are of little interest to the XML processor; however, they must be passed through to the proper application.

The PI begins with <? and ends with ?>. Because one document may contain processing instructions for several different applications, a target (PITarget) immediately follows the opening <?, identifying the application to which the instruction is directed.

The PITarget follows the same set of naming rules that elements and attributes adhere to.

One specific PI we'll encounter later is the one used to introduce a reference to an XSL style sheet into the XML document. It looks like this:

```
<?xml-stylesheet  type = "text/xsl" href  = "xslfilename.xsl"?>
```

Character References

Character references are used to introduce characters that are not standard ASCII characters and therefore cannot be entered on a keyboard. These include Latin characters with accents, umlauts, mathematical symbols, special punctuation, and non-Roman character sets. These characters are referred to by the assigned integer value of the character. For example, 163 is a hexadecimal code reference for the £ character. It can be referenced in XML using £ just like an entity reference. Like general entity references, character references are delimited with an ampersand and semicolon. The numeric value is further delimited with a preceding hash mark. XML parsers use the hash mark to tell that this is a character reference and not a general reference.

Character Range

All XML processors must accept the UTF-8 (8 bit, 1 byte) and UTF-16 (16 bit, 2 byte) encoding of ISO/IEC 10646. By way of explanation for those unfamiliar with the acronyms used in the last sentence, we will provide some brief background information. When we use the term ISO/IEC 10646, we are referring to a relatively new character set standard, published by the International Organization for Standardization (ISO). Its name is "Universal Multiple-Octet Coded Character Set" or Unicode. UTF-8/UTF-16 also known as Unicode is well on the way to replacing ASCII and Latin-1 as the international machine based encoding standard at all levels. It allows you not only to handle text in practically any script and language used on this planet, it also provides you with a comprehensive set of mathematical and technical symbols that will simplify scientific information exchange. The UTF-8 encoding allows Unicode to be used in a convenient and backwards compatible way in environments that, like Unix, were designed entirely around ASCII. UTF-8 is the way in which Unicode is used under Unix, Linux, and similar systems.

Whitespace

Whitespace is often used in XML documents in order to facilitate reading and debugging documents. It is not normally intended to be included in the delivered version of the document; however, the inclusion of whitespace may sometimes be necessary. In XML content, all whitespace is preserved, relying on the application to either handle or ignore it.

The XML processor passes all characters in the document that are not markup through to the application. Informing the application which characters constitute whitespace appearing in element content. The `xml:space` attribute is utilized to specify the intent to include whitespace. Like any other, this attribute must be declared. It must be given as a specific type with the value being either `default` or `preserve`.

```
<!ELEMENT text (#PCDATA) >
<!ATTLIST text xml:space (default|preserve) #FIXED "preserve" >
```

`preserve` means to preserve the line breaks rather than using the `default` behavior, which involves replacing line breaks with spaces before justifying the contents of the element.

Document Type Definitions (DTDs)

A DTD is used to define the structure of an XML document as well as what content is allowed. A well-written DTD will give the same look to documents that use that DTD, as well as help the browser and XML parser display the document properly.

The DTD can be used to describe all the building blocks of the document, including elements, tags, attributes, entities, PCDATA, and CDATA as well as the relationships between them. When an XML document is processed by a parser, the document is compared to the DTD to be sure it is structured correctly and all tags are used in the proper manner. This comparison process is called validation. An XML document is considered valid if it is well-formed and it conforms to its DTD. An XML document does not have to have a DTD in order to be considered a valid document.

The DTD supports the following functions, in order of priority:

1. Allows easy publication of technical information.
2. Eliminates errors from document creation and modification. The DTD should provide an intuitive, efficient interface to the creation process. The DTD should be concise and detailed enough to support information so authors will understand information.
3. Reviews content. The DTD should support the informal workflow that goes on when co-editors circulate drafts for review. To accomplish this, the DTD should provide markup for editor remarks inside of the document source.

DTD Basics

A DTD is a text file. The DTD information may either be embedded directly in the XML document or linked to an external file containing the DTD. Since an external DTD may be used by any document conforming to its definition, this method is often preferred. Each statement in a DTD uses the `<!XML DTD>` syntax.

Four kinds of markup declarations are found in the DTD: element declarations, attribute list declarations, entity declarations, and notation declarations.

Element Type Declarations

Element declarations identify the names of elements as well as the nature of their content. The following element declaration defines the name of the tag (Author, in this case), and the content model for the tag. The + notation means the `<Author>` tag must contain one or more `<Name>` tags.

```
<!ELEMENT Author (Name)+>
```

Other indicators to specify occurrence are shown in Table 16.2.

TABLE 16.2 XML Occurrence Indicators

Indicator	*Meaning*
?	The content must appear just once, or not at all.
*	The content can appear once, more than once, or not at all.
+	The content must appear once or more than once.
[none]	The content must appear exactly once, exactly as described.

Combining these indicators with parentheses in any order can create complex expressions.

After the tag that contains the data for each row in the database has been defined, individual tags can be defined. Each of these tags will look like this:

```
<!ELEMENT title          (#PCDATA)>
  <!ELEMENT author          (#PCDATA)>
```

The `#PCDATA` keyword above signifies that the tag contains parsed character data. The XML parser will find only character data, not tags or entity references. The only descriptions of allowed content between tags are `(#PCDATA)`, `EMPTY`, and `ANY`.

The `EMPTY` description means that there must not be content after the opening tag. The `ANY` means that there can be any type of text as long as it is valid XML.

Attribute Declarations

Attributes supply additional information about elements. They are created in the DTD when the elements are specified and are specified through an attribute list. Attributes identify additional data about an element. Attribute declarations define which attributes can appear inside a tag, as well as the kinds of data the attributes can contain. Here are some examples of element type declarations:

```
<!ELEMENT AnyTextHere ANY>
```

```
<!ELEMENT BR EMPTY>
```

- The `#REQUIRED` keyword in the attribute definition means that this attribute must be coded every time this element is listed.
- The `#FIXED` keyword provides a default value that cannot be modified by the document author. The attribute is not necessarily required, but if it occurs it must have a specified value.

- The `#IMPLIED` keyword is used if the attribute value is not required and a default value is not provided. If a value has not been specified, the XML processor must continue without one. When using the `IMPLIED` default, a default value is provided for the document author. If the document author does not override the default, it will be used. Attributes are implied if not otherwise specified.
- `VALUE` (default values) will provide a default value for an attribute so that any legal value can be given as a default. The attribute value is not required on each element in the document. If it is not present, the value will appear to be the specified default. If the attribute is not included in the element, the processing program assumes that this is the attribute value.

Tags Versus Attributes

A common question when writing a DTD is whether something should be a tag or an attribute. In most cases, the decision between tag and attribute doesn't make a difference; however, if data in the model needs to be reused, data in tags is easier to access.

Entity Declarations

Entities are storage units that can hold either text or non-XML data like graphics or media files. All entities used in a document must be defined with an entity declaration, where a name is assigned to the entity, and that name is used to reference the entity in a document.

Entities may be parsed or unparsed. A parsed entity's contents are referred to as its replacement text. That text is considered an integral part of the document. An unparsed entity is a resource whose contents may or may not be text and need not be XML. Parsed entities are invoked by name, utilizing entity references. Unparsed entities are invoked by name, given in the value of `ENTITY` or `ENTITIES` attributes.

Entities may also be general (simple) entities or parameter entities. General entities are used within the document content. Parameter entities are parsed entities for use within the DTD.

```
<!ENTITY   % replace_textname   "Text to be replaced">
```

Note the space between the `%` and the entity name. To use the entity within the DTD, the name must be preceded by the `%` character.

```
//Books Example of DTD
<?xml encoding='US-ASCII'?>

<!-- STYLEBOOK BOOK DTD -->
```

```
<!-- import the external source-specific dtd -->
<!ENTITY % externalEntity SYSTEM "entities.ent">
%externalEntity;

<!ELEMENT book (resources?|document|hidden|faqs|
changes|group|container|external|separator)+>
<!ATTLIST book title     CDATA #REQUIRED
          copyright CDATA #IMPLIED>

<!ELEMENT resources EMPTY>
<!ATTLIST resources source CDATA #REQUIRED>

<!ELEMENT document EMPTY>
<!ATTLIST document id     ID    #REQUIRED
                   source CDATA #REQUIRED
                   label  CDATA #REQUIRED>

<!ELEMENT hidden EMPTY>
<!ATTLIST hidden id     ID    #REQUIRED
                 source CDATA #REQUIRED>

<!ELEMENT faqs EMPTY>
<!ATTLIST faqs id     ID    #REQUIRED
               source CDATA #REQUIRED
               label  CDATA #REQUIRED>

<!ELEMENT changes EMPTY>
<!ATTLIST changes id     ID    #REQUIRED
                  source CDATA #REQUIRED
                  label  CDATA #REQUIRED>

<!ELEMENT group (entry)+>
<!ATTLIST group id    ID    #IMPLIED
                label CDATA #REQUIRED
                title CDATA #REQUIRED>

<!ELEMENT container (entry)+>
<!ATTLIST container id    ID    #IMPLIED
                    source CDATA #REQUIRED
                           label CDATA #REQUIRED>

<!ELEMENT entry EMPTY>
<!ATTLIST entry id     ID    #REQUIRED
                source CDATA #REQUIRED>

<!ELEMENT external EMPTY>
<!ATTLIST external label CDATA #REQUIRED
                   href  CDATA #REQUIRED>

<!ELEMENT separator EMPTY>
```

This example shows how the `%externalEntity` is created and used in the DTD document. The DTD displays how to specify the attributes for an element. Looking at the `book` element, you can see that the book title is required and the copyright is implied. Specifying the book title as `#REQUIRED` means that the element must be present in the XML document. If the book title is not present in the XML document, it will be marked as invalid. The parser will check each element specified in the DTD. If any element listed in the DTD does not follow the attributes specified in the DTD for that element, the document will be marked as invalid.

Notation Declarations

A notation is utilized to identify, by name, the format of unparsed entities, the format of elements that bear a notation attribute, or the application to which a processing instruction is addressed. A notation declaration provides a name as well as an external identifier for the notation. This name is used in entity and attribute-list declarations and in attribute specifications. The external identifier is used for the notation, allowing the XML processor to locate a helper application capable of processing data in the given notation.

XML Schema

A schema is a model that describes the structure of information. The term originated in the database field, describing the structure of data in relational tables (database schema). In XML, a schema describes a model for a whole class of documents. The model describes the possible arrangement of tags and text in a valid document, providing a common structure or common vocabulary for applications exchanging documents. Schemas are successors to as well as a departure from DTDs, and are expected to have a broad impact on the future of XML.

Schemas Versus DTDs

DTD functionality was passed down to XML from SGML. Although it can be used to define content models (the valid order and nesting of elements) as well as the data types of attributes to a degree, DTDs suffer from several limitations:

- They do not utilize valid XML syntax.
- There is no support for namespaces.
- Datatyping is limited. There is no facility for describing data, such as numbers, dates, and currency values nor is there the ability to express the data type of character data in elements.

- Relationships are not necessarily explicit. Two elements may have the same content models yet the content is not necessarily the same. Likewise, a group of attributes defined as a parameter entity cannot be associated as a group.

XML Schemas surmount these restrictions, allowing the exchange of XML data to occur more reliably without relying on informal validation tools. They are positioned to replace DTDs, yet DTDs remain in use due to widespread tools support and deployment.

Schema Constraints

Schemas are used to analyze data. For example, a schema could determine whether the following is a valid postal address:

```
<address>
<name>Dawn</name>
<street>6 Baby Lane</street>
<city>Gotham</city>
<state>PA</state>
<zip>08812-6326</zip>
</address>
```

For a human who reads the above document, the address presented is compared with a representation for addresses already defined in one's head. It probably goes something like this: A mailing address consists of a person, possibly at a company or organization, one or more lines of street address, a city, a state or province, a postal code, and an optional country. In that case, this address is valid.

In schemas, models are described by constraints. A constraint defines what can appear within that model. There are basically two kinds of constraints that can be given: content model constraints, which describe the order and sequence of elements, and data type constraints, which describe valid units of data.

In the preceding example, a schema might describe a valid `<address>` with the content model constraint consisting of a `<name>` element, followed by one or more `<street>` elements, followed by exactly one `<city>`, `<state>`, and `<zip>` element. The content of a `<zip>` might have a further data type constraint consisting of either a sequence of exactly five digits or a sequence of five digits, followed by a hyphen, followed by a sequence of exactly four digits. Any text not conforming to that constraint would not be considered valid.

Schemas allow the machine to validate the document structure. Using the schema informally described in the preceding paragraphs, a parser would be able to detect that the following address is not valid:

```
<address>
<name>Anthony James</name>
```

```
<street>6 Tiger Lane</street>
<city>Tiger City</city>
<state>NJ</state>
<state>LA</state>
<zip>red</zip>
</address>
```

It violates two constraints of the schema: It contains more than one `<state>` and the ZIP Code is not of the proper form.

This ability to test the validity of documents is an important aspect when dealing with large Web applications that are receiving and sending information to and from many sources. If XML transactions are being received over the Web, content should not be processed by the database if it's not in the proper schema. Errors detected earlier in the cycle are much less costly to rectify. If the faulty information is not caught before it is imported into the database, it could cause a ripple effect on the information or document.

Features of XML Schema

XML Schemas offer a range of new features including

- Richer data types, with support for Booleans, numbers, dates and times, Uniform Resource Identifiers (URIs), integers, decimal numbers, real numbers, intervals of time, and so on.
- User-defined types called archetypes that will allow the user to define her own named data type. For example, the user might define a `PostalAddress` data type and then define two elements, `ShippingAddress` and `BillingAddress` to be of that type. The shared archetype information is then available to the processor.
- Attribute grouping, which allows the schema author to explicitly define relationships between several attributes. Unlike grouping via parameter entities in DTDs, this information is passed on to the processor.
- Refinable archetypes, or inheritance, which allows more flexible content models than the closed model defined by a DTD. XML Schema admits open and refinable models. In an open content model, all required elements must be present, but it is not an error for additional elements to also be present. In a refinable content model, additional elements may be present, but only if the schema defines what they are.
- Namespace support, which enables simpler validation of documents that use namespaces.

XML Schema documents are XML documents, using elements and attributes to express the semantics of the schema. They can be edited and processed with the same tools used to process other XML documents.

Schema Vocabulary

The vocabulary of an XML Schema document contains about thirty elements and attributes. XML Schema documents are only considered valid if they conform to the schema for XML Schema. There is also a DTD regarding XML Schema.

Element Types

The content of elements and attributes are described in a schema. Using the previous example of an address, a `<name>` could be defined like this:

```
<elementType name="name">
  <mixed/>
</elementType>
```

The previous example defines the name element type. The content of the `<elementType>` element describes what content is valid for an element of that type. In this case, the content type is `<mixed/>`; therefore, the element can contain a mixture of character data and elements.

Schema Examples

The example in the following subsection will depict how a schema can declare a data type and data types can be inherited from other data types. You will see how the `CurrentTime` data type is declared and how `RequestTime` uses the `CurrentTime` data type as a model.

Current Time

XML Schemas include the ability to declare numbers with specific limits and precision: dates, times, and so on. In this example, a `CurrentTime` data type is declared as a string that can contain either exactly two digits or a colon followed by two digits:

```
<datatype name="CurrentTime">
  <basetype name="string"/>
  <lexicalRepresentation>
    <lexical>99:99</lexical>
  </lexicalRepresentation>
</datatype>
```

Once the `CurrentTime` data type is defined, it is simple to declare that a `<RequestTime>` must be of that type:

```
<elementType name="RequestTime">
  <datatypeRef name="CurrentTime"/>
</elementType>
```

An Address in Schema Notation

Basic types can be built upon to define aggregate element types such as <address>:

```
<xsd:sequence>
    <xsd:element ref = "NAME_INFO"/>
        <xsd:element name = "STREET" type = "xsd:string"/>
        <xsd:element name = "CITY" type = "xsd:string"/>
        <xsd:element name = "STATE" type = "xsd:string"/>
        xsd:element ref = "NA_LINE5"/>
        <xsd:element ref = "NA_LINE6"/>
</xsd:sequence>
```

There is little difference between this example and the preceding one. The content of the <address> element is defined in terms of other elements. It begins with a <sequence>, which is like the , separator in DTD syntax. This indicates that the things inside the sequence must occur in the order given. References to other element types are seen inside the sequence. Each element type referenced must have a corresponding <elementType> declaration elsewhere.

Occurrence qualifiers indicate how often each element can occur. A minimum occurrence of zero denotes that the element is optional. These indicators serve the same purpose as the ?, *, and + qualifiers in DTD syntax, but they are more flexible since both minimum and maximum values may be specified.

```
<group name="BookGroup">
 <sequence>
  <element name="BookGroup" minoccurs="1" maxOccurs="5"/>
</sequence>
</group>
```

In the preceding example, the element name BookGroup specifies that the minimum occurrences of this element is one and the most the element can occur is five times.

An Address Archetype in XML Schema

The following example demonstrates a major advantage of utilizing archetypes: Archetypes are refinable, meaning new yet related types can be derived from them. As an example, a return address can be created to include everything in an address plus an added element to hold a name.

```
<archetype name="address" model="refinable">
  <sequence>
    <elementTypeRef name="company" minOccur="0" maxOccur="1"/>
```

```
    <elementTypeRef name="name" minOccur="1" maxOccur="1"/>
    <elementTypeRef name="street" minOccur="1" maxOccur="2"/>
    <elementTypeRef name="city" minOccur="1" maxOccur="1"/>
    <elementTypeRef name="state" minOccur="1" maxOccur="1"/>
    <elementTypeRef name="zip" minOccur="1" maxOccur="1"/>
  </sequence>
</archetype>

<elementType name="vacation.address">
  <archetypeRef name="address"/>
</elementType>

<elementType name="shipping.address">
  <archetypeRef name="address"/>
</elementType>
```

In the preceding code, `"vacation.address"` and `"shipping.address"` are based on the `"address"` archetype.

Account Setup

For comparison, here is a complete example of an account setup using XML:

```
<?xml version = "1.0"?>
<ACCOUNT xmlns:xsi = "http://www.w3.org/2000/10/XMLSchema-instance"
xsi:noNamespaceSchemaLocation = "file:///
D:/My%20Documents/J2EEBK/XML%20example/accountsetup.xsd">
        <REQUEST_HEADER>
                <REQUEST_DATE>1999-12-31</REQUEST_DATE>
                <LOGIN_INFO>
                        <SUB>Create Account for WebSite</SUB>
                        <LOGIN_ID>DAWN23</LOGIN_ID>
                        <PASSWORD>Password</PASSWORD>
                </LOGIN_INFO>
        </REQUEST_HEADER>
        <DATA>
                        <ADDRESS>
                        <NAME_INFO>
                                <FIRST>Dawn</FIRST>
                                <LAST>Smith</LAST>
                        </NAME_INFO>
                        <STREET>61 Timberline Dr</STREET>
                        <CITY>Java</CITY>
                        <STATE>NY</STATE>
                        <ZIP_CODE>08123</ZIP_CODE>
                        <email>dawn23@yoursite.com</email>
                        <NA_LINE6/>
                        </ADDRESS>

        </DATA>
</ACCOUNT>
```

Without a schema processor, the schema DTD can be used to validate schema. All schema begin with the <schema> tag:

```
<xsd:schema xmlns:xsd = "http://www.w3.org/2000/10/XMLSchema">
<xsd:element name = "ADDRESS">
<xsd:complexType>
<xsd:sequence>
 <xsd:element ref = "NAME_INFO"/>
 <xsd:element name = "STREET" type = "xsd:string" maxOccurs = "2"/>
 <xsd:element name = "CITY" type = "xsd:string"/>
 <xsd:element name = "STATE" type = "xsd:string"/>
 <xsd:element ref = "ZIP_CODE"/>
<xsd:element ref = "E-MAIL" minOccurs = "0"/>
<xsd:element ref = "NA_LINE6" minOccurs = "0"/>
</xsd:sequence>
               </xsd:complexType>
        </xsd:element>
</xsd:schema>
```

The schema document shown here details how the address information will be validated in the previous XML example. The second line of the schema specifies the group header:

```
<xsd:element name = "ADDRESS">
               <xsd:complexType>
           <xsd:sequence>
```

The element name of the group is `ADDRESS` and it is of type `complexType` and its elements have a specified sequence. The elements of `ADDRESS` are specified in the rest of the schema:

```
<xsd:element ref = "NAME_INFO"/>
```

This specifies an element `NAME_INFO` that is broken down into more detail in the schema. The schema can specify first name, last name, and other attributes of a name.

```
<xsd:element name = "STREET"
type = "xsd:string" maxOccurs = "2"/>
```

The `STREET` element specifies that it is should be a `string` and that the field can only occur two times. The `City` and `State` attributes are specified as `string` fields. The `zip code` element is named without any field type declaration.

```
<xsd:element ref = "E-MAIL" minOccurs = "0"/>
<xsd:element ref = "NA_LINE6" minOccurs = "0"/>
```

The `E-MAIL` and `NA_LINE6` elements specify that the information is not required in the XML document. This is a basic example of an XML Schema document. A more detailed example of account setup will follow.

As previously discussed, an archetype for addresses has been defined. It can now be used to define address elements, as follows:

```
<elementType name="vacation.address">
  <archetypeRef name="ADDRESS"/>
</elementType>

<elementType name="shipping.address">
  <archetypeRef name="ADDRESS"/>
</elementType>
```

The archetype is used to define `"vacation.address"` and `"shipping.address"`.

An XML Schema for setting up a typical user account might look like this:

```
<?xml version = "1.0" encoding = "UTF-8"?>
<xsd:schema xmlns:xsd = "http://www.w3.org/2000/10/XMLSchema">
    <xsd:element name = "ACCOUNT_ADD_UPDATE_RQ_001">
        <xsd:complexType>
            <xsd:sequence>
                <xsd:element ref = "REQUEST_HEADER"/>
                                <xsd:element ref = "DATA"/>
                        </xsd:sequence>
                </xsd:complexType>
        </xsd:element>
        <xsd:element name = "REQUEST_HEADER">
                <xsd:complexType>
                        <xsd:sequence>
                                <xsd:element ref = "REQUEST_DATE"/>
                                <xsd:element ref = "LOGIN_INFO"/>
                        </xsd:sequence>
                </xsd:complexType>
        </xsd:element>
        <xsd:element name = "PASSWORD">
                <xsd:complexType mixed = "true">
                        <xsd:choice/>
                </xsd:complexType>
        </xsd:element>
        <xsd:element name = "DATA">
                <xsd:complexType>
                        <xsd:sequence>
                                <xsd:element ref = "ACCT_ADD_UPDATE_INFO"/>
                        </xsd:sequence>
                </xsd:complexType>
        </xsd:element>
<xsd:element name = "ADDRESS">
<xsd:complexType>
<xsd:sequence>
   <xsd:element ref = "NAME_INFO"/>
   <xsd:element name = "STREET" type = "xsd:string" maxOccurs = "2"/>
   <xsd:element name = "CITY" type = "xsd:string"/>
```

```
    <xsd:element name = "STATE" type = "xsd:string"/>
    <xsd:element ref = "ZIP_CODE"/>
    <xsd:element ref = "E-MAIL" minOccurs = "0"/>
    <xsd:element ref = "NA_LINE6" minOccurs = "0"/>
</xsd:sequence>
<xsd:attribute name = "namelines" use = "required" type = "xsd:string"/>
<xsd:attribute name = "irsnameline_1" use = "required" type = "xsd:string"/>
        </xsd:complexType>
    </xsd:element>
    <xsd:element name = "E-MAIL">
<xsd:complexType mixed = "true">
            <xsd:choice/>
        </xsd:complexType>
    </xsd:element>
    <xsd:element name = "ZIP_CODE">
        <xsd:simpleType>
            <xsd:list>
                <xsd:simpleType>
                    <xsd:restriction base = "xsd:string">
                        <xsd:pattern value = "99999-9999"/>
                    </xsd:restriction>
                </xsd:simpleType>
            </xsd:list>
        </xsd:simpleType>
    </xsd:element>
    <xsd:element name = "NAME_INFO">
        <xsd:complexType>
            <xsd:sequence>
                <xsd:element ref = "FIRST"/>
                <xsd:element ref = "LAST"/>
            </xsd:sequence>
        </xsd:complexType>
    </xsd:element>
    <xsd:element name = "FIRST">
        <xsd:complexType mixed = "true">
            <xsd:choice/>
        </xsd:complexType>
    </xsd:element>
    <xsd:element name = "LAST">
        <xsd:complexType mixed = "true">
            <xsd:choice/>
        </xsd:complexType>
    </xsd:element>
</xsd:schema>
```

The Future of Schema Representation

Considering the increased functionality that schemas provide, they seem like a great improvement over DTDs. Certain kinds of applications, such as information exchange between databases as well as e-commerce will be simpler yet more interoperable by increased usage of XML Schemas.

XML Parsers

An XML parser is used to read XML documents, providing access to their content and structure. The data is passed on to other applications for processing. Validating XML parsers also check the syntax and report errors. This section introduces and briefly describes two of the major XML parsers.

Xerces

Xerces, developed by a collaboration of developers worldwide, has rich generating and validating capabilities. The parser is used for building XML-savvy Web servers as well as building next generation vertical applications that use XML as their data format.

There are versions available for both Java and C++. Xerces adheres to standards including the W3C XML and DOM (Level 1 and 2) standards, as well as the SAX (version 2). In addition, initial support for XML Schema is also provided. Source code, samples, and API documentation are provided with the parser.

Document Object Model (DOM)

The Document Object Model (DOM) is a common programming interface (API) for accessing HTML and XML documents from a Web browser. DOM provides the means to implement dynamic HTML, therefore allowing animation, interaction and dynamic updating of Web pages. DOM pertains to document structures in general, providing a language and platform-neutral object model for Web pages. It may be used by any application that accesses documents.

Whereas an XML document is essentially a text file, a DOM object consists of a complex set of objects, collections, properties, methods, and events of an object model. Understanding the tree structure of an XML document is essential to understanding the DOM representation of a document.

The DOM Structure Model

The DOM presents documents as a hierarchy of node objects that implement other more specialized interfaces. Nodes may have child nodes of various types, while others are leaf nodes. Leaf nodes are bottom-most in the document structure; therefore, they cannot have child nodes. Node types supported by both XML and HTML, as well as which node types they may have as children are represented in Table 16.3.

TABLE 16.3 DOM APIs

Node Type	*Child Nodes*

`Document`	`Element` (maximum of one)
	`ProcessingInstruction`
	`Comment`
	`DocumentType` (maximum of one)

`DocumentFragment`	`Element`
	`ProcessingInstruction`
	`Comment`
	`Text`
	`CDATASection`
	`EntityReference`

`DocumentType`	No children

`EntityReference`	`Element`
	`ProcessingInstruction`
	`Comment`
	`Text`
	`CDATASection`
	`EntityReference`

`Element`	`Element`
	`Text`
	`Comment`
	`ProcessingInstruction`
	`CDATASection`
	`EntityReference`

`Attr`	`Text` `EntityReference`
`ProcessingInstruction`	No children
`Comment`	No children
`Text`	No children
`CDATASection`	No children

`Entity`	`Element`
	`ProcessingInstruction`
	`Comment`
	`Text`
	`CDATASection`
	`EntityReference`

`Notation`	No children

The DOM also specifies a `NodeList` interface that handles ordered lists of nodes, including children of a node as well as elements returned by the `getElementsByTagName` method of the `Element` interface. The `NamedNodeMap` interface handles unordered sets of nodes, referencing them by their name attribute. Changes to the underlying document structure are reflected in all relevant `NodeList` and `NamedNodeMap` objects. Therefore, any addition, subtraction, or modification made to the children of an element within a `NodeList` object are automatically reflected in the `NodeList`, without action by the user. Changes to a node in the tree are similarly reflected in all references to that node in `NodeList` and `NamedNodeMap` objects.

Memory Management

Most APIs defined by this specification are interfaces rather than classes; therefore, an implementation only needs to expose methods with the defined names and specified operation instead of implementing classes that correspond directly to the interfaces. This allows the DOM APIs to be implemented as a thin layer on top of legacy applications that have their own data structures, as well as on top of newer applications with different class hierarchies. Adversely, ordinary constructors (in the Java or C++ sense) cannot be used to create DOM objects, since the underlying objects to be constructed may have little relationship to the DOM interfaces. In object-oriented design, the conventional solution to this is to define factory methods that create instances of objects that will implement the various interfaces. For example, objects implementing the interface `X` are created by a `createX()` method on the document interface. All DOM objects live in the context of a specific Document.

Because the DOM Level 2 API does not define a standard way to create DOMImplementation objects, DOM implementations must provide some proprietary way of wrapping these DOM interfaces. All other objects can then be built from there.

The core DOM APIs are designed to be compatible with a wide range of languages, from general-user scripting languages to more challenging languages used mostly by professional programmers. Subsequently, DOM APIs need to operate across a variety of memory management philosophies, including language bindings that do not expose memory management to the user at all; those like Java that provide explicit constructors but provide an automatic garbage collection mechanism to automatically reclaim unused memory; and those like C/C++ that generally require the programmer to explicitly allocate object memory, track where it is used, then free it for reuse. To ensure a consistent API across these platforms, the DOM does not address memory management issues at all, but instead leaves these for the implementation. Neither of the explicit language bindings defined by the DOM API (for ECMAScript and Java) require memory management methods at all; however, DOM bindings for other languages (especially C or C++) may require such support. These extensions are the responsibility of those adapting the DOM API to a specific language, not the DOM Working Group.

Naming Conventions

While attribute and method names that are short, informative, consistent, and familiar to users of similar APIs are preferable, names cannot clash with the those in legacy APIs supported by DOM implementations. As a result, DOM names tend to be long and descriptive in order to be unique across all environments.

DOM Objects

The document object is the most important node object in the DOM hierarchy. It is the object from which all other objects are accessed. In essence the DOM *starts* with the document object. Creation of the document object is not specified by the W3C and therefore it relies on the implementation.

The following is an example of a DOM declaration:

```
import org.apache.xerces.parsers.DOMParser;
// other import declarations...
//create a DOM parser called 'parser'
DOMParser parser = new DOMParser();
//retrieve and parse XML document from address URL or file
parser.parse(URL);
// Create a DOM object (doc) - this represents the top-level reference
// to the whole DOM structure. Elements can be created from this object.
Document doc = parser.getDocument();
// Return the root element (node) of the document object
Element root = doc.getDocumentElement();
```

There are only three base objects in the DOM model:

- `Node`—Exposes an interface for dealing with child and parent nodes and their properties. Not all nodes have child nodes (for example, the text node does not have children). Twelve specific node types are derived from this node which supply additional properties relevant to their type.
- `NodeList`—Handles ordered sets of nodes, such as the children of an element node.
- `NamedNodeMap`—Handles unordered sets of nodes referenced by their name attribute, such as element attributes. They may also be referenced by an index.

An important property of the `NodeList` and `NamedNodeMap` objects is that they reflect *live* changes within the DOM and vice versa. A child node added to another node will be immediately reflected within the `NodeList` collection for the parent node.

Simple API for XML (SAX)

The Simple API for XML (SAX) is a standard interface for event-based XML parsing. SAX is not an XML parser; however, it is an event-driven process to identify the elements as the parser reads them. It then informs the application of events, such as the start and end of elements.

This approach is faster than using the DOM for large documents while using considerably less memory. On the other hand, it is less flexible compared to using the DOM.

SAX2, the most recent version of SAX, incorporates support for Namespaces, filter chains, and for querying and setting features and properties in the parser.

For non-interactive processing, SAX would probably be the best choice, especially if the XML document is large.

Benefits of SAX include the following:

- Handles files of any size
- Is easy to understand
- Provides small subset of document

The SAX interface is implemented for many different XML parsers (and things that pose as XML parsers), just as JDBC is a common interface implemented for many different relational databases (and things that pose as relational databases). The interfaces and classes listed and described in Tables 16.4 and 16.5 are contained in the `org.xml.sax.helpers` package.

TABLE 16.4 Sax Interface Summary

Interface	*Description*
`AttributeList`	Deprecated (replaced by the `Attributes` interface, which includes Namespace support)
`Attributes`	Interface for a list of XML attributes
`ContentHandler`	Receives notification of the logical content of a document
`DTDHandler`	Receives notification of basic DTD-related events
`EntityResolver`	Basic interface for resolving entities

TABLE 16.4 continued

Interface	*Description*
`ErrorHandler`	Basic interface for SAX error handlers
`Locator`	Associates a SAX event with a document location
`XMLFilter`	Interface for an XML filter
`XMLReader`	Reads an XML document using callbacks

TABLE 16.5 Sax Class Summary

Class	*Description*
`HandlerBase`	Works with the deprecated `DocumentHandler` interface
`InputSource`	A single input source for an XML entity

The `SAXException` Java package handles all SAX exceptions and warnings, which are listed and described in Table 16.6.

TABLE 16.6 Exception Summary

Exception Class	*Description*
`SAXException`	Encapsulates a general SAX error or warning
`SAXNotRecognizedException`	Exception class for an unrecognized identifier
`SAXNotSupportedException`	Exception class for an unsupported operation
`SAXParseException`	Encapsulates an XML parse error or warning

The `SAX` package contains some basic classes (listed and described in Table 16.7) that help developers to start using the SAX APIs.

TABLE 16.7 Class Summary

Class	*Description*
`AttributesImpl`	Default implementation of the `Attributes` interface
`DefaultHandler`	Default base class for SAX2 event handlers
`LocatorImpl`	Provides an optional convenience implementation of `Locator`
`NamespaceSupport`	Encapsulates Namespace logic for use by SAX drivers
`ParserAdapter`	Adapts a SAX1 parser to a SAX2 `XMLReader`

TABLE 16.7 continued

Class	*Description*
`XMLFilterImpl`	Base class for deriving an XML filter
`XMLReaderAdapter`	Adapts a SAX2 `XMLReader` to a SAX1 parser
`XMLReaderFactory`	Factory for creating an XML reader

Here is an example of parsing a document:

```
StringReader lsrXML = new StringReader(lsbReply.toString());
    InputSource lisXML = new InputSource(lsrXML);
    DOMParser lparser = new DOMParser();
    try
        {
        lparser.parse(lisXML);
        Document doc = lparser.getDocument();
        // Search for ERRORs
        isError = getCodeTextValues(doc, "ERROR");
        if (isError == null)
        {
        // Get values for Account Number
        String lsValue = getValue(doc, "ACCOUNT_NUMBER");
            if (lsValue != null)
            {
                isAccountNumber = lsValue;
                if (Account.length() == 12)
                {
                    //Do some processing
                }
                else
                {
                  //Display error msg account number invalid
                 liRC = -6;        // Account Number Invalid
                 isMsg = "Account number Invalid";
                }
            }
            else
            {
                liRC = -7;
             // Account Number not found in XML response
                isMsg = "Account NUMBER not found in XML response";
            }
        }
        else
        {
            liRC = -9;                       // SYSTEM_ERROR
            isMsg = "SYSTEM_ERROR: "+isError[0];
        }
```

```
        }
        catch (SAXException se)
        {
        if (se.getException() != null)
            se.getException().printStackTrace(System.err);
        else
            se.printStackTrace(System.err);
            liRC = -10;                          // SAX Exception
            isMsg = "SAX Exception during account lookup";
        }
```

This example uses both SAX and DOM methods to parse a document. The processing carried out in the parsing example takes an XML document as input. The XML document is then parsed and we extrapolate the account number using the DOM method `getValue(doc, "ACCOUNT_NUMBER")`. This account is returned to the caller. The example shows how to parse through the returned document. Moreover, the function searches for any errors in the document. If no errors are present, it starts looking for the account number. If the account number is found, it checks to see that the format is correct. If the account number is not found in the document, it displays an error message.

Java API for XML Processing (JAXP)

The Java API for XML Processing (JAXP) Optional Package, developed by Sun Microsystems, enables applications to parse and transform XML documents with a pure Java API. Since it is independent of a particular XML processor implementation, developers have the flexibility to use various XML processors without making application code changes. The latest major release of JAXP includes an XSLT framework based on TrAX (Transformation API for XML) plus updates to the parsing API to support DOM Level 2 and SAX version 2.0.

XML Output

Although XML elements explain content and markup, they do not describe the layout of the information when printed or displayed. This formatting can be accomplished using either cascading style sheets (CSS) or eXtensible Stylesheet Language (XLS).

Cascading Style Sheets (CSS)

CSS is a W3C standard for defining the formatting applied to HTML elements. These formatting rules are referred to as styles. There are various ways a style may be applied to an element. A style rule may be defined so it is associated with specific HTML or nested elements, or it may be independent of an element and have its own class name.

This class can then be associated at will with any HTML element. A full-stop character in the definition always precedes a user-defined class name or selector.

Generally, a style rule consists of a style name and a collection of property: value pairs, separated by semicolons. Style rules may be embedded inline within the HTML tag or they may be defined within special <STYLE> tags, such as the one in the upcoming example. `selector n` represents the name of the element or class.

```
<STYLE TYPE =  "text/css">  selector 1  { property:value ; property:value; ... }

selector 2  { property:value ; property:value; ... }
...
</STYLE>
```

Style rules may also be defined in a file that is linked to using a <LINK> element instead of being defined within the Web page.

```
<LINK REL = "STYLESHEET" TYPE = "text/css" HREF = "stylefile.css">
```

As with HTML elements, XML element content may be styled using cascading style sheets (CSS). A major drawback to this is that the resulting output is structured strictly according to the sequence of the XML document. There is little control over the layout of the content as well as no built-in means to filter content. Some more precise layout control can be achieved by using the following `attribute:value` pairs:

- `DISPLAY:INLINE`—The element is displayed on the same line as the preceding element.
- `DISPLAY:BLOCK`—The element is displayed on a new line. Elements may also be aligned left, center, or right.
- `DISPLAY:NONE`—This signifies that the element should not be displayed.

Examples of CSS elements:

```
 body {display:block;font-size:10pt;}
lastname {display:inline;font-size:12pt;}
```

XSL

The eXtensible Stylesheet Language (XSL) is the language that describes how XML documents should be displayed. XSL was developed by the W3C Working Group. It consists of three parts:

- XSL Transformations (XSLT)—A language for transforming XML documents (that is, converting one XML document into another format)

- XSL Formatting Objects (XSL-FO)—An XML vocabulary to define XML display
- XPath—A language used by XSLT to define XML parts or patterns

XSL documents, called XSL style sheets, are given the file extension .xsl. The style sheet is a separate file that is applied to the XML document.

XSL Transformations (XSLT)

XSLT is the mechanism within XSL that transforms an XML document into another document that will be recognized by a browser. This new document can be but is not necessarily an XML document. For example, XSLT can convert the same XML document into HTML for Web browsers or WML for cell phone browsers.

Based on template rules, XSLT specifies how the XML document should be processed. It is arguably the most important part of the XSL Standard.

XSLT is able to add completely new elements to the output file as well as remove, rearrange, and sort the elements.

XSL Formatting Objects (XSL-FO)

XSL Formatting is an XML application that describes how pages will look to the reader. The XSL-FO is used by the new document that was created by XSLT. XSL-FO supports more sophisticated formatting than HTML plus CSS does, including right-to-left and top-to-bottom text, footnotes, margin notes, and page numbers in cross-references.

XSL-FO is based on rectangular boxes called areas. Areas can contain text, empty space, images, or other formatting objects. Each area has borders and padding on the sides. An XSL formatter reads the formatting objects, determining which areas should be placed at what locations on the page. Formatting objects usually produce a single area, however they do sometimes generate more than one area.

A file containing XSL formatting objects has either the extension .fob or .fo. Since it is a well-formed XML, it may also be given the suffix .xml.

XML Path Language (XPath)

XPath is a language that finds the information within the XML document that matches predefined templates. The location of data or structure is specified so that it can then be processed by XSLT. XPath provides basic facilities for manipulation of strings, numbers, and booleans in the XML document. A compact, non-XML syntax facilitates the use of XPath within URIs and XML attribute values. It was designed to contain a natural subset that can be used for testing whether or not a node matches a pattern. XPath does not follow XML syntax, rather it follows the abstract, logical structure of an XML document. For example, instead of writing

```
xsl:template match="/firstname/lastname">
  <!--process information here -->

</xsl:template>
```

you would have to write something like this:

```
 <xsl:template>
 <xsl:select>
  <xsl:path>
   <xsl:element type = "firstname"/>
   <xsl:element type= "lastname"/>
  </xsl:path>
 </xsl:select>
<!--process information here -->
</xsl:template>
```

XPath models an XML document as a tree of nodes. The different types of nodes include element, attribute, and text nodes. A method of computing a string-value for each type of node is defined. Some types of nodes may also have names.

XSLT Namespace

An XML document contains names and attributes. Since names are local values, XML Namespace is necessary in order to put structure to this data, recognizing elements and attributes. Elements from the XSLT Namespace are only recognized in the style sheet, not in the source document. The prefix .xsl: refers to elements in the XSLT Namespace. Other prefixes can be used; however, there must be a Namespace declaration to bind the prefix to the URI (Universal Name) of the XSLT Namespace.

Elements from the XSLT Namespace may have attributes that are not from the XSLT Namespace, provided that the expanded name of the attribute has a non-null Namespace URI. These attributes cannot change the behavior of XSLT elements and functions defined in the document. The XSLT processor is able to ignore such attributes without returning an error if it does not recognize the Namespace URI. These attributes can provide unique identifiers, optimization hints, or documentation.

> **Note**
>
> Names of XSLT elements, attributes, and functions must be all lowercase, use hyphens to separate words, and use abbreviations only if they already appear in the syntax of a related language, such as XML or HTML.

Style Sheet Structure

An XSL style sheet is an XML document contained within a `stylesheet` element. The style sheet primarily contains template elements. The style sheet transforms the input/source document's tree into a structure called a result tree, which consists of result objects.

`stylesheet` Elements

The start of a style sheet is signified by the `<xsl:stylesheet` tag in the second line of an XML document. `<xsl:transform` is accepted as a synonym.

```
<xsl:stylesheet
  id = id
  extension-element-prefixes = tokens
  exclude-result-prefixes = tokens
  version = number>
  <!-- Content: (xsl:import*, top-level-elements) -->
</xsl:stylesheet>
<xsl:transform
  id = id
  extension-element-prefixes = tokens
  exclude-result-prefixes = tokens
  version = number>
  <!-- Content: (xsl:import*, top-level-elements) -->
</xsl:transform>
```

An `<xsl:stylesheet` element must have a version attribute, indicating which version of XSLT that the style sheet requires. The `<xsl:stylesheet` element may contain the following elements:

```
xsl:import
xsl:include
xsl:strip-space
xsl:preserve-space
xsl:output
xsl:key
xsl:decimal-format
xsl:namespace-alias
xsl:attribute-set
xsl:variable
xsl:param
```

```
xsl:template
xsl:script
```

Use <xsl:import> to import another style sheet into the style sheet. The format of the <xsl:import> statement is as follows:

```
<xsl:import
  href = uri-reference />
```

<xsl:include> is the same as the <xsl:import> statement but include style sheets are only allowed on the top level of the tree. The format of the <xsl:include> statement is as follows:

```
<xsl:include
  href = uri-reference />
```

<xsl:strip-space> and <xsl:preserve-space> work exactly as they are named. strip-space will remove any white space from the named element. preserve-space will not remove any white space from the named element. The syntax of <xsl:strip-space> is as follows:

```
<xsl:strip-space
  elements = tokens />
```

The syntax of <xsl:preserve-space> is shown here:

```
<xsl:preserve-space
  elements = tokens />
```

<xsl:output> specifies the output of XML, or HTML, or even plain text. <xsl:output> specifies the method by which the output will be created. The syntax of <xsl:output> is as follows:

```
<xsl:output method="xml or html or text"
version="version"
encoding="encoding"
omit-xml-declaration="yes or no"
standalone="yes or no"
cdata-section-elements="CDATA sections"
indent="yes or no"/>
```

Here is an example of <xsl:output> declaring XML output:

```
<xsl:output method="xml" version"1.0" encoding="windows-1252" standalone="yes"/>
```

The <xsl:key> element is used to declare keys in an XML document. The syntax of the <xsl:key> is as follows:

```
<xsl:key
  name = qname
```

```
  match = pattern
  use = expression />
```

`<xsl:decimal-format>` controls the format used by the XSL functionality for formatting a number. The syntax of `<xsl:decimal-format>` is shown here:

```
<xsl:decimal-format
  name = qname
  decimal-separator = char
  grouping-separator = char
  infinity = string
  minus-sign = char
  NaN = string
  percent = char
  per-mille = char
  zero-digit = char
  digit = char
  pattern-separator = char />
```

`<xsl:attribute-set>` is a handy shortcut to set attributes for a related group of attributes that always go together:

```
<xsl:attribute-set name="name of the att set"
user-attribute-sets="att set names">
```

`<xsl:template>` is the element used to define the templates which make up the XSLT style sheets. The format of `<xsl:template>` is as follows:

```
 <xsl:template match=Xpath expression"
 name="template name"
priority="number"
mode="mode name">
```

The `<xsl:variable>` element enables users to add simple constants to style sheets. For example:

```
<xsl:variable name="space">
<xsl:text> <xsl:text>
</xsl:variable>
```

An element occurring as a child of an `<xsl:stylesheet` element is referred to as a top-level element.

The following example shows the structure of a style sheet. Ellipses (…) indicate where attribute values or content have been omitted. Although this example shows one of each type of allowed element, style sheets may contain any or none of these elements.

```
<xsl:stylesheet version= "1.1"
                xmlns:xsl="http://www.w3.org/1999/XSL/Transform">
  <xsl:import href="..."/>
  <xsl:include href="..."/>
```

```
  <xsl:strip-space elements="..."/>
  <xsl:preserve-space elements="..."/>
  <xsl:output method="..."/>
  <xsl:key name="..." match="..." use="..."/>
  <xsl:decimal-format name="..."/>
  <xsl:namespace-alias stylesheet-prefix="..." result-prefix="..."/>
  <xsl:attribute-set name="...">
    ...
  </xsl:attribute-set>
  <xsl:variable name="...">.
        ...
  </xsl:variable>
  <xsl:param name="...">
        ...
  </xsl:param>
  <xsl:script implements-prefix="..." language="...">
        ...
  </xsl:script>
  <xsl:template match="...">
    ...
  </xsl:template>
  <xsl:template name="...">
    ...
  </xsl:template>
</xsl:stylesheet>
```

The order in which the children of the `xsl:stylesheet` element occur is not significant except for `xsl:import` elements. Users may put the elements in the order they prefer. Style sheet creation tools do not need to provide control over the order in which the elements occur. The `import stylesheet` template has low priority; if the imported style sheet has the same pattern, the style sheet pattern will be used. Use the `xsl:apply-import` element is used if you want to employ the functionality of the overruled template.

The `<xsl:stylesheet` element can provide

- Information that will be used by extension elements or extension functions
- Information regarding what to do with the result tree
- Information regarding how to obtain the source tree
- Metadata about the style sheet
- Structured documentation for the style sheet

Template Elements

XSL utilizes templates to define how to output XML elements. Each template contains match patterns that determine where the template applies. The resulting fragments are woven together to form the complete result tree. These match patterns are defined by the XPath language.

The beginning of the template is defined by the `<xsl:template` tag in the third line of the XML document. The template attribute `match="/"` associates that template to the root of the source document.

Applying Style Sheets

XSL must conform to the syntax of well-formed XML. All XSL elements, including the root element, must be in the qualified namespace defined in the root element and prefixed by `xsl:`. A minimal XSL document is as shown below:

```
<?xml version = "1.0"?><xsl:stylesheet xmlns:xsl ="http://www.w3.org/TR/WD-xsl">

</xsl:stylesheet>
```

To apply the style sheet, simply reference the style sheet within the XML document.

An XSL-compliant browser, such as Internet Explorer 5.0 or later will transform the XML into HTML.

XML Linking Language (XLink)

Having the ability to link to other resources on the Web is very important. The current capabilities to accomplish this tend to be too unidirectional and simple to meet the growing needs of XML-based applications. The official W3C solution for linking in XML is called XML Linking Language (XLink). The goal of XLink is to allow each Web user the ability to create links between documents that have been created by other people. The links can point to an exact document or a group of locations.

Consider the creation of an XML-based online store. Among other things, the system might be capable of performing the following actions when a user clicks on a topic:

- Opening an explanatory text (with a link back to the main index)
- Opening a window and simulating the actions that can be taken (for example, going to the Shopping Cart menu and selecting Include Item)
- Opening up a relevant dialog

XLink Structure

XLink is a recommendation of the W3C that has been created to give XML documents the ability to establish links to each other. This is similar to what HTML accomplishes through use of the <A> tag.

The Book/Categories Problem

Before discussing the details of XLink, here is an example problem. Suppose you want to express the relationship between books and categories in XML. This includes making links to lists of other books or titles in the categories and/or authors' other works. The data for each book might be written in a file like the following:

```
<?xml version="1.0"?>
<book>
 <title>Kiss the Girls</title>
 <author>James Patterson</author>
 <categories>Ficton</categories><publisher>Warner Books</publisher>
</book>
```

Also, brief descriptions of categories are included in separate files, like this:

```
<?xml version="1.0"?>
<categories>
 <type>Reference</type>
 <description>
   <p>Technical book...</p>
 </description>

 <type>biography</type>
 <description>
   <p>true life story...</p>
 </description>

</categories>
```

Fulfilling these requirements by creating a file that relates books to categories as well as authors is a task beyond a simple strategy like adding many <a> or <img> links to the previous documents. For instance:

- A single author has many books (a link points from one resource to many).
- A single publisher has associations with many titles.

The XLink Solution

In XLink there are two type of linking elements: simple (like <a> and <img> in HTML) and extended. Links are represented as elements. However, XLink does not impose any particular *correct* name for links, allowing the user to decide which elements will serve as links by means of the `xlink` attribute type. For example:

```
<?xml version="1.0"?>
<book>
 <title>Kiss the Girls</title>
 <author>James Patterson</author>
 <categories>Ficton</categories>
 <publisher xlink:type="simple"
xlink:href="http://www.twbookmark.com/index.html >
  Warner Books
 </publisher>
</book>
```

This code example shows how the `xlink` attributes are set for the home page of Time Warner Books.

XML Security

XML enables transfer of information to occur without any user intervention. Industry leaders are creating easy-to-implement, standardized, interoperable security solutions that work in conjunction with XML to minimize the risk that data will be pirated.

Two technologies that are underway now are XML Key Management Specification (XKMS) and the Security Assertion Markup Language (SAML).

XML Key Management Specification (XKMS)

As companies are increasingly exchanging information electronically, use of public key infrastructure (PKI) is rapidly growing in importance. As the implementation of PKI can be difficult, the XML Key Management Specification (XKMS) seeks to provide new levels of ease and interoperability to developers implementing public key infrastructure (PKI).

Instead of coding, PKI developers will be able to use trust utilities to perform complex tasks associated with key management, thus allowing developers to concentrate on the core application functionality. XKMS also carries the benefit of its small footprint, making this technology ideal for use in small devices and those with limited memory such as cell phones and PDAs.

Security Assertion Markup Language (SAML)

Security Assertion Markup Language (SAML) is the first industry standard for enabling secure e-commerce transactions through the XML. SAML was developed to provide a common language for the sharing of security services between companies engaged in Business-to-Business and Business-to-Consumer transactions. SAML combines two prior efforts, Security Service Markup Language (S2ML) and the specification for authentication and authorization information in XML (AuthXML).

SAML allows companies to securely exchange authentication, authorization, and profile information between customers, partners, or suppliers regardless of the security systems or e-commerce platforms that are currently in place. As a result, SAML promotes the interoperability between different security systems and provides a framework for secure e-business transactions across corporate boundaries.

Relationship Between XKMS and SAML

XKMS defines XML-based transactions for managing public keys supporting digital signature and encryption functions, such as for the authentication and confidentiality of business documents. The Security Assertion Markup Language (SAML) defines XML-based transactions for conveying information regarding the privileges or entitlements of people or organizations between different sites. XKMS and SAML are complementary, working smoothly with each other. For example, a business might use XKMS to verify a digitally signed transaction, and then use SAML to learn more about the business credentials of the signer.

Summary

This chapter has merely scratched the surface of XML, primarily providing a general overview of the technology. Some major aspects that we covered were

- The basic concepts and origins of XML
- The structure of XML documents, including the prolog and instance sections
- What makes up a well-formed XML document, including elements, tags, and attributes
- The use of DTDs and schema in XML, including the benefits and liabilities of each
- The basics of XML parsers
- How information is transformed using XSLT, XSL, and XPath
- The basics of DOM, SAX, and JAXP
- How XLink will be a crucial for XML applications in the near future
- Security in XML, including XKMS and SAML

To find more information on XML and the related technologies the best place to look is on the Web using some of the following sites:

World Wide Web Consortium (W3C)

`http://www.w3.org/`

eXtensible Markup Language (XML) 1.0

`http://www.w3.org/TR/REC-xml`

Apache XML Project

`http://xml.apache.org/`

XMLINFO

`http://www.xmlinfo.com/`

CHAPTER 17

Validating the Application

In This Chapter

- **Java and Testing** *570*
- **Quality Control Through Debugging** *572*
- **Debugging Techniques** *574*
- **Correcting an Error** *579*
- **Testing and Development Phases** *582*
- **Testing Methods and Techniques** *584*
- **Web Site Test Tools and Site Management Tools** *586*

Java and Testing

In this chapter, we will discuss the fundamentals of testing. We will address topics including problem resolution and determination, what items should be considered when locating problems, and some of the tools available for testing software.

Software is much like other physical processes; inputs are received and outputs are produced. Software and physical systems fail for many different reasons. Physical systems have different people trying to resolve different problems (for example, doctors resolve health problems, lawyers resolve legal problems). Systems can fail in many different ways, including network, server, processing, and power failures. The problems that can be encountered are countless; detecting all of these problems is generally infeasible.

Methods of testing vary widely depending on the philosophy of an organization. Most large organizations have separate testing groups while smaller organizations may use the project manager, users, or other developers as the testing team. Whatever structure is used, it's important that the testing process is defined. When testing tools and techniques are applied, the quality of the product is improved and the time to market is shortened.

Figure 17.1 shows a graphic representation of the software development cycle. This cycle is considered to be the period of time that begins with the decision to develop a software product and ends when the software is delivered. Typically, it includes a requirements phase, a design phase, an implementation phase, a test phase, and sometimes a release phase. In this chapter we will be talking mostly about the test phase, but we will be touching on all of the parts of the development cycle. We will also discuss which tools, methods, and hardware can help improve Software Quality Assurance (SQA).

It takes a wide range of tools and techniques to evaluate the quality of distributed software. The J2EE environment has unique testing challenges, as J2EE software is typically distributed across a variety of logical components such as Web Servers, Firewalls, and EJB application servers. In addition, these logical components are dispersed over different physical devices including server farms, workstations, and networks.

The first things we need to understand are the fundamental testing concepts:

- Test every component separately.
- Test during the entire project life cycle.
- Test without ego.
- Develop a plan.
- Regression test.
- Create different testing environments: development, integration, and staging areas.

- Test continuously.
- Catch bugs early in the process to save money later.

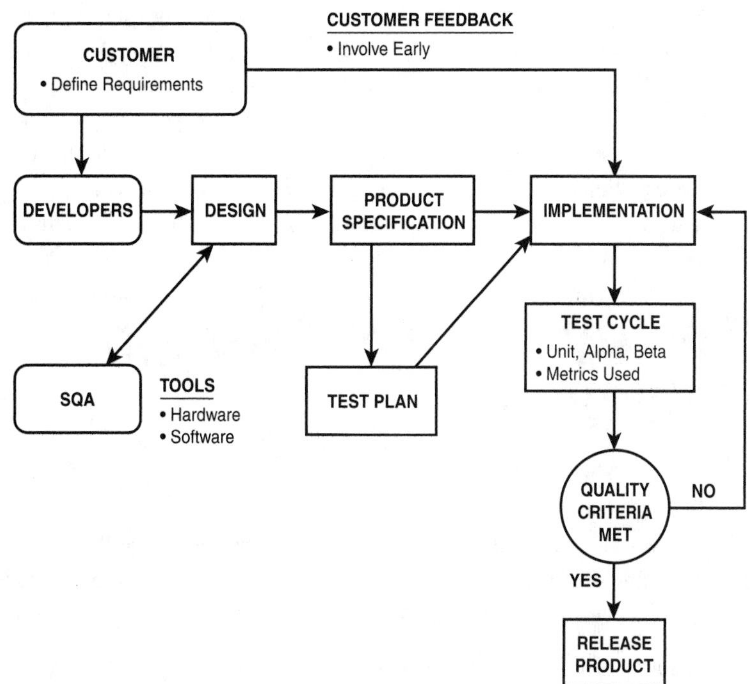

FIGURE 17.1
The software development cycle.

Involve Team Members Early

Involving people from different areas of the project from the earliest stages can be advantageous. One benefit is the creation of a sense of camaraderie. All the participants feel that they are playing on the same team. This encourages each member to be involved in learning what skills each other member possesses, as well as how those abilities can be used to promote the project. It encourages a feeling of belonging, increasing the awareness of the importance of each individual. This can really pay off in the long run.

Having users, developers, and testers working in parallel can also lead to the generation of more questions during these preliminary stages of development. More questions asked early on in the design phase contribute to a more solid design, thereby shortening the development cycle. By thoroughly exploring the testing issues, the project team comes to a better understanding of the project requirements. Finding bugs during the design phase is considerably less expensive in terms of time and money than locating them after the product has been developed.

After the design phase, the different teams split off and perform their own tasks; developers develop and testers develop test plans. Even while working on their separate pieces, it is essential that all group members continue to communicate. The objective of this type of structure is to reduce the downtime when passing the project between stages, significantly decreasing development time. As soon as the developers complete the coding, the tester/testing group is ready to begin. This model tends to refute the assumption that testing creates a bottleneck in the development cycle. Conversely, the testing team tends to get ahead when this model is used, waiting for the development team to fix the bugs they've located.

Quality Control Through Debugging

Although debugging should not be the only path to creating quality products, it is a major step toward ensuring a stable product that meets requirements.

The best systems have bugs, regardless of the technology used or the skill level of the developer. Most of these bugs are generated during the design phase of the project. Designing a perfect system is impossible.

The majority of bugs are normally found in the early stages of testing. These tend to be the most obvious, as well. As testing continues, bugs will be harder to find with the number of them falling. As the number of bugs levels off, the software should become more stable. If this does not hold true, the quality of the software is questionable.

In general, debugging is the means by which the programmer determines what is or is not a problem. Bugs are errors within code, and sooner or later the programmer will be required to fix them. The problem with applying testing solely as error detection is that software can only suggest the presence of flaws, not the absence of them.

Debugging and Experience

A study comparing programmers with only a few years of experience to experienced programmers found that there is roughly a 20-to-1 difference in the time it takes to find the same set of errors. Moreover, the experienced programmers found more errors and made more accurate corrections. Table 17.1 shows the results of the study, which examined how effectively professional programmers with at least four years of experience debugged a program with 12 errors.[1]

TABLE 17.1 Relationship Between Debugging Skills and Experience Level

Quality Characteristic	*Fastest Three Programmers*	*Slowest Three Programmers*
Average debug time (minutes)	5.0	14.1
Average number of errors not found	0.7	1.7
Average number of errors made correcting errors	3.0	7.7

This evidence supports the General Principle of Software Quality, which states that improving quality reduces development costs. The best programmers found the most errors, found them the fastest, and made the correct modifications most often.

Although debugging should not be the only path to creating a high quality application, it is a major tool in determining and ensuring the continued reliability of an application. Quality should be a consideration from the earliest design phase, and proper debugging will ensure that it is error-free. Good coding practices, careful analysis, and superior design are all part of ensuring a quality application.

Debugging Considerations

The following points should always be considered while debugging:

- Not all programs operate in the same fashion, as each programmer has a different style. Code should be examined from point to point to better understand how it is being used. It is important to understand someone else's coding style rather than attempt to change it.
- Data movement errors, such as those occurring when data is converted from one type to another or during movement of data from one variable to another, are some of the most difficult errors to resolve. It can be impossible to determine what the data looked like before the error occurred, or how the data got into the program in the first place.
- Sometimes the problem can be very simple, but can still be easily overlooked. For example, if there are two variables defined as `LSname` and `Lsname`, one might assume they are the same. The difference may not be noted until the program produces unexpected results.

[1] *J.D. Gould, "Some Psychological Evidence on How People Debug Computer Programs"* International Journal of Man-Machine Studies, *Vol. 7, No. 2, 1975, pp. 151-182.*

Debugging Techniques

When debugging an application, it is important to keep a backup copy of the original program, using a secondary copy for modifications, since making mass changes to the program can cause other problems. You should maintain a detailed record of any changes, testing after each alteration until it is apparent that a specific change fixed the problem.

Debugging is as demanding as the other parts of software development. It requires its own set of skills and procedures along with a proper mindset.

Test Without Ego

Even if an error doesn't appear to be your fault, it is often in your best interest to assume that it is. It is tricky enough to locate an error in your code when you're looking for it; the task becomes even more difficult when you assume that your code is error-free. In addition, accepting responsibility for an error will improve your credibility when you locate a problem in someone else's code, as other programmers will believe you have examined the code carefully. Assuming the error is your fault also saves you the embarrassment of claiming that an error is someone else's fault then having to take it back later when you discover the error was in fact yours.

When you are testing software that you developed, your ego will often tell you that your code is good, and is therefore error-free. To compensate, you should be methodical: forming hypotheses, collecting data, analyzing the hypotheses, and methodically rejecting the hypotheses that are proven wrong. If you are doing both code building and debugging, it is necessary to quickly switch between creative thinking for design and critical thinking for debugging. Finally, as you read your code, you must fight the effects of its familiarity, guarding against only seeing what you expect to see.

Step Away and Regroup

Have the discipline to step away from the problem. You might be staring right at it, but it's easy to overlook a simple problem if you suspect that it must be some sophisticated algorithm embedded somewhere in the code. For instance, you might not immediately realize that variables `VAR01` and `VARO1` are not the same. Or perhaps you have convinced yourself that you've narrowed down the source of the suspect code to within a few lines and haven't considered looking back to see how the variables used within those lines were populated. If you've racked your brain for hours only to discover that the culprit is something simple, don't become discouraged; just think of it as part of the learning process. It will make you a better programmer in the long run.

Adding Science to the Art of Debugging

Debugging by thinking about the problem is much more effective and interesting than debugging via guesswork. Debugging can be accomplished by following the steps of the scientific method:

1. Gather data through repeatable experiments
2. Form a hypothesis that accounts for as much relevant data as possible
3. Design an experiment that will either prove or disprove the hypothesis
4. Prove or disprove the hypothesis
5. Repeat as needed

When applied more specifically to debugging, the scientific approach for locating an error would follow these steps:

1. Stabilize the error
2. Locate the cause of the error
3. Correct the error
4. Test your program
5. Look for similar errors

Stabilize the Error

The first step is to make the error consistently repeat, therefore making the defect easier to detect. A defect that does not occur consistently is almost impossible to diagnose. Causing an irregular defect to occur predictably is one of the most challenging tasks in debugging and quality assurance.

An error that does not occur predictably is generally an initialization error or a dangling-pointer problem. If the calculation of a sum is correct sometimes and wrong sometimes, a variable involved in the calculation probably isn't being initialized properly; most of the time it just happens to start at 0. If the problem is a strange and unpredictable phenomenon and you're using pointers, you almost certainly have a pointer that was not initialized or a pointer to an area of memory that has been freed up.

Stabilizing an error usually requires more than finding a test case that produces the error. It includes narrowing the test case down to the simplest form that still produces the error. To simplify the test case, you bring the scientific method into play again.

Suppose a program has 10 factors that produce an error. First, you must form a hypothesis about which factors used in combination produce the error and which factors are irrelevant to producing the error. Change the factors assumed to be irrelevant, and rerun the test case. If the error still results, you can eliminate those factors. You can then simplify the test further. If you don't get the error, you've disproved that part of your hypothesis and you know more than you did before. It might be that some subtle change would still produce the error, but you know at least one specific change that does not. Repeat the process until the error occurs consistently.

Locate the Source of the Error

Locating the source of an error calls for using the scientific method. Gather the test data that divulged the error, analyze the data that have been produced, and form a hypothesis about the source of the error. Design a test case or an inspection to evaluate the hypothesis and then declare success or renew your efforts, as appropriate. The goal of simplifying the test case is to make it so simple that changing any aspect of it changes the behavior of the error. Then, by changing the test case carefully and watching the program's behavior under controlled conditions, you can diagnose the problem.

You might suspect that the defect is the result of a specific problem. Vary the parameter that you suspect is causing the problem. Running the application will again determine whether your hypothesis is correct.

Tips for Tracking Down Errors

Once you have stabilized an error and refined the test case that produces it, finding its source can be either trivial or challenging, depending on how well the code is written. If you are having a hard time finding an error, it's probably because the code wasn't well written. If you're having trouble, consider these tips:

- Use all available data in your analysis—When analyzing the source, try to locate your error by accounting for as much of the data as you can in your analysis. Modify the test cases that cause the error. If you still can't find the source of an error, try modifying the test cases further. Varying one parameter more than you had assumed was necessary may provide the crucial breakthrough.
- Recreate the error in several different ways—Sometimes it is instructive to try cases that are similar to the error-producing case, but not exactly the same. If you can get a fix on it from one point and a fix on it from another, you can determine exactly where it is. Errors often arise from a combination of factors; therefore, trying to diagnose the problem with only one test case can often miss the root problem.
- Use the results of negative tests—Even when a test case disproves the hypothesis, you still learn something you didn't know before. If the error is not where you thought it was, your search field has still been narrowed, as has the set of possible hypotheses.

- Brainstorm for possible hypotheses—Try to come up with several hypotheses rather than limiting yourself to the first one you thought of. Then look at each hypothesis and think about test cases that would prove or disprove it. This mental exercise is helpful in breaking the debugging logjam that can result from concentrating too hard on a single line of reasoning.
- Narrow the suspicious region of the code—Test small parts rather than the whole program, module, or routine. Systematically remove parts, determining whether the error still occurs without them. If it doesn't occur, you know it's in the part you took away. If it does, you know it's in the part you've kept.
- Divide and conquer—Use a binary search algorithm to focus your search rather than eliminating portions arbitrarily. Attempt to remove approximately half the code the first time. Determine the half the error is in, and then divide that section. Continue until you find the error.
- Use many small routines—This allows you to chop out sections of code simply by commenting out calls to the routines. Preprocessor commands and comments can be used to remove code.
- When using a debugger, you don't necessarily have to remove pieces of code—You can set breakpoints part of the way through the program and check for the error that way instead. If your debugger allows you to skip call routines, eliminate suspicious code by skipping the execution of certain routines and seeing whether the error still occurs.
- Be suspicious of routines that have had errors before—Routines that have had errors before are likely to continue to have errors. A routine that has been troublesome in the past is more likely to contain a new error than a routine that has been error-free.
- Examine code that has recently changed—If you have a new error that's hard to diagnose, it's usually related to code that's changed recently. It could be located in completely new code or in changes to old code. If you can't locate an error, run an old version of the program to see whether the error occurs. If it doesn't, you know the error is in the new version or is caused by an interaction with the new version. Scrutinize the differences between the old and new versions.
- Expand the suspicious region of the code—It's easy to focus on a small section of code if you are relatively sure the error is in a certain section. If you don't find it in the suspect section, expand the area of code you are examining, then focus on pieces of it using the binary search technique described earlier.
- Integrate incrementally—Add pieces to a system one at a time. If you add a piece to a system and subsequently encounter a new error, remove the piece and test it separately.

- Set a time limit for quick and dirty debugging—It's always tempting to try for a quick fix rather than systematically testing the code and giving the error no place to hide. The risk is that if the five-minute approach doesn't work, you get stubborn. Finding the error the "easy" way becomes a matter of principle, and hours pass unproductively.
- Check for common errors—Code quality checklists can help stimulate your thinking about possible errors. Focus on the elements that are part of the error, the data types involved, the specific area of code where the error occurs, and other modules or functions that are entered or exited at the time of error. If you keep a history of past problems that may have occurred in your environment, review them.
- Eyeball the code—Sometimes simply stepping through the code will expose the bug. If this does not work, the next step is peer code review.
- Peer code review—Reviewing the code with someone else, or with an entire team, will help you look at it more objectively. Often just explaining the code to someone else will help to find the bug.
- Give the problem a rest—Sometimes you concentrate so hard you can't think. If you're making no progress and you've tried all the options, let it rest for a while, then make a fresh start. Another benefit of giving up temporarily is that it reduces the anxiety associated with debugging.

Debugging with `print` Statements

A very basic debugging technique entails the strategic placement of `print` statements in a portion of the code to see why that part of the application is failing. This method is not very sophisticated; its power is derived from its simplicity. Since the `system` object is part of the `java` object, you can use it anywhere without installing any extra classes.

```
System.out.println(this + " Start of testing " );
```

Compared to stopping with breakpoints, writing to the `System.out` interferes very little with the normal execution flow of the application.

After the area of the error has been located, `print` statements should be added again to that general vicinity. Examine the output to determine where the error is. `System.out.println` is very useful in unit testing.

Syntax Errors

As compilers improve, providing better diagnostic messages, syntax errors are becoming less of a problem. The same compiler that can help eliminate errors can cause them as well.

Although compilers attempt to point out exactly what's wrong, the results are often unclear. It is important to read between the lines before determining what the results really mean. Errors should be resolved in the order of occurrence. Some compilers are good at detecting multiple errors but get so excited after detecting the first one that they will continue to roll out dozens of meaningless error messages. Oftentimes, a simple early error will set off a chain reaction. If you can't quickly find the source of the second or third error message, don't worry about it. Fix the first one and recompile.

Correcting an Error

Once an error has been located, correcting it is normally the easy part. However, as with many easy tasks, this simplicity makes it especially error-prone. Attempting to apply a quick fix may lead to a defective correction. The following are a few guidelines for reducing the chance of errors:

- Understand the problem before you fix it—Try to understand the problem well enough to predict its occurrence correctly every time before you attempt to fix it.
- Understand the program—If you understand the context in which a problem occurs, you're more likely to solve the problem completely rather than only one aspect of it. Try to understand at least the general vicinity of the error.
- Confirm the error diagnosis—Before you rush to fix an error, make sure that you have diagnosed the problem correctly. Take the time to run test cases that prove your hypothesis and disprove competing hypotheses. If you've only proven that the error could be the result of one of several causes, you don't yet have enough evidence to solve it.
- Don't be tempted to take shortcuts—It may take more time immediately, but it'll probably take less in the long run.
- Save the original source code—Before you begin fixing any error, be sure to make a backup copy of the code that you can return to later if necessary.
- Correct the problem, not the symptom—The focus should always be on correcting the underlying problem rather than performing cosmetic fixes that are only good for a specific case. For example:

```
int sku;
int prodnum;
double total;
double price;
for (sku = 1; sku <= prodnum; prodnum++)
   total += price;
System.out.println("Total: "+total + " Price:" + price);
```

Suppose that when prodnum equals 25, total turns out to be wrong by $9.99. Here's the wrong way to fix the problem:

```
int sku;
int prodnum;
double total;
double price;
for (sku = 1; sku <= prodnum; prodnum++)
   total += price;
if (prodnum == 25)              /*  HERE IS MY FIX  */
   total = total + 9.99;            /*  I solved this problem  */
System.out.println("Total: "+total + " Price:" + price);
```

Now suppose that when prodnum equals 49, total turns out to be off by $3.27.

```
int sku;
int prodnum;
double total;
double price;
for (sku = 1; sku <= prodnum; prodnum++)
   total += price;
if (prodnum == 25)              /*  HERE IS MY FIX  */
   total = total + 9.99;            /*  I solved this problem  */
if (prodnum == 49)              /*  HERE IS MY FIX  */
   total = total + 3.27;            /*  I solved this problem  */
System.out.println("Total: "+total + " Price:" + price);
```

If this continues along with an increase in the supply of products, the program can get very large, with potentially two lines of code for each new product. This is not a fix. It would be impossible to list all the problems that could be created by this type of coding. Instead, it is important to review why these quick fix solutions can create more problems:

- Initialization errors—Initialization errors are, by definition, unpredictable, so the fact that the total for `prodnum = 25` is off by $9.99 today doesn't tell you anything about tomorrow. It could be off by $1,000,000.00, or it could be correct. That's the nature of initialization errors.
- Workarounds—When code is special-cased to work around errors, the special cases become the code's most prominent feature. The $9.99 won't always be $9.99; the price will change and another error will show up later. If the code continues to be modified, it will become increasingly entangled with special cases until it can no longer be supported.
- Control your changes—Making changes should not be considered a trivial task, and changes should be implemented one at a time so that you can be confident about your modifications. Performing two or more changes at a time can introduce subtle errors that look like the original errors. This places you in the position of not knowing whether you simply failed to correct the error, you corrected the error but

introduced a new one that looks similar, or you didn't correct the error and you introduced a similar new error.

- Test your fix—Test the program yourself, have someone else test it for you, or walk through it with someone else. Run the same test cases you used to diagnose the problem to ensure that all aspects of the problem have been resolved.
- Rerun the whole program—Look for side effects of your changes. The easiest and most effective way to do so is to run the program through an automated suite of regression tests.
- Look for similar errors—Errors tend to occur in groups, and one of the values of paying attention to the kinds of errors you make is that you can correct all the errors of that kind.

Improving Reliability

The presence of an error generally means that the process defined does not meet user expectations. Failing to meet these specifications can be a function of not understanding the requirements, changes to the specifications, software bugs, and so on.

Most people are somewhat fallible. Even an excellent programmer can make a modest oversight. An error represents an opportunity to

- Learn about the kind of mistakes you make—Once you find the mistake, ask questions such as Why did I make it? How could I have found it more quickly? How can I prevent the error in the future? Are there similar mistakes? Can I correct them before they cause problems of their own?
- Perform code review with peers—Learn about the quality of your code from the point of view of someone who has to read it. In most cases, the person who wrote the code will not be the person fixing the problem. This is an opportunity to look critically at the quality of your code. Is it easy to read? Can it be improved? Use what you have learned to make your future programs even better.
- Improve your problem-solving techniques—Do you have confidence in your approach when attempting to debug you code? Does your approach work? Do you find errors quickly? Or are your debugging skills weak? Do you feel anguish and frustration? Do you guess randomly? What areas do you need to improve? Considering the amount of time many projects spend on debugging, it's definitely not a waste of time to evaluate how you debug. Take some time to analyze and change the way you debug. This might be the quickest way to decrease the total amount of time it takes you to develop a program.

- Learn how to fix problems quickly and efficiently—In addition to learning how to locate your errors, you can learn how to correct them. Do you make the simplest correction instead of truly eliminating the problem? Or do you systematically review, diagnose, and correct the problem?

All things considered, debugging is a valuable skill that should be fully developed, providing you with the ability to improve your application. Debugging truly begins with the application design; factors such as the readability, design, and code quality allow us to build in the reliability, availability, and serviceability that distributed applications require.

The Importance of Being a Good Debugger

Being a good debugger can reinforce good programming techniques, increasing appreciation of good formatting and insertion of meaningful comments. It can highlight the significance of naming conventions for variables and functions within programs. Establishing conventions for programs enables all developers to look at a program with an instant, basic understanding of the code. The following are several guidelines that will facilitate debugging:

- Design programs so that they have a straightforward flow, which makes it easier and faster to pinpoint the area that is at fault.
- Keep methods small and clear.
- Try to make the code self-explanatory.
- Use intuitive variable and method names.
- Use proper identification.
- Be consistent with whatever style you are using.

Testing and Development Phases

Every phase of the software development process has specific needs and requirements, not only from an engineering standpoint, but from a quality assurance standpoint as well.

A well-developed software testing routine has well-defined entry and exit criteria for each stage (see Figure 17.2).

Figure 17.2 illustrates the scope of the system testing cycle. The test should now be divided into manageable test sessions. For each test cycle, the exit criteria will be compared to the outputs. If the product passes, the next phase will be tested. If it does not pass, it will be fixed or enhanced and that phase of testing will be executed again until the product meets the exit criteria.

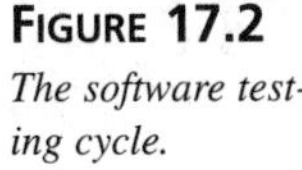

FIGURE 17.2
The software testing cycle.

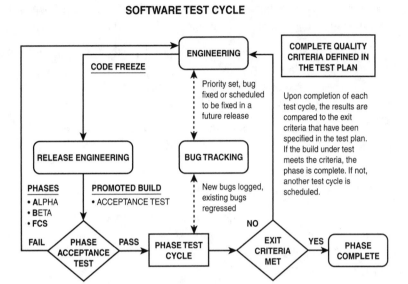

Throughout all of the testing phases, new bugs are logged while existing bugs are fixed. The Engineering department establishes priorities; they either fix the bugs or schedule them to be fixed in future releases. At that point, the exit criteria for that particular phase are achieved.

Alpha Phase

The alpha phase begins after all of the application's features have been coded. Optional entry criteria include a complete test plan, fully specified test cases, and finalized design documents and functional specs.

During this phase, the software quality assurance (SQA) group will attempt to find as many bugs as possible. This is achieved through pure nonregression testing. Tests are not rerun in the interest of maximum coverage. Test results are compared with the formal alpha exit criteria, which are normally quantitative.

When the alpha exit criteria have been satisfied, the Development department prioritizes bugs; they determine which will be fixed and tested in the beta phase, and which will wait until a future release.

Beta Phase

The beta phase occurs while preparing for the First Customer Ship (FCS). Full regression testing is used with the ultimate goal of stabilizing the product prior to final shipping.

The entry criterion for this phase may be that all documentation is in draft form. A build/test schedule similar to that of the alpha phase begins.

A common exit criterion could be that no priority one or two bugs remain. The beta exit might also entail stability measures.

FCS

FCS is the period that signifies entry into the final phase of a project. At this point, the product is feature-complete and ready for customer use.

Testing Methods and Techniques

Many QA methods and techniques can be used to improve the quality of a software product. Some of these are discussed in the following sections.

Unit Testing

This process is frequently performed by the programmer and is often the first step in the testing cycle. With unit testing, each component of the project is tested separately. For example, the JSP would be tested to ensure that input information is processed and displays the correct output.

Stress Testing and Volume Data Generation

When performing stress testing and volume data generation, the test environment is used to produce large volumes of data. This simulates how the product will react when confronted with a heavy load.

Code Complexity Analysis

Static complexity analysis is performed in order to instruct programmers as to how their coding techniques can be improved in order to make their code more reliable.

Benchmarking/Performance Testing

In this method, automated tests are constructed with timers built in, enabling the performance of the product to be judged. Benchmark results facilitate performance comparison from one build to the next as well as from your product to that of a competitor.

Stability Testing

Various tests such as flooding the controller with an artificially high load of requests are performed to destabilize the product and see how it reacts.

Regression Testing

A comprehensive suite of tests with known product coverage is performed, along with retesting of each new product build. Tests for specific bugs are incorporated to ensure they do not recur once they are fixed.

Black Box Testing

Black box testing is also known as functional testing. In this technique, the tester may only know the inputs and what outcomes are expected instead of how the program arrives at those outputs. The programming code is never examined. This method verifies that a product performs according to functional specifications.

White Box Testing

Test coverage analysis is used to pinpoint untested areas within the code, determining how effective the tests are. Opportunities for finding weak spots are also created through code walkthroughs, during which construction and stability are evaluated.

Usability Testing

In this technique, users try to use the system as a normal business process. The purpose is to ensure that the product preserves a consistent look and feel throughout the GUI. Elements such as online help and error messages are also evaluated.

Cross-Platform Testing

Cross-platform testing is constructed to ensure that the product performs properly across a variety of platforms. A J2EE application should inherently be able to run on many different platforms.

Security Testing

In security testing, proper password control, user authentication processes, private and public-key encryption, and secure messaging schemes are validated. The effectiveness of firewall and gateway protection can also be verified.

Installation Testing

It is important to verify that the program installs and uninstalls as specified.

Interrupt Testing

This method produces various interrupts at certain points during normal system processing and gauges how the system handles the interrupts.

Parallel Processing

More and more organizations are turning to parallel processing to give them the performance they need to keep up with their data processing needs. With the growth of multiprocessing machines, there is a need to check the efficiency of the parallel mechanism (the one with a closed loop). Parallel processing tests should also evaluate the system in non-parallel mode and compare the performance of the two modes.

Test Coverage Analysis

This technique is used to point out product areas that are not being tested adequately. Tools specializing in this analysis will provide ongoing evaluations as new tests are implemented.

Web Site Test Tools and Site Management Tools

Tools made specifically for debugging are typically more efficient for analyzing an application than methods such as using `print` statements scattered throughout the program. A good debugger will

- Allow you to set breakpoints when execution reaches a specific line, at a specified iteration of a specific line, when a global variable changes, or when a variable is assigned a specific value.
- Allow you to step through code line by line, returning to the point of origin of an error.
- Allow you to log the execution of specific statements. In effect, this is similar to spreading `print` statements throughout the program.
- Allow you to examine your data, monitoring it as it is read and after it is modified.
- Allow you to monitor dynamically allocated data fields as well as provide the capability of performing unplanned queries of your data.
- Provide useful reports and data tables analyzing the testing results.

The following sections provide brief descriptions of some of the tools used to test J2EE applications.

Load and Performance Test Tools

Both load and performance testing tools help to pinpoint potential performance problems by simulating, managing, and measuring complex dynamic transactions by simulated users.

Webserver Stress Tool

Webserver Stress Tool is a Web stress-testing tool from Paessler Tools that handles proxies, passwords, user agents, cookies, and ASP-session IDs. It is available as shareware for Windows 2000/NT. More information on this tool can be found at `http://www.paessler.com/tools/`.

Web Polygraph

Web Polygraph is a free benchmarking tool for caching proxies, origin server accelerators, L4/7 switches, and other Web intermediaries. Other features include realistic traffic generation and content simulation for high-performance HTTP clients and servers, ready-to-use standard workloads, a powerful domain-specific configuration language, and a portable open source implementation. The Web site for Web Polygraph is at `http://polygraph.ircache.net`.

Rational SiteLoad

Rational SiteLoad is a Web load-testing tool from Rational. The free evaluation version can emulate up to 50 users, and you can increase this number by purchasing additional "virtual testers." SiteLoad is available for Windows 2000/NT. For more information on Rational SiteLoad, go to `http://www.pts.com/siteload.cfm`.

Bean-test

Bean-test, from Empirix (formerly RSW) Software, is a tool for load testing EJB middle-tier applications. This tool is optimized for BEA WebLogic, IBM WebSphere, and Bluestone Total-e-Server and supports Unix, Solaris, Linux, Alpha, and Windows NT. Figure 17.3 displays the Bean-test Test Case selection screen.

FIGURE 17.3
The Bean-test editor.

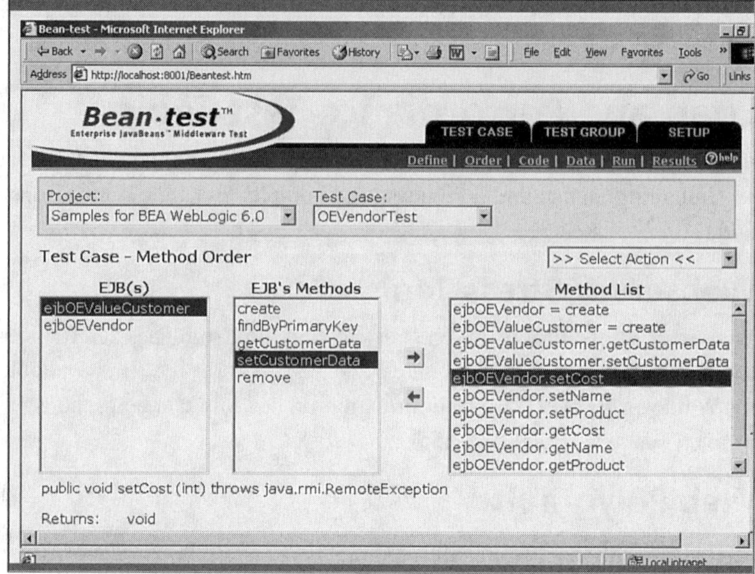

Bean-test version 4.1 has the ability to select multiple EJBs from within one test case, including passing variables between method calls. It is also capable of generating inputs for each method variable from random, data table, or static sources. The following code snippet shows some generated Bean-test code:

```
//
//EJBs under test: OEHome,OEVendor
//Description: Vendor and Home EJB
//Author:
//Creation Date: Mon Jul 02 17:10:11 EDT 2001
//Bean-test Code Generator v4.1-BetaOne
//Copyright (c) 2001 Empirix, Inc. All rights reserved.
//
package com.beantest.run;
import java.util.*;

//[Java EJB imports for BEA WebLogic Server V6.0]
//Currently there are no specific imports for this server

public class TESTCASEANDVENDOR extends Thread
    {
    int m_iClientNumber;
    String m_sUrlName;
    CDataSource m_ds;

    javax.naming.Context m_context = null;
```

```
static CFolder m_fldTest = new CFolder("Test");
static CFolder m_fldMethods = new CFolder(m_fldTest, "Methods");
static CFolder m_fldGetters = new CFolder(m_fldMethods, "Gets");
static CFolder m_fldSetters = new CFolder(m_fldMethods, "Sets");

public TESTCASEANDVENDOR (int iClientNumber, String sUrl, CDataSource ds)
    {
    m_iClientNumber = iClientNumber;
    m_sUrlName = sUrl;
    m_ds = ds;
    }

//[------> Run method for starting the EJB client test thread <------]
public void run()
    {
    CTimer timer = new CTimer(m_iClientNumber);
    CTimer timerFullTest = new CTimer(m_iClientNumber);
    timerFullTest.start(m_fldTest, "*Total");
    CLogger logger = new CLogger(m_iClientNumber);

    //[Get home references in local variables for each thread]
    com.beantest.orderentry.OrderEntryHome homeOEHome = null;
    com.beantest.vendor.VendorHome homeOEVendor = null;

    //[Get reference to the home interface for the bean(s)]
    try
        {
        timer.start(m_fldTest, "Initialize");
        m_context = getInitialContext(m_sUrlName);
        timer.stopAndLog();

        timer.start(m_fldTest, "getHome OEHome");
        homeOEHome = (com.beantest.orderentry.OrderEntryHome)
            getHomeInterface("OEHome",
    com.beantest.orderentry.OrderEntryHome.class);
        timer.stopAndLog();

        timer.start(m_fldTest, "getHome OEVendor");
        homeOEVendor = (com.beantest.vendor.VendorHome)
            getHomeInterface("OEVendor",
    com.beantest.vendor.VendorHome.class);
        timer.stopAndLog();

        }
    catch (Throwable e)
        {
        timer.stopAndLog(e);
        timerFullTest.stopAndLog();
        return;
        }
```

Bean-test generates Java code as shown here, providing the ability to update test code using the Bean-test GUI or by hand in the Bean-test editor.

Bean-test automatically generates graphs and logs of performance compared to the number of simultaneous clients. Graphs and reports represent data including response time, response time by method, number of exceptions, and transactions per second. The latest version allows the setting of baselines to view different test case results on one graph or data table. Figure 17.4 shows an example of a Bean-test report.

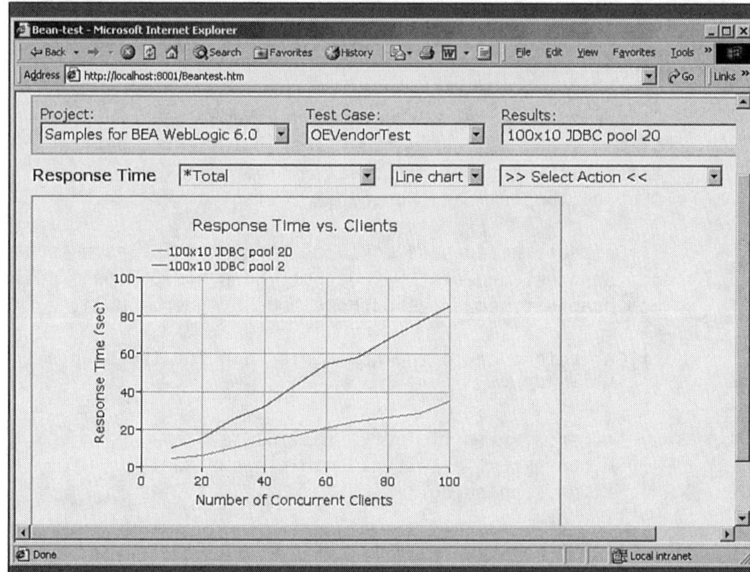

FIGURE 17.4
A Bean-test report.

For more information on Bean-test, go to `http://www.testmybeans.com`.

ApacheBench

ApacheBench is a Perl API for Apache benchmarking and regression testing intended as a foundation for a complete benchmarking and regression-testing suite for transaction-based `mod_perl` sites. This tool will stress test the server while verifying correct HTTP responses. It is based on the Apache 1.3.12 ab code. For more information on ApacheBench, go to `http://www.davin.ottawa.on.ca/archive/modperl/2000-09/msg00640.phtml`.

WebSpray

WebSpray is a load-testing tool that includes link-testing capabilities. It can simulate up to 1,000 clients from a single IP address and supports multiple IP addresses with or without aliases. It generates reports for errors and performance. WebSpray is available for Windows 98/2000/NT4.0. To get more information on WebSpray, go to `http://www.redhillnetworks.com/products/webspray.htm`.

SilkPerformer

SilkPerformer is the load- and performance-testing component of Segue's Silk testing toolset, working with their SilkTest functional testing product and SilkRealizer scenario-building tool to build complex scheduled site tests. It is available for Windows 2000/NT. For more information on SilkPerformer, go to `http://www.segue.com/html/s_solutions/s_performer/s_performer.htm`.

WebLOAD

WebLOAD, the Web site load-testing tool from RadView Software, is a scalability- and integrity-testing solution for Internet and intranet applications. WebLOAD 4.5 incorporates testing by unifying load, performance, and functional testing into a single, unified process. Each test can be run separately as well. WebLOAD delivers full Document Object Model (DOM) access, JavaScript-based test scripting, integration with most popular Web application servers, comprehensive HTTP support, automated operation, single-point management, and real-time graphical and statistical reporting for Web-based applications.

WebLOAD supports HTTP 1.0 and 1.1, including cookies, proxies, SSL, client certificates, authentications, persistent connections, and chunked transfer coding. Load is generated through the creation of virtual clients that emulate network traffic. Test script can be created by visually clicking through the Web site; the tool will create the agendas. You can also create views manually by writing the JavaScript test scripts that instruct those virtual clients about what to do. The following code snippet shows an example of WebLOAD execution JavaScript:

```
function InitAgenda() {
IncludeFile("AsmLib.js",WLExecuteScript)
wlGlobals.Proxy = "proxy.ABCXYZ.com:8080"
wlGlobals.ProxyUserName = "Userid"
wlGlobals.ProxyPassword = "Password"
}
wlHttp.Get("http://localhost:8035/SilverBooks37/app/")
Sleep(12187)
wlHttp.Type = "A"; wlHttp.ExpectedLocation = ":36";
wlHttp.ExpectedID = ""; wlHttp.ExpectedName = "";
```

```
wlHttp.ExpectedText = "Harry Potter and the Goblet of Fire";
wlHttp.Url = wlHttp.IdentifyObject
("http://localhost:8035/SilverBooks37/app/bookDetail.do?bid=277")
wlHttp.Get(wlHttp.Url)
Sleep(5978)
wlHttp.Type = "FORM"; wlHttp.ExpectedLocation = ":0";
wlHttp.ExpectedID = ""; wlHttp.ExpectedName = ""; wlHttp.ExpectedText = "";
wlHttp.Url = wlHttp.IdentifyObject
("http://localhost:8035/SilverBooks37/app/cart.do?action=update")
wlHttp.FormData["quantity1"] = "1"
wlHttp.FormData["submit"] = "update"
wlHttp.Post(wlHttp.Url)
Sleep(3265)
wlHttp.Get("http://localhost:8035/SilverBooks37/app/searchAction.do?title=T")
Sleep(5398)
wlHttp.Type = "FORM"; wlHttp.ExpectedLocation = ":0";
wlHttp.ExpectedID = ""; wlHttp.ExpectedName = "AccountDetailForm";
wlHttp.ExpectedText = "";
wlHttp.Url = wlHttp.IdentifyObject
 ("http://localhost:8035/SilverBooks37/app/updateAccount.do")
wlHttp.FormData["action"] = wlHttp.GetCurrentValue("action","create")
wlHttp.FormData["EMailAddress"] = "test@test.com"
wlHttp.FormData["password2"] = "tester"
wlHttp.FormData["password1"] = "tester"
wlHttp.FormData["firstName"] = "test"
wlHttp.FormData["lastName"] = "tester"
wlHttp.FormData["phone"] = "222222222"
wlHttp.FormData["company"] = "$WL$EMPTY$STRING$"
wlHttp.FormData["address1"] = "6 test ln"
wlHttp.FormData["address2"] = "$WL$EMPTY$STRING$"
wlHttp.FormData["address3"] = "$WL$EMPTY$STRING$"
wlHttp.FormData["city"] = "Happy City"
wlHttp.FormData["state"] = "PA"
wlHttp.FormData["zip"] = "08909"
wlHttp.FormData["country"] = "use"
wlHttp.FormData["shipradio"] = "1"
wlHttp.Post(wlHttp.Url)
Sleep(9664)
wlHttp.Type = "A"; wlHttp.ExpectedLocation = ":13";
 wlHttp.ExpectedID = ""; wlHttp.ExpectedName = "";
 wlHttp.ExpectedText = "Shopping Cart ";
wlHttp.Url = wlHttp.IdentifyObject
("http://localhost:8035/SilverBooks37/app/shoppingcart.jsp")
wlHttp.Get(wlHttp.Url)
Sleep(2584)
```

When WebLOAD runs the test, results are gathered at a per-client, per-transaction, and per-instance level from the computers that are generating the load. WebLOAD can also gather information from the application server's performance monitor. WebLOAD displays results in graphs and tables as they occur. These can be saved and exported upon completion. In Chart view, WebLOAD displays the results of your test in a line graph. Separate lines track each measurement selected in the report configuration. The lines are color-coded to match the measurements on the bottom half of the report. Measurements from two sessions, the current session and a saved Load Session, are displayed in the report.

Figure 17.5 displays the WebLOAD Console Chart view. This view gives the overall picture of the test being scripted, including the load size, transactions per second, throughput, and round time.

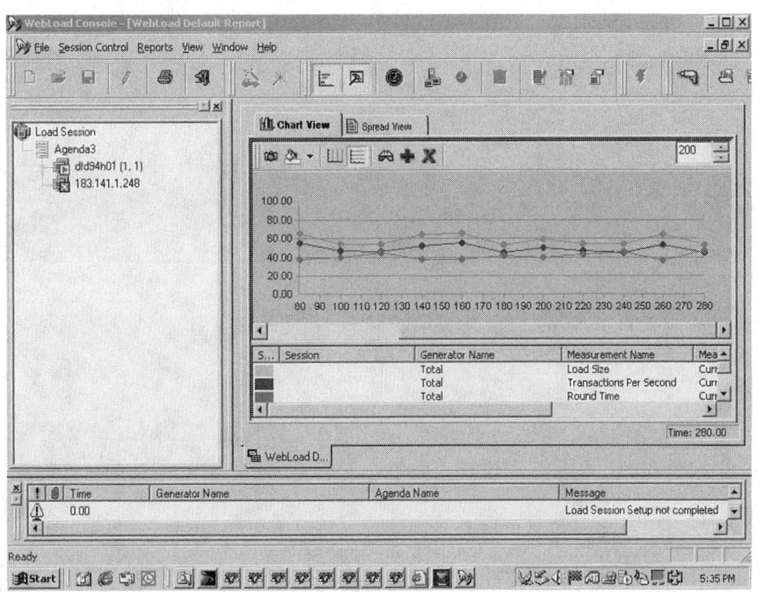

FIGURE 17.5
WebLOAD console Chart view.

To bring up a history focusing on a specific measurement, double-click on a single measurement line in the Integrated Report.

Figure 17.6 depicts how you can drill down into the different testing criteria.

The Spread view displays the data accumulated in the test session and presented in the Integrated Report Chart view in tabular format (see Figure 17.7).

For more information on WebLOAD, go to `http://www.radview.com`.

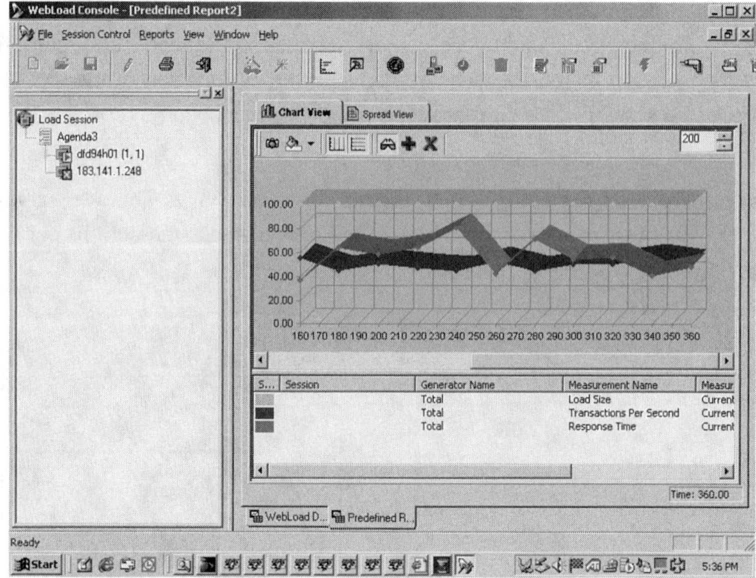

FIGURE 17.6
WebLOAD Detail view showing the number of transactions.

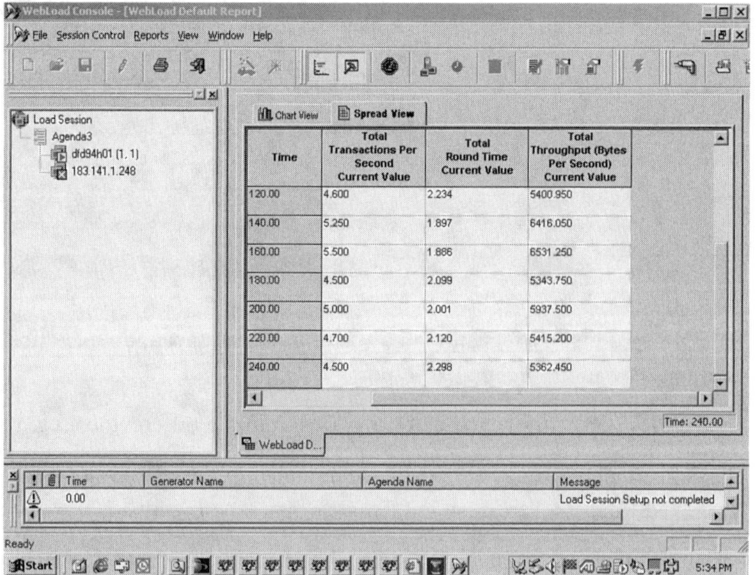

FIGURE 17.7
WebLOAD Spread view.

Astra LoadTest

Mercury Interactive's tool for Web load- and stress-testing supports Broadvision, ColdFusion, SilverStream, WebLogic, and IBM WebSphere. It includes record/playback capabilities, allows breakpoints for debugging, and enables functional and content verification checkpoints. The integrated spreadsheet parameterizes recorded input to test the application with a wide variety of data. A unique IP address is created for each virtual user. The Scenario Builder feature visually combines virtual users and host machines for tests representing real user traffic. The Content Check feature checks for failures under heavy load. Astra LoadTest also supports various security features. For more information, go to `http://www-svca.mercuryinteractive.com`.

Java Test Tools

This section discusses various Java testing tools that are currently available.

JProbe Developer Suite

This collection of Java debugging tools from Sitraka Software includes JProbe Profiler and JProbe Memory Debugger for memory leaks and performance bottlenecks, LProbe Coverage code coverage tool, and JProbe Threadalyzer for finding stalls, deadlocks, and race conditions. The ServerSide edition is available for Web server–side Java development. JProbe supports Windows 95/98/2000/NT, Solaris, and Linux. For more information on JProbe, go to `http://www.jprobe.com`.

Jtest

ParaSoft's Java testing tool performs three types of testing: black box, regression, and white box. The user can specify the inputs and other testing parameters that are fed into methods for comparison with desired results. The unique part of Jtest is that a symbolic Java virtual machine checks to see whether any potential conditions or values will cause the code to throw an exception. Developers can unit-test their code for completeness and standards compliance and conduct regression to ensure the changes they made have not introduced new errors. Jtest has "Test Generation System Technology," automating white box testing so that unexpected input will not cause the program to crash. Test cases are automatically generated and they test each class with inputs based on the class's structure. White box stubs are automatically generated to test classes using inputs from external resources (such as databases, CORBA, and EJB). Code is checked to ensure compliance with standards. Severity codes can be set for each of the rules to enable or display certain rules. Jtest is available for Windows 95/98/NT/2000 and Solaris. For more information on ParaSoft's Java Testing tool, go to `http://www.parasoft.com/products/jtest/index.htm`.

SilkPilot

Segue's SilkPilot validates Java servers through RMI public interfaces, supports EJB, and tests CORBA servers implemented in any programming language. A tool is provided to help optimize distributed objects based on industry standards for middleware implementations. SilkPilot utilizes XML to store test cases. It is available for Windows and Unix platforms. For more information on SilkPilot, go to `www.segue.com/html/s_solutions/s_corba/s_spilot_overview.htm`.

JUnit

JUnit is an open source Java unit test framework that includes a test data repository, command-line arguments, and a TestRunner class that supports a built-in repetition counter and multithreading at the command line. For more information JUnit, go to `http://www.junit.org`.

Link Checking Tools

These testing tools check for dead links on your Web pages.

Compuware WebCheck

WebCheck is a quality analysis tool that will help you proficiently test and organize your Web sites. Graphical reports provide Web quality assurance teams with detailed error reports and performance information, as well as trends on the Web sites. WebCheck has the capability to test Web sites for potential problems and errors. For more information, go to `http://www.itutils.com`.

InfoLink

BiggByte Software's link-checking program can be automatically scheduled. Features include FTP link checking and multiple page list and site list capabilities. Results can be exported to a database for easy reporting. Freeware and evaluation versions are available for Windows 95/NT. For more information on InfoLink, go to `http://www.biggbyte.com`.

CyberSpyder Link Test

CyberSpyder, a link checker by Aman Software, is available as shareware. Functionality includes specified URL exclusions, ID/password entries, test resumption at interruption point, page size analysis, and reporting. CyberSpyder is available for Windows 3.1/95/98/2000/NT. For more information, go to `http://www.cyberspyder.com`.

HTML Validators

HTML validators have been created to check your site or product to ensure that they contain valid HTML code.

RealValidator

HTML validator shareware is based on the SGML parser. RealValidator is Unicode enabled and supports documents in any language. Proprietary HTML DTDs can be added, or the existing ones can be changed. It fetches external DTDs by HTTP and caches them for faster validation. HTML 3.2 and HTML 4.0 references are included as HTML Help. RealValidator is available for Windows 95/98/NT. HTML Help 1.1 requires MSIE 4.0 or greater. For more information on RealValidator, go to `http://arealvalidator.com`.

XML Instance

XML Instance from Tibco Software is a breakthrough product for schema-driven data editing that allows for the creation, editing, and management of data-oriented XML documents, messages, and configuration files. Users are able to edit and validate XML business documents conforming to a DTD or XML schema in any prominent XML schema dialect. XML Instance offers powerful capabilities for editing XML business documents, leading the way to corporate and industry standards for XML data management. Figure 17.8 shows how XML Instance validates the XML conforming to DTDs or schemas. For more information on XML Instance, go to `http://www.extensibility.com`.

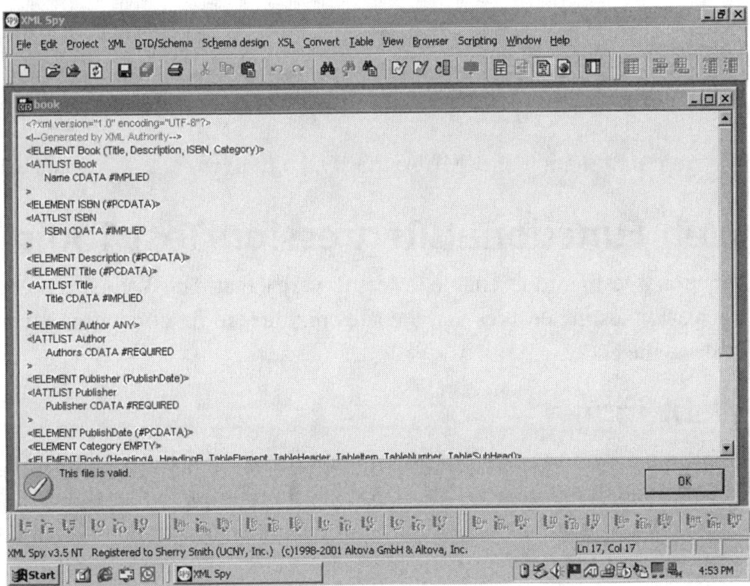

FIGURE 17.8
Overall view of XML Instance.

XML Authority

XML Authority from Tibco Software helps you see and build your schemas from a variety of different perspectives using a set of windows, panes, and menus. Each pane provides access to a different set of tools, and multiple windows may show information simultaneously, but all of them combine to present a consistent view of your schemas. The Element and Attributes panes help you lay the foundations of your schemas, describing the structure of your documents.

Figure 17.9 displays how XML Authority provides structure to XML schemas.

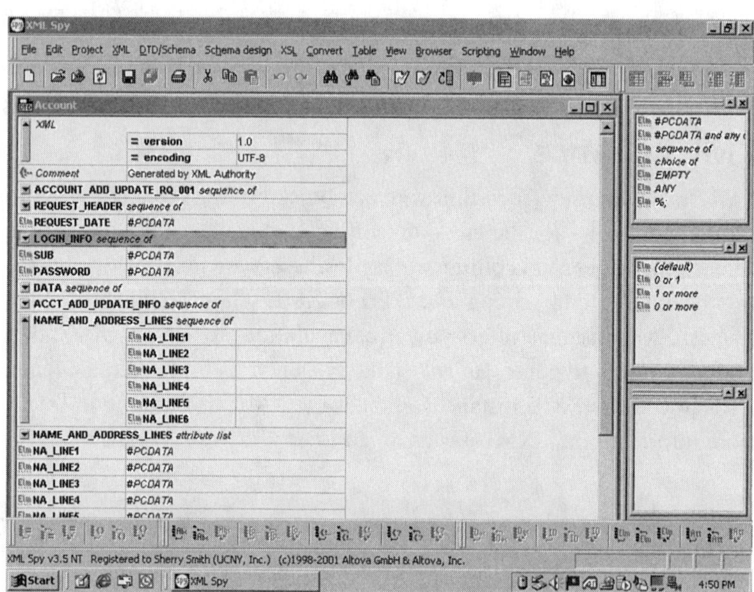

FIGURE 17.9
Overall view of XML Authority.

For more information on XML Authority, go to `http://www.extensibility.com`.

Web Functional/Regression Test Tools

Functional testing tools enable testers to verify that their Web site is operating properly. Regression testing ensures that the site continues to function after any changes have been made to the code.

WebKing

WebKing, a Web site test tool from ParaSoft, maps and tests all possible paths through a dynamic site. It enforces HTML, CSS, and JavaScript coding standards. It can be used to create rules for automatic monitoring of dynamic page content. It includes a publishing manager, a link checker, an HTML checker with custom rule selection, orphan file checking, and more. WebKing is available for Windows 95/98/2000/NT, Linux, and Solaris. For more information on WebKing or other ParaSoft products, go to `http://www.parasoft.com/products/index.htm`.

SilkTest

SilkTest is Segue's testing tool for functional and regression testing of Web, Java, or traditional client/server applications. This tool utilizes Segue's proprietary 4Test scripting language and works with HTML, JavaScript, ActiveX, Java, Windows 98 controls, Visual Basic, and C++. A recovery system that allows unattended tests to be run is also included. SilkTest works with Microsoft Internet Explorer and Netscape. For more information on SilkTest and other Segue products, go to `http://www.segue.com`.

Web Site Security Test Tools

The products discussed in this section help confirm that Web applications are secure.

SAINT (Security Administrator's Integrated Network Tool)

SAINT is a security testing service from World Wide Digital Security, Inc. The HTML interface includes TCP, UDP, and RPC service scans as well as Denial of Service Testing (DoS), which ensures the domain name has not been corrupted. Both general and customized reports can be generated. Single machine or full network scans are available. You can choose between a free version and the WebSaint paid version. For more information on SAINT, go to `http://www.wwdsi.com/saint/`.

Nmap Network Mapper

Nmap is a network audit and port scanning tool that utilizes various approaches and methods including TCP connect scanning, TCP SYN, TCP FIN, Xmas, or NULL scanning, SYN/FIN scanning using IP fragments, TCP ACK and Window scanning, direct (non-portmapper) RPC scanning, and Reverse-ident scanning. It supports several performance/reliability features including dynamic delay time calculations, packet timeout/retransmission, parallel port scanning, detection of down hosts via parallel `pings`, flexible target and port specification, and decoy scanning. Nmap works with most varieties of Unix. For more information on Nmap, go to `http://www.insecure.org`.

Secure Scanner

Secure Scanner is Cisco's product for detecting and reporting on Internet server and network vulnerabilities. It offers superior network system identification, pioneering data management, thorough security reporting capabilities, and Cisco's around-the-clock worldwide support. Secure Scanner is available for Windows NT or Solaris. For more information on Secure Scanner and other Cisco products, go to `http://www.cisco.com`.

NetRecon

NetRecon is a tool from Symantec for testing the vulnerability of network systems and resources from inside or outside the firewall. It exploits IP and non-IP-based protocols, generates HTML reports, carefully targets capabilities, and includes an Intruder Alert capability for around-the-clock monitoring. It probes any platform type. NetRecon runs on Windows NT. For more information on NetRecon and other Symantec products, go to `http://www.symantec.com`.

SATAN (Security Administration Tool for Analyzing Networks)

The SATAN Web security–testing tool includes a tutorial that explains all of the problems found, what their impact could be, and what can be done about them. Options include correcting errors in a configuration file, installing vendor bug fixes, using other means to restrict access, and disabling service. It also includes some links to related information. SATAN is available for Unix. For more information on this product, go to `http://www.fish.com/satan`.

External Site Monitoring Services

The sites discussed in this section test the Web site from an external source, monitoring the availability of the Web site as well examining its performance.

SiteAngel

SiteAngel Service from BMC Software continuously simulates and measures end-to-end customer web site experience. It compares the site's availability and performance to user-defined goals. For more information on SiteAngel and other BMC products, go to `http://www.bmc.com`.

Agilent Firehunter

Firehunter from Agilent Technologies is a service for monitoring, diagnosing, and managing Internet services. It includes performance testing, fault detection, and reporting. It supports a variety of platforms. For more information on Firehunter and other Agilent products, go to `http://www.firehunter.com`.

Atesto Automated Web Testing Service

Features of the Atesto Technologies testing service include the Automated Response Watch Service, which tracks performance of critical Web pages as well as multilayered business functions, and the Automated Load Test Service, which tests Web applications with an increasing number of concurrent users. Services are delivered via a distributed network of servers located in multiple locations across the U.S. that monitor performance over time. For more information on Atesto, go to `http://www.atesto.com`.

Web Site Management Tools

The tools described in this section aid in monitoring a Web site alerting the Webmaster when it is not working correctly.

IPCheck

IPCheck is a server-monitoring tool from Paessler Tools. It alerts Webmasters when the Web server is not working correctly, when the Web service is down, when CGI scripts return errors, and when the SQL server is not reachable. IPCheck analyzes the results and notifies the administrator when problems are identified. In addition, IPCheck can continuously monitor servers by attempting to connect through a `ping` command or through a specific port. It is available as shareware for Windows 95/98/NT. For more information on IPCheck and other Paessler Tools products, go to `http://www.web-server-tools.com`.

Rational Suite ContentStudio

ContentStudio combines software tools from Rational with Vignette's content management software for Web development team management, content and code version control, deployment control, and management. This tool integrates content and code control. For more information on Rational Suite Content Studio and other Rational products, go to `http://www.rational.com/products`.

Web Site Garage

Web Site Garage includes services for improving and maintaining Web sites. It automates site maintenance checks, optimizes graphics, and analyzes traffic. It is available as a free single-page on-the-Web tune-up or as a fee-based service for an entire site. Functionality includes Load Time Check, Dead Link Check, Link Popularity Check, Spell Check, HTML Check, and a Browser Compatibility check for 18 different browsers, platforms, and screen sizes. For more information on Web Site Garage, go to `http://websitegarage.netscape.com`.

WebSite Director

WebSite Director from CyberTeams, Inc. is a Web content workflow management system with a browser-based interface that includes configurable workflow management, e-mail submission of Web content, and e-mail notifications. It also allows defining and applying existing workflow and approval rules to the Web content management process. WebSite Director is available for Windows NT and Unix. For more information on WebSite Director, go to `http://www.cyberteams.com/`.

Other Web Test Tools

The tools discussed in this section do not fit into one of the specific categories mentioned previously, but are valuable tools nonetheless.

webfeedback

webfeedback is a Web decision support system from cyberware-neotek that combines a site's structure information and traffic information (log file analysis) and presents the combined results in full-color 3D. It also checks for problem incoming or outgoing links. It is available for Windows, Unix, and Macintosh. For more information on webfeedback, go to `http://www.cyberware-neotek.com`.

NetRaker Suite

NetRaker is a suite of usability testing and market research applications that provide real-time customer experience measurements and competitive comparisons. It gathers metrics through unobtrusive data sampling from site visitors. It provides usability and market research templates that enable you to perform competitive comparisons of sites. In addition, it monitors errors and download times across major metropolitan areas. For more information on the NetRaker Suite of products, go to `http://www.netraker.com`.

WebBug

WebBug is a debugging tool from Aman Software that monitors HTTP sends and receives, handles HTTP 0.9/1.0/1.1, and allows for entry of custom headers. You can enter a URL and WebBug displays exactly what is sent to the Web server and, when the response is received, exactly what the Web server sends back. It is available as freeware. For more information on Aman Software and WebBug, go to `http://www.cyberspyder.com`.

WebMetrics

WebMetrics is a Web usability testing and evaluation tool suite from the National Institute of Standards and Technology. It runs on Unix and Windows 95/NT and its source code is available. For more information on WebMetrics, go to `http://zing.ncsl.nist.gov/webmet/`.

Net.Medic

Net.Medic, the performance monitoring tool from VitalSoft, (a division of Lucent Technologies) assists in monitoring, isolating, and correcting bottlenecks, as well as isolating problems to the modem, ISP, backbone, or server. It can monitor the number of hops in connections, download rates, and server vs. network effects. It maintains metrics such as server availability, connection rates, and bytes transferred over time. The Net.Medic Pro version is geared toward Webmasters and ISPs, producing more detail and performing continuous monitoring. Net.Medic is available for Windows 95/98/NT. To find out more information on Net.Medic, go to `http://www.vitalsigns.com/netmedic/`.

Summary

In summation, testing J2EE software requires thorough knowledge of every aspect of multitiered Web applications. Planning is one of the most critical aspects of proper testing. Efficient debugging begins with your own train of thought.

If you experience a problem within your code, approach the problem in a methodical fashion. Understand what your program is supposed to do, read your code, find the problematic section of code, correct the offending code, and test the application. Approach problems as a learning experience. Everyone makes mistakes, so do not become discouraged. Grow as a developer or tester by not making the same mistake repeatedly.

Let technology assist in the testing. The tools mentioned in this chapter will help in debugging and analyzing the code. Use an automated tool to perform rigorous testing; this will enable you to allocate your resources for other tasks. With these tools and the testing techniques mentioned in this chapter, you should be on your way to more stable, readable code in no time. Improving testing techniques can have a lasting impact on the quality of the software and the image of the product.

CHAPTER 18

Making the Application Perform

In This Chapter

- Overview *606*
- Writing High-Performance Applications *607*
- Preparing for Performance Tuning *618*
- Guide to Diagnosis and Cure *621*
- What Affects Server Performance? *624*
- Database Monitoring and Tuning Tools *627*

Overview

The best approach to resolving performance and scalability problems is to avoid them in the first place, not to fix them after the project is developed. Performance and scalability are affected by two major factors: design and tuning.

These two issues involve two different areas of a project. The design phase is at the very beginning, and should be helped with the combination of project prototypes along with the skill and experience of the designers. People involved in the design should have experience building systems while avoiding the major pitfalls of a bad design. The tuning phase comes after the project has been developed. It is during this phase that you are able to tweak the performance of the project.

The first thing we need to discuss is what is meant by performance. Performance is considered the time that elapses between a client request and the moment a response is sent back. Throughput, another factor when discussing performance, is the number of client requests that are handled per second.

Both performance and throughput are important. To achieve high performance, you want to minimize the latency of your application while increasing throughput. In practical terms, subsecond response time is usually sufficient for Web systems. Acceptable throughput rates depend on the specific application; however, throughput of hundreds of e-commerce transactions per second is considered good.

Both latency and throughput define the performance of a system under a particular load. However, J2EE systems often operate under rapidly changing loads, at times coping with an influx of client requests numbering far greater than normal. The ability of the system to cope with such an increased load is called scalability.

Typically, system performance will degrade with an increased client load. In a poorly designed system that is confronted with an unexpectedly high load, latency may become unacceptably high while throughput falls sharply. An ideal system will maintain a constant latency regardless of the load level, while its throughput scales linearly with the load. While ideal systems don't exist, a well-designed system should scale well, maintaining low latency and high throughput under a wide range of loads.

J2EE was developed in part to help overcome shortages in developers' skill sets while still increasing productivity. One of the ways the technology achieves this is by hiding the complexity of application development from the developer, whether it's the garage collector hiding the complexity of memory management or the Enterprise JavaBeans container hiding the complexity of security and persistence. This convenience can often be detrimental to the performance of a J2EE application.

At their core, J2EE applications are Java programs that utilize a database. As such, J2EE applications are subject to the same performance principles that apply to traditional Java and database programming. Good coding techniques and efficient use of the database are a prerequisite for writing high-performance J2EE applications.

Writing High-Performance Applications

The following are key points to remember when designing a J2EE system:

- Prior experience pays off in the end. Hire a developer with a proven track record. Now that J2EE has been in use for over a year, there are qualified people available to help in the initial design of the project.
- Use an existing design pattern. There is a set of patterns available on the Sun Web site. Sun created actual system specifications or design patterns that can help in the initial creation of different Web applications. Using these patterns can help jump-start the design in the right direction.
- Understand operational requirements. Before a concrete design can be formed, requirements for security, availability, and performance should be considered.
    - Security—Determine the level of security that is required for the application. Factors such as application-level security (deployment descriptors, protection domains), network security, OS security, database security, and SAN zoning are all elements you need to consider in the design specification.
    - Availability—Determine the availability requirements for the system. Failure to meet these requirements can lead to loss of service as well as loss of user transactions. Platform reliability, application infrastructure stability, and uptime requirements must all be considered.
    - Performance—Determine response-time requirements, the expected peak-time total number of users, the number of concurrent connections, data growth rates, user-population growth rates, and storage capacity.

Sizing Factors

Another important consideration when designing an application is properly sizing the system. Key factors include

- User load—The greater the number of users accessing the system, the greater amount of hardware needed to satisfy the load. The future growth of the system should be taken into consideration; therefore, the user load should be sized greater than the expected number of users.

- Hardware requirements—The better the processor speeds, the fewer machines required; a slower processor will mean more machines will be required. Usually, cache design and memory bandwidth play a big role in determining how much extra performance is achieved, as processors are added to a server.
- Application requirements—The complexity of the system determines how much processing power is needed to run the application. If it is a simple order lookup application with a limited number of products, the application will be able to handle many requests with a given hardware. If the application will be processing many intense computations it will require more processing speed and hardware.

Performance Sizing

Once the information mentioned in the preceding sections has been gathered, a good estimate can be made about the type of performance the system will have with a particular hardware configuration. Most vendors have tools or information to help in sizing the hardware configuration needed for application performance. In addition, some guidelines that can be used are to determine performance on one machine by establishing the largest load that can be sustained with the known processing power. Also, decide how much performance can be gained by adding additional machines to the configuration. Looking at these factors in the design phase will only help in having a successful product deployment. Early discovery of problems or bottlenecks gives more time to resolve the underlying issue.

When dealing with a J2EE application, it is important to look at the different servers that are involved, including the application server and the database server. If the database server has great processing speed and lots of memory, it might be beneficial to have most of the processing completed on that server. This can be accomplished by utilizing stored procedures/packages to generate some of the application logic.

During the design phase, all the different pieces involved should be looked at, with an eye toward what piece is better suited for each particular process. Buying more and/or faster processors cannot always improve processing speed. The benefits of adding more machines often stops at a certain point, then the machines just sit idle as other parts of the systems are overwhelmed by the load. These limits are caused by bottlenecks between the system components and points of the connection.

Component Design

J2EE encourages the distribution of the logic of the system across several different components including servlets, JSP pages, entity beans, and session beans. Each component has different roles and responsibilities. J2EE leaves a lot to the developer regarding what code should be in each component. Components for a J2EE application fall into one of three areas:

- Presentation layer—Displays the results of the request. The function of this component is to display the results, not to process any business logic. Web browser and applets make up the presentation layer.
- Logic layer—Represents the core business logic. These components are the best candidates for reuse in many different applications within the project. This layer is commonly composed of JSP and servlets.
- Data layer—Controllers that contain the application data. Session beans typically make up this component but entity beans may also be used.

Figure 18.1 depicts the different components of the J2EE application. The data layer contains the EJB containers, the logic layer contains the JSP and servlets, and the presentation layer contains the applet and the application client.

FIGURE 18.1
J2EE components.

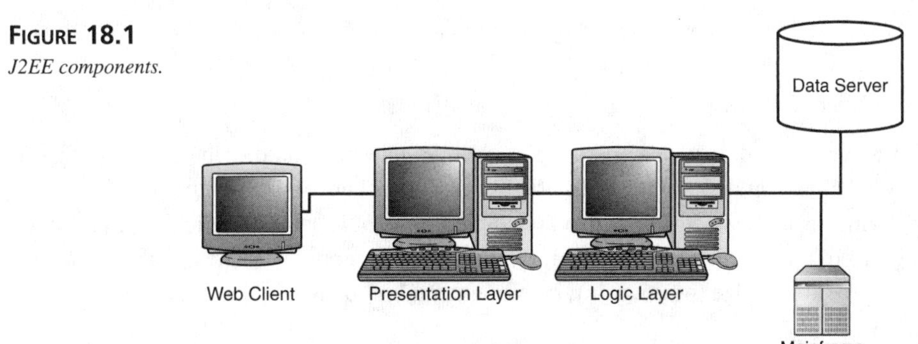

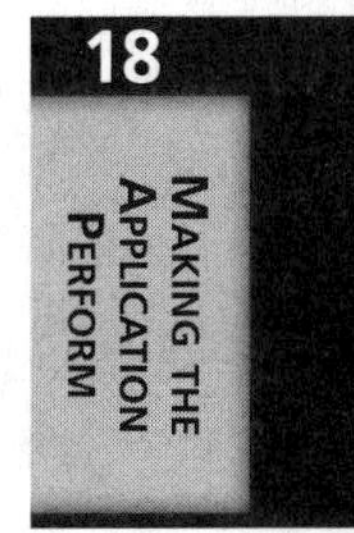

Poor Design Choices

Making the right choice at the right time is a basic factor in good design. This includes choices regarding both data structures and logic. For example, if you need to display a list of data, the type of display can be important. Factors may include the need to sort the data or having the data available for use by many different objects. Answers to such questions are essential in making proper design decisions. If the data needs to be sorted, you could sort the data on the database server. If many different objects will share the data, locking or synchronization should be considered.

When updating information that is shared, the timing of the database write lock needs to be considered, as no one else can use the table when the lock is on. All information should be processed before the database write lock is issued. For example, if information needs to be gathered from other tables before the update can be completed, read the data and process all the information first. At the last moment, issue the update to the shared information.

Environmental Factors

Understanding the underlying specifications of the application and environment it runs in is also essential to performance. These issues cannot necessarily be changed, but understanding them will help make the best of the situation. Key elements include

- Communication components such as speed and physical components of the network, access speed of disk storage, the bandwidth of input/output channels, requirements or limitations of purchased software, application server limitations, what database is used, and a version of the Java Virtual Machine
- The cost of switching environments and data transforms required between components
- Budget constraints

A broad understanding of the operating system, middleware and distributed computing in use will help when developing J2EE applications. This knowledge will help designers and architects to make design tradeoffs and build workable solutions. No system design is expected to be perfect the first time; therefore, it is important for the application team to have the knowledge to fix and find environmental problems.

Reducing Network Traffic

J2EE client applications may call EJBs directly. Each call involves a JNDI lookup and a network round-trip, both potentially causing heavy network traffic. When a J2EE client contains all the processing logic, it must perform multiple JNDI lookups and network round-trips to access the data presented by entity EJBs on the server.

This overhead can be reduced to a single lookup and round-trip if the processing logic is encapsulated in a single session bean instead. That bean, in turn, encapsulates all the entity beans that would otherwise be accessed directly by the J2EE client. In this case, a J2EE client acts as a rendering engine for the results contained in a single object returned by the session bean.

Coding Guidelines

Java is an interpreted language with a compact bytecode. Speed, or the lack of it, is often considered the main problem with Java applications. Coding techniques do affect the performance of J2EE applications, though not as much as database usage. Here are a few basic coding concepts to keep in mind when developing a J2EE application:

- Avoid unnecessary object creation. Current implementations of JVMs are much more efficient in managing object creation. Minimize object creation in commonly used functions. Creating objects costs time and CPU effort for an application; therefore, objects should be reused whenever possible.
- Presize any collection of objects. Most collection objects have similar implementations for growing the collection beyond its current capacity. Presizing a collection to its largest potential size reduces the number of objects discarded and cuts down the time needed to create new objects.
- Release all references to objects after the object has been used. Failure to release the object stops the garbage collector from reclaiming those objects. Nulling out references when finished with them makes the garbage collector's operation more efficient.
- Minimize the use of synchronization. Synchronization blocks reduce scalability of applications by forcing serialization of all concurrent threads of execution. It can also use up a large amount of resources from the JVM. For these reasons, synchronization blocks should be kept small and should be used only when absolutely needed. The same rule applies to using standard Java classes.
- Use static variables. When multiple instances of a class need to access a particular object in a variable local to those instances, using a static variable can reduce the space taken by each object while reducing the number of objects created. In other words, avoid having each instance create a separate object to populate an instance variable.
- Reuse exception instances when you do not specifically require a stack trace.
- Remove redundant calculations. Instead of writing

  ```
  double dmonthly = daypay * (numdays / daysinweek) * multiplier;
  double dmonthlybon = daypay * (numdays / daysinweek) + bonus;
  ```

  the common sub expression is calculated once and used for both calculations:

  ```
  double dpay = daypay * (numdays / daysinweek);
  double dmonthly = dpay * multiplier;
  double dmonthlybon = dpay * bonus;
  ```

Take all code that does not change in the loop and move it outside the loop. The following is an example of putting code that changes inside a `for` loop:

```
for (int j=0;j< larray.length;j++)
{
 larray[j] *=  y + x;
}
```

becomes

```
ltotal = y + x;
for (int j=0; j< larray.length; j++
   larray[j] *= ltotal;
```

- Produce content offline whenever possible. Instead of generating dynamic content, pre-cache static and dynamic HTML pages within an application server or Web server if the application is considered medium- to small-scale. With the JSP 1.1 implementation of the `BodyContent` class, the "out" or `JspWriter` object can buffer HTML to a user-defined string. At the implementation level, `pushBody()` and `popBody()` methods are used to control the "out" object.

  By default, JSP pages create a session even if your JSP pages are not using sessions. This can break down performance. Most pages served by JSP-based sites do not need to maintain sessions, yet they incur this overhead by default.

  If dynamic pages are served but there is no need to maintain session state, it is best to use a connection pooling mechanism that is optimized for short-duration, non-transactional, high-performance connections with limited synchronization-type behavior.

- Cache data at the object level. Use EJB entity beans to represent stateful persistent containers. In addition, consider using an application server for data access and caching, instead of a monolithic Web server that handles presentation, application, and data access processing.
- Use the most recent version of the applications or associated Java libraries (for example, SilverStream 3.7.2 from SilverStream). Newer versions usually have improved performance, and, in some cases, are more reliable.
- Put HTML content and HTTP logs on different disks. This will eliminate input/output(I/O) conflict, allowing these processes to work in parallel.
- Locate the processing logic in a session bean on the server. This will minimize the network overhead for J2EE clients.

Pool Management

Most container objects such as `Vectors` and `Hashtables` can be reused rather than created and thrown away. Of course, while these retained objects are not in use, more memory is being held onto than if those objects were simply discarded. This decreases the memory available to create other objects. A balance must be stricken between the need to have some free memory available and the need to improve performance by reusing objects. Generally, the space taken by retaining objects for later reuse is only a major factor for very large collections.

When recycling container objects, all the elements previously in the container should be de-referenced, otherwise they may not be garbage collected. Because extra overhead is involved in recycling, it may not always be worth recycling containers. As usual for tuning, this technique is best applied to eliminate an object-creation bottleneck that has already been identified.

A good strategy for reusing container objects is to use your own container classes, possibly wrapping other containers. This increases the control over collection objects, and these can be designed specifically for reuse. A pool manager can still be used to manage your requirements without reuse-designed classes. Although reusing classes requires extra work when you've finished with a collection object, the effort is often worth it. The following code fragment demonstrates use of a vector pool manager:


```
//An instance of the vector manager.
public static VectorManager vectorManager =
    new VectorManager(25);

...

public void someMethod( )
{
  //Get a new vector from the pool. Process information, then return the Vector
  //Use a factory method instead of 'new Vector( )'
  Vector v = vectorManager.getVector( );

  ... //Process information utilizing vector

  //tell the vector pool that you are done with the vector
  vectorManager.returnVector(v);
}
```

Note that nothing stops the application from retaining a handle on a vector after it has been returned to the pool, and obviously that could lead to a classic "inadvertent reuse of memory" bug. You need to ensure that handles to vectors are not held anywhere. Vectors should be used only internally within an application, not externally in third-party classes where a handle may be retained. The following class manages a group of vectors:

```
package tuning.reuse;

import java.util.Vector;
```

```
public class VectorManager
{

  Vector[] pool;
  boolean[] inUse;

  public VectorPoolManager(int initialPoolSize)
  {
    pool = new Vector[initialPoolSize];
    inUse = new boolean[initialPoolSize];
    for (int i = pool.length-1; i>=0; i--)
    {
      pool[i] = new Vector(  );
      inUse[i] = false;
    }
  }

  public synchronized Vector getVector(  )
  {
    for (int i = inUse.length-1; i >= 0; i--)
      if (!inUse[i])
      {
        inUse[i] = true;
        return pool[i];
      }

    //All the Vectors are in use.  Increase the number of vectors
    // in our pool by 5.
    boolean[] old_inUse = inUse;
    inUse = new boolean[old_inUse.length+5];
    System.arraycopy(old_inUse, 0, inUse, 0, old_inUse.length);

    Vector[] old_pool = pool;
    pool = new Vector[old_pool.length+5];
    System.arraycopy(old_pool, 0, pool, 0, old_pool.length);

    for (int i = old_pool.length; i < pool.length; i++)
    {
      pool[i] = new Vector(  );
      inUse[i] = false;
    }

    //and allocate the last Vector
    inUse[pool.length-1] = true;
    return pool[pool.length-1];
  }

  public synchronized void returnVector(Vector v)
  {
    for (int i = inUse.length-1; i >= 0; i--)
      if (pool[i] == v)
```

```
        {
          inUse[i] = false;
          //Can use clear( ) for java.util.Collection objects
          //Notice that setSize( ) nulls out all elements
          v.setSize(0);
          return;
        }
      throw new RuntimeException("Vector was not obtained from the pool: " + v);
    }
}
```

Because vector size is reset to `0` when it is returned to the pool, all objects previously referenced from the vector are no longer referenced. The `Vector.setSize( )` method nulls out all internal index entries beyond the new size to make certain no references are retained. All memory allocated to the vector is retained, because the current vector size is retained. A version of this class initialized using a lazy cache management strategy simply starts with zero items in the pool with the pool set to grow by one or more each time.

Many of the collection classes within the Java Developer Kit (JDK), including `java.util.Vector`, have both size and capacity attributes. Capacity refers to the number of elements the collection can hold before it needs a larger internal memory. The size refers to the number of externally accessible elements that the collection actually holds. The capacity is always greater than or equal to the size. When spare capacity is held, elements can be added to collections without the continuous need to resize the underlying memory resulting in faster and more efficient element addition.

J2EE Component Performance

Now that we have discussed general concepts of writing J2EE applications, let's look at specific performance tips for writing JSP pages, servlets, and EJBs.

A basic problem in application design is correctly deciding which object should contain the application logic. Many developers will put the code into the place they are most comfortable with, such as servlets. Choosing a particular component for this reason is a mistake. To resolve this issue, imagine that the system is not Web enabled. If the logic would be on the client side then it should be a servlet/JSP; if the logic is on the server side then it should be an EJB.

JSP Concepts

Even though JSP pages provide a sophisticated functionality built on top of servlets, the performance of JSP pages is generally comparable to that of servlets. JSP pages compile to servlets; compilation introduces a trivial amount of initialization code. Compilation happens only once and JSP pages can be precompiled, eliminating any runtime overhead.

JSP pages are slower than servlets only when returning binary data, since JSP pages always use a `PrintWriter`, whereas servlets can take advantage of a faster `OutputStream`.

Using JSP custom tag libraries can hide complex Java functionality from people who are unfamiliar with it, while enabling them to design Web pages. This allows work to be divided between Java programmers and Web designers. Adversely, the excessive use of custom tags may create unnecessary processing overhead, because it requires the Web container to retrieve the tag from the tag cache or create a new `Taghandler` object.

`BodyTags` are a special kind of custom tag with the ability to modify the content of their bodies. Using `BodyTags` causes the content between the start and end tag to be copied to memory. `BodyTags` can be nested and repeated over their bodies. Multiple levels of `BodyTags` combined with iteration will slow down the processing of the page considerably.

Servlet Performance Hints

The first factor in writing servlets for performance is to avoid the use of a `SingleThreadModel` interface, creating thread safe code instead. When using `SingleThreadModel`, the class container will create and cache numerous instances of the servlet class because the container is not thread safe. Several instances of the servlet class can be used at the same time. Marking a servlet with a `SingleThreadModel` does not certify thread-safety in an application. Several instances of the servlet class may access the same underlying classes and data at the same time. Multiple instances of the servlet incur major overhead for the Web container.

When the application returns ASCII data, you can use the `OutputStream`. This enables data to be written directly to the wire, thus skipping the character set conversion. In most cases the `PrintWriter` should be used to ensure that all character set conversions are done correctly.

The use of the `getRemoteHost()` method on a `ServletRequest` should be avoided. This method can dramatically increase the latency of your application. It performs a remote DNS lookup on the IP address of the client.

EJB Performance Hints

Session beans that update the database should be designed to prevent conflicts when updating the table. The easiest way to accomplish this is to lock the entire table when doing an update. On the other hand, this method incurs the greatest amount of overhead, reducing the scalability of the application. Instead, use of optimistic locking decreases the overhead and allows multiple updates to proceed in parallel, therefore improving the scalability of the system. Optimistic locking locks the database row when and only when the update is going to happen. Any processing of data or formatting of information should take place at the last possible moment. This will allow other users the ability to update the table at the same time. In some cases, when there are many collisions and the application spends a lot of time dealing with the failed updates the benefits of optimistic locking decreases.

Lazy loading of dependent EJBs can reduce the overhead of loading objects. In lazy loading, only the part of the EJB that is being used for the current process is loaded; otherwise, the whole EJB is loaded and taking up memory and only a small part of the object is being used. For example, suppose there is a Student Bean that refers to many different courses a student can take, and we're only interested in a computer course, not the identity of the student. Loading the Student Bean would be wasteful. Instead, we load the dependent beans only when they're actually needed.

Some application servers use optimistic locking and lazy loading internally in their container-managed persistence (CMP) implementations.

Design and Performance

Although good coding practices and efficient J2EE components are important for writing high-performance J2EE applications, application design can have a critical effect on application performance and scalability.

Read-only Web Applications

Many real-world J2EE applications such as knowledge base systems and catalogs provide read-only access to large sets of data. These applications handle a large number of queries from different users. Some of the query results are large, but all are processed quickly. Using entity EJBs is over-engineering for this type of application, as EJBs individually read each row of data and the server keeps the data in memory for a while. Instead, embedding SQL statements in JavaBeans to access the data will improve the performance of the read-only Web application.

Going from JSPs to the database without involving the EJB layer can significantly speed up the application. This approach is acceptable for read-only applications as well as those with little processing logic. This approach is not compatible with applications containing complex processing or update transactions.

Infrequently Changing Shared Data

In another type of application, a small subset of infrequently changing data is shared. A typical example of such application functionality is a list of top stories or most popular items on a shopping site. Stateless session EJBs can be used to efficiently cache and manage such data.

There are three types of objects involved in this scenario: stateless session EJBs that access and store the data; clients, such as JSPs, that use this data; and a special remote `Cursor` class that's owned by the client and used to keep track of which rows were read by that client.

To cache the data, the session EJB performs an SQL query in its `ejbCreate()` method, reads the results, and stores the individual rows as elements in a `ListArray`. To read a row of data, clients execute a business method, `readNextRow()`, on that session EJB. However, different clients need to access different rows stored by that session bean. To do that, clients pass in a special `Cursor` object that holds the number of the last row read by that client. The session bean uses that number to find the next row to give to the client. It then increments the row counter inside the `Cursor` before returning the row. A more efficient implementation results if the client manages the row number inside the `Cursor`.

To prevent the data from going stale, `readNextRow()` must implement a refresh mechanism. Data can be refreshed after it's been accessed a certain number of times. Alternatively, data can be refreshed after it's been cached for a certain amount of time.

Preparing for Performance Tuning

It is important to be properly prepared to tune the performance of an application. This project should include the following tasks:

- Establish performance improvement scope, objectives, and metrics.
- Load test the Web application.
- Profile the core application to discover hotspots.
- Perform a code review and make alternative construct recommendations.
- Compare/contrast version statistics.

Scope, Objectives, and Metrics

The objectives of the project are usually straightforward: Reduce overall average Web access time and improve performance. However, the scope might include only the home page, a certain page or all pages served. Typically, new versions of a Web application are characterized by increases in the HTML bytes per page as designers become more creative. These opposing forces should be factored into the expectations of improved performance within the new version of the application. It is also important to establish performance metrics after an application is completed in order to benchmark against previous versions.

Load Testing

It is important to determine whether any performance problems are being caused by connectivity to the ISP, the network, the HTTP server, the application server, or the DBMS as soon as possible. To discover the offending layer, load-testing tools such as Microsoft's WAS tool, Optimizeit, or custom load tests based on shell scripts should be utilized. These tools are critical for gaining an understanding of the environment.

Statistics such as Total Bytes Sent, Bytes Sent Rate, Total Bytes Received, Bytes Received Rate, or Average Number of HTML Bytes Per Page, captured through use of a tool, can be very helpful (see Table 18.1). However, response time ultimately comes down to average TTLB (Time To Last Byte) for a page.

TABLE 18.1 Useful Statistics

Measurement Attribute	*Measurement*
Average Number of HTML	In Bytes
Minimum Number of HTML	In Bytes
Maximum Number of HTML	In Bytes
Average Time To Last Byte (TTLB)	In Milliseconds
Minimum TTLB	In Milliseconds
Maximum TTLB	In Milliseconds
Average TTLB (without Secure Socket Layer)	In Milliseconds
Average time for SSL = TTLB-(TTLB without SSL)	In Milliseconds
Response Count	Number of calls with X users

Load testing a Web application from inside and outside the firewall can quickly rule out whether performance problems are application-bound or possibly related to firewall configurations to an ISP. If the performance bottleneck appears to be outside the firewall, using the same TCP Maximum Transmission Unit (MTU) as your ISP is recommended. If the application is communicating in the same size packets as the ISP, less time will be spent splitting packets or putting them back together.

In addition, look for excessive TCP retransmits, and, if possible, turn up the TCP retransmit timeout. Many servers are tuned for the small latency of a LAN and perform poorly on the Internet as a result. Also turn off reverse DNS lookups in the Web server; reverse

DNS slows the server down if it is done for each request. Once these types of things are tuned, you can then turn to the application.

Profilers

The JDK comes with a built-in profiler to help tell how time is spent in a program. The profiler will write the file java.prof displaying how much time is spent in each routine. To invoke the profiler, use the `-prof` option when invoking the Java interpreter

```
java -prof TestClass
```

or executing an applet

```
java -prof sun.applet.AppletViewer TestApplet.html
```

There are some pitfalls for using this profiler. Foremost, the output is not easy to read. Sun no longer includes documentation for the `-prof` option; however, you can use third party tools to interpret the results.

It is also possible to "profile" code by inserting explicit timing within the code, as in the following example:

```
long start = System.currentTimeMillis();
// Insert code to be tracked here****
long time = System.currentTimeMillis() - start;
```

`System.currentTimeMillis()` returns time in 1/1000ths of a second. Some systems including Windows PCs have system timers with less resolution than a 1/1000th of a second. In addition, often times 1/1000th of a second isn't long enough to accurately time many operations. In these cases, or on systems with low-resolution timers, it may be necessary to time how long it takes to repeat the operation *n* times and then divide the total time by *n* to get the actual time. This technique can be useful for timing specific tasks or operation even when profiling is available.

Here are a few closing notes on profiling:

- Always time the code before and after making any changes to ensure that your changes have improved the program, at least on the test platform.
- Generate test timings under identical conditions, such as the same time of day and same workflow. Test with the same user input. Script the test, as variations in the user input can cause the results to fluctuate, resulting in inaccurate timings.

Application Profiling

If load testing indicates that performance problems are related to the Web environment, the development team should become familiar with Java profiling tools, such as JProbe from Sitraka Software (formerly KL Group), Optimizeit from VMGEAR, and NuMega DevPartner from Compuware Corp. These tools can be used to analyze JSP pages, servlets, and Java application servers. Profiling tools allows for quick understanding of an application and immediately point out hotspots in the application code. In addition, timing code does not have to be placed within the application to gain performance instrumentation functionality.

At the bare minimum, profiling an application includes CPU utilization and elapsed time analysis as well as heap analysis. When hotspots are detected, a code review should be performed to walk through the offending construct with the creator. Some common application performance issues are memory leaks, too much memory allocation, and inefficient algorithms.

Java server-side computing performance problems can range from excessive use of `String` classes for concatenation, which can be replaced with a singular `StringBuffer` and `String` object, to excessively synchronized connection pools, which might have been engineered for OLTP rather than OLAP-type data access. These types of issues can be detected easily using a profiling tool.

Code Review

Based on profiling and code reviews, alternative coding constructs or technologies should be evaluated. Service Level Agreements (SLAs), audience analysis, and business requirements should be taken into consideration when determining how much advanced technology or engineering is warranted. For example, performance solutions, such as JSP/HTML page caching, changing thread scheduling policy, asynchronous processing, and so on, are not necessarily trivial extensions to an application.

Compare and Contrast Version Statistics

Take the time to archive performance reports at the page level by version to ensure that you are making progress. Remember, having to re-create previous versions of the applications by reinstalling the environment is never a productive use of time.

Guide to Diagnosis and Cure

There are three general levels of problems:

- Obvious problems that are easy to deal with (low-hanging fruit).
- Poor application design.
- Environmental problems that stem from the *physics* of the situation. This term refers to things that cannot be changed directly.

One feature of performance problems to continually bear in mind is that as one set of problems is resolved, additional issues may be created. This commonly occurs when the additional problems were masked by the first problem. When fixing performance problems, a full system test should be performed to ensure that the changes have not corrupted other parts of the application. You might find yourself revisiting each of the layers as you solve performance problems.

In addition, the exact approach of resolving performance problems might vary from problem to problem. In one situation, starting from the low hanging fruit to the top might work best; other times starting with the physics and the application design may be most beneficial.

Low-Hanging Fruit

Problems stemming from low-hanging fruit are often the easiest to find and fix. They are frequently caused in the implementation of the program. Problems here may range from fairly simple language misuse to outright bugs. The solution to these performance problems is often a simple substitution (a better algorithm, a more appropriate utility object) without changing the overall application structure or design.

Deployment Strategies

Just as application design and coding techniques determine the performance of the resulting systems, the manner in which an application is deployed has an effect as well:

- If possible, run the Web server and the application server in the same process. Separating the two can notably increase the response time of your application.
- Cluster machines to increase scalability. As long as your application doesn't require the servers in your cluster to communicate with each other, adding more servers keeps latency low while increasing throughput.
- Provide more than an adequate set of resources needed to run an application. Set a sufficient size for the JVM's heap, enough database connections, and reasonable size for the thread, servlet, and bean pools. Failure to provide sufficient resources results in contention and severely degrades application performance. Conversely, unreasonably high resource settings will degrade performance as well. For example, if the heap size is larger than the physical memory available, the JVM will thrash instead of doing useful work. In the same way, if the size of the database connection pool is greater than the number of available connections, the application will spend a lot of time dealing with perceived database failures.

Improving Applet Download Speed

Applet download performance is the time required for the browser to download all the files and resources needed to start the applet. A key factor affecting an applet's download performance is the number of times data must be requested from the server. Packaging the applet images into one class file or using Java Archive (JAR) files can drastically reduce that number of requests.

Packaging Images into One Class

If an applet has six images, normally that means six additional requests sent back to the Web server to load those image files. This might not seem like a lot on a local area network, but you have to think about lesser connection speeds and reliability, so those six downloads might have a huge impact. The ultimate goal is to load the applet as quickly as possible.

Using JAR Files

When an applet consists of more than one file, you can improve download performance with Java Archive (JAR) files. A JAR file contains all of the files related to an applet in a single file, leading to faster downloading. Much of the time saved stems from the reduced number of HTTP connections made by the browser.

The following HTML code uses the `CODE` tag to specify the executable for the `TestApplet` applet, and the `ARCHIVE` tag to specify the JAR file that contains all of `TestApplet`'s related files. The executable specified by the `CODE` tag is often known as the code base.

For security reasons the JAR files listed by the archive parameter must be in the same directory or a subdirectory as the applet's codebase. If no codebase parameter is given, the directory from where the applet was loaded will be used as the codebase.

The following example specifies `jarfile` as the JAR file that contains the related files for the `TestApplet.class` executable:

```
<APPLET CODE="TestApplet.class" ARCHIVE="jarfile" WIDTH="100" HEIGHT="200">
</APPLET>
```

If the applet download uses multiple JAR files as shown in the following example, the ClassLoader loads each JAR file when the applet starts. So, if your applet uses some resource files infrequently, the JAR file containing those infrequently used files is downloaded, regardless of whether the resources are actually used during that session or not:

```
<APPLET CODE="TestApplet.class" ARCHIVE="jarfile1, jarfile2" WIDTH="100"
HEIGHT="200"> </APPLET>
```

When an applet has infrequently used files, performance can be improved by putting the frequently used files into the JAR file and the infrequently used files into the applet class directory. Infrequently used files are then located and downloaded by the browser only when necessary.

Thread Pooling

The term *database thread pooling* refers to establishing a ready supply of sleeping database threads at the beginning of application execution. The thread creation process is considered the most expensive in terms of system resources. Generation of threads makes the startup process a litter slower, but improves runtime performance because sleeping (or suspended) threads are awakened only when they are needed to perform new tasks.

Thread pooling is an effective performance-tuning technique that puts the expensive thread startup process at the startup of an application. Using this method, any negative impact on performance occurs only once—at program startup where it is least likely to be noticed.

What Affects Server Performance?

To improve performance, you must first understand what server resources are used for and how they collectively affect server performance. In trying to measure the response time for a database access within an application, focus on the time that it takes for a query to be sent from the client to the database server, execute the necessary query, and return the result to the client. We can summarize the major resources that affect the server performance in the following list:

- Central Processing Unit (CPU)
- Volatile Storage (Memory)
- Persistent Storage (Disk)

Central Processing Unit (CPU)

The CPU component controls the entire application process. The CPUs processing speed greatly affects performance. There are many standard measures of relative CPU speed. The two most common are millions of instructions per second (MIPS) and millions of floating operations per second (MFLOPS).

Volatile Storage (Memory)

With the relatively low cost-to-benefit ratio of memory, making an extra investment in more memory up front will pay great dividends in the future. Memory becomes an important factor for performance either when the system does not have enough of it or it is dedicated to an unused type of processing. Performance is greatly enhanced when you have an ample amount of memory.

Persistent Storage (Disk)

Disk storage is where all the database information, or data, will reside. Disk storage consists of one or more magnetic plates, or platters accessed by one or more read/write heads. In the case of multiple heads and platter devices, the data is stored across magnetic surfaces in what is commonly known as cylinders. Disk manufactures can provide statistics for access time and comparisons of other disk storage mechanisms.

Database Performance

Database implementations can be huge, containing thousands of tables and millions of rows of data. Poor database design in any application can drastically affect performance. Keep the following points in mind when architecting the database portion of the application.

Avoid Multiple Table Joins

Every join affects the amount of work the database has to do to execute an SQL statement. Multiple table joins degrade the performance of an application once the data set becomes sufficiently large. You may not notice the performance hit on a development system because the volume of data is low, but in production the problem will manifest. Make sure any multi-table joins your application uses are really necessary.

Return Only the Data Needed

Bringing back small resultsets will speed up user display. Large sets of data will cause the server to spend an inordinate amount of resources and time storing them in memory. If you absolutely have to bring back such a large data set, consider bringing back just the primary keys first and fetching individual rows on demand. This approach doesn't reduce the total amount of work; instead, spreading it out, greatly reducing the immediate response time.

Cache Data When Reuse Is Likely

Since accessing a database is by far the most expensive operation an application server can perform, the number of such accesses should be minimized. In particular, if an application frequently refers to a certain subset of values from the database, those values should be cached.

Reduce the Number of Database Calls

Utilizing the ability stored procedures/packages have to group SQL statements and control-of-flow into one object improves the performance of the database. The objects are stored in the database, and the SQL is parsed and optimized. An execution plan is prepared and cached when a procedure is run so that subsequent execution is very fast.

Connection Pools

Use connection pools to reuse existing network connections. Bandwidth restrictions of networks worldwide make network-based operations potential bottlenecks that can have a significant impact on an application's performance. Use of connection pools permits reuse of existing network connections, therefore saving time and overhead invested in opening and closing network connections.

Adjust the Checkpoint Behavior

The checkpoint process writes out dirty pages, or those that have been modified since being brought into the buffer cache, to the SQL server data files. A buffer written to disk by checkpoint still contains the page, and user can read or update it without rereading it from the disk. If this option is set to high, excessive disk queuing will occur. You can adjust the checkpoint behavior by using the `sp_configure` option. `sp_configure` is a system stored procedure that displays or changes global configuration settings for the current server.

Adjust the Lazy Writer

The lazy writer's job is to free up cache buffers. These are 8KB data pages in the cache that contain no data. Each freed-up page is marked so that it can be used by other data. If this option is set to high, it will cause excessive disk queuing. The lazy writer can be adjusted by using the `sp_configure` option.

Partition Tables

Partitioning a database can improve performance. When you split a large table into smaller, individual tables, queries accessing only a fraction of the data will run faster.

Such tasks as index rebuilds or backup will execute quicker. You can partition your database by placing a table on one physical drive and related tables on a separate drive.

Partition Hardware

Building hardware to take advantage of multiprocessors and Redundant Array of Independent Disks (RAID) can improve the performance of the application. With a multiprocessing machine more than one query can be processed at one time. The RAID device allows data to be striped across multiple disk drives, permitting faster access to data because more read/write heads read the data at the same time. Storing tables on separate drives from related tables can significantly improve the performance of queries joining those tables.

Index Implementation

An index is a set of nodes or pages that contain index keys and pointers arranged in a hierarchy implemented through what is known as a B+ tree. The index pages contain only data from columns that make up a particular index. So, if a query is selecting rows from a table that has a `where` clause on an indexed column equal to a set of values, then the database server will read the index pages for that column and match them to the specified set of values. The choice of indexes will significantly affect the performance of the queries. Create an appropriate number of indexes; too few or too many may hurt performance. Use database tools to ascertain the correct number of indexes for your application.

Database Monitoring and Tuning Tools

The following are several tools provided by third-party software vendors that will prove invaluable when dealing with application performance.

ShowPlan (SQL Server) or Explain Plan (Oracle)

A query ShowPlan/Explain Plan displays information about what the query optimizer is doing. The report will display what indexes are being used and what path the query plan is taking to resolve the request. Using this information to optimize the SQL will greatly improve the processing speed of the application. These commands are Transact-SQL statements executed from the SQL prompt. Here is an example of the `SHOWPLAN` command:

```
SET SHOWPLAN ALL ON
```

INDEX Tuning Wizard

SQL Profiler is a graphical tool that allows system administrators to monitor events in an instance of Microsoft SQL Server. It captures and saves information about each event to analyze later.

Oracle Tuning Pack

This package automates some of the performance-increasing tasks normally handled by highly skilled consultants. The tool learns about systems and advises on where to automatically tune for optimal performance.

Oracle SQL_TRACE

This product writes a Trace File containing performance statistics for the SQL statements being executed. These include the number of parses, executes, and fetches performed; various types of CPU and elapsed times; the number of physical and logical reads performed; the number of rows processed; and the number of library cache misses. This tool provides valuable information that can be used to improve your system. More information on Oracle tuning can be found on the Oracle Web site: `http://technet.oracle.com`.

Optimizeit

The profiling solution for Java developers is to locate and fix performance issues including memory leaks and performance bottlenecks in Java applications, applets, beans, servlets, EJB, JSP, and so on. Optimizeit instantly integrates with most popular application servers. The overhead limiting features ensure scalability, and offline profiling allows testing of applications in production environments. It supports Win95/NT, Solaris, and Linux.

Optimizeit has two main components:

- The Optimizeit user interface—A window that displays profiles and controls for refining the profiles and viewing source code
- The Optimizeit audit system—A real-time detective that reports the activity on the Java Virtual Machine back to the Optimizeit user interface

Summary

Low-level optimizations in Java can increase the speed of your code. Frequently, the awareness of which operations are time consuming is enough to avoid problems in the first place. If it's necessary to optimize your code, make sure to follow a few simple guidelines:

- Don't optimize unless you know it's necessary.
- If you do need to optimize, start with the algorithm.
- Before you optimize the low-level operation of your code, profile or time the existing code to determine where the time is being spent.
- Profile the code again afterwards to see what effect any changes had.

All the suggestions mentioned above can be attempted with the goal of better application performance; however, often the bottom line is time to market—How fast does the application need to be built for the business? You need to weigh the different factors and decide what is most important for the project, including what factors need to be taken care of up front and what can be worked on as the project is being used. This is an important concern because if the competition beats you to market you may never recover.

CHAPTER 19

Deploying the Application

In This Chapter

- Java's Write Once, Run Anywhere Promise *632*
- The Assembly Process *633*
- The Deployment Process *648*

This chapter covers the various steps involved with assembling and deploying a J2EE application to an application server. It starts by discussing Java's *Write Once, Run Anywhere (WORA)* aspects and then covers the assembly phase of packaging J2EE applications into the relevant archive types. The chapter will also look at the content and role of XML deployment descriptors and the way that resource references are resolved at runtime. Finally, the chapter covers some of the deployment tools for featured J2EE application servers.

Java's Write Once, Run Anywhere Promise

From the very beginning, Sun created Java as a platform-neutral language. To achieve this, Java programs run inside the Java Virtual Machine (JVM) instead of directly on a physical machine like many other programs. As long as a compliant JVM exists for the platform that you want to run on, you will be able to use the same Java application. In other words, there are no "Mac" or "Windows" versions of a Java application.

That, at least, is the underlying premise of Java. Java is still an evolving and expanding language. With the J2EE release, Java is just now beginning to provide the functionality that designers, developers, and users need for building scalable and modular enterprise applications. As more organizations use the Java platform, the number of problems will presumably decrease, while functionality, stability, and performance continue to increase. Java's Write Once, Run Anywhere capabilities mean that computers that run Java applications should be able to work together to do what is required, regardless of the hardware or software vendors involved.

According to the Write Once, Run Anywhere promise, when a J2EE-compliant application is developed and deployed to a specific J2EE application server, it can be redeployed to another J2EE-compliant application server without any rewriting of code. The switch to another J2EE application server platform may become necessary for a variety of reasons. There may be a performance gain on the new platform, or the company may standardize on a particular vendor and want to switch all applications to a new platform.

Although there are no code changes required during a transition, there are still some changes that need to take place to allow a J2EE application to be deployed to the new J2EE platform. This chapter will cover the assembly and deployment phases, which include the changes required to deploy an application to another J2EE platform.

The Assembly Process

The following section describes how to package J2EE applications and components.

Assembly Overview

J2EE applications and components are packaged in a standard way, defined by the J2EE specifications. J2EE defines component behaviors and packaging in a generic, portable way, postponing runtime configuration until the component is actually deployed on an application server. Figure 19.1 shows the various file types that are required during the assembly and deployment phases.

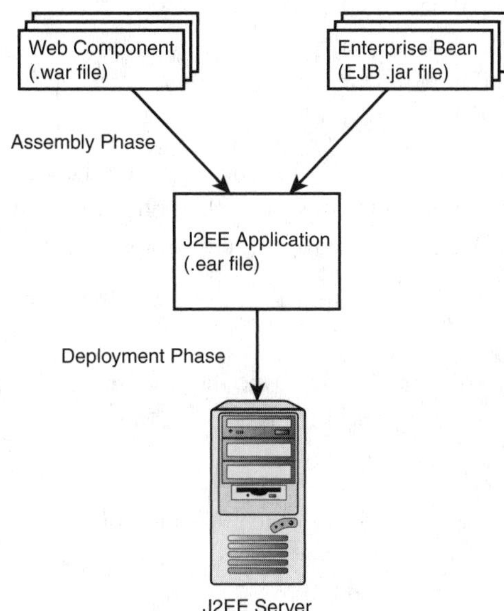

FIGURE 19.1
J2EE assembly and deployment phases.

J2EE includes deployment specifications for Web applications, EJB modules, Enterprise applications, and Client applications. J2EE does not specify how an application is deployed on the target server—only how a standard component or application is packaged.

For each component type, the specifications define the files required and their location in a directory structure. Applications and components can include Java classes for EJBs and servlets, JSP, HTML and supporting files, XML-formatted deployment descriptors, and additional JAR files containing other components.

Assembling Applications and Components

There are several types of J2EE archive files that are used when packaging a J2EE application or component. The archive file is a single file that contains one or more files.

This is very similar to a ZIP or TAR formatted file. Let's now take a look at the role of the deployment descriptors for J2EE archive files before examining each of these file types in turn and discussing how to create and populate each one.

Deployment Descriptors

Deploying Web applications requires you to create a deployment descriptor, named web.xml, for each Web application. Deployment descriptors define components and operating parameters for a Web application. Deployment descriptors are standard text files that are formatted using XML notation and packaged within the Web application. The deployment descriptor is used to deploy a Web application on any J2EE-compliant application server.

This section lists the steps you should follow in order to create the web.xml deployment descriptor. Depending on the components in your Web application, you may not need to include all of the elements listed here to configure and deploy it:

1. Using a text editor, create the web.xml file in the WEB-INF directory of the Web application.
2. Add the Document Type Definition (DTD) to the first line of the file:
   ```
   <!DOCTYPE web-app PUBLIC "-//Sun Microsystems, Inc.
   //DTD Web Application 2.2//EN"
   "http://java.sun.com/j2ee/dtds/web-app_2_2.dtd">
   ```
3. Add the opening and closing `<web-app>` tags. All subsequent elements must be added within the following tags:
   ```
   <web-app>
   </web-app>
   ```
4. Add the optional deployment-time attribute definitions. These attributes provide information to the deployment or resource management tools for the application server. This information defines the small and large icons and name to be displayed by GUI tools. There is also a tag to place descriptive text about the application. The distributable tag indicates that this Web application is suitable for deployment to a distributed servlet container. Here are attributes that you can define:

```
<small-icon>
   iconfile.gif
</small-icon>
<large-icon>
   iconfile.gif
</large-icon>
<display-name>
   application name
</display-name>
<description>
   description
</description>
<distributable/>
```

5. Define the servlets. To do this, you will need to give the servlet a name, specify the servlet class file or JSP that implements the servlet, and set the servlet-specific properties. You must list each of the servlets in the WAR file within separate `<servlet>` tags. Table 19.1 lists and describes the servlet tags.

TABLE 19.1 Servlet Tags in the web.xml File

Tag	*Description*
`<servlet>`	
`<small-icon>` `name` `</small-icon>` `<large-icon>` `name` `</large-icon>`	This is the location within the application for small and large icon images. The image file can be either .gif or .jpg format.
`<servlet-name>` `name` `</servlet-name>`	`<servlet-name>` contains the name of the servlet, which is used to reference the servlet definition elsewhere in the deployment descriptor.
`<display-name>` `Servlet Name` `</display-name>`	This tag contains a short name used by GUI tools.
`<description>` `descriptive text` `</description>`	This tag contains a description of the servlet.

TABLE 19.1 continued

Tag	Description

`<servlet-class>`
`package.name.MyClass`
`</servlet-class>`
-or-
`<jsp-file>`
`/foo/bar/myFile.jsp`
`</jsp-file>`
	This tag is the fully qualified class name of the servlet or the full path to a JSP file within the Web application, relative to the root directory. You can specify either the `<servlet-class>` tags or `<jsp-file>` tags in the servlet body, but not both.

`<init-param>`
`<param-name>`
`name`
`</param-name>`
`<param-value>`
`value`
`</param-value>`
`<description>`
`descriptive text`
`</description>`
`</init-param>`
	Initialization parameters can be accessed within the servlet using the `javax.servlet.ServletContext.getInitParameter()` and `javax.servlet.ServletContext.getInitParameterNames()` methods.

`<load-on-startup>`
`loadOrder`
`</load-on-startup>`
	This tag is optional. The contents of this element must be a positive integer indicating the order in which the servlet should be loaded. Lower integers are loaded before higher integers. If no value is specified, or if the value specified is not a positive integer, the application server can load the servlet in any order in the startup sequence.

`<security-role-ref>`
`<description>`
`descriptive text`
`</description>`
	`<security-role-ref>` is used to link a security role name defined by `<security-role>` to an alternative role name that is coded within the servlet

TABLE 19.1 continued

Tag	Description
`<role-name>` `rolename` `</role-name>` `<role-link>` `rolelink` `</role-link>` `</security-role-ref>`	`<role-name>` defines the name of the security role or principal that is used in the servlet code and `<role-link>` defines the name of the security role that is defined in a `<security-role>` element found later in the deployment descriptor.

6. Map a servlet to a URL. Once you declare your servlet or JSP using a `<servlet>` element, map it to one or more URL patterns to make it a public HTTP resource. For each mapping, use a `<servlet-mapping>` element:

```
<servlet-mapping>
     <servlet-name>
        name
     </servlet-name>
     <url-pattern>
        pattern
     </url-pattern>
</servlet-mapping>
```

7. Define the optional session timeout value. This tag defines the default session time-out interval (in minutes) for all sessions created in this Web application:

```
<session-config>
     <session-timeout>
        minutes
     </session-timeout>
</session-config>
```

8. Define optional welcome pages. These are pages that will be executed if the application is specified without an explicit page:

```
<welcome-file-list>
     <welcome-file>
        myWelcomeFile.jsp
     </welcome-file>
</welcome-file-list>
```

9. Define the error pages (optional). These elements contain a mapping between an HTTP error code (404, for example) or exception type to the path of a resource in the Web application:

```
<error-page>
      <error-code>
         HTTP error code
      </error-code>
      -or-
      <exception-type>
         Java exception class
      </exception-type>
      <location>URL</location>
</error-page>
```

10. Define the MIME mapping (optional). These elements define a mapping between an extension (for example, "txt") and a mime type (for example, "text/plain"):

```
<mime-mapping>
      <extension>
         ext
      </extension>
      <mime-type>
         mime type
      </mime-type>
</mime-mapping>
```

11. Define a JSP tag library descriptor (optional). These elements are used to describe a JSP tag library that is in use within the Web application. The `taglib-uri` describes a URI, relative to the web.xml file, that identifies the tag library. The `taglib-location` element is the location (relative to the Web application root) of the tag library descriptor (TLD) file:

```
<taglib>
      <taglib-uri>
         string_pattern
      </taglib-uri>
      <taglib-location>
         filename
      </taglib-location>
</taglib>
```

12. Reference external resources (optional). These tags declare the Web application's reference to external resources. The `<res-ref-name>` tag specifies the name of the resource factory reference name. The `<res-type>` tag specifies the type of the resource. The `<res-auth>` tag indicates whether the authentication is performed

programmatically (SERVLET) or must be performed by the container (CONTAINER), which uses information specified by the deployer at deployment time:

```
<resource-ref>
     <res-ref-name>
        name
     </res-ref-name>
     <res-type>
        Java class
     </res-type>
     <res-auth>
        CONTAINER | SERVLET
     </res-auth>
</resource-ref>
```

13. Set up the security constraints (optional). A Web application can be set up to require that the user log in. The user ID and password are verified against a security realm, and if authorized, the user will gain access to the secured resources within the application. This security feature is configured using the <login-config>, <security-constraint>, and <security-role> tags.

    The <security-constraint> tag specifies the access privileges to a set of resources defined by their URL mapping:

```
           <security-constraint>
     <web-resource-collection>
              <web-resource-name>
                 name
              </web-resource-name>
              <description>
                 descriptive text
              </description>
              <url-pattern>
                 pattern
              </url-pattern>
              <http-method>
                 GET | POST
              </http-method>
     </web-resource-collection>
     <auth-constraint>
          <role-name>
             groupname | principalname
          </role-name>
     </auth-constraint>
```

```
    <user-data-constraint>
        <description>
          descriptive text
        </description>
        <transport-guarantee>
          NONE | INTEGRAL | CONFIDENTIAL
        </transport-guarantee>
    </user-data-constraint>
</security-constraint>
```

14. Set up login authentication. The `<login-config>` tag determines how the user will be prompted to log in and sets the location of the security realm. When this tag is specified, the user must be authenticated in order to access a resource that has a `<security-constraint>` defined for it:

```
<login-config>
    <auth-method>BASIC | FORM | CLIENT-CERT</auth-method>
    <realm-name>
      realmname
    </realm-name>
    <form-login-config>
        <form-login-page>
          URI
        </form-login-page>
        <form-error-page>
          URI
         </form-error-page>
    </form-login-config>
</login-config>
```

15. Define security roles. These tags define a group or principal in the security realm. This name is placed in the `<security-constraint>` tag (see step 13) and can also be linked to by the alternative role name used in servlet code via the `<security-role-ref>` element (refer back to Table 19.1 and the discussion of servlet tags):

```
<security-role>
    <description>
      descriptive text
    </description>
    <role-name>
      rolename
    </role-name>
</security-role>
```

16. Set environment entries. These tags declare and define an application's environment variables. The `<env-entry-name>` tag contains the name of an application's environment variable. The `<env-entry-value>` tag contains the value of the environment varible. The `<env-entry-type>` tag contains the fully qualified Java type of the environment variable code. The type can be `java.lang.Boolean`, `java.lang.String`, `java.lang.Integer`, `java.lang.Double`, or

```
java.lang.Float:
<env-entry>
     <description>
        descriptive text
     </description>
     <env-entry-name>
        name
     </env-entry-name>
     <env-entry-value>
        value
     </env-entry-value>
     <env-entry-type>
        type
     </env-entry-type>
</env-entry>
```

17. Reference Enterprise JavaBeans (EJB) resources. These tags are used to declare a reference to an enterprise bean (EJB). The `<ejb-ref-name>` tag contains the internal JNDI name that the servlet uses to get a reference to the EJB. The `<ejb-ref-type>` tag contains the class type of the EJB. The `<ejb-home>` and `<ejb-remote>` tags define the fully qualified name of the EJB's home and remote interfaces. The `<ejb-link>` tag specifies that an EJB reference is linked to an EJB in an encompassing J2EE application package. The value of the tag is the `ejb-name` in the J2EE application package:

```
<ejb-ref>
     <description>
        descriptive text
     </description>
     <ejb-ref-name>
        name
     </ejb-ref-name>
     <ejb-ref-type>
        Java type
     </ejb-ref-type>
     <home>
        mycom.ejb.AccountHome
     </home>
     <remote>
        mycom.ejb.Account
     </remote>
     <ejb-link>
        ejb-name
     </ejb-link>
</ejb-ref>
```

Assembling a JAR File

A file created with the Java jar utility packages the files specified into a single file known as a Java Archive (JAR) file. Those of you who are familiar with pkzip or winzip will recognize the functionality of this command. JAR files are convenient for packaging components and applications for distribution.

The jar utility is in the bin directory of the Java Development Kit (JDK). Here are some of the more popular ways to use the jar command:

```
jar cfv archivefilename -C directory files
```

The c option tells the command to create a new archive, the f option tells the command that an archive file name is specified, and the v option tells the command to generate verbose output. This creates (or re-creates) a file named archivefilename. The jar utility will change to the specified directory and include the listed files. The directory will be included in the path for the archived file. Here are some examples with their respective output:

```
jar cfv allbeans.jar -C classes\ .
added manifest
adding: Bean1.class(in = 4236) (out= 1526)(deflated 63%)
adding: Bean2.class(in = 862) (out= 413)(deflated 52%)
adding: sub1/(in = 0) (out= 0)(stored 0%)
adding: sub1/SubBean1.class(in = 633) (out= 358)(deflated 43%)
adding: sub1/SubBean2.class(in = 1324) (out= 611)(deflated 53%)
```

The preceding code adds the files in the classes directory and any other subdirectories to a new archive file named allbeans.jar.

```
jar cfv sumbeans.jar -C classes\ Bean1.class -C classes\ Bean2.class
added manifest
adding: Bean1.class(in = 4236) (out= 1526)(deflated 63%)
adding: Bean2.class(in = 862) (out= 413)(deflated 52%)
```

The preceding code adds the Bean2.class file in the classes directory and any other subdirectories to a new archive file.

```
jar cfv subbeans.jar -C classes\ sub1\SubBean1.class
-C classes\ sub1\SubBean2.class
added manifest
adding: sub1/SubBean1.class(in = 633) (out= 358)(deflated 43%)
adding: sub1/SubBean2.class(in = 1324) (out= 611)(deflated 53%)
```

The preceding code adds the SubBean1.class and SubBean2.class files in the sub1 subdirectory of the classes directory to a new archive file.

```
jar ufv archivefilename -C directory files
```

The u option tells the command to update an existing archive. This command updates an existing file named archivefilename. The jar utility will change to the specified directory and include the listed files. The directory will be included in the path for the archived file. Here are some examples with their respective output:

```
jar ufv allbeans.jar -C classes\ .
adding: Bean1.class(in = 4236) (out= 1526)(deflated 63%)
adding: Bean2.class(in = 862) (out= 413)(deflated 52%)
adding: sub1/(in = 0) (out= 0)(stored 0%)
adding: sub1/SubBean1.class(in = 633) (out= 358)(deflated 43%)
adding: sub1/SubBean2.class(in = 1324) (out= 611)(deflated 53%)
adding: Bean3.class(in = 3071) (out= 1024)(deflated 66%)
adding: sub1/SubBean3.class(in = 2174) (out= 981)(deflated 54%)
```

The preceding code updates the files in the classes directory and any other subdirectories within the existing archive file.

```
jar ufv sumbeans.jar -C classes\ Bean3.class
adding: Bean3.class(in = 3071) (out= 1024)(deflated 66%)
```

The preceding code updates the Bean3.class file in the classes directory within the existing archive file.

```
jar ufv subbeans.jar -C classes\ sub1\SubBean3.class
adding: sub1/SubBean3.class(in = 2174) (out= 981)(deflated 54%)
```

The preceding code updates the SubBean3.class file in the sub1 subdirectory of the classes directory within the existing archive file.

The `jar` command can also be used as follows:

```
jar xfv jar-file
```

The x option tells the command to extract named (or all) files from the existing archive. This extracts the contents of the JAR file to the current directory. Here are some examples with their respective output:

```
>jar xfv allbeans.jar
  created: META-INF/
extracted: META-INF/MANIFEST.MF
extracted: Bean1.class
extracted: Bean2.class
  created: sub1/
extracted: sub1/SubBean1.class
extracted: sub1/SubBean2.class
extracted: Bean3.class
extracted: sub1/SubBean3.class
```

The following command lists the table of contents for the specified archive file:

```
jar tf jar-file
```

Here are some more examples with their respective output:

```
>jar -tfv allbeans.jar
     0 Fri Aug 03 15:46:54 EDT 2001 META-INF/
    68 Fri Aug 03 15:46:54 EDT 2001 META-INF/MANIFEST.MF
  4236 Fri Aug 03 15:30:56 EDT 2001 Bean1.class
   862 Fri Aug 03 15:30:56 EDT 2001 Bean2.class
     0 Fri Aug 03 15:47:26 EDT 2001 sub1/
   633 Fri Aug 03 15:30:56 EDT 2001 sub1/SubBean1.class
  1324 Fri Aug 03 15:30:56 EDT 2001 sub1/SubBean2.class
  3071 Fri Aug 03 15:30:56 EDT 2001 Bean3.class
  2174 Fri Aug 03 15:30:56 EDT 2001 sub1/SubBean3.class
```

Refer to the JDK documentation for more information regarding the complete set of `jar` command options.

Assembling an EJB JAR File

You can package one or more Enterprise JavaBeans in a directory and package them in an EJB JAR file.

To stage and package an Enterprise JavaBean:

1. Build a directory structure for staging purposes. For example, create the following directories:

   ```
   \ejbroot
   \ejbroot\META-INF
   ```

   The META-INF directory will hold deployment descriptors.
2. Compile or copy the bean's Java classes into the directory.
3. Create an ejb-jar.xml deployment descriptor in the META-INF directory and add the appropriate entries for the bean. These entries can also be generated automatically through fill-in wizard screens in many of the Java IDEs (for example, SilverStream WorkBench and Designer, JBuilder, Visual Café). See Listing 19.4, at the end of this chapter, for a complete example of an ejb-jar.xml file. Listing 19.4 contains the following entry:

   ```
   <ejb-name>TheInventory</ejb-name>
   ```

   This tag, which is part of an EJB resource reference, must be referred to and ultimately resolved when deployed. Take a look at the "Resolving References" section for each of the featured application servers that appear later in the deployment part of this chapter to find out how this resolution takes place.

4. Package the whole directory into a JAR file by executing the following:

```
jar cfv ejb.jar -C ejbroot .
```

The resulting JAR file is now ready either to be added to an Enterprise Archive (EAR) file or to move to the next step in the deployment process (see the section titled "The Deployment Process" later in this chapter).

Assembling a WAR File

Web applications are packaged in a single file known as a Web Archive (WAR). The following steps show how you might package a Web application:

1. Build a directory structure for staging purposes. For example, create the following directories:

   ```
   \app
   \app\images
   \app\META-INF
   \app\WEB-INF
   \app\WEB-INF\classes
   ```

   The META-INF and WEB-INF\classes directories will hold deployment descriptors and compiled Java classes. (Figure 19.2 is a diagram showing the example directory structure.)
2. Copy or create the necessary HTML, JSP, image, and any other files that are referenced. For example, put the images into the \app\images directory, put HTML or JSP files into the \app directory.
3. Copy JSP tag libraries into the WEB-INF directory.
4. Copy or compile the servlet and helper classes into the WEB-INF\classes directory.
5. Copy the `home` and `remote` interface classes for any Enterprise JavaBeans into the WEB-INF\classes directory.
6. Create a web.xml deployment descriptor in the WEB-INF directory. See the "Deployment Descriptors" section earlier in the chapter for more information on the content for this file. Listings 19.5 and 19.6, at the end of this chapter, are complete examples of the web.xml file for the Pet Store and SilverBooks applications.
7. Package the whole directory into a WAR file by executing the following:

   ```
   jar cfv app.war -C app .
   ```

The resulting WAR file is ready to either be added to an Enterprise Archive (EAR) file or to move to the next step in the deployment process (See the section titled "The Deployment Process" later in this chapter).

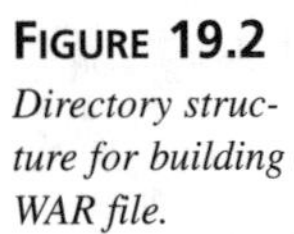

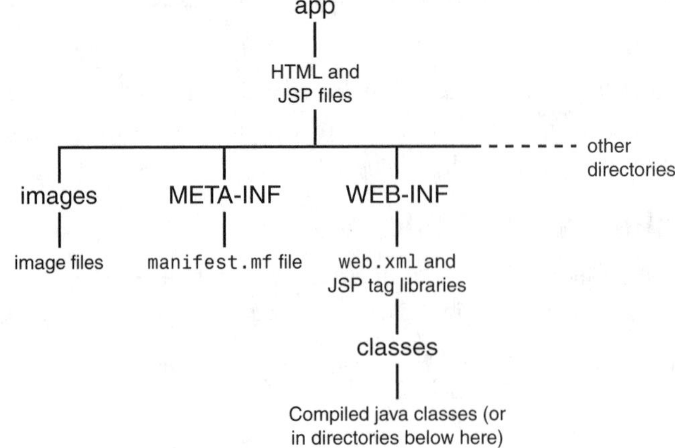

FIGURE 19.2
Directory structure for building a WAR file.

Note that the following entry appears in the example web.xml file in Listing 19.5:

```
<res-ref-name>jdbc/EstoreDataSource</res-ref-name>
```

This tag, which is part of a resource reference, must be referred to and ultimately resolved when deployed. Look at the "Resolving References" section for each of the featured application servers that appear in the deployment part of this chapter to find out how this resolution takes place.

Assembling an EAR File

The Enterprise Archive (EAR) is a file that contains Web (WAR) and EJB (JAR) archives that are part of a related application. The Web and EJB archives are bundled together in a standard archive file with a .ear extension.

To stage and package an enterprise application:

1. Build a directory structure for staging purposes. For example, create the following directories:

   ```
   \earroot
   \earroot\META-INF
   ```

   The META-INF directory will hold deployment descriptors.

2. Copy the Web (WAR) and EJB (JAR) archives into the directory.

3. Create an application.xml deployment descriptor in the META-INF directory. This file identifies the EJB and Web modules that are packaged in the Enterprise Archive (EAR). See Listings 19.1 and 19.2 for complete examples of application.xml files.

4. Package the whole directory into an EAR file by executing the following:

```
jar cfv entapp.ear -C earroot .
```

The resulting EAR file is now ready to move to the next step in the deployment process (See the section titled "The Deployment Process" later in this chapter).

LISTING 19.1 The application.xml File for Pet Store

```
<?xml version="1.0" encoding="ISO8859_1"?>
<!DOCTYPE application PUBLIC '-//Sun Microsystems, Inc.
//DTD J2EE Application 1.2//EN'
'http://java.sun.com/j2ee/dtds/application_1_2.dtd'>
<application>
  <display-name>petstore</display-name>
  <description>Application description</description>
  <module>
    <ejb>customerEjb.jar</ejb>
  </module>
  <module>
    <ejb>mailerEjb.jar</ejb>
  </module>
  <module>
    <web>
      <web-uri>petstore.war</web-uri>
      <context-root>estore</context-root>
    </web>
  </module>
  <module>
    <ejb>petstoreEjb.jar</ejb>
  </module>
  <module>
    <ejb>signonEjb.jar</ejb>
  </module>
  <module>
    <ejb>personalizationEjb.jar</ejb>
  </module>
  <module>
    <ejb>inventoryEjb.jar</ejb>
  </module>
  <module>
    <ejb>shoppingcartEjb.jar</ejb>
  </module>
</application>
```


LISTING 19.2 The application.xml File for SilverBooks

```
<?xml version="1.0" encoding="ISO8859_1"?>
<!DOCTYPE application PUBLIC '-//Sun Microsystems, Inc.
//DTD J2EE Application 1.2//EN'
```

LISTING 19.2 continued

```
'http://java.sun.com/j2ee/dtds/application_1_2.dtd'>
<application>
    <display-name>SilverBooks</display-name>
    <description>Application description</description>
    <module>
        <ejb>JDBCSource.jar</ejb>
    </module>
    <module>
        <ejb>ShoppingCart.jar</ejb>
    </module>
    <module>
        <web>
            <web-uri>silverbooks.war</web-uri>
            <context-root>app</context-root>
        </web>
    </module>
</application>
```

The Deployment Process

A J2EE application or component that is packaged and ready to deploy on an application server will also need additional server-specific deployment descriptors and, possibly, other classes generated with the server-specific compilers (for example, compilers for EJB, RMI, or JSP).

Up until this point, the J2EE archive files have the same content regardless of the destination application server. We will now take a look at the differences between the servers from this point forward in the deployment process. The essential differences are in two areas:

1. Reference resolution (also known as the XML deployment plan)
2. Tool used for deployment

The first item, reference resolution, is typically taken care of by defining elements on one or more additional XML documents. These additional deployment plans (or resource resolution files) contain information about the runtime environment regarding

- Database connection pools
- Mail sessions
- URL connections
- JMS queues and topics
- EJB references

The files map internal references along with server-specific properties to JNDI or other names that exist in the destination J2EE application server.

In this section we will examine the deployment mapping entries for the following application servers:

- J2EE Reference Implementation
- SilverStream Application Server
- BEA WebLogic Server

Once all of the files, deployment descriptors, and plans are complete, the one item remaining is the actual deployment step. On any given application server, there are one or more ways to deploy a J2EE application or component. At the very least, there is a command-line deployment tool or executable. In some cases, there is also a GUI deployment tool or administration console that can be used for visual deployment. The final section of each featured application server will examine the various deployment tools available.

Deployment Using the J2EE Reference Implementation

The J2EE Reference Implementation is a part of the Java 2 SDK, Enterprise Edition. This implementation allows the Java developer to deploy and test a J2EE application or component to the J2EE-compliant application server. The full product can be downloaded from the Sun site at `http://java.sun.com/j2ee/`.

Resolving References

There is a single file used to resolve references in the J2EE Reference Implementation. The file is named sun-j2ee-ri.xml and is placed in the META-INF directory of the archive file to be deployed. See Listing 19.7, at the end of this chapter, for the reference resolution file for the Pet Store application in the J2EE Reference Implementation environment. The following entries are contained in the file in Listing 19.7:

```
...
<res-ref-name>jdbc/EstoreDataSource</res-ref-name>
<jndi-name>jdbc/Cloudscape</jndi-name>
...
```

These two tags resolve the resource reference that was defined in the web.xml deployment descriptor file (described in the "Assembling a WAR File" section earlier in this chapter) to a JNDI database connection pool.

The following code also appears within Listing 19.7:

```
...
<ejb-name>TheInventory</ejb-name>
<jndi-name>estore/inventory</jndi-name>
...
```

These two tags resolve the EJB resource reference that was in the ejb-jar.xml deployment descriptor file (described in the "Assembling an EJB JAR File" section earlier in this chapter).

For more information regarding resource resolution, see the documentation that comes with the J2EE JDK download.

Deployment Tools

The J2EE Reference Implementation has a single tool (`deploytool`) that can be executed on a command line or started with a graphical user interface (GUI).

Here is the syntax for the command-line version of `deploytool`:

```
deploytool [-ui] [-help] [-deploy appname server jarname]
[-uninstall appname server] [-listApps server]
[-deployConnector rarname server] [-undeployConnector rarname server]
[-listConnectors server]
```

See Table 19.2 for a description of the commands available with the `deploytool` utility.

TABLE 19.2 `deploytool` Commands

`deploytool` *Command*	*Description*
`-deploy` `<ear-filename>` `<server-name>` `[<client-stub-jar>]`	Deploys the J2EE application contained in the EAR file specified by `<ear-filename>` onto the J2EE server running on the machine specified by `<server-name>`; optionally, a JAR file for a standalone Java application client may be created by specifying `<client-stub-jar>`
`-listApps` `<server-name>`	Lists the J2EE applications that have been deployed to the server running on the specified `<server-name>`
`-uninstall` `<app-name>` `<server-name>`	Removes the J2EE application `<app-name>` from the J2EE server running on the specified `<server-name>`

TABLE 19.2 continued

`deploytool` *Command*	*Description*
`-deployConnector <rar-filename> <server-name>`	Deploys the resource adapter contained in the RAR file specified by `<rar-filename>` onto the J2EE server running on the machine specified by `<server-name>`
`-listConnectors <server-name>`	Lists the resource adapters that are deployed on the J2EE server running on the machine specified by `<server-name>`
`-undeployConnector <rar-filename> <server-name>`	Undeploys the resource adapter contained in the file specified by `<rar-filename>` from the J2EE server running on the machine specified by `<server-name>`
`-help`	Displays options
`-ui`	Runs GUI version (default)

Deploying a J2EE Application

To deploy (or re-deploy) a J2EE application, you can run the command-line version of `deploytool` (see the syntax in the "Deployment Tools" section). Here is some sample output:

```
deploytool -deploy d:\jps1.1.2\petstoreadmin.ear localhost
Setting EJB version to EJB1.X...
Deploy the application in d:\jps1.1.2\petstoreadmin.ear
on the server localhost saving the client jar as null
Sender object Deploy Tool : Deploy admin on localhost
Remote message: Contacted Server....
Remote message: Application admin transferred.
Remote message: admin has 1  ejbs, 1 web components to deploy.
Remote message: Deploying Ejbs....
Remote message: Processing beans ....
Remote message: Compiling wrapper code ....
Remote message: Compiling RMI-IIOP code ....
Remote message: Making client JARs ....
Remote message: Making server JARs ....
Remote message: Contact the web server and ask it
to run: D:\j2sdkee1.3\repository\allenpa
```

```
1\applications\admin997117759943Server.jar .
Remote message: Web Components Deployed..
Remote message: Deployment of admin is complete..
Sender object Deploy Tool : client code at
http://183.141.1.248:9191/adminClient.jar
```

Alternatively, you can run the GUI version of the tool, open the Enterprise Archive (EAR) file and choose the Deploy… option from the Tools menu. See Figures 19.3 and 19.4 for an example of deploying an application using the GUI version of the tool.

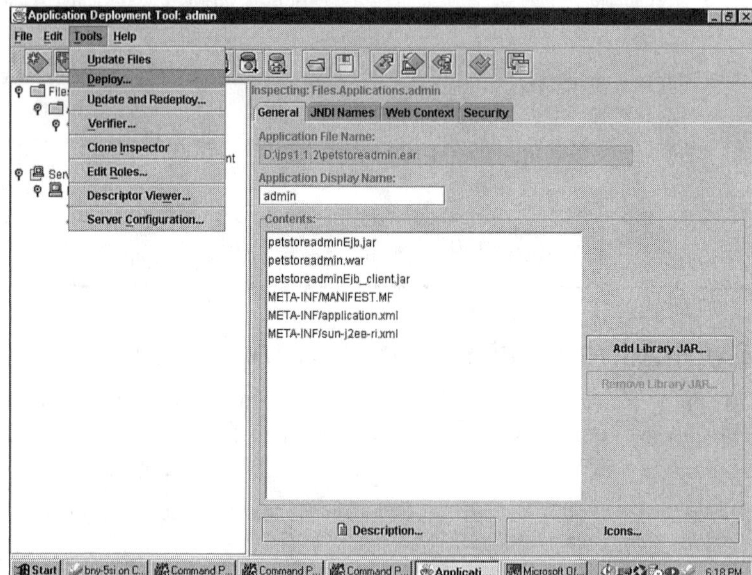

FIGURE 19.3
Deploying an application.

Listing Deployed J2EE Applications

To list the deployed J2EE applications, you can run the command-line version of `deploytool` (the syntax is shown in the "Deployment Tools" section). Here is some sample output:

```
deploytool -listApps localhost
The following apps are deployed on localhost:
        petstore
        BonusApp
        admin
```

Alternatively, you can run the GUI version of the tool, expand the Servers section, and expand the server, and the list of applications deployed in the server will be displayed. See Figure 19.5 for an example listing of applications.

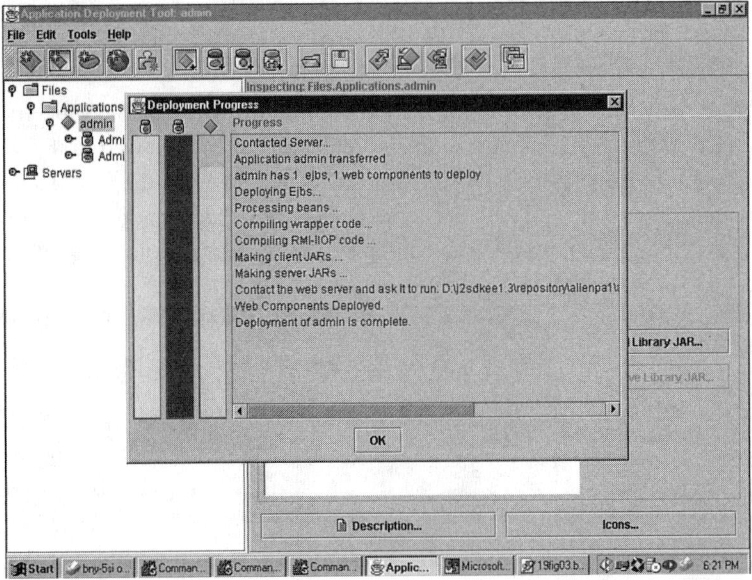

FIGURE 19.4
Result of deploying an application.

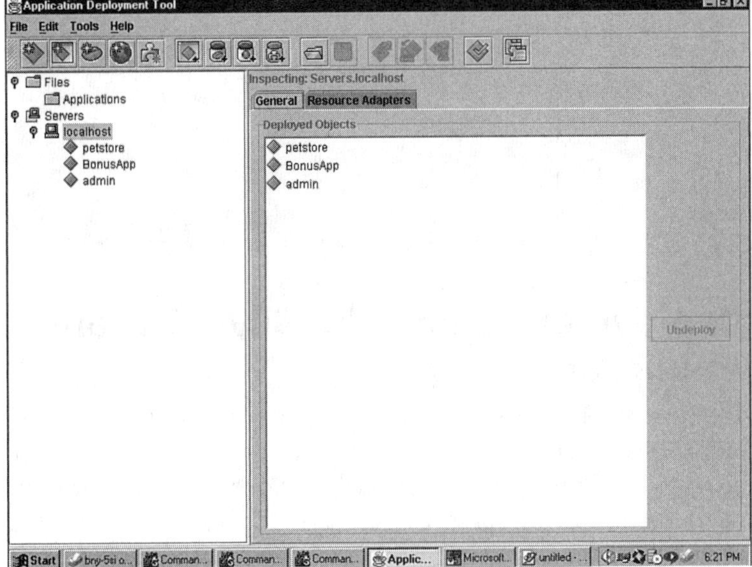

FIGURE 19.5
Listing deployed applications.

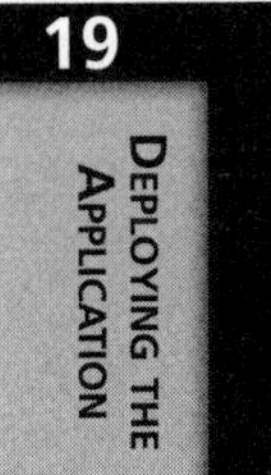

Removing a Deployed J2EE Application

To remove a deployed J2EE application, you can run the command-line version of `deploytool` (see the syntax in the "Deployment Tools" section). Here is some sample output:

```
deploytool -uninstall admin localhost
Sender object Deploytool (Main) : The application
admin was uninstalled from localhost
```

Alternatively, you can run the GUI version of the tool, expand the Servers section, and click on the server name, and the list of applications deployed in the server will be displayed. In the Deployed Objects list that is displayed on the right-hand side, click on the application name and then press the Undeploy button to remove the application from the server. See Figure 19.6 for an example of removing a deployed application.

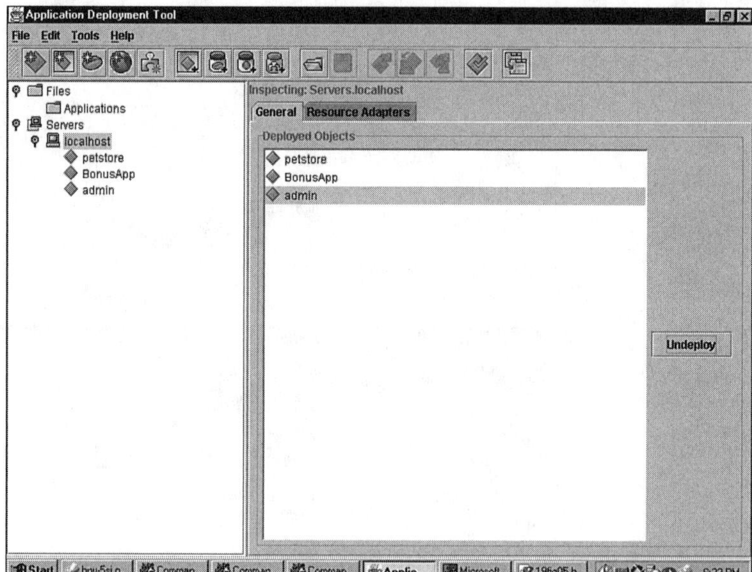

FIGURE 19.6
Removing a deployed application.

Deployment Using the SilverStream Application Server

The SilverStream Application Server is a production-quality J2EE certified application server. This implementation allows the Java developer to deploy and run J2EE applications. An evaluation version of the product can be downloaded from the SilverStream site at `http://www.silverstream.com/`.

Resolving References

There is a single file used to resolve references in the SilverStream environment. The file, known as a deployment plan, is an XML-based file that must be supplied as a parameter to the deployment tool when deploying the application or component.

We will now take a look at an example deployment plan and then take a more in-depth look at a few of the entries. See Listing 19.8 , at the end of this chapter, for the deployment plan for the Pet Store application. The deployment plan has two main sections. The first maps all modules (which are either JAR or WAR files) within the EAR file. The second section has the mapping of the security roles.

The following code appears within the resource resolution (deployment plan) file in Listing 19.8:

```
...
<name>jdbc/EstoreDataSource</name>
<dataSource>EstoreDB</dataSource>
...
```

These tags resolve the resource reference that was defined in the web.xml deployment descriptor file (described in the "Assembling a WAR File" section earlier in this chapter) to a real connection pool that exists in the deployed server.

The following code also appears within the resource resolution file in Listing 19.8:

```
...
<beanName>TheInventory</beanName>
<beanJNDIName>estore/inventory</beanJNDIName>
...
```

These two tags resolve the EJB resource reference that was in the ejb-jar.xml deployment descriptor file (described in the "Assembling an EJB JAR File" section earlier in this chapter).

For more information regarding this file, see the documentation that comes with the SilverStream product.

Deployment Tools

The SilverStream product has a single tool, `SilverCmd`, to deploy and maintain J2EE applications and components on the server. The `SilverCmd` tool has many other purposes, but we will cover just the aspects of the utility that deal with the deployment and maintenance of a J2EE application or component.

Deploying a J2EE Application or Component

There are three types of J2EE archives that can be deployed. The first is the Enterprise Archive, the second is the JAR or EJB Archive and the third is the Web Archive.

To deploy an Enterprise Archive (EAR), the syntax is

```
SilverCmd DeployEAR server[:port] database [EARFile]
-f deploymentPlan [options]
```

Here is an example:

```
SilverCmd DeployEAR localhost:80 EStoreDB petstore.ear
-f petstore-depl-plan.xml -o -i -U system
-P j2eeucny -v 5
```

See Tables 19.3 and 19.4 for an explanation of the arguments and options for the `DeployEAR` command.

TABLE 19.3 Arguments for the `DeployEAR` Command

`DeployEAR` *Argument*	*Description*
`server`	The name of the server to which the EAR file is to be deployed
`port`	The destination port number (default is 80)
`database`	The name of the database to which the EAR file is to be deployed
`EARFile`	The name of the EAR file to deploy (this can also be specified in the deploymentPlan options file); the command-line name supersedes the name specified in the deployment plan file
`-f deploymentPlan`	XML file specifying deployment information

TABLE 19.4 Options for the `DeployEAR` Command

`DeployEAR` *Option*	*Description*
`-?`	Print the usage and syntax
`-U userid`	Username
`-P password`	Password
`-l deployname`	Name of deployed EAR object on server; archive name is used by default
`-o`	Overwrite existing deployed object
`-i`	Ignore errors when compiling JSP pages and deploy whatever builds successfully (passed to WAR deployer)
`-v verboseLevel`	The level of messages to output—0 for no messages (default) to 5 for the most messages

To deploy an Enterprise JavaBeans (EJB) Archive, the syntax is

```
SilverCmd DeployEJB server[:port] database [ejbJar] [-d  ejbDeployedObject]
[-r ejbRemoteJar] -f deploymentPlan [-R remoteJarPath] [options]
```

Here is an example:

```
SilverCmd DeployEJB localhost:80 EStoreDB petstoreEjb.ear
-f petstore-depl-plan.xml -o -i -U system -P j2eeucny -v 5
```

See Tables 19.5 and 19.6 for an explanation of the arguments and options for the `DeployEJB` command.

TABLE 19.5 Arguments for the `DeployEJB` Command

`DeployEJB` *Argument*	*Description*
`server`	The name of the server to which the EJB JAR file is to be deployed
`port`	The destination port number (default is 80)
`database`	The name of the database to which the EJB JAR file is to be deployed
`ejbJar`	The name of the JAR file to deploy (if this argument is not specified, the jarname must be specified in the deployment plan file; if this argument is given, it supersedes the name specified in the deployment plan file)
`-f deploymentPlan`	XML file specifying deployment information

TABLE 19.6 Options for the `DeployEJB` Command

`DeployEJB` *Option*	*Description*
`-?`	Print the usage and syntax.
`-U userid`	Username.
`-P password`	Password.
`-d ejbDeployedObject`	The name to use for the deployed object. If this argument is not specified, the name may be specified in the deployment plan file (if the name is not specified in the deployment plan file, a deployed object name will be generated). If this argument is given, it supersedes the name specified in the deployment plan file.

TABLE 19.6 continued

DeployEJB *Option*	*Description*
`-r ejbRemoteJar`	The name to use for the remote stubs JAR. If this argument is not specified, the name may be specified in the deployment plan file (if the name is not specified in the deployment plan file, a remote JAR name will be generated). If this argument is given, it supersedes the name specified in the deployment plan file.
`-R remoteJarPath`	Create a copy of the generated ejbRemoteJar on the local drive in the directory path given. The JAR will have the same name as the remote JAR generated on the server.
`-o`	Overwrite the existing deployed object.
`-v verboseLevel`	The level of messages to output—0 for no messages (default) to 5 for the most messages.

To deploy a Web Archive (WAR), the syntax is

```
SilverCmd DeployWAR server[:port] database [WARFile]
-f deploymentPlan [options]
```

Here is an example:

```
SilverCmd DeployWAR localhost:80 EStoreDB petstore.war
-f petstore-war-depl-plan.xml -o -i -U system -P j2eeucny -v 5
```

See Tables 19.7 and 19.8 for an explanation of the arguments and options for the `DeployWAR` command.

TABLE 19.7 Arguments for the `DeployWAR` Command

DeployWAR *Argument*	*Description*
`server`	The name of the server to which the WAR file is to be deployed
`port`	The destination port number (default is 80)
`database`	The name of the database to which the WAR file is to be deployed
`WARFile`	The name of the WAR file to deploy (if this argument is not specified, the WAR filename must be specified in the deployment plan file; if this argument is given, it supersedes the name specified in the deployment plan file)
`-f deploymentPlan`	XML file specifying deployment information

TABLE 19.8 Options for the `DeployWAR` Command

`DeployWAR` *Option*	*Description*
`-?`	Print the usage and syntax
`-U userid`	Username
`-P password`	Password
`-l deployname`	Name of deployed EAR object on server; archive name is used by default
`-o`	Overwrite existing deployed object
`-i`	Ignore errors when compiling JSP pages and deploy whatever builds successfully (Passed to WAR deployer)
`-v verboseLevel`	The level of messages to output—0 for no messages (default) to 5 for the most messages

Deleting a Deployed J2EE Component

To remove a J2EE component from the server, run the following command:

```
SilverCmd Delete server[:port] database [item] [options]
```

Here is an example:

```
SilverCmd Delete localhost:80 EStoreDB Media/Jars/petstore.war
-U system -P j2eeucny
```

To delete multiple entries, use the following:

```
SilverCmd Delete locahost:80 EStoreDB -f jarlist.txt
-U system -P j2eeucny
```

The content of the jarlist.txt file is

```
<?xml version="1.0" encoding="UTF-8"?>
<!DOCTYPE ItemList PUBLIC "-//SilverStream Software, Inc.
//DTD SilverCmd ItemList//EN" "itemlist.dtd">
<ItemList>
    <Items>
        <el>Media/Jars/petstore.ear</el>
        <el>Media/Jars/petstoreadmin.ear</el>
    </Items>
</ItemList>
```

Tables 19.9 and 19.10 list and describe the arguments and options for the `Delete` command.

TABLE 19.9 Arguments for the `Delete` Command

`Delete` *Argument*	*Description*
`server`	The name of the server containing the component to be deleted
`port`	The destination port number (default is 80)
`database`	The name of the database containing the component to be deleted
`item`	Specifies the name of the item to delete. The format is Media/Jars/archivename Example: `Media/Jars/petstore.ear`
`-f multfile`	A text input file specifying multiple items to delete

TABLE 19.10 Options for the `Delete` Command

`Delete` *Option*	*Description*
`-?`	Print the usage and syntax
`-U userid`	Username
`-P password`	Password

The input file format is based on the ItemList DTD; see the delete_sample.xml file in the DTDs directory for an example.

The filename must include a string array of item names. The file can have any extension and can reside in any directory accessible to `SilverCmd`.

Deployment Using the BEA WebLogic Server

The BEA WebLogic Server is a production-quality J2EE certified application server. This implementation allows the Java developer to deploy and run J2EE applications. An evaluation version of the product can be downloaded from the BEA site at `http://www.bea.com/`.

Resolving References

The weblogic.xml file contains WebLogic-specific attributes for a Web application. It contains the attributes for the following: HTTP session parameters, HTTP cookie parameters, JSP parameters, resource references, and security role assignments. This deployment descriptor is located in the WEB-INF directory of the WAR file.

If you define external resources such as DataSources, EJBs, or a security realm in the web.xml deployment descriptor, you can use any descriptive name to define the resource. To access the resource, you then map this resource name to the actual name of the resource in the JNDI tree using a file called weblogic.xml. Place this file in the WEB-INF directory of your Web application.

The ordering of the tag elements within the weblogic.xml file must follow the ordering specified here. Follow these steps to create the weblogic.xml file:

1. With a simple text editor, create the weblogic.xml file.
2. Add the following DTD reference:
```
<!DOCTYPE weblogic-web-app PUBLIC "-//BEA Systems, Inc.
//DTD Web Application 6.0//EN"
"http://www.bea.com/servers/wls600/dtd/weblogic-web-jar.dtd">
```
3. Add the opening and closing `<weblogic-web-app>` tags. All subsequent elements must be added within the following tags:
```
<weblogic-web-app>
</weblogic-web-app>
```
4. Add the following `weblogic-web-app` tags:
```
     <description>
        Text description of the Web App
     </description>
     <weblogic-version>
       version number
     </weblogic-version>
```
5. Map security role names to a security realm:
```
<security-role-assignment>
        <role-name>
           name
        </role-name>
        <principal-name>
            name
        </principal-name>
</security-role-assignment>
```
If multiple roles are required, add each pair of `<role-name>` and `<principal-name>` tags within a separate `<security-role-assignment>` tag.
6. Resolve the resources reference. This is where you map resources used in your application to the real JNDI tree. When you define `<res-ref-name>` or `<ejb-ref-name>` in the web.xml deployment descriptor, you need to resolve these names in weblogic.xml and map them to an actual JNDI name that is present in the server. For example, if you have a `javax.sql.DataSource` that is referenced in a servlet with `jdbc/EStoreDataSource`, this reference must be defined, along with its data

type, in the web.xml file. The `jdbc/EStoreDataSource` reference is then resolved (or mapped) in the weblogic.xml file by mapping it to a real name in the JNDI tree.

Similarly, if an EJB is referenced via `ejb/Account` in the same servlet, this reference must be defined in the web.xml file. The `ejb/Account` reference is then resolved (or mapped) in the weblogic.xml file by mapping it to a real name in the JNDI tree. The following example shows snippets of servlet code along with the relevant entries in the web.xml and weblogic.xml files, with the resource reference being resolved to `jdbc.EstoreDB` and the EJB reference being resolved to `estore/account`.

Here is the Servlet code:

```
javax.sql.DataSource ds = (javax.sql.DataSource)
    ctx.lookup ("jdbc/EstoreDataSource");
Object objref = ctx.lookup("java:comp/env/ejb/Account");
CustomerHome custHome = (CustomerHome)
    PortableRemoteObject.narrow(objref, CustomerHome.class);
```

Here is the web.xml code:

```
<resource-ref>
    <res-ref-name>jdbc/EstoreDataSource</res-ref-name>
    <res-type>javax.sql.DataSource</res-type>
    <res-auth>Container</res-auth>
</resource-ref>
...
<ejb-ref>
    <description>no description</description>
    <ejb-ref-name>ejb/account</ejb-ref-name>
    <ejb-ref-type>Entity</ejb-ref-type>
    <home>com.sun.estore.account.ejb.AccountHome</home>
    <remote>com.sun.estore.account.ejb.Account</remote>
</ejb-ref>
```

Here is the weblogic.xml code:

```
<reference-descriptor>
...
    <resource-description>
        <res-ref-name>jdbc/EstoreDataSource</res-ref-name>
        <jndi-name>jdbc.EstoreDB</jndi-name>
        </resource-description>

    <ejb-reference-description>
        <ejb-ref-name>ejb/account</ejb-ref-name>
        <jndi-name>estore/account</jndi-name>
    </ejb-reference-description>
...
</reference-descriptor>
```

7. Define session parameters. These are coded within `<session-param>` tags, which are nested inside `<session-descriptor>` tags. For each `<session-param>` you need to supply a `<param-name>` tag that names the parameter being defined and a `<param-value>` tag that provides the value of the parameter:

```
<session-descriptor>
     <session-param>
          <param-name>
             session param name
          </param-name>
          <param-value>
              my value
          </param-value>
     </session-param>
</session-descriptor>
```

8. Define JSP parameters. These are coded within `<jsp-param>` tags, which are nested inside `<jsp-descriptor>` tags. For each `<jsp-param>` you need to supply a `<param-name>` tag that names the parameter being defined and a `<param-value>` tag that provides the value of the parameter:

```
<jsp-descriptor>
     <jsp-param>
          <param-name>
            jsp param name
          </param-name>
          <param-value>
             my value
          </param-value>
     </jsp-param>
</jsp-descriptor>
```

The WebLogic Server also requires a deployment descriptor for each EJB JAR in the deployment package. You must create the weblogic-ejb-jar.xml file, add the necessary entries for the bean, and place the file in the META-INF directory or the archive, along with the J2EE standard ejb-jar.xml file. See Listing 19.9, at the end of this chapter, for the complete weblogic-ejb-jar.xml file for the Pet Store application. The following code appears within the resource resolution file in Listing 19.9:

```
...
<res-ref-name>jdbc/EstoreDataSource</res-ref-name>
<jndi-name>jdbc.EstoreDB</jndi-name>
...
```

These two tags resolve the resource reference that was defined in the web.xml deployment descriptor file (described in the “Assembling a WAR File” section earlier in this chapter) to a JNDI database connection pool.

The following code also appears within the resource resolution file in Listing 19.9:

```
...
<ejb-name>TheInventory</ejb-name>
<jndi-name>estore/inventory</jndi-name>
...
```

These two tags resolve the EJB resource reference that was in the ejb-jar.xml deployment descriptor file (described in the "Assembling an EJB JAR File" section earlier in this chapter).

For more information regarding the resource resolution file, see `http://e-docs.bea.com/wls/docs61/webapp/webappdeployment.html`.

Also note that if the application uses an EJB entity bean running with container-managed persistence (CMP), the WebLogic Server requires an additional deployment descriptor. You must create the weblogic-rdbms-cmp-jar.xml file, map the bean to this CMP deployment descriptor with a `<type-storage>` attribute, and place the file in the META-INF directory of the archive, along with the J2EE standard ejb-jar.xml and WebLogic-specific file weblogic-ejb-jar.xml file.

The Pet Store application installed with WebLogic does not have an example of this file; see Listing 19.3 for an example from an alternate application:

LISTING 19.3 Example CMP EJB Deployment Descriptor for the WebLogic Environment

```
<?xml version="1.0" encoding="UTF-8"?>
<!DOCTYPE weblogic-rdbms-jar PUBLIC '-//BEA Systems, Inc.
//DTD WebLogic 6.1.0 EJB//EN'
'http://www.bea.com/servers/wls600/dtd/weblogic-rdbms20-persistence-600.dtd'>
<weblogic-rdbms-jar>
  <weblogic-rdbms-bean>
    <ejb-name>TheAccount</ejb-name>
    <data-source-name>financeDB</data-source-name>
    <table-name>ACCOUNT</table-name>
    <field-map>
        <cmp-field>accountID</cmp-field>
        <dbms-column>ACCOUNT_NUMBER</dbms-column>
    </field-map>
    <weblogic-query>
       <query-method>
         <method-name>findFatCatAccounts</method-name>
         <method-params>
           <method-param>double</method-param>
         </method-params>
       </query-method>
       <weblogic-ql>WHERE BALANCE>500000</weblogic-ql>
```

LISTING 19.3 continued

```
    </weblogic-query>
    <delay-database-insert-until>ejbPostCreate</delay-database-insert-until>
    <automatic-key-generation>
       <generator-type>SQL_SERVER</generator-type>
    </automatic-key-generation>
  </weblogic-rdbms-bean>
  <weblogic-rdbms-relation>
      <relation-name>account-rep</relation-name>
      <weblogic-relationship-role>
          <relationship-role-name>account</relationship-role-name>
          <column-map>
              <foreign-key-column>rep-id</foreign-key-column>
              <key-column>id</key-column>
          </column-map>
      </weblogic-relationship-role>
  </weblogic-rdbms-relation>
  <create-default-dbms-tables>True</create-default-dbms-tables>
</weblogic-rdbms-jar>
```

For more information regarding the CMP deployment descriptor, visit `http://e-docs.bea.com/wls/docs61/ejb/EJB_reference.html`.

Deployment Tools

The WebLogic product has two ways to deploy J2EE applications and components. The tools available are

- Administration Console (GUI)
- `weblogic.deploy` utility (command line)

Here are the steps involved in deploying an application using the Administration Console:

1. Start the Administration Console.
2. In the left pane, expand Deployments.
3. Under Deployments, click Applications.
4. In the right pane, click Install a new Application (see Figure 19.7). Then click Browse, and find the .ear, .jar, or .war file containing the component or application you want to install.
5. Click Upload (see Figure 19.8). This copies the file to the Administration Server's applications directory.
6. Expand the new application under the Applications node to reveal the components.

7. For each of the components in the application, click the component name in the left pane, then complete the information on the Configuration and Targets tabs in the right pane. Consult the online help to find details about the values of these tabs.
8. Click on the application name under the Applications node, and check the Deployed check box in the right pane.
9. Click Apply.

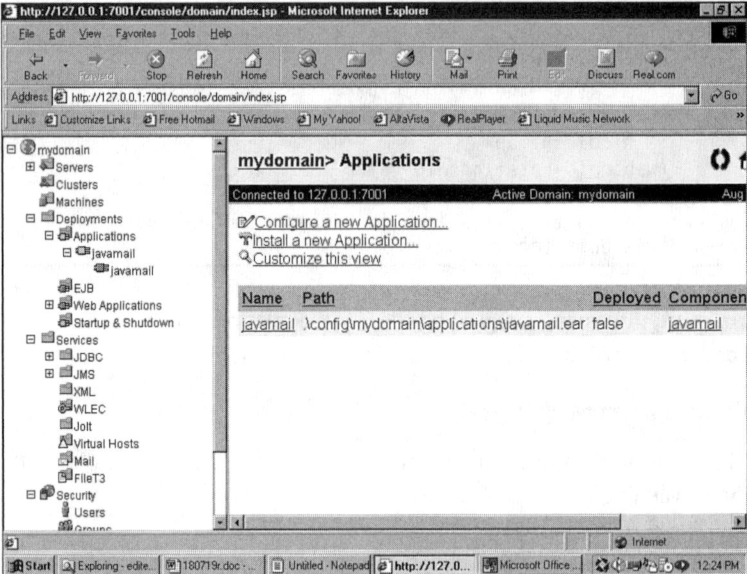

FIGURE 19.7
Installing a new application.

Depending on your choices, you may need to restart WebLogic Server. The Administration Console displays a restart message in the right pane.

The `weblogic.deploy` command-line utility allows you to deploy, undeploy, update, and list components on the server. Here is the syntax for the `weblogic.deploy` command-line utility:

```
java weblogic.deploy [options] [list|deploy|undeploy|update]
password {application} {source}
```

See Tables 19.11 and 19.12 for a description of the arguments and options for the `weblogic.deploy` utility.

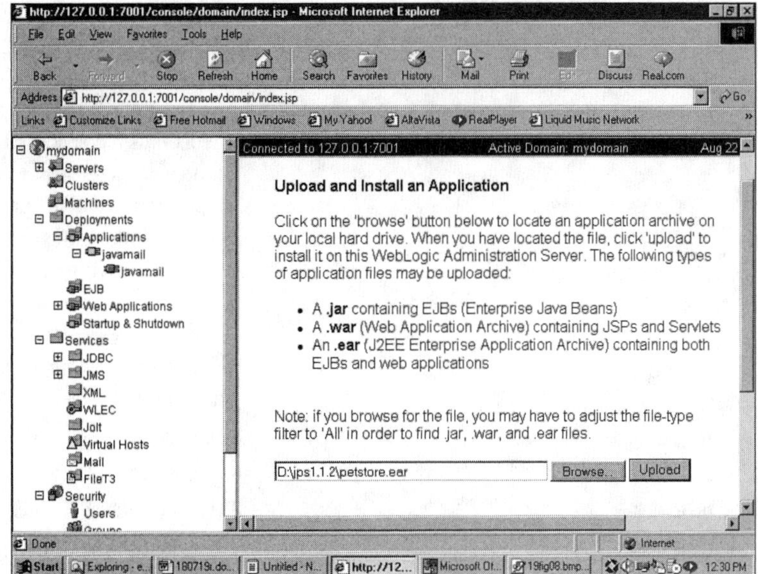

FIGURE 19.8
Uploading the new application.

TABLE 19.11 `weblogic.deploy` Arguments

Argument	*Required*	*Description*
`application`	Yes	The name of the application (the application name can be specified at deployment time with either the deployment or console utilities)
`deploy`	No	Deploy a J2EE .jar, .war, or .ear to the server
`list`	No	List the applications in the server
`password`	Yes	The system password
`source`	Yes	The location of the archive file (.jar, .war, or .ear), or the path to the top level of an application directory
`undeploy`	No	Mark an existing application as undeployed (this will not remove it)
`update`	No	Re-deploy an application

TABLE 19.12 `weblogic.deploy` Options

Option	*Description*
`-component` *`componentname`*`:target1,target2`	The component to be deployed on various targets must be specified as *`componentname`*`:target1,target2`, where *`componentname`* is the name of the .jar or .war file without the extension. This option can be specified multiple times for any number of components (.jar or .war). A .ear file cannot be deployed. Each of its components must be deployed separately using this option.
`-debug`	Prints debugging information out on the console.
`-help`	Prints options available.
`-host` *`host`*	Hostname of the destination server (default is `localhost`).
`-port` *`port`*	Port number of the destination server (default is `7001`).
`-url` *`url`*	URL of the server (default is `localhost:7001`).
`-username` *`username`*	Server administrator user ID (default is `system`).
`-version`	Prints version number of the utility.

Viewing a Deployed J2EE Component

To view an application that is deployed on a local WebLogic Server, enter the following command:

```
java weblogic.deploy list password
```

The value of `password` is the password for the WebLogic Server system account.

To list a deployed application on a remote server, specify the `port` and `host` options, as follows:

```
java weblogic.deploy -port port_number -host host_name list password
```

For example:

```
java weblogic.deploy -port 7001 -host allenpa1 list j2eeucny
```

Deploying a New J2EE Component

To deploy a J2EE application file (.jar, .war, or .ear) or application directory that is not deployed to WebLogic Server, enter the following command:

```
java weblogic.deploy -port port_number
-host host_name deploy password application source
```

The values are as follows:

`application` is the string you want to assign to this application.

`source` is the full pathname of the J2EE application file (.jar, .war, .ear) you want to deploy, or the full pathname of the application directory.

For example:

```
java weblogic.deploy -port 7001
-host localhost deploy j2eeucny javamail
d:\j2ee\javamaildemo\javamail.ear
```

The J2EE application file (.jar, .war, .ear) copied to the applications directory of the Administration Server is renamed with the name of the application. Therefore, in the previous example, the name of the application archive in the /config/mydomain/applications directory is changed from BasicStatefulTraderBean.jar to Basic_example.jar.

Removing a Deployed J2EE Component

To remove a deployed J2EE component, you must use the `undeploy` parameter along with the assigned application name, as shown in the following example:

```
java weblogic.deploy -port 7001
-host localhost undeploy j2eeucny javamail
```

Removing a J2EE application does not remove the application from the WebLogic Server, it simply sets the status of the application to undeployed. You can, however, reuse the application name via the `update` parameter, as described in the following section.

Updating an Existing J2EE Component

To update a J2EE component, use the `update` argument and specify the name of the active J2EE application as follows:

```
java weblogic.deploy -port 7001
-host localhost update j2eeucny javamail
d:\j2ee\javamaildemo\javamail.ear
```

To update a specific component on one or more servers, enter the following command:

```
java weblogic.deploy -port 7001 -host localhost
-component javmailear:server1,server2
update j2eeucny javamail
d:\j2ee\javamaildemo\javamail.ear
```

LISTING 19.4 The ejb-jar.xml File for Pet Store

```
<?xml version="1.0" encoding="Cp1252"?>
<!DOCTYPE ejb-jar PUBLIC '-//Sun Microsystems, Inc.
//DTD Enterprise JavaBeans 2.0//EN'
'http://java.sun.com/dtd/ejb-jar_2_0.dtd'>
<ejb-jar>
 <description>This component is used to maintain
the quantity of items in inventory.</description>
 <display-name>Inventory Component</display-name>
 <enterprise-beans>
  <entity>
   <description>The Inventory EJB keeps track of items in stock</description>
   <display-name>TheInventory</display-name>
   <ejb-name>TheInventory</ejb-name>
   <home>com.sun.j2ee.blueprints.inventory.ejb.InventoryHome</home>
   <remote>com.sun.j2ee.blueprints.inventory.ejb.Inventory</remote>
   <ejb-class>com.sun.j2ee.blueprints.inventory.ejb.InventoryEJB</ejb-class>
   <persistence-type>Bean</persistence-type>
   <prim-key-class>java.lang.String</prim-key-class>
   <reentrant>False</reentrant>
   <env-entry>
    <env-entry-name>ejb/inventory/InventoryDAOClass</env-entry-name>
    <env-entry-type>java.lang.String</env-entry-type>
    <env-entry-value>
     com.sun.j2ee.blueprints.inventory.dao.InventoryDAOImpl
    </env-entry-value>
   </env-entry>
   <security-identity>
    <description/>
    <use-caller-identity/>
   </security-identity>
   <resource-ref>
    <res-ref-name>jdbc/InventoryDataSource</res-ref-name>
    <res-type>javax.sql.DataSource</res-type>
    <res-auth>Container</res-auth>
    <res-sharing-scope>Shareable</res-sharing-scope>
   </resource-ref>
  </entity>
 </enterprise-beans>
 <assembly-descriptor>
  <container-transaction>
   <method>
    <ejb-name>TheInventory</ejb-name>
    <method-intf>Remote</method-intf>
    <method-name>addQuantity</method-name>
    <method-params>
     <method-param>int</method-param>
    </method-params>
   </method>
   <trans-attribute>Required</trans-attribute>
```

LISTING 19.4 continued

```
  </container-transaction>
  <container-transaction>
   <method>
    <ejb-name>TheInventory</ejb-name>
    <method-intf>Remote</method-intf>
    <method-name>getDetails</method-name>
    <method-params/>
   </method>
   <trans-attribute>Required</trans-attribute>
  </container-transaction>
  <container-transaction>
   <method>
    <ejb-name>TheInventory</ejb-name>
    <method-intf>Remote</method-intf>
    <method-name>reduceQuantity</method-name>
    <method-params>
     <method-param>int</method-param>
    </method-params>
   </method>
   <trans-attribute>Required</trans-attribute>
  </container-transaction>
  <container-transaction>
   <method>
    <ejb-name>TheInventory</ejb-name>
    <method-intf>Home</method-intf>
    <method-name>remove</method-name>
    <method-params>
     <method-param>javax.ejb.Handle</method-param>
    </method-params>
   </method>
   <trans-attribute>Required</trans-attribute>
  </container-transaction>
  <container-transaction>
   <method>
    <ejb-name>TheInventory</ejb-name>
    <method-intf>Home</method-intf>
    <method-name>remove</method-name>
    <method-params>
     <method-param>java.lang.Object</method-param>
    </method-params>
   </method>
   <trans-attribute>Required</trans-attribute>
  </container-transaction>
  <container-transaction>
   <method>
    <ejb-name>TheInventory</ejb-name>
    <method-intf>Remote</method-intf>
    <method-name>remove</method-name>
```

LISTING 19.4 continued

```
    <method-params/>
   </method>
   <trans-attribute>Required</trans-attribute>
  </container-transaction>
  <container-transaction>
   <method>
    <ejb-name>TheInventory</ejb-name>
    <method-intf>Home</method-intf>
    <method-name>findByPrimaryKey</method-name>
    <method-params>
     <method-param>java.lang.String</method-param>
    </method-params>
   </method>
   <trans-attribute>Required</trans-attribute>
  </container-transaction>
 </assembly-descriptor>
 <ejb-client-jar>inventoryEjb_client.jar</ejb-client-jar>
</ejb-jar>
```

LISTING 19.5 The web.xml File for Pet Store

```
<?xml version="1.0" encoding="ISO8859_1"?>
<!DOCTYPE web-app PUBLIC '-//Sun Microsystems, Inc.
//DTD Web Application 2.2//EN'
'http://java.sun.com/j2ee/dtds/web-app_2.2.dtd'>
<web-app>
    <display-name>WebTier</display-name>
    <description>Web Tier DD for the PetStore application</description>
    <servlet>
        <servlet-name>webTierEntryPoint</servlet-name>
        <display-name>centralServlet</display-name>
        <description>no description</description>
        <servlet-class>
         com.sun.j2ee.blueprints.petstore.control.web.MainServlet
        </servlet-class>
    </servlet>
    <servlet>
        <servlet-name>populateServlet</servlet-name>
        <display-name>Populate Servlet</display-name>
        <description>no description</description>
        <servlet-class>
         com.sun.j2ee.blueprints.tools.populate.web.PopulateServlet
        </servlet-class>
    </servlet>
    <servlet-mapping>
        <servlet-name>webTierEntryPoint</servlet-name>
        <url-pattern>/control/*</url-pattern>
    </servlet-mapping>
```

LISTING 19.5 continued

```
<servlet-mapping>
    <servlet-name>populateServlet</servlet-name>
    <url-pattern>/populate</url-pattern>
</servlet-mapping>
<session-config>
    <session-timeout>54</session-timeout>
</session-config>
<welcome-file-list>
    <welcome-file>index.html</welcome-file>
</welcome-file-list>
<resource-ref>
    <description>no description</description>
    <res-ref-name>jdbc/EstoreDataSource</res-ref-name>
    <res-type>javax.sql.DataSource</res-type>
    <res-auth>Container</res-auth>
</resource-ref>
<env-entry>
    <description>no description</description>
    <env-entry-name>ejb/catalog/CatalogDAOClass</env-entry-name>
    <env-entry-value>
     com.sun.j2ee.blueprints.shoppingcart.catalog.dao.CatalogDAOImpl
    </env-entry-value>
    <env-entry-type>java.lang.String</env-entry-type>
</env-entry>
<env-entry>
    <description>no description</description>
    <env-entry-name>ejb/profilemgr/ProfileMgrDAOClass</env-entry-name>
    <env-entry-value>
    com.sun.j2ee.blueprints.personalization.profilemgr.dao.ProfileMgrDAOImpl
    </env-entry-value>
    <env-entry-type>java.lang.String</env-entry-type>
</env-entry>
<env-entry>
    <description>no description</description>
    <env-entry-name>server/ServerType</env-entry-name>
    <env-entry-value>
     Java 2 Enterprise Edition Reference Implementation
    </env-entry-value>
    <env-entry-type>java.lang.String</env-entry-type>
</env-entry>
<ejb-ref>
    <description>no description</description>
    <ejb-ref-name>ejb/catalog/Catalog</ejb-ref-name>
    <ejb-ref-type>Session</ejb-ref-type>
    <home>
     com.sun.j2ee.blueprints.shoppingcart.catalog.ejb.CatalogHome
    </home>
    <remote>
     com.sun.j2ee.blueprints.shoppingcart.catalog.ejb.Catalog
    </remote>
```

LISTING 19.5 continued

```
    </ejb-ref>
    <ejb-ref>
        <description>no description</description>
        <ejb-ref-name>ejb/cart/Cart</ejb-ref-name>
        <ejb-ref-type>Session</ejb-ref-type>
        <home>
         com.sun.j2ee.blueprints.shoppingcart.cart.ejb.ShoppingCartHome
        </home>
        <remote>
         com.sun.j2ee.blueprints.shoppingcart.cart.ejb.ShoppingCart
        </remote>
    </ejb-ref>
    <ejb-ref>
        <description>no description</description>
        <ejb-ref-name>ejb/customer/Customer</ejb-ref-name>
        <ejb-ref-type>Session</ejb-ref-type>
        <home>com.sun.j2ee.blueprints.customer.customer.ejb.CustomerHome</home>
        <remote>com.sun.j2ee.blueprints.customer.customer.ejb.Customer</remote>
    </ejb-ref>
    <ejb-ref>
        <description>no description</description>
        <ejb-ref-name>ejb/profilemgr/ProfileMgr</ejb-ref-name>
        <ejb-ref-type>Entity</ejb-ref-type>
        <home>
         com.sun.j2ee.blueprints.personalization.profilemgr.ejb.ProfileMgrHome
        </home>
        <remote>
         com.sun.j2ee.blueprints.personalization.profilemgr.ejb.ProfileMgr
        </remote>
    </ejb-ref>
    <ejb-ref>
        <description>no description</description>
        <ejb-ref-name>ejb/scc/Scc</ejb-ref-name>
        <ejb-ref-type>Session</ejb-ref-type>
        <home>
      com.sun.j2ee.blueprints.petstore.control.ejb.ShoppingClientControllerHome
        </home>
        <remote>
         com.sun.j2ee.blueprints.petstore.control.ejb.ShoppingClientController
        </remote>
    </ejb-ref>
    <ejb-ref>
        <description>no description</description>
        <ejb-ref-name>ejb/inventory/Inventory</ejb-ref-name>
        <ejb-ref-type>Entity</ejb-ref-type>
        <home>com.sun.j2ee.blueprints.inventory.ejb.InventoryHome</home>
        <remote>com.sun.j2ee.blueprints.inventory.ejb.Inventory</remote>
    </ejb-ref>
</web-app>
```

LISTING 19.6 The web.xml File for SilverBooks

```
<?xml version="1.0" encoding="ISO-8859-1"?>
<!DOCTYPE web-app PUBLIC "-//Sun Microsystems, Inc.
//DTD Web Application 2.2//EN"
  "http://java.sun.com/j2ee/dtds/web-app_2_2.dtd">
<web-app>
    <!-- Action Servlet Configuration -->
    <servlet>
        <servlet-name>action</servlet-name>
        <servlet-class>org.apache.struts.action.ActionServlet</servlet-class>
        <init-param>
            <param-name>application</param-name>
            <param-value>
             com.sssw.demo.silverbooks.res.ApplicationResources
            </param-value>
        </init-param>
        <init-param>
            <param-name>config</param-name>
            <param-value>/WEB-INF/action.xml</param-value>
        </init-param>
        <init-param>
            <param-name>debug</param-name>
            <param-value>2</param-value>
        </init-param>
        <init-param>
            <param-name>detail</param-name>
            <param-value>2</param-value>
        </init-param>
        <load-on-startup>2</load-on-startup>
    </servlet>
    <servlet>
        <servlet-name>imagesdb</servlet-name>
        <servlet-class>com.sssw.demo.silverbooks.ImageServlet</servlet-class>
    </servlet>
    <!-- Action Servlet Mapping -->
    <servlet-mapping>
        <servlet-name>action</servlet-name>
        <url-pattern>*.do</url-pattern>
    </servlet-mapping>
    <servlet-mapping>
        <servlet-name>imagesdb</servlet-name>
        <url-pattern>/imagesdb/*</url-pattern>
    </servlet-mapping>
    <!-- The Welcome File List -->
    <welcome-file-list>
        <welcome-file>booklist.jsp</welcome-file>
    </welcome-file-list>
    <!-- Struts Tag Library Descriptor -->
    <taglib>
        <taglib-uri>/WEB-INF/struts.tld</taglib-uri>
        <taglib-location>/WEB-INF/struts.tld</taglib-location>
    </taglib>
</web-app>
```

LISTING 19.7 The Pet Store Resource Resolution File in the J2EE Reference Implementation Environment

```
<?xml version="1.0" encoding="Cp1252"?>
<j2ee-ri-specific-information>
   <server-name/>
   <rolemapping/>
   <web>
      <module-name>petstore.war</module-name>
      <context-root>estore</context-root>
      <resource-ref>
         <res-ref-name>jdbc/EstoreDataSource</res-ref-name>
         <jndi-name>jdbc/Cloudscape</jndi-name>
         <default-resource-principal>
            <name>estoreuser</name>
            <password>estore</password>
         </default-resource-principal>
      </resource-ref>
      <ejb-ref>
         <ejb-ref-name>ejb/catalog/Catalog</ejb-ref-name>
         <jndi-name>estore/catalog</jndi-name>
         <use-ssl>false</use-ssl>
      </ejb-ref>
      <ejb-ref>
         <ejb-ref-name>ejb/cart/Cart</ejb-ref-name>
         <jndi-name>estore/cart</jndi-name>
         <use-ssl>false</use-ssl>
      </ejb-ref>
      <ejb-ref>
         <ejb-ref-name>ejb/customer/Customer</ejb-ref-name>
         <jndi-name>estore/customer</jndi-name>
         <use-ssl>false</use-ssl>
      </ejb-ref>
      <ejb-ref>
         <ejb-ref-name>ejb/profilemgr/ProfileMgr</ejb-ref-name>
         <jndi-name>estore/profilemgr</jndi-name>
         <use-ssl>false</use-ssl>
      </ejb-ref>
      <ejb-ref>
         <ejb-ref-name>ejb/scc/Scc</ejb-ref-name>
         <jndi-name>estore/scc</jndi-name>
         <use-ssl>false</use-ssl>
      </ejb-ref>
      <ejb-ref>
         <ejb-ref-name>ejb/inventory/Inventory</ejb-ref-name>
         <jndi-name>estore/inventory</jndi-name>
         <use-ssl>false</use-ssl>
      </ejb-ref>
   </web>
   <enterprise-beans>
      <module-name>mailerEjb.jar</module-name>
      <unique-id>0</unique-id>
```

LISTING 19.7 continued

```
      <ejb>
         <ejb-name>TheMailer</ejb-name>
         <jndi-name>estore/mailer</jndi-name>
         <resource-ref>
            <res-ref-name>mail/MailSession</res-ref-name>
            <jndi-name>mail/Session</jndi-name>
            <mail-configuration>
               <name>YourName</name>
               <mail-from>orders@javapetstoredemo.com</mail-from>
               <mail-host>YourMailServer</mail-host>
            </mail-configuration>
         </resource-ref>
      </ejb>
   </enterprise-beans>
   <enterprise-beans>
      <module-name>signonEjb.jar</module-name>
      <unique-id>0</unique-id>
      <ejb>
         <ejb-name>TheSignOn</ejb-name>
         <jndi-name>estore/signon</jndi-name>
         <resource-ref>
            <res-ref-name>jdbc/SignOnDataSource</res-ref-name>
            <jndi-name>jdbc/Cloudscape</jndi-name>
            <default-resource-principal>
               <name>estoreuser</name>
               <password>estore</password>
            </default-resource-principal>
         </resource-ref>
      </ejb>
   </enterprise-beans>
   <enterprise-beans>
      <module-name>personalizationEjb.jar</module-name>
      <unique-id>0</unique-id>
      <ejb>
         <ejb-name>TheProfileMgr</ejb-name>
         <jndi-name>estore/profilemgr</jndi-name>
         <resource-ref>
            <res-ref-name>jdbc/EstoreDataSource</res-ref-name>
            <jndi-name>jdbc/Cloudscape</jndi-name>
            <default-resource-principal>
               <name>estoreuser</name>
               <password>estore</password>
            </default-resource-principal>
         </resource-ref>
      </ejb>
   </enterprise-beans>
   <enterprise-beans>
      <module-name>shoppingcartEjb.jar</module-name>
      <unique-id>0</unique-id>
      <ejb>
```

LISTING 19.7 continued

```
        <ejb-name>TheCart</ejb-name>
        <jndi-name>estore/cart</jndi-name>
        <ejb-ref>
          <ejb-ref-name>ejb/catalog/Catalog</ejb-ref-name>
          <jndi-name>estore/catalog</jndi-name>
          <use-ssl>false</use-ssl>
        </ejb-ref>
      </ejb>
      <ejb>
        <ejb-name>TheCatalog</ejb-name>
        <jndi-name>estore/catalog</jndi-name>
        <resource-ref>
          <res-ref-name>jdbc/EstoreDataSource</res-ref-name>
          <jndi-name>jdbc/Cloudscape</jndi-name>
          <default-resource-principal>
            <name>estoreuser</name>
            <password>estore</password>
          </default-resource-principal>
        </resource-ref>
      </ejb>
    </enterprise-beans>
    <enterprise-beans>
      <module-name>petstoreEjb.jar</module-name>
      <unique-id>0</unique-id>
      <ejb>
        <ejb-name>TheShoppingClientController</ejb-name>
        <jndi-name>estore/scc</jndi-name>
        <ejb-ref>
          <ejb-ref-name>ejb/mail/Mailer</ejb-ref-name>
          <jndi-name>estore/mailer</jndi-name>
          <use-ssl>false</use-ssl>
        </ejb-ref>
        <ejb-ref>
          <ejb-ref-name>ejb/catalog/Catalog</ejb-ref-name>
          <jndi-name>estore/catalog</jndi-name>
          <use-ssl>false</use-ssl>
        </ejb-ref>
        <ejb-ref>
          <ejb-ref-name>ejb/cart/Cart</ejb-ref-name>
          <jndi-name>estore/cart</jndi-name>
          <use-ssl>false</use-ssl>
        </ejb-ref>
        <ejb-ref>
          <ejb-ref-name>ejb/profilemgr/ProfileMgr</ejb-ref-name>
          <jndi-name>estore/profilemgr</jndi-name>
          <use-ssl>false</use-ssl>
        </ejb-ref>
```

LISTING 19.7 continued

```
        <ejb-ref>
          <ejb-ref-name>ejb/signon/Signon</ejb-ref-name>
          <jndi-name>estore/signon</jndi-name>
          <use-ssl>false</use-ssl>
        </ejb-ref>
        <ejb-ref>
          <ejb-ref-name>ejb/customer/Customer</ejb-ref-name>
          <jndi-name>estore/customer</jndi-name>
          <use-ssl>false</use-ssl>
        </ejb-ref>
        <ejb-ref>
          <ejb-ref-name>ejb/inventory/Inventory</ejb-ref-name>
          <jndi-name>estore/inventory</jndi-name>
          <use-ssl>false</use-ssl>
        </ejb-ref>
      </ejb>
    </enterprise-beans>
    <enterprise-beans>
      <module-name>inventoryEjb.jar</module-name>
      <unique-id>0</unique-id>
      <ejb>
        <ejb-name>TheInventory</ejb-name>
        <jndi-name>estore/inventory</jndi-name>
        <resource-ref>
          <res-ref-name>jdbc/InventoryDataSource</res-ref-name>
          <jndi-name>jdbc/Cloudscape</jndi-name>
          <default-resource-principal>
            <name>estoreuser</name>
            <password>estore</password>
          </default-resource-principal>
        </resource-ref>
      </ejb>
    </enterprise-beans>
    <enterprise-beans>
      <module-name>customerEjb.jar</module-name>
      <unique-id>0</unique-id>
      <ejb>
        <ejb-name>TheCustomer</ejb-name>
        <jndi-name>estore/customer</jndi-name>
        <ejb-ref>
          <ejb-ref-name>ejb/account/Account</ejb-ref-name>
          <jndi-name>estore/account</jndi-name>
          <use-ssl>false</use-ssl>
        </ejb-ref>
        <ejb-ref>
          <ejb-ref-name>ejb/order/Order</ejb-ref-name>
          <jndi-name>estore/order</jndi-name>
          <use-ssl>false</use-ssl>
```

LISTING 19.7 continued

```
            </ejb-ref>
        </ejb>
        <ejb>
            <ejb-name>TheAccount</ejb-name>
            <jndi-name>estore/account</jndi-name>
            <resource-ref>
                <res-ref-name>jdbc/EstoreDataSource</res-ref-name>
                <jndi-name>jdbc/Cloudscape</jndi-name>
                <default-resource-principal>
                    <name>estoreuser</name>
                    <password>estore</password>
                </default-resource-principal>
            </resource-ref>
        </ejb>
        <ejb>
            <ejb-name>TheOrder</ejb-name>
            <jndi-name>estore/order</jndi-name>
            <resource-ref>
                <res-ref-name>jdbc/EstoreDataSource</res-ref-name>
                <jndi-name>jdbc/Cloudscape</jndi-name>
                <default-resource-principal>
                    <name>estoreuser</name>
                    <password>estore</password>
                </default-resource-principal>
            </resource-ref>
            <ejb-ref>
                <ejb-ref-name>ejb/account/Account</ejb-ref-name>
                <jndi-name>estore/account</jndi-name>
                <use-ssl>false</use-ssl>
            </ejb-ref>
        </ejb>
    </enterprise-beans>
</j2ee-ri-specific-information>
```

LISTING 19.8 The Pet Store Resource Resolution File in the SilverStream Environment

```
<?xml version="1.0" encoding="UTF-8" standalone="yes"?>
<?AgMetaXML 1.0?>
<earJarOptions isObject="true" >
  <earJar isObject="true" >
    <earJarName>petstore.ear</earJarName>
    <moduleList isObject="true" >
      <module isObject="true" >
        <ejbJar isObject="true" >
          <ejbJarName>customerEjb.jar</ejbJarName>
          <isEnabled type="Boolean">true</isEnabled>
          <remoteAccessJar>customerEjbRemote.jar</remoteAccessJar>
```

LISTING 19.8 continued

```
    <addManifest type="Boolean">false</addManifest>
    <addDescriptor type="Boolean">true</addDescriptor>
    <addDeploymentInfo type="Boolean">true</addDeploymentInfo>
    <beansList isObject="true" >
      <session isObject="true" >
        <bean isObject="true" >
          <beanName>TheCustomer</beanName>
          <beanJNDIName>estore/customer</beanJNDIName>
          <beanReferenceList isObject="true" >
            <beanReference isObject="true" >
              <name>ejb/account</name>
              <beanLink>estore/account</beanLink>
            </beanReference>
            <beanReference isObject="true" >
              <name>ejb/order</name>
              <beanLink>estore/order</beanLink>
            </beanReference>
          </beanReferenceList>
        </bean>
      </session>
      <entity isObject="true" >
        <bean isObject="true" >
          <beanName>TheAccount</beanName>
          <beanJNDIName>estore/account</beanJNDIName>
          <resourceReferenceList isObject="true" >
            <resourceReference isObject="true" >
              <name>jdbc/EstoreDataSource</name>
              <dataSource>EstoreDB</dataSource>
            </resourceReference>
          </resourceReferenceList>
        </bean>
      </entity>
      <entity isObject="true" >
        <bean isObject="true" >
          <beanName>TheOrder</beanName>
          <beanJNDIName>estore/order</beanJNDIName>
          <beanReferenceList isObject="true" >
            <beanReference isObject="true" >
              <name>ejb/account</name>
              <beanLink>estore/account</beanLink>
            </beanReference>
          </beanReferenceList>
          <resourceReferenceList isObject="true" >
            <resourceReference isObject="true" >
              <name>jdbc/EstoreDataSource</name>
              <dataSource>EstoreDB</dataSource>
            </resourceReference>
          </resourceReferenceList>
        </bean>
```

LISTING 19.8 continued

```
        </entity>
      </beansList>
    </ejbJar>
  </module>
  <module isObject="true" >
    <ejbJar isObject="true" >
      <ejbJarName>petstoreEjb.jar</ejbJarName>
      <isEnabled type="Boolean">true</isEnabled>
      <remoteAccessJar>petstoreEjbRemote.jar</remoteAccessJar>
      <addManifest type="Boolean">false</addManifest>
      <addDescriptor type="Boolean">true</addDescriptor>
      <addDeploymentInfo type="Boolean">true</addDeploymentInfo>
      <beansList isObject="true" >
        <session isObject="true" >
          <bean isObject="true" >
            <beanName>TheShoppingClientController</beanName>
            <beanJNDIName>estore/scc</beanJNDIName>
            <beanReferenceList isObject="true" >
              <beanReference isObject="true" >
                <name>ejb/mailer</name>
                <beanLink>estore/mailer</beanLink>
              </beanReference>
              <beanReference isObject="true" >
                <name>ejb/catalog</name>
                <beanLink>estore/catalog</beanLink>
              </beanReference>
              <beanReference isObject="true" >
                <name>ejb/cart</name>
                <beanLink>estore/cart</beanLink>
              </beanReference>
              <beanReference isObject="true" >
                <name>ejb/profilemgr</name>
                <beanLink>estore/profilemgr</beanLink>
              </beanReference>
              <beanReference isObject="true" >
                <name>ejb/customer</name>
                <beanLink>estore/customer</beanLink>
              </beanReference>
              <beanReference isObject="true" >
                <name>ejb/inventory</name>
                <beanLink>estore/inventory</beanLink>
              </beanReference>
            </beanReferenceList>
          </bean>
        </session>
        <entity isObject="true" >
          <bean isObject="true" >
            <beanName>TheProfileMgr</beanName>
```

Listing 19.8 continued

```
<beanJNDIName>estore/profilemgr</beanJNDIName>
          <beanReferenceList isObject="true" >
            <beanReference isObject="true" >
              <name>ejb/catalog</name>
              <beanLink>estore/catalog</beanLink>
            </beanReference>
          </beanReferenceList>
          <resourceReferenceList isObject="true" >
            <resourceReference isObject="true" >
              <name>jdbc/EstoreDataSource</name>
              <dataSource>EstoreDB</dataSource>
            </resourceReference>
          </resourceReferenceList>
        </bean>
      </entity>
    </beansList>
  </ejbJar>
</module>
<module isObject="true" >
  <ejbJar isObject="true" >
    <ejbJarName>inventoryEjb.jar</ejbJarName>
    <isEnabled type="Boolean">true</isEnabled>
    <remoteAccessJar>inventoryEjbRemote.jar</remoteAccessJar>
    <addManifest type="Boolean">false</addManifest>
    <addDescriptor type="Boolean">true</addDescriptor>
    <addDeploymentInfo type="Boolean">true</addDeploymentInfo>
    <beansList isObject="true" >
      <entity isObject="true" >
        <bean isObject="true" >
          <beanName>TheInventory</beanName>
          <beanJNDIName>estore/inventory</beanJNDIName>
          <resourceReferenceList isObject="true" >
            <resourceReference isObject="true" >
              <name>jdbc/InventoryDataSource</name>
              <dataSource>InventoryDB</dataSource>
            </resourceReference>
          </resourceReferenceList>
        </bean>
      </entity>
    </beansList>
  </ejbJar>
</module>
<module isObject="true" >
  <ejbJar isObject="true" >
    <ejbJarName>mailerEjb.jar</ejbJarName>
    <isEnabled type="Boolean">true</isEnabled>
    <remoteAccessJar>mailerEjbRemote.jar</remoteAccessJar>
    <addManifest type="Boolean">false</addManifest>
    <addDescriptor type="Boolean">true</addDescriptor>
```

LISTING 19.8 continued

```
        <addDeploymentInfo type="Boolean">true</addDeploymentInfo>
        <beansList isObject="true" >
          <session isObject="true" >
            <bean isObject="true" >
              <beanName>TheMailer</beanName>
              <beanJNDIName>estore/mailer</beanJNDIName>
              <resourceReferenceList isObject="true" >
                <resourceReference isObject="true" >
                  <name>mail/MailSession</name>
                  <mailRefProperties type="StringArray">
                    <el>mail.name</el>
                    <el>j2ee</el>
                    <el>mail.from</el>
                    <el>orders@javapetstoredemo.com</el>
                    <el>mail.host</el>
                    <el>shorter.eng.sun.com</el>
                  </mailRefProperties>
                </resourceReference>
              </resourceReferenceList>
            </bean>
          </session>
        </beansList>
      </ejbJar>
    </module>
    <module isObject="true" >
      <ejbJar isObject="true" >
        <ejbJarName>shoppingcartEjb.jar</ejbJarName>
        <isEnabled type="Boolean">true</isEnabled>
        <remoteAccessJar>shoppingcartEjbRemote.jar</remoteAccessJar>
        <addManifest type="Boolean">false</addManifest>
        <addDescriptor type="Boolean">true</addDescriptor>
        <addDeploymentInfo type="Boolean">true</addDeploymentInfo>
        <beansList isObject="true" >
          <session isObject="true" >
            <bean isObject="true" >
              <beanName>TheCart</beanName>
              <beanJNDIName>estore/cart</beanJNDIName>
              <beanReferenceList isObject="true" >
                <beanReference isObject="true" >
                  <name>ejb/catalog</name>
                  <beanLink>estore/catalog</beanLink>
                </beanReference>
              </beanReferenceList>
            </bean>
          </session>
          <session isObject="true" >
            <bean isObject="true" >
              <beanName>TheCatalog</beanName>
              <beanJNDIName>estore/catalog</beanJNDIName>
```

LISTING 19.8 continued

```
          <resourceReferenceList isObject="true" >
            <resourceReference isObject="true" >
              <name>jdbc/EstoreDataSource</name>
              <dataSource>EstoreDB</dataSource>
            </resourceReference>
          </resourceReferenceList>
        </bean>
      </session>
    </beansList>
  </ejbJar>
</module>
<module isObject="true" >
  <warJar isObject="true" >
    <warJarName>petstore.war</warJarName>
    <isEnabled type="Boolean">true</isEnabled>
    <URL>estore</URL>
    <usesJars type="StringArray">
      <el>petstoreEjbClient.jar</el>
      <el>petstoreEjbRemote.jar</el>
      <el>mailerEjbRemote.jar</el>
      <el>mailerEjb.jar</el>
      <el>customerEjbRemote.jar</el>
      <el>customerEjb.jar</el>
      <el>inventoryEjbRemote.jar</el>
      <el>inventoryEjb.jar</el>
      <el>shoppingcartEjbRemote.jar</el>
      <el>shoppingcartEjb.jar</el>
    </usesJars>
    <excludedJSPs type="StringArray">
      <el>changeaddressform.jsp</el>
      <el>changepreferencesform.jsp</el>
      <el>ja/search.jsp</el>
      <el>mylist.jsp</el>
    </excludedJSPs>
    <beanReferenceList isObject="true" >
      <beanReference isObject="true" >
        <name>ejb/catalog</name>
        <beanLink>estore/catalog</beanLink>
      </beanReference>
      <beanReference isObject="true" >
        <name>ejb/cart</name>
        <beanLink>estore/cart</beanLink>
      </beanReference>
      <beanReference isObject="true" >
        <name>ejb/customer</name>
        <beanLink>estore/customer</beanLink>
      </beanReference>
      <beanReference isObject="true" >
        <name>ejb/scc</name>
```

LISTING 19.8 continued

```
              <beanLink>estore/scc</beanLink>
            </beanReference>
            <beanReference isObject="true" >
              <name>ejb/inventory</name>
              <beanLink>estore/inventory</beanLink>
            </beanReference>
          </beanReferenceList>
          <resourceReferenceList isObject="true" >
            <resourceReference isObject="true" >
              <name>jdbc/EstoreDataSource</name>
              <dataSource>EstoreDB</dataSource>
            </resourceReference>
          </resourceReferenceList>
        </warJar>
      </module>
    </moduleList>
    <roleMap isObject="true" >
      <roleMapping isObject="true" >
        <name>gold_customer</name>
        <userOrGroupName>gold</userOrGroupName>
      </roleMapping>
      <roleMapping isObject="true" >
        <name>administrator</name>
        <userOrGroupName>admin</userOrGroupName>
      </roleMapping>
      <roleMapping isObject="true" >
        <name>customer</name>
        <userOrGroupName>cust</userOrGroupName>
      </roleMapping>
    </roleMap>
  </earJar>
</earJarOptions>
```

LISTING 19.9 The Pet Store Resource Resolution File in the WebLogic Environment

```
<?xml version="1.0"?>
<!DOCTYPE weblogic-ejb-jar PUBLIC '-//BEA Systems, Inc.
//DTD WebLogic 6.1.0 EJB//EN'
'http://www.bea.com/servers/wls600/dtd/weblogic-ejb-jar.dtd'>
<weblogic-ejb-jar>
    <weblogic-enterprise-bean>
      <ejb-name>TheInventory</ejb-name>
      <reference-descriptor>
    <resource-description>
      <res-ref-name>jdbc/InventoryDataSource</res-ref-name>
      <jndi-name>jdbc.InventoryDB</jndi-name>
```

LISTING 19.9 continued

```
</resource-description>
  </reference-descriptor>
  <jndi-name>estore/inventory</jndi-name>
</weblogic-enterprise-bean>
<weblogic-enterprise-bean>
  <ejb-name>TheCatalog</ejb-name>
  <reference-descriptor>
<resource-description>
  <res-ref-name>jdbc/EstoreDataSource</res-ref-name>
  <jndi-name>jdbc.EstoreDB</jndi-name>
</resource-description>
<ejb-reference-description>
  <ejb-ref-name>ejb/inventory</ejb-ref-name>
  <jndi-name>estore/inventory</jndi-name>
</ejb-reference-description>
  </reference-descriptor>
  <jndi-name>estore/catalog</jndi-name>
</weblogic-enterprise-bean>
<weblogic-enterprise-bean>
  <ejb-name>TheCart</ejb-name>
  <reference-descriptor>
<ejb-reference-description>
  <ejb-ref-name>ejb/catalog</ejb-ref-name>
  <jndi-name>estore/catalog</jndi-name>
</ejb-reference-description>
  </reference-descriptor>
  <jndi-name>estore/cart</jndi-name>
</weblogic-enterprise-bean>
<weblogic-enterprise-bean>
  <ejb-name>TheMailer</ejb-name>
  <reference-descriptor>
<resource-description>
  <res-ref-name>mail/MailSession</res-ref-name>
  <jndi-name>mail/Session</jndi-name>
</resource-description>
<ejb-reference-description>
  <ejb-ref-name>ejb/order</ejb-ref-name>
  <jndi-name>estore/order</jndi-name>
</ejb-reference-description>
<ejb-reference-description>
  <ejb-ref-name>ejb/account</ejb-ref-name>
  <jndi-name>estore/account</jndi-name>
</ejb-reference-description>
  </reference-descriptor>
  <jndi-name>estore/mailer</jndi-name>
</weblogic-enterprise-bean>
<weblogic-enterprise-bean>
  <ejb-name>TheAccount</ejb-name>
```

LISTING 19.9 continued

```
    <persistence-descriptor>
  <delay-updates-until-end-of-tx>false</delay-updates-until-end-of-tx>
    </persistence-descriptor>
    <reference-descriptor>
  <resource-description>
    <res-ref-name>jdbc/EstoreDataSource</res-ref-name>
    <jndi-name>jdbc.EstoreDB</jndi-name>
  </resource-description>
    </reference-descriptor>
    <jndi-name>estore/account</jndi-name>
  </weblogic-enterprise-bean>
  <weblogic-enterprise-bean>
    <ejb-name>TheShoppingClientController</ejb-name>
    <reference-descriptor>
  <ejb-reference-description>
    <ejb-ref-name>ejb/catalog</ejb-ref-name>
    <jndi-name>estore/catalog</jndi-name>
  </ejb-reference-description>
  <ejb-reference-description>
    <ejb-ref-name>ejb/mailer</ejb-ref-name>
    <jndi-name>estore/mailer</jndi-name>
  </ejb-reference-description>
  <ejb-reference-description>
    <ejb-ref-name>ejb/order</ejb-ref-name>
    <jndi-name>estore/order</jndi-name>
  </ejb-reference-description>
  <ejb-reference-description>
    <ejb-ref-name>ejb/cart</ejb-ref-name>
    <jndi-name>estore/cart</jndi-name>
  </ejb-reference-description>
  <ejb-reference-description>
    <ejb-ref-name>ejb/inventory</ejb-ref-name>
    <jndi-name>estore/inventory</jndi-name>
  </ejb-reference-description>
  <ejb-reference-description>
    <ejb-ref-name>ejb/account</ejb-ref-name>
    <jndi-name>estore/account</jndi-name>
  </ejb-reference-description>
    </reference-descriptor>
    <jndi-name>estore/scc</jndi-name>
  </weblogic-enterprise-bean>
  <weblogic-enterprise-bean>
    <ejb-name>TheOrder</ejb-name>
    <reference-descriptor>
  <resource-description>
    <res-ref-name>jdbc/EstoreDataSource</res-ref-name>
    <jndi-name>jdbc.EstoreDB</jndi-name>
  </resource-description>
```

LISTING 19.9 continued

```
    <ejb-reference-description>
      <ejb-ref-name>ejb/account</ejb-ref-name>
      <jndi-name>estore/account</jndi-name>
    </ejb-reference-description>
      </reference-descriptor>
      <jndi-name>estore/order</jndi-name>
    </weblogic-enterprise-bean>
    <security-role-assignment>
      <role-name>gold_customer</role-name>
      <principal-name>gold</principal-name>
    </security-role-assignment>
    <security-role-assignment>
      <role-name>customer</role-name>
      <principal-name>cust</principal-name>
      <principal-name>customer</principal-name>
      <principal-name>j2ee</principal-name>
    </security-role-assignment>
  </weblogic-ejb-jar>
```

Summary

This chapter covered various topics related to the process of assembling and deploying a J2EE application to a J2EE application server:

- Java's Write Once, Run Anywhere promise
- The contents of the J2EE archive types and how to create and populate them
- How XML is used for the deployment descriptor and plan files
- Different files that are used to resolve references on several application servers
- Deployment tools used by the featured J2EE application servers

APPENDIX

Documentation for Sample Applications

IN THIS APPENDIX

- SilverBooks *692*
- Java Pet Store *702*

This chapter documents the sample applications developed according to J2EE (Java 2 Platform, Enterprise Edition) specifications.

- SilverBooks, provided by SilverStream, is a Web-based e-commerce application simulating an online bookstore. SilverBooks uses the Struts Framework architecture, an open-source framework for Web applications that implements the Model-View-Controller (MVC) design paradigm.
- Java Pet Store is the standard J2EE sample application from Sun Microsystems.

SilverBooks

SilverBooks is an online bookstore that allows users to purchase books from SilverBooks Corporation, a fictitious bookseller.

This sample application resides in the SilverBooks37 database and is part of the installation for the SilverStream Application Server. To download a copy of the SilverStream software, visit `http://www.silverstream.com`, click on the Downloads section, and then click on the Light Download (J2EE Server + Cloudscape).

SilverBooks is implemented using J2EE standards and the Struts Framework architecture. Struts Framework is an open-source framework for Web applications that implement the MVC design paradigm. As an application that conforms to this paradigm, SilverBooks includes a few components, which you will find in Table A.1.

TABLE A.1 Components Included in SilverBooks

Component	*Description*
Model	A set of form classes that hold the data that is updated by JavaServer Pages (JSPs).
View	JSPs that render the front-end interface. These JSPs insert dynamic content based on the interpretation of action tags at page request time.
Controller	An action servlet that dispatches requests to action classes to perform business logic, such as searching for a book or displaying book details when a user clicks a book title. The action servlet also provides the View component with the user interface to be displayed after the action is completed.

The major benefit of this approach is that it logically separates the key functions of the application—actions, data access, and presentation—to allow role-specific assignments, ease of maintenance, and efficient debugging.

Tour of the SilverBooks Site

After installing the SilverBooks database, open your browser and enter the following URL:

```
http://your-server-name/SilverBooks37/app
```

Figure A.1 shows the page that should be displayed. You can now interact with the SilverBooks application by clicking on the various links.

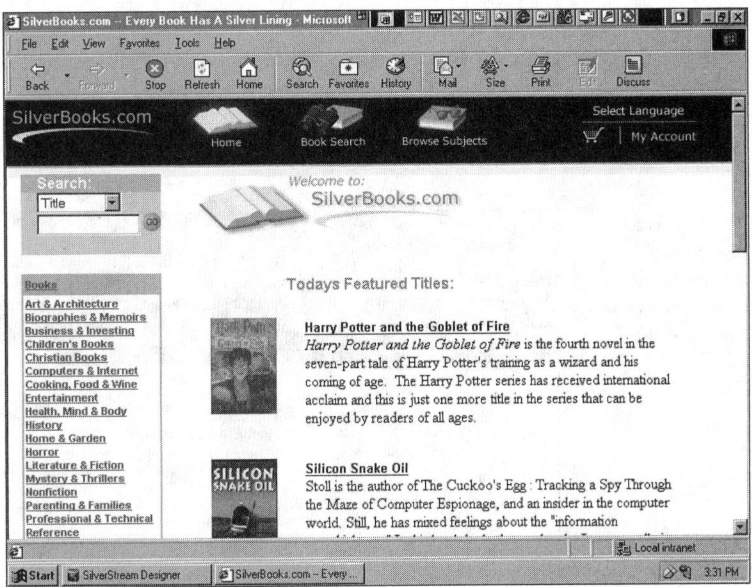

FIGURE A.1
The SilverBooks home page, displayed after launching the application.

From the home page, we see several different navigation options. Figure A.2 shows the result of choosing Select Language. As you can see, we have selected English.

Another option that can be chosen from the home page is My Account. This selection will bring you to the screen shown in Figure A.3.

If you do not already have an account you must create one, as demonstrated in Figure A.4, in order to place orders with SilverBooks.

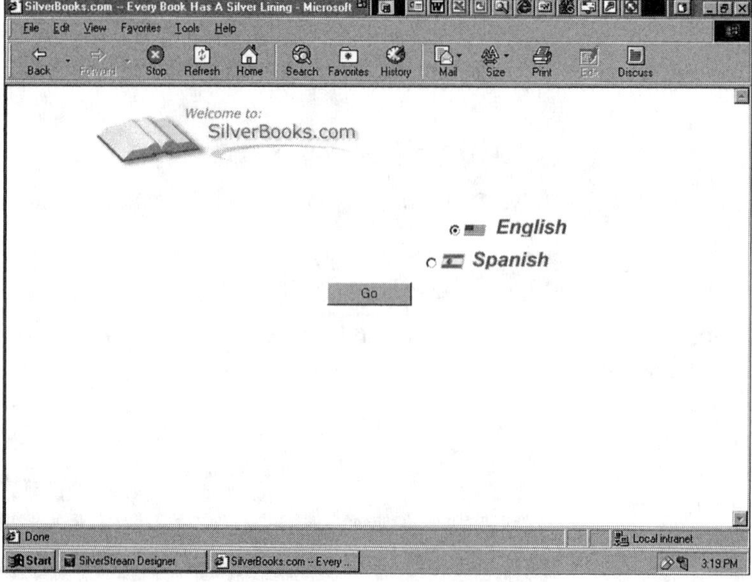

FIGURE A.2
Selecting a language for displaying static text.

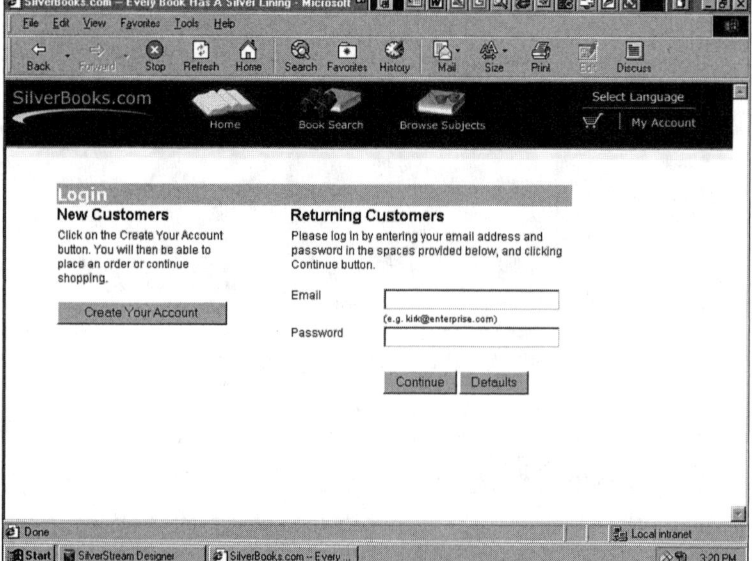

FIGURE A.3
The My Account screen allows you to either log in or create a new account.

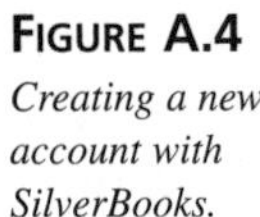

FIGURE A.4
Creating a new account with SilverBooks.

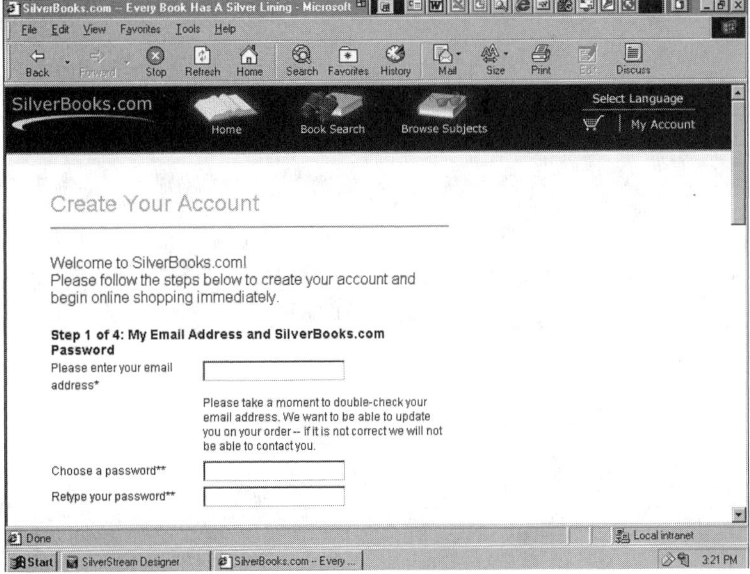

Now that we have created an account, we are ready to shop. Navigation choices include searching by book titles, authors, and subjects. Figure A.5 shows the interface upon choosing Browse Subjects.

FIGURE A.5
The Browse Subjects interface in SilverBooks displays a list of topics, with subdivisions of each.

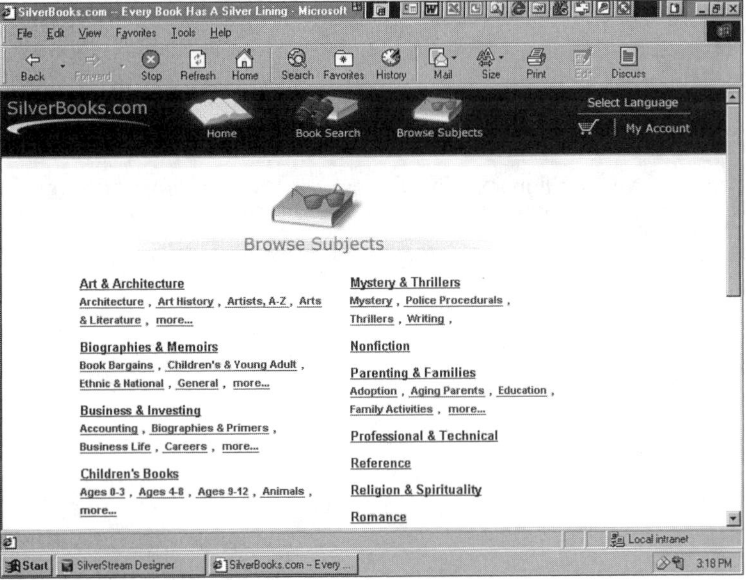

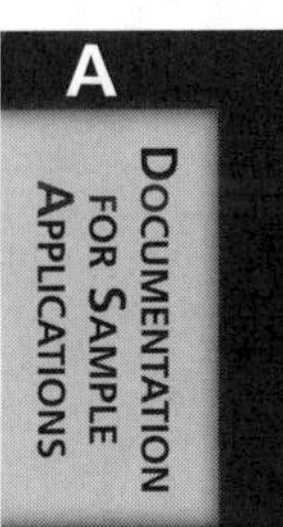

The option for searching for individual titles also exists. Figure A.6 shows the Book Search interface. Here, you can enter any amount of information including a specific book title, author, or publisher. In addition, categorical information can be included to further narrow the search results.

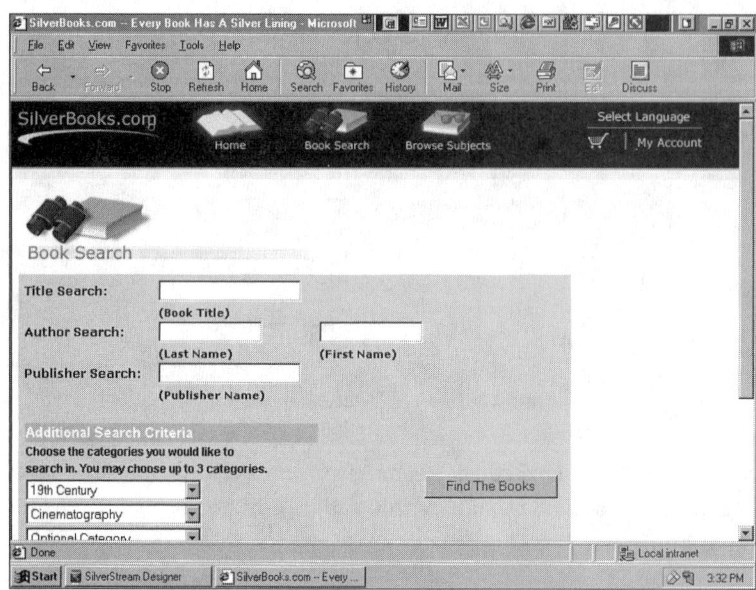

FIGURE A.6
The Book Search screen, with fields including book title, author, or publisher and category drop boxes.

A search for Children's Books has yielded the results seen in Figure A.7.

Clicking Get More Information About This Book brings us to a more detailed description, shown in Figure A.8, of the selected title.

Selecting Add to Shopping Cart brings us to the cart information, displayed in Figure A.9.

FIGURE A.7
Results of a book search, with hyperlinks to further information on fields such as Author and Publisher.

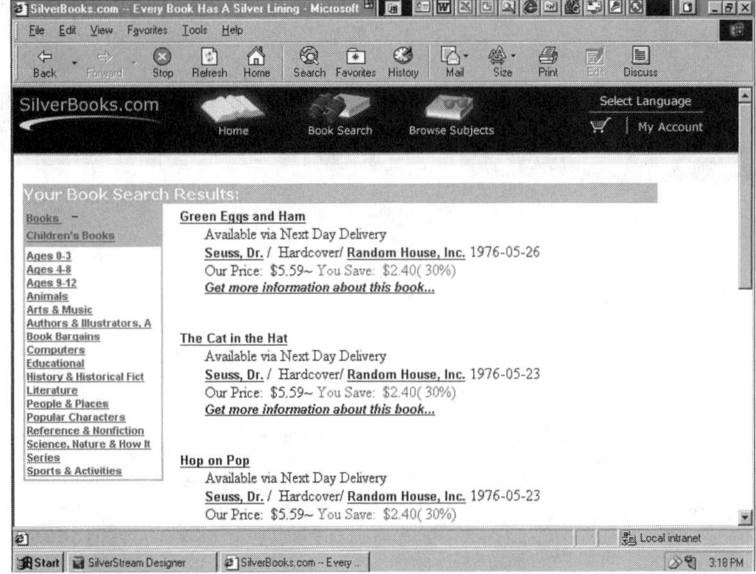

FIGURE A.8
Available book information includes the format of the book, delivery and pricing information, and a brief description.

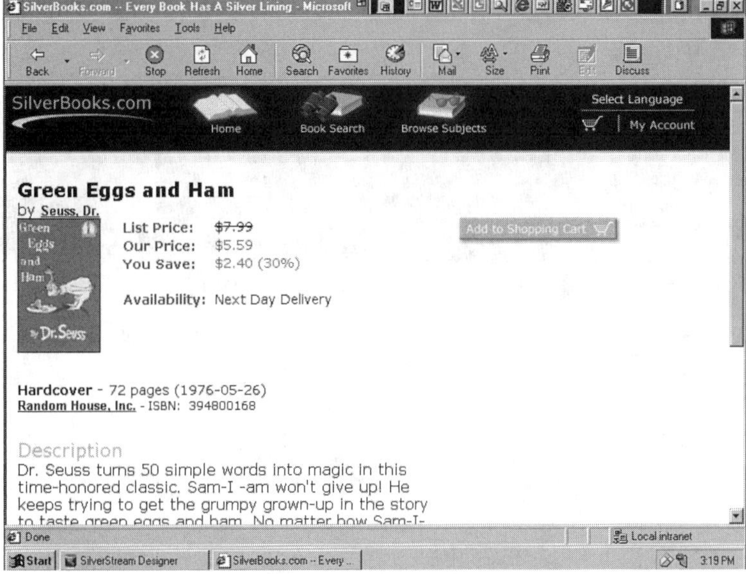

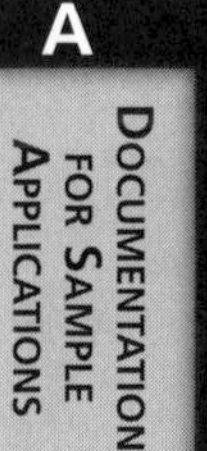

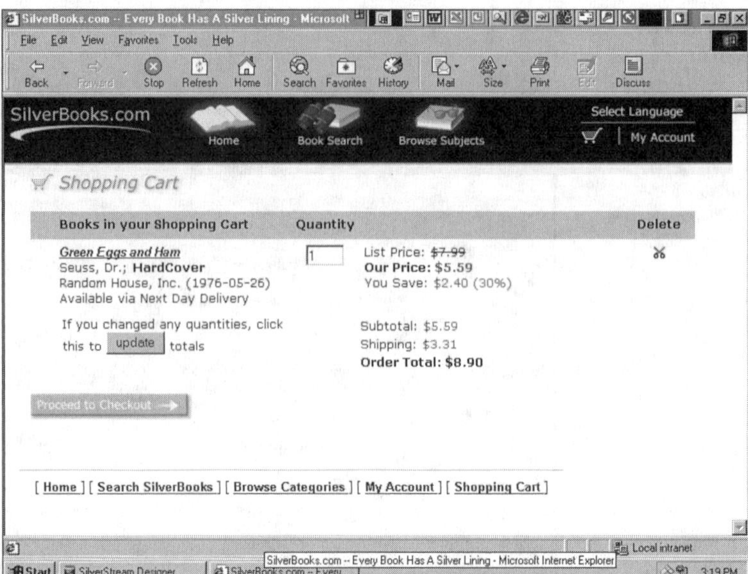

FIGURE A.9
The Shopping Cart screen, with options including changing the quantity ordered, deleting the title from your order, continuing to shop, or proceeding to checkout.

After proceeding to checkout, as seen in Figure A.10, you are given one more opportunity to change your order, as well as confirm delivery information.

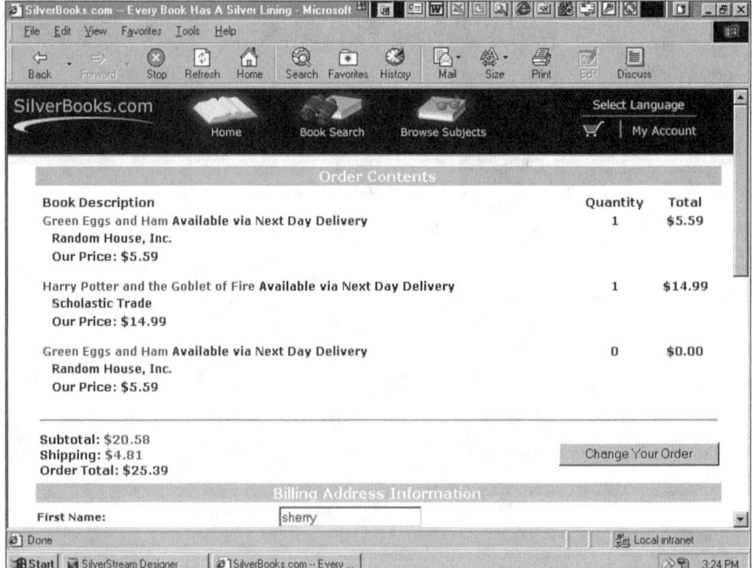

FIGURE A.10
The Checkout screen provides a final chance to alter an order as well as confirm delivery information.

Upon successful submission of the order, a confirmation screen, shown in Figure A.11, will result.

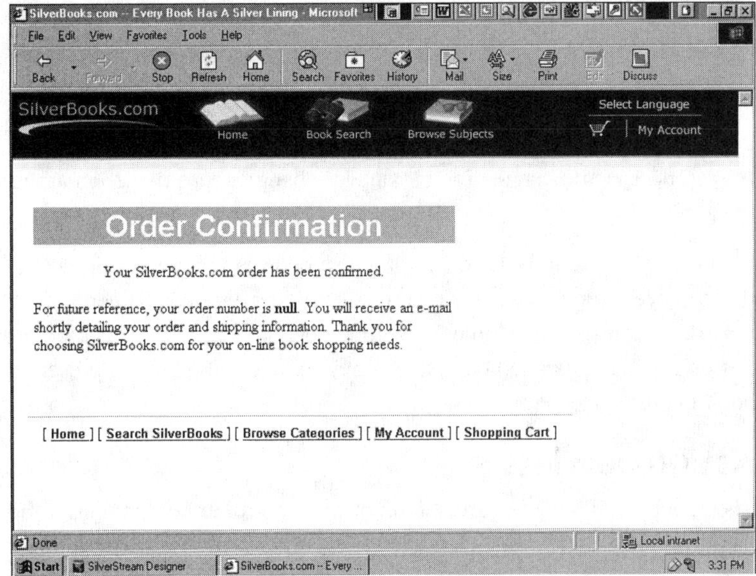

FIGURE A.11
The Confirmation screen verifies successful submission of the order.

Technologies Used in SilverBooks

SilverBooks incorporates J2EE standard technologies to implement the Struts Framework and Model-View-Controller (MVC) design paradigm. The following technologies are described:

- JavaServer Pages (JSP)
- Action servlets
- Form classes
- Enterprise JavaBeans (EJB)

More information about the Struts Framework and the MVC design paradigm can be found in Chapter 10, "Building the User Interface to the Application."

JavaServer Pages (JSP)

JavaServer Pages (JSP) are used to implement the View component of the MVC design paradigm. SilverBooks uses JSPs to present both the static and the dynamic content of the bookstore application.

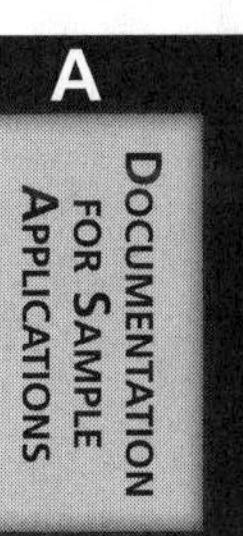

The following JSPs display data considered static, therefore changing infrequently if at all in SilverBooks:

- Top navigation bar
- Bottom navigation bar
- Book category list
- Featured book list

In fact, because the navigation bars never change, these two JSPs are reused throughout the application.

SilverBooks presents a more dynamic use of JSPs for presenting details about a book that has been selected from search results by the end user. When a user clicks a book title hyperlink, control passes to a JSP called `bookdetail.jsp`. This JSP in turn calls properties on a JavaBean called `BookBean.java` to determine how to present data about the book the user selected.

Action Servlets

The action servlet is the cornerstone of the Controller component of the MVC design paradigm. In SilverBooks, the action servlet performs three key functions:

1. Receives requests from the client—in this case, a user interacting with the SilverBooks application in a Web browser
2. Determines the action to perform
3. Delegates to an appropriate View component the responsibility for producing the next part of the user interface

Two XML specifications are used to configure the action servlet. The specification in `web.xml` associates the URL pattern `*.do` with the action servlet. This association means that any URL request or post ending in `.do` will go to the action servlet for processing. The specification in `action.xml` maps each possible client request to an action class that performs the appropriate business logic or handles the possible exceptions.

For example, this snippet is one of the URL mappings in `action.xml`:

```
<action path="/bookDetail"
  actionClass="com.sssw.demo.silverbooks.action.DetailAction">
  <forward name="success" path="/bookdetail.jsp" />
  </action>
```

This mapping means that when the URL `bookDetail.do` is requested, the action servlet instantiates the `DetailAction` class (or uses one that has already been instantiated) to display the detail data about a book selected by the user. The book identifier is passed as a parameter on the URL. This action class has access to a forward-mapping address called `success`, which is mapped to the relative URL `bookdetail.jsp`.

The `DetailAction` class services the client request as follows:

1. Gets a reference to the book in the EJB data source, based on the book identifier. Each book is represented by a book bean.
2. Retrieves the book data and places the book in the session.
3. If no exceptions occur, passes control to the JSP page `bookdetail.jsp`, which calls properties on the book bean to determine how to display the page.

The shopping cart works in a similar way. When a user decides to add a book to the shopping cart, the URL `cart.do` is requested, causing the action servlet to pass control to the `AddCartAction` class along with two parameters on the URL: add as the action and the book identifier.

Form Classes

Form classes represent the Model component of the MVC design paradigm. For example, the checkout and account detail pages use the form classes `PaymentForm.java` and `AccountDetailForm.java` to store data about customers' orders. When the data is updated, the application calls the `validate()` method on these form classes to ensure the accuracy of the information.

Enterprise JavaBeans (EJB)

Enterprise JavaBeans (EJB) represent business logic and manage data access in the MVC paradigm. EJBs are referenced by action servlets and form classes.

In SilverBooks, EJBs perform two key functions:

1. Retrieve and maintain book data from an external JDBC data source. An EJB session bean interacts with this database, which contains pertinent data about each book (including book identifier, title, author, description, price, publisher, and ISBN).
2. Manage the shopping cart. An EJB session bean keeps track of shopping cart values from page to page. Two entity beans are used to process orders.

The application server provides a connection pool to these databases.

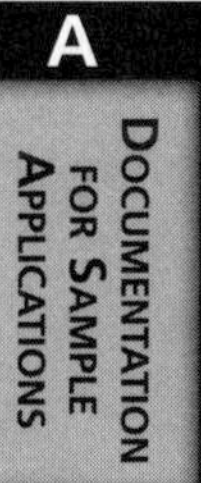

E-mail Verification

SilverBooks provides an e-mail verification option. When you enable this option, you will receive confirmation via e-mail when your book orders have been processed.

To enable e-mail verification, follow these steps:

1. In your favorite text editor, open the file SilverBooksConstants.java located at SilverStreamInstallDir\samples\SilverBooks\src\silverbooks\src\com\sssw\demo\silverbooks\SilverBooksConstants.java.
2. In the section `//Mail` Options, enter values for `MAIL_SERVER` and `MAIL_FROM`, and set `MAIL_ENABLED` to new `Boolean(true)`.
3. Save your changes and close SilverBooksConstants.java.
4. Rebuild the application by running buildSilverBooksAll.bat located at SilverStreamInstallDir\samples\SilverBooks\buildSilverBooksAll.bat.
5. Make sure your SilverStream server is running and redeploy the application by running deploySilverBooksEar.bat located at SilverStreamInstallDir\samples\SilverBooks\deploySilverBooksEar.bat.
6. Restart the SilverStream server.

Internationalization

The Struts Framework provides a methodology for internationalizing prompts and messages in a Web application. SilverBooks implements this feature by using Java resource bundles that use name/value pairs to translate static text labels to the language selected by the user. Each language supported by SilverBooks has its own resource bundle.

To select a new language

1. Start the SilverBooks application by entering the following URL in your browser: `http://server/SilverBooks37/app`.
2. In the top navigation bar, click Select Language.
3. Select the radio button associated with your language of choice and click Go.

The page refreshes to display static text labels in the language you selected.

Java Pet Store

Java Pet Store is a sample application developed by Sun Microsystems to illustrate the J2EE programming model. It is a very basic e-commerce Web site. It is part of J2EE Blueprints, a collection of design patterns and documentation illustrating best practices for J2EE applications.

Technologies Used in Java Pet Store

Java Pet Store is a multitier Web application that uses the Model-View-Controller (MVC) architecture. The MVC architecture, user scenarios for the application, the use of EJBs, and the implementation of the Model, View, and Controller are all discussed within other chapters of this book.

The Version of Java Pet Store That We Used

If you download the Java Pet Store application from the Sun Microsystems Web site, you will find it needs some server-specific modifications to run on a J2EE application server. In the version provided with the SilverStream Application Server, the server-specific code is provided.

This version has the following modifications:

- Implemented a security adapter class called `SilverSecurityAdapter.java`.
- Modified the return value from `getCallerPrincipal()` and `getUserPrincipal()` to remove the security domain from the login ID.
- Changed the paths for the error and login pages in the web.xml deployment descriptor to conform with the Servlet 2.2 specification.
- Customized a variable so that the pages display the application server name.
- The data tables are provided in a Cloudscape database.

Files Provided

The Java Pet Store sample application includes source code, ready-to-deploy archives, and databases with the archives already installed. You'll find these files in the SilverStream\samples\Petstore directory listed in Table A.2.

TABLE A.2 The SilverStream\samples\Petstore Directory

File or Directory	*Description*
EStoreDB.db	Database containing the deployed Java Pet Store application with a DSN of EStoreDB
InventoryDB.db	Database containing inventory tables for the store with a DSN of InventoryDB
petstore.ear	Archive containing the individual archives for the EJBs and the Web application
petstore-depl-plan.xml	Server-specific deployment plan for the store module

TABLE A.2 continued

File or Directory	*Description*
petstoreadmin.ear	Archive containing the individual archives for the administration module
petstoreadmin-depl-plan.xml	Server-specific deployment plan for the administration module
AddPetstoreUsers.bat AddPetstoreUsers.sh	Windows and Unix command files that add users and groups to Silver Security
deployPetStore.bat deployPetStoreAdmin.sh	Windows and Unix command files that install the Pet Store Admin EAR on the server
src directory	A directory containing ZIP files that have the SilverStream version of the Pet Store application's source code

Running the Command Files

The command files SilverStream provides for installing and redeploying the Java Pet Store application have versions for Windows and Unix systems. The arguments they take are listed in Table A.3.

TABLE A.3 Parameters for Deploying the Applications Using the Command Files

Argument	*Description*
`server`	The name of the SilverStream server where you installed the Java Pet Store databases. For a local server, specify `localhost`.
`userid`	An administrative user ID for the server (required only for a secure server).
`password`	The password for the administrative ID (required only for a secure server).

For example, if your `server` is `localhost`, you can specify

```
AddPetStoreUsers localhost
```

If your `server` is `secure` and the administrative ID is `serveradmin`, you can specify

```
AddPetStoreUsers localhost serveradmin myadminpassword
```

Running the Java Pet Store Application

The Java Pet Store application uses two databases: EStoreDB and InventoryDB. You need to install these databases, install user IDs in SilverStream security, and use your browser to run the Java Pet Store application. You can also use the supplied source code and deployment files to redeploy the application.

Installation types for the EStoreDB and InventoryDB databases are shown in Table A.4.

TABLE A.4 Installation Options

Type of Install	*What Happens*
Typical install	Installs all sample applications and creates their ODBC settings, but does not add them to your server. This option is recommended to conserve space on the server.
Full install	Installs all sample applications, creates their ODBC settings, and adds all sample applications to your server at once.
Custom install	If you select Sample Databases, installs sample applications you select, creates their ODBC settings, and adds them to your server.

You can run the Pet Store example by following these steps:

1. Install the SilverStream Application Server by selecting one of the installation types found in Table A.4. By default, you can access these databases with the username `dba` and password `sql`.
2. If you chose Typical install, add sample applications of your choice to your server by selecting Add Database from the Main Designer or by using the `SilverCmd AddDatabase` command-line tool.
3. Make sure the SilverStream server is running and start your browser.
4. Interact with the Java Pet Store application using one of the URLs listed in Table A.5.

TABLE A.5 URLs That Can Invoke Application Modules

Application Module	*URL*
Information page	`http://server/EStoreDB/estore/index.html`
Shopping for pets	`http://server/EStoreDB/estore/control/main`

TABLE A.5 continued

Application Module	*URL*
Shopping with annotations about the application design	`http://server/EStoreDB/estore/annotated-index.html`
Store administration	`http://server/EStoreDB/admin`

In case you want to set up a user ID to try the sample application, see the suggestions that follow:

- User IDs for shopping—When you fill your shopping cart and are ready to finalize the sale, the application displays the login screen. You can add a new user or log in with the user ID `j2ee` and password `j2ee`.
- User ID for store administration—To log in to the administration module, specify the user ID `admin` and password `admin`.

To Redeploy Java Pet Store

This procedure assumes you have installed the EStoreDB and InventoryDB databases:

1. Rebuild the WAR and EAR files using the appropriate Java tools.
2. Deploy the Pet Store EAR by running the appropriate command file for your system.

   For example, on Windows, at a command prompt in the SilverStream\samples\Petstore directory, type

   `deployPetStore localhost`

   or

   `deployPetStore localhost serveradmin myadminpassword`
3. Deploy the Pet Store Admin EAR by running the appropriate command file for your system.

   For example, on Windows, at a command prompt in the SilverStream\samples\Petstore directory, type

   `deployPetStoreAdmin localhost`

   or

   `deployPetStoreAdmin localhost serveradmin myadminpassword`
4. Run the shopping or administration module.

The deployment plans for the two EARs include a section labeled `<excludedJSPs>`. The SilverStream Application Server compiles JSPs during deployment, but some JSPs are fragments that are included in other JSPs and won't compile successfully by themselves. These fragments get compiled with the JSPs that include them. By putting these fragments on the list of excluded JSPs, the deployment plan prevents the server from displaying error messages for these uncompilable fragments. If the server tries to compile the fragments, you will see error messages, which can be ignored.

To Install User IDs for Java Pet Store

Run the AddPetStoreUsers command file appropriate to your operating system.

For example, on Windows, at a command prompt in the SilverStream\samples\Petstore directory, type

```
AddPetStoreUsers localhost
```

or

```
AddPetStoreUsers localhost serveradmin myadminpassword
```

Summary

These sample applications are a really good way to delve into the code and supporting files required to develop with J2EE. They are also helpful when reading the other chapters of this book, which concentrate on individual J2EE APIs.

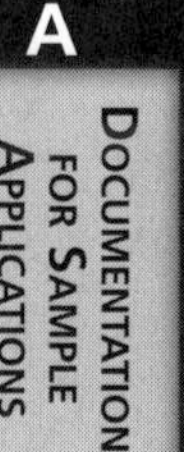

APPENDIX B

Related Tools

IN THIS APPENDIX

- Development Tools *710*
- Application Servers *725*
- Modeling and Object/Report Generation Tools *736*
- Messaging and XML Tools *744*
- Validation and Performance Monitoring Tools *748*

This appendix contains details about a number of products that combine with J2EE standards to provide benefits including platform independence, reduced time-to-market, increased developer productivity through the reusability of EJB components, and standardization across platforms. These factors allow developers to focus on writing business logic and addressing business-critical issues. Periodic updates on the following products can be found at `http://www.ucny.com/j2ee_tools_resource_center.htm`.

Development Tools

To be productive, especially with a comprehensive technology like J2EE, analysts and programmers need visual development tools for building applications. J2EE involves developing Java, archiving classes, and other objects as well as describing these objects in XML deployment files. These actions must be coordinated among multiple developer roles. At this time there are not very many mature tools to help with J2EE development. However, certain vendors (the old familiar ones like Borland) are in the process of evolving tools to facilitate the coding, testing, and deployment of Java objects in the form of applets, JSP/Servlets, JavaBeans, Enterprise JavaBeans, and distributed J2EE applications for the Java 2 Platform.

When the J2EE tools technology reaches maturity, developers will be able to deliver a full spectrum of platform-independent solutions, from applets to applications. Tools must be available to provide open, scalable, and standards-based development, especially when it comes to large scale, mission-critical, enterprise-wide, distributed Internet solutions, or networked database and client/server connectivity. Only when this infrastructure is in place will the time-to-market for J2EE applications be acceptable for the majority of enterprise development teams.

SilverStream eXtend Workbench

SilverStream Software

Two Federal Street

Billerica, MA 01821

Tel: +1 978-262-3000 or +1 888-823-9700

Fax: +1 978-262-3499

`http://www.silverstream.com`

The SilverStream eXtend Workbench is an open and extensible integrated development environment (IDE) designed specifically to help you build applications for the Java 2 Platform, Enterprise Edition (J2EE). The exTend Workbench is a powerful IDE for creating J2EE-compliant applications with either experienced or inexperienced Java programming resources.

With the visual WYSIWYG environment, drag-and-drop tools enable the developer to easily create complex applications that include JavaServer Pages, Servlets, JavaBeans, JDBC JavaBeans, and Enterprise JavaBeans.

Key features include

- Support for J2EE roles
- Ability to maintain J2EE projects at the project, archive, and source filesystem levels
- Automated assistance in creating and maintaining J2EE components, including JavaServer Pages, Servlets, JavaBeans, JDBC JavaBeans, Enterprise JavaBeans, and other Java class files
- Source editors for Text, JSPs, and XML
- Automated compiling, building, and archiving of J2EE modules, including Enterprise archives (EARs), Web archives (WARs), EJB archives (EJB JARs), client application archives (client JARs or CARs), and Java class archives (JARs)
- Automated assistants for creating J2EE deployment descriptors and deployment plans for the modules and components in your project

Artistic Systems' JCanvas Studio

Artistic Systems, Inc.

7031 Albert Pick Road, Suite 100

Greensboro, NC 27409

Tel: +1 336-668-4106

Fax: +1 336-662-8415

`http://www.artisticsystems.com`

JCanvas Studio is a powerful IDE for creating J2EE-compliant applications with minimal Java programming experience. With the visual WYSIWYG environment, drag-and-drop tools enable the developer to easily create complex applications that include JavaServer Pages, Servlets, JavaBeans, JDBC JavaBeans, and Enterprise JavaBeans.

Key features include

- Wizards and editors—JCanvas provides a set of tightly integrated visual wizards and editors that facilitate intuitive development while minimizing necessary coding. They are listed here:
    - VisualPage Editor
    - Visual HTML Frame Editor

    - Dynamic VisualPage Editor
    - Visual DataBean Editor
    - Servlet Editor
    - Java Class Editor
    - JMS Message Editor

- JSP/Servlet application server—A lightweight JSP/Servlet container is included for instant testing and debugging of visual JSP pages. This enables quick viewing of complex pages.
- Instant deployment to JAR files—JCanvas Studio offers one-click deployment of projects to a JAR file that can be run in any compliant application server.
- Data-aware HTML beans—DataBeans created with the Visual DataBean editor can be visually bound to data-aware visual HTML page beans. Data-aware beans contain controls that encapsulate the access language (SQL) as well as data type–specific formatting.
- Built-in EJB container—This enables testing and debugging of EJBs.
- Server-side debugger—This facilitates debugging of server-side classes including JSP pages, EJBs, and Servlets and enables the viewing of the states of Servlet requests and responses, EJB activity, and transactions.
- Client-side EJB support—This allows the developer to bind client-side pages and controls. Through EJB accessing client-side JavaBeans, complex activities such as JNDI, RMI, and narrowing are abstracted from the developer.

JCanvas Studio supports J2SE SDK version 1.3.

Borland JBuilder 5

Borland Software Corporation

100 Enterprise Way

Scotts Valley, CA 95066

Tel: +1 831-431-1000

Fax: +1 831-431-4122

`http://www.borland.com/jbuilder/`

JBuilder is an integrated, scalable Java development suite that seeks to facilitate the creation and management of multitier, Web, and e-commerce applications. It adheres to the latest Java standards, including Java 2, Java 2 Swing/JFC, XML, Java2D, Message Queue, Java Collections, Accessibility APIs, and Speech API. Cross-platform development is supported for Solaris, Linux, and Windows 98/NT/2000.

JBuilder is a complete, integrated environment for the development of Enterprise-scale applications. New features and significant improvements over previous versions include support for the leading application servers (Borland AppServer, WebLogic, and WebSphere), three version control systems (ClearCase, Visual SourceSafe, and CVS) and three development platforms (Windows, Linux, and Solaris).

It brings Java and XML together and takes advantage of the latest technology for data exchange and presentation. JBuilder includes fully-integrated and comprehensive XML development support for the entire development cycle including creation, manipulation, transformation/presentation, and integration. The new release improves group productivity, offering integration with the leading version control systems: Rational ClearCase and Microsoft Visual SourceSafe.

Additional features are available in several key areas:

Environment:

- Customization of Java Layout Managers for faster user interface development.
- Visual Java designers and wizards for drag-and-drop JFC/Swing application development.
- Visual menu designer and customizable toolbars.
- Open Tools API for customizing and adding to the current environment.
- Cascading style sheet layout viewer.
- AppBrowser combines design, code, debugger, and explorer windows into one screen.
- Advanced search/replace options.
- Keymap editor for assigning actions to user-defined keystrokes.

Wizards and JavaBean Components:

- Wizards enable rapid development of applications, applets, and JavaBeans.
- Make or Rebuild command automatically creates a single JAR from an EJB group.
- Existing EJBs can be migrated into new groups.
- Multiple EJBs can be contained in one application.
- EJBs can be run and tested in a local container or application server. They may be deployed automatically when run or debugged.

- Entity Bean Modeler allows entity beans to be mapped to existing tables.
- InternetBeans Express Components allow for seamless data transfer between Java and HTML.

Smart Debugging:

- Web Debug and Web Run enable testing directly from the AppBrowser.
- Debug configurations for managing multiple debug sessions per project.
- Floating windows to view multiple debug views simultaneously.
- Debug through JSP and Java Servlets.
- Integrated AppServer.
- DataStore embeddable database.

The current release of JBuilder supports JDK 1.1 and J2SE SDK version 1.2.

Compoze's Harmony Component Suite

Compoze Software, Inc.

1554 Paoli Pike, Suite 228

West Chester, PA 19380

Tel: +1 866-COMPOZE or +1 610-862-1104

Fax: +1 610-862-1180

`http://www.compoze.com/`

The Harmony Component Suite contains technologies designed to promote rapid development and deployment of applications, specifically those that require collaboration such as such as Customer Relationship Management (CRM), sales force automation, time tracking, and groupware. Written in 100% Java and developed on the J2EE platform, Harmony Suite will run on any platform supported by the application server. Compatible servers currently include BEA WebLogic 5.1 and Allaire JRun 3.0, but support by additional application servers such as iPlanet Application Server 6.0, Iona Application Server, and SilverStream 3.0 will be added in the near future.

Harmony Suite facilitates the creation of components by a process referred to as Automatic Bean-Managed Persistence (ABMP). Abstract classes for writing components are provided, reducing the amount of code required for creation of EJBs. ABMP combines the flexibility of bean-managed persistence (BMP) with the convenience of container-managed persistence (CMP).

In addition, Harmony Component Suite includes the following functionality:

- Calendaring and scheduling—provides scheduling management entities and workflow components necessary to create, detail, and manage events for use by multiple users
- Content management—handles posting and retrieval of content such as hypertext links, text, and files; shares information and manages access control on a user/role basis
- Contacts and contact groups—manages a list of contacts and their relevant information
- Task management—creates and prioritizes task lists for a user or a group of users
- Journal—tracks events and milestones

The current release of Harmony Suite supports JDK 1.2 and 1.3.

Elixir IDE

Elixir Technology

50 Armenian Street, #04-04

Wilmer Place, Singapore 179938

Republic of Singapore

Tel: +65 532-4300

Fax: +65 532-4255

`http://www.elixirtech.com/ElixirIDE/`

Elixir IDE provides a flexible Java development environment intended for experienced Java code developers. All tools are written entirely in Java, allowing applications to be built, rebuilt, or debugged on any platform. Project files are either plain text or XML, eliminating the need to re-enter information when utilizing Elixir tools with other custom tools. Elixir IDE's file-based project structure preserves performance without increasing RAM requirements regardless of project size.

Elixir IDE provides features intended to enhance the development process. These include

- Visual File Management—The color-coded feedback produced by this tool indicates compilation status.
- Auto-Complete—This feature allows previous lines to be duplicated without copy/paste.
- Scripting—IDE allows the definition of a scripting interface, thereby enabling the user to choose the scripting language.

- Auto-Expand—This allows the user to create macros that can be expanded into code with dialog-driven prompting as needed.
- Build Engine—This feature enables automation of the project build cycle. The user may define a sequence of steps for each build type including preprocessing, post-processing, obfuscation, and JAR-ing.
- Bookmarks—The ability to mark and comment lines of code enables faster navigation of the project file. Collapsible code blocks also facilitate navigation.
- Debugger—IDE builds upon the Java Platform Debugger Architecture (JPDA) defined for Java 2. It supports multithreaded debugging, breakpoints, and watchpoints.

Elixir IDE runs on all JDK 1.x– and Java 2–compliant platforms.

Flashline.com's Component Manager

Flashline.com, Inc.

1300 East 9th Street, Suite 1600

Cleveland, OH 44114

Tel: +1 216-861-4000

Fax: +1 216-861-1861

`http://www.flashline.com`

Flashline's Component Manager Enterprise Edition (CMEE) is a comprehensive component reuse solution. Developer productivity is increased and time-to-market is decreased through the availability of quality software components across the Enterprise. CMEE supports Enterprise JavaBeans and Java Foundation Classes.

Features include

- A shared component repository—This allows for faster creation and deployment of applications by cataloging tested, reusable components in a centralized repository that consolidates information such as code reviews and usage histories in order to streamline the process of selecting the best component for the situation. Over 200 documented and tested open source components are available for immediate use.
- Quality assurance standards—The component cannot be published in the repository until organizational standards are met and testing is complete. Flashline's QA Lab is included for additional testing.
- Tracking and reporting tools—The CMEE repository contains code and usage reviews for each component. Additional tracking features allow organizations to

highlight successful projects, developers, and components. Subjective component evaluations and predefined reports are available.

CMEE supports J2SE SDK version 1.3.

IBM VisualAge for Java

IBM

New Orchard Road

Armonk, NY 10504

Tel: +1 800-426-2255

`http://www.ibm.com/software/ad/vajava/`

IBM VisualAge for Java is an integrated development environment suitable for both beginners and experts, delivering advanced, scalable pure Java applications. The object-oriented development environment enables organization into logical elements such as packages, classes, and methods.

Visual Programming support utilizing user-friendly window panes, packages, classes, interfaces, management, and problem panes is available.

Using these graphical drawing tools and templates allows the developer to build Java classes that are automatically generated and prepared for testing.

JavaBean information is integrated directly into the drawing surface. Direct access to tools is possible with a right-click. VisualAge for Java provides helpful features in several key areas:

Repository:

- VisualAge offers a multiuser environment created via tight integration with WebSphere Studio. Programmers can share and maintain source code as well as remotely test and debug applications.
- The repository uses code versioning to maintain multiple versions of classes and methods. (Users can revert to any version.)

Coding:

- VisualAge provides help with methods.
- Data access beans allow developers to access JDBC-enabled relational databases from a single Java application.
- Scrapbook allows ideas to be organized, developed, and tested without specifying which class they belong to.

- Smartguides, comparable to wizards, generate Java application elements and perform administrative tasks.
- Users can set bookmarks.
- VisualAge enables generation of Java documents.

High performance compilers and a remote debugger:

- VisualAge employs incremental compilation. Java code is automatically generated and compiled upon transition from one major task to another.
- Any problems that are identified are placed on a problem page for resolution. Alternatives are presented in a fix list.
- The debugger can work with multiple active programs simultaneously as well as debugging client and server portions of the application.

VisualAge for Java supports reuse and connectivity through database access (UDB, Oracle, Sybase), message and queuing systems (MQ Series), systems management (Tivoli), collaborative computing/groupware (Lotus Notes), and object connection standards (CORBA, RMI, JDBC).

VA Assist Enterprise

Instantiations, Inc.

7618 SW Mohawk

Tualatin, OR 97062

Tel: +1 503-612-9337

Fax: +1 503-612-9499

`http://www.instantiations.com/assist/home.htm`

VA Assist Enterprise provides a host of productivity tools and commands created to enhance IBM's VisualAge.

Key features and areas of improvement include

- Browser—color highlighting, drag and drop, component name direct editing, view filtering, problem filtering, menu keys, bookmarks, intra-repository broadcast messaging, recently modified and visited methods, exit without saving, exception sets, inspector/debugger field sorting
- Source code—font style control, auto save text changes, code metrics, code assist, field and method creation

- Library management—version renaming, version name templates, edition descriptions/comments, repository query window, repository explorer, management query
- Task automation—task scheduler, export tasks, management query task, global tasks, load components, sequential tasks, and external program tasks
- Import/export function—Search dialog, text Search/Replace dialog, GoTo dialog, Type search, references, and declarations
- User management—Super User and Group modes, group member management, set/change user on startup
- VCE—connect filtering, dynamic linking, component direct edit, enhanced selection mode, auto size, move, and size by pixel

Macromedia Dreamweaver UltraDev

Macromedia, Inc.
600 Townsend Street
San Francisco, CA 94103
Tel: +1 415-252-2000
Fax: +1 415-626-0554
`http://www.macromedia.com/software/ultradev/`

Dreamweaver UltraDev 4 adds features to Macromedia's popular Dreamweaver, creating a WYSIWYG environment for development of server-side code and database-driven Web applications.

Key features include

- Simple GUI—The clean workspace features a toolbox where the developer can switch between tools with a mouse-click. A properties inspector displays tool properties along with any other available information.
- Text editor—This includes ASP, JSP, CFML, JavaScript, and HTML with keyword color-coding, auto-indenting, and line numbers.
- Split view—This feature enables simultaneous viewing of code and design with immediate reflection of any changes.
- Server Behavior Builder—This enables users to generate reusable libraries of server-side scripts by writing new behaviors or editing existing ones.
- User Authentication Wizard—This feature offers User logon and password protection and can create different levels of user access.

- Live Object function for automatic dataform creation—A prebuilt behavior can automatically create an update and insert a record form or Master/Detail display page.
- Data Bindings Inspector—This allows users to register any JavaBean as an UltraDev Data Source. Once JavaBeans are registered, users have drag-and-drop access to JavaBean properties.
- Database connectivity—Dreamweaver UltraDev can access data directly through application server and allows developers to view the actual data while designing the application.
- Macromedia Exchange—This is a centralized location where a user may download and install UltraDev extensions or share objects, behaviors, and commands with a group.

Dreamweaver UltraDev currently supports ASP, ColdFusion, and JSP servers including Microsoft IIS, Allaire ColdFusion, IBM WebSphere, Allaire JRun, and Netscape iPlanet. UltraDev can also be extended to support other servers. UltraDev supports any relational database that can be connected via ODBC, JDBC, or ADO, including Oracle, Sybase, mySQL, MS SQL Server, and Microsoft Access.

Pramati Studio 2.5

Pramati Technologies

2570 North First Street, Suite 200

San Jose, CA 95131

Tel: +1 877-PRAMATI or +1 408-965-5513

Fax: +1 408-965-5305

`http://www.pramati.com`

Pramati Studio 2.5 is a server-side Java development and testing platform that utilizes a unique set of tools and wizards to expedite development throughout creation, assembly, and deployment while minimizing the complexity of compliance with J2EE standards.

Key features include

- Framework Development Environment—This provides configurable framework, pluggable tools, and APIs to automate tools and customize workflow. Toolbars can be docked and configured with only the required tools for streamlined startups and resource usage.

- Service Manager—Pramati Studio provides a registry for tool-related services that is created when the tool plugs into the framework. Other tools may look up those services using the unique key string given by the tool provider.
- File Manager—This serves as a registry for file-related tools that utilizes the extension of the file on which the tool is operating. The file manager will search the list of all registered tools for the proper one to handle a file with that extension.
- Event Manager—This manager is a registry where tools publish changes or events to other tools. It maintains a list of tools that should be notified of a particular event.
- Bean Wizard—This enables users to automatically create skeletons for entity and session beans with CMP/BMP.
- Editor—This feature provides a Java-specific source display for working with bean code.
- Import Bean—This Studio element repackages components for use of third-party beans.
- Packaging Tool—This tool assembles beans, JSPs, and servlets into portable packaged applications.
- Pramati Converter API—The Converter API enables developers to write tools that read Pramati XML deployment descriptors and convert them to target server XML DDs.
- Open API—This interface enables power users to write Java classes as macros, thus enabling them to automate tasks. Third party tools can be plugged in by writing "stitch" classes.
- Query designer—This feature grants users access to database tables via JDBC to prepare query statements.
- User manager—This manager defines user roles for beans and maps them to the realm.
- Templates—Web components such as JSPs and Servlets can be built on ready-to-code templates.
- Enterprise security—Through the integration of JAAS, developers are provided with a real-world security framework for testing applications.
- Smart enterprise class debugger—This is a J2EE application-specific debugger that allows seamless movement between EJBs and JSPs. JSPs can be debugged while servlets are running. The debugger works on all tiers of the application simultaneously as well as on remote VMs.

- Embedded database—Pramati Studio 2.5 ships with the Cloudscape database for creation of databases, tables, and embedded data sources.
- Deploy tool—This tool reads the environment properties of the target server, resolves references of enterprise beans, and makes sure the package is ready for deployment. Developers are also able to write their own tools for converting Pramati XML deployment descriptors to target server DDs.

Pramati Studio ships with Pramati Server 2.5 and a converter that enables Pramati deployable components to be run on the WebLogic application server. A simple GUI guides the user through cross-platform deployment. It provides an example of how tools can be plugged into the Studio framework regardless of the differences in its functionality.

Sitraka's JClass Enterprise Suite

Sitraka Software

260 King Street East

Toronto, Ontario, Canada

M5A 4L5

Tel: +1 800-663-4723 or +1 416-594-1026

Fax: +1 416-594-1919

`http://www.sitraka.com/software/jclass/`

JClass is a suite of Java class libraries and applets that provide a wide range of interface functionality. Developers are able to quickly create applications with high quality Java components. 100% Pure Java GUI JavaBeans ensure integration with any JavaBeans-compliant IDE.

Key features include

- JClass Chart—JClass Chart is a data-aware tool used to generate graphs and charts in applications. Most popular chart types are supported, including line, bar, pie, and stacked. Rich text format allows for label customization and mixing images and URLs with text.
- JClass LiveTable—JClass LiveTable can easily be configured to act as a spreadsheet, data-entry form, multicolumn list, or data grid for the development of virtually any Java GUI. Built-in formula abstractions facilitate customization of spreadsheet functionality. It supports data-intensive environments through automatic data-binding and XML support, and allows a wide variety of user interactions.

- JClass Field—Using JavaBeans technology, JClass Field gives the developer a wide variety of components for data entry and validation.
- JClass PageLayout—PageLayout adds printing and reporting functionality, with sophisticated and easy-to-use APIs for adding text, images, and tables to any document. This facilitates creation of complex layouts incorporating columns, frames, multiple fonts and styles, automatic page numbering, headers and footers, and sophisticated tables.
- JClass Elements—JClass Elements provides a set of valuable tools and components, enabling the developer to improve the look and functionality of Java applications and applets. It is also ideal for developers who need to extend and enhance Swing-based applications.
- JClass HiGrid—JClass HiGrid is a unique front end for database-driven Java applications. Using JClass HiGrid in combination with JClass DataSource, the developer can display and update hierarchical data with one user-friendly component. The built-in customizer enables configuration of data selection and display with no additional programming required. JClass HiGrid automatically generates SQL statements needed to access data. The developer has complete control over input and display with cell editors and easily modified fonts, borders, styles, and colors.
- JClass DataSource—JClass DataSource is a flexible and customizable hierarchical multiple-platform data source, written in 100% pure Java. It enables users to access multiple tables in multiple databases by expressing a hierarchy of queries. It permits modification of the properties of DataSource components to determine how data entry elements will look and behave. Developers can control the appearance of the GUI components, as well as the types of operations end users are permitted to perform on the records. JClass DataSource includes data-bound versions of popular Swing components such as TextField, ListBox, and Label.
- JClass JarMaster—JClass JarMaster allows the developer to quickly package and manage Java classes for rapid download. Only the Java classes required to create a single compact JAR or ZIP file are selected, facilitating the optimization of JAR files before deployment. The advanced hierarchical interface gives the developer more flexibility to add or delete classes, transfer between archives, or refresh the contents of an existing archive based on the contents of the CLASSPATH. The bean manifest editor enables customization of the JAR's manifest. Version information or file dependencies can be modified as well. The easy-to-use wizard walks the developer through the process of building a JAR for an application or library.

WebGain Studio 4.5 Professional Edition

WebGain, Inc.

5425 Stevens Creek Blvd.

Santa Clara, CA 95051

Tel: +1 408-517-3700

Fax: +1 408-517-3701

`http://www.webgain.com/products/webgain_studio/professional_edition/`

WebGain Studio 4.5 Professional Edition is an integrated e-commerce development solution that streamlines processes from design and development to deployment of Java applications. Wizards, tools, and utilities facilitate rapid development of EJBs and servlets. WebGain Studio 4.5 provides universal J2EE application server architecture for simplified integration with leading application servers. Developers can deploy applications locally or remotely to test them in a real-world environment prior to operational deployment. Studio 4.5 Professional combines multiple products to create an end-to-end solution:

- Macromedia Dreamweaver—Dreamweaver is one of the leading HTML/Web authoring tools. JSP extensions have been added, enabling the developer to view and edit JSP pages from within Dreamweaver. It works in conjunction with the VisualCafé source editor, providing an integrated solution for editing HTML, JavaScript, and Java for JSP pages.
- WebGain StructureBuilder—StructureBuilder is a model-based tool that can be used to visually create Java applications, as well as design, develop, and deploy EJB components. Developers can visually specify and display objects and the relationships between them, develop complex object models graphically, and create customized Java code. The object model and Java code can be viewed simultaneously while modification is reflected immediately. Existing code can be loaded into StructureBuilder, automatically creating an object model. The Enterprise Edition also allows you to build the following diagram types:
  - Sequence diagrams—As classes and methods are defined, they are automatically associated with the objects and messages within sequence diagrams. StructureBuilder also supports sequence methods to generate code necessary to implement an object interaction represented in a sequence diagram.
  - Use case diagrams—These diagrams capture requirements and behavior of systems and attach annotations to each use case. Any text annotations are displayed when the diagram imagemap is clicked.

- VisualCafé—This offers a complete solution for rapid development and debugging of Java and EJB applications. VisualCafé enables both local and remote debugging and provides multiple wizards and utilities to increase productivity. EJB development capabilities allow for multiple beans per project with support for development of entity and session beans. Generic EJB deployment can be used on a variety of platforms. Distributed debugging allows the developer to debug applications running on different machines and different Java Virtual Machines. All server-side code running on the server can be debugged. Servlets can be debugged in real time while connected to a browser.VisualCafe supports industry-leading application servers such as BEA WebLogic, iPlanet Application Server, and IBM WebSphere.
- BEA WebLogic Server 6.0—This is a Java application server that provides services specifically for building e-commerce applications. It delivers comprehensive implementation of J2EE standards, allowing the developer to utilize the full range of Java-compatible tools on the market.
- TopLink—TopLink is a database integration tool that seeks to bridge the gap between objects and relational technology. It provides an advanced object-to-relational container-managed persistence solution and enables entity beans and Java business objects to be stored in relational databases. Toplink supports multiple databases, including Oracle, DB2, Sybase, Informix, and Microsoft SQL Server.
- TurboXML—TurboXML is an IDE for developing and managing XML that supports the XML Schema Recommendation. It facilitates the creation, validation, conversion, and management of XML schemas, files, and DTDs.
- Quality Analyzer—Quality Analyzer is a set of products (Audit, Cover, and Metrics) for improving the quality and performance of enterprise Java applications. Audit checks the quality of source code. Cover measures the coverage of Java code, collecting method and statement execution counts from applets, servlets, and applications running on any JVM on a network. Metrics calculates global complexity and quality metrics on portions of code.

Application Servers

The World Wide Web has vaulted the application server from relative obscurity to a mainstream form of computing with literally scores of companies jumping in to develop products for this market. However, these companies do not see the role of the application server in exactly the same way and have developed a broad range of products with somewhat similar features. Fortunately, with the advent of Sun's J2EE specification, the functionality for this fairly broad range of products will become standardized, with performance and flexibility probably being the deciding factors in vendor selection.

Essentially, application servers provide a framework for developing complex, dynamic Web sites. This framework provides features required in most Web applications, such as security (authentication and authorization), transaction support, database and client connection pooling, and caching of objects. Most noticeably, application servers connect database information (typically coming from a database server) and the end-user or client program (most often in a Web browser). This allows developers to decrease the size and complexity of client programs, reduces the need to cache and control the data flow for better performance, and establishes a requirement to provide security for both data and user traffic.

SilverStream Application Server

SilverStream Software

Two Federal Street

Billerica, MA 01821

Tel: +1 978-262-3000 or +1 888-823-9700

Fax: +1 978-262-3499

`http://www.silverstream.com/website/staticpages/solutions/products/ApplicationServer.html`

Since the release of SilverStream 1.0, SilverStream has been a leader in the application server field. Version 3.7 is Certified J2EE compliant, meeting support specifications including Enterprise JavaBeans 1.1, JavaServer Pages 1.1, Servlets 2.2, JNDI 1.2, JDBC 2.0, JavaMail 1.1, and XML 1.0. Archive formats for including EAR, CAR, JAR, and WAR files are also supported. Other features include database connection pooling, application object caching, server-based transaction management, multithreaded load balancing, and a server-based automatic restart feature.

SilverStream 3.7 features an object-oriented HTML programming environment. Applications can be built using wizards to determine factors such as data sources and display specifications. Drag-down controls are available for data-management tasks. The developer can work in WYSIWYG or HTML display mode.

In addition, a QuickDeploy feature is included to compile and redeploy only the JARs and WARs that have been changed since the last full deployment.

SilverStream has excellent database connectivity, with drivers for Microsoft SQL Server and Access, Oracle, Sybase, IBM DB/2, and Informix.

SilverStream operates on Windows 2000/NT 4.0, Solaris 2.6 or higher, AIX 4.3.3.10, and Linux 6.2.

Allaire-Macromedia JRun 3.0

Allaire
275 Grove Street
Newton, MA 02466
Tel: +1 617-219-2000 or +1 888-939-2545
`http://www.allaire.com/products/jrun/`

JRun is an easy-to-use application server that is designed for corporate intranets and mid-sized companies. With JRun's modular architecture, developers can use only the specific components they need, including EJB 1.1, JTA 1.0, JMS 1.0, JSP 1.1, and Servlets 2.2.

The JRun Management Console (JMC) is a Web-based interface that gives the user complete control of the server environment. It can also be utilized to load EJB components to the server for deployment.

JRun supports the XA protocol and the JTA specification. It can be integrated with most major Web servers and runs on Microsoft, Solaris, Linux, and MacOS platforms.

BEA WebLogic Server 6.1

BEA Systems, Inc.
2315 North First Street
San Jose, CA 95131
Tel: +1 408-570-8000
Fax: +1 408-570-8901
`http://www.beasys.com/products/weblogic/server/`

BEA WebLogic Server 6.1 is J2EE certified, fully complying with the J2EE JDK 1.3 specifications including EJB 2.0, JMS 1.1, JDBC 2.0, JNDI 1.2, JTS/JTA 1.01, Servlet 2.3, JSP 1.2, RMI/IIOP 1.0, JavaMail 1.1, JAAS 1.0, and Java RMI 1.0. WebLogic also provides support for the latest XML technologies for parsing, transformation, and Web services with compliance to JAXP 1.1, SAX V2.0, DOM level 2, and W3C Schema.

BEA WebLogic Server offers core platform services that deliver increased reliability and scalability for transaction-intensive applications.

Key features include

- Distributed transaction manager—Enterprise JavaBeans servers facilitate the development of middleware by providing automatic support for middleware services including transactions, security, and database connectivity.
- Centralized management—BEA WebLogic Server offers simplified manageability, usability, and installation through a pure Java, Web-based console for managing the distribution of applications to remote users. It also provides dynamic application partitioning and cluster membership and enables system administrators to configure and manage individual or multiple servers (including remote servers) from a single interface. Zero Administration Client (ZAC) supports automatic distribution of software applications and Java applets.
- E-commerce-ready security—WebLogic includes Secure Sockets Layer (SSL) support for integration of encryption and authentication security into e-commerce solutions.
- Enterprise Messaging—WebLogic provides an integrated messaging platform based on JMS, which has the ability to perform database, file, or in-memory persistence. Developers can use both Publish/Subscribe and Point-to-Point messaging, as well as either Multicast or TCP/IP transport protocols.
- Advanced clustering—This feature allows a group of WebLogic Servers to work together for a more scalable and available application platform. Clustering is available for Java Messaging Services (JMS), EJB components , and Web pages. Web page clustering handles transparent replication, load balancing, and failover for the presentation logic that generates responses to Web clients, while EJB component clustering handles the complexities of replication, load balancing, and failover for the application's business logic, as well as the recovery of stateful objects such as EJB entity beans. Both Web page and component clustering are critical for delivering global scalability and high availability for e-commerce systems.

WebLogic 6.1 is optimized for Oracle 8.1.7 and integrates easily with industry-leading databases, as well as providing support for Microsoft Visual Basic, Visual C++, Active Server Pages, and COM.

Gemstone/J Application Server

Gemstone Systems, Inc.

20575 N.W. Von Neumann Drive

Beaverton, OR 97006

Tel: +1 800-243-9369 or +1 503-533-3000

Fax: +1 503-629-8556

`http://www.gemstone.com/products/j/`

GemStone/J is a middle-tier server that provides an integrated set of services and tools for building and deploying server-side, multiuser Java applications. Utilizing Extreme Clustering architecture, Gemstone/J is dedicated to scaling complex sites, simplifying application design, and maintaining system availability. Available prebuilt components reduce the amount of lower-level foundation work required for the application. Services and tools include capabilities for JavaBeans component deployment and partitioning, multiuser Java application execution, standard CORBA integration, enterprise integration, and shared, transactional, and persistent Java objects.

Key features include

- Multi-VM architecture—A single instance of GemStone/J software can be deployed on one or more physical machines, creating a virtual server cluster. These VMs are capable of seamless communication, thereby increasing the scalability of the application. VMs on the same server can be configured independently of each other, enabling multiple applications to run concurrently on the same GemStone/J server. Each application can have its own VM and namespace.
- Smart Load Balancing technology—This feature integrates load balancing at the server level, thereby eliminating the need to write that functionality into the application.
- Pooled resources—VMs, HTTP sessions, EJBs, CORBA objects, threads, and JDBC connections maintained within one GemStone/J server are easily accessible upon initiation of a transaction. The workload of each VM is constantly monitored, ensuring that requests will be assigned to other VMs should performance begin to degrade. Adapters in each Web server balance the assignment of JSP pages and servlets across pooled servlet engines. Beans and components are dynamically assigned to executable threads running in a VM. JDBC sessions are dynamically assigned as necessary to permit optimal access to back-end databases.
- Persistent Cache Architecture—GemStone/J provides a shared object cache, an object repository, and a repository management system. All VMs have seamless access to this cache. EJBs written to third-tier data stores are also written into the Persistent Cache Architecture, eliminating mapping calls to the RDBMS.
- Object Transaction Monitor (OTM)—This feature provides a standard infrastructure for building J2EE applications that can initiate or participate in transactions with third-tier data or with the Persistent Cache Architecture. The OTM allows data from disparate sources to be stored as objects, thereby allowing transactions to be performed across heterogeneous databases.

- Universal Application Model (UAM)—This model uses standardized XML-based descriptors and includes the Universal Deployment Model, which enables easy deployment of EJB, CORBA, Web/servlets, and JavaBeans applications. XML parsing and support is embedded into the deployment tools. In addition, upgrades and new applications can be deployed remotely as well as while transactions are still being executed.
- Security—Gemstone/J offers protection at the application code, user, and method levels. Pluggable interfaces are provided for SSL and PKI protocols.

GemStone/J 4.0 is a J2EE licensee, compliant with standards including JSP 1.1, servlets 2.2, EJB 1.1, JDK 1.2, JMS 1.0, JNDI 1.2, JDBC 2.0, JSA, JCA, JCE, and JAAS.

IBM WebSphere

IBM

New Orchard Road

Armonk, NY 10504

Tel: +1 800-426-2255

`http://www.ibm.com/software/info/websphere/`

Seeking to provide all the necessary tools to successfully build complete Web applications (more specifically, e-commerce applications), IBM's WebSphere features *application accelerators*, services and tools such as portal servers, application host connectors, and business components built around the core server. Modules can be registered across multiple servers, making large-scale development projects possible. Versioning is made manageable via server-side distributed debugging, which enables source code to be debugged across multiple servers through a single point.

Performance-boosting features include Fragment Caching, used with JSPs, Servlets, and EJBs and a Fast Response Cache Accelerator to cache static HTML pages.

Management of the server's component assets is completed in the WebSphere Studio. Clustering services are provided by Edge server, which can scale machines through a network dispatcher and maintain load balancing on a geographic scale. A vast range of security options is provided through an LDAP server built on top of DB2.

Other features include load balancing, failover, XSL support, and XML server tools including a parser and data transformation tools.

WebSphere is compatible with most Web servers and has excellent cross-platform support.

IONA iPortal Application Server 3.0

IONA Technologies PLC

The IONA Building

Shelbourne Road

Dublin 4

Ireland

Tel: +353-1-637-2000

Fax: +353-1-637-2888

http://www.iona.com/products/ip_ipas_home.htm

iPortal Application Server is a J2EE server/container coupled with a simple graphic interface for the assembly, deployment, and administration of J2EE applications. Simple installation and ease-of-use are key features of iPortal. This latest release has also focused on adding to and improving the developer's toolset.

Version 3.0 is for use with JDK 1.3 and includes support for EJB 1.1 standards such as session and entity beans, JNDI, EJB Security, and RMI-IIOP. Container- and bean-managed persistence is supported as well as JDBC 2.0 technology for connectivity with over 100 databases. CORBA Object Transaction Service (OTS) provides transaction support, including 2-phase commit via Java Telephony API (JTAPI). XML is automatically generated to further reduce necessary coding. This release features the addition of a Cloudscape database with the administration client Cloudview.

iPlanet Application Server

iPlanet E-Commerce Solutions

901 San Antonio Rd.

Palo Alto, CA 94303

Tel: +1 888-786-8111 or +1 650-254-1900

Fax: +1 650-254-1900

http://www.iplanet.com/products/iplanet_application/home_2_1_1n.html

The iPlanet 6.0 Application Server provides an integrated approach to implementing enterprise-class applications. It was the first product to pass the J2EE certification suite, with support for Java 2 SDK, EJB 1.1, JDBC, JNDI 1.2, Servlet 2.2, JSP 1.1, JavaMail, JAF 1.1, RMI/IIOP, and Java Transaction API. The Kiva Engine, a major component of iPlanet 6.0, provides support for C++; however, this support has diminished in favor of Java. The iPlanet Application Server is available in Standard Edition, Enterprise Edition, and Enterprise Pro Edition.

Standard Edition is designed for developers who require high performance JSP and Servlet functionality with monitoring and session management services. Monitoring capabilities include live and historical graphs for reporting and analysis. Standard Edition integrates with LDAP-based directory servers, and includes iPlanet Directory Server for managing password policies and user groups.

Enterprise Edition provides a J2EE-certified e-commerce platform for delivering application services to a broad range of servers, clients, and devices. Application failover eliminates single points of failure at multiple levels, creating high transaction integrity and continuous uptime.

Enterprise Pro Edition provides enterprises with a J2EE-certified Java development and deployment platform for building e-commerce applications. The business process automation runtime services and legacy system integration enable companies to increase revenue and reduce costs while leveraging existing information technology investments.

The iPlanet Application Builder is positioned for entry-level development, (iPlanet recommends their FortZ product for more complex applications.) Wizards are provided to manage complex tasks such as building database forms, displaying resultsets, and generating session/entity beans. Interfaces for IDEs such as JBuilder, VisualAge, and WebGain are also included.

iPlanet has many features within the server itself, including XML parsers and an XSLT engine. A Process Manager, Messaging Services, and a Wireless and iPlanet Portal Server make this a complete server suite.

Pramati Java Application Server

Pramati Technologies

2570 North First Street, Suite 200

San Jose, CA 95131

Tel: +1 877-PRAMATI or +1 408-965-5513

Fax: +1 408-965-5305

`http://www.pramati.com`

The Pramati Server 2.5 strives to be an industrial-strength solution for building large-scale enterprise systems. It implements and supports the J2EE standards including EJB 1.1, JavaServer Pages 1.1, Servlets 2.2, Java Transaction APII 1.0, JAXP 1.1, JMS 1.0.2, RMI-JRMP, JDBC 1.0/2.0 Extensions, Java Naming and Directory Interface (JNDI) 1.2, JavaMail 1.1, and JavaBeans Activation Framework 1.0.

Key features include

- The Enterprise JavaBeans container—The EJB container fully supports EJB 1.1, with partial EJB 2.0 compliance. It handles stateless and stateful session beans as well as entity beans with container-managed persistence (CMP) and bean-managed persistence (BMP). It generates smart `EJBObject` code at deployment and provides pluggable bean handlers for customizable bean life cycle support. The container's fast RMI (Remote Method Indication) enables high-speed intra-VM calls.
- The Web container—This container provides custom handling of requests via pre- and postprocessors. Its customer processing modules are written in Java to eliminate the necessity of recompiling or rebuilding the server. It enables easy integration of WAP Gateway collaboration and includes a WML generator, a JSP 1.0–compliant compiler, and a Servlet 2.1 implementation with session management, thread pooling, scheduling, and security features.
- Pramati Cluster—Consisting of Web nodes, EJB nodes, and compound nodes, the cluster is a self-organizing system that works on a peer-to-peer model. Multiple nodes can exist on a single server, thereby increasing application scalability by overcoming JVM resource limits. No additional programming is needed to utilize clustering. Web nodes automatically discover the EJB nodes of the cluster and detect any failures of those nodes. The cluster's autorecovery feature ensures that another node will take over if a delegated lock server fails.
- Extensive management console—The management console allows applications and resources to be managed from both local and remote servers on a single console. It displays real-time information including the properties of archives currently deployed on the server, EJB container details including the status of each bean, Web container details such as deployed Servlets and JSPs with servlet-URL mapping, transaction logs, resource usage, security aspects, and naming services complete with a view of all objects in the namespace along with their properties and references.
- Optimized performance—Pramati server is designed to perform even under critical system resource constraints. It offers entity bean caching, database connection and statement pooling, and a network connection pooling server to improve performance and scalability.

Sitraka DeployDirector

Sitraka Software

260 King Street East

Toronto, Ontario, Canada

M5A 4L5

Tel: +1 800-663-4723 or +1 416-594-1026

Fax: +1 416-594-1919

`http://www.sitraka.com/software/deploydirector/`

DeployDirector offers a scalable solution for deploying Java applets and applications to end users. It can be run from any server that supports a Java VM and Servlets in both Windows and Solaris environments. Key elements include

- Vault—This stores applications, JREs, and associated properties. Changes made to packages are stored and automatically replicated to other servers in the cluster if necessary.
- Server Application Manager—This manager handles inbound requests for new or updated components. It authenticates the user and identifies and delivers any missing and/or updated components to the user.
- Client Application Manager—This manages the installation and execution of the application on the client's computer. It communicates with the Server Application Manager, ensuring that policies such as automatically updating the program upon startup are administered.
- Remote Administration Tool—This tool enables developers/administrators to define which Java packages should be deployed to users as well as to create rules for that deployment.

Unify eWave Engine

Unify Corporation

2101 Arena Boulevard

Sacramento, CA 95384

Tel: +1 800-GO-UNIFY or +1 916-928-6400

`http://www.unifyewave.com/`

Unify eWave Engine is a scalable enterprise-caliber application server designed to run under the most demanding conditions.

Key features include

- Replicated Application Services—Session beans can be replicated across multiple application servers and multiple machines, enabling increased throughput. This feature also replicates system services including JNDI and security, guarding against failure in a deployed system.

- Load balancing—Optimized resources and response time are achieved through the automatic balancing of load across each application server.
- High availability—Messages destined for an unavailable server are rerouted to other servers that provide the same services.
- Optimized Wire Level Communication Protocol—An optimized implementation of the RMI specification reduces network load and server load while increasing responsiveness.
- Database connection pooling—This feature limits the number of physical connections in use to any single database, preserving performance.
- Thread pooling—This type of pooling limits the maximum physical number of threads within the application server, eliminating the need for the application server to constantly spawn new threads for each new request.
- Network connection pooling—This limits the amount of network resources used for communication and enables all messages between two computers to be transmitted across a single network socket.
- Integrated performance management—Unify eWave Engine automatically provides detailed information such as response times, data flow, and resource utilization, enabling faster analysis and correction of problems.
- Security Manager—This manager enables the creation of roles, each with access to particular job functions.
- JMS integration—This feature provides for both Point-to-Point and Publish/Subscribe capabilities. Additionally, eWave Engine extends the EJB specification to allow inbound JMS messages to trigger the invocation of EJB component methods.
- Advanced container-managed persistence support—By offering this support, Unify eWave Engine facilitates the task of developing and managing entity beans. Caching occurs upon deployment, minimizing database server load and maximizing throughput.

In addition to supporting EJB 1.1 specifications, Unify eWave Engine supports COM, DCOM, RMI, HTTP, clustering, automatic load balancing, automatic failover, role-based security, and an integrated JSP engine.

Unify eWave Engine Enterprise Edition supports all major Web servers and operating systems, including Microsoft IIS, Netscape Enterprise Server, iPlanet Web Server, and Apache Web Server across Unix, Microsoft Windows, and Linux.

The Enterprise Edition also extends the standard Access Edition by supporting advanced features of Enterprise JavaBeans required in multiserver configurations (those that use replication, failover, and load balancing).

Modeling and Object/Report Generation Tools

As SQL has evolved as the standard for database deployment, data modeling for SQL-based database management systems has matured as well. Unfortunately, until recently, there was a paucity of process modeling languages and tools that provided a common notation for software process modeling. For data modeling, Erwin (most recently owned by Computer Associates) set the standard.

For process modeling, a consortium of companies developed the Unified Modeling Language (UML). This UML is widely accepted and has recently become an international standard. Now two software developers, even if they speak different languages, have a way to describe and talk about their software. With the UML, software engineers can draw complex diagrams to represent their software, just the way electrical engineers can draw complex diagrams to represent their circuits. UML is helping to bring the world's most influential software development firms (IBM, Microsoft, HP, Oracle, and so on) to agreement on process modeling. This is a major step. This section will identify the new wave of modeling tools as well as reintroduce some old favorites that have been upgraded for Java development.

Cape Clear CapeConnect XML Business Server

Cape Clear Software Ltd.

7-8 Mount Street Crescent

Dublin 2, Ireland

Tel: +353-1-241-9900

Fax: +353-1-241-9901

`http://www.capeclear.com/products/capeconnect/`

CapeConnect is an EJB-based application that enables J2EE, EJB components, and CORBA systems to be reused for e-business. The product provides the capability to automatically generate standards-based HTML and XML (SOAP) e-clients for EJB and CORBA components. The development capability is supported by end-to-end secure-session connectivity from Internet client to back-end server.

Cerebellum eCom Integrator and Portal Integrator

Cerebellum Software, Inc.

600 Waterfront Drive

Pittsburgh, PA 15222

Tel: +1 888-862-9898 or +1 412-208-6500

Fax: +1 412-208-6521

`http://www.cerebellumsoft.com/products/ecom/`

Cerebellum eCom Integrator and Portal Integrator are Java technology–based tools designed to provide real-time data integration.

eCom Integrator

Cerebellum eCom Integrator is a Java technology–based product designed to enable seamless, real-time integration of data between e-commerce applications and back-end data systems. Mapping to a variety of data sources including Oracle, Sybase, SQL Server, Informix, DB2, SAP R/3 System, VSAM, Access, and MySQL can be achieved out of the box.

The eCom Integrator graphic interface provides UML tools that allow developers to visually model the application requirements with object-oriented design. A bean-managed persistence layer is generated automatically upon the mapping of EJB components to relational, legacy, and SAP data.

Portal Integrator

Cerebellum Portal Integrator is a Java technology–based tool that enables real-time collection of corporate data for use in Enterprise Information Portal applications. A variety of data sources including Oracle, Sybase, SQL Server, Informix, DB2, SAP R/3 System, VSAM, Access, and MySQL can be easily accessed.

The visual environment facilitates the bridging of the application with relational, legacy, and ERP data. Drag-and-drop query language supplants manual coding. Developers are able to access, integrate, update, and delete information quickly and easily.

Multiple development environments including Java, C++, and EJBs are supported. Cerebellum integrates with most major application servers.

Embarcadero Technologies' DBArtisan

Embarcadero Technologies

425 Market Street, Suite 425

San Francisco, CA 94105

Tel: +1 415-834-3131

Fax: +1 415-434-1721

`http://www.embarcadero.com/products/administer/dbdatasheet.htm`

DBArtisan is a database administration solution designed to facilitate concurrent management of multiple databases from a single graphic console.

Tasks such as creating user accounts, altering objects, migrating schemas, and managing security have been simplified. Object editors and wizards enable simple manipulation and creation of database objects such as tables, constraints, indexes, procedures, functions, and packages. Visual tools allow straightforward creation of SQL statements.

DBArtisan requires only client-side installation, allowing administrators to manage multiple databases without the inconvenience of lengthy server-side installations and version incompatability.

Computer Associates' ERwin 4.0

Computer Associates International, Inc.

One Computer Associates Plaza

Islandia, NY 11749

Tel: +1 631-342-6000

Fax: +1 631-342-6800

`http://www.cai.com/products/alm/erwin.htm`

ERwin is designed to support a structured approach to managing information. The data requirements and database designs can be defined, managed, and implemented across database platforms including Ingres II, CA-Clipper, DB2, dBASE, FoxPro, HiRDB, Informix, InterBase, MS Access, MS SQL Server, ODBC 2.0/3.0, Oracle, Paradox, Rdb, Red Brick Warehouse, SAS, SQL Anywhere, SQL Base, Sybase, and Teradata.

Key features of ERwin include

- Design Layer Architecture—This structure consists of Logical Only and Physical Only models for capturing data requirements, transform technology for optimizing designs while maintaining traceability, and a Model Synchronizer for managing the impact of change across your designs.

- Glossary—This tool aids in the establishment and implementation of naming standards. Glossary entries containing the full business term and abbreviations are created, then the user can utilize a Glossary Checker, which operates much like spell checker for validation.
- Datatype Mapping Facility—This feature works with the Glossary to transform data requirements into physical designs. The user has the ability to define custom datatype mappings between datatypes and target database environments.
- Model Explorer—This assists in managing large and complex models using drag-and-drop diagram operations and easy-to-access object editors. Objects are organized into Model view for references in the entire contents, Subject Area view for referencing contents according to predefined business views, and Domain view for referencing domains within the model.
- Alignment, spacing, and grouping tools—ERwin 4.0 includes tools for graphically arranging models. Users can select multiple objects for easy manipulation in the diagramming environment.
- Drawing objects—ERwin 4.0 enables users to place drawing objects into their models to improve legibility.

HiT's Allora for Java

HiT Software, Inc

4020 Moorpark Avenue, Suite 100

San Jose, CA 95117

Tel: +1 408-345-4001

Fax: +1 408-345-4899

`http://www.hitsw.com`

HiT Allora for Java is a middleware tool designed to maintain an XML-consistent interface across any relational databases supporting JDBC by allowing both read and write integration. Allora uses standard JAXP interfaces to build W3C DOM objects, update node values, and apply XML data changes back to the underlying DBMS. It can also function as a SAX parser, treating database selections as XML infosets. Allora supports JDK 1.2 and later and is compatible with all major Web application development platforms.

PointBase Network Server and Embedded Server

PointBase, Inc.

1965 Charleston Road

Mt. View, CA 94043

Tel: +1 877-238-8798 or +1 650-230-7200

Fax: +1 650-230-7230

`http://www.pointbase.com`

PointBase Server Edition is a 100% Java object-relational database designed for networked Java servers and Java-based packaged applications. It is platform independent and offers advanced features for self-management, extensibility, and compatibility with enterprise database systems. It supports industry standards including SQL, JDBC, TCP/IP, and HTTP.

Rational Rose

Rational Software Corporation

18880 Homestead Rd.

Cupertino, CA 95014

Tel: +1 800-728-1212 or +1 408-863-9900

`http://www.rational.com/products/rose/index.jsp`

Rational Rose 2000 is a graphical component modeling and development tool that enables developers to graphically visualize their applications using the industry-standard UML. Developers may visualize and refine the application throughout the development life cycle without committing the architecture to code.

Rational Rose offers the following features:

- Rational RequisitePro—This feature enables users to manage use case artifacts, specify documents, attributes, traceability, and diagrams.
- Round-trip engineering—This ensures that the model always coordinates with the code.
- Data modeler—Comprehensive database support is provided for Windows developers, including object-relational mapping, schema generation, and round-trip engineering.

- XML support—XML support is provided through UML-based Web application extentions, round-trip engineering of JSP and ASP pages, and advanced modeling features. Rational is also a member of the W3C, ensuring adherence to the latest XML standards.
- Component testing—Problems may be located and fixed while components are still isolated. Test code is automatically generated.

Together ControlCenter

TogetherSoft

920 Main Campus Drive, Suite 410

Raleigh, NC 27606

Tel: +1 919-833-5550

Fax: +1 919-833-5533

`http://www.togethersoft.com/`

Together ControlCenter 5 is designed to accelerate enterprise application development using Java- and J2EE-compliant application servers. ControlCenter is targeted toward large development organizations, striving to be a centerpiece tool that will facilitate massive parallel development at all stages.

Features include

- XML structure editor
- UML-diagram editor
- Programming editor
- EJB Deployment Expert
- Enhanced audit and metrics
- Pattern-builder expert
- Improved compile/make/run/debug
- Improved forward and reverse engineering of database schemas
- WLE CORBA Expert for working with BEA WebLogic Enterprise

TogetherSoft Open Platform API is shipped as part of the platform, enabling users to develop Java plug-ins that will suit their needs. A building block community for the sharing of building class, link, or member patterns and templates is available at TogetherCommunity.com.

The program also supports C++, IDL, and XML.

Elixir Report

Elixir Technology

50 Armenian Street, #04-04

Wilmer Place, Singapore 179938

Republic of Singapore

Tel: +65 532-4300

Fax: +65 532-4255

`http://www.elixirtech.com/ElixirReport/`

Elixir Report is coded entirely in Java for increased flexibility, enabling report generation on any Java-compliant platform. Reports can be either created on the fly or graphically constructed using elements from supporting data sources including XML, Java Objects, JDBC, LDAP, Crosstab, and Text. Version 1.6 generates reports in CSV file format so the user may import data into a variety of applications, such as MS Excel or other spreadsheet and database applications as well as the Portable Document Format (PDF) and Java Graphics Format (.jgf) output file formats.

Report templates and data source schemas are stored in XML 1.0 format. In addition to report templates, there is a wizard for report creation, multiple functions for report manipulation, and an end user–friendly Visual Report Designer.

The Project Manager enables categorizing and managing of reports and provides version control ability, which is important for larger projects.

Elixir Report runs on all JDK 1.x– and Java 2–compliant platforms.

InetSoft Style Report

InetSoft Technology

559 Buckingham Dr

Piscataway, NJ 08854

Tel: +1 908-755-0200

Fax: +1 908-756-1888

`http://www.inetsoftcorp.com/`

Style Report is a Java technology toolkit for report generation from both application and external data sources. Style Report is based on a Java class/Java bean library that allows easy integration of any Java data source through an API.

A GUI designer is included for WYSIWYG report building. Swing JTables are also supported. Advanced features such as charting, grouping/summarization, and high resolution printing drivers are included.

The Enterprise Edition of Style Report enables interactive reports that can be viewed in a browser, electronically stored, and transmitted. Style Report/EE can also be integrated into an Internet/intranet infrastructure via Java servlet–, RMI-, or Corba-based deployment options. Other server-side features include Demand-paging, load balance, open security API, scheduling, and remote administration.

Tidestone Technologies' Formula One iReporting Engine

Tidestone Technologies

12980 Metcalf Avenue, Suite 300

Overland Park, KS 66213

Tel: +1 800-884-8665 or +1 913-851-2200

Fax: +1 913-851-1390

`http://www.tidestone.com/products/formulaone.jsp`

Formula One iReporting Engine uses server-based technology to manage the vast amount of data collected on servers in Web-based applications. Formula One can generate Excel reports (assuming that Excel is present on the user's desktop), applet-based reports, or HTML-based reports. This ensures that users can access data from virtually anywhere. No client-side software installation is necessary, as reports can be received, read, and manipulated using either Excel or a Web browser. Reports are generated in forms that are already familiar to most users. Additional training is not required for end users to utilize the data that is delivered to them.

Quadbase Systems' EspressChart

Quadbase Systems, Inc.

2855 Kifer Road #203

Santa Clara, CA 95054

Tel: +1 408-982-0835

Fax: +1 408-982-0838

`http://www.quadbase.com/espresschart/index.html`

EspressChart is a 100% Java-based charting tool that enables the publishing of dynamic 2D and 3D charts on the Web from data sources including ODBC/JDBC databases, XML files, text data files, and arguments in API calls.

Charts can be created from a visual design/editing tool or with a flexible object-oriented API. They may be displayed as Java applets or JPE/PNG/GIF images. A comprehensive set of customizable chart types is available.

Data analysis options include Time-Series Data Zooming, Histogram, Control Line, Data Drill Down, Trend Lines, and Normal Distribution curves.

EspressChart can be used with most major IDEs and application servers. Platforms supported are Windows NT/95 +, Solaris, AIX, AS/400, RS/6000, and OS/390.

Messaging and XML Tools

In essence, a messaging system enables separate, uncoupled applications to reliably communicate asynchronously. The messaging system architecture generally replaces the client/server model with a peer-to-peer relationship between individual components, where each peer can send and receive messages to and from other peers.

Messaging systems provide a host of powerful advantages over other, more conventional distributed computing models. Primarily, they encourage "loose coupling" between message consumers and message producers. There is a high degree of anonymity between producer and consumer: To the message consumer, it doesn't matter who produced the message, where the producer lives on the network, or when the message was produced.

Distributed applications are proliferating, as are a host of previously unexplored synchronization, reliability, scalability, and security problems. One solution is a messaging system built from loosely coupled components communicating through messages.

The Java Message Service (JMS) provides a consistent API set that gives developers access to the common features of many messaging system products. Java Message Service, part of the J2EE (Java 2 Platform, Enterprise Edition) suite, provides standard APIs that Java developers can use to access the common features of enterprise message systems. JMS supports the Publish/Subscribe and Point-to-Point models and enables the creation of message types consisting of arbitrary Java objects.

In this section we have identified vendors who provide messaging systems/servers that support the J2EE JMS. (Of course, this list is not exhaustive. You can visit our Web site at `http://www.ucny.com` or other sources such as `http://developer.java.sun.com` to find descriptions of other vendors and their products.) Also in this section we briefly discuss the eXtensible Markup Language (XML). XML was developed to address the

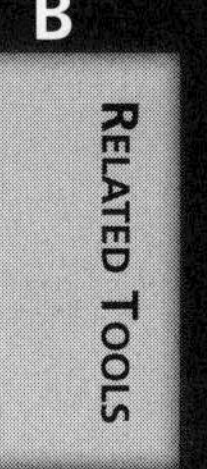

requirements of commercial Web publishing and enable the further expansion of Web technology into new domains of distributed document processing beyond the Hypertext Markup Language (HTML). Chapter 16, "Data Exchange with XML," discusses the eXtensible Markup Language technology in detail.

FioranoMQ 5 Message Server

Fiorano Software, Inc.

718 University Avenue, Suite 212

Los Gatos, CA 95032

Tel: +1 408-354-3210

Fax: +1 408-354-0846

`http://www.fiorano.com/products/products.htm`

FioranoMQ 5 Message Server is a messaging service infrastructure solution implemented entirely in Java on both the server and client sides. This maximizes cross-platform support, reduces client administration, and increases application accessibility across enterprise intranets and the Internet.

The latest release of FioranoMQ contains a Scalable Connection Management Module (SCM) to maximize the number of concurrent users and throughput. Utilizing the Publish/Subscribe communications model, FioranoMQ automatically disseminates events to the relevant subscribers as they happen. Other key features include support for security, remote administration, guaranteed message delivery, scalability, and language interoperability. The Administration API allows servers to be monitored remotely.

FioranoMQ software implements all of the JMS Pub/Sub and PTP APIs. Support is included for security, remote administration, guaranteed message delivery, scalability, and language interoperability. Additions and enhancements with the latest release provide support for Client/Server communication via HTTP and HTTPS protocols, support for Object Messages, LDAP integration for all named objects, integration with LDAP's security manager, and interoperability with other messaging services such as IBM MQSeries and MSMQ.

SonicMQ

Sonic Software Corporation

`http://www.sonicsoftware.com/`

SonicMQ Enterprise Edition is a fully JMS-compliant Java Messaging infrastructure for the reliable transport of data over the Internet. It offers asynchronous messaging, guaranteed message delivery, security, and transaction capabilities. The Dynamic Routing

Architecture provides a high degree of scalability. Applications based on SonicMQ can handle disconnected users, network outages, and other software or hardware failures. SonicMQ Java messaging server can also be remotely monitored and reconfigured.

Interbroker clustering allows multiple servers to operate as one unit, eliminating single failure-points in the system.

SonicMQ also provides full access control and certificate-based authentication for server-to-server and client-to-server security. End-to-end secure communication is achieved via message payload and channel encryption. Flexible HTTP/HTTPS maximizes existent Internet security mechanisms and allows messages to travel through firewalls.

SilverStream jBrokerMQ

SilverStream Software

Two Federal Street

Billerica, MA 01821

Tel: +1 978-262-3000 or +1 888-823-9700

Fax: +1 978-262-3499

`http://www.silverstream.com/jbroker/`

SilverStream's jBrokerMQ 1.1 is a 100% pure Java implementation of the Java Messaging Service (JMS) API. jBrokerMQ is fully compliant with the JMS specification version 1.0.2. It implements all the required features as well as some of the optional and value-added features like built-in system namespace, security, and administration.

Softwired's iBus//MessageServer

Softwired Inc.

Technoparkstrasse1

Zurich, 8005

Switzerland

Tel: +41 (0)1 445 2370

Fax: +41 (0)1 445 2372

`http://www.softwired-inc.com/`

Softwired iBus//MessageServer Business Edition 4.1 is an enterprise messaging middleware product that supports multiple transport protocols (TCP/IP, SSL, IP multicast, HTTP, Wireless) and conforms to the JMS open standard. Written in 100% Java, iBus is designed to run on any type of device including PCs, servers, and PDAs. iBus provides fault-tolerance and load-sharing features, as well as integration support for applications written in C, C++, CORBA, and EJB.

iBus//MessageServer supports applications using XML to represent their data structures. XML documents can be sent or received without being converted to an available JMS message type.

For applications that require privacy, iBus//MessageServer offers the SSL transport protocol with full strength cryptography.

An administration client is available as a free download to simplify iBus//MessageServer administration. It consists of a graphical user interface, a text user interface, and an administration API. The graphical user interface, which is installed as a standalone application, can be used to administer a server remotely via TCP/IP.

Remote server configuration as well as a JMS message-browser and an online help function are supported.

Xerces and Xalan

The Apache Software Foundation

1901 Munsey Drive

Forest Hill, MD 21050-2747

Fax: +1 410-803-2258

`http://xml.apache.org`

Xerces is a highly modular and configurable standards-based XML solution. The current release, 1.3.0, supports XML 1.0 and offers preliminary support for the W3C XML Schema language including DOM Level 2 specifications for core, events, and traversal and range modules. The finalized SAX Version 2 APIs are also supported.

The Apache Project is a collaborative effort between developers worldwide. Xerces-J 1.3.0 is available as source code, as well as in JAR file form. Feedback and participation are encouraged.

Xalan is an XSLT processor for transforming XML documents into HTML, text, or other XML document types. It implements the W3C Recommendations for XSL Transformations (XSLT) and the XML Path Language (XPath). It can be used from the command line, in an applet or a servlet, or as a module in another program.

Java API for XML Processing 1.1 (JAXP)

Sun Microsystems, Inc.

901 San Antonio Rd.

Palo Alto, CA 93403

Tel: +1 650-960-1300

`http://java.sun.com/xml/xml_jaxp.html`

Java API for XML Processing (JAXP) is a lightweight API that enables integration of any XML-compliant parser with a Java application. It allows for reading, manipulating, and generating XML documents through pure Java APIs.

JAXP 1.1 conforms to specifications including XML 1.0 Second Edition, XML Namespaces, SAX 2.0, SAX2 Extensions 1.0, DOM Level 2, and XSLT 1.0.

JAXP was created under the Java Community Process, which provides full public participation for definition and development. It is available as a free download. The user must have any version of the Java 2 Software Development Kit (SDK) or version 1.1.8 (or above) of the Java Development Kit (JDK).

Altova's XML Spy

Altova, Inc.

900 Cummings Center

Suite 306-T

Beverly, MA 01915-6181

`http://www.xmlspy.com`

XML Spy is an Integrated Development Environment for the eXtensible Markup Language. XML Spy is centered around a validating XML editor that provides five advanced views of your documents: an Enhanced Grid view for structured editing, a Database/Table view that shows repeated elements in a tabular fashion, a Text view with syntax-coloring for low-level work, a graphical XML Schema design view, and an integrated Browser view that supports both CSS and XSL style sheets.

Validation and Performance Monitoring Tools

We have seen how we can model and develop, but how do we test the stuff? It is also important to leverage improvements in the management of code and system validation to make testing as effective and efficient as possible. In large-scale development, automated software validation tools and performance monitoring tools can improve quality and cut back on the time, effort, and cost involved in testing an application's integrity and responsiveness. Before procuring a validation/performance tool, it's a good idea to consider the following:

- Whether you really need an automated code and system validation/testing tool
- Why it is necessary to perform a formal evaluation
- The process of identifying and documenting your code and system validation requirements
- How to research the market and generate a short list of tools
- Why you should invite suppliers to come to your site for presentations

When should you use an automated code and system validation tool? Such products are particularly appropriate if you have any of the following:

- Frequent builds and releases of the software for code and system validation
- A requirement for thorough regression code and system validation, and particularly for business-critical, safety-critical, and secure or confidential software systems
- Software involving complex graphical user interfaces
- A requirement for rigorous, thorough, and repeatable code and system validation
- A need to deliver software that can perform across many different platforms
- A need to reduce timescales, effort, and cost

In this section we provide a starting list of tools that can provide help. Each must be reviewed to determine if it can help you with your particular needs.

VMGEAR's Optimizeit

VMGEAR
1479 Saratoga Avenue
San Jose, CA 95129
Tel: +1 888-655-0055 or +1 408-865-1915
Fax: +1 408-865-1946
`http://www.vmgear.com`

Optimizeit 4.0 allows Java developers to quickly discover and rectify performance issues in any type of Java environment, including servlets, EJBs, JSPs, or JavaBeans. Java programs can be launched from the Optimizeit user interface. In addition to profiling applications locally, the developer may profile remotely on any system that matches the development and deployment environment. Overall, Optimizeit reduces development time while improving overall performance of the program.

Optimizeit includes several means of analyzing performance issues. Data can be saved offline using Snapshots for analysis at another time, enabling applications to be tested while live traffic is being served.

Optimizeit offers the following key features:

- CPU profiling—CPU consumption can be quickly and accurately evaluated to determine and fix performance bottlenecks and inefficient algorithms. This profiling can be instrumentation-based (for small or fast parts of code) or sample-based (for large servers or client applications).
- Memory leak debugging—Optimizeit displays a comprehensive object reference graph that lists all references on each instance. References that need to be cleared are highlighted for fast and easy garbage collection.
- Monitoring of object allocations—Many features are specifically designed for monitoring object allocations. Developers may monitor in real time to detect issues such as excessive allocations. In addition, Optimizeit has the functionality of garbage collection control and temporal mark setting.

Integration wizards automatically integrate Optimizeit with most popular application servers and servlet engines. Performance data is displayed in graphs and measurements, allowing for simple detection of problems.

Optimizeit is available for Windows NT/98/2000, Sparc Solaris, Solaris Intel, and Linux.

ParaSoft's Jtest

ParaSoft

2031 S. Myrtle Ave.

Monrovia, CA 91016

Tel: +1 888-305-0041 or +1 626-305-3036

Fax: +1 626-305-0041

`http://www.parasoft.com/products/jtest/`

Jtest 3.2 is a Java error prevention and detection tool designed to detect runtime exceptions from the earliest stages of development. Jtest automatically performs white box and black box testing as well as static code analysis and regression testing on Java classes and EJBs.

White box testing is automatically generated and executed based on a class's structure. White box stubs can also be generated to test classes using inputs from resources such as external databases, CORBA, and EJBs. Jtest reports the arguments, stack trace, and calling sequence for input generating an uncaught runtime exception.

Black box testing checks code using test cases based on the program's specifications. Test cases can be created by adding method inputs to simple test cases or by creating test classes for more complex test cases. Outcomes are verified with a mouse-click.

Regression testing occurs at the class level, ensuring that regression errors are detected at the earliest possible stage of development.

Static analysis enables the user to automatically enforce a vast array of industry standards as well as more tailored standards designed for a particular project through RuleWizard.

Benefits that Jtest offers include the following:

- Eliminates problems that result in crashing
- Ensures structurally sound code
- Prevents errors from returning to code
- Streamlines development
- Reduces development and support costs

Jtest currently runs on Windows, Solaris, and Linux.

RadView Software's WebLoad

RadView Software, Inc.
7 New England Executive Park
Burlington, MA 01803
Tel: +1 1-888-RADVIEW or +1 781-238-1111
Fax: +1 781-238-8875
`http://www.radview.com/`

WebLoad is a user-friendly testing solution that analyzes both hardware and software to validate the performance of Web applications. Scalability, performance, and functional testing can be combined into a single process.

An *agenda* (A script file defining the test to be executed) is created using the Agenda Authoring Tool. Testing can be performed from a single machine, or among many machines on a network. *Host* workstations or servers launch multiple simultaneous

TCP/IP connections to the target site, each simulating a separate user. Test complexity can be increased by accelerating the number of simultaneous tests or by diversifying the simulated browsers by type, bandwidth, and so on.

Automatic verification wizards enable important functional tests on data returned from the server to be created and run without manual scripting.

The results of each execution time and details of any errors that have occurred are reported back to the WebLoad console in real time. While the console presents graphs of those results, the tester retains the ability to examine individual nodes on the graph or even the raw data.

WebLoad delivers full DOM access, JavaScript-based test scripting, and HTTP support. It is easily integrated with leading Web application servers.

Empirix Bean-test

Empirix, Inc.

`http://www.ejbtest.com/ejbad/`

Bean-test is a straightforward tool designed specifically for conducting functionality and performance tests on EJB components both throughout the development cycle and after deployment.

Synchload technology generates thousands of test client threads to emulate the load of real clients on the EJB application. The DataWizard can apply user-supplied data, or Bean-test can populate the test with random data.

Test results such as response time, transactions per second, and exceptions can be viewed graphically.

The program is optimized for BEA WebLogic and IBM WebSphere application servers. Bean-test uses all Java technology, and supports Windows NT/2000, UNIX, Solaris, and Linux platforms.

Segue Software's SilkPilot

Segue Software, Inc.

201 Spring St.

Lexington, MA 02421

Tel: +1 800-287-1329 or +1 781-402-1000

Fax +1 781-402-1099

`http://www.segue.com`

SilkPilot is a standards-based tool designed to automate the testing of distributed objects behavior. Support is provided for CORBA and Java interface descriptions, IIOP and RMI communication protocols, and EJB component standards. Test cases are stored in XML.

The graphic GUI allows navigation of interface descriptions, connection to objects, creation and editing of arguments and attributes, and invocation of methods.

SilkPilot is available for Windows and Unix platforms and supports Java platform and C++ servers.

Sitraka Software's JProbe

Sitraka Software

260 King Street East

Toronto, Ontario, Canada

M5A 4L5

Tel: +1 800-663-4723 or +1 416-594-1026

Fax: +1 416-594-1919

`http://www.sitraka.com/software/jprobe/`

JProbe is an integrated suite consisting of tools that optimize the performance, scalability, and reliability of Java Enterprise applications. Version 3.0 also supports profiling of EJBs, servlets, and client-side applets. Included are JProbe Profiler with Memory Debugger, JProbe Threadalyzer, and JProbe Coverage, each of which is described here:

- JProbe Profiler with Memory Debugger—The profiler detects bottlenecks and loitering objects in the Java code. Data is gathered on either a per-line or per-method basis. Statistics including number of calls, cumulative time for each method, and average method time are available in several levels of detail. Memory Debugger runs whenever the user is profiling code. Reports include the Runtime Heap Summary, which displays the available and allocated heap space, and the Instance Summary, which tracks object creation and deletion.
- JProbe Threadalyzer—This component monitors thread execution as the JVM runs, detecting deadlocks, stalls, and race conditions. It identifies not only where problems are occurring, but where potential problems may occur. Results are displayed by class name and line number.
- JProbe Coverage—This tracks the executed lines of code in the program, locating and measuring untested code. Results are grouped by classname. Coverage provides data such as the number of methods and lines hit or missed and the total percentage of hits and misses.

Each of these tools allows users to specify which classes to include or exclude, which JVM the tool should use, and when to collect data during execution. The data is displayed graphically, and is therefore easy to read. Profiler utilizes color-coding to display the execution time of each node. Memory Debugger displays a moving graph in which instances of garbage collection are shown with a saw-tooth pattern.

JProbe supports major IDEs including IBM VisualAge for Java, WebGain VisualCafé, and Borland JBuilder.

Quick Reference Material

APPENDIX C

IN THIS APPENDIX

- J2EE APIs *756*
- J2EE Software Development Kit (SDK) Installation Instructions *759*
- Naming Conventions for J2EE *763*

J2EE APIs

This appendix provides an overview of the entire J2EE specification, and how all components fit together.

Required APIs

As we hope you have determined from reading this book, J2EE is composed of core Java APIs. These are as follows:

- Java IDL (Java Interface Definition Language) API—This provides interoperability and connectivity with services that exist outside the J2EE environment. It is used to define interfaces to objects. In addition, it defines the types of objects according to the operations that may be performed on them and the parameters of those operations.
- JDBC (Java Database Connectivity) Core API—JDBC is critical because it allows developers to take advantage of the Write Once, Run Anywhere (WORA) capabilities of the Java platform, facilitating cross-platform applications that require access to enterprise data. JDBC enables connection to corporate data in a heterogeneous environment. JDBC can be used to access a database on the same machine, on a server on a LAN, or on a server across the Internet. In our years of experience, accessing data residing on various vendor databases is the key to success in development.
- RMI-IIOP (Remote Method Invocation over Internet InterORB Protocol) API—This allows objects defined using Remote Method Invocation–style interfaces to be accessed using the Internet InterORB Protocol, delivering Common Object Request Broker Architecture (CORBA) distributed computing capabilities via J2EE. Subsequently, developers are able to pass any serializable Java objects (Objects by Value) between application components.
- JNDI (Java Naming and Directory Interface) API—This is an integrated interface utilized by other APIs that gives connectivity to naming and directory services in the enterprise. Version 1.2 includes new features such as event notification and Lightweight Directory Access Protocol (LDAP) version 3 extensions and controls.

  JNDI comprises several packages, including the following:

  - `javax.naming` package—defines classes and interfaces for accessing naming services
  - `javax.naming.directory` package—defines classes and interfaces for accessing directory services

- `javax.naming.event` package—defines classes and interfaces for event notification when accessing naming and directory services
- `javax.naming.ldap` package—defines classes and interfaces that provide support for LDAP version 3 extended operations and controls
- `javax.naming.spi` package—defines classes and interfaces used to access existing naming and directory services using JNDI's SPI

Optional Packages

Formerly released as Java Standard Extensions, the following are optional in relation to J2SE, but are required for J2EE:

- JDBC 2.0 Extension—This extends JDBC functionality for typical access patterns used on data.
  - Rowsets—These are JavaBeans components containing sets of rows that have the ability to pass data to a client or provide scrollability to a resultset.
  - DataSource interface for working with JNDI—This Allows the data source to be defined as an object with specific properties and registered with a JNDI naming service, thereby simplifying connection to that data source. This makes code even more portable.
  - Connection pooling—This is critical, as it allows reuse of connections as opposed to creation of a new connection every time. This greatly improves performance.
  - Distributed transactions—These allow multiple database servers to be included in a transaction. We hope that this will be implemented properly. It is an important package. Historically, distributed transaction functionality has been difficult to implement because there are so many failure points in committing distributed database updates.
- EJB 2.0—This includes all specifications of the EJB interoperability protocol based on RMII-IIOP. All containers that support EJB clients must be able to use the EJB interoperability protocol to invoke enterprise beans. EJB 2.0 integrates with JMS, allowing EJBs to participate in loosely connected systems as well as send messages via the JMS API. It utilizes Container-Managed Persistence (CMP) to expedite application development, extending the capabilities for modeling and supporting dependent objects. In addition, it introduces a standard query language. It is based on CMP bean definitions, not the underlying database schema.

- Servlets 2.3—This defines the packaging and deployment of Web applications, addresses security, and includes requirements for Web containers. Servlets have been commonly used for years as an efficient platform-independent replacement for antiquated common gateway interface (CGI) scripts.
- JSP 1.2 (JavaServer Pages)—As befits development trends, JSP separates the user interface from content generation, thus enabling changes to the overall page layout to be made without altering the underlying dynamic content. Tags and scriptlets written in the Java programming language encapsulate the logic that generates the content for the page. These tags and scriptlets access the server-based application logic. Tags are more desirable than scriptlets, as proper tag deployment will promote reuse.
- JMS 1.0 (Java Message Service)—JMS is made up of a set of classes that provide support that enables independent applications to communicate via reliable, scalable, asynchronous messages over a network. JMS supports the sending and receiving of both text-based messages and object messages using either Point-to-Point or Publish/Subscribe messaging models. You must ensure that the vendor message server supports JMS. Predictably, as Microsoft does not go out of its way to support Java interoperability, their messaging software MSMQ does not offer JMS compatibility.

  JMS defines a specific type of object called an administered object that constitutes JMS configuration information. These objects are created by a JMS administrator and are registered so they can be accessed through JNDI. Configuration parameters are defined by an administrator and are used by a JMS client to create a connection with a particular provider.
- JTA 1.0 (Java Transaction API)—This specifies standard Java interfaces between a transaction manager and the parties involved in a distributed transaction system (the resource manager, the application server, and the transactional applications). We hope that the Java Transaction API will provide a way for distributed application components to interact with each other in a reliable manner.
- JavaMail 1.2—This is a set of abstract classes that model a mail system, providing a platform-independent framework to build Java technology-based mail and messaging applications.
- JAF 1.0 (JavaBeans Activation Framework)—This determines the type of data and what operations are available on it, and engages the appropriate JavaBeans component to perform the operation(s).
- JAXP 1.1 (Java API for XML Parsing)—This enables developers to add essential XML functionality to Java applications, facilitating the reading, manipulating, and generating of XML documents through pure Java APIs.

- Connector 1.0—This holds the promise of enabling integration with existing Enterprise Information Systems (EIS). Many large organizations still maintain "books and records" on legacy mainframe applications. The Connector architecture defines the following set of system-level contracts between an application server and EIS:
  - A Connection Management contract—This enables an application server to pool connections to an underlying EIS and permits application components to connect to an EIS. This leads to a scalable application environment that can support a large number of clients requiring access to EISs.
  - A Transaction Management contract—This exists between the transaction manager and an EIS and supports transactional access to EIS resource managers. This contract allows an application server to use a transaction manager to manage transactions across multiple resource managers. It also supports transactions that are managed within an EIS resource manager without the necessity of involving an external transaction manager.
  - A Security Contract—This enables secure access to an EIS. This contract provides support for a secure application environment, reducing security threats to the EIS and protecting valuable information resources managed by the EIS.
  - Common Client Interface (CCI)—This defines a standard client API for application components. This interface enables application components and Enterprise Application Integration (EAI) frameworks to direct interactions across heterogeneous EISs using a common client API.
- JAAS 1.0 (Java Authentication and Authorization Service)—This enables services to authenticate and enforce access controls on users. It decides whether or not to grant individual access permissions to running code based on the code's characteristics, such as where it is coming from, whether it is signed, and if so by whom.

J2EE Software Development Kit (SDK) Installation Instructions

You can download all the items you need from `http://java.sun.com/j2ee/` as well as the J2EE development kit that fits your environment. Before installing the software or documentation onto your system, you must also download the appropriate software bundle from the Sun Web site. You will need to install the JDK 1.2 to develop with J2EE.

Installation for Windows

Depending on your system resources, choose a drive space with adequate storage to house the downloaded components as well as any ancillary components such as the database or connector add-ons.

1. Skip this first step if you downloaded the software as a single bundle. If you downloaded the software into multiple files, you must concatenate them together. There must be enough available disk space for all the individual files plus an equal amount for the resulting self-extracting archive. Execute the following command to concatenate the downloaded files into a single file (you may find it easier to copy this command into a batch file, which you will then run):

   ```
   copy /b j2sdkee-1_2_1-win-a.exe +
   j2sdkee-1_2_1-win-b.exe + j2sdkee-1_2_1-win-c.exe +
   j2sdkee-1_2_1-win-d.exe + j2sdkee-1_2_1-win-e.exe +
   j2sdkee-1_2_1-win-f.exe + j2sdkee-1_2_1-win-g.exe +
   j2sdkee-1_2_1-win-h.exe + j2sdkee-1_2_1-win-i.exe
   j2sdkee-1_2_1-win.exe
   ```

   The resulting file (j2sdkee-1_2_1-win.exe) is a self-extracting InstallShield setup program.

2. Run the setup program by double-clicking on the icon of the j2sdkee-1_2_1-win.exe file. Instructions will be provided by the setup program, which installs the software in C:\j2sdkee1.2.1 by default. If you install the software after installing the documentation, the software should be installed in the parent directory of the documentation.

3. Edit the user configuration script, found in the userconfig.bat file of the bin directory of your installation. The userconfig.bat file sets the following environment variables:

   `J2EE_CLASSPATH`—This is the classpath referenced by the J2EE server. `J2EE_CLASSPATH` must include the location of JDBC driver classes (except for those used by the Cloudscape DBMS included in this download bundle) delimited by a semicolon. `J2EE_CLASSPATH` need not include the Java 2 SDK, Enterprise Edition classes (`j2ee-jar`) or the Java 2 SDK, Standard Edition software.

   `JAVA_HOME`—This is the directory where the Java 2 SDK, Standard Edition is installed.

   The following is an example of how the userconfig.bat file may be edited:

   ```
   set J2EE_CLASSPATH=C:\oracle\jdbc;C:\db\driver.zip
   set JAVA_HOME=C:\jdk1.2.2
   ```

4. Set the environment variables by executing the `bin\userconfig.bat` script in your shell window or by using the Environment tab of the System Properties window.

The System Properties window can be accessed from the Settings menu: Select Control Panel and from there select System.

5. Install the Windows Documentation Bundle.

   If you downloaded the documentation as one large .exe file, run the setup program by double-clicking on the icon of the j2sdkee-1_2_1-doc-win.exe file, and then follow the instructions provided by the setup program. If you install the documentation after you install the software, the setup program will choose the proper directory in which to install the documentation.

   If you downloaded the documentation into multiple .zip files, then you must concatenate the files together. There must be enough available disk space for all the individual files plus an equal amount for the resulting self-extracting archive. Execute the following command to merge the downloaded files into a single file (you may find it easier to copy this command into a batch file, which you will then run):

   ```
   copy /b j2sdkee-1_2_1-doc-a.zip +
   j2sdkee-1_2_1-doc-b.zip + j2sdkee-1_2_1-doc-c.zip +
   j2sdkee-1_2_1-doc-d.zip + j2sdkee-1_2_1-doc-e.zip
   j2sdkee-1_2_1-doc.zip
   ```

   Use an unzip utility to extract the documentation from the j2sdkee-1_2_1-doc.zip file. The documentation should end up in the j2sdkee1.2.1/doc directory.

Installation for Linux

Depending on your system resources, choose a drive space with adequate storage to house the downloaded components as well as any ancillary components such as the database or connector add-ons.

1. Change to the directory where you want to install the software. To illustrate, to install the software under /usr/local you would type this command:

   ```
   cd /usr/local
   ```

   A subdirectory called j2sdkee1.2.1 is automatically created upon unpacking the bundle.

2. If you did not download the software as a single bundle, concatenate the downloaded files into a single file by executing the following command:

   ```
   cat j2sdkee-1_2_1-linux-* > j2sdkee-1_2_1-linux.tar.gz
   ```

   There must be enough available disk space for all the individual files plus an equal amount for the resulting self-extracting archive.

3. Unpack the download bundle located in the j2sdkee-1_2_1-linux.tar.gz file. Run the following command to uncompress and unpack the download bundle:

   ```
   tar xvzf j2sdkee-1_2_1-linux.tar.gz
   ```

   After you agree to the license, the j2sdkee1.2.1 directory will be created and the software will be installed into it.

4. Edit the user configuration script located in the userconfig.sh file of the bin directory of your installation. The userconfig.sh file sets the following environment variables:

   `J2EE_CLASSPATH`—This is the classpath referenced by the J2EE server. `J2EE_CLASSPATH` is required to include the location of JDBC driver classes (except for those used by the Cloudscape DBMS included in the download bundle). Each location is delimited by a colon. `J2EE_CLASSPATH` is not required to include the J2EE classes (`j2ee-jar`, the J2SE classes, or the classes contained in the enterprise application).

   `JAVA_HOME`—This is the absolute path of the directory in which the Java 2 SDK, Standard Edition is installed.

   The following is an example of how the userconfig.sh file may be edited:

   ```
   J2EE_CLASSPATH=/opt/oracle/jdbc:/usr/local/db/driver.zip
   export J2EE_CLASSPATH
   JAVA_HOME=/usr/local/java/jdk1.2.2
   export JAVA_HOME
   ```

5. Install the Linux Documentation Bundle.

   Change to the directory above the one in that the software is installed in. For example, you would type the following command if you installed the software in /usr/local/j2sdkee1.2.1:

   ```
   cd /usr/local
   ```

   If you downloaded the documentation as one large .exe file, the download bundle can be unpacked as follows. The download bundle for the documentation is in the j2sdkee-1_2_1-doc-linux.tar.gz file. Run this command to uncompress and unpack the bundle:

   ```
   tar xvzf j2sdkee-1_2_1-doc-linux.tar.gz
   ```

   The j2sdkee1.2.1/doc directory is created, with the documentation installed into it.

   If you downloaded the documentation into multiple .zip files, then concatenate the files together by executing the following command:

   ```
   cat j2sdkee-1_2_1-doc*.zip > j2sdkee-1_2_1-doc.zip
   ```

   There must be enough available disk space for all the individual files plus an equal amount for the resulting self-extracting archive.

Use the jar utility to extract the documentation from the j2sdkee-1_2_1-win.zip file.

```
jar xvf j2sdkee-1_2_1-doc.zip
```

Common Installation Notes for All Platforms

After you've installed the documentation, you should read the following HTML files:

- The Release Notes list software requirements, supported platforms, and current limitations. The Release Notes are in the doc/release/ReleaseNotes.html file.
- The Configuration Guide explains how to configure JDBC drivers and various J2EE properties. If you are using the Cloudscape DBMS included with the J2EE software bundle, you do not have to configure the Cloudscape JDBC drivers. This guide is located in the doc/release/ConfigGuide.html file.
- The Getting Started chapter gives instruction on coding, deploying, and running a simple client/server application that uses an enterprise bean. This chapter is located in the doc/guides/ejb/html/Started.fm.html file.
- The main page of the J2EE SDK documentation bundle is in the doc/index.html file. We recommend that you add a bookmark to this file in your browser.
- The Code Examples appendix lists the sample enterprise beans documented and shipped with this release. The appendix is in the doc/guides/ejb/html/ZExamplesAppend.fm.html file. The source code for the examples can be found in the doc/guides/ejb/examples directory.

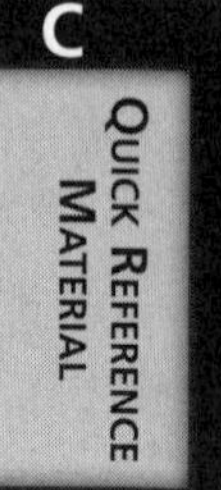

Naming Conventions for J2EE

The naming requirements for the J2EE platform address the following two objectives, which help to promote portability and interoperability:

- The application assembler and deployer should be able to customize an application's business logic without accessing the application's source code.
- Applications must be able to access resources and external information in their operational environment without knowledge of how the external information is named and organized in that environment.

Required Access to the JNDI Naming Environment

Sun Microsystems has released JNDI as a Java Standard Extension. Sun has also released service providers that plug in seamlessly behind JNDI for a number of naming and

directory services: LDAP, NIS, CORBA (COS) Naming, and files. These service providers as well as service providers produced by other vendors are available for download.

J2EE application clients, enterprise beans, and Web components are required to have access to a JNDI naming environment. The Java Naming and Directory Interface (JNDI) Naming Context defines the interfaces that specify and access the application component's naming environment.

Deployment descriptors are the main vehicle for conveying access information to the application assembler and deployer about application components' requirements for customization of business logic and access to external information. The deployment descriptor entries described here are present in identical form in the deployment descriptor DTDs for each of these application component types.

Responsibilities of the Application Component Provider

J2EE applications depend on the J2EE container (Servlet, EJB, and so on) to configure the application component environment (things such as database connections) and they use JNDI to look it up. This model allows the application deployer to configure the database properties from a central place, and gives the J2EE container the ability to manage distributed transactions across multiple data sources.

Access to the Application Component's Environment

An application component instance locates the environment-naming context using JNDI. An instance creates a `javax.naming.InitialContext` object by using the constructor with no arguments, and looks up the naming environment via the `InitialContext` under the name `java:comp/env`. The application component's environment entries are stored directly in the environment-naming context, or in its direct or indirect subcontexts.

Environment entries have the Java programming language type declared by the application component provider in the deployment descriptor.

The following code example illustrates how an application component accesses its environment entries:

```
public void setTaxInfo(int numberOfExemptions,...)
throws InvalidNumberOfExemptionsException {
...
// Obtain the application component's
// environment naming context.
Context initCtx = new InitialContext();
Context myEnv = (Context)initCtx.lookup("java:comp/env");
```

```
// Obtain the maximum number of tax exemptions
// configured by the deployer.
Integer max = (Integer)myEnv.lookup("maxExemptions");

// Obtain the minimum number of tax exemptions
// configured by the deployer.
Integer min = (Integer)myEnv.lookup("minExemptions");

// Use the environment entries to
// customize business logic.
if (numberOfExemptions > max.intValue() ||
        numberOfExemptions < min.intValue())
throw new InvalidNumberOfExemptionsException();

// Get some more environment entries. These environment
// entries are stored in subcontexts.
String val1 = (String)myEnv.lookup("foo/name1");
Boolean val2 = (Boolean)myEnv.lookup("foo/bar/name2");

// The application component can also
// lookup using full pathnames.
Integer val3 = (Integer)initCtx.lookup("java:comp/env/name3");
Integer val4 =
(Integer)initCtx.lookup("java:comp/env/foo/name4");
...
}
```


Java Naming and Directory Interface (JNDI)

The application component's naming environment is a mechanism that allows customization of the application component's business logic during deployment or assembly. Use of the environment allows the application component to be customized without the need to access or change its source code.

The container implements the application component's environment, and provides it to the application component instance as a JNDI naming context. The environment is used as follows:

1. The application component's business methods access the environment using the JNDI interfaces. The application component provider declares in the deployment descriptor all the environment entries that the application component expects to be provided in its environment at runtime.
2. The container provides an implementation of the JNDI naming context that stores the application component environment. The container also provides the tools that allow the deployer to create and manage the environment of each application component.

3. The deployer uses the tools provided by the container to initialize the environment entries that are declared in the application component's deployment descriptor. The deployer can set and modify the values of the environment entries.
4. The container makes the environment-naming context available to the application component instances at runtime. The application component's instances use JNDI to obtain the values of the environment entries.

Each application component defines its own set of environment entries. All instances of an application component within the same container share the same environment entries. Application component instances are not allowed to modify the environment at runtime.

The application component's *environment* should not be confused with the *environment properties*. The JNDI environment properties are used to initialize and configure the JNDI naming context itself. The application component's environment is accessed through a JNDI naming context for direct use by the application component.

Declaration of Environment Entries

The application component provider must declare all the environment entries accessed from the application component's code. The environment entries are declared using the `env-entry` elements in the deployment descriptor. Each `env-entry` element describes a single environment entry. The `env-entry` element consists of an optional description of the environment entry, the environment entry name relative to the `java:comp/env` context, the expected Java programming language type of the environment entry value (the type of the object returned from the JNDI `lookup` method), and an optional environment entry value.

The environment entry values may be one of the following Java types: `String`, `Character`, `Byte`, `Short`, `Integer`, `Long`, `Boolean`, `Double`, and `Float`. If the application component provider provides a default value for an environment entry, the value can be changed later by the application assembler or deployer.

The value must be a string that is valid for the constructor of the specified type that takes a single `String` parameter, or in the case of `Character`, a single character.

The following example is the declaration of environment entries used by the application component whose code was illustrated in the previous subsection:

```
...
<env-entry>
 <description>
 The maximum number of tax exemptions
 allowed to be set.
 </description>
 <env-entry-name>maxExemptions</env-entry-name>
```

```
 <env-entry-type>java.lang.Integer</env-entry-type>
 <env-entry-value>15</env-entry-value>
</env-entry>
<env-entry>
 <description>
 The minimum number of tax exemptions
 allowed to be set.
 </description>
 <env-entry-name>minExemptions</env-entry-name>
 <env-entry-type>java.lang.Integer</env-entry-type>
 <env-entry-value>1</env-entry-value>
</env-entry>
<env-entry>
 <env-entry-name>foo/name1</env-entry-name>
 <env-entry-type>java.lang.String</env-entry-type>
 <env-entry-value>value1</env-entry-value>
</env-entry>
<env-entry>
 <env-entry-name>foo/bar/name2</env-entry-name>
 <env-entry-type>java.lang.Boolean</env-entry-type>
 <env-entry-value>true</env-entry-value>
</env-entry>
<env-entry>
 <description>Some description.</description>
 <env-entry-name>name3</env-entry-name>
 <env-entry-type>java.lang.Integer</env-entry-type>
</env-entry>
<env-entry>
 <env-entry-name>foo/name4</env-entry-name>
 <env-entry-type>java.lang.Integer</env-entry-type>
 <env-entry-value>10</env-entry-value>
</env-entry>
...
```

Responsibilities of the Application Assembler

The application assembler is allowed to modify the values of the environment entries set by the bean provider, and is allowed to set the values of those environment entries for which the bean provider has not specified any initial values.

Responsibilities of the Deployer

The deployer must ensure that all the environment entries declared by an application component are set to meaningful values.

The deployer can modify the values of the environment entries that have been previously set by the application component provider and/or application assembler, and must set the values of those environment entries for which no value has been specified.

Responsibilities of the J2EE Product Provider

The J2EE product provider has the following responsibilities:

- Provide a deployment tool that allows the deployer to set and modify the values of the application component's environment entries.
- Implement the `java:comp/env` environment naming context, and provide it to the application component instances at runtime. The naming context must include all of the environment entries declared by the application component provider, with their values supplied in the deployment descriptor or set by the deployer. The environment-naming context must allow the deployer to create subcontexts if they are needed by an application component.
- The container must ensure that the application component instances have only read access to their environment variables. The container must throw the `javax.naming.OperationNotSupportedException` from all the methods of the `javax.naming.Context` interface that modify the environment naming context and its subcontexts.

Enterprise JavaBeans (EJB) References

This section describes the programming and deployment descriptor interfaces that allow the application component provider to refer to the homes of enterprise beans using logical names called EJB references. The EJB references are special entries in the application component's naming environment. The deployer binds the EJB references to the enterprise bean's home in the target operational environment.

The deployment descriptor also allows the application assembler to link an EJB reference declared in one application component to an enterprise bean contained in an ejb-jar file in the same J2EE application. The link is an instruction to the tools used by the deployer describing the binding of the EJB reference to the home of the specified target enterprise bean.

Responsibilities of the Application Component Provider

This subsection describes the application component provider's view and responsibilities with respect to EJB references. It does so in two sections, the first describing the API for accessing EJB references, and the second describing the syntax for declaring the EJB references.

Programming Interfaces for EJB References

The application component provider must use EJB references to locate the `home` interfaces of enterprise beans as follows:

- Assign an entry in the application component's environment to the reference.
- This specification recommends, but does not require, that all references to enterprise beans be organized in the EJB subcontext of the application component's environment (that is, in the `java:comp/env/ejb` JNDI context).
- Look up the `home` interface of the referenced enterprise bean in the application component's environment using JNDI.

The following example illustrates how an application component uses an EJB reference to locate the `home` interface of an enterprise bean:

```
public void changePhoneNumber(...) {
...
// Obtain the default initial JNDI context.
Context initCtx = new InitialContext();
// Look up the home interface of the EmployeeRecord
// enterprise bean in the environment.
Object result = initCtx.lookup("java:comp/env/ejb/EmplRecord");
// Convert the result to the proper type.
EmployeeRecordHome emplRecordHome = (EmployeeRecordHome)
javax.rmi.PortableRemoteObject.narrow(result,
EmployeeRecordHome.class);
...
}
```

In the example, the application component provider assigned the environment entry `ejb/EmplRecord` as the EJB reference name to refer to the home of an enterprise bean.

Declaration of EJB References

Although the EJB reference is an entry in the application component's environment, the application component provider must not use an `env-entry` element to declare it. Instead, the application component provider must declare all the EJB references using the `ejb-ref` elements of the deployment descriptor. This allows the consumer of the application component's jar file (the application assembler or deployer) to discover all the EJB references used by the application component.

Each `ejb-ref` element describes the interface requirements that the referencing application component has for the referenced enterprise bean. The `ejb-ref` element contains an optional description element and the mandatory `ejb-ref-name`, `ejb-ref-type`, `home`, and `remote` elements.

The `ejb-ref-name` element specifies the EJB reference name; its value is the environment entry name used in the application component code. The `ejb-ref-type` element specifies the expected type of the enterprise bean; its value must be either `Entity` or `Session`. The `home` and `remote` elements specify the expected Java types of the referenced enterprise bean's `home` and `remote` interfaces.

The following example illustrates the declaration of EJB references in the deployment descriptor:

```
...
<ejb-ref>
 <description>
 This is a reference to the entity bean that encapsulates access to employee
records.
 </description>
 <ejb-ref-name>ejb/EmplRecord</ejb-ref-name>
 <ejb-ref-type>Entity</ejb-ref-type>
 <home>com.wombat.empl.EmployeeRecordHome</home>
 <remote>com.wombat.empl.EmployeeRecord</remote>
</ejb-ref>
<ejb-ref>
 <ejb-ref-name>ejb/Payroll</ejb-ref-name>
 <ejb-ref-type>Entity</ejb-ref-type>
 <home>com.aardvark.payroll.PayrollHome</home>
 <remote>com.aardvark.payroll.Payroll</remote>
</ejb-ref>
<ejb-ref>
 <ejb-ref-name>ejb/PensionPlan</ejb-ref-name>
 <ejb-ref-type>Session</ejb-ref-type>
 <home>com.wombat.empl.PensionPlanHome</home>
 <remote>com.wombat.empl.PensionPlan</remote>
</ejb-ref>
...
```

Responsibilities of the Application Assembler

The application assembler can use the `ejb-link` element in the deployment descriptor to link an EJB reference to a target enterprise bean. The link will be observed by the deployment tools.

The application assembler specifies the link to an enterprise bean as follows:

- The application assembler uses the optional `ejb-link` element of the `ejb-ref` element of the referencing application component. The value of the `ejb-link` element is the name of the target enterprise bean. (It is the name defined in the `ejb-name` element of the target enterprise bean.) The target enterprise bean can be in any ejb-jar file in the same J2EE application as the referencing application component.

- Alternatively, to avoid the need to rename enterprise beans in order to have unique names within an entire J2EE application, the application assembler may use the following syntax in the `ejb-link` element of the referencing application component. The application assembler specifies the pathname of the ejb-jar file containing the referenced enterprise bean and appends the `ejb-name` of the target bean separated from the pathname by a pound sign (#). The pathname is relative to the referencing application component jar file.
- The application assembler must ensure that the target enterprise bean is type-compatible with the declared EJB reference. This means that the target enterprise bean must be of the type indicated in the `ejb-ref-type` element, and that the `home` and `remote` interfaces of the target enterprise bean must be Java type–compatible with the interfaces declared in the EJB reference.

The following example illustrates the use of the `ejb-link` element in the deployment descriptor. The enterprise bean reference should be satisfied by the bean named `EmployeeRecord`. The `EmployeeRecord` enterprise bean may be packaged in the same module as the component making this reference, or it may be packaged in another module within the same J2EE application as the component making this reference:

```
...
<ejb-ref>
 <description>
 This is a reference to the entity bean
 that encapsulates access to employee records.
 It has been linked to the entity bean named
 EmployeeRecord in this application.
 </description>
 <ejb-ref-name>ejb/EmplRecord</ejb-ref-name>
 <ejb-ref-type>Entity</ejb-ref-type>
 <home>com.wombat.empl.EmployeeRecordHome</home>
 <remote>com.wombat.empl.EmployeeRecord</remote>
 <ejb-link>EmployeeRecord</ejb-link>
</ejb-ref>
...
```

The following example illustrates using the `ejb-link` element to indicate an enterprise bean reference to the `ProductEJB` enterprise bean that is in the same J2EE application unit but in a different ejb-jar file:

```
...
<ejb-ref>
 <description>
 This is a reference to the entity bean that encapsulates access to a product.
It has been linked to the entity bean named ProductEJB in the product.jar file
in this application.
 </description>
```

```
 <ejb-ref-name>ejb/Product</ejb-ref-name>
 <ejb-ref-type>Entity</ejb-ref-type>
 <home>com.acme.products.ProductHome</home>
 <remote>com.acme.products.Product</remote>
 <ejb-link>../products/product.jar#ProductEJB</ejb-link>
</ejb-ref>
...
```

Responsibilities of the Deployer

The deployer is responsible for the following:

- The deployer must ensure that all of the declared EJB references are bound to the homes of enterprise beans that exist in the operational environment. The deployer may use, for example, the JNDI `LinkRef` mechanism to create a symbolic link to the actual JNDI name of the target enterprise bean's home.
- The deployer must ensure that the target enterprise bean is type-compatible with the types declared for the EJB reference. This means that the target enterprise bean must be of the type indicated in the `ejb-ref-type` element, and that the `home` and `remote` interfaces of the target enterprise bean must be Java type-compatible with the `home` and `remote` interfaces declared in the EJB reference.
- If an EJB reference declaration includes the `ejb-link` element, the deployer must bind the enterprise bean reference to the home of the enterprise bean specified as the link's target.

Responsibilities of the J2EE Product Provider

The J2EE product provider must provide the deployment tools that allow the deployer to perform the tasks described in the previous subsection. The deployment tools provided by the J2EE product provider must be able to process the information supplied in the `ejb-ref` elements in the deployment descriptor.

At the minimum, the tools must be able to

- Preserve the application assembly information in the `ejb-link` elements by binding an EJB reference to the `home` interface of the specified target enterprise bean.
- Inform the deployer of any unresolved EJB references, and allow him or her to resolve an EJB reference by binding it to a specified compatible target enterprise bean.

Resource Manager Connection Factory

A resource manager connection factory is an object that is used to create connections to a resource manager. For example, an object that implements the `javax.sql.DataSource` interface is a resource manager connection factory for `java.sql.Connection` objects that implement connections to a database management system.

This section describes the application component programming and deployment descriptor interfaces that allow the application component code to refer to resource factories using logical names called resource manager connection factory references. The resource manager connection factory references are special entries in the application component's environment. The deployer binds the resource manager connection factory references to the actual resource manager connection factories that exist in the target operational environment. Because these resource manager connection factories enable the container to affect resource management, the connections acquired through the resource manager connection factory references are called managed resources (for example, these resource manager connection factories allow the container to implement connection pooling and automatic enlistment of the connection with a transaction).

Resource manager connection factory objects accessed through the naming environment are only valid within the component instance that performed the lookup. See the individual component specifications for additional restrictions that may apply.

Responsibilities of the Application Component Provider

This subsection describes the application component provider's view of locating resource factories and defines his or her responsibilities.

Programming Interfaces for Resource Manager Connection Factory References

The application component provider must use resource manager connection factory references to obtain connections to resources as follows:

- Assign an entry in the application component's naming environment to the resource manager connection factory reference.
- This specification recommends, but does not require, that all resource manager connection factory references be organized in the subcontexts of the application component's environment, using a different subcontext for each resource manager type. For example, all JDBC DataSource references should be declared in the `java:comp/env/jdbc` subcontext, all JMS connection factories in the `java:comp/env/jms` subcontext, all JavaMail connection factories in the `java:comp/env/mail` subcontext, and all URL connection factories in the `java:comp/env/url` subcontext.

- Look up the resource manager connection factory object in the application component's environment using the JNDI interface.
- Invoke the appropriate method on the resource manager connection factory object to obtain a connection to the resource. The factory method is particular to the resource type. You can obtain multiple connections by calling the factory object multiple times.

The application component provider has two choices with respect to associating a principal with the resource manager access:

1. Allow the deployer to set up principal mapping or resource manager sign-on information. In this case, the application component code invokes a resource manager connection factory method that has no security-related parameters.
2. Sign on to the resource from the application component code. In this case, the application component invokes the appropriate resource manager connection factory method that takes the sign-on information as method parameters.

The application component provider uses the `res-auth` deployment descriptor element to indicate which of the two resource authentication approaches is used.

We expect that the first form (that is, letting the deployer set up the resource sign-on information) will be the approach used by most application components.

The following code sample illustrates the process of obtaining a JDBC connection:

```
public void changePhoneNumber(...) {
...
// obtain the initial JNDI context
Context initCtx = new InitialContext();
// perform JNDI lookup to obtain resource manager
// connection factory
javax.sql.DataSource ds = (javax.sql.DataSource)
initCtx.lookup("java:comp/env/jdbc/EmployeeAppDB");
// Invoke factory to obtain a resource. The security
// principal for the resource is not given, and
// therefore it will be configured by the deployer.
java.sql.Connection con = ds.getConnection();
...
}
```

Declaration of the Resource Manager Connection Factory

Although a resource manager connection factory reference is an entry in the application component's environment, the application component provider must not use an `env-entry` element to declare it.

Instead, the application component provider must declare all the resource manager connection factory references in the deployment descriptor using the `resource-ref` elements. This enables the consumer of the application component's jar file (the application assembler or deployer) to discover all the resource manager connection factory references used by an application component.

Each `resource-ref` element describes one resource manager connection factory reference. The `resource-ref` element consists of the description element as well as the mandatory `res-ref-name`, `res-type`, and `res-auth` elements.

The `res-ref-name` element contains the name of the environment entry used in the application component's code. The name of the environment entry is relative to the `java:comp/env` context (for example, the name should be `jdbc/EmployeeAppDB` rather than `java:comp/env/jdbc/EmployeeAppDB`). The `res-type` element contains the Java type of the resource manager connection factory that the application component code expects. The `res-auth` element indicates whether the application component code performs resource sign-on programmatically, or whether the container signs on to the resource based on the principal mapping information supplied by the deployer. The application component provider indicates the sign-on responsibility by setting the value of the `res-auth` element to `Application` or `Container`.

A resource manager connection factory reference is scoped to the application component whose declaration contains the `resource-ref` element. This means that the resource manager connection factory reference is not accessible from other application components at runtime, and that other application components may define `resource-ref` elements with the same `res-ref-name` without causing a name conflict.

The type declaration allows the deployer to identify the type of the resource manager connection factory.

Note that the indicated type is the Java programming language type of the resource manager connection factory, not the type of the connection.

The following example is the declaration of resource references used by the application component illustrated in the previous subsection:

```
...
<resource-ref>
 <description>
 A data source for the database in which the EmployeeService
 enterprise bean will record a log of all transactions.
 </description>
 <res-ref-name>jdbc/EmployeeAppDB</res-ref-name>
```

```
  <res-type>javax.sql.DataSource</res-type>
  <res-auth>Container</res-auth>
</resource-ref>
```

Resource Manager Connection Factory Types

The application component provider must use the `javax.sql.DataSource` resource manager connection factory type for obtaining JDBC API connections.

The application component provider must use `javax.jms.QueueConnectionFactory` or `javax.jms.TopicConnectionFactory` for obtaining JMS connections.

The application component provider must use the `javax.mail.Session` resource manager connection factory type for obtaining JavaMail connections.

The application component provider must use the `java.net.URL` resource manager connection factory type for obtaining URL connections.

It is recommended that the application component provider name JDBC API data sources in the `java:comp/env/jdbc` subcontext, all JMS connection factories in the `java:comp/env/jms` subcontext, all JavaMail API connection factories in the `java:comp/env/mail` subcontext, and all URL connection factories in the `java:comp/env/url` subcontext.

The J2EE Connector Extension enables an application component to use the API described in this section to obtain resource objects that provide access to additional back-end systems.

Responsibilities of the Deployer

The deployer uses deployment tools to bind the resource manager connection factory references to the actual resource factories configured in the target operational environment.

The deployer must perform the following tasks for each resource manager connection factory reference declared in the deployment descriptor:

- He or she must bind the resource manager connection factory reference to a resource manager connection factory that exists in the operational environment. The deployer may use, for example, the JNDI `LinkRef` mechanism to create a symbolic link to the actual JNDI name of the resource manager connection factory. The resource manager connection factory type must be compatible with the type declared in the `res-type` element.
- The deployer must provide any additional configuration information that the resource manager needs for opening and managing the resource. The configuration mechanism is resource manager–specific, and is beyond the scope of this specification.

- If the value of the `res-auth` element is `Container`, the deployer is responsible for configuring the sign-on information for the resource manager. This configuration is done in a manner specific to the container and resource manager.

For example, if principals must be mapped from the security domain and principal realm used at the application component level to the security domain and principal realm of the resource manager, the deployer or system administrator must define the mapping. The mapping is performed in a manner specific to the container and resource manager; it is beyond the scope of this specification.

Responsibilities of the J2EE Product Provider

The J2EE product provider is responsible for the following:

- He or she must provide the deployment tools that allow the deployer to perform the tasks described in the previous subsection.
- He or she must provide the implementation of the resource manager connection factory classes that are required by this specification.
- If the application component provider set the `res-auth` of a resource reference to `Application`, the container must allow the application component to perform explicit programmatic sign-on using the resource manager's API.
- The container must provide tools that allow the deployer to set up resource sign-on information for the resource manager references whose `res-auth` element is set to `Container`. The minimum requirement is that the deployer must be able to specify the user/password information for each resource manager connection factory reference declared by the application component, and the container must be able to use the user/password combination for user authentication when obtaining a connection by invoking the resource manager connection factory.

  Although not required by this specification, we expect that containers will support some form of a single sign-on mechanism that spans the application server and the resource managers. The container will allow the deployer to set up the resources such that the principal can be propagated (directly or through principal mapping) to a resource manager, if required by the application.

While not required by this specification, most J2EE products will provide the following features:

- A tool to allow the system administrator to add, remove, and configure a resource manager for the J2EE server.
- A mechanism to pool resources for the application components and otherwise manage the use of resources by the container. The pooling must be transparent to the application components.

Responsibilities of the System Administrator

The system administrator is typically responsible for adding, removing, and configuring resource managers in the J2EE server environment.

In some scenarios, these tasks can be performed by the deployer.

Resource Environment References

This section describes the programming and deployment descriptor interfaces that enable the application component provider to refer to administered objects that are associated with a resource (for example, JMS Destinations) by using logical names called resource environment references. The resource environment references are special entries in the application component's environment. The deployer binds the resource environment references to administered objects in the target operational environment.

Responsibilities of the Application Component Provider

This subsection describes the application component provider's view and responsibilities with respect to resource environment references.

Resource Environment Reference Programming Interfaces

The application component provider is required to use resource environment references to locate administered objects such as JMS Destinations (which are associated with resources) as follows:

- Assign an entry in the application component's environment to the reference.
- This specification recommends, but does not require, that all resource environment references be organized in the appropriate subcontext of the component's environment for the resource type (for example, in the `java:comp/env/jms` JNDI context for JMS Destinations).
- Look up the administered object in the application component's environment using JNDI.

The following example illustrates how an application component uses a resource environment reference to locate a JMS Destination:

```
// Obtain the default initial JNDI context.
Context initCtx = new InitialContext();
// Look up the JMS StockQueue in the environment.
Object result = initCtx.lookup("java:comp/env/jms/StockQueue");
// Convert the result to the proper type.
javax.jms.Queue queue = (javax.jms.Queue)result;
```

In the example, the application component provider assigned the environment entry `jms/StockQueue` as the resource environment reference name to refer to a JMS queue.

Declaration of Resource Environment References in the Deployment Descriptor

Although the resource environment reference is an entry in the application component's environment, the application component provider must not use an `env-entry` element to declare it. Instead, the application component provider must declare all references to administered objects associated with resources using the `resource-env-ref` elements of the deployment descriptor. This allows the application component's jar file consumer to discover all the resource environment references used by the application component.

Each `resource-env-ref` element describes the requirements that the referencing application component has for the referenced administered object.

The `resource-env-ref` element contains an optional description element and the mandatory `resource-env-ref-name` and `resource-env-ref-type` elements.

The `resource-env-ref-name` element specifies the resource environment reference name; its value is the environment entry name used in the application component code. The name of the environment entry is relative to the `java:comp/env` context (for example, the name should be `jms/StockQueue` rather than `java:comp/env/jms/StockQueue`). The `resource-env-ref-type` element specifies the expected type of the referenced object. For example, in the case of a JMS Destination, its value must be either `javax.jms.Queue` or `javax.jms.Topic`.

A resource environment reference is scoped to the application component whose declaration contains the `resource-env-ref` element. This means that the resource environment reference is not accessible to other application components at runtime, and that other application components may define `resource-env-ref` elements with the same `resource-env-ref-name` without causing a name conflict.

The following example illustrates the declaration of resource environment references in the deployment descriptor:

```
...
<resource-env-ref>
 <description>
 This is a reference to a JMS queue used in the
 processing of Stock info
 </description>
 <resource-env-ref-name>jms/StockInfo</resource-env-ref-name>
 <resource-env-ref-type>javax.jms.Queue</resource-env-ref-type>
</resource-env-ref>
...
```

Responsibilities of the Deployer

The deployer is responsible for the following:

- The deployer must ensure that all the declared resource environment references are bound to administered objects that exist in the operational environment. The deployer may use, for example, the JNDI `LinkRef` mechanism to create a symbolic link to the actual JNDI name of the target object.
- The deployer must ensure that the target object is type-compatible with the type declared for the resource environment reference. This means that the target object must be of the type indicated in the `resource-env-ref-type` element.

Responsibilities of the J2EE Product Provider

The J2EE product provider must provide the deployment tools that allow the deployer to perform the tasks described in the previous subsection. The deployment tools provided by the J2EE product provider must be able to process the information supplied in the `resource-env-ref` elements in the deployment descriptor.

At the minimum, the tools must be capable of informing the deployer of any unresolved resource environment references, and enabling him or her to resolve a resource environment reference by binding it to a specified compatible target object in the environment.

`UserTransaction` References

Certain J2EE application component types are allowed to use the JTA `UserTransaction` interface to start, commit, and abort transactions. Such application components can find an appropriate object implementing the `UserTransaction` interface by looking up the JNDI name `java:comp/UserTransaction`. The container is only required to provide the `java:comp/UserTransaction` name for those components that can validly make use of it. Any such reference to a `UserTransaction` object is only valid within the component instance that performed the lookup. See the individual component definitions for further information.

The following example illustrates how an application component acquires and uses a `UserTransaction` object:

```
public void updateData(...) {
...
// Context initCtx = new InitialContext();
// Look up the UserTransaction object.
UserTransaction tx = (UserTransaction)initCtx.lookup(
"java:comp/UserTransaction");
// Start a transaction.
tx.begin();
```

```
...
// Perform transactional operations on data.
...
// Commit the transaction.
tx.commit();
...
}
```

Responsibilities of the Application Component Provider

The application component provider is responsible for using the defined name to look up the `UserTransaction` object.

Only some component types within the application need to have access to a `UserTransaction` object.

Responsibilities of the Deployer

The deployer has no specific responsibilities associated with the `UserTransaction` object.

Responsibilities of the J2EE Product Provider

The J2EE product provider is responsible for providing an appropriate `UserTransaction` object as required by this specification.

Responsibilities of the System Administrator

The system administrator has no specific responsibilities associated with the `UserTransaction` object.

INDEX

Numbers & Symbols

% (percent) character, 538
%> markers, 233
& (ampersand), 205, 532-533
*** (asterisk) notation, 537**
; (semicolon), 533
? (question mark) notation, 537
-? option, 656-657, 659-660
+ (plus) notation, 536-537
< (less than) character, 532-533
<% markers, 233
... (ellipsis), 562
100-500 status codes, Hypertext Transfer Protocol (HTTP), 187
3NF (third normal form), 105

A

abstract persistence schema, 420
accessing
- cookies, 208
- data, 21
- databases, 144-148
  - *Java Database Connectivity (JDBC), 172-178*
  - *Java Naming and Directory Interface (JNDI), 169-170*
- directory listings, local file systems, 133-134
- directory services, 131
- Java Database Connectivity (JDBC), from session beans, 174-175
- request parameters, HttpServletRequest object, 197
- table of contents, Web Application Archive (WAR), 214

accessor method, 267
account setup, schema, 545-548
accounts, creating to place orders with SilverBooks, 693
ACID (Atomic, Consistent, Isolated, and Durable), 349
acknowledge() method, 495
ACTION elements, Hypertext Markup Language (HTML), 193
action objects, 251
action servlets, SilverBooks sample application, 700-701
ActionForm beans, 303, 310
ActionMapping class, 254
ActionMapping interface, 315
actions, JavaServer Pages (JSP), 267-275, 277-280
ActionServlet class, 254
addBatch() method, 164
addCookie() method, 204, 207
addFrom() message, 461
adding
- connections
  - *DataSource objects, 126, 135, 169*
  - *naming services, 133*
- controls to pages and subpages, 116-117
- cookies, 207
- Destination Queues and Topics, Java Message Service (JMS), 518-520, 522
- environment entries, 177-178
- InitialDirContext class, 131
- messages, 500-501
- non-triggered business objects, 219-220
- rows, databases, 163
- sessions, 208
- updateable resultsets, 161-162
- Web Archive (WAR) files, 214

addRecipients() method, 461
addresses
- Internet Protocol (IP), 200
- schema, 544

AddressStringTerm class, 456
AddressTerm class, 456
administered objects, Java Message Service (JMS), 491, 498-499
Administration Console, 665, 667-668
afterBegin method, 349
afterCompletion method, 349
AgiDatabase interface, 173

AgiHttpServletRequest object, 223
AgiHttpServletResponse object, 223
Agilent Firehunter, 600
AgoBusinessObjectEvent class, 223
ALIGN attribute, 530
Allaire Corporation, 14
Allaire-Macromedia JRun 3.0, 727
Allora for Java, 739
alpha phase, testing applications, 583
Altova, 748
Aman Software, 596, 602
amorphous beans, 336
ampersand (&), 205, 532-533
AndTerm class, 456
ANY description, 537
Apache Software Foundation, 185, 747
Apache Software Foundation license, Struts framework, 252
ApacheBench, 590
API. *See* application programming interfaces
API drift, 293
APPID (application identification code), 208-209
applet containers, 50
APPLET property, 130
applets, 46, 620, 623
application argument, 667
application assembler, 355
application assembly phase, 56-60
application client containers, 50
application clients, 45
application deployment, 60-61
application entities, 102-103
application frameworks, 52
application identification code (APPID), 208-209
Application implicit object, 281
application life cycle events, 223
application programming interfaces (APIs)
- certification and, Java 2 Enterprise Edition (J2EE), 30-31
- described, 139
- Document Object Model (DOM), 550
- Internet Server (ISAPI), 183-184
- Java Database Connectivity (JDBC)
  - *accessing databases, 172-178*
  - *architecture, 139-141, 143*
  - *batch statements, 164-165*
  - *benefits of, 139*
  - *data types, 166-168*
  - *described, 125-126, 139*
  - *exceptions, 157-158*
  - *javax.sql package, 168-169, 171*
  - *metadata, 158-159*
  - *packages, 143-148*
  - *retrieving and updating data, 148-156*
  - *scrollable resultsets, 159-160, 162*
  - *SilverStream Application Server case study, 171, 173-178*
  - *transaction support, 163-164*
  - *updating columns and rows, resultsets, 162-163*
- Java Message Service (JMS)
  - *components required by applications using, 498-499*
  - *creating and destroying Destination Queues and Topics, 518-520, 522*
  - *described, 126-127, 488-490*
  - *implementation and deployment issues, 522-523*
  - *interfaces, message-oriented middleware (MOM), 490-494, 496-497*
  - *Point-to-Point model, 491-492, 502-504*
  - *Point-to-Point Queue model, 507-518*
  - *producing and consuming messages, 500-501*
  - *Publish/Subscribe model, 492-494, 504-507*
- Java Naming and Directory (JNDI)
  - *accessing databases, 169-170*
  - *architecture, 128*

- *benefits of, 125*
- *described, 124*
- *Enterprise JavaBeans (EJB), 125*
- *Java Database Connectivity (JDBC), 125-126*
- *Java Message Service (JMS), 126-127*
- *Lightweight Directory Access Protocol (LDAP), 132-135*
- *obtaining handles to DataSource objects, 211-213*
- *operations, 131-132*
- *service providers, 127*
- Java Servlet 2.2, 208-209
- Java Transaction (JTA), 347, 349-351
- JavaMail, 447
  - *architecture, 450-451*
  - *JAF (Java Activation Framework), 451-456, 459-466*
  - *JavaServer Pages, 474-479, 481-483*
  - *primary classes, 450-451*
  - *Provider Registry, 448-450*
- JDBC 2.1 Core, 143-148
- Netscape Web (NSAPI), 183-184
- required for Java 2 Enterprise Edition (J2EE), 756-757
- servlets, 184, 188-189, 223-224

application scope, 302

application server provider, 356

application servers, 14, 725-734, 736, 654-660

application user interface styles, choosing, 112

Application/msword MIME type, 217

Application/octet-stream MIME type, 217

Application/pdf MIME type, 217

Application/vnd.ms-excel MIME type, 217

Applications
- assembling, 633-634, 636-638, 640-641, 643-646, 648
- component-based, 26-27
- components required, Java Message Service (JMS), 498-499
- contents of, 53-54
- deploying, 622, 648-650, 652, 654-665, 667-680, 682, 684-689
- designing and developing
  - *building pages, 114-117*
  - *computer aided software engineering (CASE) tools, 67, 69-70*
  - *creating back-end interfaces, 110-112*
  - *creating data access objects, 117-118*
  - *creating interfaces, 112, 114*
  - *creating models, 65, 67*
  - *creating tables and columns, 104-108*
  - *database support, 76-77*
  - *databases, 102-104*
  - *defining, 108-110*
  - *EJB UML mapping, 92, 94*
  - *entity modeling, 72-73*
  - *entity relationships, 67-68*
  - *modeling tools, 64*
  - *modeling Web applications, 77-79*
  - *modeling Web pages, 87, 89-90, 92*
  - *preparations for, 98-99, 101*
  - *refining code, 119-121*
  - *relationship modeling, 73, 76*
  - *reverse engineering, 70-71*
  - *system modeling, 79-80*
  - *tool support, 94-95*
  - *Unified Modeling Language (UML), 82-87*
  - *validating code, 118-119*
  - *Web application architecture, 81-82*
- developing
  - *challenges in, 17-20*
  - *distributed programming, Enterprise JavaBeans (EJB), 330*
  - *effects of eXtensible Markup Language (XML) on, 36-37*
  - *with Java, 12-14*
  - *roles of developers in, Enterprise JavaBeans (EJB), 353-356*
- Internet, life cycles of, 22-26, 28, 30
- Java 2 Enterprise Edition (J2EE), 38-40

Java Message Service (JMS) in, 491-494
multitier, 9
partitioning, 140
performance, 606-607
database monitoring and tuning tools, 627-628
diagnoses and cures for, 621-624
factors affecting, 624-627
preparing for performance tuning, 618-621
writing high-performance applications, 607-612, 614-618
profiling, 620-621
rapid application development (RAD), 234
samples, 61
Java Pet Store, 702-704, 706-707
SilverBooks, 692-693, 696, 698, 700-702
server, JavaServer Pages (JSPs), 229
testing, 570, 572
correcting errors, 579-582
debugging, 572-579
methods and techniques, 584-586
phases of, 582, 584
repairs to, 581
tools for, 586-587, 589, 591-593, 595-597, 599-603
Web
architecture, 81-82
modeling, 77-79
servlets, 213-217
Write Once, Run Anywhere (WORA), 632

archetypes, schema, 542, 544-545
architecture
component-based, 27-28
containers and services, 49-50
Java 2 Enterprise Edition (J2EE), 25-26
Java Database Connectivity (JDBC), 139-141, 143
Java Naming and Directory Interface (JNDI), 128-131
JavaMail, 447, 450-451
JavaServer Pages (JSP), 240-248, 250, 252-254
Model-View-Controller (MVC), 703
architecture of, 24-25
overview of, 49
requirements for Internet, 20, 22
Web applications, 81-82
archives. *See* Enterprise Archive, Java Archive, Web Archive
ArgoUML, 94
arguments
application, 667
Database, 221, 656-658, 660
Delete command, 660
deploy, 667
DeployEAR command, 656
DeployEJB command, 657
DeployWAR command, 658
EARfile, 656
ejbJar, 657
-f deploymentPlan, 221, 656-658
-f multifile, 660
item, 660
javax.jms.Message, 343
list, 667
password, 667, 704
port, 656-658, 660
RootDir, 221
Server, 221, 656-658, 660, 704
SilverCmd BuildWAR command, 221
SilverCmd DeployWAR command, 221
source, 667
undeploy, 667
update, 667
Userid, 704
WARFile, 221, 658
weblogic.deploy, 667
arithmetic operators, MessageSelector objects, 501
ARRAY data type, 166-168
Artistic Systems, 711-712
assembly, J2EE applications, 633-634, 636-638, 640-641, 643-646, 648
assignments, Internet Protocol (IP) addresses, 200
asterisk (*) notation, 537
Astra LoadTest, 595
asynchronous communication, 490
Atesto Automated Web Testing Service, 601
Atomic, Consistent, Isolated, and Durable (ACID), 349
Attr interface, 550
attribute attribute, 285
attribute declarations, document type definitions (DTDs), 537-538

AttributeImpl class, 554
AttributeList interface, 553
attributes
- attribute, 285
- bodycontent, 285
- Enterprise JavaBeans (EJB), 335-336
- errorPage, 281
- eXtensible Markup Language (XML) documents, 529-530
- include directives, 260-261
- info, 284-285
- isErrorPage, 281
- <jsp:forward> action, 276
- <jsp:getProperty> action, 272
- <jsp:include> action, 275
- <jsp:plugin> action, 277-279
- <jsp:setProperty> action, 272
- <jsp:useBean> action, 268-271
- jspversion, 284
- Mandatory, 350
- name, 275, 285
- Never, 350
- NotSupported, 350-352
- page directives, 262-264
- refining, 68, 103
- Remote interface, 351
- Required, 344, 350-351
- RequiresNew, 350
- retrieving, 131
- shortname, 284
- special, 68
- StateManagementType, 336
- Supports, 350
- tagclass, 285
- taglib declaration, 284
- tags vs., 538
- teiclass, 285
- tlibversion, 284
- uri, 284
- value, 275

Attributes class, 134-135
Attributes interface, 553
audio/midi MIME type, 217
audio/x-pn-realaudio MIME type, 217
audio/x-pn-realaudio-plugin MIME type, 217
AUTHORITATIVE property, 130
AUTO_ACKNOWLEDGE method, 344, 495
Auxiliary Elements subpackage, 85

B

back-end interfaces, creating, 110-112
backups
- databases, batching utilities, 112
- original applications, 574

BASE pages, 116
Basic Mapping Support (BMS), 245
batch statements, Java Database Connectivity (JDBC), 164-165
batching utilities, databases, 112
BATCHSIZE property, 130
BatchUpdateException, 165
BEA Systems, 14
BEA WebLogic Server, deploying applications, 660-665, 667-680, 682, 684-689
BEA WebLogic Server 6.1, 727-728
Bean class, 420
bean deployer, 355
bean life cycle management service, 331
bean transaction management service, 332
bean writer, 354-355, 417-420
bean-managed persistence (BMP), 340, 348, 415
Bean-test, 587, 589-590, 752
beans
- entity, 12, 22, 334-335, 345
- Message-Driven (MDB), 342-345, 351-352
- parts of, 336
- session, 11, 22, 333-335, 345
  - *accessing Java Database Connectivity (JDBC) from, 174-175*
  - *defining resource reference lookups, 176*
- stateful, 336
- stateless, 336
- userInfo, 270-271

beforeCompletion method, 349
benchmarks, testing, 584
beta phase, testing applications, 583-584
Binary Large Objects (BLOBs), 166-167
binary messages, 471-472, 474
bind operation, 131
black box testing, 585
BLOB. *See* Binary Large Objects, 166

Bluestone Software Inc., 14
BMC Software, 600
BMP (bean-managed persistence), 340, 348, 415
BMS (Basic Mapping Support), 245
body formats, Java Message Service (JMS), 497
bodycontent attribute, 285
BodyTags, 616
BodyTerm class, 456
boolean absolute(int row) method, 160
boolean first() method, 160
boolean last() method, 160
boolean previous() method, 160
Borland, 712-714
bound objects, retrieving, 132
breakpoints, choosing, 119
browse clients, Point-to-Point Queue model, 507-511
browsers, retrieving information about, 200-203
bugs, 572
building
- business logic layer, 44
- calls, Java Database Connectivity (JDBC), 176
- client layers, 42-43
- JavaServer Pages (JSPs), 233, 236-240
- non-triggered business objects, 219-220
- pages, 114-117
- presentation layers, 43
- servlet-triggered business objects, 222-223
- servlets, SilverStream Application Server, 218, 220-223
- SQL select statements, 176-177
- srvltTest servlets, 210

business components, 48
business logic
- component support, 28, 30
- in data layer, 45
- Model-View-Controller (MVC), 252-253, 291
- separating from presentation, Web pages, 230
- Struts, 296-297, 303-304

business logic layer, 44
business method (session beans), 367
Business Object Wizard, 219-220, 222
business objects, rendering, 253
businessMethod2() method, 372
Button control, 116
ByteMessage body format, Java Message Service (JMS), 497

C

c option, 642
CachedRowSet objects, 171
caching data, 626
CallableStatement object, 148, 151-152, 166
calling session beans from clients, 405
calls
- databases, reducing number of, 626
- Java Database Connectivity (JDBC), constructing, 176

CapeConnect XML Business Server, 736
Cascade option, 76
Cascading Style Sheets (CSS), 526, 556-557
CASE (computer aided software engineering) tools, 67, 69-70
case sensitivity, column names, 153
case studies, SilverStream Application Server, 171, 173-178
CCI (Common Client Interface), 759
CDATA (Character Data), eXtensible Markup Language (XML) documents, 533-534
CDATASection interface, 550
central processing units (CPUs), 624
Cerebellum eCom Integrator and Portal Integrator, 737
certification, application programming interfaces (APIs) and, 30-31
CGI (Common Gateway Interface), 81, 182-183
changing columns and rows, resultsets, 162-163

Character Data (CDATA), eXtensible Markup Language (XML) documents, 533-534
Character Large Objects (CLOBs), 166-167
character ranges, Processing Instructions (PIs), 535
character references, Processing Instructions (PIs), 534
characters, escape, 532-533
Chart view, WebLOAD, 593
CheckBox control, 116
checkpoints, databases, 626
choosing
- application user interface styles, 112
- breakpoints, 119
- data types, 105-106

CICS, 8
CICS DB2, 245
class libraries, Java Naming and Directory Interface (JNDI), 128
Class.forName() method, 145
classes. *See also* servlets
- ActionMapping, 254
- ActionServlet, 254
- AgoBusinessObjectEvent, 223
- Attributes, 134-135
- Bean, 420
- DetailAction, 701
- DriverManager, 144, 146-148
- EJBHome, 361, 402, 420
- EJBLocalHome, 420
- EJBObject, 361, 402, 420
- Enterprise JavaBeans (EJB), creating, 111-112
- EntityBean, 430-437
- form, SilverBooks sample application, 701
- GenericServlet, 189
- Handle, 334
- HandlerBase, 554
- home object, 382-384
- home stub, 374-378
- home tie, 378-382
- HttpJspBase, 241
- HttpServlet, 189
- InitialContext, 129, 403
- InitialDirContext, 131
- InputSource, 554
- interface, Java Message Service (JMS), 499
- JavaMail, 450-451
  - *JAF (Java Activation Framework), 451*
  - *javax.mail.Address, 459*
  - *javax.mail.Folder, 454-455*
  - *javax.mail.internet. InternetAddress, 459*
  - *javax.mail.internet. MimeMessage, 460-465*
  - *javax.mail.search, 456, 459*
  - *javax.mail.Session, 452*
  - *javax.mail.Store, 453*
  - *javax.mail.Transport, 466*
  - *javax.Message.search, 460*
- javax.servlet package, 189
- org.omg.PortableServer. Servant, 378, 394
- packaging images into one, 623
- remote object, 398-400
- remote stub, 385-393
- remote tie, 394-398
- retrieving, 132
- servlets, packaging in Web Archive (WAR) files, 221
- Simple API for XML (SAX), 554-555
- stub, 361
- tie, 361

classes directory, 642-643
classes subdirectory, 236
classpaths, J2EE, 760, 762
clauses
- <jsp:param> , 274-275
- ORDER BY, 173
- WHERE, 173

clearBatch() method, 164
ClearCase, 95
client components
- applets, 46
- application clients, 45
- JavaBeans component architecture, 46
- overview of, 45
- server communications, 47
- thin clients, 47
- Web browsers, 46

client JAR files, 402
client layer, 42-43
CLIENT_ACKNOWLEDGE method, Java Message Service (JMS), 495
clients
- component support, 28
- e-mail, as asynchronous communication, 490
- EJB clients, 437-439

Java Message Service (JMS) messaging applications, 491
MessageListener class, 512-514
publishing, Publish/Subscribe model, 504-505
receiving, Point-to-Point model, 503-504
receiving browse, Point-to-Point Queue model, 508-511
receiving MessageListener, Point-to-Point Queue model, 512
receiving MessageSelector, Point-to-Point Queue model, 516-518
retrieving browser information, 200-203
sending, Point-to-Point model, 502-503
sending browse, Point-to-Point Queue model, 507-508
sending MessageSelector, Point-to-Point Queue model, 514-518
session beans
calling, 405
EJBs, 405
enterprise beans, 408
finding, 402-405
J2EE, 408
JSP, 408
loop-back calls, 405
reentrance, 405
removing, 406
servlets, 406-407
standalone Java applications, 408
standalone non-Java applications, 408
Unix, 408
updating, 402
Windows, 408
streaming data to, 190
subscribing, Publish/Subscribe model, 506-507

CLOB. (Character Large Objects), 166-167
close() method, 150
closing ResultSet and Statement objects, 150
clusters, servers, 622
CMP. *See* container-managed persistence
code
guidelines for writing, 611-612
readmail.jsp, 484-485
refining, 119-121
send.html, 483-484
sendmail.jsp, 484
session beans, 367-372
static complexity analysis, 584
validating, 118-119
Code Examples appendix, Java 2 Enterprise Edition (J2EE) Software Development Kit (SDK) documentation, 763
code listings
application.xml
Pet Store, 647
SilverBooks, 647-648
attributes, page directives, 263
CMP EJB deployment descriptor example, WebLogic environment, 664-665
CorpBanner.jsp, 287
CorpBannerTag.java, 286-287
CorpTagLib.tld, 286
creating Queue destinations, 518-519
creating Topic destinations, 520-521
destroying Queue destinations, 519-520
destroying Topic destinations, 521-522
ejb-jar.xml, Pet Store, 670-674, 677-689
jspDateTime.jsp, 261
jspIncludeDirective.jsp, 261
MessageListener class, clients, 512-514
Point-to-Point model
receiving clients, 503-504
sending clients, 502-503
Point-to-Point Queue model
receiving browse clients, 508-511
receiving MessageListener clients, 512
receiving MessageSelector clients, 516-518
sending browse clients, 507-508
sending MessageSelector clients, 514-518
Publish/Subscribe model
publishing clients, 504-505
subscribing clients, 506-507

resource resolution files, Pet Store, 676-680, 682, 684-689
syntax
<jsp:plugin> action, 277
<jsp:useBean> action, 268
tag handlers, 284
Tag Library Descriptors (TLDs), 285-286
userInfo bean, 270-271
web.xml
Pet Store, 672-674
SilverBooks, 675
code reviews, 581, 621
codes, application identification (APPID), 208-209
Column Editor, 73
column names, case sensitivity of in ResultSet objects, 153
columns
creating, 104-108
resultsets, printing names and data types, 158
resultsets, updating, 162-163
command files, running in Java Pet Store sample application, 704
commands
Delete, 660
DeployEAR, 656
DeployEJB, 657-658
deploytool, 650-651
DeployWAR, 658-659
jar, 642-644
SilverCmd BuildWAR, 221
SilverCmd DeployWAR, 221
Comment interface, 550
comments
eXtensible Markup Language (XML) documents, 533
JavaServer Pages (JSP), 258-259
commit() method, 164, 494
Common Behavior package, 85-87
Common Client Interface (CCI), 759
Common Gateway Interface (CGI), 81, 182-183
Common Object Request Broker Architecture (CORBA), 44, 347
communication, asynchronous and synchronous, 490
comparison operators, MessageSelector objects, 501
ComparisonTerm class, 457
compatibility, SilverStream Application Server, 218
Compatibility Test Suite (CTS), 30, 32
competition
in the Internet Economy, 14-17
promoting with standards, 19
speed of on the Internet, 20
compiled pages, 82
compilers, diagnosing syntax errors with, 578-579
compiling
JavaServer Pages (JSP), 279-280
non-triggered business objects, 220
SQL select statements, 176-177
Component Manager, 716-717
-component option, 668
component-based applications, 26-27
component-based architecture, 27-28
component option, 668
components
assembling, 634, 636-638, 640-641, 643-646, 648
business type, 48
client type, 45-47
deploying, 655
described, 45
designing, 608, 610
Java Message Service (JMS) messaging applications, 491
JavaServer Pages (JSP), 231
location of, 42
packaging, hierarchies, 353
performance of, 615
required by applications using Java Message Service (JMS), 498-499
reusable, 230
support for, 28, 30
Web type, 47-48
Compoze, 714-715
Computer Associates, 738-739
Compuware Corporation, 621

Compuware WebCheck, 596
concerns, separation of, 89
CONCUR_READ_ONLY resultset, 161
CONCUR_UPDATABLE resultset, 161
concurrency, message-driven beans (MDB), 344
concurrent processing, message-driven beans (MDB), 343-344
CONCUR_READ_ONLY resultset, 161
CONCUR_UPDATABLE resultset, 161
Config implicit object, 281
Configuration Guide, Java 2 Enterprise Edition (J2EE) Software Development Kit (SDK) documentation, 763
configuring
- development database environment, 108
- Multipurpose Internet Mail Extension (MIME) types, 190, 192
- response status, HttpServletResponse object, 204-205

connecting databases, 144-148
- Java Database Connectivity (JDBC), 172-178
- Java Naming and Directory Interface (JNDI), 169-170

connection factories, finding, 126-127
Connection interface, 144
Connection Management contract, 759
Connection object, 144, 163, 174, 212-213, 498
Connection Pool Manager, 174
connection pools, 169-170, 622, 626, 757
connection.prepareStatement() method, 177
ConnectionFactory object, 498
connections
- creating
  - *DataSource objects, 126, 135, 169*
  - *naming services, 133*
- methods for servlets, 198, 200

Connector 1.0, 759
Console Chart view, WebLOAD, 593
constants, status, 204
constraints, schema, 541-542
constructing
- business logic layer, 44
- calls, Java Database Connectivity (JDBC), 176
- client layers, 42-43
- JavaServer Pages (JSP), 233, 236-240
- non-triggered business objects, 219-220
- pages, 114-117
- presentation layers, 43
- servlet-triggered business objects, 222-223
- servlets, SilverStream Application Server, 218, 220-223
- SQL select statements, 176-177
- srvltTest servlets, 210

consumers, responding to demands by, 18
consuming
- clients
  - *browse, Point-to-Point Queue model, 508-511*
  - *MessageListener, Point-to-Point Queue model, 512*
  - *MessageSelector, Point-to-Point Queue model, 516-518*
  - *Point-to-Point model, 503-504*
- e-mail messages
  - *binary, 472, 474*
  - *multipart, 470-471*
- messages, 500-501
  - *Point-to-Point model, 491-492, 502-504*
  - *Point-to-Point Queue model, 507-518*

container services, message-driven beans (MDB), 344-345
container-managed persistence (CMP), 332, 339, 348, 416
containers
- described, 27-28, 49-50
- Enterprise JavaBeans (EJB), 331-333
- message-driven beans (MDB), 343
- servlets, 188
- types of, 50

content, retrieving from servlets, 197-198
ContentHandler interface, 553
ContentStudio, 601
<context-param> tag, 216
contexts, Java Naming and Directory Interface (JNDI), 129-130
contracts, 339, 759
ControlCenter, 86-87
controllers, 113
Model-View-Controller (MVC), 248, 253-254
servlet, 184-185, 248
controls, adding to pages and subpages, 116-117
converting data types, 153-155
cookies, 200
CORBA (Common Object Request Broker Architecture), 44, 347
CORBA Object Service (COS), 127
core logic, 230
Core subpackage, 85
COS (COBRA Object Service), 127
CPU (central processing units), 624
create() method, 366, 405, 454
createServletResource() method, 223
createStatement method, 149
createTopicConnection() method, 493
createX() method, 551
creating
accounts, placing orders with SilverBooks, 693
back-end interfaces, 110-112
columns, 104-108
connections
DataSource objects, 126, 135, 169
naming services, 133
cookies, 207
custom tag libraries, 286-287
data access objects, 117-118
deployment descriptors, 634, 636-638, 640-641
Destination Queues and Topics, Java Message Service (JMS), 518-520, 522
Enterprise JavaBeans (EJB) classes, 111-112
entity beans, 334
entity relationships, 67
environment entries, 177-178
executables, 120-121
handles to naming services, 129
high-performance applications, 607-612, 614-618
InitialDirContext class, 131
instances, EJBHome, 405
interfaces, 112, 114
JavaServer Pages (JSP), 233, 236-240
keys, 106
messages, 500-501
models, J2EE applications, 65, 67
non-triggered business objects, 219-220
relationships, 74
servlet-triggered business objects, 222-223
servlets, SilverStream Application Server, 218, 220-223
session beans, home interface, 364-365
sessions, 208
srvltTest servlets, 210
stored procedures, 111-112
tables, 104-108
updateable resultsets, 161-162
Web Archive (WAR) files, 214
cross-platform testing, 585
CSS (Cascading Style Sheets), 526, 556-557
CTS (Compatibility Test Suite), 30, 32
Cursor object, 153, 618
custom installs, Java Pet Store sample application, 705
CyberSpyder, 596
CyberTeams, Inc., 602
cyberware-neotek, 602

D

-d ejbDeployedObject option, 657
data
accessing, 21
caching, 626
data types, Java Database Connectivity (JDBC), 166-168
loading, 111
metadata, Java Database Connectivity (JDBC), 158-159

posting, Hypertext Markup Language (HTML), 193-195
retrieving and updating, Java Database Connectivity (JDBC), 148-156
returning small amounts of, 625
sharing, effects on performance, 617-618
streaming to clients, 190
structure of, 533-534
unparsed, eXtensible Markup Language (XML)
volume data generation, 584

Data access control, 116

data access objects, creating, 117-118

data entry, introduction of, 8

data entry elements, Hypertext Markup Language (HTML), 193, 195

data layer, 44, 609

data sources, finding, 145-146

data types
ARRAY, 166-168
Binary Large Objects (BLOBs), 166-167
Character Large Objects (CLOBs), 166-167
choosing, 105-106
Java, converting to Structured Query Language (SQL) data types, 153-155
Java Database Connectivity (JDBC), 166-168
REF, 166, 168
resultset columns, printing, 158
schema, 543-544
STRUCT, 166, 168
Structured Query Language (SQL), converting to Java data types, 153-155

Data Types subpackage, 85

Database argument, 221, 656-658, 660

database drivers, 141, 143, 145

database modeling, 64-65, 70

DatabaseMetaData object, 159

DatabaseMetaData.supportsBatchUpdates() method, 164

databases
accessing
Java Database Connectivity (JDBC), 172-178
Java Naming and Directory Interface (JNDI), 169-170
batching utilities, 112
connecting, 144-148
designing, 102-104
development, configuring, 108
estimating sizes of, 107
mapping resources references to, 178
monitoring and tuning tools, 627-628
performance of, 625-627
retrieving structures of, 159
rows, 162-163
Struts, accessing with, 323-326
support, J2EE applications, 76-77

DataSource interface, 757

DataSource objects, 126, 169, 211-213

DataTruncation, 158

datatype() method, 153

DateTerm class, 457

DBArtisan, 738

DCOM (Distributed Component Object Model), 79

dead links, tools for testing, 596

-debug option, 668

Debugger, 118-119

debugging applications, 572-579

declarations
document type definitions (DTDs), 536-538, 540
entities, 532
environment entries, 766-767
initialization paramaters in Web applications, 216
JavaServer Pages (JSP), 238, 265-266
notation, document type definitions (DTDs), 540
references
Enterprise JavaBeans (EJB), 769-770
resource environment, 779
resource manager connection factories, 774-776
servlets in Web applications, 215
tag libraries, 282-283

DefaultHandler class, 554
defining
mappings, ServletContainer object, 216
resource reference lookups in session beans, 176
shared constant parameters, Web applications, 216
uniform resource locators (URLs), 145-146
Delete command, 660
DELETE method, 186
delete() method, 454
deleteRow() method, 163
deleting
deployed J2EE applications, 653-654
deployed J2EE components, 659-660, 669
Destination Queues and Topics, Java Message Service (JMS), 518-520, 522
rows, databases, 163
delivery of messages, 492, 496
demands of consumers, responding to, 18
dependent object, 338
deploy argument, 667
DeployDirector, 733-734
DeployEAR command, 656
DeployEJB command, 657-658
deployer, 60-61
deploying
applications, 622, 648-650, 652, 654-665, 667-680, 682, 684-689
assembling, 633-634, 636-638, 640-641, 643-646, 648
Write Once, Run Anywhere (WORA), 632
Enterprise JavaBeans (EJB), 352-353
issues with, Java Message Service (JMS), 522-523
JavaServer Pages (JSP), 218, 233, 236-240
servlets, 218
Web Archive (WAR) files to SilverStream Application Servers, 221
deployment descriptors, 38, 53, 337, 352-353, 420, 634, 636-638, 640-641
JAR files, 400-401
mapping requests to servlets, 215-216
Struts, 318-319, 321-323
deployment JAR files, 402
deployment tools
deploytool, 650-651
SilverCmd, 655
WebLogic, 665, 667-668
DeploymentDescriptor object, 336
deploytool, 650-651
DeployWAR command, 658-659
descriptors, deployment, 38, 215-216, 337, 352-353, 634, 636-638, 640-641
design phase, 606
designing
applications
building pages, 114-117
computer aided software engineering (CASE) tools, 67, 69-70
creating back-end interfaces, 110-112
creating data access objects, 117-118
creating interfaces, 112, 114
creating models, 65, 67
creating tables and columns, 104-108
database support, 76-77
databases, 102-104
defining, 108-110
effects on performance, 617-618
EJB UML mapping, 92, 94
entity modeling, 72-73
entity relationships, 67-68
modeling tools, 64
modeling Web applications, 77-79
modeling Web pages, 87, 89-90, 92
Model-View-Controller, 110, 112, 184-185, 290
preparations for, 98-99, 101
refining code, 119-121
relationship modeling, 73, 76
reverse engineering, 70-71
system modeling, 79-80

tool support, 94-95
Unified Modeling Language (UML), 82-87
validating code, 118-119
Web application architecture, 81-82
components, 608, 610
databases, 102-104
menu interactions, 117
Destination object, 498
Destination Queues and Topics, creating and destroying, Java Message Service (JMS), 518-520, 522
destroy() method, 196
destroying Destination Queues and Topics, Java Message Service (JMS), 518-520, 522
destruction phase, servlets, 196
DetailAction class, 701
developers
increasing productivity of, 17-18
roles of, Enterprise JavaBeans (EJB) programming, 353-356
developing
applications
building pages, 114-117
challenges in, 17-20
creating back-end interfaces, 110-112
creating data access objects, 117-118
creating interfaces, 112, 114
creating tables and columns, 104-108
defining, 108-110
designing databases, 102-104
distributed programming, Enterprise JavaBeans (EJB), 330
effects of eXtensible Markup Language (XML) on, 36-37
with Java, 12-14
preparations for, 98-99, 101
refining code, 119-121
roles of developers in, Enterprise JavaBeans (EJB), 353-356
validating code, 118-119
entity beans, 421-437
entity relationships, 67
JavaServer Pages (JSP), 233, 236-240
development database environments, configuring, 108
development methodology
contents of applications, 53-54
development tools, 52
iterative development, 24-25
modeling tools, 51-52
overview of, 51
role-based development, 22-24
two- and three-tier development, 99
development phases
application assembly, 56-60
application deployment, 60-61
enterprise bean creation, 56
eXtensible Markup Language (XML) and, 55-56
overview of, 54-55
software development cycle, 582, 584
Web component creation, 56
development tools, 52, 710-725
DirContext interface, 132
directives
include, 231
JavaServer Pages (JSP), 231, 259-261, 263-265, 282-283
language, 231
page, 231
taglib, 231-233, 238
directories
classes, 642-643
JAVA HOME, 760, 762
root, 236
Web Archive (WAR), 213
directory listings, accessing, local file systems, 133-134
directory services, 124-125, 131
disks, persistent storage, 625
dispatching requests, servlets, 209-211
displaying
cookies, 200
deployed J2EE components, 668
histories on specific measurements, WebLOAD, 593
table of contents, Web Archive (WAR), 214

Distributed Component Object Model (DCOM), 79
distributed programming, Enterprise JavaBeans (EJB), 330
distributed programming services, 346
distributed remote access service, 332
distributed transactions, 170-171, 349-350, 757
distribution JAR files, 401
DNS (Domain Name Service), 124-125, 129
DNS_URL property, 130
doAfterBody() method, 283
Document interface, 550
Document Object Model (DOM), 34-35, 37, 549, 551-553
document type definitions (DTDs), 34
- deployment descriptors, version and location of, 215
- described, 528
- eXtensible Markup Language (XML), 535-540
- schema vs., 540-541

documentation
- Java 2 Enterprise Edition (J2EE) Software Development Kit (SDK), 763
- Java Naming and Directory Interface (JNDI), 129

DocumentFragment interface, 550
documents
- eXtensible Markup Language (XML), structure of, 527, 529-531, 533
- Microsoft Word, opening in servlets, 217

DocumentType interface, 550
doEndTag() method, 283
doGet() method, 189, 191
doInitBody() method, 283
DOM (Document Object Model), 34-35, 37, 549, 551-553
Domain Name Service (DNS), as naming service, 124-125, 129
doPost() method, 189, 194
doStartTag() method, 283
doWait value, 173
downloading applets, improving speed of, 623
Dreamweaver UltraDev, 719-720
DriverManager class, 144, 146-148
drivers
- database, 141, 143, 145
- Java Database Connectivity (JDBC), 139-141, 143
- JDBC-ODBC Bridge, 141-142
- middleware, 142
- partial Java, 142
- pure Java, 143
- support for scrolling, 159-160

DropDownListBox control, 116
DTD. *See* document type definitions
DTDHandler interface, 553
dummy Internet Protocol (IP) addresses, 200
duplicated message sessions, Java Message Service (JMS), 494
DUPS_OK_ACKNOWLEDGE method, 344, 495

E

e-commerce, 35-38
e-mail, 446-447
- as asynchronous communication, 490
- binary messages, 471-472, 474
- flags, 455-456
- JavaMail, 447
  - *architecture, 450-451*
  - *JAF (Java Activation Framework), 451-456, 459-466*
  - *JavaServer Pages, 474-479, 481-483*
  - *primary classes, 450-451*
  - *Provider Registry, 448-450*
- multipart messages, 469
  - *receiving, 470-471*
  - *sending, 469-470*
- receiving messages, 468
  - *binary, 472, 474*
  - *multipart, 470-471*
- sending messages, 467
  - *binary, 471-472*
  - *multipart, 469-470*

e-mail verification, SilverBooks sample application, 702
EAI (Enterprise Application Integration), 36
EAR. *See* Enterprise Archive
EARfile argument, 656
EAserver, 14
ECS. *See* Element Construction Set, 195
EDI (Electronic Data Interchange), 35
Edit mask control, 116
editing columns and rows, resultsets, 162-163
EJB. *See* Enterprise JavaBeans
ejb-jar.xml, 670-674, 677-689
ejbActivate() method, 360, 414, 433
ejbCreate() method, 430-431, 434, 618
ejbFind() method, 432
EJBHome class, 361, 402, 405, 420
EJBHome interface, 346
EJBHome object, 337
ejbJar argument, 657
ejbLoad() method, 340, 414, 432-433
EJBLocalHome class, 420
EJBLocalObject class, 420
EJBObject class, 361, 402, 420
EJBObject interface, 337, 341
ejbPassivate() method, 360, 414, 433
ejbPostCreate() method, 430-432, 434
ejbRemove() method, 360, 414, 432, 435-436
ejbStore() method, 340, 414, 433
Electronic Data Interchange (EDI), 35
Element Construction Set (ECS), 195
element declarations, document type definitions (DTDs), 536-537
Element interface, 550-551
element types, schema, 543
elements
<embed>, 277
eXtensible Markup Language (XML), 33, 528-529
Hypertext Markup Language (HTML), 193, 195
<object>, 277
scripting, JavaServer Pages (JSP), 265-267
stylesheet, 560-563
template, 563-564
Elixir IDE, 715-716
Elixir Report, 742
ellipsis (...), 562
Embarcadero Technology, 738
<embed> element, 277
Empirix Bean-test, 752
Empirix Software, 587
EMPTY description, 537
empty elements, eXtensible Markup Language (XML) documents, 529
enabling e-mail verification, SilverBooks sample application, 702
encapsulating entity beans inside session beans, 335
engineering, reverse, 70-71
engines
JavaServer Pages (JSP), 227, 231, 240
Servlet, 188
Enterprise Application Integration (EAI), 36
Enterprise Archive (EAR), 29, 39, 476, 482-483, 646, 648
Enterprise Bean Creation phase, 54, 56
enterprise beans, 48, 53, 408
enterprise information system (EIS) tier, 48
Enterprise JavaBeans (EJB)
advantages of, 22
assembling Java Archive (JAR) files, 644-645
bean attributes, 335-336
bean-managed persistence (BMP), 340
benefits of, 330-331
clients, 437-439
Common Object Request Broker Architecture (CORBA), 347
container provider, 356
container-managed persistence (CMP), 339
containers, 50, 331-333
dependent and fine-grained objects, 338
deploying, 352-353
deployment descriptors, 337
described, 11, 28-29, 328-330

distributed programming, 330
distributed programming services, 346
EJBObject interface, 337
entity beans, 334-335
  bean-managed persistence, 415
  components, 416-421
  container-managed persistence, 416
  deployment descriptor, 420
  developing, 421-437
  instances, 413
  life cycle states, 413-414
  tools for configuring, packaging, and deploying, 439-444
  uses, 412-413
files, Java Archive (JAR) compression, 400
growth of, 22
handles, objects, 363
Home interface, 337
input forms, 251-252
internal state, 253
Java Message Service (JMS), 341-342
life cycle of, 340
message-driven beans (MDB), 342-345
performance of, 616-617
protocol requirements, 346
references, 768-772
Remote Method Invocation (RMI), 347-349
roles for developers, 353-356
security, 352
session beans, 333-335
  clients, 405
  enterprise beans, 408
  finding, 402-405
  J2EE, 408
  JSP, 408
  servlets, 406-407
  standalone Java applications, 408
  standalone non-Java applications, 408
  Unix, 408
  updating, 402
  Windows, 408
SessionContext and EntityContext objects, 337-338
SilverBooks sample application, 701
transaction management, 349-352
Unified Model Language (UML) mapping, 92, 94
version 2.0, 757

entities
  application, 102-103
  database, building data access objects, 118
  determining relationships for, 103-104
  eXtensible Markup Language (XML) documents, 530-532
  refining, 103

entity bean developers, 354

entity beans, 12, 22, 48, 334-335, 345
  components, 416-421
  deployment descriptor, 420
  developing, 421-437
  instances, 413
  life cycle states, 413-414
  persistence
    bean-managed persistence, 415
    container-managed persistence, 416
  tools for configuring, packaging, and deploying, 439-444
  uses, 412-413

entity declarations, document type definitions (DTDs), 538, 540

Entity interface, 550

entity modeling, 72-73

entity relationships, 67-68

Entity-Attribute Editor, 73

EntityBean class, 430-437

EntityContext object, 337-338

EntityReference interface, 550

EntityResolver interface, 553

entries, environment, 177-178, 766-767

environment entries
  creating, 177-178
  declaring, 766-767

EnvironmentContext object, 338

environments, 610

equals() method, 430

erasing
  deployed J2EE applications, 653-654
  deployed J2EE components, 659-660, 669
  Destination Queues and Topics, Java Message Service (JMS), 518-520, 522
  rows, databases, 163

error handling, JavaServer Pages (JSP), 281-282
ErrorHandler interface, 554
errorPage attribute, 281
errors
- assuming responsibility for, 574
- correcting in applications, 579-582
- finding sources of, 576-578
- initialization, 575, 580
- stabilizing, 575-576
- syntax, 578-579

ERwin, 68-71, 73, 76-77, 738-739
escape characters, eXtensible Markup Language (XML) documents, 532-533
event-driven user interfaces, disadvantages of, 290
events, application life cycle, 223
exception handling, message-driven beans (MDB), 344
Exception implicit object, 281
exceptions
- BatchUpdateException, 165
- DataTruncation, 158
- Handling, Java Message Service (JMS) in, 494
- Java Database Connectivity (JDBC), 157-158
- javax.servlet package, 189
- ServletException, 189, 196
- Simple API for XML (SAX), 554
- SQLException, 157
- SQLWarning, 157-158
- Struts, 315
- UnavailableException, 189, 196

executables, creating, 120-121
execute() method, 149-150, 152, 156
executeBatch() method, 164
executeQuery() method, 149-153, 156, 162, 177
executeUpdate() method, 149-151
executing
- applets, 620
- Java interpreters, 620
- SQL select statements, 176-177
- stored procedures, 152

Explain Plan, 627
ExpressChart, 743-744
expressions
- JavaServer Pages (JSP), 266-267
- MessageSelector objects, 501

expunge() method, 455
eXtensible Markup Language (XML), 32, 55-56, 253, 526
- Document Object Model (DOM), 549, 551-553
- document type definitions (DTDs), 535-540
- eXtensible Stylesheet Language (XSL), 557-559
- features of, 526-527
- history of, 526
- Java 2 Enterprise Edition (J2EE) and, 32-38
- in Java code, 253
- output, 556-557
- parsers, 549
- Processing Instructions (PIs), 534-535
- rendering business objects in, 253
- schema, 540-549
- security, 566-567
- Security Assertion Markup Language (SAML), 566-567
- Simple API for XML (SAX), 553-556
- structure of documents, 527, 529-531, 533
- style sheets, 527, 560-564
- tools, 744-748
- unparsed data, 533-534
- XML Key Management Specification (XKMS), 566-567
- XML Linking Language (XLink), 564, 566

eXtensible Stylesheet Language (XSL), 557-564
extension mapping, 321
Extension Mechanisms subpackage, 85
external entities, 532
external files, including JavaScript in servlets, 210-211
external site monitoring services, 600-601

F

-f deploymentPlan argument, 221, 656-658
-f multifile argument, 660
f option, 642
factories, connection, 126-127
FCS (First Customer Ship), 584
fieldLevelValidation interface, 398
fieldLevelValidationHome interface, 382
fields
- headers, Java Message Service (JMS), 496-497
- hidden form, 205
- redelivery flag, 495

FIFO (first-in, first-out), message delivery, 492
file systems, accessing directory listings, 133-134
files
- command, running in Java Pet Store sample application, 704
- deployment descriptors, mapping requests to servlets, 215-216
- ejb-jar.xml, Pet Store, 670-674, 677-689
- Enterprise Archive (EAR), assembling, 646, 648
- external, including JavaScript in servlets, 210-211
- Java Archive (JAR), 213-214, 353, 623-624, 642-645
- PDF, opening in servlets, 217
- resource resolution, Pet Store, 676-680, 682, 684-689
- Tag Library Descriptor (TLD), 214, 238
- used in J2EE applications, 54
- Web Archive (WAR), 213-214, 218, 221, 236
  - *assembling, 645-646*
- web.xml, 214-216
  - *Pet Store, 672-674*
  - *servlet tags, 635-637*
  - *SilverBooks, 675*

filters, 223, 501
findByPrimaryKey() method, 434-435
finding
- book titles, SilverBooks sample application, 696
- connection factories, 126-127
- data sources, Uniform Resource Locators (URLs), 145-146
- DataSource objects, 126, 135
- session beans, clients, 402-405
- sources of errors, 576-578
- table of contents, Web Archive (WAR), 214

fine-grained object, 338
FioranoMQ 5 Message Server, 745
Firehunter, 600
First Customer Ship (FCS), 584
first-in, first-out (FIFO), message delivery, 492
#FIXED keyword, 537
flags
- e-mail messages, 455-456
- redelivery, 495

FlagTerm class, 457
Flashline, 716-717
folders, 454. *See also* directories
for loops, 237
foreign key constraints, 45
form classes, SilverBooks sample application, 701
form elements (HTML), Struts, 307
form fields, hidden, 205
<FORM> tag, Hypertext Markup Language (HTML), 192-193, 195
formats, body, 497
forms
- Hypertext Markup Language (HTML), 192-193, 195, 474-475, 478
- input, 251-252
- Struts implementation of, 305-307, 309-310
- validation of input, 312-313
- Web pages, 91

Formula One iReporting Engine, 743
forward tag, JavaServer Pages (JSP), 232
forwarding requests to servlets, 209-211
Foundation package, 85
frame pages, 116
frames, Web pages, 92
frameworks, 52, 185, 248, 250, 252-254
FromStringTerm class, 457

FromTerm class, 457
full installs, Java Pet Store sample application, 705
functional testing, 585, 598-599

G

Gemstone/J Application Server, 728-730
general entities, 532
General Principle of Software Quality, 573
generated remote stubs, 332
generating
  data during testing phase, 584
  Hypertext Markup Language (HTML) pages, 190
GenericServlet class, 189
GET method, 186, 189, 193, 197, 271
getAgaData() method, 223
getAllHeaderLines() method, 461
getAllHeaders() method, 461
getAllRecipients() method, 461
getArray() method, 167
getAttribute() method, 208-209
getAttributes() method, 131
getBlob() method, 166
getCharacterEncoding() method, 197-198
getConcurrency() method, 161
getConnection() method, 146-147, 173
getContent() method, 461
getContentLength() method, 197
getContentType() method, 197
getContextPath() method, 196
getCookies() method, 206-208
getDatabase() method, 223
getDataHandler() method, 461
getEJBHome() method, 363
getEJBMetaData() method, 364, 436
getElementsByTagName method, 551
getErrorCode() method, 157
getFlags() method, 462
getFolder() method, 462
getFrom() method, 462
getHandle() method, 363
getHeader() method, 200-203
getHomeHandle() method, 364
getInitParameter() method, 216
getInitParameterNames() method, 216
getInputStream() method, 462
getInvalidAddresses() method, 466
getMessageID() method, 462
getMessageNumber() method, 462
getMoreResults() method, 152
getNextException() method, 157
getObject() method, 168
getObject(index) method, 177
getParameter() method, 206
getParameterNames() method, 206
getParameterValues() method, 206
getPrimaryKey() method, 363
getPrimaryKeys() method, 159
getProcedureColumns() method, 159
getProcedures() method, 159
getProperty tag, 232, 238
getReceivedDate() method, 462
getRecipients() method, 462
getRef() method, 168
getRemoteHost() method, 616
getReplyTo() method, 463
getRequestAttributes() method, 203
getRequestDispatcher() method, 209-210
getRequestHeader() method, 203
getRequestInfo() method, 203
getSchemas() method, 159

getSentDate() method, 463
getSession() method, 208
getSize() method, 463
getString() method, 166
getSubject() method, 463
getTables() method, 159
getter method, 267
Getting Started chapter, Java 2 Enterprise Edition (J2EE) Software Development Kit (SDK) documentation, 763
getUser() method, 223
getValidSentAddresses() method, 466
getValidUnsentAddresses() method, 466
getValue() method, 556
getWarning() method, 157
getWriter() method, 192
get*XXX*() methods, 152-153, 155-156
Giga Information Group, 13
Gilpin, Mike, 13
Graph control, 116
graphics, packaging into one class, 623
Group presentation tool box control, 116

H

Handle class, 334
HandlerBase class, 554
handlers, tag, 283-286
handles
creating to naming services, 129
EJB objects, 363
obtaining to Connection and DataSource objects, 211-213
removing, 365
handling
errors, JavaServer Pages (JSP), 281-282
exceptions
Java Message Service (JMS) in, 494
message-driven beans (MDB), 344
nulls, Java Database Connectivity (JDBC), 155
hardware, partitioning, 627
Harmony Component Suite, 714-715
Hartman, Amir, 15
hashCode() method, 430
Hashtables object, 612
HEAD method, 186
headers
fields, Java Message Service (JMS), 496-497
retrieving information from, 200-203
web.xml, 215-216
HeaderTerm class, 457
help, SilverStream Application Servers, 222
-help option, 668
hidden comments, JavaServer Pages (JSP), 259
hidden form fields, 205
hidden Internet Protocol (IP) addresses, 200
hierarchies
applications, 53-54
packaging components, 353
HiT Software, 739
home interfaces, 334, 337, 345, 351, 353, 433-436
methods, 364-365
references, 363
session beans, 361, 364-365
home references, 405
Horizontal ScrollBar control, 117
-host option, 668
HTML. *See* Hypertext Markup Language
htmlKona package, 195
HTTP. *See* Hypertext Transfer Protocol
HttpJspBase class, 241
HttpServlet class, 189
HttpServlet object, 191-192
HttpServletRequest object, 189, 196-198, 200-208
HttpServletResponse object, 189
HttpSession object, 223
HttpSessionRequest object, 208-209
hybrid HTML/Dynamic HTML/JavaScript clients, 43
hyperlink tags, Struts for, 312
Hypertext Markup Language (HTML), 32
comments, JavaServer Pages (JSP), 258-259
described, 526
<FORM> tag, 192-193, 195
forms, 192-193, 195, 474-475, 478
in Java code, 240-244, 253

rendering business objects in, 253
validators, 597-598
Hypertext Transfer Protocol (HTTP), 406
Servlet Container support, 188
servlets, 184-188

I

-i option, 656, 659
IBM, 245
early advances in computer technology by, 8
eXtensible Markup Language (XML) support, 33
introduces OS MVT/MFT, 8
WebSphere, 14
IBM VisualAge for Java, 717-718
IBM WebSphere, 730
ID attribute, 530
ID. *See* identifiers
IDE (Integrated Development Environments), 19
identifiers (IDs), 501
application identification (APPID), 208-209
MessageSelector objects, 501
uniform resource (URI), 238
user, Java Pet Store sample application, 707
IIOP (Internet InterORB Protocol), 332, 346-348
illegal entities, 532
images, packaging into one class, 623
IMAP4 (Internet Message Access Protocol), 447
implicit objects, 238, 280-281
implicit request variable, 238
implicit variables, 238
#IMPLIED keyword, 538
import stylesheet template, 563
IN parameter, 152
include directives, 231, 260-261
include tag, JavaServer Pages (JSP), 232, 239
include() method, 210, 247
INDEX Tuning Wizard, 628
indexes, implementing for databases, 627
InetSoft Technology, 742-743
info attribute, 284-285
InfoLink, 596
inheritance, session beans, 360
init() method, 195-196
INITIAL_CONTEXT_FACTORY property, 130
InitialContext class, 129, 403
InitialDirContext class, 131
initialization errors, 575, 580
initialization paramaters
declaring in Web applications, 216
retrieving from Web applications, 216
initialization phase, servlets, 195-196
INOUT parameter, 152, 156
input elements, Struts, 307
input forms, 251-252
InputSource class, 554
inserting rows, databases, 163
insertRow() method, 163
installation testing, 585
installing
Java 2 Enterprise Edition (J2EE) Software Development Kit (SDK), 759-763
user IDs, Java Pet Store sample application, 707
instance pooling, 331
instances
creating, EJBHome, 405
eXtensible Markup Language (XML) documents, 528
Instantiations, Inc., 718-719
IntegerComparisonTerm class, 457
Integrated Development Environments (IDEs), 19
Integrated Report Chart view, WebLOAD, 593
integrity, referential, 75
interfaces. *See also* objects
AgiDatabase, 173
application programming (API). *See* application programming interfaces
back-end, creating, 110-112
classes, Java Message Service (JMS), 499

Common Client (CCI), 759
Common Gateway (CGI), 81, 182-183
Connection, 144
creating, 112, 114
DataSource, 757
DirContext, 132
EJBHome, 346
EJBObject, 337, 341
fieldLevelValidation, 398
fieldLevelValidationHome, 382
home, 334, 337, 345, 351, 353, 433-436
Java Database Connectivity (JDBC), accessing databases, 172-178
Java Naming and Directory (JNDI)
accessing databases, 169-170
architecture, 128
benefits of, 125
described, 124
Enterprise JavaBeans (EJB), 125
Java Database Connectivity (JDBC), 125-126
Java Message Service (JMS), 126-127
Lightweight Directory Access Protocol (LDAP), 132-135
obtaining handles to DataSource objects, 211-213
operations, 131-132
service providers, 127
java.jms.MessageListener, 342-343
javax.rmi.CORBA.Tie, 394
JNDI Service Provider, 127
local, 436-437
message-oriented middleware (MOM), 490-494, 496-497
MessageListener, 342
NamedNodeMap, 551
NodeList, 551
OutputStream, 616
Remote, 332, 334-335, 345-347, 351, 353, 436
RequestDispatcher, 209-211
session beans, 360-362, 372-373
SessionSynchronization, 336, 349
Simple API for XML (SAX), 553-554
SingleThreadModel, 616
Stuctured Query Language (SQL) Call-Level, 140
styles, setting up TAGLIB class library, 114
UserTransaction, 351
See also objects
internal entities, 532
International Organization for Standardization (ISO), 535
internationalization
messages, 304-305
SilverBooks sample application, 702
Internet
architecture requirements, 20, 22
life cycles, applications, 22-26, 28, 30
Internet Economy, ability to compete in, 14-17
Internet InterORB Protocol (IIOP), 332, 346-348
Internet Message Access Protocol 4. *See* IMAP4
Internet Protocol (IP) addresses, 200
Internet Quotient self-assessment test, 15-16
Internet Server Application Programming Interface (ISAPI), 183-184
interrupt testing, 586
Intuitive Systems, 750
Iona Technologies, 14, 731
IP (Internet Protocol) addresses, 200
IPCheck, 601
iPlanet, 14
iPlanet Application Server, 731-732
iPortal Application Server 3.0, 731
ISAPI. *See* Internet Server Application Programming Interface, 183
isErrorPage attribute, 281
isExpunged() method, 463
isIdentical() method, 429-430
isIdentical() method (remote interface), 363
ISO (International Organization for Standardization), 535
isSet() method, 463

isValid() method, 372
item argument, 660
iterative development, 24-25

J

J2EE. *See* Java 2 Enterprise Edition
JAAS 1.0, 759
JAF (Java Activation Framework), 451, 758
Jakarta Project, 185, 228, 293
JAR. *See* Java Archive
Java 2 Enterprise Edition (J2EE)
- application programming interfaces (APIs) and certification, 30-31
- architecture of, 25-26
- CLASSPATH, 760, 762
- eXtensible Markup Language (XML) and, 32-38
- features of, 9-10
- installing Software Development Kit (SDK), 759-763
- JavaMail application, 476, 481
  - *archives, 476, 482-483*
  - *creating HTML forms, 474-475, 478*
  - *creating receiving JSP file, 475, 479, 481*
  - *creating sending JSP file, 475, 478-479*
  - *deployment descriptor, 476*
  - *deployment plan, 476, 482*
  - *testing, 476-477, 483*
- naming conventions, 763-780
- optional packages, 757-759
- packaging applications, 38-39
- Reference Implementation, 31, 649-650, 652, 654
- released by Sun Microsystems, 8
- required application programming interfaces (APIs), 756-757
- sample applications, 39-40
- session beans, clients, 408

Java 2 Platform, Enterprise Edition Specification, 31-32
Java Activation Framework, 451, 758
Java API for XML Processing (JAXP), 556, 748, 758
Java Archive (JAR), 213-214, 353, 400, 623-624, 642-645
Java Community Process (JCP), 38, 328
Java Conformance Kit (JCK), 30
Java Database Connectivity (JDBC), 341, 349, 756
- accessing databases, 172-178
- architecture, 139-141, 143
- batch statements, 164-165
- benefits of, 139
- data types, 166-168
- described, 139
- exceptions, 157-158
- javax.sql package, 168-169, 171
- metadata, 158-159
- packages, 143-148
- retrieving and updating data, 148-156
- scrollable resultsets, 159-160, 162
- servlets, 211-213
- SilverStream Application Server case study, 171, 173-178
- transaction support, 163-164
- updating columns and rows, resultsets, 162-163

Java data types, converting to Structured Query Language (SQL) data types, 153-155
JAVA HOME directory, 760, 762
Java Interface Definition Language (Java IDL), 30, 756
Java interpreters, executing, 620
Java Message Service (JMS), 230, 341-342, 345, 758
- components required by applications using, 498-499
- creating and destroying Destination Queues and Topics, 518-520, 522
- described, 126-127, 488-490
- implementation and deployment issues, 522-523

interfaces, message-oriented middleware (MOM), 490-494, 496-497
Point-to-Point model, 491-492, 502-504
Point-to-Point Queue model, 507-518
producing and consuming messages, 500-501
Publish/Subscribe model, 492-494, 504-507
standard protocols, 345

Java Naming and Directory Interface (JNDI), 30, 404, 438, 756, 763-767
accessing databases, 169-170
architecture, 128
benefits of, 125
described, 124
Enterprise JavaBeans (EJB), 125
Java Database Connectivity (JDBC), 125-126
Java Message Service (JMS), 126-127
Lightweight Directory Access Protocol (LDAP), 132-135
obtaining handles to DataSource objects, 211-213
operations, 131-132
service providers, 127

java object, 578

Java Pet Store sample application, 61, 702-704, 706-707

Java Platform Extension for XML technology, 37-38

Java programming language
advantages and disadvantages of, 12-14
session beans, 408
tools for testing, 595-596

Java Remote Method Invocation (RMI), 79, 127, 332, 346-349

Java Servlet 2.2 Application Programming Interface (API), 208-209

Java servlets
described, 11
Struts, 293, 296

Java Transaction API (JTA), 30, 347, 349, 351, 758

Java Transaction Service (JTS), 350

java.jms.MessageListener interface, 342-343

java.naming package, 756

java.naming.directory package, 756

java.naming.event package, 757

java.naming.ldap package, 757

java.naming.spi package, 757

java.sql package, 143-148

java.util.Collection, 335

java.util.Set, 335

JavaBeans component architecture, 46

JavaMail, 30, 447
architecture, 450-451
JavaServer Pages, 474
archives, 476, 482-483
creating HTML forms, 474-475, 478
creating receiving file, 475, 479, 481
creating sending file, 475, 478-479
J2EE deployment descriptor, 476
J2EE deployment plan, 476, 482
J2EE file, 476, 481
testing, 476-477, 483
primary classes, 450-456, 459-466
Provider Registry, 448-450

JavaMail 1.2, 758

JavaScript, external files, including in servlets, 210-211

engine, 227, 231, 240

JavaServer Pages (JSP), 11, 46-47, 474
advantages of, 254-255
architecture, 240-248, 250, 252-254
deploying, 218
described, 11, 226-227, 229
developing and deploying, 233, 236-240
directives, 231
engine, 227, 231, 240
features of, 229-231
interactions between servlets and, 185
JavaMail, 474
creating HTML forms, 474-475, 478
creating receiving file, 475, 479, 481
creating sending file, 475, 478-479
J2EE file, 476-477, 481-483

passing control to, 210
performance of, 615-617
session beans, clients, 408
SilverBooks sample application, 699-700
Struts, 293, 296
syntax, 258-261, 263-275, 277-282
tag libraries, 282-287
tags, 228, 231-232
version 1.2, 758

javax.ejb.MessageDrivenContext, 344
javax.jms.Message argument, 343
javax.mail.Address class, 459
javax.mail.Folder class, 454-455
javax.mail.internet.InternetAddress class, 459
javax.mail.internet.MimeMessage class, 460-465
javax.mail.Message class, 460
javax.mail.search class, 456, 459
javax.mail.Session class, 452
javax.mail.Store class, 453
javax.mail.Transport class, 466
javax.naming package, 129
javax.rmi.CORBA.Tie interface, 394
javax.servlet package, 189
javax.sql package, 143, 168-169, 171
JAXP. *See* Java API for XML Processing
JBuilder 5, 712-714
JCanvas Studio, 711-712
JCK (Java Conformance Kit), 30
JClass Enterprise Suite, 722-723
JCP (Java Community Process), 328
JDBC. *See* Java Database Connectivity
JDBC 2.0 Extension, 757
JDBC 2.1 Core Application Programming Interface (API), 143-148
JDBC-ODBC Bridge drivers, 141-142
JDBCRowSet objects, 171
JMS. *See* Java Message Service
JMS provider component, Java Message Service (JMS) messaging applications, 491
JMSDeliveryMode header field, 496
JMSExpiration header field, 496
JMSMessageID header field, 496
JMSPriority header field, 496
JMSRedelivered header field, 497
JMSReplyTo header field, 497
JNDI. *See* Java Naming and Directory Interface
JNDI lookup services, 49
JNDI Service Provider Interface (SPI), 127
JNDI Software Development Kit (SDK), 127
joins, tables, 625
JProbe, 620, 753
JProbe Developer Suite, 595
JRun 3.0, 727
JSP. *See* JavaServer Pages
<jsp:forward> action, 275-276
jsp:forward tag, 232
<jsp:getProperty> action, 271-272
jsp:getProperty tag, 232, 238
<jsp:include> action, 274-275
jsp:include tag, 232, 239
<jsp:param> clause, 274-275
<jsp:plugin> action, 276-279
<jsp:setProperty> action, 272-274
jsp:setProperty tag, 232
<jsp:useBean> action, 267-271
jsp:useBean tag, 232, 238
jspDestroy() method, 241
jspInit() method, 241
jspService() method, 241, 281
jspversion attribute, 284
JSR-000026 UML profile for EJB, 93
JTA. *See* Java Transaction API
Jtest, 595, 750-751
JTS (Java Transaction Service), 350
JUnit, 596

K

keys
creating, 106
primary, entities, 68
keywords, 537-538
KL Group, 621

L

-l deployname option, 656, 659
language directives, 231
LANGUAGE property, 130
latency
applications, 606
MVC design effect on, 293
lazy writers, 626
LDAP (Lightweight Directory Access Protocol), 127, 132-135
LEFT attribute, 530
legacy systems, integration of, 18-19
less than (<) character, 532-533
lib subdirectory, 236
libraries
classes
Java Naming and Directory Interface (JNDI), 128
TAGLIB, 114
tag, 232, 282-287
licenses, Apache Software Foundation, 252
life cycles
application life cycle events, 223
Enterprise JavaBeans (EJB), 340
Internet applications, 22-26, 28, 30
JavaServer Pages (JSP), 280
managing, beans, 331, 344
servlets, 195-196
Lightweight Directory Access Protocol (LDAP), 127, 132-135
links, tools for testing, 596
Linux, installing Java 2 Enterprise Edition (J2EE) Software Development Kit (SDK), 761-763
list argument, 667
list operation, 132
ListArray object, 618
ListBox control, 117
listing deployed J2EE applications, 652-653
listings
application.xml
Pet Store, 647
SilverBooks, 647-648
attributes, page directives, 263
CMP EJB deployment descriptor example, WebLogic environment, 664-665
CorpBanner.jsp, 287
CorpBannerTag.java, 286-287
CorpTagLib.tld, 286
creating Queue destinations, 518-519
creating Topic destinations, 520-521
destroying Queue destinations, 519-520
destroying Topic destinations, 521-522
ejb-jar.xml, Pet Store, 670-674, 677-689
jspDateTime.jsp, 261
jspIncludeDirective.jsp, 261
MessageListener class, clients, 512-514
Point-to-Point model
receiving clients, 503-504
sending clients, 502-503
Point-to-Point Queue model
receiving browse clients, 508-511
receiving MessageListener clients, 512
receiving MessageSelector clients, 516-518
sending browse clients, 507-508
sending MessageSelector clients, 514-518
Publish/Subscribe model
publishing clients, 504-505
subscribing clients, 506-507
resource resolution files, Pet Store, 676-680, 682, 684-689
syntax
<jsp:plugin> action, 277
<jsp:useBean> action, 268
tag handlers, 284
Tag Library Descriptors (TLDs), 285-286
userInfo bean, 270-271

web.xml
- *Pet Store, 672-674*
- *SilverBooks, 675*

literals, MessageSelector objects, 501
loading
- data, 111
- database drivers, 145

loads
- effects on system performance, 606
- testing, 619-620
- tools for testing, 587, 589, 591-593, 595

local file systems, accessing directory listings, 133-134
local interfaces, 436-437
localization
- messages, 304-305
- SilverBooks sample application, 702

Locator interface, 554
LocatorImpl class, 554
logic
- business
  - *Model-View-Controller (MVC), 252-253*
  - *separating from presentation, Web pages, 230*
- core, 230

logic layer, 609
logical operators, MessageSelector objects, 501
logins, Struts login function, 316
logistics, designing J2EE applications, 98-99, 101
lookup operation, 132
lookups, resource reference, 176
loop-back calls, session beans, 405
loops, for, 237
Lotus Domino, 14
Lucent Technologies, 603

M

Macromedia Dreamweaver UltraDev, 719-720
mail. *See* e-mail
maintenance, MVC design effect on, 293
managing sessions, servlets, 205-209
Mandatory attribute, 350
MapMessage body format, Java Message Service (JMS), 497
mapping
- EJB UML, 92, 94
- requests to servlets, deployment descriptors, 215-216
- resource references to databases, 178

mappings, defining for ServletContainer object, 216
markers, <% and %>, 233
match() method, 463
Maximum Transmission Unit (MTU), 619
MDB. *See* message-driven beans
memory
- managing, Document Object Model (DOM), 551-552
- volatile storage, 625

menus, designing interactions for, 117
message acknowledgments
- Java Message Service (JMS), 495
- message-driven beans (MDB), 344

Message Service, Java (JMS), 30
message-driven beans (MDBs), 48, 342-345, 351-352
message-oriented middleware (MOM)
- described, 489
- interfaces, Java Message Service (JMS), 490-494, 496-497

MessageConsumer object, 500
MessageIDTerm class, 457
MessageListener clients, Point-to-Point Queue model, 512
MessageListener interface, 342
MessageListener object, 495, 501, 510, 512-514
MessageNumberTerm class, 457
MessageProducer object, 500
messages. *See also* e-mail
- delivery of
  - *first-in, first-out (FIFO), 492*
  - *non-persistent, 496*
  - *persistent, 496*
- described, 488
- Java Message Service (JMS), 495-497, 491

producing and consuming, 500-501
publishing and subscribing, Publish/Subscribe model, 492-494
sending and receiving
Point-to-Point model, 491-492, 502-504
Point-to-Point Queue model, 507-518

MessageSelector clients, Point-to-Point Queue model, 514-518
MessageSelector object, 497, 501, 514-518
messaging tools, 744-748
metadata, Java Database Connectivity (JDBC), 158-159
metamodels, 83, 85
METHOD elements, Hypertext Markup Language (HTML), 193
method pooling, session beans, 358
methods
accessor, 267
acknowledge(), 495
addBatch(), 164
addCookie(), 204, 207
addFrom, 461
addRecipients(), 461
afterBegin, 349
afterCompletion, 349
AUTO_ ACKNOWLEDGE, 344
beforeCompletion, 349
boolean absolute(int row), 160
boolean first(), 160
boolean last(), 160
boolean previous(), 160
businessMethod2(), 372
Class.forName(), 145
clearBatch(), 164
close(), 150
commit(), 164, 494
connection, servlets, 198, 200
connection.prepareStatement(), 177
create(), 405, 454
createServletResource(), 223
createStatement, 149
createTopicConnection(), 493
createX(), 551
DatabaseMetaData. supportsBatchUpdates(), 164
datatype(), 153
DELETE, 186
delete(), 454
deleteRow(), 163
destroy(), 196
doAfterBody(), 283
doEndTag(), 283
doGet(), 189, 191
doInitBody(), 283
doPost(), 189, 194
doStartTag(), 283
DUPS_OK_ACKNOWLEDGE, 344
ejbActivate(), 414, 433
ejbCreate(), 430-431, 434, 618
ejbFind(), 432
ejbLoad(), 340, 414, 432-433
ejbPassivate(), 414, 433
ejbPostCreate(), 430-432, 434
ejbRemove(), 414, 432, 435-436
ejbStore(), 340, 414, 433
equals(), 430
execute(), 149-150, 152, 156
executeBatch(), 164
executeQuery(), 149-153, 156, 162, 177
executeUpdate(), 149-151
expunge(), 455
findByPrimaryKey(), 434-435
GET, 186, 189, 193, 197, 271
getAgaData(), 223
getAllHeaderLines(), 461
getAllHeaders(), 461
getAllRecipients(), 461
getArray(), 167
getAttribute(), 208-209
getAttributes(), 131
getBlob(), 166
getCharacterEncoding(), 197-198
getConcurrency(), 161
getConnection(), 146-147, 173
getContent(), 461
getContentLength(), 197
getContentType(), 197
getContextPath(), 196
getCookies(), 206-208
getDatabase(), 223
getDataHandler(), 461
getEJBMetaData(), 436
getElementsByTagName, 551

getErrorCode(), 157
getFlags(), 462
getFolder(), 462
getFrom(), 462
getHeader(), 200-203
getInitParameter(), 216
getInitParameterNames(), 216
getInputStream(), 462
getInvalidAddresses(), 466
getMessageID(), 462
getMessageNumber(), 462
getMoreResults(), 152
getNextException(), 157
getObject(), 168
getObject(index), 177
getParameter(), 206
getParameterNames(), 206
getParameterValues(), 206
getPrimaryKeys(), 159
getProcedureColumns(), 159
getProcedures(), 159
getReceivedDate(), 462
getRecipients, 462
getRef(), 168
getRemoteHost(), 616
getReplyTo(), 463
getRequestAttributes(), 203
getRequestDispatcher(), 209-210
getRequestHeader(), 203
getRequestInfo(), 203
getSchemas(), 159
getSentDate(), 463
getSession(), 208
getSize(), 463
getString(), 166
getSubject(), 463
getTables(), 159
getter, 267
getUser(), 223
getValidSentAddresses(), 466
getValidUnsentAddresses(), 466
getValue(), 556
getWarning(), 157
getWriter(), 192
get*XXX*(), 152-153, 155-156
hashCode(), 430
HEAD, 186
Home interface, 351
  getEJBMetaData(), 364
  getHomeHandle(), 364
  remove(Handle h), 365
  remove(Object primaryKey), 365
Hypertext Transfer Protocol (HTTP), 186
include(), 210, 247
init(), 195-196
insertRow(), 163
isExpunged(), 463
isIdentical(), 429-430
isSet(), 463
isValid(), 372
jspDestroy(), 241
jspInit(), 241
jspService(), 281
_jspService(), 241
match(), 463
MimeMessage(), 460
moveToInsertRow(), 163
newInstance(), 344
next(), 152-153
onException(), 494
onMessage(), 342-344, 351, 501
open(), 455
out.println(), 192
POST, 186, 189, 193, 197
prepareCall(), 152
println(), 194
public void updateString(), 162
publish(), 496
PUT, 186
readNextRow(), 618
receive(), 500
receiveNoWait(), 500
registerOutParameter(), 152, 156
releaseConnection(), 174
Remote interface
  getEJBHome(), 363
  getHandle(), 363
  getPrimaryKey(), 363
  IsIdentical(), 363
  remove(), 363
reply(), 463
resultSet.getObject(), 177
rollback(), 164, 494
saveChanges(), 464
search(), 455
send(), 466, 496
sendError(), 204
sendMessage(), 466
service(), 189-190, 192, 196
ServletRequest object, 206
session beans
  business, 367
  create(), 366
  ejbActivate(), 360
  ejbPassivate(), 360
  ejbRemove(), 360
  setSessionContext(SessionContext), 360
set, 271
setAttribute(), 208
setAutoCommit(false), 164-165

setBlob(), 166
setContent(), 464
setContentLength(), 204
setContentType(), 190, 192, 204
setDateHeader(), 204
setDeliveryMode(), 500
setEntityContext(), 432
setExceptionListener(), 494
setExpunged(), 464
setFetchSize(), 160
setFlags(), 455, 464
setFrom(), 465
setHeader(), 204
setIntHeader(), 204
setMessageDriven-Context(), 344
setMessageListener(), 501
setNull(), 151
setPriority(), 500
setRecipients(), 465
setReplyTo(), 465
setSentDate(), 465
setStatus(), 204
setSubject(), 465
setter, 267, 272
setText(), 465
setTimeToLive(), 500
set*XXX*(), 150, 152, 156
Start(), 501
unsetEntityContext(), 432
updateAsciiStream(), 162
updateBigDecimal(), 162
updateBinaryStream(), 162
updateBoolean(), 162
updateByte(), 162
updateNull(), 162
update*XXX*(), 162
wasNull(), 155

Microsoft
eXtensible Markup Language (XML) support, 33
introduces personal computer (PC), 8
releases client server platform, 8

Microsoft Internet Server Application Programming Interface (ISAPI), 183

Microsoft Word documents, opening in servlets, 217

middleware
described, 488-489
message-oriented (MOM)
described, 489
interfaces, Java Message Service (JMS), 490-494, 496-497

middleware drivers, 142

MIME. *See* Multipurpose Internet Mail Extension protocol

MimeMessage() method, 460

MimeMessages, 467-471

mod perl sites, 590

Model-View-Controller (MVC)
ActionServlet and ActionMapping classes, 254
architecture, 24-25, 703
design of, 110, 112
redirecting requests, JavaServer Pages (JSP), 245-247
Struts framework, 248, 250, 252-254
system state, 252-253
Web page presentation, 253

Model-View-Controller (MVC) patterns, 184-185
advantages, 290, 292-293
appropriate uses, 292
components of, 290-292
Controller, 291-292, 298-301
JavaServer Pages (JSP), 115
Model, 290-292, 297-298
problems with, 293
Struts framework. *See* Struts
View, 290-292, 298

modeling
databases, 64-65, 70
entity, J2EE applications, 72-73
process, 66
relationship, J2EE applications, 73, 76
system, 79-80
tools for, 51-52, 64, 736-744
Web applications, 77-79
Web pages, 87, 89-90, 92

modifying columns and rows, resultsets, 162-163

MOM. *See* message-oriented middleware

monitoring tools
databases, 627-628
performance, 748-753

moveToInsertRow() method, 163

MTU (Maximum Transmission Unit), 619

MultiLineEdit control, 117

multipart e-mail messages, 469
receiving, 470-471
sending, 469-470
multiple transactions, 350
Multipurpose Internet Mail Extension (MIME) protocol, 187, 190, 192, 217
multitier applications, 9
multitiered distribution application model
business logic layer, 44
client layer, 42-43
data layer, 44
overview of, 42
presentation layer, 43
three-tiered, 42
MVC. *See* Model-View-Controller

N

name attributes, 275, 285
named objects, retrieving, 134
NamedNodeMap interface, 551
NamedNodeMap object, 552-553
names
resultset columns, printing, 158
retrieving, 132
uniform resource (URN), 238
namespaces
described, 131
XSL Transformations (XSLT), 559
NamespaceSupport class, 554
naming conventions
Document Object Model (DOM), 552
Java 2 Enterprise Edition (J2EE), 763-780
naming services
creating handles to, 129
described, 124-125
Java Naming and Directory Interface (JNDI), 129
namespaces, 131
narrowing objects types, 403-404
***Net Ready*, 15**
Net.Medic, 603
NetRaker Suite, 602
NetRecon, 600
Netscape Web Application Programming Interface (NSAPI), 183-184
networks, reducing traffic, 610
Never attribute, 350
newInstance() method, 344
next() method, 152-153
Nmap, 599
Node object, 552
NodeList interface, 551
NodeList object, 552-553
non-Java applications, session beans, 408
non-persistent delivery, 496
non-triggered business objects, creating, 219-220
non-Web-based components, 45
[none] notation, 537
None option, 76
not null constraints, 45
notation declarations, document type definitions (DTDs), 540
Notation interface, 550
NotSupported attribute, 350-352
NotTerm class, 458
Novell, eXtensible Markup Language (XML) support, 33
NSAPI. *See* Netscape Web Application Programming Interface
nulls, handling, 155
numbers, Internet Protocol (IP) addresses, 200
NuMega DevPartner, 621

O

-o option, 656, 658-659
Object Constraint Language (OCL), 80
object equality, 429
object generation tools, 736-744
Object Management Group (OMG), 36, 347
Object Request Broker (ORB), 44, 347-348
object scope, JavaServer Pages (JSP), 280
Object Transaction Service (OTS), 347
<object> element, 277
OBJECT_FACTORIES property, 130
ObjectMessage body format, Java Message Service (JMS), 497

objects. *See also* interfaces
action, 251
administered
Java Message Service (JMS), 498-499
Java Message Service (JMS) messaging applications, 491
AgiHttpServletRequest, 223
AgiHttpServletResponse, 223
Binary Large (BLOB), 166-167
bound, retrieving, 132
business, rendering, 253
CachedRowSet, 171
CallableStatement, 148, 151-152, 166
Character Large (CLOB), 166-167
Connection, 144, 163, 174, 211-213, 498
ConnectionFactory, 498
Cursor, 153, 618
data access, creating, 117-118
DatabaseMetaData, 159
DataSource, 126, 169, 211-213
dependent, 338
DeploymentDescriptor, 336
Destination, 498
Document Object Model (DOM), 552-553
EJBHome, 337
EntityContext, 337-338
EnvironmentContext, 338
fine-grained, 338
Hashtables, 612
home object class, 382-384
home stub class, 374-378
home tie class, 378-382
HttpServlet, 191-192
HttpServletRequest, 189, 196-198, 200-208
HttpServletResponse, 189
HttpSession, 223
HttpSessionRequest, 208-209
implicit, 238, 280-281
java, 578
JDBCRowSet, 171
ListArray, 618
MessageConsumer, 500
MessageListener, 495, 501, 510, 512-514
MessageProducer, 500
MessageSelector, 497, 501, 514-518
named, retrieving, 134
NamedNodeMap, 552-553
Node, 552
NodeList, 552-553
non-triggered business, creating, 219-220
passing by reference, 338
PreparedStatement, 148, 150-151, 166
PrintWriter, 190, 192
Properties, 147, 452
QueueConnectionFactory, 492
recycling, 612, 614-615
remote object class, 398-400
remote stub class, 385-393
remote tie class, 394-398
RequestDispatcher, 209, 211
ResultSet, 150, 152-153, 159-160, 162, 166
ResultSetMetaData, 158
returning, 403-404
RowSet, 171
Serializable, 488
servlet-triggered business, 222-223
ServletConfig, 195
ServletContext, 196, 210, 216, 223
ServletOutputStream, 190
ServletRequest, methods, 206
session, 348-349, 498
session beans, removing, 363
SessionContext, 337-338
Statement, 148-150
system, 578
Taghandler, 616
TopicConnectionFactory, 493
types, narrowing, 403-404
UserTransaction, 352
utilServlet, 203
Vectors, 612
WebRowSet, 171
XSL Formatting (XSL-FO), 558

OCL (Object Constraint Language), 80

ODBC. *See* Open Database Connectivity, 139

OMG (Object Management Group), 36, 347

onException() method, 494

online help, SilverStream Application Servers, 222

onMessage() method, 342-344, 351, 501
Open Database Connectivity (ODBC), 139
open() method, 455
opening
 Microsoft Word documents in servlets, 217
 PDF files in servlets, 217
operations
 bind, 131
 Java Naming and Directory Interface (JNDI), 131-132
 list, 132
 lookup, 132
 rebind, 131
 rename, 132
 unbind, 131
operators, MessageSelector objects, 501
Optimizeit, 621, 628, 750
options
 -?, 656-657, 659-660
 c, 642
 Cascade, 76
 -component, 668
 -d ejbDeployedObject, 657
 -debug, 668
 Delete command, 660
 DeployEAR command, 656
 DeployEJB command, 657-658
 DeployWAR command, 659
 ERwin actions, 76
 f, 642
 -help, 668
 -host, 668
 -i, 656, 659
 -l deployname, 656, 659
 None, 76
 -o, 656, 658-659
 -P password, 656-657, 659-660
 -port, 668
 -prof, 620
 -r ejbRemoteJar, 658
 -R remoteJarPath, 658
 Restrict, 76
 Set Default, 76
 Set Null, 76
 sp_configure, 626
 u, 643
 -U userid, 656-657, 659-660
 -url, 668
 -username, 668
 v, 642
 -v verboseLevel, 656, 658-659
 -version, 668
 weblogic.deploy, 668
 x, 643
Oracle, 33, 627-628
ORB (Object Request Broker), 44, 347-348
ORDER BY clause, 173
org.omg.PortableServer.Servant class, 378, 394
OrTerm class, 458
OTS (Object Transaction Service), 347
Out implicit object, 281
OUT parameter, 152
out.println() method, 192
output, eXtensible Markup Language (XML), 556-557
OutputStream interface, 616
overhead, reducing in networks, 610

P

-P password option, 656-657, 659-660
packager tool, 57-59
packages
 Common Behavior, 85-87
 Foundation, 85
 htmlKona, 195
 Java Database Connectivity (JDBC), 143-148
 Java Naming and Directory Interface (JNDI), 128-129
 java.naming, 756
 java.naming.directory, 756
 java.naming.event, 757
 java.naming.ldap, 757
 java.naming.spi, 757
 java.sql, 143-148
 javax.servlet, 189
 javax.sql, 143, 168-169, 171
 jazax.naming, 129
 optional, Java 2 Enterprise Edition (J2EE), 757-759
 SAXException, 554
 servlets, 188-189
packaging
 applications, 38-39, 633-634, 636-638, 640-641, 643-646, 648
 components, hierarchies, 353
 images into one class, 623
 servlets, Web Archive (WAR) files, 221
Paessler Tools, 601
Page A's View, 113
page directives, 231, 262-264

Page implicit object, 281
page scope, 268-269, 302
PageContext implicit object, 281
pages
BASE, 116
building, 114-117
compiled, 82
frame, 116
Hypertext Markup Language (HTML), generating, 190
JavaServer (JSP)
advantages of, 254-255
architecture, 240-248, 250, 252-254
deploying, 218
described, 11, 226-227, 229
developing and deploying, 233, 236-240
directives, 231
features of, 229-231
interactions between servlets and, 185
passing control to, 210
performance of, 615-617
SilverBooks sample application, 699-700
syntax, 258-261, 263-275, 277-282
tag libraries, 282-287
tags, 228, 231-232
MVC JSP, 115
presentation, Model-View-Controller (MVC), 253
scripted, 81
separating business logic and presentation, 230
Web, modeling, 87, 89-90, 92
parallel processing, 586
parameter entities, 532
parameters
IN, 152
initialization, 216
INOUT, 152, 156
OUT, 152
request, accessing, 197
shared constant, defining for Web applications, 216
ParaSoft, 595, 598, 750-751
Parsed Character Data (PCDATA), eXtensible Markup Language (XML) documents, 534
parsed entities, 532
ParserAdapter class, 554
parsers, eXtensible Markup Language (XML), 549
partial Java drivers, 142
partitioning
applications, 140
hardware, 627
tables, 626-627
passing objects by reference, 338
password argument, 667, 704
passwords, Struts to implement, 307
patterns, 51
PC (personal computer), introduction of, 8
PCDATA (Parsed Character Data), eXtensible Markup Language (XML) documents, 534
PDF files, opening in servlets, 217
percent (%) character, 538
performance
applications, 606-607
database monitoring and tuning tools, 627-628
diagnoses and cures for, 621-624
factors affecting, 624-627
preparing for performance tuning, 618-621
writing high-performance applications, 607-612, 614-618
databases, 625-627
MVC design effect on, 293
session beans, 359
tools for monitoring, 748-753
tools for testing, 587, 589, 591-593, 595
performance testing, 584
persistence
bean-managed (BMP), 340, 348, 415
container-managed (CMP), 332, 339, 348, 416
MVC Model, 291
session objects, 348-349
persistence managers, 339
persistence schema, 339
persistent cookies, tracking sessions, 206, 208
persistent delivery, 496

persistent storage, 625
personal computer (PC), introduction of, 8
Picture control, 117
PIs (Processing Instructions), eXtensible Markup Language (XML), 534-535
PKI (public key infrastructure), 566
platform independence, JavaServer Pages (JSP), 230
plus (+) notation, 536-537
Point-to-Point model, Java Message Service (JMS), 491-492, 502-504
Point-to-Point Queue model, Java Message Service (JMS), 507-520, 522
PointBase Server Edition, 740
pools
- connection, 169-170, 622, 626, 757
- instance, 331
- managing, 612, 614-615
- threads, 624

POP3 (Post Office Protocol 3), 447
port argument, 656-658, 660
-port option, 668
POST method, 186, 189, 193, 197
Post Office Protocol 3 (POP3), 447
posting
- data, Hypertext Markup Language (HTML), 193-195
- messages, Publish/Subscribe model, 492-494

PowerBuilder, 68
PowerDesigner, 68-70
Pramati Java Application Server, 732-733
Pramati Studio 2.5, 720-722
predefined entities, 532
prefix matching, 321
prepareCall() method, 152
PreparedStatement object, 148, 150-151, 166
presentation
- separating from business logic, Web pages, 230
- Web pages, Model-View-Controller (MVC), 253

presentation layer, 43, 609
primary classes in JavaMail, 450-451
- JAF (Java Activation Framework), 451
- javax.mail.Address, 459
- javax.mail.Folder, 454-455
- javax.mail.internet.InternetAddress, 459
- javax.mail.internet.MimeMessage, 460-465
- javax.mail.Message, 460
- javax.mail.search, 456, 459
- javax.mail.Session, 452
- javax.mail.Store, 453
- javax.mail.Transport, 466

primary keys
- entitites, 68
- session beans, 363

print statements, debugging with, 578
printing names and data types, resultset columns, 158
println() method, 194
PrintWriter object, 190, 192
procedures, stored, 111-112, 152, 155-156
process modeling, 66
processing
- concurrent, message-driven beans (MDB), 343-344
- parallel, 586

Processing Instructions (PIs), eXtensible Markup Language (XML), 534-535
ProcessingInstruction interface, 550
producing. *See* creating
productivity, increasing for developers, 17-18
-prof option, 620
profilers, 620-621
profiling applications, 620-621
programmers. *See* developers
programming. *See* developing
programs. *See* applications
projects, design phase, 606
prologs, eXtensible Markup Language (XML) documents, 528
properties
- APPLET, 130
- AUTHORITATIVE, 130
- BATCHSIZE, 130

contexts, 130
DNS_URL, 130
INITIAL_CONTEXT_FACTORY, 130
Java Message Service (JMS), 497
LANGUAGE, 130
OBJECT_FACTORIES, 130
PROVIDER_URL, 130
REFERRAL, 130
SECURITY_AUTHENTICATION, 130
SECURITY_CREDENTIALS, 130
SECURITY_PRINCIPAL, 130
SECURITY_PROTOCOL, 130
Session, 452
STATE_FACTORIES, 130
URL_PKG_PREFIXES, 130

Properties object, 147, 452

protocols

Common Object Request Broker Architecture (CORBA), 347
Internet InterORB (IIOP), 346-348
Internet Message Access Protocol 4. *See* IMAP4
Java Message Service (JMS), 345
Lightweight Directory Access (LDAP), 127, 132-135
Multipurpose Internet Mail (MIME), 187, 190, 192, 217
Post Office Protocol 3. *See* POP3
Remote Method Invocation over Internet InterORB (RMI-IIOP), 756
requirements for, Enterprise JavaBeans (EJB), 346
Simple Mail Transfer Protocol. *See* SMTP

Provider Registry, 448-450

PROVIDER_URL property, 130

proxies. *See* stubs

public key infrastructure (PKI), 566

public void updateString() method, 162

publish() method, 496

Publish/Subscribe model, Java Message Service (JMS), 492-494, 504-507

publishing clients, Publish/Subscribe model, 504-505

publishing messages, Publish/Subscribe model, 492-494

pure HTML-only clients, 43

pure Java drivers, 143

PUT method, 186

Q

Quadbase Systems, 743-744

query strings, URL-encoded, 205-206

question mark (?) notation, 537

QueueConnectionFactory object, 492

queues, Destination, 518-520, 522

R

-r ejbRemoteJar option, 658

-R remoteJarPath option, 658

RAD (rapid application development), 234

RadioButton control, 117

RadView Software, 591, 751-752

RAM (Random Access Memory), volatile storage, 625

Random Access Memory (RAM), volatile storage, 625

ranges, character, 535

rapid application development (RAD), 234

Rational Rose, 94, 740-741

Rational Rose 2000, 86

Rational SiteLoad, 587

Rational Suite ContentStudio, 601

read-only Web applications, effects on performance, 617

readmail.jsp, 484-485

readNextRow() method, 618

realMethods framework, 52

RealValidator, 597

rebind operation, 131

receive() method, 500

ReceiveDateTerm class, 458

receiveNoWait() method, 500
receiving
clients
browse, Point-to-Point Queue model, 508-511
MessageListener, Point-to-Point Queue model, 512
MessageSelector, Point-to-Point Queue model, 516-518
Point-to-Point model, 503-504
e-mail messages
binary, 472, 474
multipart, 470-471
messages, 500-501
Point-to-Point model, 491-492, 502-504
Point-to-Point Queue model, 507-518
RecipientStringTerm class, 458
RecipientTerm class, 458
recovering databases, batching utilities, 112
recycling objects, 612, 614-615
redelivery flag field, 495
redirecting requests, JavaServer Pages (JSP), 244-247
reentrance, client session beans, 405
REF data type, 166, 168
references
character, Processing Instructions (PIs), 534
Enterprise JavaBeans (EJB), 768-772
home, instances, 405
home interface, 363
passing objects by, 338
resolving, application deployment, 649-650, 654-655, 660-665
resource, 176, 178
resource environments, 778-780
UserTransaction, 780
referential integrity, 75
REFERRAL property, 130
registerOutParameter() method, 152, 156
registration, EJBHome interface, 346
regression testing, 585, 598-599
Relationship Management Methodology (RMM), 78
relationships
determining roles of entities in, 103-104
entity, 67-68
modeling, J2EE applications, 73, 76
Release Notes, Java 2 Enterprise Edition (J2EE) Software Development Kit (SDK) documentation, 763
releaseConnection() method, 174
reliability, improving in applications, 581-582
Remote interface, 332, 334-335, 345-347, 351, 353
remote interfaces, 360, 363, 372-373, 436
Remote Method Invocation (RMI), 79, 127, 332, 346-349
Remote Method Invocation over Internet InterORB Protocol (RMI-IIOP), 756
Remote SessionContext, 334
remove connectivity model, 50
remove() method, 363
remove(Handle h) method, 365
remove(Object primaryKey) method, 365
removing
deployed J2EE applications, 653-654
deployed J2EE components, 659-660, 669
Destination Queues and Topics, Java Message Service (JMS), 518-520, 522
handles, 365
rows, databases, 163
session beans
clients, 406
objects, 363
rename operation, 132
rendering business objects, 253
repairing databases, batching utilities, 112
reply() method, 463
report generation tools, 736-744
Request implicit object, 280
request parameters, accessing with HttpServletRequest, 197

request scope, 302
request-processing phase, JavaServer Pages (JSP), 240
RequestDispatcher interface, 209-211
RequestDispatcher object, 209, 211
Requests
- redirecting, JavaServer Pages (JSP), 244-247
- servlets, 209-211, 215-216

Required attribute, 344, 350-351
#REQUIRED keyword, 537
RequiresNew attribute, 350
resource environment references, 778-780
resource manager connection factory, 772-778
resource references, 176, 178
resource resolution files, Pet Store, 676-680, 682, 684-689
Response implicit object, 281
response status, setting with HttpServletResponse object, 204-205
Restrict option, 76
ResultSet object, 150, 152-153, 159-160, 162, 166
resultSet.getObject() method, 177
ResultSetMetaData object, 158
resultsets, 158-163
retrieving
- attributes, 131
- browser information from clients, 200-203
- content, servlets, 197-198
- data, Java Database Connectivity (JDBC), 148-156
- database structures, 159
- initialization paramaters from Web applications, 216
- named objects, 134
- names, classes, and bound objects, 132
- values, ResultSet objects, 153

return on invested capital (ROIC), 16
returning objects, 403-404
reusability, MVC patterns, 292
reusable components, 230
Reverse Engineer—Select Target Server dialog, 76
reverse engineering, J2EE applications, 70-71
rewriting Uniform Resource Locators (URLs), 205-206
RMI. *See* Java Remote Method Invocation
RMI-IIOP (Remote Method Invocation over Internet InterORB Protocol), 756
RMM (Relationship Management Methodology), 78
ROIC (return on invested capital), 16
role-based development, 22-24
rollback() method, 164, 494
root directories, 236
RootDir argument, 221
rows of resultsets, updating, 162-163
RowSet objects, 171
rowsets, 757
RSW Software, 587
running Java Pet Store sample application, 704-707

S

SAINT (Security Administrator's Integrated Network Tool), 599
SAML (Security Assertion Markup Language), 566-567
sample applications, 61
- Java Pet Store, 702-704, 706-707
- SilverBooks, 692-693, 696, 698, 700-702

SATAN (Security Administration Tool for Analyzing Networks), 600
saveChanges() method, 464
SAX. *See* Simple API for XML
SAXException, 554
SAXNotRecognized-Exception, 554

SAXNotSupported-Exception, 554
SAXParseException, 554
SC_ACCEPTED status constant, 204
SC_BAD_REQUEST status constant, 204
SC_FORBIDDEN status constant, 204
SC_NOT_FOUND status constant, 204
SC_OK status constant, 204
SC_UNAUTHORIZED status constant, 204
scalability
 MVC design effect on, 293
 session beans, 359
schema, eXtensible Markup Language (XML), 540-549
scientific method, applying to debugging applications, 575-578
scope, 268-269, 280, 302
scripted pages, 81
scripting elements, JavaServer Pages (JSP), 265-267
scriptlets, 230, 233, 238, 266
scripts, Common Gateway Interface (CGI), 182
scrollable resultsets, Java Database Connectivity (JDBC), 159-160, 162
SDK (Software Development Kits), Java 2 Enterprise Edition (J2EE), 759-763
search() method, 455
searching
 book titles, SilverBooks sample application, 696
 connection factories, 126-127
 data sources, uniform resource locators (URLs), 145-146
 DataSource objects, 126, 135
 session beans, clients, 402-405
 sources of errors, 576-578
 table of contents, Web Archive (WAR), 214
SearchTerm class, 458
Secure Scanner, 599-600
security
 Enterprise JavaBeans (EJB), 352
 eXtensible Markup Language (XML), 566-567
 integrated systems, 19-20
 Internet InterORB Protocol (IIOP), 348
 message-driven beans (MDB), 345
 tools for testing, 599-600
Security Administration Tool for Analyzing Networks (SATAN), 600
Security Administrator's Integrated Network Tool (SAINT), 599
Security Assertion Markup Language (SAML), 566-567
security constraint enforcement service, 332
Security contract, 759
security model, 49
security testing, 585
SECURITY_AUTHENTICATION property, 130
SECURITY_CREDENTIALS property, 130
SECURITY_PRINCIPAL property, 130
SECURITY_PROTOCOL property, 130
Segue Software, 599, 752-753
selecting
 application user interface styles, 112
 breakpoints, 119
 data types, 105-106
semicolon (;), 533
send() method, 466, 496
send.html, 483-484
sendError() method, 204
sending
 messages
  Point-to-Point model, 491-492, 502-504
  Point-to-Point Queue model, 507-518
sending browse clients, Point-to-Point Queue model, 507-508
sending clients, Point-to-Point model, 502-503
sending e-mail messages, 467
 binary, 471-472
 multipart, 469-470
sending MessageSelector clients, Point-to-Point Queue model, 514-518
sendmail.jsp, 484
sendMessage() method, 466

SentDateTerm class, 458
separating
business logic and presentation, Web pages, 230
concerns, 89
Serializable objects, 488
server applications, JavaServer Pages (JSP), 229
Server argument, 221, 656-658, 660, 704
server communications, 47
server JAR files, 402
servers
application, 14, 725-734, 736
BEA WebLogic, deploying applications, 660-665, 667-680, 682, 684-689
case studies, SilverStream Application Server, 171, 173-178
clustering, 622
SilverStream Application
deploying applications, 654-660
servlets, 218, 220-223
WebLogic Application, 195
service phase, servlets, 196
service providers, Java Naming and Directory Interface (JNDI), 127
service() method, 189-190, 192, 196
services
availability of, 20
container, 331-332
message-driven beans (MDB), 344-345
CORBA Object (COS), 127
directory
accessing, 131
described, 124-125
distributed programming, 346
Domain Name (DNS), 124-125, 129
external site monitoring, 600-601
Java Message (JMS)
components required by applications using, 498-499
creating and destroying Destination Queues and Topics, 518-520, 522
described, 126-127, 488-490
implementation and deployment issues, 522-523
interfaces, message-oriented middleware (MOM), 490-494, 496-497
Point-to-Point model, 491-492, 502-504
Point-to-Point Queue model, 507-518
producing and consuming messages, 500-501
Publish/Subscribe model, 492-494, 504-507
standard protocols, 345
naming
creating handles to, 129
described, 124-125
Java Naming and Directory Interface (JNDI), 129
namespaces, 131
Object Transaction (OTS), 347
transaction, message-driven beans (MDBs), 351-352
Servlet 2.3 Application Programming Interface (API), 223-224
Servlet Container, 188
servlet controller
Struts framework, 248
Servlet Engine, 188
servlet tags, 215, 635-637
servlet-triggered business objects, 222-223
ServletConfig object, 195
ServletContext object, 196, 210, 216, 223
ServletException, 189, 196
ServletOutputStream object, 190
ServletRequest object, 206
servlets, 47. *See also* classes
action, SilverBooks sample application, 700-701
application programming interface (API) packages, 188-189
benefits of, 184
containers, 188

as controllers in Model-View-Controller (MVC) patterns, 184-185
described, 182, 184
dispatching requests, 209-211
HttpServletRequest object, 197-198, 200-205
Hypertext Markup Language (HTML), 192-193, 195
Hypertext Transfer Protocol (HTTP), 184-188
Java, 11
Java Database Connectivity (JDBC), 211-213
JavaServer Pages (JSP), 255
life cycles of, 195-196
managing sessions, 205-209
performance of, 616
service() method, 189-190, 192
Servlet 2.3 Application Programming Interface (API), 223-224
ServletContext object, 196
session beans, clients, 406-407
SilverStream Application Server, 218, 220-223
Web applications, 213-217

Servlets 2.3, 758

session beans, 11, 22, 48, 333-335, 345
accessing Java Database Connectivity (JDBC) from, 174-175
clients
calling, 405
EJBs, 405
enterprise beans, 408
finding, 402-405
J2EE, 408
JSP, 408
loop-back calls, 405
reentrance, 405
removing, 406
servlets, 406-407
standalone Java applications, 408
standalone non-Java applications, 408
Unix, 408
updating, 402
Windows, 408
defining resource reference lookups, 176
deployment descriptors, JAR files, 400-401
home interface, 361
creating, 364-365
references, 363
home object class, 382-384
home stub class, 374-378
home tie class, 378-382
inheritance, 360
instances, creating, 405
interface, 360-362, 372-373
Java Archive (JAR), 400-402
Java Naming and Directory Interface (JNDI), 404
method pooling, 358
methods
business, 367
create(), 366
ejbActivate(), 360
ejbPassivate(), 360
ejbRemove(), 360
setSessionContext(SessionContext), 360
objects
removing, 363
types, 403-404
performance, 359
primary keys, 363
remote interface, 360
remote object class, 398-400
remote stub class, 385-393
remote tie class, 394-398
sample code, 367-372
scalability, 359
stateful, 358-359
stateless, 358-359

Session implicit object, 281

session objects, 348-349, 498

session scope, 302

SessionContext object, 334, 337-338

sessions
Java Message Service (JMS), 494-495
managing, servlets, 205-209

SessionSynchronization interface, 336, 349

Set Default option, 76

set method, 271

Set Null option, 76

setAttribute() method, 208

setAutoCommit(false) method, 164-165

setBlob() method, 166

setContent() method, 464

setContentLength() method, 204

setContentType() method, 190, 192, 204
setDateHeader() method, 204
setDeliveryMode() method, 500
setEntityContext() method, 432
setExceptionListener() method, 494
setExpunged() method, 464
setFetchSize() method, 160
setFlags() method, 455, 464
setFrom() method, 465
setHeader() method, 204
setIntHeader() method, 204
setMessageDriven-Context() method, 344
setMessageListener() method, 501
setNull() method, 151
setPriority() method, 500
setProperty tag, JavaServer Pages (JSP), 232
setRecipients() method, 465
setReplyTo() method, 465
setSentDate() method, 465
setSessionContext-(SessionContext) method (session beans), 360
setStatus() method, 204
setSubject() method, 465
setter method, 267, 272
setText() method, 465
setTimeToLive() method, 500
setting
  Multipurpose Internet Mail Extension (MIME) types, 190, 192
  response status, HttpServletResponse object, 204-205
set*XXX*() methods, 150, 152, 156
SGML (Standard Generalized Markup Language), 526
shared constant parameters, defining for Web applications, 216
sharing data, effects on performance, 617-618
shopping, SilverBooks sample application, 695-696, 699, 701
shortname attribute, 284
ShowPlan, 627
Sifonis, John, 15
SilkPerformer, 591
SilkPilot, 596, 752-753
SilkTest, 599
SilverBooks sample application, 61, 692-693, 696, 698, 700-702
SilverCmd, 655
SilverCmd BuildWAR command, 221
SilverCmd DeployWAR command, 221
SilverStream Application Server, 421, 726-727
  case study, 171, 173-178
  deploying applications, 654-660
  Pet Store resource resolution file, 680, 682, 684-686
  servlets, 218, 220-223
SilverStream eXtend Workbench, 710-711
SilverStream jBrokerMQ, 746
SilverStream Software Inc., 14
Simple API for XML (SAX), 34, 37, 553-556
Simple Mail Transfer Protocol. *See* SMTP
SingleLineEdit control, 117
SingleThreadModel interface, 616
SiteAngel, 600
SiteLoad, 587
sites. *See* Web sites
Sitraka Software, 595, 621, 722-723, 733-734, 753
sizes of databases, estimating, 107
SizeTerm class, 458
sizing applications, 607-608
skeletons. *See* ties
SMTP (Simple Mail Transfer Protocol), 446
software. *See* applications
software development cycle, 570, 582, 584
Software Development Kits (SDKs), 127, 759-763
Softwired iBus//Message Server, 746-747
SonicMQ, 745-746
source argument, 667

sp_configure option, 626
spaces, Processing Instructions (PIs), 535
special attributes, 68
specifications, applications, 610
speed
competition on the Internet, 20
downloading applets, improving, 623
SPI (JNDI Service Provider Interface), 127
SpinBox control, 117
Spread view, WebLOAD, 593
SQL (Structured Query Language), 8, 153-155
SQL Call-Level Interface. *See* Structured Query Language
SQL data types. *See* Structured Query Language
SQL select statements, 176-177
SQL Server, ShowPlan, 627
SQL_TRACE, 628
SQLException, 157
SQLWarning, 157-158
SQL_TRACE, 628
srvltJust servlet, 191-192
srvltTest servlets, 210
stability testing, 584
stabilizing errors, 575-576
standalone Java applications, session beans, 408
standalone non-Java applications, session beans, 408
Standard Generalized Markup Language (SGML), 526
standards
integrating legacy systems while using, 18-19
promoting competition and choices with, 19
Start() method, 501
state, Struts, 297, 303
state management service, 332
STATE_FACTORIES property, 130
stateful beans, 336, 358-359
stateless beans, 336, 358-359
StateManagementType attribute, 336
Statement object, 148-150
statements
batch, 164-165
eXtensible Stylesheet Language, 561-563
Java Database Connectivity (JDBC), 148-153, 164-165
print, debugging with, 578
SQL select, constructing, compiling, and executing, 176-177
static complexity analysis, code, 584
Static Text control, 117
statistics
application versions, 621
load testing, 619
status, response, 204-205
status codes, Hypertext Transfer Protocol (HTTP), 187
status constants, HttpServletResponse object, 204
stereotypes, 80
storage, persistent and volatile, 625
stored procedures, 111-112, 152, 155-156
streaming data to clients, 190
StreamMessage body format, Java Message Service (JMS), 497
stress testing, 584
strings
query, URL-encoded, 205-206
username, 274
StringTerm class, 459
STRUCT data type, 166, 168
Structured Query Language (SQL)
Call-Level Interface, 140
data types, converting to Java data types, 153-155
introduction of, 8
structures, retrieving from databases, 159
Struts, 114-115
action mapping configuration files, 315-318
action objects, 297, 313-315
action servlet instance descriptors, 318-319
ActionForm beans, 302-303, 310
ActionForward objects, 314
ActionMapping class, 298
ActionMapping interface, 315

ActionServlet class, 298, 301
adding components to applications, 323
advantages of, 326
business logic, 296-297, 303-304
client requests, handling, 298
Controller, 296, 298-301, 313-319, 321-323
controller servlets, 294, 314
custom tags, 297
data storage with, 296
databases, accessing, 323-326
deployment descriptors, 318-319, 321-323
exceptions, 315
extension mapping, 321
form beans, 297, 305-307, 309-310
functional areas of, 294
hyperlink tags, 312
initialization parameters, table of, 319, 321
input field HTML tags, 311-312
installing, 294-295
internationalized messages, 304-305
JavaBean scope, 302
Locale objects, 307
login function, 316
mappings, 296, 313
message tags, 306
Model, 296-298, 302-304
multipart forms, 307
origins at Jakarta Project, 293
passwords, 307
prefix matching, 321
prerequisite software, 294-295
presentation tags, 312
process flow, 296
request URIs, 315
state, 297, 303
tag libraries, 306, 322-323
utility clases, 294
ValidatingActionForm beans, 309
validation of input, 312-313
View, 296, 298, 304-307, 310-313
Web application deployment descriptor file, 313

Struts framework, 52, 185, 248, 250, 252-254
SilverBooks sample application, 702

struts-config.xml, 316-317
stub class, 361
stubs, 330, 332
Style Report, 742-743
style sheets, eXtensible Markup Language (XML), 527, 560-564
styles, 112, 114
stylesheet elements, 560-563
subdirectories, 236
subpages, adding controls to, 116-117
subscriptions, Publish/Subscribe model, 492-494, 506-507
Sun BluePrints Design Guidelines, 32
Sun Microsystems, 8, 14, 33, 748
Sun's J2EE BluePrints, 52
support
components
business logic, 28, 30
clients, 28
databases, J2EE applications, 76-77
JavaServer Pages (JSP), 230
scrolling, drivers, 159-160
Servlet Containers, Hypertext Transfer Protocol (HTTP), 188
SilverStream Application Server, 218
tools for providing, J2EE applications, 94-95
transactions, Java Database Connectivity (JDBC), 163-164

Supports attribute, 350
surrogates. *See* stubs, 330
Sybase, 14
Symantec, 600
synchronous communication, 490
syntax, JavaServer Pages (JSP), 258-261, 263-275, 277-282
syntax errors, 578-579
system modeling, 79-80
system object, 578
system state, Model-View-Controller (MVC), 252-253

T

table of contents, viewing in Web Archive (WAR), 214
tables, 104-108, 625-627
tag handlers, 283-286
tag libraries, 232, 282-287
Tag Library Descriptors (TLDs), 214, 238, 284-286
tagclass attribute, 285
Taghandler object, 616
TAGLIB class library, 114
taglib directive, 231-233, 238, 264-265, 282-283
tags
- attributes vs., 538
- BodyTags, 616
- <context-param>, 216
- eXtensible Markup Language (XML), 33, 529
- <FORM>, 192-193, 195
- JavaServer Pages (JSP), 228, 231-232
- servlet, 215, 635-637
- <web-app>, 215

teiclass attribute, 285
templates
- elements, 563-564
- import stylesheet, 563
- text in, 253
- trigger, 76

test coverage analysis, 586
testing applications, 570, 572
- correcting errors, 579-582
- debugging, 572-579
- J2EE, 476-477, 483
- loads, 619-620
- methods and techniques, 584-586
- phases of, 582, 584
- repairs to, 581
- tools for, 586-587, 589, 591-593, 595-597, 599-603

testing phase, software development cycle, 582, 584
text in templates, 253
Text interface, 550
text/gif MIME type, 217
text/plain MIME type, 217
TextMessage body format, Java Message Service (JMS), 497
thin clients, 47
third normal form (3NF), 105
thread pooling, 624
threading message-driven beans (MDB), 344
three-tier development, 99
three-tiered applications, 42
throughput, applications, 606
Tibco Software, 597-598
Tidestone Technologies, 743
tie class, 361
ties, 330
TLD. ***See*** **Tag Library Descriptors**
tlibversion attribute, 284
Together ControlCenter, 741
TogetherSoft, 86
tools
- batching, databases, 112
- computer aided software engineering (CASE), 67, 69-70
- database monitoring and tuning, 627-628
- deployment
  - *deploytool, 650-651*
  - *SilverCmd, 655*
  - *WebLogic, 665, 667-668*
- development, 710-725
- messaging and eXtensible Markup Language (XML), 744-748
- modeling, 64, 736-744
- object/report generation, 736-744
- support, J2EE applications, 94-95
- testing applications, 586-587, 589, 591-593, 595-597, 599-603
- validation and performance monitoring, 748-753

TopicConnectionFactory object, 493
topics
- Destination, creating and destroying, Java Message Service (JMS), 518-520, 522
- publishing messages to, 493-494

tracking sessions, persistent cookies, 206, 208
traffic, reducing in networks, 610
transacted sessions, Java Message Service (JMS), 494

Transaction Management contract, 759
transaction management systems, 10
transaction model, 49
transactions
- distributed, 170-171, 349-350, 757
- managing, 349-352
- multiple, 350
- support, Java Database Connectivity (JDBC), 163-164

translation phase, JavaServer Pages (JSP), 240
transmitting
- messages
  - *Point-to-Point model, 491-492, 502-504*
  - *Point-to-Point Queue model, 507-518*

trigger templates, 76
triggered business objects, 222-223
tuning
- databases
  - *batching utilities, 112*
  - *tools for, 627-628*
- performance, 618-621

turning on e-mail verification, SilverBooks sample application, 702
two-tier development, 99
TYPE_FORWARD_ONLY resultset, 159
TYPE_SCROLL_INSENSITIVE resultset, 159
TYPE_SCROLL_SENSITIVE resultset, 159
types, objects, 403-404
typical installs, Java Pet Store sample application, 705

U

u option, 643
-U userid option, 656-657, 659-660
UCNY, Inc., 14
UML. *See* Unified Modeling Language
UnavailableException, 189, 196
unbind operation, 131
undeploy argument, 667
Unicode standard, 34
Unified Modeling Language (UML), 36, 51, 64, 77-79, 82-87
uniform resource identifier (URI), 238
uniform resource locators (URLs), 238
- finding data sources, 145-146
- rewriting, 205-206

uniform resource name (URN), 238
Unify eWave Engine, 734, 736
unit testing, 584
Unix, client session beans, 408
unparsed data, eXtensible Markup Language (XML), 533-534
unparsed entities, 532
unsetEntityContext() method, 432
update argument, 667
updateable resultsets, 161-162
updateAsciiStream() method, 162
updateBigDecimal() method, 162
updateBinaryStream() method, 162
updateBoolean() method, 162
updateByte() method, 162
updateNull() method, 162
update*XXX*() methods, 162
updating
- columns and rows, resultsets, 162-163
- data, Java Database Connectivity (JDBC), 148-156
- deployed J2EE components, 669-680, 682, 684-689
- session beans, clients, 402

uri attribute, 284
URI (uniform resource identifier), 238
URL. *See* uniform resource locators
-url option, 668
URL-encoded query strings, 205-206
URL_PKG_PREFIXES property, 130
URN (uniform resource name), 238
usability testing, 585
useBean tag, JavaServer Pages (JSP), 232, 238

user IDs, installing in Java Pet Store sample application, 707
user interfaces, MVC Controller, 292
User Object control, 117
Userid argument, 704
userInfo bean, 270-271
-username option, 668
username string, 274
UserTransaction interface, 351
UserTransaction object, 352
UserTransaction references, 780
utilities
batching, databases, 112
computer aided software engineering (CASE), J2EE applications, 67, 69-70
database monitoring and tuning, 627-628
deployment
deploytool, 650-651
SilverCmd, 655
WebLogic, 665, 667-668
development, 710-725
messaging and eXtensible Markup Language (XML), 744-748
modeling, J2EE applications, 64
modeling and object/report generation, 736-744
support, J2EE applications, 94-95
testing applications, 586-587, 589, 591-593, 595-597, 599-603
validation and performance monitoring, 748-753
utilServlet object, 203

V

v option, 642
-v verboseLevel option, 656, 658-659
VA Assist Enterprise, 718-719
validating code, 118-119
validation tools, 748-753
validators, Hypertext Markup Language (HTML), 597-598
value attribute, 275
VALUE keyword, 538
values
doWait, 173
MessageSelector objects, 501
retrieving, ResultSet objects, 153
variables
implicit, 238
implicit request, 238
Vectors object, 612
vendor-specific containers, 333
verifier, 59-60
-version option, 668
version statistics, 621
Vertical ScrollBar control, 117
viewing
cookies, 200
deployed J2EE components, 668
histories on specific measurements, WebLOAD, 593
table of contents, Web Archive (WAR), 214
views
Chart, WebLOAD, 593
Console Chart, WebLOAD, 593
Integrated Report Chart, WebLOAD, 593
MVC View, 291
Spread, WebLOAD, 593
Visio, 65
VisualAge for Java, 717-718
VitalSoft, 603
VMGEAR, 621
volatile storage, 625
volume data generation, 584
VSAM, 8

W

W3C (World Wide Web Consortium), 33
WAI. *See* Netscape Web Application Programming Interface
WAR. *See* Web Archive
WAR (Web Archive) files, assembling, 645-646
WARFile argument, 221, 658
wasNull() method, 155
Web Archive (WAR), 213-214, 218, 221, 236
Web applications
architecture, 81-82
modeling, 77-79
read-only, effects on performance, 617
servlets, 213-217

Web Archive (WAR) files, assembling, 645-646
Web browsers, 46
Web component creation phase, 56
Web components, 47-48
Web containers, 50
Web Logic, 421
Web pages
modeling, 87, 89-90, 92
presentation, Model-View-Controller (MVC), 253
separating business logic and presentation, 230
Web Polygraph, 587
Web Site Garage, 601
Web sites
Allaire-Macromedia JRun 3.0, 727
Allora for Java, 739
ApacheBench, 590
ArgoUML, 94
Astra LoadTest, 595
Atesto Automated Web Testing Service, 601
BEA WebLogic Server, 660, 727
Bean-test, 590
CapeConnect XML Business Server, 736
Cerebellum eCom Integrator and Portal Integrator, 737
Component Manager, 716
ContentStudio, 601
CyberSpyder, 596
DBArtisan, 738
DeployDirector, 734
documentation, Java Naming and Directory Interface (JNDI), 129
Element Construction Set (ECS), 195
Elixir IDE, 715
Elixir Report, 742
Empirix Bean-test, 752
ERwin, 68, 738
ExpressChart, 743
FioranoMQ 5 Message Server, 745
Firehunter, 600
Formula One iReporting Engine, 743
Gemstone/J Application Server, 729
Giga Information Group, 13
Harmony Component Suite, 714
header field list, Java Message Service (JMS), 496
help, SilverStream Application Servers, 222
IBM VisualAge for Java, 717
IBM WebSphere, 730
InfoLink, 596
Internet Quotient self-assessment test, 15
IPCheck, 601
iPlanet Application Server, 731
iPortal Application Server 3.0, 731
J2EE Reference Implementation, 649
J2EE-compliant application servers, 10
Jakarta, 228
Java API for XML Processing 1.1 (JAXP), 748
Java Community Process (JCP), 328
JBuilder 5, 712
JCanvas Studio, 711
JClass Enterprise Suite, 722
JNDI Software Development Kit (SDK), 127
JProbe, 753
JProbe Developer Suite, 595
JSR-000026 UML profile for EJB, 93
Jtest, 595, 750
JUnit, 596
Macromedia Dreamweaver UltraDev, 719
mod perl, 590
Net.Medic, 603
NetRaker Suite, 602
NetRecon, 600
Nmap, 599
Object Management Group (OMG), 36
Optimizeit, 749
Oracle, 628
PointBase Server Edition, 740
PowerDesigner, 68
Pramati Java Application Server, 732
Pramati Studio 2.5, 720
Rational Rose, 86, 740
RealValidator, 597
Secure Scanner, 600
Security Administration Tool for Analyzing Networks (SATAN), 600
Security Administrator's Integrated Network Tool (SAINT), 599

SilkPerformer, 591
SilkPilot, 596, 752
SilkTest, 599
SilverStream, 692
SilverStream Application Server, 218, 726
SilverStream eXtend Workbench, 710
SilverStream jBrokerMQ, 746
SiteAngel, 600
SiteLoad, 587
Softwired iBus//Message Server, 746
SonicMQ, 745
Struts Framework, 185, 248
Style Report, 742
testing and management tools, 586-587, 589, 591-593, 595-597, 599-603
Together ControlCenter, 741
TogetherSoft, 86
UCNY, Inc., 14
Unify eWave Engine, 734
VA Assist Enterprises, 718
Visio, 65
Web Polygraph, 587
Web Site Garage, 601
WebBug, 602
WebCheck, 596
webfeedback, 602
WebGain Studio 4.5 Professional Edition, 724
WebKing, 599
WebLOAD, 593, 751
WebMetrics, 603
Webserver Stress Tool, 587
WebSite Director, 602
WebSpray, 591
Xerces and Xalan, 747
XML Authority, 598
XML Instance, 597
XML Spy, 748

<web-app> tag, 215

Web-based components, 45

WEB-INF subdirectory, 236

WEB-INF/classes directory, 214

WEB-INF/lib directory, 214

web.xml, 214-216
- Pet Store, 672-674
- servlet tags, 635-637
- SilverBooks, 675

WebBug, 602

WebCheck, 596

webfeedback, 602

WebGain Studio 4.5 Professional Edition, 724-725

WebKing, 598-599

WebLOAD, 591-593, 751-752

WebLogic, 14, 686-689
- Server, 195, 727-728
  - *deploying applications, 660-665, 667-680, 682, 684-689*

weblogic.deploy, 665, 667-668

WebMetrics, 603

WebRowSet objects, 171

Webserver Stress Tool, 587

WebSite Director, 602

WebSphere, 14, 421

WebSpray, 591

WHERE clause, 173

white box testing, 585

whitespaces, Processing Instructions (PIs), 535

Windows operating systems
- installing Java 2 Enterprise Edition (J2EE) Software Development Kit (SDK), 760-761
- session beans, clients, 408

Wireless Markup Language (WML) pages, 46

wizards
- Business Object, 219-220, 222
- INDEX Tuning, 628

WML (Wireless Markup Language) pages, 46

WORA (Write Once, Run Anywhere), 632

Word documents, opening in servlets, 217

workarounds, correcting errors, 580

World Wide Web
- architecture requirements, 20, 22
- life cycles, applications, 22-26, 28, 30

World Wide Web Consortium (W3C), 33

Write Once, Run Anywhere (WORA), 632

writers, lazy, 626

writing
- Destination Queues and Topics, Java Message Service (JMS), 518-520, 522

high-performance applications, 607-612, 614-618
JavaServer Pages (JSP), 233, 236-240
messages, 500-501
servlet-triggered business objects, 222-223
servlets, SilverStream Application Server, 218, 220-223
srvltTest servlets, 210

X–Z

x option, 643
Xalan, 747
Xerces, 549, 747
XKMS (XML Key Management Specification), 566-567
XLink (XML Linking Language), 564, 566
XMI (XML Metadata Interchange), 36, 93
XML. *See* eXtensible Markup Language
XML Authority, 598
XML Instance, 597
XML Key Management Specification (XKMS), 566-567
XML Linking Language (XLink), 564, 566
XML Metadata Interchange (XMI), 36, 93
XML Spy, 748
XMLFilter interface, 554
XMLFilterImpl class, 555
XMLReader interface, 554
XMLReaderAdapter class, 555
XMLReaderFactory class, 555
XPath (XSL Path Language), 558-559
XSL (eXtensible Stylesheet Language), 557-564
XSL Formatting Objects (XSL-FO), 558
XSL Path Language (XPath), 558-559
XSL Transformations (XSLT), 558-559
<xsl:apply-import> statement, 563
<xsl:attribute-set> statement, 562
<xsl:decimal-format> statement, 562
<xsl:import> statement, 561, 563
<xsl:include> statement, 561
<xsl:key> statement, 561
<xsl:output> statement, 561
<xsl:preserve-space> statement, 561
<xsl:strip-space> statement, 561
<xsl:stylesheet> statement, 562-563
<xsl:template> statement, 562
XSL-FO (XSL Formatting Objects), 558
XSLT (XSL Transformations), 558-559